McDOUGAL LITTELL

GEORGIA

in the American Experience

Patricia Klein

Assistant Professor of Education
Georgia College and State University, Milledgeville

Craig Pascoe

Assistant Professor and Director of the Center for Georgia Studies
Georgia College and State University, Milledgeville

W0009570

McDougal Littell
A HOUGHTON MIFFLIN COMPANY

Authors

Dr. Patricia "Trish" Klein

Dr. Klein's interest in state histories began when she was a fourth-grade student in a small rural school, where she studied her state's history. As an adult educator, she tries to transmit that interest in her writing and her teaching. Dr. Klein holds a Ph.D. in Social Studies Education. Since 1993, she has been instructing pre-service teachers in social studies methods and middle-level education, first at Georgia State University and currently at Georgia College and State University in Milledgeville. She is past president of the Georgia Council for the Social Studies and a former coordinator of the Georgia Geographic Alliance. Dr. Klein has authored or co-authored several state and county social studies programs. When she is not teaching and writing, she enjoys spending time with her husband, their pets, children, and grandchildren.

Dr. Craig Pascoe

Craig Pascoe received his M.A. degree at the University of North Carolina, Charlotte in 1992. He went on to earn his Ph.D. in history at the University of Tennessee, Knoxville, in 1998. He taught at Georgia Southern University and the University of Georgia before taking the position of Director of the Center for Georgia Studies at Georgia College and State University in Milledgeville. Dr. Pascoe is currently working on a book about the development of Fort Stewart, Georgia, and is co-editing a collection of essays about the South in the 20th century. Dr. Pascoe is the editor of *Atlanta History: A Journal of Georgia and the South*. He lives in an antebellum Greek Revival cottage in Eatonton with his wife and daughter.

Maps on pages 528–536 © Rand McNally & Company. All rights reserved.

Acknowledgments begin on page 574.

ISBN 0-618-42248-X

Printed in the United States of America.
1 2 3 4 5 6 - DWO - 09 08 07 06 05 04

Content Reviewers

Dr. Andy Ambrose
Atlanta History Center

Dr. Eddie Bennett
Cobb County Public Schools

Dr. Deborah Daniel
Gwinnett County Public Schools

Cathy Geis
Fayette County Public Schools

William Greene
Clayton County Public Schools

Dr. Pat Guillory
Fulton County Schools

Rosanne MacCauley
Savannah-Chatham County Public
    Schools

Lynn McCoy
Southwest Georgia RESA

Chris Pratt-Consoletti
Harris County Schools

Larry Smith
Massie Heritage Interpretation Center

Roger Smith
Georgia Historical Society

Dorothy Taylor
Bibb County Schools

William Walker
Savannah-Chatham County Public
    Schools

Dr. Lois Wolfe
Henry County Public Schools

UNIT 1

The Land and Original Peoples of Georgia

▼ Tchow-Ee-Put-O-Kaw

▲ Hernando de Soto

The Georgia Colony Comes of Age

▲ John Locke

▲ James Madison

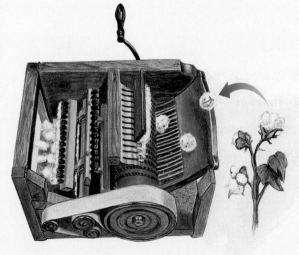

Georgia and the Nation Go to War

▲ African-American Congressmen

Growth in Georgia and the Nation

▲ Alfred Holt Colquitt

I WANT YOU
FOR U.S. ARMY
NEAREST RECRUITING STATION

Modern America
Takes Shape

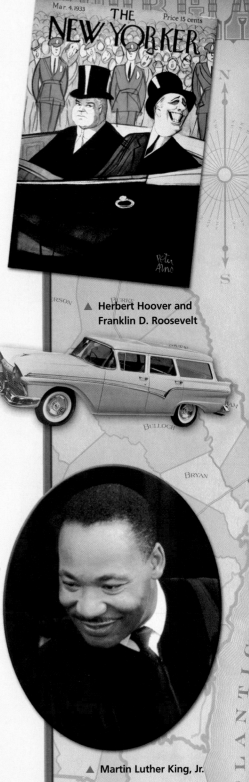

▲ Herbert Hoover and Franklin D. Roosevelt

▲ Martin Luther King, Jr.

UNIT 7

Building the Future

▲ Hank Aaron

GRAPHS, CHARTS, TABLES, DIAGRAMS

PRIMARY SOURCES

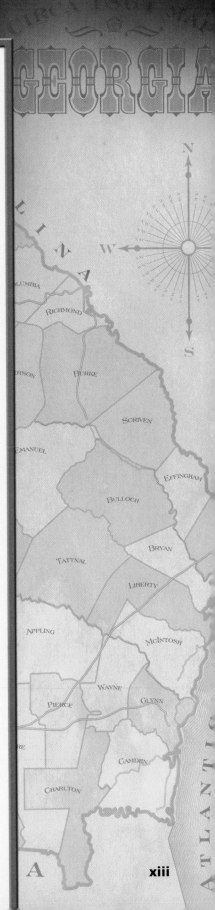

SPECIAL FEATURES

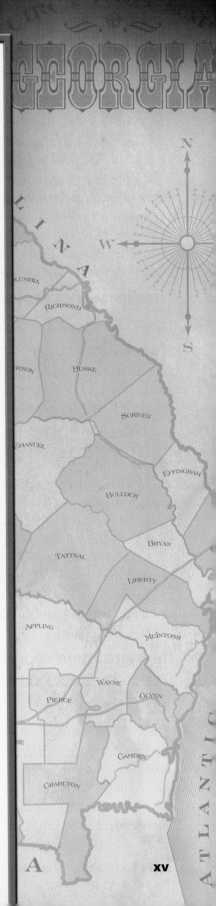

Themes of Geography

One useful way to think about geography is in terms of major themes or ideas. These pages examine the five major themes of geography and show how they apply to Georgia. Recognizing and understanding these themes will help you to understand all the different aspects of geography.

Location

"Where am I?" Your answer to this question is your location. One way to answer it is to use absolute location. That means you'll use the coordinates of longitude and latitude to give your answer. For example, if you are in Atlanta, its absolute location is approximately 33° north latitude and 84° west longitude.

Like most people, however, you'll probably use relative location to answer the question. Relative location describes where a certain area is in relation to another area. For example, Georgia is in the southern part of the United States and lies on the Atlantic coast between South Carolina and Florida.

THINKING ABOUT GEOGRAPHY What is the relative location of your school?

▲ Georgia has four geographic regions.

Place

"What is Georgia like?" Place can help you answer this question. Place refers to the physical and human factors that make one area different from another. Physical characteristics are natural features, such as physical setting, plants, animals, and weather. For example, Georgia's Stone Mountain is one of the largest masses of exposed granite in the world.

Human characteristics include cultural diversity and the things people have made—including language, the arts, and architecture. For instance, Georgia's population includes descendants of the earliest people in North America—Native Americans. Descendants of people who arrived during colonial times include Africans, English, Scots–Irish, and Germans. Recent immigration has brought people from Asia and Latin America to Georgia's diverse population.

THINKING ABOUT GEOGRAPHY What physical and human characteristics make where you live unique?

Region

Geographers can't easily study the whole world at one time. So they break the world into regions. A region can be as large as a continent or as small as a neighborhood. A region has certain shared characteristics that set it apart. These characteristics might include political divisions, climate, language, or religion. Georgia is a part of the region in the United States known as the South. Within Georgia there are four

▲ Teens in Americus, Georgia, work together on a service project with Habitat for Humanity.

◀ Georgia's population continues to grow. Issues such as air quality and land use are affected by increasing population.

physical regions: the Outer Coastal Plain, the Inner Coastal Plain, the Piedmont, and the Appalachian Mountains.

THINKING ABOUT GEOGRAPHY What characteristics does your city or town share with nearby cities or towns?

Movement

Movement refers to the shifting of people, goods, and ideas from one place to another. People constantly move in search of better places to live, and they trade goods with one another over great distances. Movement also causes ideas to travel from place to place. In recent years, technology has quickened the movement of ideas and goods.

The Atlanta metropolitan area provides a good example of many types of movement. As business and industry moved to Atlanta, newcomers moved into the surrounding areas. Metropolitan Atlanta now encompasses 10 counties. Henry County is the third fastest-growing county in the nation. Not only are many people moving into the area, but ideas and products flow freely into and out of the region.

THINKING ABOUT GEOGRAPHY What are some of the different ways you can spread information and ideas?

▼ The Okefenokee Swamp is the largest swamp in North America.

Human-Environment Interaction

Human-environment interaction refers to ways people interact with their environment, such as building a dam, cutting down a tree, or even sitting in the sun. The environment sometimes forces people to find ways to protect themselves from natural disasters or extreme weather.

Georgia's Okefenokee Swamp encompasses 650 square miles of wetlands. Before it was protected by presidential order, humans had attempted to drain the water from parts of it. Logging also destroyed some areas of the wetlands. Today, the varied plant and animal life are protected, while humans enjoy recreation such as hiking and canoeing. However, overuse of water resources and air pollution threaten the delicate balance of the swamp.

THINKING ABOUT GEOGRAPHY What are the ways that people in your city or town have changed their environment?

Themes of Geography Assessment

MAIN IDEAS

1. What is the relative location of your home?

2. What are three characteristics of the region in which you live?

3. What are at least three ways in which you have recently interacted with the environment?

FORMING AND SUPPORTING OPINIONS

Which aspect of geography described in these themes do you think has most affected your life? Explain.

THINK ABOUT

- ways you interact with your environment
- how you travel from place to place

Georgia's Physical Geography

A kayaker maneuvers through the rapids of the Tallulah Gorge in north Georgia.

→INTERACT←
with HISTORY

You are planning a driving trip across Georgia, and will be stopping frequently to do some camping and hiking. You have prepared a tour that will take you across each of the different land regions in Georgia. As you travel across the state, you notice the differences in the landscape, as well as the different activities of the people.

How are your activities affected by the environment around you?

WHAT DO YOU THINK?

• What kinds of outdoor sports or activities do people enjoy in the different regions of Georgia?

• Some kinds of businesses are located in specific regions, others are not. What types of businesses depend on the physical environment? What types of businesses do not?

• How does the environment affect the lives of people in Georgia?

For more information on this chapter, visit . . .

RESEARCH LINKS
CLASSZONE.COM

Reading Strategy: Finding Main Ideas

What Do You Know?

What do you know about how the weather, climate, and terrain change across the state of Georgia? Why do you think these regions vary?

THINK ABOUT

- what you have learned about Georgia as you've traveled across the state
- what you have heard about the state from local news

What Do You Want to Know?

What questions do you have about the different parts of Georgia? What would you like to know about environmental challenges facing your state? Record these questions in your notebook before you read the chapter.

Finding Main Ideas

The main idea summarizes the most important point of a passage or section you read. For each major section of this chapter, identify what you think may be one main idea. (Note that some sections may have more than one main idea.) Often you will find the main idea at the opening of a section. Then identify at least four details that explain or give examples of the main idea. What do you learn about Georgia's land regions, weather, and water supply as you read?

 See Skillbuilder Handbook, page 549.

Taking Notes

	Georgia's Land Regions	Georgia's Weather and Climate	Georgia's Water Supply
Main Idea			
Supporting Idea			
Supporting Idea			
Supporting Idea			
Supporting Idea			

Georgia's Land Regions

MAIN IDEA	WHY IT MATTERS NOW	TERMS & NAMES
Dividing Georgia into specific regions assists in studying the state.	Georgia's regions contribute to the state's economy.	Sunbelt region Piedmont Coastal Plain Appalachian fall zone Mountains

SETTING THE STAGE

If you had to "live off the land," where would you like to live? Would you want to live on a farm and grow crops? Would you prefer to live in the mountains and hunt game? Would you like to live near a stream and reel in fish?

What kind of landscape would you like to see out your kitchen window? Would you like to see the rolling ocean? Would you prefer to see flat, open fields? What kinds of outdoor activities do you enjoy? Do you like canoeing or waterskiing? Or do you prefer hiking? Our physical surroundings affect our work and leisure activities.

◀ Recreational fishing in Georgia's lakes and rivers is a popular pastime. This girl is enjoying fishing for spotted bass in Lake Burton.

Where We Are

How many ways are there to answer the question, "Where do you live?" You could begin by saying that you live on planet Earth. To be more specific, you could say that you live in the Western Hemisphere, on the continent of North America, in the country of the United States of America. You live in the southeastern region of that country, in a state called Georgia.

Georgia is bordered by South Carolina, North Carolina, and Tennessee on the north. To the west are Alabama and a small part of Florida. Florida forms the southern border. The Atlantic Ocean forms about 100 miles of the eastern border. Georgia has a number of small barrier islands on its coast.

Georgia is a Southern state. It is part of the Deep South, the southernmost tier of states that also includes South Carolina, Florida, Alabama, Mississippi, and Louisiana. Georgia is also part of the **Sunbelt**. The Sunbelt is a group of Southern states that stretches from the East Coast all the way to California. The Sunbelt is a popular place for businesses and people to locate because of its moderate climate.

Taking Notes

Use your chart to take notes about Georgia's land regions.

	Georgia's Land Regions	Georgia's Weather and Climate
Main Idea		
Supporting Idea		

Georgia's Physical Geography **5**

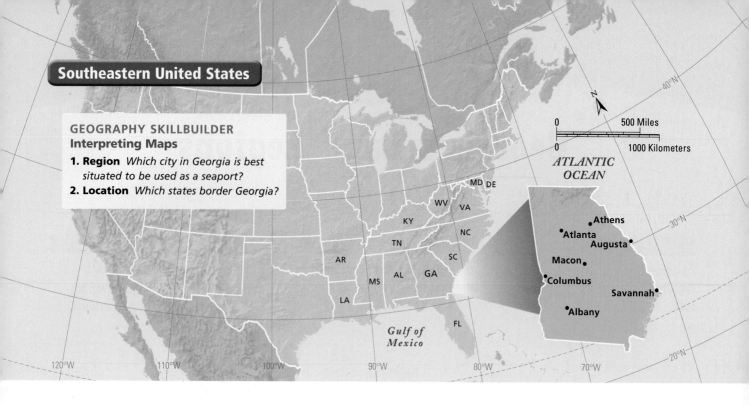

ATLANTIC OCEAN

Athens
Atlanta
Augusta
Macon
Columbus
Savannah
Albany

Gulf of Mexico

Georgia's Natural Regions

Georgia is the largest state east of the Mississippi River. At its widest points, Georgia is 318 miles north to south and 278 miles east to west. Because of its size, the climate, elevation, vegetation, soils, and terrain vary from one part of the state to another. Geographically, the state is divided into natural **regions**—areas in which the climate, elevation, terrain, soils, and vegetations are similar.

Georgia's natural regions are the Coastal Plain, the Piedmont, and the Appalachian Mountain region. The Coastal Plain is the largest natural region and includes about 60 percent of the state. It is further divided into the Inner Coastal Plain and the Outer Coastal Plain. The Piedmont is an area of gently rolling hills. The Appalachian Mountain region also includes smaller regions: the Blue Ridge Mountains in the northeast, the Ridge and Valley region in the northwest, and the Appalachian Plateau region in the northwestern corner of the state.

Outer Coastal Plain

The **Coastal Plain** is the southernmost geographic region in Georgia. It consists of the Outer Coastal Plain and the Inner Coastal Plain. The Outer Coastal Plain includes the Okefenokee Swamp, the marshes of Glynn, and the Golden Isles (the barrier islands). These barrier islands are especially important to Georgia's coast because they protect the coastal zone from the storms and waves of the Atlantic Ocean.

Thousands of years ago, the higher waters of the Atlantic covered the Coastal Plain. During that time, several rows of barrier islands topped with sand dunes ran along the coast. As the ocean waters receded and

Reading History

A. Summarizing Why are the barrier islands important to Georgia?

exposed more land, the barrier islands became low ridges. Between the ridges were broad belts of tidal marshes. These marshes and ridges are still evident.

Inner Coastal Plain

Most of Georgia's farmland is located in the Inner Coastal Plain. This region ranges from level land to gently sloping, well-drained sandy loam soil. Most of the farmers in this region irrigate their land to ensure adequate moisture for their crops. The combination of moisture and long days of warm sun make it one of the most productive farming regions in the nation.

The transition from the Outer Coastal Plain to the Inner Coastal Plain is gradual. The land rises steadily from the beaches and marshlands to a belt of hills known as the fall line.

The Fall Zone The fall line stretches across Georgia from Augusta in the northeast, through Macon and Milledgeville, to Columbus in the southwest. Perhaps **fall zone** is a more appropriate title for this region. The fall zone is several miles wide and marks the transition from the Coastal Plain to the Piedmont region.

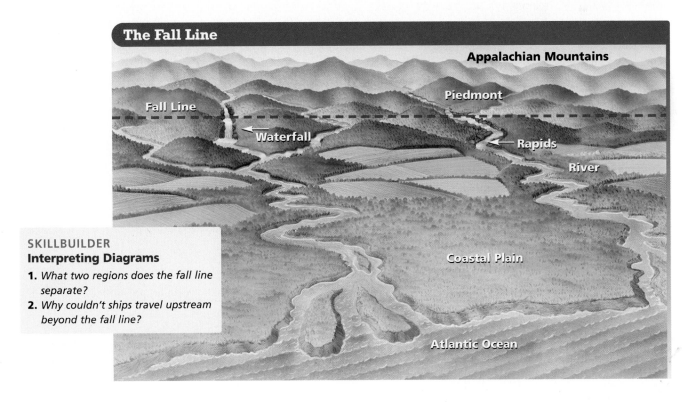

The Fall Line

Appalachian Mountains

Piedmont

Fall Line

Waterfall

Rapids

River

Coastal Plain

Atlantic Ocean

SKILLBUILDER
Interpreting Diagrams
1. *What two regions does the fall line separate?*
2. *Why couldn't ships travel upstream beyond the fall line?*

The land here has hills and valleys with steep slopes and little level land. Rivers flow over the hard, rocky granite beds of the higher elevation. The water drops down onto the lower elevations and softer sandstone and limestone rocks of the Coastal Plain. The water forms rapids or waterfalls. Northern Georgia has many waterfalls. The largest is Amicalola Falls in Dawson County.

The fall zone is the home of Georgia's most important mining operations. Long ago, the receding waters of the Atlantic Ocean left rich mineral deposits. Georgia has the world's largest deposit of kaolin, a clay used in many products such as paints, rubber, plastics, cement, detergents, and fertilizers. The largest and most important use for kaolin is in papermaking. Kaolin provides the material for the glossy coating of magazines and other slick-finished papers.

Reading History

B. Recognizing Effects What caused the rich mineral deposits in the fall zone?

The Piedmont

Piedmont means "at the foot of the mountains." The **Piedmont** is a rolling, hilly plateau at the base of the Appalachian Mountains. In this region, elevations range from about 600 feet above sea level near the fall zone to over 2,000 feet above sea level near the mountains. The Piedmont region not only divides the mountainous region from the coastal region, but it also divides the species of plants found in Georgia.

▼ The Piedmont is the beginning point, or source, for Georgia's large rivers.

Stone Mountain is one of the most prominent features of the Piedmont region. Stone Mountain is a large mass of granite formed from molten rock that pushed through the existing rock layers about 300 million years ago. About 15 million years ago, the surface material covering the Piedmont eroded. With the weight and pressure of the eroded material gone, the granite expanded upward into the domed shape that Stone Mountain has today. Quarrying was done at Stone Mountain in the 1800s. Some of the granite was used in the United States Capitol and in the locks of the Panama Canal.

Appalachian Mountains

The **Appalachian Mountain** region of Georgia is the highest and most rugged area of the state. The Appalachians stretch from Canada in the northeast to Alabama in the southwest.

The Blue Ridge Mountains are part of the Appalachian Mountain system and run through the northwest corner of the state.

The Blue Ridge Mountains were once higher than the Rockies, but erosion over millions of years has worn them down to about one-fourth of their original height. Fertile valleys are separated by rocky ridges. The highest point in Georgia is in this region. It is Brasstown Bald Mountain at 4,784 feet above sea level.

Many counties in this region have large areas of commercial forests. Other counties have marble quarries. In Pickens County, the marble industry is one of the largest employers.

The Appalachian Mountain region is a popular tourist spot. The Blue Ridge Mountain area is the beginning of the Appalachian Trail, a 2,100-mile hiking trail that ends in Maine. Fishermen and hunters enjoy the natural forests. Tourists enjoy the mountain village hotels and shops.

Fault Line   The Appalachian Mountain region features an interesting geologic formation—a fault line that sometimes results in earthquake activity. In March and April of 2003, earthquake tremors registered up to 4.6 on the Richter scale. The tremors were the result of activity of the Brevard Fault that runs along one of the ridges of the

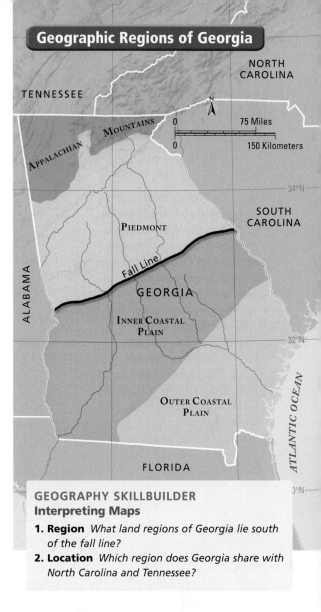

Geographic Regions of Georgia

GEOGRAPHY SKILLBUILDER
Interpreting Maps
1. **Region** What land regions of Georgia lie south of the fall line?
2. **Location** Which region does Georgia share with North Carolina and Tennessee?

Earthquakes

The East Coast's solid rock does not absorb shock waves as well as the West Coast's fractured rock. Earthquakes on the East Coast are felt over a much larger geographic area than in the West.

When a magnitude 7.0 earthquake struck Charleston, S.C. in 1886, its shock waves rocked Savannah's streets and buildings, cracked Tybee Island's 6-foot-thick lighthouse walls, and toppled nearly 1000 chimneys in Augusta.

mountain region. The ridge begins in the northeast corner of White County. The fault line follows the ridge toward Marietta and then runs westward close to highways I-20, I-575, and Georgia 515.

The Chattahoochee River flows through the Brevard Fault area. The rocks of the fault area are very fractured. These large fractured rocks often determine which way the Chattahoochee River is going to bend and turn. The broken rocks are also easy to excavate and are a good source of material for large construction projects.

Sidney Lanier was a Georgia poet who was born in Macon in 1842. He is perhaps best noted for his poems that describe some of the physical terrain of Georgia. In *The Marshes of Glynn*, he describes the woods and marshes of Georgia's southern coastal region. In *The Song of the Chattahoochee*, he depicts the rushing river's path through the hills and valleys of the Piedmont to the Coastal Plain.

The environment affects how people live. Geographic regions are part of the environment. In the next section, you will learn how the weather and climate in those regions also affect how we live.

Reading History

C. Recognizing Effects What makes the fault line a good source of material for construction projects?

Section 1 Assessment

1. TERMS & NAMES

Explain the significance of:

a. Sunbelt

b. region

c. Coastal Plain

d. fall zone

e. Piedmont

f. Appalachian Mountains

2. TAKING NOTES

Use a diagram like the one below to note the features of Georgia's three main geographic regions.

Regions	Features
Coastal Plain	
Piedmont	
Appalachian Mountains	

3. MAIN IDEAS

a. What are the three main regions of Georgia? How can the Appalachian Mountains and Coastal Plains be further divided?

b. Why are barrier islands important?

c. Why is the fall zone important to Georgia's economy?

4. CRITICAL THINKING

Analyzing Causes

Why is the Georgia Inner Coastal Plain one of the most productive farming regions in the country?

Think About
- the benefit of rich soil
- the benefit of a long growing season
- the impact of irrigation

ACTIVITY -OPTIONS-

Art/Language Arts Make a **collage** that illustrates the different geographic regions in Georgia, or write a **poem** that celebrates a geographic feature of Georgia.

Georgia's Weather and Climate

<table>
<tr><td>MAIN IDEA</td><td>WHY IT MATTERS NOW</td><td>TERMS & NAMES</td></tr>
<tr><td>Several factors influence Georgia's climate.</td><td>Weather and climate are important influences on the activities of Georgians.</td><td>weather
climate
tornadoes

hurricanes
ozone</td></tr>
</table>

SETTING THE STAGE

Weather is always in the news. When weather is severe or extremely unusual, it can become headline news. Weather affects our daily lives. From sunshine to tornadoes, the weather affects what we do, where we go, even what we wear. On a larger scale, our economic activities are affected by our climate. The warm days and long growing season of Georgia's moderate climate help farmers grow many crops. From prehistoric times to the present, people who have occupied the land now called Georgia have learned to use the climate to their advantage.

▲ Severe weather, such as hurricanes and tornadoes, is often headline news. But damage from acid rain and pollution can be just as devastating.

Influences on Weather and Climate

<u>Weather</u> is the condition and temperature of the atmosphere. Weather can change from day to day and season to season. When we describe a region, we talk about its climate. <u>Climate</u> is the average weather conditions over a long period.

Weather Georgia's weather is affected by winds that tend to blow from the west toward the east in winter. The air masses carried by these winds form fronts that can cause snow or rainstorms and sharp changes in temperature in short periods of time. In the summer months, warm, moist air masses from the Gulf of Mexico often influence Georgia's weather. Frequent thunderstorms form in the summer when the sun warms the land and the heated surface air rises. As the warm, moist air cools at higher altitudes, clouds form and heavy precipitation occurs along with thunder and lightning.

Climate Georgia is in the warm temperate subtropical zone. This zone has a year-round warm, moist climate with hot summers, and where most precipitation is in the form of rain. Winters are generally cool and can be cold depending on the elevation and latitude.

Taking Notes

Use your chart to take notes about Georgia's weather and climate.

<table>
<tr><td></td><td>Georgia's Land Regions</td><td>Georgia's Weather and Climate</td></tr>
<tr><td>Main Idea</td><td></td><td></td></tr>
<tr><td>Supporting Idea</td><td></td><td></td></tr>
</table>

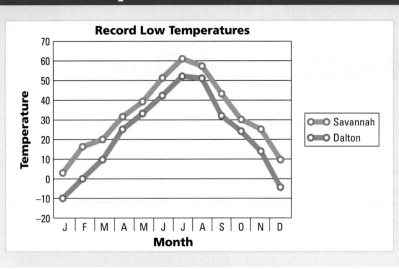

Record Low Temperatures

Savannah
Dalton

SKILLBUILDER
Interpreting Graphs

1. *Which city has the lower record low temperatures?*

2. *Using the temperatures in the table, which city do you think is located near the coast? Which is located inland?*

Different regions of Georgia have some differences in climate. The Outer Coastal Plain has a moist, warm climate because it is so close to the Atlantic Ocean. Oceans and other large bodies of water heat up and cool off much more gradually than landmasses. As a result, places near oceans tend to be warmer in winter and slightly cooler in summer.

Winter temperatures are lower in the Piedmont than in the Coastal Plain, because the Piedmont is at a higher elevation. Also, the Piedmont receives a bit less rainfall than the Coastal Plain because of its greater distance from the ocean. Georgia's northern mountains have frequent light snowfalls, but snow is rare in other parts of the state.

Georgia's warm temperate subtropical climate has played an important role in making agriculture a major economic activity throughout the state's history. Long growing seasons and adequate moisture in most years allow a wide variety of crops to be grown.

Reading History

A. Recognizing Effects How does the climate of Georgia affect the state's economy?

Dangerous Weather

Most of the time, Georgia's weather and climate provide comfortable conditions. Sometimes, however, severe weather can be dangerous.

Tornadoes Many Georgians are familiar with tornadoes. When warm, moist air rises rapidly and a front pushes under it, severe thunderstorms can result. **Tornadoes** occur when strong fast winds form funnel-shaped spirals. These winds move unpredictably across the land, causing devastating damage.

Hurricanes Another type of severe weather that sometimes occurs along Georgia's coast is the hurricane. **Hurricanes** are a much larger type of spiraling wind system that can cause great damage. Hurricanes form in the warm, moist air above the tropical waters of the southern Atlantic Ocean.

▲ A tornado struck the town of Camilla in February 2000, killing 11 and damaging 200 homes. Three years later, another tornado ripped a mile-wide swath of destruction.

Tornadoes and hurricanes are big news when they occur. However, there are other weather conditions that occur more frequently and are just as dangerous, even though they do not make the news.

Air Quality

Georgia, like other Sunbelt states, faces the problems that come with a warm climate and rapid population growth.

Unhealthy Air Pollution <u>Ozone</u> is a gas made up of three atoms of oxygen that form in the air when certain chemicals react with sunlight. Ozone in the upper levels of Earth's atmosphere is helpful, because it reduces the sun's harmful rays. At ground level, a high ozone level (usually seen as smog) is hazardous to human health and the environment. Several counties in the Atlanta area have levels of ozone that are higher than what the federal government considers safe.

In recent years, the metropolitan Atlanta area has posted air pollution alerts. These alerts warn people with breathing problems to stay indoors. They are also a reminder that people should drive their cars only if absolutely necessary. New data indicates that other cities in Georgia are suffering from increased air pollution also.

Monitoring Particulate Matter Particulate matter is solid matter or liquid droplets from smoke, dust, ash, or condensing vapors that

Reading History

B. Compare and Contrast Under what conditions is ozone helpful or harmful?

can be suspended in the air for long amounts of time. Particulates can come from wood burning stoves, power plants, diesel engines, cars and trucks, as well as industrial sources. Too much particulate matter results in haze over a region that can reduce visibility and make the air appear dirty. Long periods of increased particulate matter can result in heart, lung, and respiratory problems.

Reading History

C. Recognizing Effects Besides vehicle emissions, what sources contribute to particulate matter in the air?

Cleaning the Air Cars and light trucks are one of the main contributors to the ozone problem. In the 1990s, Georgia supported the Federal Clean Air Act. One goal of this act is to identify the vehicles that cause the most pollution and have them fixed. Many counties require a vehicle emissions test to determine which vehicles are giving off too many harmful particles. The emissions problems have to be corrected before license plates are issued.

Georgians may soon need to make decisions about lifestyle and about regulations to govern air quality. In the next section, you will learn about another immediate problem with long-term consequences that Georgians face—a shortage of clean water.

▲ Cars and light trucks create smog over Atlanta and other urban areas in Georgia.

Section 2 Assessment

1. TERMS & NAMES

Explain the significance of:

a. weather

b. climate

c. tornadoes

d. hurricanes

e. ozone

2. TAKING NOTES

Use a cluster diagram like the one below to take notes on dangerous weather patterns that occur in Georgia.

Georgia Weather

3. MAIN IDEAS

a. What is the difference between weather and climate?

b. How does Georgia's climate contribute to its economy?

c. How do tornadoes form? How do hurricanes form?

d. What is one step many counties in Georgia have taken to help clean the air?

4. CRITICAL THINKING

Making Decisions

How does air pollution negatively affect life in Georgia?

Think About
- the effect on people
- the effect on plants
- the effect on animals

Art/Math Draw a **diagram** that shows how a thunderstorm can develop, or create a **chart** of the average monthly temperatures for the past year in your town.

Georgia's Water Supply

MAIN IDEA	WHY IT MATTERS NOW	TERMS & NAMES
Water is an important resource.	A growing population in Georgia puts demands on the state's water supply.	aquifers hazardous wastes

SETTING THE STAGE

Twenty or thirty years ago, Georgians could bathe, water lawns, wash cars, fill swimming pools, and irrigate large fields with little thought to the water supply. As the population has grown, present-day Georgians are faced with a very real concern: Will there be enough clean water to meet our needs?

Our Fresh Water Supply

As Georgia's population increases, concern for its fresh water supply grows. Georgia has many rivers and artificial lakes. In most years, there is adequate rainfall. Keeping our water clean and conserving the water supply have become important topics to all Georgians.

In an average year, most of Georgia receives about 50 inches of rainfall. Plants take up much of this water. Some of the water seeps deeper into the ground. The water that seeps down into the ground goes to underground layers of rocks and gravel called __aquifers__. Aquifers are important because they supply the ground water used by farmers and manufacturers. In some areas, though, sewage, excess fertilizers, and __hazardous wastes__ have polluted water supplies and caused serious problems. Another problem occurs in some low-lying areas where swampland has been drained. The rainwater runs quickly off the land rather than seeping into the soil to replenish ground water supplies.

Rivers and Lakes

All of Georgia's rivers are formed either within the state or along its boundaries. No river flows into Georgia from another state. Georgia's largest rivers are the Altamaha, the Chattahoochee, the Flint, and the Savannah. Dams have been built on many of the rivers to generate hydroelectric power. The waterpower at these dams provides energy for the people who live in those areas. The lakes provide recreation.

▲ Restrictions on water usage may cause changes in our daily lives.

Taking Notes

Use your chart to take notes about demands on Georgia's water supply.

	Georgia's Land Regions	Georgia's Weather and Climate
Main Idea		
Supporting Idea		

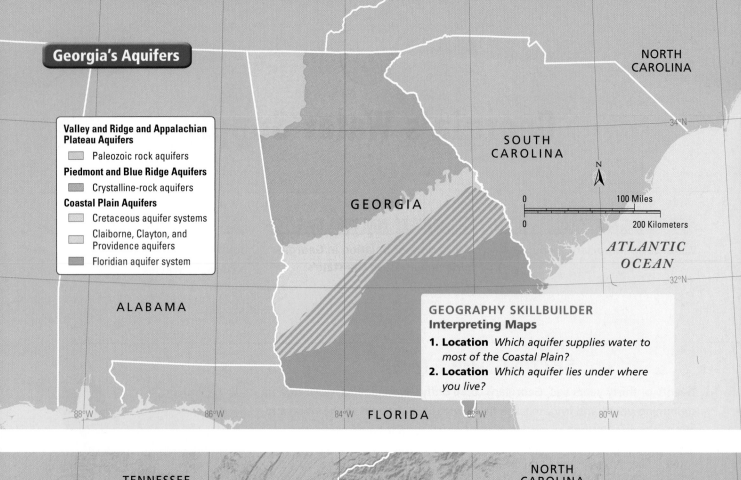

Georgia's Aquifers

Valley and Ridge and Appalachian Plateau Aquifers
  Paleozoic rock aquifers
Piedmont and Blue Ridge Aquifers
  Crystalline-rock aquifers
Coastal Plain Aquifers
  Cretaceous aquifer systems
  Claiborne, Clayton, and Providence aquifers
  Floridian aquifer system

NORTH CAROLINA

SOUTH CAROLINA

GEORGIA

ALABAMA

FLORIDA

ATLANTIC OCEAN

GEOGRAPHY SKILLBUILDER
Interpreting Maps
1. **Location** Which aquifer supplies water to most of the Coastal Plain?
2. **Location** Which aquifer lies under where you live?

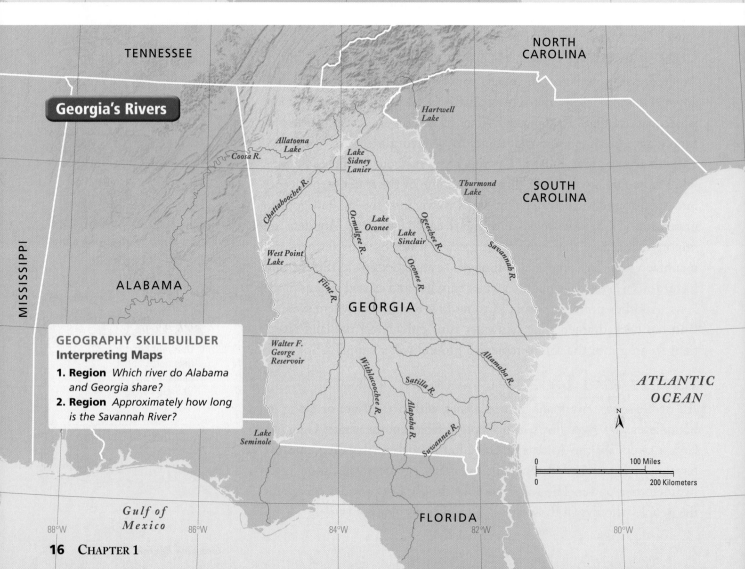

Georgia's Rivers

TENNESSEE

NORTH CAROLINA

MISSISSIPPI

ALABAMA

SOUTH CAROLINA

GEORGIA

ATLANTIC OCEAN

FLORIDA

Gulf of Mexico

Hartwell Lake
Allatoona Lake
Coosa R.
Lake Sidney Lanier
Thurmond Lake
Chattahoochee R.
Ocmulgee R.
Lake Oconee
Ogeechee R.
Lake Sinclair
Savannah R.
West Point Lake
Oconee R.
Flint R.
Walter F. George Reservoir
Altamaha R.
Withlacoochee R.
Satilla R.
Alapaha R.
Suwannee R.
Lake Seminole

GEOGRAPHY SKILLBUILDER
Interpreting Maps
1. **Region** Which river do Alabama and Georgia share?
2. **Region** Approximately how long is the Savannah River?

Reading History

A. Analyzing Points of View
Why do Georgia farmers believe they shouldn't have to restrict their water usage?

In recent years, Georgia has become involved in a "water war" with Florida and Alabama. Florida and Alabama are charging that Georgia is taking too much water from rivers that the states share.

Within Georgia, there is disagreement about who should get most of the water. Metropolitan Atlanta is growing so fast that builders there say that more water should be made available for the personal consumption of the many people moving to Atlanta. In rural Georgia, farmers say that they have to use water to irrigate crops to produce food to feed people. They believe that more water should be reserved for agricultural uses.

The water issue has been a critical one for several years and will continue to be for many more. We will need new solutions to ensure enough water for all our needs.

Guarding Our Water Supply

The United States Geological Survey program helps Georgia's political and economic leaders make informed decisions about our water supply. In recent decades, severe strains have been put on the resources of Georgia's rivers and lakes. Leaders will need to make decisions as to whether or not to pump water from underground aquifers in certain areas. In the metropolitan areas, citizens have become accustomed to temporary water restrictions. Those water restrictions may become permanent if we cannot find ways to protect our current water resources.

Section 3 Assessment

1. TERMS & NAMES

Explain the significance of:

a. aquifers

b. hazardous wastes

2. TAKING NOTES

Use a diagram like the one below to identify the threats to Georgia's fresh water supply.

Threats to Fresh Water Supply

3. MAIN IDEAS

a. What is the connection between a growing population and the water supply?

b. Why are aquifers important to Georgia?

c. How do artificial lakes help the people of Georgia?

4. CRITICAL THINKING

Making Decisions

What kinds of changes will Georgians need to make in order to conserve the supply of clean water?

Think About
- how water is used now
- how water will be needed in the future
- what pollutes the water

ACTIVITY -OPTIONS-

Science/Language Arts Create a cross-section **diagram** of one of the aquifer systems in Georgia or write a **news article** about water issues facing Georgians today.

VISUAL SUMMARY

The Land Regions of Georgia

OUTER COASTAL PLAIN
A part of the southernmost region in Georgia, this area includes the Okefenokee Swamp, the marshes of Glynn, and the Golden Isles barrier islands.

INNER COASTAL PLAIN
Moisture and warm sun make this region one of the most productive farming regions in the United States.

THE PIEDMONT
This rolling, hilly region sits "at the foot of the mountains"—the Appalachian Mountains. Elevations here range from 600 to 2,000 feet above sea level.

APPALACHIAN MOUNTAINS
This mountainous region is the highest and most rugged area of the state. The area supports commercial forests and marble quarries.

TERMS & NAMES

Briefly explain the significance of the following.

1. Sunbelt
2. region
3. Coastal Plain
4. Piedmont
5. Appalachian Mountains
6. fall zone
7. weather
8. climate
9. aquifers
10. hazardous wastes

REVIEW QUESTIONS

Georgia's Land Regions (pages 5–10)

1. Which states border Georgia?
2. What is the largest natural region in Georgia?
3. Which region in Georgia is one of the most productive farming regions in the country?
4. Which region in Georgia is the most popular for tourism?

Georgia's Weather and Climate (pages 11–14)

5. What factors affect the climate in Georgia?
6. What affect has the climate had on the state's economy?
7. What types of severe weather affect Georgia?

Georgia's Water Supply (pages 15–17)

8. Why are aquifers important to Georgia's water supply?
9. What are the names of Georgia's four largest rivers?
10. What is the cause of Georgia's "water war" with Florida and Alabama?

CRITICAL THINKING

1. USING YOUR NOTES: FINDING MAIN IDEAS

	Georgia's Land Regions	Georgia's Weather and Climate	Georgia's Water Supply
Main Idea			
Supporting Idea			
Supporting Idea			
Supporting Idea			
Supporting Idea			

Using your completed chart, answer the questions.

a. What is the main idea of the section titled "Georgia's Land Regions"?
b. What points support the idea that concern for Georgia's fresh water supply is growing?

2. ANALYZING LEADERSHIP

What role do Georgia's political and economic leaders play in the future of Georgia's water supply?

3. APPLYING CITIZENSHIP SKILLS

How can citizens play a role in improving air quality in Georgia?

4. THEME: CITIZENSHIP

What steps can you as a citizen of Georgia take to address environmental issues in your state?

5. COMPARING AND CONTRASTING

Compare and contrast the regions of Georgia. How do they differ?

INTERACT with HISTORY

Based on your interests and likes, which Georgia region would you choose for your future home?

Use the map and your knowledge of Georgia aquifers to answer questions 1 through 3.

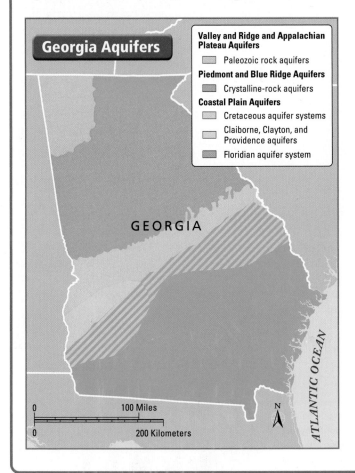

Georgia Aquifers

Valley and Ridge and Appalachian Plateau Aquifers
☐ Paleozoic rock aquifers

Piedmont and Blue Ridge Aquifers
☐ Crystalline-rock aquifers

Coastal Plain Aquifers
☐ Cretaceous aquifer systems
☐ Claiborne, Clayton, and Providence aquifers
☐ Floridian aquifer system

GEORGIA

ATLANTIC OCEAN

0 ——— 100 Miles

0 ——— 200 Kilometers

N

1. The Paleozoic rock aquifer supplies which areas of the state?

   A. Valley and Ridge and Appalachian Plateaus
   B. Piedmont and Blue Ridge
   C. Inner Coastal Plain
   D. Outer Coastal Plain

2. Which aquifer system supports the largest part of the Coastal Plain area?

   A. Crystalline-rock aquifers
   B. Paleozoic rock aquifer
   C. Floridian aquifer system
   D. Cretaceous aquifer systems

3. What aquifer systems lie above the Claiborne, Clayton, and Providence aquifers?

   A. Crystalline-rock
   B. Cretaceous
   C. Floridian
   D. Paleozoic

TEST PRACTICE
CLASSZONE.COM

ALTERNATIVE ASSESSMENT

1. CREATE A BROCHURE

Georgia has many beautiful regions that attract visitors to the state. Choose one region, and create a brochure to encourage travel and tourism. Research attractions in your region. Then develop text, graphics, and photos to complete your package.

2. COOPERATIVE LEARNING

Participate in a debate about Georgia's water war. You may debate for Georgia, or for Florida and Alabama. Research the issues, and develop persuasive arguments to support your position.

INTEGRATED TECHNOLOGY ACTIVITY

CREATE A DATABASE

Research the climate, elevation, vegetation, and industries of each of the regions of the state. Compile the information you find in a database. For each region, use the following categories.

- Average temperature
- Average rainfall
- Average elevation
- Common vegetation
- Industries

RESEARCH LINKS
CLASSZONE.COM

The First People of North America

10,000 B.C.– A.D. 1500

Archaeologists work carefully to remove bones from surrounding dirt and rock without damaging them.

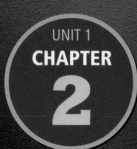

10,000 B.C.
Paleo-Indians may have passed through Georgia.

10,000–8000 B.C.
Archiac Indians settle in Georgia.

6000 B.C.
Archaic Indians develop the atlatl, a spear throwing device.

GEORGIA USA

| 10,000 B.C. | 8000 B.C. | 6000 B.C. | 4000 B.C. |

10,000 B.C.
The last Ice Age ends.

7000 B.C.
Agriculture develops in Mexico.

4000 B.C.
Archaic Indians begin making stone axes.

You are an archaeologist working in central Georgia, excavating a prehistoric town, possibly of the Woodland period. You and your staff have uncovered two fragments of large storage pots within a structure that had been surrounded by fence posts. It appears to be a food storage shed. You will be writing up your results at the end of the dig.

What can you learn about prehistoric cultures?

WHAT DO YOU THINK?

- How would farming affect the lives of a nomadic people?

- How would the ability to store food change daily life?

For more information on this chapter, visit . . .

RESEARCH LINKS
CLASSZONE.COM

1000 B.C.–A.D. 800
Woodland Indians build structures such as the Kolomoki Mounds in Georgia.

A.D. 100–1000
Ancestors of the Creek Indians migrate to the Chattahoochee River Valley.

| 2000 B.C. | 0 | 2000 A.D. |

100 B.C.
People settle in the deserts of the American Southwest.

A.D. 1492
Columbus arrives in the Americas.

Reading Strategy: Categorizing

What Do You Know?

What do you know about the history of the earliest people in America? How advanced must a society be to develop pottery, art, and tools like the one to the right?

THINK ABOUT

• what you know about Native American cultures
• books you've read and pictures you've seen

What Do You Want to Know?

What questions do you have about the earliest inhabitants of what is now Georgia? What would you like to know about how they lived and what they believed? Record those questions in your notebook before you read the chapter.

Categorizing

Categorizing information as you read can help you identify and understand patterns and developments in historic events. When you categorize, you sort people, objects, ideas, or other information into groups. What information can you record in these categories as you read about the earliest people in America?

 See Skillbuilder Handbook, page 550.

Taking Notes

	Lifestyle	Technology	Food	Trade	Religion
Paleo-Indian Period					
Archaic Period					
Woodland Period					
Mississippian Culture					
Creek					
Cherokee					

The First People in America

Ancient peoples came from Asia to the Americas and over time developed complex civilizations.

Knowledge of early cultures helps us to understand how societies develop and become successful.

archaeologist
artifact
prehistoric
culture

Paleo-Indians
Archaic Indians
Woodland Indians

SETTING THE STAGE

Many scientists think that ancient peoples crossed a land bridge that joined Asia and North America during the last Ice Age, about 12,000 years ago. The Ice Ages were a time of extreme cold that lasted for thousands of years. Glaciers, or huge masses of ice, trapped so much water that ocean levels dropped. When this happened, a bridge of land, now called Beringia, appeared where the Bering Strait is now. Many scientists believe that the earliest Americans crossed this bridge from Asia to the Americas 12,000 years ago. Other scientists believe humans came to the Americas much earlier and by other routes, including by boat.

What do we know of ancient Americans? How did we get the information? How did ancient Americans survive? What happened to them?

▲ Beringia appeared when water levels dropped. When Earth warmed, the glaciers melted and flooded Beringia.

Prehistoric Cultures

Archaeologists are scientists who study **artifacts.** Artifacts are objects from the past that contribute to our understanding of prehistoric cultures. **Prehistoric** means the time before written history. A **culture** is a way of life shared by people with similar arts, beliefs, and customs. It is impossible to know exactly how many years ago a prehistoric culture existed. In fact, scientists themselves disagree about the dates of prehistoric cultures.

Scientists do agree, however, on the order of prehistoric cultures in North America. They also generally agree on the characteristics of these cultures. Three significant archaeological museums in Georgia help us

Taking Notes

Use your chart to note characteristics of earliest American peoples.

	Lifestyle	Technology
Paleo-Indian Period		

◀ Paleo-Indians used spears made by attaching a stone tip to a wooden stick to hunt large game animals.

learn about early cultures. They are the Ocmulgee National Monument at Macon, the Etowah Mounds Archaeological Area at Cartersville, and Kolomoki State Park near Blakely.

The Paleo-Indian Period

The earliest known inhabitants of North America lived during the **Paleo-Indian** period. This period was approximately 10,000 years ago, when glaciers of the Ice Age started melting. The Paleo-Indians adapted well to climates that were wetter and cooler than today's. Archaeologists believe that Paleo-Indians hunted animals that are now extinct or absent from the East Coast. These included big game animals such as woolly mammoths, large bison, wild horses, moose, and elk. Paleo-Indians used these animals for food, clothing, and tools. In order to track these large animals, the Paleo-Indians lived nomadic lives. That is, they moved from place to place, following the animal herds.

Hunters used spears made by attaching a stone tip to a wooden stick. In addition to hunting large game, the Paleo-Indians probably gathered wild plant foods and fished when they were close to water.

The extinction of large game animals brought an end to the Paleo-Indian way of life. Herds of the largest game animals dwindled as ice sheets melted away. Scientists have not found any settlements in Georgia from the Paleo-Indian period. However, a spear point known as a "Clovis" point from this period was found on the Ocmulgee site. Because the Paleo-Indians were nomads, there is no evidence of any long-term settlements. But the spear point indicates that they probably passed through Georgia.

Vocabulary

paleo: early or primitive. Paleo-Indians lived during the Pleistocene era

Reading History

A. Drawing Conclusions
Why didn't Paleo-Indians establish villages?

The Archaic Period

Around 8000 B.C., Earth's climate was warmer. The big game animals disappeared. Forests replaced the open land of the Ice Ages.

Vocabulary

archaic: surviving from an earlier period. It is the period from 8000 B.C. to 1000 B.C. in North America

The descendants of the Paleo-Indians are called the **Archaic Indians.** Most scientists estimate that they occupied eastern North America from about 8000 B.C. to around 1000 B.C. Scientists believe that they were the first culture of Georgia.

Archaic Indians developed improved techniques for fishing, gathering, and hunting in changing environments. They used a wide variety of small, crudely fashioned spear points. They also ground tools from stone, including stone axes. These tools show that the people of this era had begun to hunt small animals and grow some crops. Other artifacts show that the people of the Archaic culture lived under rock shelters or in pithouses. These were circular or rectangular structures built of clay and logs with rooms entirely or partially underground.

▼ The ax was invented during the Archaic period. It was used to chop trees into firewood and construct homes.

During this period, cultures began to stay in one spot, establish villages, and trade with one another. Artifacts suggest that the people of this culture in Georgia carved large bowls out of soapstone boulders. They traded the bowls to people in other regions for tools and utensils.

The Archaic people did not have three things: bows and arrows, well-developed pottery, and plant agriculture (or farming). The people of the next period developed these three elements.

The Woodland Period

The period that followed the Archaic period is known as the Woodland period. The rise of the Woodland culture began after 1000 B.C. and continued to about A.D. 800. The **Woodland Indians** also developed agriculture, or farming. They began to clear fields and plant and harvest crops like sunflowers, squash, gourds, beans, and maize, an early type of corn. Farming produced more than enough food for one season, so the people could store excess food for winter and early spring months.

Reading History

B. Making Inferences What kinds of activities could develop once food production became less time consuming?

Hunting   To hunt more effectively, the Woodland Indians developed bows and arrows. Bows and arrows were highly effective weapons. With them, a single hunter could bring down game animals such as white tail deer.

Settlements   Native Americans of the Woodland period built villages along stream valleys, where the soil was soft and moist. The people could use hoes and sticks to dig holes and plant seeds. Evidence suggests that the Woodland Indians built protective walls around their villages and storage facilities. Patterns on pottery fragments suggest

▲ The Rock Eagle effigy in Eatonton is made of white quartzite rock and has a wingspan of 100 feet.

that the people of the Woodland period had begun to develop differences from one area to another.

Mounds Some of the best-known structures left by the Woodland Indians are large mounds of earth. The mounds contain skeletons and elaborate grave articles, such as pottery, jewelry, and beads, which were buried with the dead. Woodland Indians built several mounds in what is now Georgia. The Kolomoki Mounds near Blakely are a group of ceremonial burial mounds. Another significant structure from this period is the Rock Eagle stone effigy in Putnam County.

In the 1500s, most of the early Native American groups who first met European explorers were Woodland Indians. However, archaeologists believe that some Native Americans from the period were from a later prehistoric culture—the Mississippians. You will read about this culture in the next section.

Reading History

C. Summarizing
What was the purpose of mounds?

Section 1 Assessment

1. TERMS & NAMES

Explain the significance of:

a. archaeologist

b. artifact

c. prehistoric

d. culture

e. Paleo-Indians

f. Archaic Indians

g. Woodland Indians

2. TAKING NOTES

Use a diagram like the one below to compare the characteristics of the three cultures discussed in this section.

	Paleo-Indians	Archaic Indians	Woodland Indians
Food Source			
Settlements			
Artifacts Left Behind			

3. MAIN IDEAS

a. What are the disagreements about how and when prehistoric cultures lived?

b. How did early cultures use the environment for survival?

c. Why is there little evidence of Paleo-Indian settlement?

4. CRITICAL THINKING

Making Inferences

What does the presence of burial mounds suggest about a culture?

Think About
• the contents of the mounds
• possible purposes of the mounds
• where and how the mound builders lived

ACTIVITY -OPTIONS-

Art/Language Arts Research the Swift Creek pottery designs of the Woodland period. Create your own Swift Creek **design** or write a **paragraph** about how pottery was marked with the designs.

The Development of the Mississippian Culture

MAIN IDEA

When Europeans arrived, complex cultures occupied the land that became the United States.

WHY IT MATTERS NOW

The impact of early cultures is still present in Georgia today.

TERMS & NAMES

Mississippian culture
civilization
hierarchy
anthropologist

SETTING THE STAGE

By the time Europeans arrived, they found well-established Native American cultures. The people had become master farmers and had developed large towns with well-defined political and religious structures. They lived in small villages and grew crops of maize, tobacco, beans, and squash. They hunted and fished, and gathered nuts and berries.

The Mississippian culture began along the Ohio and Mississippi River valleys, but stretched from Georgia north to Minnesota, and west into the Great Plains.

What allowed this culture to develop? What resources were available to them that allowed them to be successful? What artifacts did they leave behind that let us know about their culture?

▲ A shortened pyramid at the Ocmulgee Site near Macon reveals a connection to Mexican and Guatemalan cultures.

Improved Agriculture

The period that followed the Woodland period is characterized by important advancements in agriculture. The **Mississippian culture** began along the Mississippi and Ohio Rivers. Mississippian sites in Georgia are located along the Ocmulgee, Savannah, Chattahoochee, and Coosa Rivers. These fertile growing conditions allowed them to produce a new kind of corn from Mexico. The new corn needed a shorter growing season and could grow in places farther north.

The Mississippian people grew another important crop from Mexico—beans. Beans added protein to the diet. As a source of protein, beans were much easier to obtain than animals. Beans could also feed more people over a longer period of time. Now there were three main staples—corn, squash, and beans. These three contained the important nutrients for a healthy diet.

Taking Notes

Use your chart to note characteristics of the Mississippian culture.

	Lifestyle	Technology
Paleo-Indian Period		

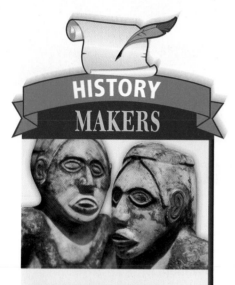
THE ETOWAH INDIANS
The Etowah Indian Mounds give us a glimpse into the lives of Native Americans who thrived from about A.D. 900 to A.D. 1500. They traded widely, as seen by the Florida shells, Tennessee flint, North Georgia copper, and Mississippi River clay.

The Etowah people fished, and they hunted turkey, deer, and other game as far away as the Piedmont area. From their trash pits we learn that they used river cane and corn husks to make mats, baskets, and arrow shafts.

The Etowah people appreciated art, as we see from the remains of jewelry, masks, and handicrafts fashioned from bones, clay, wood, copper, stones, and shells. They honored their dead with carved marble figures.

A More Complex Culture

The improvements in agriculture, which produced a sufficient and reliable source of food, enabled the Mississippians to develop civilizations, which earlier cultures had not. The people of the Mississippian period kept many of the practices of the Woodland culture, such as agriculture and the bow and arrow.

They also developed new social, political, and religious structures that made their culture different. The Mississippian culture demonstrated all of the features that characterize a **civilization**:

1. cities that are centers of trade
2. specialized jobs for different people
3. organized forms of government and religion
4. a system of record keeping
5. advanced tools

Temple Mounds Mississippian culture had true towns—social, political, and economic activity centers. Most Mississippian towns had temple mounds. These were earthen mounds with ramps leading up the side. Towns had from 1 to 20 flat-topped temple mounds with ceremonial buildings or other public structures built on top. Wooden palisades or earthen moats often surrounded the towns. Homes were located both inside and outside the stockade walls.

The flat-topped pyramids of the Mississippian culture are also found in Mexico and Guatemala. These pyramids, along with the introduction of corn and beans, indicate that there was contact between Mexico, Guatemala, and Mississippian cultures in North America.

Mississippian Societies European explorers described Mississippian societies as organized into social **hierarchies,** or levels of importance. The person at the top level might be determined by heredity or by bravery in wars. The Mississippian culture used war to gain and defend territories.

Shell carving was also an important part of the Mississippian culture. Common designs engraved on shells included a sunburst, an elaborate cross, a human eye in the palm of an open hand, arrows, a weeping eye, and some abstract designs. These designs also appeared on wood, carved stone, painted fabrics, and copper sheets. The designs provide a record of some of the beliefs and practices of the culture.

Mississippian artifacts include stone axes, bowls, and pipes. Pottery incorporated new ideas, such as pots shaped like human or animal heads, long-necked water jugs, round-bottomed pots, and other forms suggesting Mexican influence. Later sites include painted pottery artifacts.

The End of the Mississippian Culture

The Mississippian culture was the one that the first Europeans met when they set foot in North America. It was also the first to be devastated by diseases brought by the Europeans.

However, artifacts of the period suggest that entire towns were uninhabited as early as 1540. Archaeological records do not provide the answers as to why Mississippian sites were abandoned. The Ocmulgee site near Macon was abandoned within 200 years of its settling. Some scholars suggest that Mississippian towns became overcrowded. Others suggest that rulers lost their power over the tightly organized societies.

Anthropologists have provided some of the most recent evidence on the disappearance of whole towns. **Anthropologists** study the science of human beings through their physical characteristics, culture, and environment. Their study of human bones at Mississippian sites has found evidence of tuberculosis and other diseases. Tuberculosis is a disease that spreads rapidly in crowded conditions. Other possible diseases are those caused by intestinal parasites from poor sanitary conditions.

In the next section, you will learn about the cultures that descended from the Mississippian culture.

Reading History

A. Recognizing Effects How would overcrowding in a town lead to a decrease in population?

Section 2 Assessment

1. TERMS & NAMES

Explain the significance of:

a. Mississippian culture

b. civilization

c. hierarchy

d. anthropologist

2. TAKING NOTES

Use a diagram like the one below to identify the five characteristics of a civilization.

Civilization

3. MAIN IDEAS

a. How did beans and corn allow the Mississippian culture to flourish?

b. What evidence do we have that Mississippian cultures had contact with Mexico and Guatemala?

c. Why were the rich river valleys important to the Mississippian culture?

4. CRITICAL THINKING

Drawing Conclusions

Why would a civilization need to develop agriculture before it could develop a civilization?

Think About

• how the five features of a civilization would depend on a stable food supply

Science/Language Arts Research the growing of corn. Draw a **diagram** of a corn plant with its parts labeled or write a **description** of how corn grows.

Creek, Cherokee, and Seminole

MAIN IDEA	WHY IT MATTERS NOW	TERMS & NAMES
The Creek culture was the dominant culture when Europeans arrived in what is now Georgia.	Remnants of the Creek culture remain in Georgia today, especially in place names.	confederacy matrilineal Creek Cherokee Confederacy Seminole clan

SETTING THE STAGE

Diseases or other factors caused the Mississippian culture to weaken and eventually decline. Those who survived from the Mississippian culture banded together and created new cultures. These cultures were present when written history began. They kept many of the traditions and practices of the Mississippian culture, including town and home building practices, some political, social, and religious ceremonies, language, farming, and family systems.

All of the southeastern Indian tribes—the Creek, Cherokee, Seminole, Choctaw, and Chickasaw—descended from the Mississippian culture. They are known as the Five Civilized Tribes. The Creek were the dominant culture in early Georgia. Their territory included most of present-day Georgia. The Cherokee moved south into Georgia in the early 1700s. What were their cultures like? How would their cultures deal with Europeans as they arrived?

▲ Tchow-Ee-Put-O-Kaw, a Creek Indian woman painted by George Catlin.

From Mississippian to Creek

Ancestors of the Creek Indians migrated from the Mississippi Valley into the Chattahoochee Valley around A.D. 100–1000. They came from the northern Mississippian territories and moved into the Carolinas, eastern Tennessee, and northern Georgia in the mid-1400s.

There are no written records to tell exactly how these tribes and cultures developed. However, the first European explorers recorded how they lived. Based on pottery and other artifacts, the social groups of Georgia in the 1500s belonged to the same Mississippian culture. Most of these native tribes, including the group that became the Creek, spoke the Muskhogean language.

The Creek were more than a tribe. They were a group of several Mississippian chiefdoms that had banded together to form a **confederacy**. The **Creek Confederacy** became the largest group in the Southeast. They originally occupied most of what is now Georgia.

Taking Notes

Use your chart to note characteristics of the Native American cultures in Georgia.

	Lifestyle	Technology
Paleo-Indian Period		

Creek Culture

According to European records, 7,000 to 8,000 Creek lived in 50 to 80 towns. The towns were divided into two groups: the Lower Creek and the Upper Creek. There were about twice as many Upper Creek as Lower Creek.

The name "Creek" comes from the English. Some Indians lived at the headwaters of the Ocmulgee River, which was called the Ochese Creek during the 1600s. English traders called them the Ochese Creek Indians. After a time, they dropped "Ochese" and simply called the Indians the Creek.

Creek Towns Every major Creek town had a center for ceremonial and political functions. Buildings with open fronts surrounded a large open rectangular space. In warm months, the town leaders held important functions there. In cold months, Creek leaders met in a community house nearby that contained the ceremonial fire. This building was called a *chakofa*. It could accommodate up to 500 people.

Most Creek lived in large family compounds near the square grounds or spread out along a stream or river. The compounds had clusters of gardens, large fields, and several buildings.

A family, which included all members of the same clan, owned each compound. A **clan** is a group of people with a common ancestor. Clan members were required to help each other in time of need and to defend each other when threatened.

The Creek were a **matrilineal** society, meaning that ancestry was traced through the mother's family. After marriage, a young man moved into the compound of his wife's family. Children belonged to their mother's clan and were not considered related to their father's clan.

Creek Government Creek towns were actually groups of small farming communities inhabited by groups of clan relatives. A chief governed each town. The position of chief was usually inherited and always held by a member of a specific clan. A group of elders made up

Reading History

A. Analyzing
How did Creek culture demonstrate the five characteristics of a civilization?

Background

Creek clans included the Wind clan, the Bird clan, the Alligator clan, and the Bear clan.

GEOGRAPHY SKILLBUILDER
Interpreting Maps

1. **Location** Which Native American tribe in what is now Georgia was located farthest south?
2. **Location** What tribes are located west of the Creek?

Early Native Americans of the Southeast

The Upper Creek lived along the Coosa, Tallapoosa, and Alabama Rivers.

The Lower Creek lived primarily along the Chattahoochee and Flint Rivers.

31

a town council. This council assisted the chief in his official duties and in making decisions for the town.

Creek Religion   Religion was important to the Creek. The Green Corn ceremony was the most significant festival in the year. In late summer, the Creek gave thanks for the new corn crop, honored the renewal of life, and retold the history and laws of the town.

An important event of the festival involved extinguishing the old council fire and lighting a new fire. The women of the tribe would start new fires in their homes with coals from the new ceremonial fire. Then the feasting would begin. The two elements of the ceremony—fire and corn—celebrated life, health, happiness, friendship, and kinship.

▲ Cherokee dancers perform at the Chehaw National Indian Festival held annually at Chehaw Park in Albany, Georgia.

The Cherokee

The **Cherokee** were the second largest group of Native Americans in early Georgia. However, they did not arrive in any large numbers until the 1700s. They migrated from western North Carolina and occupied the northwest portion of Georgia.

Cherokee culture was similar to Creek culture because both tribes were descended from the Mississippians. Their towns and buildings were alike. Children belonged to the mother's clan. They both practiced the Green Corn ceremony.

Maintaining Balance   The Cherokee believed that maintaining harmony and order would keep the world balanced. If they did not maintain balance, droughts, storms, disease, or other disasters might destroy their crops or villages.

The Cherokee practiced many of the same rituals as the Creek during the Green Corn ceremony, with perhaps a greater focus on harmony. The villagers cleaned their houses, as well as the council house. They threw away broken items. They dissolved any unhappy marriages and forgave any old wrongs except murder. They began the year with a clean slate, believing that order had been restored.

Women were responsible for farming and furnishing the house. They were good farmers and made benches, baskets, pottery, and clothing. Men were responsible for hunting. The most important game animal to the Cherokee was the deer. The people ate the deer's meat, wore the skins, and made tools and ornaments from bones and antlers. They used ligaments for thread and hooves for glue. They tried not to waste anything, and they did not kill more than they needed.

Cherokee Government Cherokee government differed from the Creek government. The Cherokee did not have a chief or national council until the 1700s. Town council meetings were run democratically, and people debated an issue until they reached an agreement. Women and men were allowed to voice their opinions.

The most important question debated at council meetings was whether to go to war. Cherokee did not fight for territory, only to pay back enemies who had killed Cherokee.

The Seminole

Various other tribes that descended from the Mississippian culture lived in the area that became Florida. A small number of them lived in what became Georgia territory. Just like the Creek, they spoke the Muskhogean language, and they had many of the cultural practices of the Creek, but the Europeans gave them a different name—**Seminole**. The name came from their word *yat'siminoli* meaning "free people." The Seminole culture was very similar to that of the Creek.

The arrival of Europeans changed everything for Native Americans. You will read about that in the next chapter.

▲ This painting is of the Seminole hero Osceola Nick-A-No-Chee, as a boy. He later led his people in the Seminole Wars in the 1830s.

Section ❸ Assessment

1. TERMS & NAMES
Explain the significance of:

a. confederacy

b. Creek Confederacy

c. clan

d. matrilineal

e. Cherokee

f. Seminole

2. TAKING NOTES

Use a diagram like the one below to help you take notes on the differences and similarities between the Creek and Cherokee.

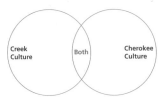

3. MAIN IDEAS

a. Why do we know more about how the Creek of Georgia lived in the 1500s?

b. How do we know that the tribes of the Southeast were of the same original culture?

c. Compare elements of the Creek culture to similar elements in our present-day lives.

4. CRITICAL THINKING
Drawing Conclusions

What aspects of the Creek culture made a confederacy?

Think About
• their organized government
• their common language
• their clan system

ACTIVITY -OPTIONS- **Language Arts/Art** Research early myths of the Creek and Cherokee. Write a **skit** or draw a **poster** of the story.

The First People of North America

10,000 B.C.
The Paleo-Indian Period begins.

8000 B.C.
The Archaic Indian culture arises.

1000 B.C.
The Woodland Indian culture arises.

800 A.D.
The Mississippian culture arises.

1400 A.D.
The Creek Confederacy, Cherokee, and Seminole cultures arise.

TERMS & NAMES

Briefly explain the significance of the following.

1. Paleo-Indians
2. Archaic Indians
3. Woodland Indians
4. Mississippian culture
5. confederacy
6. clan
7. matrilineal
8. Creek Confederacy
9. Cherokee
10. Seminole

REVIEW QUESTIONS

The First People in America (pages 23–26)

1. The earliest known inhabitants of North America lived during what period?
2. What was the first culture believed to occupy Georgia?
3. What culture developed after 1000 B.C. and continued to about A.D. 800?
4. What three new things did the Woodland Indians develop?

The Development of the Mississippian Culture (pages 27–29)

5. The Mississippian culture was influenced by what country?
6. What features characterize a civilization?
7. What caused the end of the Mississippian culture?

Creek, Cherokee, and Seminole (pages 30–33)

8. What are the Five Civilized Tribes?
9. What is a *chakofa*?
10. What religious ceremony was practiced by both the Creek and Cherokee peoples?

CRITICAL THINKING

1. USING YOUR NOTES: CATEGORIZING

	Lifestyle	Technology	Food	Trade	Religion
Paleo-Indian Period					
Archaic Period					
Woodland Period					
Mississippian Culture					
Creek					
Cherokee					

Using your completed chart, answer the questions.

a. Which culture was the first to farm?
b. Which culture had the first significant political structures in place?

2. ANALYZING LEADERSHIP

What values influenced decisions made by leaders in Cherokee town council meetings?

3. APPLYING CITIZENSHIP SKILLS

Which government, Creek or Cherokee, is most like the U.S. government today? Why?

4. THEME: DIVERSITY AND UNITY

How have Native Americans influenced American culture? Give examples from your own experience.

5. DRAWING CONCLUSIONS

Review the five characteristics of a civilization. Which of these characteristics would a culture need to be able to build something like the Great Serpent Mound?

INTERACT with HISTORY

As a visitor to a Cherokee town, what might you have gained observing their culture?

Use the map and your knowledge of early cultures to answer questions 1 through 3.

Georgia Native Americans

1. Which cultures lived west of Georgia?

   A. Timacua

   B. Cherokee

   C. Yamasee

   D. Choctaw

2. Which river ran through Cherokee land?

   A. Chattahoochee

   B. Tennessee

   C. Mississippi

   D. None

3. Which states were home to Creek cultures?

   A. Georgia and Alabama

   B. Georgia and South Carolina

   C. Alabama and Tennessee

   D. Georgia and North Carolina

TEST PRACTICE
CLASSZONE.COM

ALTERNATIVE ASSESSMENT

1. RETELLING A FOLK TALE

Many North American Indian tales give insight into the relationships between Native Americans and their environment. Select a tale from a collection of Native American literature, and retell the tale for the class.

2. COOPERATIVE LEARNING

North American Indian story, art, music, and culture have strongly influenced our culture today. Select a particular Indian culture to research. Gather copies of folk tales and art, recordings of music, and video that represents the culture you've chosen. Decide how to display your materials, and write descriptive captions for each item. Display your interactive exhibit for the class.

INTEGRATED TECHNOLOGY ACTIVITY

CREATING A MULTIMEDIA DISPLAY

Use your computer to prepare an electronic presentation on a North American Indian culture. Use the folk tales, art, music, and video that you selected for your museum exhibit (see Alternative Assessment Activity 2). Write text or record narrative to guide viewers through your interactive exhibit. Present your multimedia display to the class.

RESEARCH LINKS
CLASSZONE.COM

Contact and European Explorations 1450–1730

Columbus's three ships—the Niña, the Pinta, and the Santa Maria—approach the New World in 1492.

1498
Cabot explores Georgia coastline.

1526
First American colony established by De Ayllon on Sapelo Island.

1540
De Soto travels through Georgia.

GEORGIA USA — 1450 — 1520 — 1590

1492
Columbus lands in the Americas.

1585
First English colony established at Roanoke.

The year is 1510. You live in a European port town and have heard exciting tales about mysterious lands across the sea. You decide to board a ship and explore these lands in search of fortune.

Would you join a voyage to explore new lands?

WHAT DO YOU THINK?

- Why do you think people explored distant lands?

- Why would you want to join a voyage of exploration?

- What reasons would keep you from joining such a voyage?

For more information on this chapter, visit . . .

RESEARCH LINKS
CLASSZONE.COM

1696
James Oglethorpe is born.

1715
Yamasee War

1717
Azilia is proposed.

1732
James Oglethorpe founds colony of Georgia.

1660

1730

1620
Pilgrims land at Plymouth.

1692
Salem witchcraft trials are held.

Reading Strategy: Sequencing Events

What Do You Know?

What comes to mind when someone uses the word *explorer*? Why do you think people explored different territories?

THINK ABOUT

• what you've learned about explorers from movies, school, or your parents

• reasons that people travel throughout the world today

What Do You Want to Know?

What questions do you have about exploration or the early colonization of the Americas? Record those questions in your notebook before you read the chapter.

Sequencing Events

By following the sequence (or order) of events in history, you can get a better sense of the relationship among events. Look for dates and clues about time that can help you put events in a sequence. As you read the chapter, put early American explorers and settlers in sequence and complete the time line below. What do you learn about early Spanish, French, and English explorers?

S *See Skillbuilder Handbook, page 549.*

 Taking Notes

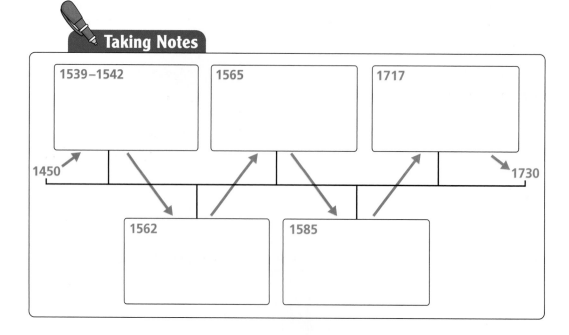

Spanish Explorations in North America

MAIN IDEA	WHY IT MATTERS NOW	TERMS & NAMES
Europeans, in their quest for better trade routes, landed in the Americas.	European exploration was the beginning of the culture and society that we know in the United States today.	Renaissance Christopher Columbus conquistador Juan Ponce de León Gulf Stream Hernando de Soto Pedro Menéndez de Avilés

SETTING THE STAGE

Europeans knew little about North America in the 15th century. They knew even less about the people there. They thought the land might contain precious metals, jewels, and other treasure. It might also provide a shorter route to their trading partners.

What would happen when explorers from Spain arrived on the North American continent? Would they see the continent as a place that could provide a new home for some of Spain's people? Would they see the inhabitants of North America as future trading partners? What would happen when two opposing cultures collided?

▲ This picture is an artist's idea of the first meeting between European explorers and Native Americans.

Why Exploration?

While early civilizations were learning to survive in North America, older civilizations in Europe were experiencing a time of "rebirth" called the **Renaissance.** The Renaissance lasted from the 1300s to 1600 and was a time of increased interest in art and learning. The Renaissance began in Italy, which was thriving from successful trade, and spread throughout all of Europe.

The Renaissance brought changes in learning, religion, and trade. Merchants began to focus on making a profit—not just meeting their needs. Since most of the trading involved Europe and Asia, merchants began to wonder if there was a shorter route to Asia—a water route that went west, instead of the land route to the east that was controlled by the Muslims.

Use your time line to put events of the Spanish Exploration in North America in order.

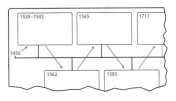

Finding a Water Route to Asia

Portuguese explorers Bartolomeu Dias and Vasco da Gama attempted to sail south around Africa and then northeast to Asia. Da Gama was successful in 1497.

Christopher Columbus had a different plan. He had read the writings of Marco Polo and of a geographer named Paolo Toscanelli. Columbus believed that he could sail west across the Atlantic and reach Asia. He did not know that Polo and Toscanelli had made some mistakes, however. Asia was not as large as they believed and the distance around Earth was more than Columbus had believed. Columbus expected that, after a short trip across the water, he would land in Asia.

What Columbus found, instead, were the Americas, not Asia. Europeans had considered the ocean a barrier, but Columbus showed that the ocean was a bridge connecting Europe, Africa, and the Americas. Columbus's explorations began an era of great wealth and power for Spain.

Reading History

A. Making Inferences
How did the Atlantic become a bridge connecting Europe, Africa, and the Americas?

Spanish Explorers in the New World

The Spanish were known for their **conquistadors,** or conquerors. As their name implies, they sought to destroy and take over the existing culture. They did not wish to live peacefully with those who were

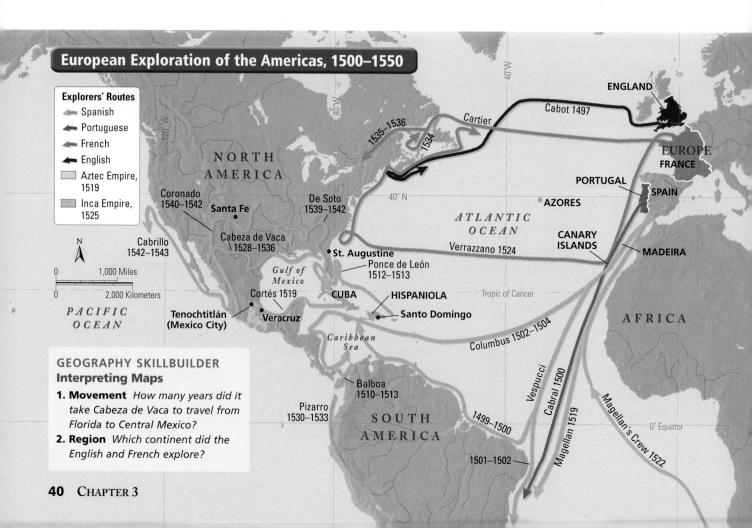

European Exploration of the Americas, 1500–1550

Explorers' Routes
- Spanish
- Portuguese
- French
- English
- Aztec Empire, 1519
- Inca Empire, 1525

NORTH AMERICA

Coronado 1540–1542
Santa Fe
Cabeza de Vaca 1528–1536
Cabrillo 1542–1543

De Soto 1539–1542
St. Augustine
Ponce de León 1512–1513

Cortés 1519
Tenochtitlán (Mexico City)
Veracruz

Gulf of Mexico
CUBA
HISPANIOLA
Santo Domingo
Caribbean Sea

Balboa 1510–1513
Pizarro 1530–1533
SOUTH AMERICA

PACIFIC OCEAN

ATLANTIC OCEAN

Cartier
Cabot 1497
ENGLAND
EUROPE
FRANCE
PORTUGAL
SPAIN
AZORES
CANARY ISLANDS
MADEIRA
AFRICA

1535–1536
1534

Verrazzano 1524
Columbus 1502–1504
Tropic of Cancer

Vespucci
Cabral 1500
Magellan 1519
Magellan's Crew 1522
1499–1500
1501–1502
0° Equator

N

0   1,000 Miles
0   2,000 Kilometers

GEOGRAPHY SKILLBUILDER
Interpreting Maps

1. **Movement** How many years did it take Cabeza de Vaca to travel from Florida to Central Mexico?
2. **Region** Which continent did the English and French explore?

already there. As the conquistadors explored the Americas, they used superior weapons, such as guns, to defeat Native Americans. European diseases also killed millions of Native Americans and weakened their resistance to conquest.

Between 1539 and 1542, three expeditions set out to find cities of gold rumored to be in the Americas. Francisco Vasquez de Coronado traveled through present-day Arizona and New Mexico. Hernando de Soto set out from Florida to explore the southeast, including present-day Georgia. Juan Rodriguez Cabrillo sailed up the California coast. All three failed to find any cities of gold, but they did steal treasure from the tribes they encountered. As Spain grew rich, England, France, and other European countries wanted the same thing, so they began to send ships to the Americas.

Spanish Explorers in Florida **Juan Ponce de León** made the second voyage with Columbus. He did not return with Columbus but stayed in the Caribbean islands, where he became governor of Puerto Rico after brutally conquering the local people. He was interested in their stories of a nearby land with a fountain that restored youth to those who bathed in it. Determined to find the fountain, the aging governor paid for ships and soldiers and set sail with high hopes.

Ponce de León's expedition explored the east and west coasts of Florida as the soldiers searched for the magic fountain. Because of the shape of Florida, the soldiers thought they were exploring an island, so Ponce de León claimed the "Isle of Florida" for Spain before he returned to Puerto Rico.

▲ Juan Ponce de León landed on Easter Sunday, called *Pasqua Florida* in Spanish. He named his discovery *Isla de Florida* ("Island of Flowers").

Reading History

B. Reading a Map Use the map on page 40 to trace Juan Ponce de León's route.

Of course, Ponce de León never discovered a magic fountain of youth. But he did discover something of value to Spanish explorers. In his written accounts, Ponce de León told of a strong current in the ocean near the east coast of Florida. He reported that, as he traveled south, his ship was pushed backward, even though he had a good wind. He was pushed backward by the **Gulf Stream,** a powerful ocean current that flows from the Gulf of Mexico north along the eastern coast before turning east toward Europe. Spanish explorers used the force of the Gulf Stream to speed their voyage home from explorations in Mexico, Central America, and the Caribbean.

Other Explorations in the Southeast

Another Spanish explorer who explored the area that now includes Georgia was Lucas Vásquez de Ayllón. Vásquez de Ayllón was notable because he tried to establish the first Spanish settlement along the east coast. He settled first at the mouth of the Cape Fear River in North Carolina. Since that site was swampy and full of insects, Vásquez de

Ayllón and his settlement moved south into what is now South Carolina.

Some historians think that Vásquez de Ayllón moved to a site in the Sapelo Sound area off the coast of present-day Georgia. He started a colony named San Miguel de Gualdape there. Like the settlement in North Carolina, this was also unsuccessful and lasted less than a year. Many of the settlers died, including Vásquez de Ayllón. The survivors left for Hispaniola.

Hernando De Soto in Georgia

Hernando de Soto and his expedition entered what is now the southwestern corner of Georgia in 1540. The Native Americans in the area were friendly and provided food for the Spanish expedition as they traveled across the state toward the northeast.

The expedition continued northeast into what is now South Carolina. After traveling northwest through present-day North Carolina, de Soto and his men became the first Europeans to cross the Appalachian Mountains. From what is now Tennessee, they turned southwest and once more entered Georgia in the northwest corner into the Chiefdom of Coosa, according to some historians. Other historians argue that de Soto never reentered Georgia—that his route kept him in Tennessee and then into Alabama.

De Soto's Conflicts with Native Americans

The Spanish described Coosa as "thickly settled in numerous and large towns with fields between, extending from one to another." As in other places, de Soto treated the Native Americans there cruelly and captured their chief. He took the chief with him into what is now Alabama. De Soto's reputation had made the southeastern Native Americans angry. At a town in Alabama, they attempted to massacre de Soto's expedition. They wounded de Soto and some of his soldiers, but were no match for the advanced weapons of the Spaniards. One estimate of Native American deaths during this battle was between 2,500 and 3,000. After the battle, de Soto's party then turned west and never returned to Georgia.

Possibly because of the injuries he received in the battle, de Soto became ill and died. When he died, the expedition was close to the Mississippi River. De Soto's soldiers weighted his body with sand bags and sank it in the river. They feared the Native Americans might find the body and mutilate it.

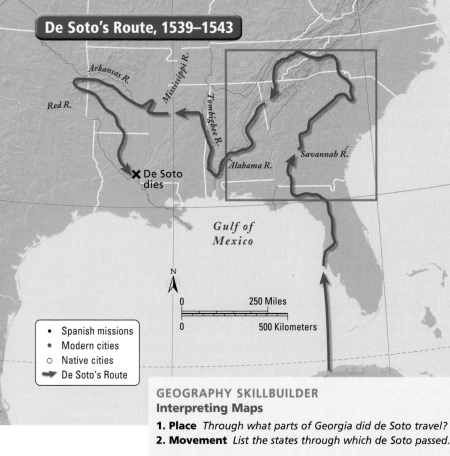

De Soto's Route, 1539–1543

Arkansas R.
Red R.
Mississippi R.
Tombigbee R.
Alabama R.
Savannah R.

✗ De Soto dies

Gulf of Mexico

Chiaha
Xuala
Chattanooga
Coosa
Rome
Ulibahali
Itaba
Cofitachaqui
Piachi
Athens
Atlanta
Cofaqui
Augusta
Talisi
Ocute
Macon
Columbus
Ichisi
Savannah
Toa
Santa Catalina de Guale
Albany
Zapala
Capachequi
Asao
Gualquini
Valdosta
San Pedro
Apalachee

ATLANTIC OCEAN

- • Spanish missions
- • Modern cities
- ○ Native cities
- ➡ De Soto's Route

0   250 Miles
0   500 Kilometers

GEOGRAPHY SKILLBUILDER
Interpreting Maps
1. Place *Through what parts of Georgia did de Soto travel?*
2. Movement *List the states through which de Soto passed.*

Only about 300 men survived the expedition. They returned to Spain penniless and lucky to be alive. They had spent four years searching for gold and riches that did not exist in the Southeast. Other Spanish explorers decided to focus their efforts in Mexico and South America.

De Soto's cruel treatment of the Native Americans of the Southeast made them resentful and suspicious of other European explorers. Worse, his soldiers brought European diseases such as chicken pox and measles. These were deadly to the Native Americans who had never been exposed to these diseases and had no immunity.

A Spanish Colony

In 1565, King Phillip II of Spain sent **Pedro Menéndez de Avilés** to Florida. Menéndez de Avilés was sent to prevent the French from building a fort in the territory claimed by Spain. He crushed the French settlers and built a fort he named St. Augustine, not far from present-day Georgia. St. Augustine was the base for many Spanish explorations.

Spanish Missions in Georgia   Spain built missions, or churches with small settlements around them, along the Atlantic coast in an attempt to bring Christianity to the Indians. Their main purpose, however, was to keep the French off the coast.

Contact and European Explorations **43**

The mission district known as Guale (pronounced "Wally") covered the Outer Coastal Plain and barrier islands of what is now Georgia. Guale was named for the Native Americans who lived there.

Menéndez de Avilés began a mission in 1566 on St. Catherine's Island. It was called the mission of Santa Catalina de Guale. The mission priests cleared fields and built houses, churches, and fortifications to protect the mission. They tried to persuade the Indians to become full-time farmers and live in permanent villages around the churches. Other missions extended as far as present-day Valdosta and Statenville, as well as along the coastal islands.

The Spanish controlled the coast and southern part of Georgia for over 100 years through their missions and the military posts that accompanied them.

Spanish Claims in the Americas

By 1700, Spain controlled much of the Americas. They were most successful in South America, Central America, and Mexico. In Mexico, Spain had conquered the great Aztec and Inca empires and claimed their lands and fortunes. Spain had wealth and superior military power. What competition would they face from other European nations eager to gather the riches of the new land?

In the next section, you will learn about the French and their explorations and attempts to establish colonies during this time.

Reading History

C. Making Inferences Explain how "God, gold, and glory" motivated Spanish exploration of North America.

Section 1 Assessment

1. TERMS & NAMES

Explain the significance of:

a. Renaissance

b. Christopher Columbus

c. conquistador

d. Juan Ponce de León

e. Gulf Stream

f. Hernando de Soto

g. Pedro Menéndez de Avilés

2. TAKING NOTES

Use a diagram like the one below to take notes on the Spanish explorers discussed in this section.

Explorer	Area Explored	Results
Christopher Columbus		
Juan Ponce de León		
Lucas Vásquez de Ayllón		
Hernando de Soto		
Pedro Menéndez de Avilés		

3. MAIN IDEAS

a. How did the Renaissance contribute to exploration?

b. How did the Gulf Stream affect Spanish exploration?

c. What impact did Hernando de Soto have on Native Americans in Georgia?

4. CRITICAL THINKING

Evaluating

Why did early explorers want a water route to Asia?

Think About

• the location of Western European countries

• the size of Europe

• trade routes that developed during the Crusades

 Language Arts/Arts Imagine you are a soldier with de Soto's expedition. Write a **journal entry** about your experience or draw an **illustrated map** of your travels.

2

French Explorations in North America

MAIN IDEA	WHY IT MATTERS NOW	TERMS & NAMES
The French tried to establish colonies in what is now Georgia and nearby Florida, but were unsuccessful.	The success of the first colony in Georgia determined our history, including where we are today.	Jean Ribault René de Laudonnière Huguenot New France

SETTING THE STAGE

Some French explorers had motives similar to those of the Spanish explorers. They were looking for riches and fame. Other French explorers were searching for a place to live where they could enjoy more freedom.

The French did not abuse the Native Americans as the Spanish had. They were looking for a place to live peacefully. They wanted to find a place to bring their families, but they were not equipped to handle the harsh environment of unsettled America. Could they learn how to survive in the new country? Could they find a site where they could be successful? Would the Native Americans be willing to help them?

▲ Jean Ribault established a settlement in what is now South Carolina in 1562.

Jean Ribault

France hoped to gain riches by exploring and settling in North America. The French wanted to establish a colony on the Atlantic coast. From there they could attack Spanish ships that were traveling north on the Gulf Stream sending treasure back to Spain.

France sent **Jean Ribault** (re BOW) in 1562 to explore the Southeast coast and find a suitable place to start a colony. Ribault and his crew traveled in 3 ships, bringing 150 people to the new land. His lieutenant was **René de Laudonnière** (lo don YAIR). The settlers were French Protestants called **Huguenots** (HYOOH gu nots). France was officially Catholic, but there were many Protestants in the country who wanted the freedom to worship their own way. Like the Spanish, one of the Huguenots' goals was to bring their religion to North America.

Ribault landed in Florida but soon sailed farther north. He explored the barrier islands and made maps of the area. Ribault gave French names

Taking Notes

Use your time line to put events of the French Explorations in North America in order.

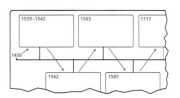

This engraving, made in 1591, shows Ribault and his men sailing up the St. Johns River in what is now Florida.

to the rivers that he explored. He built a fort in present-day South Carolina and named it Charlesfort in honor of the French king. But soon his supplies ran out, and Ribault sailed back to France to gather more equipment and provisions.

When he and de Laudonnière returned to France, they found that the Huguenots and Roman Catholics were fighting a religious war. Ribault was unable to get the money and supplies he needed, so he went to England and asked Queen Elizabeth for help. She did not like the idea of a French colony in Spanish territory, so she had Ribault imprisoned until 1565. When help did not arrive, the colonists of Charlesfort returned to France.

René de Laudonnière

In 1564, France sent René de Laudonnière back to Florida. He took 304 Huguenot colonists with him who were interested in finding a place of religious freedom.

This group built a fort at the mouth of the St. Johns River in Florida, near present-day Jacksonville. They named it Fort Caroline. De Laudonnière explored the interior of this new territory. At first he had good relations with the Native Americans there, and they helped him with food supplies. Soon, though, his supplies ran short, and they were no longer willing to help. The colonists lost faith in de Laudonnière's leadership. They stole boats and sailed south to become pirates and steal from Spanish ships. De Laudonnière and the rest of the colonists waited at Fort Caroline for help from France.

Reading History

A. Summarizing Why did the French Huguenots settle in America?

France Abandons the Southeast

When Ribault was released from prison, the king of France sent him with reinforcements and supplies to rescue what was left of Fort Caroline. King Phillip II of Spain, however, was angry that France had tried to establish a colony so near its territory in Florida. He sent a fleet of warships commanded by Pedro Menéndez de Avilés to stop the French colony. Menéndez de Avilés and his men landed in Florida at what is now St. Augustine. He and 500 of his men marched north and destroyed Fort Caroline. They found Ribault and his soldiers and killed them too. De Laudonnière was wounded but managed to get back to France, where he wrote the history of what had happened. After this attack, the French ended their colonization efforts in the area.

Reading History

B. Making Inferences
Why did the French want to establish a colony near the Spanish settlement?

French Claims

The French explored the interior of North America while the English settled the coast. By the late 1600s, French explorers had claimed the Ohio River valley, the Mississippi River valley, and the entire Great Lakes region. The French territory of Louisiana stretched from the Appalachian Mountains to the Rocky Mountains.

By 1760, the French colony of **New France** had a population of 80,000 and France controlled most of the land in the interior of North America. In the next section, you will learn about England's efforts to explore and acquire more territory for its colonists in the New World.

Section Assessment

1. TERMS & NAMES
Explain the significance of:

a. Jean Ribault

b. René Laudonnière

c. Huguenot

d. New France

2. TAKING NOTES
Use a diagram like the one below to take notes on the French explorers discussed in this section.

Explorer	Area Explored	Results
Jean Ribault		
René Laudonnière		

3. MAIN IDEAS

a. Why did the French want colonies on the coast of North America?

b. What major problem made the Spanish and French colonies unsuccessful?

c. In what ways did the French and Spanish contribute to future explorations and colonies?

4. CRITICAL THINKING
Recognizing Effects

What impact did religion have on French attempts to colonize the Americas?

Think About
• Huguenots who left France
• Huguenots who remained in France
• Roman Catholics

ACTIVITY -OPTIONS-

Geography/Math Draw a **map** of French settlements in North America as of 1750 or measure the distances between settlements to include in a **chart**.

Early English Colonies in North America

MAIN IDEA	WHY IT MATTERS NOW	TERMS & NAMES
The English had different plans for settlement that enabled them to be successful in North America.	The success of the first colony in Georgia has helped shape the history of the state.	mercantilism indentured joint-stock servant company monopoly charter Azilia

SETTING THE STAGE

People from England had more pressing reasons than the Spanish and the French for wanting to find a new home in America. Conditions in England were not good. Cities were crowded, and the countryside could not produce enough food for all the people. Some felt oppressed by the Church of England. They looked to America as a place for new economic opportunities and religious freedom.

Neither the Spanish nor the French had been successful in starting colonies. What could the English do that would be different? Could they discover how to use America's resources? Could they make friends with the Native Americans? Could they establish a place where families could live successfully?

▲ Early settlers build the fort at Jamestown.

Spain Loses Power

Spain and England had been at odds for many reasons. Spain was Catholic, and England was Protestant. When Queen Elizabeth I became queen of England in 1558, Spain tried to remove her. England fought back.

The major defeat for Spain came in 1588 at sea. Although England's navy was not as large as Spain's, the English had a fleet of fast ships and skillful sailors. The smaller, speedier English ships defeated the heavier, slower ships of the Spanish fleet, known as the Spanish Armada. The English victory was important for two reasons. First, England remained independent and Protestant. Second, Spain's image as a major power suffered. The world saw that Spain could be beaten.

English adventurers began directing their resources to attacking Spain's territories overseas. England wanted to establish its own colonies and challenged Spanish claims in North America.

Taking Notes

Use your time line to put events of the early English colonies in North America in order.

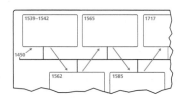

▲ The English navy used its smaller, quicker ships to defeat the larger, slower galleons of the Spanish Armada.

In addition to Spain's problems at sea, their manufacturing centers were struggling. Spaniards were moving in large numbers to Mexico and Central America, where people found better economic opportunities.

Conditions in England

The English population—especially in the cities—was growing. Some political leaders in London thought that their country was becoming overcrowded. Overseas colonies might be one way to solve the population problem and make the economy stronger. Lack of economic opportunities in England and the lure of fortunes in the New World made many people eager to become colonists.

Richard Hakluyt (HAK lyoot) was an English geographer who urged England to start a colony in the New World. Hakluyt thought colonies would provide a market for English exports. The colonies would also provide raw materials for England's manufacturing centers. By having colonies, England hoped to increase its trade and build up its supply of gold. This economic theory is called **mercantilism**. In mercantilism, government controls trade and attempts to transfer wealth from colonies to the parent country. Hakluyt also thought that English colonies would help to establish the Protestant faith in the Americas.

England's First Attempts

In 1585, Queen Elizabeth I gave permission to Sir Walter Raleigh to begin a colony on Roanoke Island in present-day Virginia. This colony

Contact and European Explorations **49**

lasted only as long as their food supply did. When the local natives discovered that the settlers wanted to take their land, they stopped supplying food. The surviving colonists returned to England in 1586.

John White, one of the survivors of the first Roanoke colony, encouraged Raleigh to try again. In 1587, Raleigh established a second colony at Roanoke. Raleigh named White governor of the new colony. When the colony ran out of supplies, White returned to England for more.

What follows next remains one of America's mysteries. Because of the war at sea between England and Spain, White did not return to the colony until 1590. When he arrived, the colonists had completely disappeared. The only clues left were the letters *CRO* carved in a tree and

Reading History

B. Drawing Conclusions Why did the colony of Roanoke fail?

ECONOMICS *in* HISTORY

Mercantilism

The main goal of mercantilism is to increase the money in a country's treasury by creating a favorable balance of trade. A country has a favorable balance of trade if it has more exports than imports. Colonies were a source of goods and raw materials the "mother country" needed to maintain a favorable balance of trade.

For example, say the American colonies sold $500 in lumber and $500 in tobacco to England. England manufactured $1,000 in furniture from the raw lumber, which it sold back to the colonies. England sold the tobacco for twice its original value to the Dutch. England would then have a favorable balance of trade because the value of its exports (tobacco and furniture) was greater than the value of its imports (tobacco and lumber). England would become richer because of the raw materials it received from the colonies.

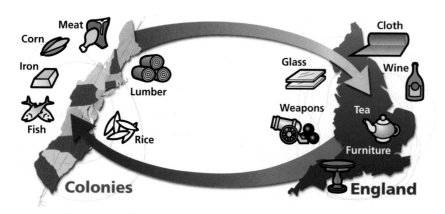

CONNECT TO HISTORY

1. **Finding Main Ideas** Under mercantilism, what did a country need to do to become rich? Discuss the way colonies enriched a country according to mercantilism.

   See Skillbuilder Handbook, page 549.

CONNECT TO TODAY

2. **Making Inferences** Think about your own family budget. What do you think would happen if your family collected less money than it paid for goods for several years? Do you think this situation would be the same for a nation as it would for a family?

For more about mercantilism . . .

RESEARCH LINKS
CLASSZONE.COM

the word *Croatoan* carved in a doorpost. Some historians believe that the colonists became part of the neighboring tribes. Others believe that they moved to the Chesapeake Bay area, where they died.

A Colony at Jamestown

The English had learned some important lessons from Raleigh's attempts at starting colonies. Raleigh had paid for the ventures himself. He lost all of his investment when the colonies failed. Through Raleigh's experiences, the English learned that one person could not finance an entire colony. To raise money, they turned to the **joint-stock company.** Joint-stock companies were backed by investors, people who put money into a project to earn profits. Each investor owned a piece of the company, called a share of stock. In this way, the investors split any profits and divided any losses.

Merchants organized the Virginia Company of London and the Virginia Company of Plymouth. King James I of England granted charters to both companies in 1606. A **charter** was a written contract, issued by a government, giving the holder the right to establish a colony.

A Difficult First Year   In 1607, the Virginia Company of London financed a colony at Jamestown with more than 100 colonists. The first year was extremely difficult for the colonists. They faced a hard climate, malaria, and poor drinking water. Also, they spent their days searching for gold rather than building houses and growing food. By January 1608, only 38 colonists remained alive.

Then John Smith took control. He made a rule: "He that will not work shall not eat." Smith built a wall around Jamestown and persuaded the Powhatan tribe to trade their corn to the colonists. In 1609, 800 additional English settlers came to Jamestown.

In 1612, John Rolfe developed a type of tobacco that grew well in the area. It quickly became popular in England. Tobacco changed Jamestown in many ways. The Virginia Company had thought of the settlers as employees. The colonists, however, wanted to share in the profits. In response, the company allowed the settlers to own land. The settlers worked harder knowing that the land was their own. The company offered 50 acres of land to any person who could pay his or her own way to the colony.

Those who could not afford to pay their own way came as **indentured servants.** These men and women sold their labor to the person who paid their passage to the colony. After working for a number of years,

CONNECTIONS to Technology

Navigation

To calculate the distance they traveled each day, "New World" sailors would drop overboard a small wooden triangle at the end of a knotted rope. Speed was gauged by the number of knots that went out during a short amount of time measured on an hourglass. The term "knot" came to mean one nautical mile per hour. Top speed for the vessels of early explorers was about 8 knots. Sailing 100 miles a day was typical. With favorable winds, a voyage from Spain to the New World could be accomplished in 2 months.

Reading History

C. Solving Problems   If you had been John Smith, how would you have forced colonists to work?

they were free to farm or take up a trade of their own. The first enslaved Africans were brought to Jamestown in 1619. Dutch traders put into port to resupply their ship on the way to the West Indies. They traded their cargo of 20 slaves for the supplies they needed.

By 1621, the population of the colony was over 2,000. Finally, the English had a successful colony.

▲ Early English colonists depended on supplies brought by ship from London.

Other Early English Colonies

England continued to establish colonies along the eastern shore. Carolina was founded as a colony in 1663. English settlers built Charles Town, later called Charleston, in 1670. After 1685, Charles Town became a refuge for Huguenots seeking religious freedom.

By the 1700s, the English settlers used the Indian trails through Georgia to make surprise attacks on the Spanish forts that remained in Florida. In turn, the Spanish attacked Charles Town. The Spanish were no match for the stronger English fort there. They retreated to Florida.

Georgia's Native American tribes were also involved in the fighting. The Creek, who traded with the English, fought against the tribes who sided with the Spanish.

The Yamasee War

The English were soon the only strong trading force in the colonies. Both the French and the Spanish had lost power. The English controlled all the supplies of guns and other manufactured goods the local Native Americans wanted. They had a **monopoly**. English traders began to cheat and mistreat the Native Americans.

In 1715, the Yamasee tribe led an uprising against traders in what is now South Carolina. The Creek and other Native American tribes joined the Yamasee. They massacred most of the traders and began attacking the frontier settlements. The frontier colonists fled to the safety of Charles Town.

The English settlers rallied their forces and used their superior weapons and military power against the Yamasee, pushing them south through what is now Georgia and into Florida. As the Yamasee retreated, the Creek left their home around Macon and moved to land west of the Chattahoochee River in what is now Alabama.

Plans for a Georgia Colony

Leaders in England were afraid that the Spanish in Florida would grow strong again after the Native Americans left. The land between Spanish Florida and English Carolina needed to be a buffer to protect plantations in Carolina.

Vocabulary

buffer: a protective barrier

In 1717, a Scottish nobleman proposed a new settlement in what is now Georgia. The Lord Proprietors of Carolina gave Sir Robert Montgomery permission to settle "all that Tract of Land which lies between the Rivers Allatamaha and Savanna." Montgomery called the proposed colony the Margravate of **Azilia**. Montgomery tried to attract colonists by calling Azilia a "future Eden."

Apparently the English people thought that the risks in such a place were too great. The possibility of attacks from Native Americans and the Spanish was very real. For three years, Montgomery was unable to convince enough people to start the colony, so he lost his charter.

Primary Source

▲ This is the plan for the Margravate of Azilia, 1717.

Azilia Is Not Forgotten Azilia was never built, but many maps printed in that period showed it. These maps, along with the landowners in Carolina, reminded the English government that it needed to claim the land between South Carolina and Florida. By 1730, the English government acted to create a new colony there. In the next chapter, you will learn about how England's North American colonies grew and prospered.

Section ③ Assessment

1. TERMS & NAMES

Explain the significance of:

a. mercantilism

b. joint-stock company

c. charter

d. indentured servant

e. monopoly

f. Azilia

2. TAKING NOTES

Use a diagram like the one below to compare and contrast the reasons Spain, France, and England had for exploring the New World.

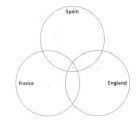

3. MAIN IDEAS

a. Do you think sending families made English colonies successful? Why or why not?

b. Why was the land that became Georgia important to the colonists in South Carolina?

c. Analyze this statement: "Azilia paved the way for Georgia."

4. CRITICAL THINKING

Drawing Conclusions

What advantages did the English have over the Spanish in starting new colonies?

Think About
• British military
• Spain's economy

ACTIVITY -OPTIONS- **Art/Language Arts** Draw a **poster** or write an **advertisement** that will attract sailors and soldiers to join your voyage to explore the New World.

TERMS & NAMES

Briefly explain the significance of the following.

1. Renaissance
2. Christopher Columbus
3. conquistador
4. Gulf Stream
5. Jean Ribault
6. René de Laudonnière
7. Huguenot
8. mercantilism
9. charter
10. Azilia

REVIEW QUESTIONS

Spanish Explorations (pages 39–44)

1. Why did Europeans explore different territories?
2. Why did Spain succeed in its conquests?
3. What was significant about Ponce de León's explorations?
4. How did Hernando de Soto's explorations affect relations with Native Americans?

French Explorations (pages 45–47)

5. What motivated the French to explore North America?
6. Why did Jean Ribault's attempted colony fail?
7. Why did France control most of North America by 1750?

Early English Colonies (pages 48–53)

8. Why did the English want to settle in America?
9. Why was England's defeat of the Spanish Armada important?

CRITICAL THINKING

1. USING YOUR NOTES: SEQUENCING EVENTS

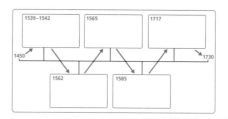

Using your chart, answer the questions below.

a. How did Spain's level of exploration evolve?
b. How did England colonize North America with more success than the French or Spanish?

2. ANALYZING LEADERSHIP

Compare the leadership of René de Laudonnière and John Smith.

3. APPLYING CITIZENSHIP SKILLS

What kind of values did Hernando de Soto demonstrate in his actions? How effective was he in improving the New World?

4. THEME: IMMIGRATION AND MIGRATION

What were the causes and effects of the migration of Europeans to the Americas?

INTERACT with HISTORY

Would you join an expedition to a new world across the ocean? What might keep you from being a part of the voyage?

VISUAL SUMMARY

European Exploration of the Americas

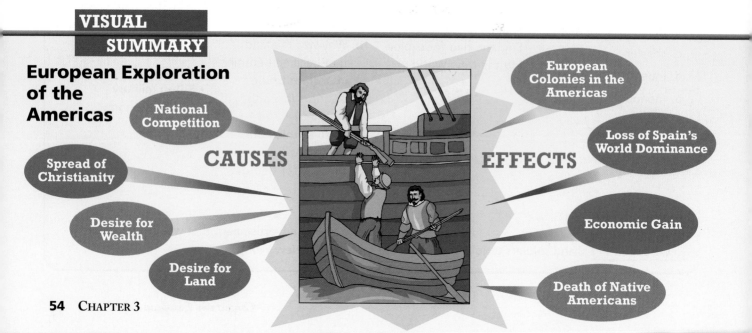

CAUSES

- National Competition
- Spread of Christianity
- Desire for Wealth
- Desire for Land

EFFECTS

- European Colonies in the Americas
- Loss of Spain's World Dominance
- Economic Gain
- Death of Native Americans

Use the map and your knowledge of early European exploration and settlements to answer questions 1 through 3.

French Explorers on the Mississippi

Marquette and Joliet, 1673

La Salle 1679–1682

Present-day state boundary

1. Where did La Salle's explorations end?

   A. New Orleans
   B. Ontario
   C. Ft. Detroit
   D. Lake Michigan

2. Where did Marquette and Joliet begin their explorations?

   A. Lake Huron
   B. Fort Detroit
   C. Lake Michigan
   D. Lake Ontario

3. Approximately how many miles did La Salle travel?

   A. 600 miles
   B. 1200 miles
   C. 1500 miles
   D. 1800 miles

TEST PRACTICE
CLASSZONE.COM

ALTERNATIVE ASSESSMENT

1. WRITING A NEWS REPORT

Research an event in the conquest of the Americas. Write a news report about the event that explains what happened and who was involved. You should also explain when, where, why, and how the event occurred. Add a photograph or visual to your story. Then publish the story for the class.

2. COOPERATIVE LEARNING

With a group of classmates, research the communities of Spanish America in the 1600s. Then create a diorama of one of those settlements, including a mission, a *hacienda,* roads, and mines or sugar mills. Use elements such as drawings, maps, and written text to show significant features of life there. Display your diorama and discuss it in class.

INTEGRATED TECHNOLOGY ACTIVITY

USING AN ELECTRONIC CARD CATALOG

Choose an early American explorer you would like to research. Then use your library's computerized search program to find information about your explorer. Enter your explorer's name, and print out the list of library materials you find. This information is called bibliographic information. Locate one of the books on your list, and take it to class. Identify two or three interesting excerpts from the book to share with your classmates.

RESEARCH LINKS
CLASSZONE.COM

The English Colonies 1600–1753

The *Mayflower* brought the Pilgrims to Plymouth in 1620.

GEORGIA
USA

1600

1650

1607
John Smith and other English settlers establish Jamestown.

1620
The Pilgrims land at Plymouth.

1630
Puritans found Massachusetts Bay Colony.

1663
The colony of Carolina established.

1670
Charles Town is established in Carolina.

It is the early 1700s when you arrive in one of America's larger port cities. After nearly a month of ocean travel, you are thrilled to see land. As you leave the ship, you wonder where you will live and how you will make a living.

Would you settle on a farm or in a town?

WHAT DO YOU THINK?

- Will you choose to live where other people from your homeland live? Or will you try to live somewhere new?

- How did you make a living in your old country? Will this influence your choice of where to live?

For more information on this chapter, visit . . .

RESEARCH LINKS
CLASSZONE.COM

1717
The colony of Azilia is proposed.

1732
James Oglethorpe receives a charter for the colony of Georgia.

1733
The colonists land in Georgia and establish Savannah.

1736
Augusta is established.

1700

1750

1712
Carolina splits into North Carolina and South Carolina.

1730–1740s
The Great Awakening religious revivals spread.

Reading Strategy:
Analyzing Causes and Recognizing Effects

What Do You Know?

What do you already know about the American colonies? What sort of person might choose to leave his or her native country and cross the ocean to settle in a new land?

THINK ABOUT

• what you've learned about American settlers from movies, television, historical fiction, or science fiction about space travel

• opportunities and challenges offered in a new land

What Do You Want to Know?

What questions do you have about the Europeans who settled in North America? About those who were already here? Record these questions in your notebook before you read the chapter.

Analyzing Causes and Recognizing Effects

A single event in history can have many causes. And one action or cause may result in many effects. Analyzing cause-and-effect relationships can help you understand more of what you read about history. Use the chart below to list causes that contributed to the different economic developments in each of the colonial regions.

S *See Skillbuilder Handbook, page 551.*

Taking Notes

	New England	Middle	Southern	Backcountry
Cause: Climate				
Cause: Resources				
Cause: People				
Effect: Economic Development				

The English Establish 13 Colonies

MAIN IDEA	WHY IT MATTERS NOW	TERMS & NAMES
Each region of the English colonies developed a distinct regional identity.	The political and economic regions of the colonial era are still evident in U.S. culture today.	Pilgrim cash crop Puritan plantation commonwealth economy triangular trade

SETTING THE STAGE

Many English settlers came to the colonies hoping to make a fresh start. Some wanted land so they could provide for their families. Some wanted to make their fortune. Many wanted the freedom to worship as they pleased.

The land was different from what they had known in England. Could the colonists work together to build a new way of life in this new land? Could they discover how to work the land successfully? Could they survive the challenges and demands of a new way of life?

The New England Colonies

The founders of the colonies of New England were primarily English religious groups who disagreed with many of the practices of the Church of England. The Church persecuted them for their faith, so many chose to leave England and establish colonies elsewhere. Connecticut, Rhode Island, Massachusetts, and New Hampshire were New England colonies. Present-day Maine and Vermont were part of other colonies at that time.

▲ John and Priscilla Alden were among the 102 passengers on the *Mayflower*.

The Pilgrims Establish Plymouth   The **Pilgrims** were part of a group called the Separatists. They wanted to separate themselves from the Church of England. At first, they went to Holland. Dissatisfied with life there, they decided to leave and establish their own settlement in the colonies.

The Virginia Company, which had financed the Jamestown colony, gave the Pilgrims permission to settle on land within its charter in Virginia. The Pilgrims set sail on the *Mayflower* for the colonies. In November 1620, the Pilgrims finally landed. But a storm had blown them north of their course, and they landed at a site which had been named Plymouth off the Massachusetts coast in an area called New England.

Taking Notes

Use your chart to note causes of the establishment of the 13 colonies.

	New England	Middle
Cause: Climate		

▲ Squanto taught the Pilgrims to use fish as fertilizer to grow corn.

The first winter was a hard one. Starvation and disease killed half the Pilgrims. The next year Squanto, a Native American who spoke English, befriended them. Squanto showed them how to hunt, fish, and plant, and he helped negotiate a peace treaty with the Native American neighbors.

With his help, the colony prospered. They were able to trade with the Native Americans for furs, and they cut lumber to ship back to England to sell for a profit. The success of Plymouth inspired other groups to make the journey.

The Massachusetts Bay Colony

Between 1630 and 1640, members of another religious group, the **Puritans,** left England to start new settlements in the Americas. The Puritans did not want to break with the Church of England entirely. They hoped to "purify" Church practices. About 20,000 Puritans eventually came to New England.

Many Puritan merchants had invested in the Massachusetts Bay Company. The company gave them a charter to settle in New England. In 1630, 1,000 Puritans set sail for Massachusetts. Their plan was to start a **commonwealth**—a community in which people worked together for the good of the whole.

Puritan Town Organization

The congregation was the basic unit of the commonwealth. The congregation usually bought a large plot of land and divided it among its members. The meetinghouse was usually the focal point of a central square, called a green. Individual farmhouses surrounded the green. Fields and pastures lay behind the farmhouses.

Puritan law required everyone to attend church. The Puritans emphasized duty, godliness, hard work, and honesty. They called this the "New England Way." They believed that activities such as dancing and playing games would lead to laziness. This Puritan work ethic and the abundant natural resources of the region led to the rapid growth and success of the New England colonies.

Northern Agriculture and Resources

The New England soil was very rocky, and winters were long and cold. This made farming difficult, and often families produced just enough to feed themselves, with perhaps a small amount left over for trading. Producing just enough to survive is called subsistence farming.

However, New England had abundant natural resources. The waters of the Atlantic Ocean were full of fish. Thick forests provided lumber

Reading History

A. Making Inferences
Why do you think Squanto was so helpful to the Pilgrims?

Reading History

B. Summarizing
What were some important elements of the New England Way?

for building ships and homes and sheltered abundant fur-bearing animals. The soil was rich in iron deposits.

New England Grows   As Massachusetts grew, colonists began to move inland or settle outside the colony. Growing Puritan congregations established new colonies. Other colonies were founded by religious leaders expelled by church leaders for views that opposed Puritans' beliefs.

In the 1600s, Puritanism was widespread among the colonists. But by the early 1700s, Puritanism had started to decline. One reason for the decline was that the drive to make a profit became more important than the original Puritan ideals. Another reason was that other religions such as Baptists and Anglicans were attracting new converts. Political changes also weakened the Puritan community. A new royal charter in 1691 granted religious freedom for all Protestants, not just Puritans.

Triangular Trade   The New England colonies were involved in three kinds of trade. The first was trade with other colonies. The second was direct trade with Europe. The third was **triangular trade** between Europe, Africa, and the Americas. A typical trade might include the New England colonies sending rum and iron to Africa. In Africa, the captain would trade his cargo for slaves. He would take the slaves to the West Indies, where he would exchange them for sugar and molasses. Then he would take the sugar and molasses to New England. These ingredients were used in making rum, and the trade cycle started over.

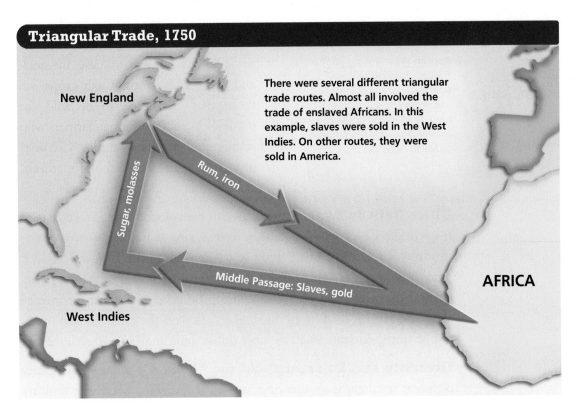

Triangular Trade, 1750

New England

There were several different triangular trade routes. Almost all involved the trade of enslaved Africans. In this example, slaves were sold in the West Indies. On other routes, they were sold in America.

Sugar, molasses

Rum, iron

Middle Passage: Slaves, gold

West Indies

AFRICA

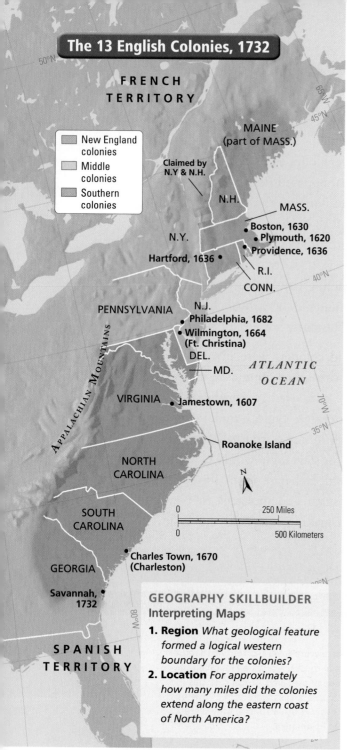

The 13 English Colonies, 1732

Legend:
- New England colonies
- Middle colonies
- Southern colonies

FRENCH TERRITORY

MAINE (part of MASS.)

Claimed by N.Y & N.H.

N.H.

MASS.
- Boston, 1630
- Plymouth, 1620
- Providence, 1636

N.Y.

Hartford, 1636

R.I.

CONN.

PENNSYLVANIA

N.J.
- Philadelphia, 1682
- Wilmington, 1664 (Ft. Christina)

DEL.

MD.

ATLANTIC OCEAN

VIRGINIA
- Jamestown, 1607

Roanoke Island

NORTH CAROLINA

SOUTH CAROLINA

GEORGIA

Charles Town, 1670 (Charleston)

Savannah, 1732

SPANISH TERRITORY

APPALACHIAN MOUNTAINS

0 250 Miles
0 500 Kilometers

GEOGRAPHY SKILLBUILDER
Interpreting Maps
1. **Region** What geological feature formed a logical western boundary for the colonies?
2. **Location** For approximately how many miles did the colonies extend along the eastern coast of North America?

Africans in New England There were very few enslaved people in the New England colonies. With only small farms, there was not much need for slave labor. Farmers could not afford to feed and house slaves when there was no work for them. Some New Englanders in larger towns had slaves to work as house servants, cooks, gardeners, and stable-hands. Sometimes slave owners hired out their slaves to work on the docks or in shops or warehouses. Sometimes the slaves were allowed to keep a portion of their wages.

The Middle Colonies

New York, New Jersey, Pennsylvania, and Delaware formed the Middle Colonies, between New England to the north and the Chesapeake region to the south. Religious freedom attracted many groups. Protestants, Catholics, Quakers, and Jews all settled in this area.

Agriculture and Resources The Hudson and Delaware River valleys supported shipping and commerce. The broad valleys, rich soil, and milder winters allowed farmers to raise livestock and grow cash crops. **Cash crops** are those that are raised to be sold for money. Dutch and German farmers who immigrated to the Middle Colonies brought advanced agricultural methods, skills, and knowledge with them.

Cities Built on Trade Wealthy cities developed along the coasts of the Middle Colonies. New York City was situated at the mouth of the Hudson River, and Philadelphia was founded on the Delaware River. The thriving wheat trade caused these cities to grow rapidly. It was only natural that shipyards and shipbuilding became important businesses also. The wealth from these businesses allowed the cities to add many public improvements, such as large public buildings and streetlights.

Diversity and Tolerance As the Middle Colonies grew, many different immigrant groups migrated to the region. Soon, the region's

Reading History

C. Analyzing Causes Why were there relatively few enslaved workers in New England?

Reading History

D. Forming Opinions Why might the promise of religious freedom encourage a diverse population in a colony?

population showed a great diversity, or variety in its people. By the mid-1600s the Middle Colonies were home to English, Germans, Dutch, Scots-Irish, Africans, Irish, Scottish, Welsh, Swedish, and French.

One of the notable groups of settlers in the Middle Colonies was the Quakers. William Penn created a colony where Quakers could live according to their beliefs. They believed that all people should live in peace. They welcomed people of different religions and nationalities to their colony. Penn wanted all people treated equally in his colony. This included equal treatment for women and Native Americans. His policies helped make Pennsylvania one of the wealthiest American colonies because many people were able to freely pursue their businesses there.

Africans in the Middle Colonies   About seven percent of the Middle Colonies' population was enslaved. Most lived in New York City. They worked as manual laborers, servants, drivers, and assistants to craftspeople.

There were also free African men and women who worked as laborers, servants, or sailors. Tension between the races sometimes led to violence. Slaves who revolted were punished severely. Such punishment showed that slaveholders would resort to force and violence to control their slaves.

The Southern Colonies

The Southern Colonies consisted of Maryland, Virginia, the Carolinas, and Georgia. The Appalachian Mountains bordered parts of these colonies in the west. To the east lay the Atlantic Ocean. You read about the founding of Virginia in chapter 3. You will learn about the founding of Georgia in chapter 5.

Maryland and the Carolinas   Maryland was the first Southern Colony to be established. Lord Baltimore founded Maryland in 1632 as a place where Roman Catholics could escape persecution.

Carolina was established in 1663. English settlers from Barbados built Charles Town (later known as Charleston) in 1670. After 1685, Charles Town became a refuge for French Protestants who were seeking religious freedom. In 1712, Carolina split into North Carolina and South Carolina.

Southern Agriculture   The broad coastal plains, numerous streams, and long growing season made the Southern Colonies ideal for cash crops such as tobacco,

Reading History

E. Comparing and Contrasting
How did Penn's policies toward Native Americans compare with those of other colonies you have read about?

Reading History

F. Finding Main Ideas   How did the search for religious freedom affect the establishment of the Southern colonies?

THINK AS A
GEOGRAPHER

Rice Plantations

Fresh-water rivers such as the Altamaha are affected by the rise and fall of the tides from the coast to about 30 miles inland. The ebb and flow of fresh and salt-water tides, long growing season, and semitropical climate are ideal conditions for cultivating rice.

Africans from the "Rice Coast" (Senegal to Liberia) were experienced in growing rice in this environment and knew how to build and operate the floodgates and drains that were needed.

In the peak decade of the 1850s, 2,800 slaves worked on Altamaha valley rice plantations. The Geechee community in Georgia is descended from these Africans.

indigo, and rice. Maryland's economy was based on tobacco, which was backbreaking work. Every few years the soil was exhausted and new land had to be prepared. Carolina settlers grew indigo, a plant which yields a blue dye, on higher ground. They grew rice along the swampy marshlands of the coast. Some of the wealthiest people in the world were South Carolina rice planters. (Cotton would not become an important cash crop until the invention of the cotton gin in 1793.)

A Plantation Economy   The conditions were right for a **plantation economy** in the Southern Colonies. Very large farms or plantations produced just about everything that their families and workers needed. Because the large farms were self-sufficient, there was little need for large cities like those found in the Middle Colonies. But there was a need for many workers to run the plantation.

During the first half of the 1600s, indentured servants provided much of the labor. Around the mid-1600s, many indentured servants paid off their passage, saved money, and bought their own land. As a result, planters tried to force the Native Americans to work for them. European diseases caused many of the native population to die. Others knew the country well enough to escape.

Landowners began buying people brought from Africa to work on their plantations. Toward the end of the 1600s, planters relied almost completely on enslaved Africans for their labor force. The growth of slavery allowed plantation farming to expand in the Southern Colonies.

Reading History

G. Drawing Conclusions
Why did white settlers choose not to remain on the plantations as laborers?

▶ This watercolor sketch by Henry Latrobe shows two African women clearing tree stumps on a Virginia plantation while an overseer looks on.

Africans in the Southern Colonies By 1750, more than 235,000 enslaved people lived in the American colonies. About 85 percent of them lived in the Southern Colonies. They made up about 40 percent of the South's population. Most enslaved Africans tried to maintain their own culture. They often resisted their enslavement. At times they rose up in rebellion or revolts. Such revolts led planters to tighten the restrictions, which were called slave codes, even more. These codes forbade slaves to leave plantations without permission. It was illegal for enslaved blacks to meet with free blacks.

A Planter Class Emerges The plantation economy, the widespread use of slave labor, the large percentage of slaves compared to white settlers, and the strict slave codes made the Southern Colonies distinctly different from the other colonies.

The plantation economy produced a powerful planter class that controlled much of the rich land along the coast. This upper class soon took control of the political and economic power in the South. A traveler in the South commented that the planters "think and act precisely as do the nobility in other countries."

Small landowners with only one or two slaves just could not compete with the wealthy upper class. Many of them gave up their land and started moving to the Backcountry. You will learn about that colonial region in the next section.

Reading History

H. Recognizing Effects How did the growth of slavery affect political power in the South?

Section 1 Assessment

1. TERMS & NAMES

Explain the significance of:

a. Pilgrims

b. Puritans

c. commonwealth

d. triangular trade

e. cash crop

f. plantation economy

2. TAKING NOTES

Use a diagram like the one below to review how the different colonial regions developed.

Regions	New England Colonies	Middle Colonies	Southern Colonies
Who Lived There			
Agriculture			
Type of Economy			

3. MAIN IDEAS

a. How did the Puritan work ethic affect the New England Colonies?

b. What natural resources helped the Middle Colonies succeed?

c. How did the climate of the Southern Colonies affect their economy?

4. CRITICAL THINKING

Analyzing Causes

Why did the colonists in the Southern Colonies enslave Native Americans and use African slaves?

Think About

• the crops that were grown

• the size of the farms

• the growing season

Art/Language Arts Draw a **poster** or write a **newspaper article** describing one of the geographic regions and persuading colonists to leave Europe and settle in America.

The Backcountry

SETTING THE STAGE

Many colonists came to America for the opportunity to own their own land. The king of England granted most of the land along the Atlantic coast to companies or individuals as favors. Wealthier settlers soon owned the most desirable areas.

What about those people who were not wealthy or who came as indentured servants? Would there be land available for them? The rugged land between the coast and the Appalachian Mountains seemed to provide the answer. But what kind of person would want to tackle that wilderness? What kind of natural resources would they find there? Would the land yield what they needed? Would the Native Americans be hostile or friendly to them? Could they survive the "Backcountry"?

▲ Settlers in the Backcountry built their homes from local timber.

Geography of the Backcountry

The rougher, more mountainous region farther inland from the coast was called the **Backcountry**. In the South, the Backcountry began at the fall line, where the rivers form waterfalls as the hilly piedmont drops to the lower elevations of the coastal plain.

The natural resources of the Backcountry made it relatively easy for a family to start a small farm. The many springs and streams provided fresh water. Abundant forests provided wood for log cabins and fences. Augusta was a Backcountry town in Georgia. It was established in 1736 as a trade center for settlers in Charles Town and Savannah.

The Great Wagon Road

The English knew very little about the areas inland past the navigable rivers. But Native Americans knew of a north-south route called the "Warriors' Path." This trail ran along the eastern edge of the Appalachian Mountains. The Iroquois controlled the route and used it to come south to trade or to make war on other Native American tribes.

Taking Notes

Use your chart to note causes of the growth of the Backcountry.

	New England	Middle
Cause: Climate		

In 1744, the English signed a series of treaties with the Five Nations of the Iroquois for use of the path. After 1744, the English took over the land. The Warriors' Path became the **Great Wagon Road,** the main highway of the colonial Backcountry. Great numbers of English, Scots-Irish, and Germans traveled down the road to claim land and a new life in America.

The People of the Backcountry

The people who settled the Backcountry were different from the landowners of the coastal plantations. With the exception of Georgia, trading companies and wealthy European families settled most of the colonial coastal regions. The cities, businesses, plantations, and new ideas there could produce great wealth.

Backcountry settlers were neither wealthy nor well connected. But they were honorable people who were willing to work hard. Their measure of success was not money. It was land ownership. And there was plenty of open land in the Backcountry.

The first European settlers in the Backcountry made a living by trading with the Native Americans. Newly arrived colonists and former indentured servants settled there. Some became small subsistence farmers, raising enough for their families with a small amount to trade. The farmers often clashed with the Native Americans, because the farmers were taking Native American land.

The Scots-Irish The Scots-Irish came from the borderland between Scotland and England. Most of them had lived for a time in northern Ireland. Persecution, poverty, and crop failures made life hard in Scotland and Ireland. As a result, thousands of Scots-Irish moved to America. Many of them headed for the Backcountry. The terrain there was familiar to them because it was geographically similar to what they had known at home.

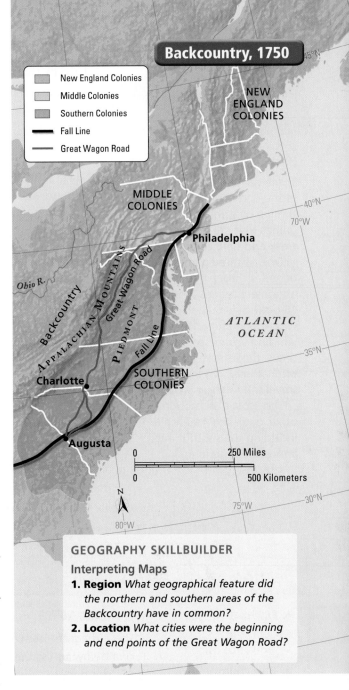

Backcountry, 1750

Legend:
- New England Colonies
- Middle Colonies
- Southern Colonies
- Fall Line
- Great Wagon Road

NEW ENGLAND COLONIES

MIDDLE COLONIES

Philadelphia

Ohio R.

Backcountry

APPALACHIAN MOUNTAINS

Great Wagon Road

PIEDMONT

Fall Line

ATLANTIC OCEAN

Charlotte

SOUTHERN COLONIES

Augusta

0   250 Miles
0   500 Kilometers

N

GEOGRAPHY SKILLBUILDER
Interpreting Maps
1. **Region** What geographical feature did the northern and southern areas of the Backcountry have in common?
2. **Location** What cities were the beginning and end points of the Great Wagon Road?

Reading History

A. Summarizing How did Backcountry settlers make a living?

Backcountry Sports Today

Three centuries ago, crowds in the Backcountry were thrilled by some of the same games that are now part of track and field competitions.

One of these games is the hammer throw. In this event, an athlete swings around a 16-pound metal ball on a wire-rope handle. After whirling around several times, the athlete lets go of the hammer, hoping it will travel the farthest distance.

The Scots-Irish brought other games to America, including the shotput, high jump, and long jump.

Backcountry Life

Life in the Backcountry was very different from life on the coast. Settlers along the coast carried on a lively trade with England. But in the Backcountry, rough roads, swift rivers, and rocky mountains made it almost impossible to trade with other regions.

As a result, Backcountry farmers quickly learned to depend on themselves. They built log cabins and furnished them with corn husk mattresses and homemade benches and tables. They fed their families the hogs and cattle they raised and the fish and game they killed. They grew yellow corn to feed their livestock and white corn to eat. Women in the Backcountry worked in the cabin, but they also worked the fields and used guns and axes to establish their homestead.

New England, the Middle Colonies, the Southern Colonies, and the Backcountry differed in many ways. Varying geography and climate, population, and economic systems led to regional differences. But the colonists shared the experience of living in a new land, far from the settled life they left behind. That shared experience became part of a unique colonial culture that you will learn about in the next section.

Reading History

B. Making Inferences
How would you describe the way people in the Backcountry lived?

Section 2 Assessment

1. TERMS & NAMES

Explain the significance of:

a. Backcountry

b. Great Wagon Road

2. TAKING NOTES

Use a diagram like the one below to list the reasons people came to settle in the Backcountry.

Reasons to Settle in the Backcountry

3. MAIN IDEAS

a. Explain how the people who settled the Backcountry were different from the people who owned the coastal plantations.

b. Why did settlers move to the Backcountry?

c. Why did women have different roles in the Backcountry than along the coast?

4. CRITICAL THINKING

Making Inferences

What advantage might there be in living near the coastal regions?

Think About

• how colonists traveled

• the kind of land available for farming

Language Arts/Art Write a **journal entry** in the voice of a settler traveling the Great Wagon Road or draw a **picture** of a typical Backcountry farm.

3

Colonial Culture

MAIN IDEA	WHY IT MATTERS NOW	TERMS & NAMES
As the traditions of the different colonists merged with the realities of colonial life, a new culture formed.	The laws and customs of the colonies were the starting point for an American identity that is still developing today.	apprentice Enlightenment dame school John Locke Great Awakening

SETTING THE STAGE

The opportunities to build a new life attracted many colonists. But unknown hardships were also a part of that life. Living in an unfamiliar land meant facing these problems with fresh solutions. Although they brought their skills and traditions with them, survival in the new country meant finding new ways to work together.

The struggle for survival required the energy of all settlers: men, women, and children. How would their lives be different in the new country? How would they meet the new challenges? What different ways of living would develop? How did these unique ways of living and looking at the world affect what became the "American culture"?

▲ On many colonial farms, women worked in the fields with their husbands.

The Importance of Land Ownership

For European settlers, owning land was a powerful attraction. In England, fewer than 5 percent of the people owned land. England was a small, well-populated country; land was not offered for sale frequently. In America, land was plentiful—once settlers persuaded Native Americans to leave or forced them off the land. Most Europeans did not recognize the Native Americans' rights to the land. If the Indians could be persuaded to give up the land, settlers could claim it. Many colonists believed that God meant for land to be cultivated. If Native Americans did not improve the land, they thought, it should be taken by those who would.

Land ownership also granted political rights. Generally, only white male landowners had the right to vote. Land ownership also determined social rank. Large landholders were the highest on the social ladder. Small farmers who owned land were in the middle. Most colonists were in this social class. People who did not own land were at the lowest rank. Women held the same rank as their husbands or fathers. Unskilled

Taking Notes

Use your chart to note causes that led to colonial culture.

	New England	Middle
Cause: Climate		

Colonial Social Ranks

HIGH

- large landowners
- church officials
- government officials
- wealthy merchants

UPPER MIDDLE

- small farmers
- tradespeople

LOWER MIDDLE

- renters
- unskilled workers

LOW

- indentured servants
- slaves

laborers, indentured servants, and enslaved workers might attain other rights, such as being admitted to a church congregation. Rarely, however, did they gain political rights.

Colonial Women

Women played an important part in the success of the English colonies. In Virginia, where the first group of settlers to a site was usually unmarried men, women soon followed. A man would agree to pay the cost of a woman's transportation to America. The woman would either become his wife or agree to work for him for five to seven years as an indentured servant.

Women's Responsibilities At that time, most people believed that a wife was the property of her husband. But marriage was very important to women because it was the most common way to achieve any status.

Women's contributions were critical to the settlers' survival in the early years of the colonies. Most white women were farm wives, who cooked, churned butter, made soap and candles, spun fibers, wove cloth, and sewed and knitted clothes. They usually tended the animals that were food for the family. They kept a small garden. At harvest time, they often helped gather the crops.

Since cash was scarce, women might exchange goods and services with one another. For example, one woman might take care of a sick neighbor in exchange for sugar or cloth. Women who lived in well-populated towns might become seamstresses or run boardinghouses. A few women, usually the wives or widows of tradesmen, practiced trades themselves. In areas where enslaved workers were held, women helped raise cash crops such as rice, tobacco, and indigo.

Other Roles for Women Women were the first to establish schools and homes for orphaned children in the colonies. They provided medical care when a doctor was not available. Some, such as Anne Hutchinson, became religious leaders. She believed people should make their own moral choices. She also thought that women had the same rights as men. Church leaders felt she was "disruptive" and forced her to leave the colony. She moved to Rhode Island, which was more tolerant of religious differences.

Despite their real contributions, women had few rights in colonial society. The husband owned everything—even the wife's clothes. A woman could not own property without her husband's permission, and even any money she earned belonged to the husband.

Reading History

A. Finding Main Ideas In what ways was women's work essential to the economy?

Colonial Children

Children also contributed to the economic life and success of the colonies. Large families meant more workers. Children as young as three or four years old had simple jobs to do. They might tend farm animals, gather fruits and vegetables, or watch younger children.

Reading History

B. Contrasting
How did the training of boys and girls differ?

Learning a Trade Families expected boys to start helping their fathers at work around the age of six. Sons of farmers helped clear land and tend the crops. In this way, they learned how to farm. Sons of craftsmen learned their trade by helping their fathers. Young boys often left their families around age 11 to become apprentices. An **apprentice** learned a trade from an experienced craftsman. He worked for free in exchange for food, clothing, lodging, and a general education along with learning the craft.

Home Skills Girls rarely became apprentices. They learned sewing, cooking, and household management at home from their mothers. Sometimes in the New England colonies, girls of 13 or 14 years of age might go to another household. There they would learn special tasks, such as weaving or cheese making.

If children were orphans, they usually went to work as servants for other families. In exchange, the family housed, fed, and clothed them until they reached adulthood. Often there were more orphans than there were families who could take them in. Orphanages were one way to deal with this problem. George Whitefield originally established The Bethesda School in Savannah as an orphanage.

▼ Apprentices worked for four to seven years to learn a trade. Girls learned the skills they would need at home.

Colonial Education

Colonists valued education, but education then was different from what is taught today. Most children were taught to read so they could understand the Bible. In 1647, Massachusetts passed a law that required towns with at least 50 families to hire a teacher of reading and writing. Towns with at least 100 families had to establish a grammar school.

Reading and Writing Young children usually attended a **dame school,** where they learned the alphabet and basic reading and writing skills. An older woman, or dame, taught the school, usually in her own home. Most children finished their formal education by the age of six or seven, when they left to learn a trade or homemaking skills.

Children from wealthier families had private tutors or attended private schools called Latin grammar schools. A minister or teacher usually taught the classes. In addition to reading, writing, and arithmetic, the students learned Latin and Greek. There was a lot of memorization, and discipline was very strict.

Higher Education Colleges in the colonial period were located in the northeast (with the exception of William and Mary College in

Reading History

C. Contrasting
How was colonial education different from education today?

▼ In a dame school, children learned to read, write, and say their prayers.

Virginia). Colleges such as Harvard, Yale, and Princeton trained young men who would become political leaders, ministers, and wealthy landowners or merchants. Colleges did not admit women. A young man had to know Latin and Greek to attend college. They studied the classics and liberal arts. Unlike today, college students did not go to school to prepare for a particular profession. They went for a general education.

Most colonists thought schooling was more important for males. It was rare for Africans to receive an education. If they were enslaved, teaching them to read was illegal. If they were free, they were often kept out of schools.

The Great Awakening and the Enlightenment

King James II was king of England when the first English colonies were established. He believed in a heavy-handed rule with little input from his subjects. James was also Catholic when most of England belonged to the Church of England. The English Parliament grew unhappy with King James and overthrew him in 1688. His daughter and her husband, William and Mary, came to the throne in 1689. They agreed to uphold the English Bill of Rights, which limited the power of royalty and made them obey the laws passed by Parliament.

Reading History

D. Recognizing Effects What were some of the effects in the colonies of the Great Awakening?

The Great Awakening In the 1730s and 1740s, a religious movement called the <u>**Great Awakening**</u> swept through the colonies, stirring up intense religious enthusiasm. Ministers traveled the colonies, preaching that inner religious emotion was more important than outward religious behavior.

As religion became more personal and emotional, people developed differing views about how to express their religious ideas. These differences often caused congregations to split apart. People left and established new congregations and even new churches. Sometimes these new congregations welcomed the Native Americans and African Americans into their membership.

The renewed religious feeling encouraged the colonists to help others. In Georgia, the well-known preacher George Whitefield raised money to start his Bethesda Home for orphans. Others raised money for seminaries to train ministers. Some ministers educated Native Americans and African Americans.

The Great Awakening lasted for several years and changed colonial culture. It gave the people ideas about equality and the right to challenge authority. It contributed

▼ George Whitefield preaching to a crowd.

73

▲ John Locke believed that a government's power comes from the consent of the people who are governed.

to the movement for independence that prepared the way for the American Revolution.

The Enlightenment   Another 18th-century cultural movement was known as The Age of **Enlightenment.** The Enlightenment, like the Great Awakening, also influenced people to think differently. But Enlightenment thinkers emphasized reason and science as the path to knowledge, rather than religion. Traditionally, religious authorities had been looked to for answers on how to live, even how to be governed. Followers of the Enlightenment believed that human rights were being neglected under the traditional rules. This was revolutionary thinking. Enlightenment ideas caused cultural and political upheavals that led to the American Revolutionary War, the French Revolution, as well as the Industrial Revolution. The Enlightenment movement appealed mostly to wealthy, educated men, but its ideas affected all the colonists.

One English philosopher, **John Locke,** wrote that people have natural rights. These included rights to life, liberty, and property. He further believed that people create governments to protect their natural rights. If a government fails to protect the rights, the people have a right to change the government. In other words, Locke was challenging the ideas of kings being allowed to rule people. Locke's ideas inspired the writers of America's Declaration of Independence years later.

Colonial Africans

In all aspects of colonial life, enslaved Africans were treated differently. Except in certain cases, they were not allowed to read or write. They could not own property or earn wages. They had no political voice. In spite of often brutal living conditions, Africans preserved many customs and beliefs from their homelands. These included music, dances, stories, and, for a time, African religions—including Islam. African kinship customs became the basis of African-American family culture. A network of kin was a source of strength even when families were separated.

The Stono Rebellion   While enslaved Africans struggled to maintain their own culture, they fought against their enslavement. Sometimes slaves would attempt to run away, even if it meant risking their lives. In a few cases, slaves became so angry and frustrated by their loss of freedom that they rose up in rebellion. Although it lasted only a day, the Stono Rebellion was one of the most famous incidents.

On September 9, 1739, about 20 slaves broke into a store near the Stono River in South Carolina. They killed two people, stole weapons and supplies, and headed toward St. Augustine. The Spanish there prom-

Reading History

E. Forming Opinions   Why do you think that force was needed to keep Africans enslaved?

ised freedom to any escaped slave. Fort Mose, near St. Augustine, was a settlement of nearly 100 Africans who had escaped from South Carolina. Along the road, they attacked and burned plantations. At each farm, more slaves joined them, until they were between 60 and 80 people.

When a group of slaveholders pursuing the slaves caught up with them, they fought. About 20 white South Carolinians and 40 black South Carolinians were killed in the battle.

Reading History

F. Analyzing Cause and Effect
How did white colonists react to the Stono Rebellion?

After the Stono Rebellion, white colonists became fearful of more revolts. Fearful lawmakers enacted harsh slave codes. Slaves were prohibited from growing their own food, assembling in groups, keeping any money they earned, or learning to read. Some of these limitations were already law, but had not been strictly enforced in many places. These codes made life for slaves even harder than before.

Plans for a Different Colony

Twelve of the original thirteen colonies were well established by the 1700s. The last English colony to be added was Georgia. The founders of Georgia had plans for a different kind of colony. This colony would have no large plantations, no liquor, and no slaves. It would offer poor, but worthy, people a chance for a fresh start in a new country. It would help protect the colony of South Carolina and more firmly establish England's rights in North America. In the next chapter, you will learn more about the founding of Georgia.

Section 3 Assessment

1. TERMS & NAMES
Explain the significance of:

a. apprentice

b. dame school

c. Great Awakening

d. Enlightenment

e. John Locke

2. TAKING NOTES
Create a chart like the one below to review how women and children contributed to the success of their colonies.

Contribution	Women	Children
Home		
Economy		
Community		

3. MAIN IDEAS
a. Why was land ownership especially important to colonists?

b. Explain how new religions resulted from the Great Awakening.

c. How did the Enlightenment contribute to the move for independence?

d. How did slave rebellions affect slave codes?

4. CRITICAL THINKING
Contrasting

How were the Great Awakening and the Enlightenment different?

Think About
• the ideas each movement promoted
• the people to whom each movement appealed

Language Arts/Art Research and write a **paragraph** about the different trades a colonial child could be apprenticed to or create an **illustrated chart** of social ranks in the colonies.

The Colonies Develop

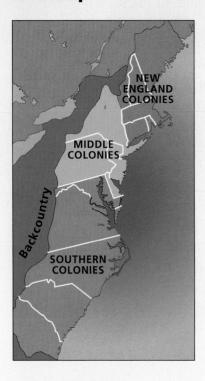

NEW
ENGLAND
COLONIES

MIDDLE
COLONIES

Backcountry

SOUTHERN
COLONIES

■ **NEW ENGLAND: COMMERCE AND RELIGION**

New England was distinguished by its small farming towns and profitable fishing and trade.

■ **THE MIDDLE COLONIES: FARMS AND CITIES**

The Middle Colonies' farms produced large cash crops that fueled trade in its coastal cities.

■ **THE SOUTHERN COLONIES: PLANTATIONS AND SLAVERY**

The South's plantation economy and large number of enslaved Africans made it different from the other regions.

■ **THE BACKCOUNTRY**

The Backcountry was distant from the denser coastal populations, so settlers there developed an independent and rugged way of life.

TERMS & NAMES

Briefly explain the significance of the following.

1. Pilgrim
2. Puritan
3. commonwealth
4. cash crop
5. triangular trade
6. plantation economy
7. Backcountry
8. apprentice
9. Great Awakening
10. Enlightenment

REVIEW QUESTIONS

The English Establish 13 Colonies (pages 59–65)

1. What role did the Church of England play in the Colonies?
2. How did the Puritan work ethic affect the Colonies?
3. What three kinds of trade did the New England Colonies participate in?
4. Why did the Middle Colonies become home to large urban trading centers?
5. What made the Southern Colonies different from the other colonies?

The Backcountry (pages 66–68)

6. What was the Great Wagon Road?
7. What types of people settled in the Backcountry?

Colonial Culture (pages 69–75)

8. Why was land ownership important to the colonists?
9. What role did education play in the colonies?
10. What two movements of the 1730s and 1740s paved the way to revolution?

CRITICAL THINKING

1. USING YOUR NOTES: ANALYZING CAUSES AND RECOGNIZING EFFECTS

	New England	Middle	Southern	Backcountry
Cause: Climate				
Cause: Resources				
Cause: People				
Effect: Economic Development				

Using your completed chart, answer the questions below.

a. How did the resources of New England affect its economy?
b. How did the South's labor system differ from the North's?

2. ANALYZING LEADERSHIP

How did the leaders of the Great Awakening influence early American culture and values?

3. APPLYING CITIZENSHIP SKILLS

What key values of American citizenship are reflected in John Locke's Enlightenment philosophy?

4. THEME: ECONOMICS IN HISTORY

What factors influenced the economic development of each of the four colonial regions?

5. ANALYZING CAUSES

What factors caused the growth of slavery in the South?

INTERACT with HISTORY

Having read about the differences in the colonies, where do you think you would have chosen to settle? What type of life would you have chosen for yourself and your family?

A. Use the chart to answer questions 1 and 2.

	1601–1810	
Slaves Imported to the Americas *(in thousands)*		
REGION/COUNTRY	*1601–1700*	*1701–1810*
British N. America	*	348
British Caribbean	263.7	1,401.3
French Caribbean	155.8	1,348.4
Spanish America	292.5	578.6
Dutch Caribbean	40	460
Danish Caribbean	4	24
Brazil (Portugal)	560	1,891.4

*=less than 1,000

1. Which region or country had the largest increase in slaves imported to the Americas?

   A. British Caribbean
   B. French Caribbean
   C. Dutch Caribbean
   D. Brazil (Portugal)

2. Which region imported fewer than 1,000 slaves before 1700?

   A. Danish Caribbean
   B. Dutch Caribbean
   C. British North America
   D. Spanish America

B. Jonathan Edwards' sermon *Sinners in the Hands of an Angry God* led to renewed religious commitment for many in the Great Awakening. Use your knowledge of the Great Awakening to answer question 3.

PRIMARY SOURCE

How awful is it to be left behind at such a day! To see so many others feasting, while you are pining and perishing! To see so many rejoicing and singing for joy of heart, while you have cause to mourn for sorrow of heart, and howl for vexation of spirit!

3. According to Edwards, what will happen to those who are left behind?

   A. They will feast.
   B. They will rejoice and sing.
   C. They will flock to Christ.
   D. They will mourn and howl.

TEST PRACTICE
CLASSZONE.COM

ALTERNATIVE ASSESSMENT

1. DRAWING A MAP

Draw a map of the New England, Middle, and Southern Colonies. Locate the major cities and rivers of each colony. Also show where people of different racial and ethnic groups settled. Explain how each region's geographic location contributed to the colonies' economic activities.

2. COOPERATIVE LEARNING

Do some more research on the Backcountry and the history of log cabins. Work with others to record details about the location where you will build your log cabin. Then design and construct a model of a log cabin that could be compared to the cabins in which Backcountry settlers lived.

INTEGRATED TECHNOLOGY ACTIVITY

1. MAKING A CLASS PRESENTATION

Life on the farm in colonial New England was a real challenge. Use the library or Internet to find accounts of how New England farm families lived. Then design a multimedia presentation about a typical New England farmer and his family. Be sure to include the social and economic contributions of women in your presentation.

RESEARCH LINKS
CLASSZONE.COM

Trustee Georgia 1730–1761

An illustration from a pamphlet about Georgia published by the trustees shows the town of Savannah being built.

1730
Oglethorpe proposes new kind of colony between South Carolina and Florida.

1738
Minister George Whitefield arrives in Georgia.

1739
War of Jenkins' Ear

1742
Battle of Bloody Marsh

1743
Oglethorpe returns to England. William Stephens becomes president of Georgia.

GEORGIA USA   1730   1740

1732
Benjamin Franklin publishes Poor Richards' Almanack.

1739
Enslaved Africans revolt in Stono Rebellion.

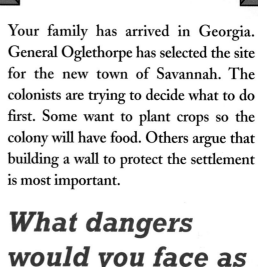

Your family has arrived in Georgia. General Oglethorpe has selected the site for the new town of Savannah. The colonists are trying to decide what to do first. Some want to plant crops so the colony will have food. Others argue that building a wall to protect the settlement is most important.

What dangers would you face as a settler?

WHAT DO YOU THINK?

- What do you need to survive in the wilderness?

- The men of the colony need to be "soldier-farmers." What kind of skills are needed for these roles? Can one person be both?

- What kind of settlement would you build?

For more information on this chapter, visit . . .

RESEARCH LINKS
CLASSZONE.COM

1747
Mary Musgrove claims ownership to most of Georgia.

1751
First legislative assembly meets. Slavery becomes legal.

1754
John Reynolds appointed first royal governor.

1761
James Wright becomes third royal governor.

1750

1760

1752
Benjamin Franklin invents the lightning rod.

1754
French and Indian War begins.

Reading Strategy:
Identifying and Solving Problems

What Do You Know?

What do you already know about the first Georgia colonists? What sort of people first came to Georgia and why did they come? What challenges did they face? What did they hope to find here?

THINK ABOUT

• what you've learned about early Georgia history from school, from your parents, or from your travels in the state

• opportunities and challenges faced by the colonists

What Do You Want to Know?

What questions do you have about the Europeans who settled in Georgia? About those who were already here? Record those questions in your notebook before you read the chapter.

Identifying and Solving Problems

The first colonists in Georgia faced many challenges. How did these problems affect the colonists and their leaders? How did they attempt to solve their problems? As you better understand the choices made by the colonists and their leaders, you can learn new ways to solve problems today. Use the chart below to list the problems faced by the Georgia colonists. Note how the different parties viewed these problems and the solutions they attempted.

S *See Skillbuilder Handbook, page 553.*

Taking Notes

Differing Points of View	Problem	Solution
Trustees: Colonists:		
Trustees: Colonists:		
Trustees: Colonists:		
Trustees: Colonists:		
Trustees: Colonists:		
Trustees: Colonists:		

Creating a Buffer Colony

MAIN IDEA	WHY IT MATTERS NOW	TERMS & NAMES
Georgia was created for different reasons than other English colonies. Unique rules made Georgia different from the start.	Savannah was the first permanent European settlement in Georgia. It is one of the state's leading cities today.	James Edward Oglethorpe trustee Yamacraw Bluff John and Mary Musgrove Tomochichi Treaty of Savannah

SETTING THE STAGE

The English settlement at Charles Town, South Carolina, was successful and growing. But the Spanish in Florida encouraged the Native Americans to make regular attacks on Charles Town. In between was "debatable land" not claimed by either country.

When Sir Robert Montgomery advertised his plans for Azilia in 1717, he saw the need for a "buffer colony" to protect Charles Town from the Spanish. Montgomery gave up his charter in 1720. His ideas were not forgotten, however.

In 1721, South Carolinians built Fort King George at the mouth of the Altamaha River to protect their southern border. But attacks from the Spanish and Native Americans, disease, and the harsh environment forced them to abandon it in 1728.

In 1730, James Oglethorpe proposed a new kind of colony for the area between Charles Town and Florida. The colony would solve several problems for England. The scheme sounded ideal, but would it work? Could he attract enough colonists? Could they grow and prosper in the new land?

▲ The bustling seaport at Charles Town needed protection from Spanish and Native American attacks.

Reasons for the Colony

<u>James Edward Oglethorpe</u> was born in 1696. He became a member of the British Parliament in 1722. In Parliament, he argued for prison reform and spoke out against any kind of slavery. Oglethorpe was known for his benevolence, or kind deeds.

Hard Times in England England was experiencing serious agricultural problems. People were leaving the farms and going to the cities. The remaining farmers could not produce enough food. Cities were overcrowded, and many people were homeless and without work. People who could not pay their debts went to prison, where the conditions were

Taking Notes

Use your chart to note problems and solutions offered in the creation of a buffer colony.

Differing Points of View	Problem	Solution
Trustees: Colonists:		
Trustees: Colonists:		

JAMES EDWARD OGLETHORPE
1696–1785

James Edward Oglethorpe was a natural leader. In Parliament, he argued for the rights of the poor and against slavery. He championed the idea of a new colony for debtors.

As "Resident Trustee," Oglethorpe was responsible for the colonists. He was strict, but cared about the colonists' physical and spiritual welfare. He made frequent trips to England to obtain money, supplies, advice, and even ministers for the colony.

In 1775, Oglethorpe was asked to lead the British Army against America, but he refused because he thought Britain should compromise with, not fight, the colonists.

horrible. Oglethorpe served on the Prison Discipline Committee in Parliament, and it was there that he heard about the idea of a colony created for debtors.

A few leaders thought that creating a debtors' colony might solve many problems. It would give debtors a chance to start over. It would also ease overcrowding, homelessness, and unemployment in England. The colony could support itself financially by selling the raw materials of the new land to England. England would save money by purchasing from the colony instead of from other countries. In addition, the new colony would protect the settlement at Charles Town from an attack by Spanish Florida.

The Creation of Georgia After a friend died in debtor's prison, Oglethorpe became a strong advocate for creating a colony for debtors. In 1730, Oglethorpe and 20 other prominent men who were called **trustees** drafted a charter that requested the king to give them "a grant of lands on the southwest of Carolina for settling poor persons of London." They would name the new colony "Georgia" in honor of King George II.

The trustees requested in their charter "all land between the Altamaha and Savannah Rivers and from the headwaters of these rivers to the south seas." The charter also outlined the three purposes for the new colony:

1. **charitable:** relief for debtors and "worthy poor";
2. **economic:** a self-supporting colony that would provide cheap natural resources for Britain;
3. **defensive:** a protective barrier between Florida and the settlement at Charles Town.

Oglethorpe used his connections to get the charter to the king, who signed it on June 9, 1732.

To encourage colonists, the trustees offered each man free passage, 50 acres of land, and support for his family for up to a year until he could start making his own way. A colonist who paid for his passage would receive 500 acres that would be tax-free for 10 years.

While Parliament gave some money to establish the colony, most money came from private sources.

When the time came to select the colonists, many people who were not debtors applied for the trip. The trustees decided to start the new colony with these "worthy poor" instead of debtors. The trustees

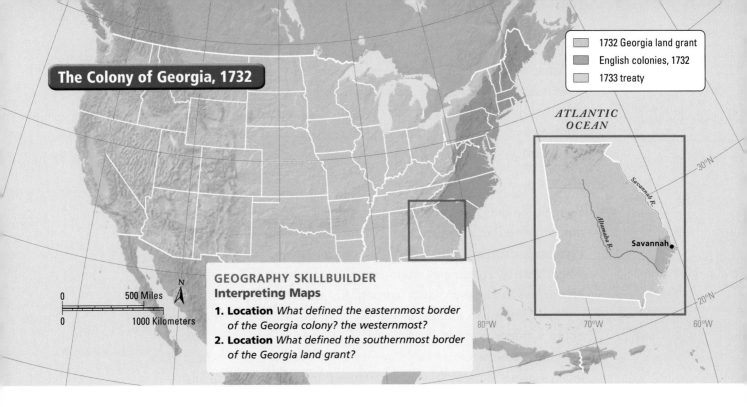

1732 Georgia land grant
English colonies, 1732
1733 treaty

ATLANTIC OCEAN

Savannah R.

Altamaha R.

Savannah

GEOGRAPHY SKILLBUILDER
Interpreting Maps

1. **Location** What defined the easternmost border of the Georgia colony? the westernmost?
2. **Location** What defined the southernmost border of the Georgia land grant?

carefully screened the applicants to make sure they were of good character. Most were artisans or small businessmen.

Oglethorpe paid his own way for the trip across the Atlantic. The trustees named him "Resident Trustee," meaning that he would be the trustee who lived in the new colony. They did not name a colonial governor, so Oglethorpe was in charge. On November 17, 1732, 115 men, women, and children boarded the *Ann*, bound for the new colony.

New Rules for a New Colony

Reading History

A. Finding Main Ideas What rules made Georgia different from other colonies?

The Georgia trustees established several rules that made Georgia quite different from other American colonies. The trustees could not own land in Georgia. They could not make a profit from the colony. This was unlike other colonies that were designed to make a profit for the investors. The trustees claimed that the new colony could pay for itself by supplying England with silk, wine, oil, dyes, and medicines.

In other colonies, the king gave large land claims to people he favored. As a result, social classes developed, with differences between large landowners, small landowners, and those who did not own land. In Georgia, however, the trustees gave all colonists the same amount of land so that distinct classes would not develop. The trustees chose people who were poor and likely to benefit from a new start in the colony.

The trustees would not allow rum or other hard liquor in the new colony. They believed that drinking would interfere with working.

They also banned slavery. This was because residents of other colonies had starved to death because they did not farm the land. Oglethorpe and the other trustees believed that white settlers became lazy when they relied on enslaved labor to do their work.

Another rule had to do with land inheritance. Only male heirs could inherit land. The trustees made this rule because they expected the colonists to defend the colony, as well as farm it. A widow could continue to live on her husband's land, but she and her daughters could never own it.

Sailing to Georgia

By the time the Georgia colonists set sail in 1732, travel conditions had not improved much since the *Mayflower* brought the Pilgrims to Plymouth Rock in 1620. It still took two months to cross the Atlantic. There was barely enough room for the passengers. They slept as a group, and had only a canvas "curtain" for privacy.

After almost two months at sea, the colonists reached Charles Town, South Carolina. Oglethorpe met with Robert Johnson, Royal Governor of South Carolina. Governor Johnson wanted the Georgians to help protect his colony from attacks by the Yamasee Indians and the Spanish.

Establishing the Colony

After docking at Charles Town, the *Ann* sailed to Port Royal, near present-day Beaufort. The Georgia colonists stayed behind while Oglethorpe sailed south, looking for a site for the new colony. Colonel William Bull and Peter Gordon of Charles Town went with him, along with members of the new military unit, the Georgia Guard. They selected a spot beside the Savannah River called **Yamacraw Bluff**. This became the town of Savannah. The site gave an excellent view of the surrounding area, including a nearby Yamacraw Indian village and a trading post run by a husband and wife, **John and Mary Musgrove.**

Reading History

B. Analyzing Causes Why was Yamacraw Bluff chosen as the new colony site?

▼ Tomochichi gave Oglethorpe permission to establish a settlement on Yamacraw Bluff, which became Savannah.

John and Mary Musgrove John Musgrove was the son of Colonel John Musgrove of South Carolina. Mary was born "Cousaponakeesa" in Coweta Town on the Ocmulgee River. She was the daughter of a white South Carolina trader and a Creek Indian.

The Musgroves had a trading monopoly since other whites were not allowed to settle in that area. Both the Indians and the merchants of Charles Town traded with the Musgroves. Mary supplied the colonists with meat, bread, and other supplies.

Chief Tomochichi John introduced Oglethorpe to **Tomochichi,** chief of the Yamacraw Indians, part of the Creek Confederacy. The Musgroves advised the colonists to make a treaty with Tomochichi in order to settle at Yamacraw Bluff. John translated during the negotiations between Oglethorpe and Tomochichi. Tomochichi agreed to allow the colonists to settle there.

Oglethorpe left the Georgia Guard there to prepare the area, including building steps up the bluff. Oglethorpe then returned to Port Royal to collect the colonists. They left Port Royal and arrived at the site of their new colony on February 1, 1733.

Negotiating with the Creek About three months after the colonists' arrival, Oglethorpe met with a group of Creek chiefs to establish peace and friendship. After three days of talking and dealing, they signed the **Treaty of Savannah.** The Creek agreed to give the land to the colonists. The colonists agreed to trade with the Creek at set prices. The Creek would return escaped slaves to their masters in South Carolina. Oglethorpe promised that the colonists would not move into other areas of Creek land.

Continued Help from the Musgroves and Tomochichi Both Mary and John served as translators between the colonists and the Native Americans. John also served as interpreter for John Wesley, a minister Oglethorpe had brought over from England, and for Tomochichi. Mary allowed Oglethorpe to use her employees, both traders and Native American runners, as his assistants. John Musgrove died in June 1734. Mary continued to serve as trader and negotiator between the settlers and the Native Americans. She died in 1763.

▼ Tomochichi's help in negotiating land and peace treaties between Native Americans and colonists was critical to the colony's early success.

Tomochichi was an important ally for Oglethorpe. Oglethorpe respected him so much that he asked Tomochichi to accompany him to England in 1734. Oglethorpe took John Musgrove, Tomochichi, and Tomochichi's nephew, Tooanahowi. Tomochichi met the king and the trustees while he was in London. He was impressed by what he saw and by what he heard. He was convinced that the Creek Confederacy should be the allies of England.

Reading History

C. Forming Opinions Why was Tomochichi an important ally?

In 1739, Oglethorpe visited the Creek capital in present-day Alabama and signed the Treaty of Coweta. In this treaty, the chiefs reaffirmed their vows of loyalty to King George II. They also reconfirmed their land grant of 1733 to Oglethorpe that gave him permission to settle.

PRIMARY SOURCE

All the lands upon Savannah River as farr as the River Ogechee and all lands along the Sea Coast as farr as the River Saint Johns & as high as the Tide Flows and All the Islands of Frederica, Cumberland & Amelia to which they have given the names of his Majesty King Georges Family out of gratitude to him.

Treaty of Coweta

Once the colonists had received permission from Tomochichi and the Creek to establish their colony, the real work began. Living and farming in forested wilderness was challenging. In the next section, you will learn more about how early Georgians met that challenge.

Section 1 Assessment

1. TERMS & NAMES

Explain the significance of:

a. James Edward Oglethorpe

b. trustee

c. Yamacraw Bluff

d. John and Mary Musgrove

e. Tomochichi

f. Treaty of Savannah

2. TAKING NOTES

Use a diagram like the one below to note the three laws made by the trustees for the new colony in Georgia.

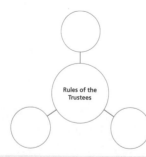

Rules of the Trustees

3. MAIN IDEAS

a. What conditions in England made people want to come to America?

b. Why was the colony of Georgia important to the South Carolina colony?

c. Why was Yamacraw Bluff a good site for the new colony?

4. CRITICAL THINKING

Supporting Opinions

Why do you think the Creek negotiated a treaty to give land to the colonists?

Think About
• previous contact with the Spanish
• who served as translator
• trade agreements

Art/Technology Create a **wall plaque** or design a **web page** that pays tribute to James Oglethorpe's, Tomochichi's, or Mary Musgrove's contributions to Georgia.

Life in the New Colony

MAIN IDEA	WHY IT MATTERS NOW	TERMS & NAMES
The noble ideals Georgia was founded on quickly gave way to the difficult realities of life in a new land.	Many different groups settled in Georgia. Their impact is apparent in Georgia today.	palisade George Whitefield Scots Highlander Augusta John Wesley

SETTING THE STAGE

The colonists were aware of the trustees' rules for the new colony when they applied to come to Georgia. They were eager to start a new life where they could own land.

They did not know, however, how hard that new life would be. The hot, humid climate of Georgia was uncomfortable. Very few colonists were farmers. Would the colonists be able to grow the crops they needed and England wanted? Would they be willing to live under the strict rules and high expectations of the trustees? Could they make a success of this new kind of colony?

▲ The colonists built a crane atop the bluff to lift their supplies to the site of Savannah.

Establishing Savannah

When the colonists arrived at the site for their new colony, they set up tents and began building a **palisade** around the settlement. A palisade is a strong wooden wall that surrounds a compound for defense. When the colonists finished building the palisade, they built a crane at the top of the bluff. The crane lifted supplies from ships. The colonists worked "in common," meaning they all worked as a group until they completed one task, before starting the next one.

Planning for a City   Oglethorpe and Colonel Bull began laying out the city. Oglethorpe based the layout of Savannah on designs for Azilia.

The original plan for Savannah called for four districts called wards. In the center of a ward was an open public space called a square. At the four corners of the square were large lots for public buildings such as churches or government offices. Around the square were four blocks of 10 house lots each.

In early May 1733, the *James* brought more colonists to Port Royal, who then made their way to Savannah. The colony needed the new

Taking Notes

Use your chart to note problems and solutions offered in establishing a new life in a new colony.

Differing Points of View	Problem	Solution
Trustees: Colonists:		
Trustees: Colonists:		

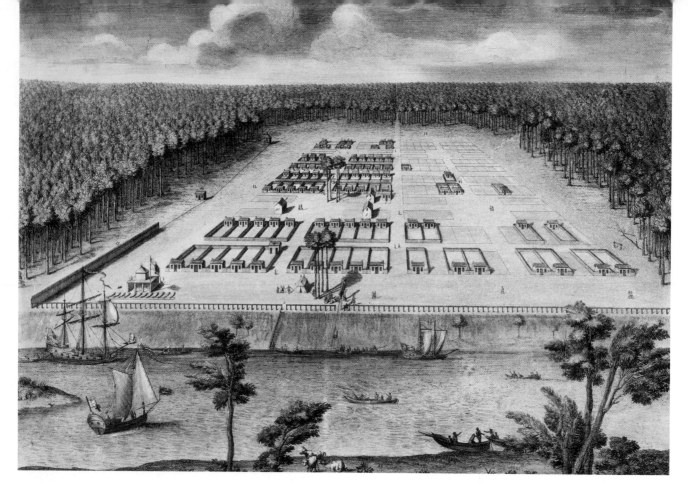

▲ This 1734 view of Savannah shows the orderly plan of wards, public squares, and house lots. The palisade to the left soon surrounded the town.

arrivals to fill out the population. Living conditions in Savannah had been difficult. Contaminated water and disease-carrying insects had killed many of the original settlers during the first two years.

When the palisade was finished and the edge of the new town was safe, Oglethorpe built forts to defend Savannah from the west and south. The first was Fort Argyle, built along the Ogeechee River. Fort Argyle was finished in September 1733.

In February 1736, Hugh Mackay led 166 **Scots Highlanders** to settle on the northern bank of the Altamaha River. They built a fort there to protect Savannah, called the area Darien, and named the town New Inverness.

Fort Frederica on St. Simons Island was built in early 1736. By September, 200 men, women, and children were living there. In March 1736, Oglethorpe selected sites for three more forts: Forts St. Andrew and William on Cumberland Island and Fort St. George on Amelia Island. In June, Fort Augusta was authorized. These forts would protect the colony on all sides.

More Residents for the Colony Settlers continued to arrive in the new Georgia colony. They included three religious groups that had been heavily persecuted in their original countries: Moravians (Protestants from Czechoslovakia), Salzburgers (from Austria near the German border), and Jews.

Reading History

A. Making Inferences Why did Oglethorpe lead the colonists in building forts?

Initially the trustees had not allowed Jewish settlers in Georgia. But in 1733, a ship of Jewish colonists from Portugal arrived in Savannah, with physician Dr. Samuel Nunes among them. The colony desperately needed his services, as the only doctor had died earlier. Oglethorpe allowed the Jewish settlers to disembark.

Religion in the Colony   Oglethorpe and other trustees welcomed all religions except Roman Catholics. Threatened by Florida to the south, they did not want to risk that Catholic settlers might ally with Spanish Catholics there.

When Oglethorpe returned from his trip to London in 1736, he brought back two ministers: **John Wesley,** who later founded the Methodist movement, and his brother Charles. John was to minister to the colonists in Savannah, while Charles was to serve as Oglethorpe's secretary and chaplain at Fort Frederica. Charles returned to England in August 1736. John remained in Georgia until December 1737.

On a later trip, Oglethorpe brought another minister from England, **George Whitefield** (HWIT feeld). Among other actions, Whitefield founded the Bethesda Home for Boys near Savannah in 1740. He wanted it to be a place where orphans "might learn to labor, read and write, and at the same time be brought up in the nurture and admonition of the Lord." The Bethesda school still operates today.

▲ The faith of John Wesley (above) was strongly influenced by the Moravian community in Georgia. His successor, George Whitefield (left), arrived in Georgia in mid-1737.

Another Town for Georgia

Regular communications between Savannah and Charles Town began in October 1734. As trade among settlers and Native Americans grew, there was need for a secure settlement between the two colonies. In June 1736, Oglethorpe approved the site for a way station north of Savannah along the Savannah River. He named the site **Augusta** in honor of Princess Augusta, who had recently married the Prince of Wales. By December 1738, the fort was completed, and the young community was launched. Oglethorpe visited Augusta in 1739 and called it the "Key of the Indian Country."

Life in the New Colony

Although he was not the official governor, Oglethorpe acted as protector for the new colony. From the beginning, the trustees intended Georgia to be different from the Carolinas or Virginia.

Georgia's First Jobs

The trustees hoped the colony could produce wine and silk, two precious commodities in England. So it's clear why two vintners (wine-makers) and one man who "understands raw silk" were chosen for the first passage.

The farmers, gardeners, and sawyers, joiners, and other carpenters would certainly prove useful. Even a cordwainer (shoemaker) and men who could turn flax and hemp into cloth and rope would be valuable.

But why include a peruke (wigmaker) in the founding of a new colony? Luckily, the colony soon found him work as a bailiff (sheriff or deputy).

A small book titled *Some Account of the Designs of the Trustees for Establishing the Colony of Georgia in America* told of some of the trustees' plans for the colony. In it, the trustees promised "good Discipline" and said that the colony would make its people better Christians.

Responsibilities of the Trustees The trustees fed and clothed the colonists for one year and provided seeds and tools so they could begin farming. The men received military training before they left England so they could help defend the colony.

The trustees gave each settler and his family a total of 50 acres and a small town lot for the family home in one of the wards. The 50 acres consisted of a 5-acre garden plot on the edge of town for growing food for the family and a 45-acre farm plot farther out in the countryside for growing larger crops.

The trustees had planned for Georgia to produce silk that they would send back to England. They required everyone to plant mulberry trees because silkworms feed on mulberry leaves. The colonists soon found that they did not know how to take care of silkworms, and they certainly could not make a profit from them.

Discontent Among the Colonists

The colonists began to complain about the trustee rules. In particular, they were upset with restrictions on land ownership, the use of slavery, and the prohibition of rum.

Land Even though colonists received 50 acres of free land, many of the farms were located in areas of poor soil not suited to farming. Some land was even under water at high tide. Many colonists found it difficult to grow the crops that England wanted. But the trustees would not trade the poor land for better. Colonists were also upset that they could not sell or lease their land. Another problem was that women could not inherit. If a family left the colony or the male head of household died, their land went back to the trustees.

Slaves The colonists were also unhappy with the way the trustees wanted them to farm. The trustees had banned slavery so that colonists had to work their own land. While the land was not very good for farming, farmers were able to grow some crops such as rice and indigo. However, these crops were very labor-intensive, and settlers felt they could not prosper without the use of enslaved workers. African slaves in

Reading History

B. Finding Main Ideas Why did the colonists become discontented with their colony?

South Carolina knew the land and had made these crops profitable there. Many South Carolinians had grown rich. Georgians wanted to be able to do the same.

Rum   A third source of discontent was the ban on rum and liquor. Rum was cheap and readily available in other colonies. It was also an item of trade between colonists and Native Americans. The colonists did not understand why they were not allowed to drink it. In fact, officials could not enforce the law.

Hardships Take a Toll   A large reason for the unhappiness of the colonists was that they were not prepared for life in the new colony. The trustees tried to help them. They brought in experts from Italy to teach the colonists how to produce raw silk. They brought in experts from Portugal to teach about the production of indigo for dyes and grapes for wine. What everyone tended to forget, however, is that Georgia's soil and climate were not suited for the crops the colonists were required to grow.

The trustees called the unhappy colonists "Grumbletonians" and "Clamorous Malcontents." In 1738, some of the loudest complainers left for South Carolina. This took care of the problem for a short time, but other problems were waiting for Oglethorpe and the trustees. In the next section, you will read how this discontent led to radical changes in the colony's structure.

▲ Eliza Lucas, a 17-year-old South Carolina girl, was the first colonist to grow indigo.

Section ❷ Assessment

1. TERMS & NAMES
Explain the significance of:

a. palisade

b. Scots Highlanders

c. John Wesley

d. George Whitefield

e. Augusta

2. TAKING NOTES
Use a diagram like the one below to identify what the trustees gave to each colonial family.

Trustees to Give Each Family:

3. MAIN IDEAS
a. What were the causes of death for some of the colonists?

b. Who were the groups that added to the diversity of the colony?

c. What factors prevented the Georgia colonists from producing what the trustees expected?

4. CRITICAL THINKING
Identifying Problems

What problems did the colonists blame on the trustees' laws they had to live under?

Think About
- how land was distributed
- the crops they had to grow
- the value of rum in the colonies

ACTIVITY -OPTIONS-   **Geography/Art** Research the forts that Oglethorpe had built to protect Savannah. Create a **map** indicating where the forts were or build a **model** of one of the forts.

3

The End of Trustee Georgia

MAIN IDEA

Defending the new colony and making a profit for England proved to be too great a task for Oglethorpe. In 1752, Britain took back Georgia and made it a royal colony.

WHY IT MATTERS NOW

Georgia was able to grow when it became more like the other colonies. As a royal colony, the colonists assumed some leadership in the government of the colony.

TERMS & NAMES

Battle of Bloody Marsh
John Reynolds
Commons House of Assembly
parish

▲ The Scots Highlanders of Darien were known for their fighting ability.

SETTING THE STAGE

One of the main purposes of the Georgia colony was to serve as a buffer between Spanish Florida and English Carolina. Even as Oglethorpe tried to keep his colonists happy, he did not forget about protecting Savannah and Charles Town from Spanish attacks. Colonists received only brief military training before leaving England. They had a much smaller militia than the Spanish had in Florida. How could they successfully defend the colony?

The young colony had not been able to make a profit yet. The colonists were unhappy and frustrated because the trustees did not allow them the same privileges as other colonies. The trustees were growing tired of funding the struggling colony. How could they survive?

Defending the New Colony

Oglethorpe had to deal with unhappy settlers from within the colony, as well as unhappy trustees back in England. In 1736, the trustees had sent William Stephens to assist Oglethorpe. In April 1741, they divided Georgia into two counties—Savannah and Frederica. They put Stephens in charge of Savannah. Oglethorpe was in charge of Frederica.

In addition to colonists' discontent, Oglethorpe had to worry about attacks from the Spanish and unfriendly Native Americans from without. From the beginning, he was concerned about improving the colony's defenses. He traveled regularly to the various settlements to keep an eye on their safety.

The rivalry between England and Spain continued, even though England had established its dominance over Spain. An ongoing area of dispute was the border between British Georgia and Spanish Florida. In 1739, Britain declared war on Spain.

Taking Notes

Use your chart to note the problems and solutions offered in making Georgia a royal colony.

Differing Points of View	Problem	Solution
Trustees: Colonists:		
Trustees: Colonists:		

European Conflicts Carried to the Colonies
In the colonies, fighting broke out between the Spanish colonists in Florida and the West Indies and the English colonists in South Carolina and Georgia. In May 1740, Oglethorpe took the offensive and invaded Florida, marching to attack St. Augustine. Native American allies protected him on the west. From May to July, his forces attacked St. Augustine, but he ordered a retreat when Spanish reinforcements arrived. He and his troops fell back to Fort St. Simons.

Minor fighting broke out over the next two years. Then in June 1742, the Spanish sent a fleet of 36 boats to the mouth of the Altamaha River. A week later, the fleet moved up the river behind Fort St. Simons and forced Oglethorpe to evacuate. On July 6, the Spanish marched into the fort that Oglethorpe had built to protect the Georgia colony.

British Establish Control

Oglethorpe commanded only about 650 British and Scots Highlander colonists/soldiers and their Native American allies. The Spanish forces numbered over 2,000. Oglethorpe knew he was outnumbered, but he also knew he had to defeat the Spanish to save the colony. On July 7, he planned to ambush the Spanish troops as they traveled from Fort St. Simons to Fort Frederica. He placed a company of about 60 British soldiers on the left side of the road and about 60 Darien Highlanders and their Native American allies on the right side of the road. A surprise attack from both sides would make the Spanish think there was a large army.

Spain Is Turned Back   When the Spanish troops passed through, Oglethorpe's troops attacked. The **Battle of Bloody Marsh** lasted less than an hour. The Spanish captain was wounded, and his troops ran out of ammunition. He gave the order to retreat. Oglethorpe and his few men had tricked the Spanish into believing that Oglethorpe had many more soldiers than he actually did. Three days later, the Spanish retreated to St. Augustine. This battle gave the British a clear claim to Georgia land. It settled the question of debatable land.

Changes in Leadership   While Oglethorpe led the troops to victory, he was not as successful in leading the colony. The other trustees and the settlers were unhappy with him. After a last unsuccessful attempt to invade Florida in 1743, Oglethorpe left for England and never returned to Georgia. The two counties merged back into one, Savannah. On July 11, 1743, Stephens became president of the Georgia colony.

Reading History

A. Evaluating
Why were Oglethorpe's troops able to triumph over the Spanish troops?

STRANGE BUT TRUE

War of Jenkins' Ear
In October 1739, England declared war against the Spanish because of an incident involving a British officer's ear. Captain Robert Jenkins claimed that Spanish guards had cut off his ear in 1731. When he returned to England and told his story, the House of Commons told him to produce the ear. He did! He had it pickled in a bottle. The ear became a symbol of English pride. They said the Spanish must be taught a lesson—that they could not be allowed to cut off an Englishman's ear. The "War of Jenkins' Ear" began.

▶ In the Battle of Bloody Marsh, Oglethorpe led a force of 650 to victory against 2,000 Spanish forces. Yet only a year later, the colonists' unhappiness with his leadership convinced him to return to England.

The reunited colony grew quickly after the defeat of the Spanish. William Stephens asked for and received permission to establish a legislative assembly. The legislative assembly, however, could only make recommendations. It could not enact laws. The first assembly met on January 14, 1751. It consisted of 16 deputies. They elected Francis Harris, a merchant, as speaker. They also elected Henry Parker to succeed William Stephens as president of the colony on April 8, 1751.

Changing the Rules

The trustees had made three laws for Georgia: limits on land ownership, a ban on rum, and a prohibition on slavery. Many colonists blamed these laws for the colony's problems. Under pressure from the colonists, and wanting to make the colony a success, the trustees began reversing these laws.

Land One of the early rules of the trustees was that no man could own more than 50 acres. This rule was to discourage the growth of large plantations. But the colonists looked to their neighbors who had large plantations, and they wanted the same opportunities for large farms and larger profits. In the mid-1740s, the trustees increased the limit on land ownership to 2,000 acres. Another change allowed women to inherit property left to them in a will.

Reading History

B. Making Inferences Why did the trustees want to discourage the growth of large plantations?

Rum   The colonists had also complained because the trustees prohibited rum. Not only did the colonists want the rum to drink, but rum was valuable for trading with the Native Americans and with the West Indies. The trustees allowed the drinking and sale of rum in 1742.

Slavery   Almost from the beginning, some colonists had petitioned the trustees to allow slavery. In 1749, James Habersham, a successful merchant, and several others asked the trustees to allow slavery in the colony. The following year, the trustees granted his request. Slavery became legal on January 1, 1751. However, two groups of Georgia settlers opposed slavery—the Scots Highlanders at Darien and the German-speaking Salzburgers at Ebenezer.

Reading History

C. Finding Main Ideas   How had the rules for the Georgia colony changed by 1751?

Becoming a Royal Colony

By 1752, the trustees had lost interest in the Georgia colony. They no longer had the money to keep the struggling colony going. The trustees returned the colony to the king in 1752, one year before their 21-year charter expired. King George II appointed **John Reynolds** the first royal governor. He arrived in Georgia on October 30, 1754.

The new royal government consisted of the governor, his council, and a legislature. The 12 men of the Governor's Council advised the

Flags Over Georgia, 1513–1775

Many different flags have flown over Georgia since European settlers landed in the New World. These are just a few.

▲ **1513**   Juan Ponce de León would have carried the flag of Ferdinand and Isabella of Spain when he sailed through the coastal waters of Georgia to claim Florida.

▲ **1562**   Jean Ribault would have carried the French National flag when he founded Port Royal, just north of present-day Savannah.

▲ **1540**   Hernando de Soto would have carried the Spanish cross of Burgundy as he explored Georgia.

▲ **1665 to 1775**   From its early days as part of Carolina to its status as a royal colony, the British Union flag, or Union Jack, would have flown over Georgia.

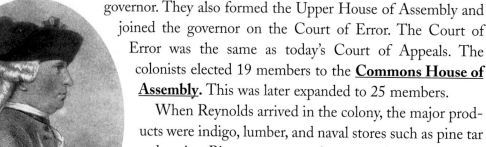

governor. They also formed the Upper House of Assembly and joined the governor on the Court of Error. The Court of Error was the same as today's Court of Appeals. The colonists elected 19 members to the **Commons House of Assembly**. This was later expanded to 25 members.

When Reynolds arrived in the colony, the major products were indigo, lumber, and naval stores such as pine tar and resin. Rice was a popular crop along the coast. Farmers farther inland grew wheat and other products whose hulls needed to be cracked before the grain could be used. One story has it that these poor upcountry farmers earned the name "Crackers" because of these crops.

▲ John Reynolds was the first royal governor of Georgia.

The Assembly Takes Action   The first royal assembly met on January 7, 1755. It approved several acts in that session. The first reorganized the militia. The second provided funding for roads and bridges. The third created paper bills of credit. Another established a list of 10 crimes that would be punished by death. Finally, they approved the first slave code for Georgia. This code became the basis for all future legislative acts on slavery in the colony and the state.

A Change of Governors   Despite this activity, Governor Reynolds was not popular. He tried to move the capital from Savannah to a new town he founded called Hardwicke. This irritated the colonists, and Reynolds gave up the idea. However, he did not accept advice from the council on other issues and soon angered many of the colonists. Dislike and disapproval of Governor Reynolds grew. After an investigation in London, Reynolds was removed.

Lieutenant governor Henry Ellis became the next royal governor of Georgia in May 1758. James Wright became lieutenant governor. Ellis inherited a weak colony with political infighting and an empty treasury. Over the course of three years, he restored the colony to good order. He reformed the government, divided Georgia into parishes, settled land claims, and kept the Creek Indians neutral during the French and Indian War. He was well liked and respected when he resigned in early 1761. James Wright became the third royal governor on May 4, 1761.

Reading History

D. Drawing Conclusions How did Reynolds fail the colonists?

A Voice in Government

When Oglethorpe and the Georgia trustees first established Georgia, it had a very loose local government. Colonists could express their complaints to Oglethorpe, but they did not have a voice in the running of the colony. But when Georgia became a royal colony, the Commons House of Assembly gave the colonists a representative voice in their local government. The Advisory Council, although appointed by the governor, also expressed opinions on the affairs of the colony.

Forming Parishes In 1758, Georgia was divided into eight districts called **parishes,** which were similar to the counties of today. Parishes were mostly for religious and military organization, however, rather than for government purposes. Parish members paid taxes to the church and to help the poor.

For over one hundred years, England had let the colonies take care of their own affairs. This hands-off policy was called "salutary neglect." Colonists learned to handle their own problems, for the most part. When Parliament passed laws that affected the colonies, the colonies rarely enforced them. In the next chapter, you will learn how England started to enforce those laws and made the colonists very unhappy.

Colonial Government in Georgia

BRITISH CROWN

ROYAL GOVERNOR
- appointed by the crown
- oversaw colonial trade
- had final approval on laws
- could dismiss colonial assembly

COUNCIL
- appointed by governor
- advisory board to governor
- acted as highest court in each colony

COLONIAL ASSEMBLY
- elected by eligible colonists
- made laws
- had authority to tax
- paid governor's salary

SKILLBUILDER Interpreting Charts
1. *Which officials were appointed, and which were elected?*
2. *How were lawmaking powers shared?*

Section ③ Assessment

1. TERMS & NAMES
Explain the significance of:

a. Battle of Bloody Marsh

b. John Reynolds

c. Commons House of Assembly

d. parishes

2. TAKING NOTES
Use a diagram like the one below to take notes about the different elements of royal government in Georgia.

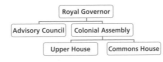

3. MAIN IDEAS
a. How was Oglethorpe able to defeat the Spanish troops?

b. How had the rules of the colony changed by 1751?

c. How did Georgia change and grow under the royal governors?

4. CRITICAL THINKING
Recognizing Effects

How did the colonists' unhappiness with the trustees' rules change how the colony was run?

Think About
- the original type of colony
- the original leadership
- the original rules of the trustees

Language Arts/Speech Read more about the idea of a "utopian society." Write a school newspaper **article** or give a **speech** in support of a new utopian colony.

The Colony of Georgia Is Established

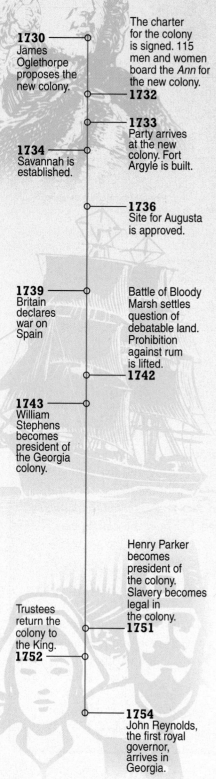

1730
James Oglethorpe proposes the new colony.

The charter for the colony is signed. 115 men and women board the *Ann* for the new colony.
1732

1733
Party arrives at the new colony. Fort Argyle is built.

1734
Savannah is established.

1736
Site for Augusta is approved.

1739
Britain declares war on Spain

Battle of Bloody Marsh settles question of debatable land. Prohibition against rum is lifted.
1742

1743
William Stephens becomes president of the Georgia colony.

Henry Parker becomes president of the colony. Slavery becomes legal in the colony.
1751

Trustees return the colony to the King.
1752

1754
John Reynolds, the first royal governor, arrives in Georgia.

TERMS & NAMES

Briefly explain the significance of the following.

1. James Edward Oglethorpe
2. trustee
3. John and Mary Musgrove
4. Tomochichi
5. Yamacraw Bluff
6. palisade
7. Augusta
8. Battle of Bloody Marsh
9. John Reynolds
10. Commons House of Assembly

REVIEW QUESTIONS

Creating a Buffer Colony (pages 81–86)

1. What English problems influenced the plan for the colony of Georgia?
2. What incentives encouraged colonists to settle in Georgia?
3. What rules made the new colony different from others?

Life in the New Colony (pages 87–91)

4. What religious groups settled in Georgia?
5. Why did the trustees found the colony of Georgia?
6. Why were colonists unhappy with their life in Georgia?

The End of Trustee Georgia (pages 92–97)

7. What role did the Battle of Bloody Marsh play in the life of the new colony?
8. Why did the colony not prosper under the trustees?
9. What acts were passed by the first royal assembly?
10. Why was the Commons House of Assembly important to the colonists?

CRITICAL THINKING

1. USING YOUR NOTES: IDENTIFYING AND SOLVING PROBLEMS

Differing Points of View	Problem	Solution
Trustees: Colonists:		
Trustees: Colonists:		
Trustees: Colonists:		
Trustees: Colonists:		
Trustees: Colonists:		
Trustees: Colonists:		

Using your completed chart, answer the questions below.

a. In what way was slavery a solution to a problem in the Georgia colony?
b. In what ways did the charitable interests of the colony's founders become problems for the colony?

2. ANALYZING LEADERSHIP

Give an example of bad military or political leadership from the chapter. What mistake was made?

3. APPLYING CITIZENSHIP SKILLS

Compare the new royal government of Georgia with our state government today. What similarities do you see?

4. THEME: DEMOCRATIC IDEALS

What democratic ideals did Americans inherit from England?

5. MAKING GENERALIZATIONS

What generalization or broad judgment would you make about the role of Tomochichi in the founding of the state?

INTERACT with HISTORY

Having read about the challenges faced by the Georgia colonists, do you think you would have wanted to stay in Georgia? Why or why not?

Use the map and your knowledge of American history to answer questions 1 through 3.

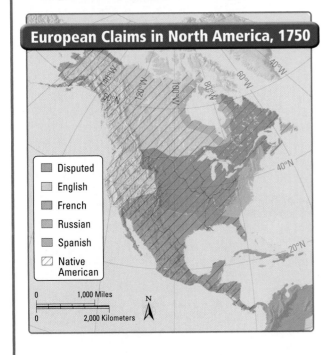

European Claims in North America, 1750

Legend:
- Disputed
- English
- French
- Russian
- Spanish
- Native American

0   1,000 Miles
0   2,000 Kilometers

N

1. Which of the groups shown inhabited the largest area of North America?

   A. Spanish
   B. Russian
   C. English
   D. French

2. Which groups claimed the northernmost territory?

   A. Native American
   B. Russian
   C. French
   D. English

3. In what area did the English claim the most land?

   A. Along the Mississippi River
   B. Around the Great Lakes
   C. Along the east coast
   D. North of Georgia

TEST PRACTICE
CLASSZONE.COM

ALTERNATIVE ASSESSMENT

1. WRITING A JOURNAL ENTRY

Research the lives of the early Georgia colonists. Then put yourself in their place for a day. What work do you do? What is your life like? What do you think about your experience? Write a journal entry about a day in your life as a Georgia colonist.

2. COOPERATIVE LEARNING

In 1730, Oglethorpe and 20 other men drafted a charter requesting "all land between the Altamaha and Savannah Rivers and from the headwaters of these rivers to the south seas." The charter stated the charitable, economic, and defensive purposes of the new colony. Work with a team and use your knowledge of the early Georgia colony to write your own proposal to King George II. Persuade him to grant you the authority to establish the colony of Georgia. Include your plans for the colony and the benefits of the colony to the king. Share your proposal with the class.

INTEGRATED TECHNOLOGY ACTIVITY

DESIGNING A WEB SITE

Use the Internet, your library, and a computer to design a web site that tells the story of the founding of Georgia. Look for primary and secondary sources that reveal what life was like for the colonists. Organize your information into an outline showing the content to appear on each web site page. Write the text, and develop graphics and links for each page. Try to include the following in the plan for your site:

- Reasons for the founding of Georgia
- Important people and places
- Colony organization and government
- Life in the colony

RESEARCH LINKS
CLASSZONE.COM

Discontent in the Colonies 1754–1775

Sons of Liberty march through the streets of Boston carrying an image of a hated tax collector.

GEORGIA USA 1750   1760

1754
French and
Indian War begins.

JOIN, or DIE.

1763
French and Indian
War ends. Proclamation
of 1763 becomes law.

1763
Treaty of Augusta
is negotiated.

1765
Stamp Act
is passed.

→INTERACT←

with HISTORY

The year is 1765. Your neighbors are enraged by Britain's attempts to tax them without their consent. Britain has never done this before. Everyone will be affected by the tax. There are protests in many cities. You have to decide what you will do.

Will you join the protest?

WHAT DO YOU THINK?

- What is the best way to show opposition to policies you consider unjust?

- Is there anything to be gained by protesting? Anything to be lost?

- Does government have the right to tax without consent of the people? Why or why not?

For more information on this chapter, visit . . .

RESEARCH LINKS
CLASSZONE.COM

1773
Treaties with Native Americans add two million acres to Georgia.

August 1774
The Committee of Thirty forms.

1770

1780

1770
Boston Massacre

1774
First Continental Congress meets.

1775
Battle of Lexington and Concord

Reading Strategy: Sequencing Events

What Do You Know?

What do you already know about the time before the Revolution? What were the issues that caused the colonists to choose independence?

THINK ABOUT

• what you've learned about this period from movies, television, or historical fiction

• reasons people in history have chosen to fight for freedom from oppression

What Do You Want to Know?

What questions do you have about the issues and events that pushed the American colonists toward rebellion? Record these questions in your notebook before you read the chapter.

Sequencing Events

Sequencing means putting events in the order in which they happen in time. In learning how the American colonies moved toward independence, it would be helpful to list the important events. Place them in the order in which they occurred. You might record the event and its date in a graphic organizer like the one below. Copy this organizer into your notebook, and fill it in as you read the chapter.

 See Skillbuilder Handbook, page 549.

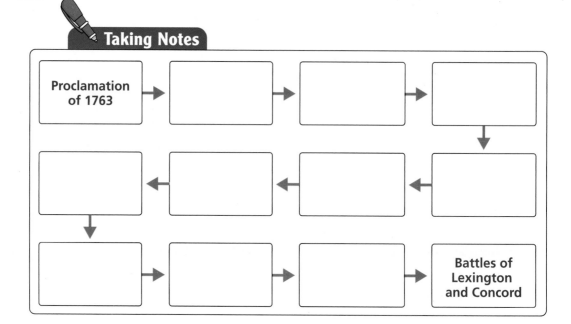

Taking Notes

Proclamation of 1763 → ☐ → ☐ → ☐

☐ ← ☐ ← ☐

☐ → ☐ → ☐ → Battles of Lexington and Concord

The French and Indian War

SETTING THE STAGE

While English colonists settled the eastern coast, French explorers claimed the interior. By the late 1600s, France claimed the Mississippi River Valley, the Ohio River Valley, and the Great Lakes region. The French formed alliances with the Huron and Algonquin Indians of the Great Lakes region, with whom they usually traded. The Iroquois of upper New York often were allies of the Dutch and the English. The Cherokee and Creek in the Southeast were usually the allies of the English.

Alliances between Europeans and Native Americans led them to become involved in each other's wars. When Native American groups made war against each other, their European allies provided weapons. The Europeans used their Native American allies to attack the other's forts. During the 1700s, two wars between France and England led to wars between their colonies. Neither side won a clear victory. A final war would decide which nation would control territory in North America.

▲ La Salle and his expedition travelled south from Canada down the Mississippi River to the Gulf of Mexico in 1682.

War Breaks Out

Beginning in 1754, the British and French fought several small battles in North America over their territories. The British colonists called this conflict the **French and Indian War** because they were fighting the French and their Native American allies. This war became part of a larger worldwide conflict between France and Britain called the Seven Years' War, which lasted from 1756 to 1763.

By 1759, the British controlled most of the French forts in North America. Spain entered the conflict in 1761 on the side of France, but it did not make much difference in the outcome. When the war ended in 1763, Britain had won.

Taking Notes

Use your graphic organizer to note important events of the French and Indian War.

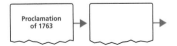

Georgia was relatively calm during this time, because most of the fighting was in the North. The war began the year John Reynolds became governor. It remained calm through two more governors. Georgia remained peaceful while Governor Ellis worked to stabilize the colony. And Georgia continued to grow and prosper under the skillful diplomacy of Governor James Wright.

The War Ends The **Treaty of Paris** ended the Seven Years' War. In the treaty, Britain claimed all of North America east of the Mississippi River. In return for their help in the war, France gave Spain New Orleans and Louisiana, the territory west of the Mississippi River. Britain had captured Cuba and the Philippines during the war. In the treaty, Britain traded them to Spain in return for Florida. The treaty ended French power in North America.

The Proclamation of 1763

Although it had won the French and Indian War, Great Britain faced several problems. To fight the war, Britain had incurred a large war debt. The British government felt the colonies should help pay the debt since the war had made the colonies more secure.

Reading History

A. Reading a Map
Find the Proclamation Line of 1763 on the map below.

IN 1754
European Claims in North America

British territory
French territory
Spanish territory
Russian territory
Disputed territory

Hudson Bay
NEW-FOUNDLAND
Great Lakes
St. Lawrence R.
Quebec
40°N
ATLANTIC OCEAN
Mississippi R.
New Orleans
FLORIDA
Tropic of Cancer
20°N
Gulf of Mexico
CUBA
HAITI
JAMAICA
SANTO DOMINGO
Caribbean Sea
PACIFIC OCEAN

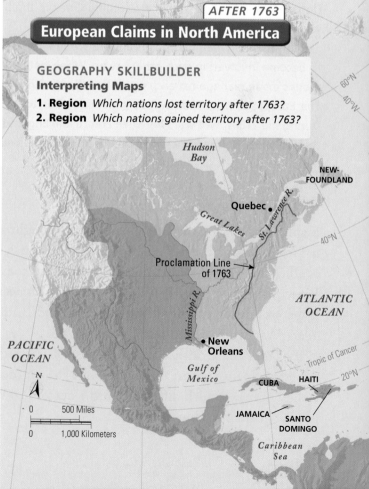

AFTER 1763
European Claims in North America

GEOGRAPHY SKILLBUILDER
Interpreting Maps
1. **Region** Which nations lost territory after 1763?
2. **Region** Which nations gained territory after 1763?

Hudson Bay
NEW-FOUNDLAND
Great Lakes
St. Lawrence R.
Quebec
40°N
Proclamation Line of 1763
ATLANTIC OCEAN
PACIFIC OCEAN
N
Mississippi R.
New Orleans
Gulf of Mexico
Tropic of Cancer
20°N
CUBA
HAITI
JAMAICA
SANTO DOMINGO
Caribbean Sea
0   500 Miles
0   1,000 Kilometers

In addition, colonists started moving into the newly won territory west of the Appalachian Mountains. Native American groups living there responded by attacking settlers and destroying British forts. Settlers reacted brutally, killing Native Americans who had not attacked them. Obviously defending the new territory would be expensive.

The **Proclamation of 1763** attempted to solve some of those problems. The proclamation stated that American colonists could not settle west of the Appalachian Mountains. Britain wanted to avoid conflict with the Native Americans there. But the proclamation angered many colonists who had hoped to settle in the fertile Ohio River Valley. As a result, settlers continued to move into the area. However, since colonial governments did not want to spend the money to defend the settlers, they ordered the settlers to return to the eastern settlements.

The colonists believed they had won the right in the war to settle in the West. For years, the colonies had managed their own affairs without British interference. It became almost impossible for King George and Parliament to enforce the proclamation, so many colonists ignored it. In addition, the colonies had largely ignored the different taxes that Britain had tried to impose for many years.

Reading History

B. Making Inferences Why was the Ohio River Valley important to the French and British governments?

Reading History

C. Summarizing Who was upset by the Proclamation of 1763?

Georgia Changes Shape

Georgia was different from the other colonies in several ways. It was the youngest colony, with the smallest population, and a nonprofit group had established it. Georgia did not have the political structures of older colonies such as Virginia. However, with the end of the French and Indian War, Georgia was ready and able to grow.

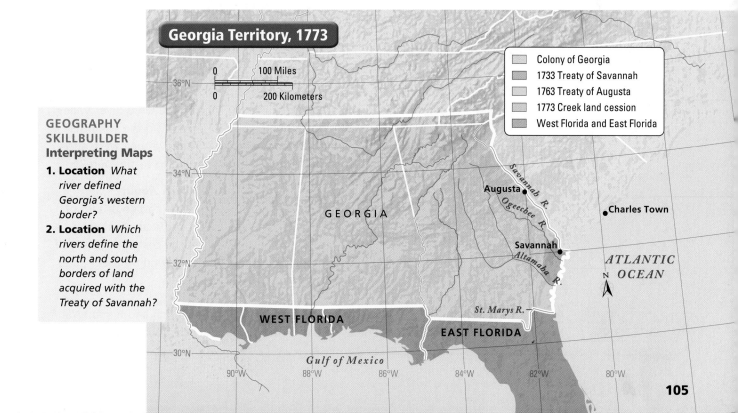

Georgia Territory, 1773

Colony of Georgia
1733 Treaty of Savannah
1763 Treaty of Augusta
1773 Creek land cession
West Florida and East Florida

GEOGRAPHY SKILLBUILDER
Interpreting Maps

1. **Location** What river defined Georgia's western border?
2. **Location** Which rivers define the north and south borders of land acquired with the Treaty of Savannah?

British Control Protects Georgia The threat of raids on Georgia from Florida to the south or from Native Americans allied with the French to the west ended. The British now controlled all land east of the Mississippi, including Florida. Under its 1732 charter, Georgia had extended to present-day California. Under the Treaty of Paris, the western border became the Mississippi River. A year later, the southern border was changed to the St. Marys River.

Georgia Grows and Prospers In 1763, Governor Wright negotiated the **Treaty of Augusta** with the Creek, which almost tripled the size of Georgia. It confirmed earlier agreements and fixed a definite boundary between the colony and the Creek territory.

After the Treaty of Augusta, Georgia controlled the entire coast south of the Savannah River, and along the Savannah inland to Augusta. The treaty was negotiated in 1763. The land was not surveyed until 1768, but settlers began moving in before that.

Another treaty in 1773 added two million acres in two areas, one section north of Augusta and the other between the Ogeechee and the Altamaha Rivers. By 1766, almost 50,000 people lived in Georgia.

While Georgians were generally optimistic about the future, residents of other colonies were not so happy. And Britain was beginning to think the colonies needed to be reined in. In the next section, you will learn about British efforts to gain control over the colonies and make them profitable for the mother country.

Reading History

D. Reading a Map Use the map on page 105 to locate the land given in the Treaty of Augusta.

Section 1 Assessment

1. TERMS & NAMES
Explain the significance of:

a. French and Indian War

b. Treaty of Paris

c. Proclamation of 1763

d. Treaty of Augusta

2. TAKING NOTES
Use a diagram like the one below to note how three events in 1763 affected Georgia territorial claims.

Event	Georgia Territory
Treaty of Paris	
Treaty of Augusta	
Proclamation of 1763	

3. MAIN IDEAS
a. How did the French and British use the Native Americans of the region?

b. What was the cause of the French and Indian War?

c. Who was fighting against whom in the war?

4. CRITICAL THINKING
Analyzing Points of View

Why did the British government close expansion to the Ohio River Valley? Why did the colonists believe they were entitled to settle there?

Think About
• the cost to Britain of protecting colonists
• the cost to colonists of defending themselves

Geography/Language Arts Research one of the battles of the French and Indian War. Make a three-dimensional **model** or write a short **newspaper article** about the battle.

Britain Tightens Control

 MAIN IDEA	WHY IT MATTERS NOW	TERMS & NAMES
Americans saw British efforts to tax them and to increase control over the colonies as violations of their rights.	Colonial protests were the first steps on the road to American independence.	Acts of Trade Sons of Liberty Sugar Act Daughters of Quarterling Act Liberty Stamp Act Townshend Acts

◄ The Quartering Act enacted by the British Parliament required colonists to house British soldiers and provide certain supplies.

SETTING THE STAGE

During the French and Indian War, Britain and the colonies fought together to defeat the French. After the war, however, differences arose between the former allies. Britain wanted to gain greater control over the colonies and enforce laws that colonists had been ignoring. For some time the colonists had been allowed to develop without British control. Now they felt that Britain was limiting their freedom and restricting their rights.

How could Britain regain command of the colonies? How would it pay for the thousands of soldiers needed to carry out British laws and protect its citizens? Could Britain rule the colonies from across the Atlantic Ocean?

Trade, Taxes, and Troops

To help pay the debt from the French and Indian War and other costs associated with their Empire, the British government began to look for ways to raise money in the colonies.

The Trade and Navigation Acts Trade and navigation laws, formally called the **Acts of Trade,** had existed for many years but the colonists had largely ignored them. The acts dictated that certain products from the colonies, such as tobacco, sugar, cotton, and indigo, could be sold only to Britain or British colonies. These laws also controlled what could be made and sold outside a colony.

These acts also restricted trade between the colonies and other countries. When a foreign nation shipped goods to the colonies, it now had to pass them through a British port, or use British or colonial ships. Then, Britain taxed these products when they arrived in Britain. And British ships added a charge for carrying the goods to the colonies. This

▶ Taking Notes

Use your graphic organizer to note important events as Britain tightens control.

raised prices, making the colonists pay more for goods. Colonists tried to go around the system, but customs agents could break into ware- h uses and homes of the colonists to look for illegal trade goods. The colonists were especially angry about this. They thought that Britain was supposed to be helping them, not punishing them.

The Sugar Act   The British government wanted the colonists to buy sugar from British planters in the West Indies instead of from the French and Dutch. To do that, Parliament passed the **Sugar Act** in 1764. This law actually reduced the tax on Dutch and French molasses, but the British enforced the tax more strictly. This made it harder for colonists to smuggle molasses and avoid the tax as they had before.

Most resistance to the Sugar Act came from New England. Georgia was mainly concerned with how the Sugar Act might affect their sale of timber to the Caribbean. Customers in the Caribbean used money from exporting molasses to pay for timber from Georgia. Since many colonists protested, Parliament reduced the tax in 1766.

ECONOMICS *In* HISTORY

Free Enterprise

One cause of the Revolution was the colonists' resentment of British mercantilism. Parliament passed laws to discourage the colonists from developing their own manufacturing and to force them to buy British goods. When British economic control weakened, the colonists were able to make more economic choices—for example, they could choose to manufacture wool clothing.

The end of Britain's mercantilist control allowed free enterprise to begin to develop in the United States. In a free-enterprise system, business can be conducted freely based on the choices of individuals. The government does not control the system, but only protects and regulates it.

A Competition encourages businesses to improve goods and services and to keep prices down.

B Property is owned by individuals and businesses.

C The desire to make a profit motivates businesspeople.

D Individuals, not the government, decide what to buy and what to manufacture and sell.

E The government protects private property and makes sure businesses operate fairly.

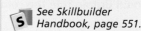

CONNECT TO HISTORY

1. **Analyzing Causes** Why do you think the colonists were able to manufacture their own wool clothing during the war?

   See Skillbuilder Handbook, page 551.

CONNECT TO TODAY

2. **Comparing** Think about a mall where you shop. Name examples of businesses that compete with each other. Compare the methods they use to attract customers.

For more about free enterprise . . .

RESEARCH LINKS
CLASSZONE.COM

The Quartering Act   Britain stationed ten thousand troops in the colonies to enforce British laws and keep peace with Britain's Native American allies. Parliament passed the **Quartering Act** in 1765. This act forced colonial assemblies to provide housing, food, and supplies for the troops. The colonists believed that this violated their rights.

The Stamp Act

Reading History

A. Drawing Conclusions Why was it important for the colonists to be represented in Parliament?

Parliament also enacted the **Stamp Act** in 1765. The Sugar Act had affected only merchants, but the Stamp Act affected almost everyone. Under this act, all legal and commercial documents had to carry an official stamp that showed that the tax had been paid.

Colonists began to ask how the British Parliament could impose taxes on them when the colonists were not represented in Parliament. Colonists everywhere began to shout, "Taxation without representation is tyranny." In October 1765, nine colonies sent delegates to an assembly in New York called the Stamp Act Congress. They declared the Stamp Act illegal and unfair and asked King George to repeal it.

Vocabulary

tyranny: absolute power in the hands of a single ruler

The Stamp Act in Georgia   Governor Wright supported Parliament. He refused to convene the Georgia Assembly, so Georgia did not send any delegates to the Stamp Act Congress. However, members of the Assembly who opposed the Stamp Act sent an unofficial letter of support. When the stamps arrived in Georgia, people bought a few. Georgia was the only colony in which any stamps were purchased. Most people decided to see if Parliament was going to repeal the act. Some angrily threatened to destroy the stamps, so Governor Wright moved the stamps to Fort George on Cockspur Island for safety.

Britain Repeals the Stamp Act   The British Parliament grew more fearful of a revolt in the colonies. They repealed the Stamp Act in 1766 but passed the Declatory Act. This stated that Britain had complete control over the colonies. The situation between Britain and America calmed. But this calm did not last long.

The Townshend Acts

In 1767, Charles Townshend became the finance minister of Britain. Townshend proposed a tax on goods imported into the colonies and collected at the ports.

DAILY LIFE

Women and Protest

Women were not allowed to participate in political life in the colonies, so their role in protesting British actions was not as prominent as that of men. However, women made their beliefs known by taking part in demonstrations.

Also, some women formed the Daughters of Liberty. This was a patriotic organization that joined in the boycott of British tea and other goods. The refusal of these colonial women to use British imports caused them personal hardship. They were forced to make many of the boycotted items, such as clothing, themselves.

▲ This is an example of stamps colonists were expected to use on paper items.

Among other things, the **Townshend Acts** placed taxes on tea, paper, lead, glass, and paint brought into the colonies. The money raised would be used to pay the salaries of British governors and other colonial officials. Townshend thought no one would protest since the taxes were paid before the items reached the final buyer.

He was wrong. Protests broke out immediately. Colonists refused to buy these items. The **Sons of Liberty** pressured merchants not to sell these goods. The **Daughters of Liberty** persuaded colonists to weave their own cloth (called homespun) and use products made in the colonies. Later, colonists organized a boycott of British goods. Georgia began to import goods from other trading partners.

Georgia Prepares for Independence

A group of concerned Georgia colonists began to think about what would happen if they could not depend on Britain for supplies and trade. They met on September 12, 1769 to consider their options. The group proposed ways for Georgians to become more independent. They encouraged colonists to manufacture more of what they needed themselves and to reduce the number of imported items from England or Europe. The group suggested colonists not do business with any merchants who did not sign the pledge to decrease dependence on England.

The colonists hoped that actions like these would persuade Britain to relax the restrictive taxes it had imposed. When it did not, the conflict escalated, as you will read in the next section.

Vocabulary

boycott: a refusal to buy certain goods

Reading History

B. Solving Problems If you were a Georgian in 1769, what steps would you take to reduce your dependence on Britain?

Section 2 Assessment

1. TERMS & NAMES

Explain the significance of:

a. Acts of Trade

b. Sugar Act

c. Quartering Act

d. Stamp Act

e. Townshend Acts

f. Sons of Liberty

g. Daughters of Liberty

2. TAKING NOTES

Use a cluster diagram like the one below to review the different laws and taxes Britain enacted that the colonists objected to.

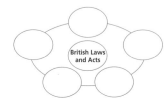

British Laws and Acts

3. MAIN IDEAS

a. Why did more people object to the Stamp Act than to the Sugar Act?

b. Why did colonists think it was unfair for Britain to place taxes on them?

c. What steps did Georgia take to reduce its dependence on Britain?

4. CRITICAL THINKING

Analyzing Points of View

Why did Britain feel it was justified in passing the different taxes on the colonies?

Think About

• what Britain had done during the French and Indian War

• how Parliament viewed the colonies

ACTIVITY -OPTIONS- **Art/Language Arts** Draw a **political cartoon** or write a short **speech** exposing the dangers of one of the taxes discussed in this section.

Colonial Resistance Grows

MAIN IDEA	WHY IT MATTERS NOW	TERMS & NAMES

MAIN IDEA

Many colonists organized to oppose British policies. The tensions between Britain and the colonies led to armed conflict.

WHY IT MATTERS NOW

Americans continue to protest what they view as wrongs and injustice. At times, Americans still find themselves called upon to fight for their principles.

TERMS & NAMES

committee of correspondence
Boston Tea Party
Intolerable Acts
First Continental Congress
Lexington and Concord
Loyalist
Patriot

SETTING THE STAGE

Most colonists protested British laws by boycotting the goods that were taxed or the merchants that sold them. Some people made emotional speeches against taxes. Others turned to violent acts to express their anger. While colonial leaders called for peaceful protests and newspaper articles asked people to remain calm, tempers ran high. A riot broke out when customs officials attempted to seize a ship carrying smuggled supplies.

Officials called for more British troops. Colonial leaders threatened violence. Britain was angry. The colonies were also angry. Could they reach a compromise? Or were the two sides heading for a confrontation?

▲ Colonists protest the Stamp Act.

Shots in Boston

Boston was a center of protest and resistance. British soldiers quartered there were regularly harassed. Crowds would gather around the soldiers, calling them names and insulting them. One name that stuck was "redcoat" because of their bright red uniforms. On March 5, 1770, tensions exploded into violence. A group of youths and soldiers started trading insults in front of the Customs House. About 50 colonists surrounded one soldier. Other soldiers came to help him. Someone gave the order to fire. Five colonists were killed.

The Sons of Liberty called the shooting the Boston Massacre. The incident was publicized in newspaper articles, pamphlets, and posters. The people of Boston were outraged. Citizens demanded that the soldiers be tried for murder and that all remaining troops leave Boston. The British authorities agreed to their demands.

Taking Notes

Use your graphic organizer to note important events as colonial resistance grows.

Proclamation of 1763

▲ This engraving, *The Bloody Massacre Perpetrated in King Street* by Boston silversmith Paul Revere (above), appeared in the *Boston Gazette* (right).

Problems Within Georgia

Governor Wright, as a royal governor and representative of the king, tried to keep Georgians loyal and discouraged attempts to weaken ties to Britain. In 1771, a new Commons House met and chose Noble W. Jones as speaker. Wright rejected Jones because he had spoken out strongly against the British. Archibald Bulloch was then elected. Bulloch also objected to British actions but not as strongly. Wright accepted him.

Georgia colonists and their governor knew of the acts that angered other colonies. Georgians were just as outraged. But Georgia was the youngest colony and still very dependent on England. Wright believed that English laws should be obeyed. He also believed that changes in policy should be made by negotiating with the British parliament.

Disagreements between the house and the governor occurred regularly. Sessions usually ended when the governor dismissed them. He would end a session early, rather than let the representatives have their way.

The Tea Act and Tea Parties

On the same day as the Boston Massacre, Parliament proposed the repeal of the Townshend Acts. One month later, Parliament repealed all the acts except for the tax on tea. The colonists' boycott had worked—British trade had been hurt. However, Parliament kept the tax on tea to show that it still had the authority to tax the colonists. For many colonists, things were once again peaceful—for a short time.

Committees of Correspondence   Samuel Adams of Boston urged the colonists to use peaceful measures against England. He called for boycotts, rather than violence. Adams proposed forming **committees**

Reading History

A. Making Inferences What did Samuel Adams hope the committees of correspondence would accomplish?

of correspondence in towns across Massachusetts. These would spread news from town to town. Soon Virginia, Rhode Island, Connecticut, New Hampshire, and South Carolina formed committees. Thomas Jefferson and Patrick Henry of Virginia served on a central committee that coordinated all the committees.

Aiding the British East India Company   Tea was a popular drink in the colonies. Many colonists stopped drinking English tea to protest the Townshend Act. Instead, they smuggled in Dutch tea. As a result, the British East India Tea Company became almost bankrupt. To help the company, the British government passed the Tea Act in 1773, which gave the company control of the American tea trade. Colonists who had not been paying any tax on smuggled tea now had to pay a tax on the regulated tea. The East India Tea Company sold its tea through merchants in New York City, Boston, Philadelphia, and Charleston.

Angry Colonists React   The Sons of Liberty in New York City refused to buy the tea. In New York and Philadelphia, colonists blocked tea ships from landing. In Boston, the Sons of Liberty organized a protest that came to be known as the **Boston Tea Party**.

HISTORY MAKERS

SAMUEL ADAMS
1722–1803

Samuel Adams was a Harvard graduate. But unlike his cousin John, also a Harvard graduate, he showed little skill for the law. Later when he took control of the family business, he lost his father's fortune. Yet he succeeded in one important undertaking—moving America toward independence from Britain.

Adams's true talent lay in rousing people to action in support of a cause. A fiery orator and a master of propaganda, he used words as a weapon. One British official said that "every dip of his pen stings."

JOHN ADAMS
1735–1826

John Adams, unlike Samuel, was considered a moderate in the struggle against Britain. He was an important voice of reason and at first opposed resisting by force.

Adams believed in the rule of law. He called his defense of the soldiers in the Boston Massacre "one of the best pieces of service I ever rendered my country."

Eventually, Adams became convinced that only outright resistance would gain liberty for America. He said, "Britain has at last driven America, to the last Step, a compleat Seperation from her."

► Colonists dumped hundreds of chests of tea into Boston Harbor in 1773 to protest the Tea Act.

On the evening of December 16, 1773, a group of more than 100 men disguised as Mohawk Indians boarded three tea ships and threw the entire load of 342 chests of tea into the Boston Harbor. Similar "tea parties" took place in other cities.

Protestors in Charleston, South Carolina, used a different tactic. They unloaded the tea but left it on the docks. Later, some of it was sold to help pay for the American Revolution. Georgia colonists felt just as much resentment as other colonists, but since no tea had been shipped to Savannah, they did not protest.

King George III and members of Parliament were angry, especially with the New England colonies where most protests occurred. Parliament wanted to punish Massachusetts and warn the other colonies.

Reading History

B. Recognizing Effects How did Britain react to the Boston Tea Party?

The Intolerable Acts

To bring the colonies under control, Parliament passed several acts in 1774. The British called these acts the Coercive Acts. They were so harsh that colonists named them the **Intolerable Acts.**

One act closed Boston Harbor until the tea was paid for. Another act outlawed groups such as the Sons of Liberty and committees of correspondence and allowed colonists to gather for only one town meeting each year.

Parliament also passed a new Quartering Act. This act required colonists to feed and shelter British troops in their homes, not just in public places. To enforce these acts, Parliament appointed General Thomas Gage as governor of Massachusetts.

Committees of correspondence quickly spread the word about what was happening in Boston. Citizens of Rhode Island, Pennsylvania, and New York sent food and supplies in support. The committees of

Vocabulary

coercive: to force someone by threats

intolerable: unbearable

CAUSE AND EFFECT: Growing Conflict Between Britain and America

DATE	BRITISH ACTION	COLONIAL REACTION
1763	Proclamation of 1763 issued	▶ Proclamation leads to anger
1765	Stamp Act passed	▶ Boycott of British goods; Stamp Act Resolves passed
1766	Stamp Act repealed; Declatory Act passed	▶ Boycott ended
1767	Townshend Acts passed	▶ New boycotts; Boston Massacre (March 1770)
1770	Townshend Acts repealed (April)	▶ Tension between colonies and Britain reduced
1773	Tea Act passed	▶ Boston Tea Party
1774	Intolerable Acts passed	▶ First Continental Congress bans trade; militias organized
1775	Troops ordered to Lexington and Concord, Massachusetts	▶ Militia fights British troops; Second Continental Congress; Continental Army established

SKILLBUILDER Interpreting Charts

1. *What British action caused the first violence in the growing conflict between Britain and America?*
2. *How might the Intolerable Acts be seen as a reaction as well as an action?*

correspondence also called for a meeting of colonial representatives to discuss how they should respond.

The First Continental Congress

In September 1774, representatives of all the colonies except Georgia and Florida met in Carpenters' Hall in Philadelphia. At this meeting, called the **First Continental Congress,** the delegates passed a series of resolutions that came to be known as the Declaration of Resolves.

These resolves included boycotting all trade with Britain until Britain repealed the Intolerable Acts. They urged the people of Massachusetts to form a government to collect taxes and hold those taxes until the repeal. They also advised people in all colonies to arm themselves and form militias, or companies of armed civilians.

The First Continental Congress marked an important step in American history. While most delegates were not ready to call for independence from Britain, they were ready to insist on colonial rights. The Congress adjourned on October 22 and agreed to meet again on May 10, 1775, if Parliament had not repealed the acts.

Between Peace and War   The petitions and Declaration of Resolves reached Parliament in January 1775. Parliament responded by proposing a harsher bill that would stop colonial trade with countries other than England. Both sides had reached the point where there could be no compromise.

▼ In the Petition of Grievances and Declaration of Resolves, the Continental Congress asked that the "unjust and cruel" acts of Parliament be repealed. They were not.

THE
PETITION
OF THE
GRAND AMERICAN CONTINENTAL
CONGRESS,
TO THE
KING's
Most Excellent Majesty.
———
AMERICA:
Boston, Printed and sold at the Printing-Office, near
the Mill-Bridge.

Vocabulary

militia: companies of armed civilians pledged to defend their community

Reading History

C. Evaluating
Why do you think the First Continental Congress was important?

Georgians Consider the Intolerable Acts

Although it did not send delegates to the Congress, a small group of Georgians met on July 27, 1774, at Peter Tondee's tavern in Savannah. Businessmen, politicians, and wealthy planters were at the meeting to discuss the issues facing the colonies. They were not a radical group. Their main interest was to keep good relations with the British troops protecting their frontier from Native American attacks. They also wanted to continue importing goods for trade with the Creek and Cherokee.

▲ Lyman Hall could not gain enough support to attend the First Continental Congress. He was at the Second Continental Congress and signed the Declaration of Independence.

These Georgians met again on August 10. They called themselves the Committee of Thirty. At this meeting, representatives from every parish officially objected to the Intolerable Acts. They also formed a small group to correspond with other colonies on an official basis. But they rejected the idea of sending delegates to the First Continental Congress. Lyman Hall of St. John's Parish was strongly in favor of going, but he could not get enough support. Georgians were divided on whether or not to support the Continental Congress.

Georgia Support for the First Continental Congress

Support for the First Continental Congress grew in the parishes of Georgia. The Scots in Darien and others spoke out strongly against Britain. A few, however, still disagreed. Elijah Clarke, William Few, and George Wells signed a petition stating their disagreement.

The Committee of Thirty called for another meeting, a provincial congress, to take place during the next Georgia Assembly in January 1775. In his opening address to the Assembly, Governor Wright begged the members to consider the consequences of adopting measures that would anger England.

> **PRIMARY SOURCE**
>
> . . . it grieves me that a Province that I have been so long in, and which I have seen nurtured by the Crown . . . and grew up from mere infancy . . . should, by the imprudence and rashness of some inconsiderate people, be plunged into a state of distress and ruin.
>
> Governor James Wright, quoted in *A History of Georgia* by Kenneth Coleman

Reading History

D. Using Primary Sources What did Governor Wright think would be the result of rebellion against Great Britain?

His speech did little good. The Assembly convened and began discussing their rights as Americans.

The provincial congress met also, but only five of the twelve parishes sent delegates. They discussed the resolutions of the First Continental

Congress and elected Noble W. Jones, Archibald Bulloch, and John Houstoun to represent the colony at the next Continental Congress. With delegates from only five parishes, the men did not represent all of Georgia. Even so, they hoped the Assembly would allow them to attend the Continental Congress in Philadelphia. But Wright adjourned the Assembly before it could take that action.

The Midnight Ride

In Boston, General Gage had orders to keep the peace, even if he had to use force. Gage learned that the Massachusetts militia stored weapons and ammunition in Concord, about 21 miles northwest of Boston. He also discovered that two colonial leaders, John Hancock and Samuel Adams, were in the nearby town of Lexington. On the night of April 18, 1775, Gage sent about 700 British troops to arrest Hancock and Adams and destroy the supplies at Concord.

The colonists were concerned about Gage's troops. Paul Revere had arranged a system of signals to alert colonists in Charlestown, across the harbor from Boston, about troop movements. If one lantern burned in the steeple of the Old North Church in Boston, the British were coming by land. Two lanterns meant they were coming by water.

Background

The signals were a backup system in case Revere was captured.

When Gage's troops set out, someone lit the signal: one lantern. The British were coming by land. Paul Revere and William Dawes set off to warn Hancock, Adams, and the citizens of Lexington and Concord. They took different routes to Lexington and alerted citizens along the

▲ American artist Grant Wood painted this rendition of Paul Revere's midnight ride in 1931.

way that British soldiers were coming. When they reached Lexington, they warned Adams and Hancock. A third man, Dr. Samuel Prescott, joined the ride in Lexington. When a British patrol stopped Revere and Dawes, Prescott broke away to carry the message to Concord.

Lexington and Concord

The British reached Lexington around dawn on April 19 and found the colonial militia waiting for them. The British commander ordered the militiamen to drop their muskets. They refused. Shots rang out. Eight colonists were killed and ten were wounded. The British marched on to Concord, where they burned the courthouse and destroyed the weapons and ammunition.

At Concord's North Bridge, a battle broke out, forcing the British troops back. Only the arrival of 1,000 reinforcements saved the British from defeat. **Lexington and Concord** were the first battles of the American Revolution.

"The Shot Heard Round the World"   Ralph Waldo Emerson's poem "The Concord Hymn" described the battle at Concord as the "shot heard round the world." Certainly, it was the beginning of major changes for the colonies. Colonists now had to decide whether they would be Loyalists or Patriots. **Loyalists** were those who remained loyal to Britain. They were also called Tories. **Patriots** were those who rebelled against Britain. They were also called Whigs.

Loyalists and Patriots in Georgia

In 1775, public opinion in Georgia was divided. Georgians had good reason to remain loyal to Britain. Britain had been generous over the years. It had bought huge tracts of Native American land and opened it for settlement. The colony was doing well, despite the constant threat of an attack from the Creek Indians. However, if an attack occurred, the colonists knew they would need help from British troops.

Many other reasons, however, led Georgia to join the other colonies in breaking from Britain. Georgians hated the British taxes just as much as other colonists. Younger Georgians wanted a larger and more representative legislature to run the colony.

Some Georgians were Quakers and did not believe in war because of their religious beliefs. The New England Congregationalists around Midway and Sunbury were strong Whigs. In fact, St. John's Parish was nicknamed Liberty County, and colonists there had voted to send Lyman Hall to the First Continental Congress although he did not actually attend. The Scots around Darien were vehemently against the English. The Jews in Savannah, particularly the Sheftall family, were also Patriots. The Germans at Ebenezer were largely Loyalists.

Reading History

E. Summarizing
Why did some Georgians want to remain loyal?

Older Georgians and recent immigrants wanted to remain loyal to Britain. Those who had been born in America were more likely to want independence. The conflict divided communities, families, and friends. In the next chapter, you will learn how this conflict was fought and resolved.

Section 3 Assessment

1. TERMS & NAMES
Explain the significance of:

a. committee of correspondence

b. Boston Tea Party

c. Intolerable Acts

d. First Continental Congress

e. Lexington and Concord

f. Loyalist

g. Patriot

2. TAKING NOTES

Create a time line like the one below to show the significant people and events described in this section.

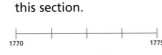

1770   1775

3. MAIN IDEAS

a. Why were some Georgians reluctant to rebel against Britain?

b. What was the purpose of "tea parties"?

c. What was Governor Wright's position on war with Britain?

4. CRITICAL THINKING
Drawing Conclusions

Do you think colonial outrage over the Boston Massacre was justified? Explain your answer.

Think About
• how colonists treated the British troops
• whether troops have the right to fire on citizens

Speech/Technology Research the Boston Massacre or the Boston Tea Party. Prepare an **oral report** or plan a **multimedia presentation** about the event.

VISUAL SUMMARY

The Road to Revolution

1763 — Proclamation of 1763

1764 — Sugar Act

1765 — Quartering Act; Stamp Act; Sons of Liberty; Stamp Act Congress

1766 — Repeal of Stamp Act; Declaratory Act

1767 — Townshend Acts

1768 — Occupation of Boston by British troops

1769 — Daughters of Liberty

1770 — Boston Massacre; Repeal of all Townshend Acts except tea tax

1772 — Committees of Correspondence

1773 — Tea Act; Boston Tea Party

1774 — Intolerable Acts; Georgia's Committee of Thirty; First Continental Congress; Boycott of British goods

1775 — Battles of Lexington and Concord; "The Shot Heard Round The World"; Georgia provincial congress

TERMS & NAMES

Briefly explain the significance of the following:

1. Treaty of Paris
2. Treaty of Augusta
3. Sugar Act
4. Quartering Act
5. Stamp Act
6. Townshend Acts
7. Boston Massacre
8. committees of correspondence
9. Boston Tea Party
10. Lexington and Concord

REVIEW QUESTIONS

The French and Indian War (pages 103–106)

1. What resulted from the Treaty of Paris?
2. How did the Treaty of Paris and the Treaty of Augusta affect Georgia?
3. Why did the British government pass the Proclamation Act of 1763?

Britain Tightens Control (pages 107–110)

4. How did Governor Wright respond to the Stamp Act?
5. What role did the Sons of Liberty play in the colonies?

Colonial Resistance Grows (pages 111–119)

6. Why was Georgia slow to join in resisting the British?
7. What acts were included in the Coercive Acts?
8. Why was the First Continental Congress significant?
9. What was the Committee of Thirty?

CRITICAL THINKING

1. USING YOUR NOTES: SEQUENCING EVENTS

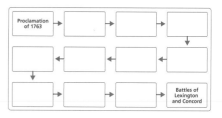

Using your completed chart, answer the questions below.

a. What city was the site of early protest activities?
b. What event happened after the Tea Act?

2. ANALYZING LEADERSHIP

What impact did Samuel Adams's leadership have on the colonies?

3. APPLYING CITIZENSHIP SKILLS

How did women work together to influence the future of the American colonies?

4. THEME: IMPACT OF THE INDIVIDUAL

How did individual protests affect the future of the country? Pick one individual from the chapter to use as an example.

5. MAKING INFERENCES

Why would Emerson use the phrase "the shot heard round the world" in his poem about the battle at Concord?

6. ANALYZING CAUSES

What factors led the colonists to develop a new, common American identity?

INTERACT with HISTORY

Having read about the acts passed by Britain, do you think you would have joined in the protests? How would you have participated?

Use the map and your knowledge of American history to answer questions 1 through 3.

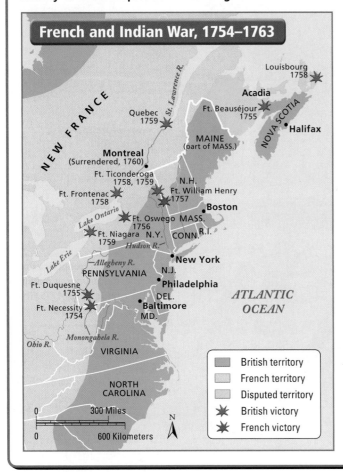

French and Indian War, 1754–1763

NEW FRANCE

St. Lawrence R.

Louisbourg 1758

Acadia
Ft. Beauséjour 1755

Quebec 1759

NOVA SCOTIA

• Halifax

MAINE (part of MASS.)

Montreal (Surrendered, 1760) •
Ft. Ticonderoga 1758, 1759
Ft. Frontenac 1758
N.H.
Ft. William Henry 1757
Lake Ontario
• Boston
Ft. Oswego MASS.
1756
Ft. Niagara N.Y.
1759
CONN. R.I.
Lake Erie
Hudson R.
—Allegheny R.
• New York
PENNSYLVANIA
N.J.
• Philadelphia
Ft. Duquesne 1755
DEL.
Ft. Necessity 1754
• Baltimore
MD.
ATLANTIC OCEAN
Monongahela R.
Ohio R.
VIRGINIA

NORTH CAROLINA

	British territory
	French territory
	Disputed territory
✶	British victory
✶	French victory

0   300 Miles
0   600 Kilometers
N

1. Which of the following was the site of a French victory?

   A. Ft. Beauséjour
   B. Ft. Duquesne
   C. Ft. Niagara
   D. Quebec

2. Where did the British have a victory in 1758 and 1759?

   A. Ft. Frontenac
   B. Ft. Niagara
   C. Ft. William Henry
   D. Ft. Ticonderoga

3. Which fort was located in the colony of New York?

   A. Ft. Necessity
   B. Ft. Beauséjour
   C. Ft. William Henry
   D. Ft. Duquesne

TEST PRACTICE
CLASSZONE.COM

ALTERNATIVE ASSESSMENT

1. DRAWING A POLITICAL CARTOON

As newspapers grew and spread throughout the colonies, political cartoons began to play an important role in colonial propaganda. View historical and contemporary political cartoons. Then draw your own political cartoon expressing your view about actions taken by Great Britain.

2. COOPERATIVE LEARNING

Newspapers helped to unite the colonies. View articles published by Benjamin Franklin and others during colonial times. Then work with a team to create your own colonial newspaper. Choose a name and design your logo. Write articles and include your own political cartoons.

INTEGRATED TECHNOLOGY ACTIVITY

USING TECHNOLOGY FOR RESEARCH

The colonists and the people of Georgia were divided in their opinions about how best to deal with Great Britain. Some were loyalists. Some were patriots. Use the Internet and the electronic database in your library to research speeches and articles written during this period. Find quotes that support both loyalist and patriot views. Then prepare a brief report comparing and contrasting the views. Share your report with the class.

RESEARCH LINKS
CLASSZONE.COM

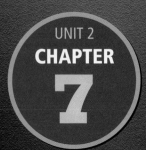

UNIT 2
CHAPTER
7

The War for Independence 1775–1783

Section 1
Moving Toward Independence

Section 2
Declaring Independence

Section 3
Fighting for Independence

British troops fire on the Lexington militia on April 19, 1775. The war has begun.

July 1775
Georgia elects representatives to the Second Continental Congress.

March 1776
Battle of the Rice Boats

December 1778
British troops capture Savannah.

January 1779
British troops capture Augusta.

February 1779
Battle of Kettle Creek

GEORGIA USA

1775

June 1775
Battle of Bunker Hill.

July 1776
The Declaration of Independence is adopted.

October 1777
Battle of Saratoga

122

It is 1777. Your brother is an American soldier. In his last letter to you, he wrote that the army has no shoes or bullets and little food. But he plans to keep fighting. Now, a British army is coming toward your farm. You've heard that the soldiers are stealing crops to feed themselves and their horses.

What would you sacrifice to win freedom?

WHAT DO YOU THINK?

- What sacrifices do soldiers make?

- What sacrifices do civilians make during wartime?

- Is it worth such sacrifices to win independence for your country? Why or why not?

For more information on this chapter, visit . . .

RESEARCH LINKS
CLASSZONE.COM

June 1781
American troops recapture Augusta.

June 1782
British troops leave Savannah.

1780 — 1785

May 1780
British troops take Charles Town.

October 1781
Cornwallis surrenders to Washington at Yorktown.

1783
Treaty of Paris ends the American Revolution.

Reading Strategy: Taking Notes

What Do You Know?

What stories do you know about the people or events of the Revolutionary War? How do people display courage and self-sacrifice during wartime?

THINK ABOUT

- what you've learned about the American Revolution from books, movies, historical fiction, or other classes
- news stories you've heard about revolutions or civil wars in other countries today

What Do You Want to Know?

What questions do you have about the steps that people took to win the American Revolution? Record those questions in your notebook before you read the chapter.

Taking Notes

Writing down important ideas, names, dates, and events can help you remember more of what you read. A chart or an outline can help you organize your notes so you can use them to study in the future. Write notes from your reading related to the dates listed in the chart below.

S *See Skillbuilder Handbook, page 549.*

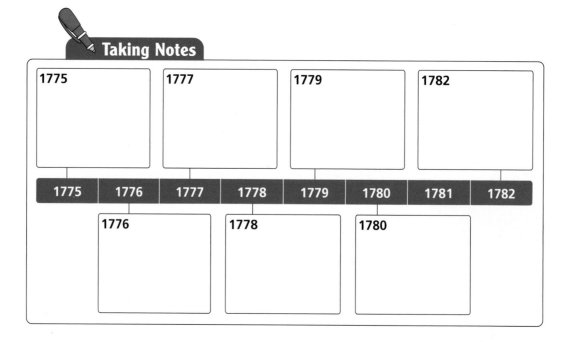

| Taking Notes |

Moving Toward Independence

MAIN IDEA	WHY IT MATTERS NOW	TERMS & NAMES
Fighting between American and British troops convinced most colonists that they should seek independence from England.	Americans fought for rights that are guaranteed by the U.S. Constitution today.	Second Continental Congress Continental Army George Washington Battle of Bunker Hill *Common Sense*

SETTING THE STAGE

After Lexington and Concord, militiamen in the colonies began training in earnest. Fighting continued in Massachusetts and broke out in New York. Ethan Allen and a group of Patriots called the Green Mountain Boys attacked Fort Ticonderoga. They captured the fort and its large supply of cannons and large guns. These guns would be used later to drive the British out of Boston.

Georgians were late in joining the other colonies in their resistance to British rule. But Georgians, like the other colonies, were ready to pool their resources to fight for independence. They would spend the early years of the Revolution regulating their new government and raising up leaders from among its citizens.

Most colonists did not want to fight, but they did not want to live under a government that did not represent them. Could the two sides resolve their differences? Or was conflict inevitable? Would "common sense" prevail?

▲ The militia was a small force of armed civilians that defended their community. Each militiaman was equipped with a musket, a bayonet, and ammunition.

The Second Continental Congress

During this period of conflict, the **Second Continental Congress** opened in Philadelphia on May 10, 1775. They took several actions.

Taking Action Against Georgia The Congress noted that Georgia had supported the Congressional resolutions, but Georgia had not joined the Continental Association, a boycott of trade with Great Britain and colonies that did business with Great Britain. Congress voted to cut off trade with Georgia.

Forming the Continental Army Representatives voted on June 14, 1775, to create an American army called the **Continental Army**. They asked **George Washington**, a colonial officer with the British

Taking Notes

Use your chart to organize important dates in America's move toward independence.

The War for Independence **125**

army during the French and Indian War, to command the colonial army. Washington accepted and offered to serve without pay.

Georgia Takes Action

News of Lexington and Concord reached Savannah on May 10, 1775. Noble W. Jones held a meeting at his house to discuss the events. As a result of that meeting, the first open act of rebellion in Georgia took place. Nobel W. Jones and Joseph Habersham, along with some other Patriots, broke into the royal powder magazine in Savannah and stole 600 pounds of gunpowder. The government offered a reward for information about the incident, but no one came forward.

Governor Wright knew he no longer had any authority in Georgia. In June, he sent a letter to England asking for more troops. His letter was intercepted in South Carolina, and a forged letter took its place. The forged letter said that everything was under control.

The Second Provincial Congress Convenes   On July 4, 1775, Georgia's second provincial congress began. This congress was very different from the first. This time 102 delegates from 10 of the 12 parishes attended. The delegates elected five representatives to the Second Continental Congress that was meeting in Philadelphia. They voted to join the Continental Association's boycott of British goods and formed the Council of Safety to coordinate Georgia's boycott efforts with those in other colonies. The delegates advised the Second Continental Congress that Georgia was ready to join fully with the other colonies.

The provincial congress also adopted a set of resolutions that claimed their rights as British subjects. They threatened to declare independence if these rights were not respected.

The Battle of Bunker Hill

Meanwhile, the situation in Boston in June 1775 grew worse. Patriot militia seized Bunker Hill and Breed's Hill outside of Boston and built fortifications on Breed's Hill. The British decided to attack.

General William Howe led 2,200 British soldiers up Breed's Hill. Colonel William Prescott told his American soldiers, "Don't fire until you see the whites of their eyes." When the British came within musket

▲ **His courageous service in the French and Indian War made Washington a popular hero. As commander of the Continental Army, Washington's popularity helped unite Americans.**

range, the Patriot militia opened fire. The British fell back, but then charged again. They finally forced the American militia off the hill.

The British had won the **Battle of Bunker Hill,** but "[t]he loss we have sustained is greater than we can bear," wrote General Thomas Gage, royal governor of Massachusetts. American losses were 100 dead, 267 wounded, and 30 captured. British losses were 1,054 men killed or captured. Even though the colonial militia had lost the battle, they had proven they could stand up to the British army.

A Last Attempt at Peace

Even while General Washington prepared his troops, Congress still hoped to find a peaceful solution. In July 1775, Congress wrote the Olive Branch Petition and sent it to the king. In the petition they asked the king to restore peace between Britain and the colonies.

Congress adopted another resolution—the Declaration of the Causes and Necessities of Taking Up Arms. Written by Thomas Jefferson, this stated that Americans would give up the idea of being independent from England, but they would rather die than be enslaved to England.

Background

The olive branch is considered a symbol of peace.

Reading History

A. Using Primary Sources
According to the Declaration of the Causes and Necessities of Taking Up Arms, why were the colonists fighting?

> **PRIMARY SOURCE**
>
> Our cause is just. Our union is perfect. . . . With . . . the arms we have been compelled by our enemies to assume, we will . . . employ for the preservation of our liberties; being with one mind resolved to die freemen rather than live slaves.
>
> We have not raised armies with ambitious designs of separating from Great Britain . . . We shall lay them down when hostilities shall cease on the part of the aggressors.
>
> The Declaration of the Causes and Necessities of Taking Up Arms, from the Journals of the Continental Congress

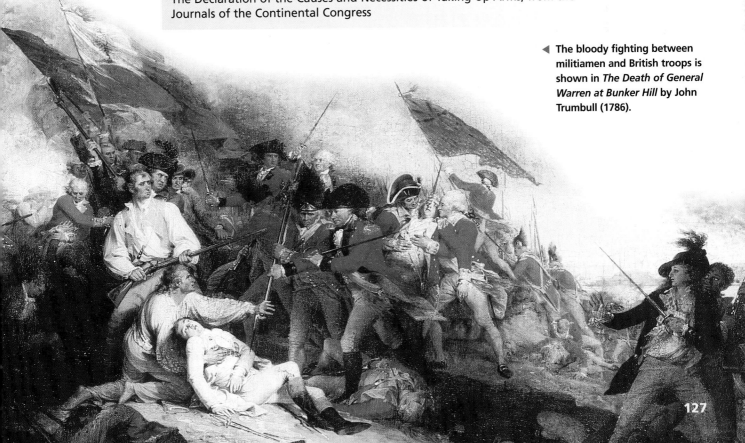

◀ The bloody fighting between militiamen and British troops is shown in *The Death of General Warren at Bunker Hill* by John Trumbull (1786).

THINK AS A GEOGRAPHER

A Smaller World

Distance between England and the 13 colonies helped weaken ties with the home country and pave the way for a distinctly American identity. Today, air travel and electronic communication mean that geographic distances no longer separate people as they did in the 1700s.

Reading History

B. Analyzing Points of View Why did King George reject the petition?

King George III rejected the Olive Branch Petition. Instead, he announced new acts to punish the colonies. He would use the British navy to block American ships from leaving their ports. He would also send 10,000 hired German soldiers, called Hessians, to fight in America. The king said, "When once these rebels have felt a smart blow, they will submit."

Fighting Spreads through the Colonies

After the Battle of Bunker Hill, small battles erupted in other places, north and south. There were clashes from Maine to Georgia. In North Carolina and Boston, Patriots forced British troops out of their cities. And the fighting in Georgia ended the royal government's reign.

The Battle of Moores Creek   North Carolina's governor planned to unite his Loyalist troops from the interior of the colony with British soldiers on the coast, near Wilmington. To prevent this, Patriots took planks off a bridge over Moores Creek and greased its supporting logs with soap and animal fat (lard). Patriots surprised the Loyalists trying to cross the slippery bridge. In a battle that lasted only three minutes, 50 Loyalists were killed or wounded and more than 850 captured. The Patriots lost only one man. This battle was called the "Lexington and Concord of the South."

The British Retreat from Boston   In Boston, the Continental Army had surrounded the British forces and neither side would back down. But the situation changed as the cannons from Fort Ticonderoga arrived. Soldiers had hauled about 50 heavy cannons by sled for hundreds of miles, floated them on rafts down the icy Hudson River, and dragged them up the hills surrounding Boston.

When the British saw the cannons pointed at them, they decided to withdraw. On March 17, 1776, about 9,000 British soldiers departed on over 100 ships from Boston Harbor and headed toward Canada.

The Battle of the Rice Boats   The first fighting in Georgia began in March 1776. The British had sent a fleet of ships to Savannah Harbor to buy supplies. Governor Wright wanted Georgians to cooperate.

The British wanted several ships that were loaded with rice and anchored near Savannah. The colonists set fire to some of the rice boats rather than let the British have the rice. The British sailed away, taking Governor Wright with them. The Council of Safety and the Committee of Thirty took control. Royal government had come to an end in Georgia.

Common Sense Is Published

Even as the fighting increased, most Americans wanted to avoid a break with Britain. In January 1776, though, Thomas Paine published ***Common Sense,*** a pamphlet that explained the issues from the Patriots' point of view. Paine urged fellow Americans to declare independence immediately. He wrote that America could be the beginning of a "new world."

> **PRIMARY SOURCE**
>
> The cause of America is, in great measure, the cause of all mankind. We have in our power to begin the world over again. A situation similar to the present hath not happened since the days of Noah until now. The birthday of the New World is now at hand.
>
> Thomas Paine, *Common Sense*

Citizens across the colonies read *Common Sense.* Many who had hesitated about joining the Revolution became convinced after reading the pamphlet. The call for independence became deafening, as you will read in the next section.

▶ **The document at the right is the front page of *Common Sense* by Thomas Paine (pictured above). It was one of the most influential political documents in history.**

Section 1 Assessment

1. TERMS & NAMES

Explain the significance of:

a. Second Continental Congress

b. Continental Army

c. George Washington

d. Battle of Bunker Hill

e. *Common Sense*

2. TAKING NOTES

Use a diagram like the one below to note how Georgia's second provincial congress moved to fully participate in the Second Continental Congress.

Georgia Convenes Second Provincial Congress

Georgia Joins the Second Continental Congress

3. MAIN IDEAS

a. How was Georgia's second provincial congress different from the first?

b. What was the purpose of the Olive Branch Petition?

c. What happened after the Battle of the Rice Boats that changed Georgia's government?

4. CRITICAL THINKING

Supporting Opinions

Do you think the fighting between Britain and the colonies could have been avoided? Why or why not?

Think About

• the king's attitude toward the colonies

• colonial feelings about Britain

ACTIVITY -OPTIONS-   **Geography/Math** Research the Battle of Bunker Hill. Draw a **map** of key events or create a **chart** showing statistics from the battle.

2

Declaring Independence

MAIN IDEA

The Declaration of Independence stated the colonies' intention to be free of British control.

WHY IT MATTERS NOW

With the Declaration of Independence, our country took the first steps to becoming the United States of America.

TERMS & NAMES

Declaration of Independence
Thomas Jefferson

▲ Jefferson wrote the Declaration of Independence in two weeks. In it, he explained the colonists' reasons for separating from Britain.

SETTING THE STAGE

Common Sense convinced many to call for independence. But the Continental Congress remained undecided about whether or not it was the right thing to do. On June 7, 1776, Richard Henry Lee of Virginia introduced a resolution calling for independence.

PRIMARY SOURCE

That the United Colonies are, and of right ought to be, free and independent States, that they are absolved from all allegiance to the British Crown, and that all political connection between them and the State of Great Britain is, and ought to be, totally dissolved.

Richard Henry Lee, Lee Resolution of Independence (1776)

Could the colonies come together to declare their independence? Would England accept the declaration without a fight? Or did this mean war?

The Decision for Independence

When Lee introduced his resolution at the Second Continental Congress, most delegates were in favor of the resolution. However, not all were ready to vote on it. They postponed the discussion until July 1. In the meantime, however, they appointed a committee to prepare a **Declaration of Independence**.

The committee chose **Thomas Jefferson** to write the document for two reasons. First, he was from Virginia. Virginia's support for the Declaration of Independence was critical for success. Second, he had a reputation as an excellent writer. John Adams and Benjamin Franklin made some minor changes, but most of the work was Jefferson's.

On July 1, Congress reconsidered Lee's resolution. Seven colonies favored it, including Georgia. Even though they had been one of the last to join the move for independence, most Georgians were now in favor of

Taking Notes

Use your chart to organize important dates in America's pursuit of independence.

1775	1777	1779

| 1775 | 1776 | 1777 | 1778 | 1779 |

▲ The artist John Trumbull tried to capture the mood of the American leaders as they presented the Declaration of Independence to the Continental Congress.

it. Georgia's three delegates, Button Gwinnett, George Walton, and Lyman Hall, were unanimous in their support for independence.

The Colonies Agree   At first the vote on Lee's resolution of independence did not pass. Nine colonies voted for it, two against it, one colony abstained, and one delegation split its vote. Delegates in favor of independence worked to convince their colleagues to vote for the resolution. Late on July 2, the resolution passed, with New York abstaining. Then they turned to Jefferson's Declaration of Independence.

Congress made two minor changes in Jefferson's document. One change was about the blame Jefferson had placed on the British people. Jefferson agreed to that change. He did not agree to the second change.

Slavery Threatens Their Unity   The second change was about a passage Jefferson had included in the Declaration that blamed King George III for slavery and for the slave trade. The delegates from South Carolina and Georgia did not want this passage included. It also offended shippers from New England. Congress deleted the passage about slavery.

Congress Accepts the Declaration   On July 4, 1776, Congress adopted the Declaration of Independence. Four days later, the Declaration was read publicly for the first time. People cheered, bells rang, soldiers paraded, fireworks exploded, and guns were fired in celebration. The Sons of Liberty in New York pulled down a statue of King George III. They later melted the statue and made it into bullets.

Reading History

A. Analyzing Points of View
Why did some colonies reject Jefferson's first Declaration?

THOMAS JEFFERSON
1743–1826

Jefferson was just 33 years old when chosen to write the Declaration of Independence. He was already a brilliant thinker and writer and a highly respected political leader. Jefferson came from a wealthy Virginia family. As a child, he was interested in everything, and he became an inventor, scientist, and architect, among other things. In 1769, he began his political career in the House of Burgesses.

Jefferson felt that writing the Declaration was a major achievement of his life. He had that fact carved on his tombstone.

Signing the Declaration of Independence

The official signing took place on August 2. John Hancock signed first. According to legend, he wrote his name in large letters so that King George could read it easily. The remaining delegates signed in the order in which they had voted in Congress. This was by colony from north to south, making Georgia delegates Walton, Gwinnett, and Hall the last to sign.

These men fully expected to be hanged as traitors. But none died at the hands of the British. The homes of 20 of the signers were damaged or destroyed. Most were poorer at the end of the war than when they had signed. Several had sold personal property to help pay for the war.

The Declaration closed with this pledge: "[W]ith a firm reliance on the protection of divine Providence, we mutually pledge to each other our Lives, our Fortunes, and our sacred Honor."

Americans had declared their independence. In the next section you'll learn how they had to fight a war to win their freedom.

Reading History

B. Finding Main Ideas Why did the signers of the Declaration worry about the consequences of signing?

Section 2 Assessment

1. TERMS & NAMES
Explain the significance of:

a. Declaration of Independence

b. Thomas Jefferson

2. TAKING NOTES

Use a time line like the one below to note some events from Lee's resolution to the signing of the Declaration of Independence.

June 7, 1776
Lee proposes independence to Congress

August 2, 1776
Declaration is signed

3. MAIN IDEAS

a. Who were Georgia's signers of the Declaration of Independence?

b. Why was the paragraph on slavery deleted from the Declaration?

c. What did the signers of the Declaration gain or lose by signing the document?

4. CRITICAL THINKING

Drawing Conclusions

Why did it take the colonists so long to declare their independence?

Think About
• the colonists' ties to Britain
• the risk of revolution

ACTIVITY -OPTIONS-

Art/Language Arts Find out more about a person discussed in this section. Create a **trading card** or write a short **biography** of that person.

Fighting for Independence

MAIN IDEA	WHY IT MATTERS NOW	TERMS & NAMES

MAIN IDEA
The poorly trained and equipped Continental Army defeated a much stronger British army to win independence for America.

WHY IT MATTERS NOW
The United States of America established itself as a free and independent country.

TERMS & NAMES
The American Crisis
Marquis de Lafayette
Battle of Kettle Creek
General Cornwallis
Battle of Yorktown

SETTING THE STAGE

Many colonists hoped that Britain would give up control of the colonies without a fight. But the colonies were too important for Britain to give up easily. The colonists did not know what was ahead. In the French and Indian War, they had fought *with* Britain against a common enemy. Now they were fighting *against* the country that had been their protector.

Georgia's Assembly had met to discuss their rights as Americans in spite of their royal governor's pleas to consider the terrible consequences of seeking independence. Governor Wright was convinced that Georgians would be "plunged into a state of distress and ruin" if they joined the other colonies in rebellion against the Crown. Georgia's parishes were divided in their loyalties.

How could a loosely joined group of colonies expect to defeat a well-established army? What would happen to them if they lost? What would happen if they won?

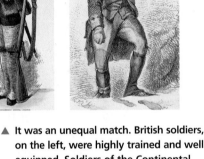

▲ It was an unequal match. British soldiers, on the left, were highly trained and well equipped. Soldiers of the Continental Army, on the right, were inexperienced, lacked adequate food and clothing, and were poorly paid.

War in the Middle States

When Washington's army forced the British out of Boston in March 1776, General William Howe and his British troops went to Canada to wait for reinforcements. Washington expected Howe to attack New York, so he stationed the Continental Army on Long Island. Washington was right. Howe sailed for New York and arrived in July 1776 with a large army, including several thousand Hessian soldiers. Even more British soldiers arrived in August.

For several months, Washington and Howe's armies clashed in New York. Eventually, Howe forced Washington to retreat. Washington led his army through New Jersey and across the Delaware River into Pennsylvania. Many of Washington's troops had been killed or

Taking Notes
Use your chart to organize important dates in America's fight for independence.

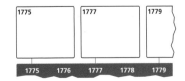

wounded. Others had become discouraged and deserted. Only 3,000 soldiers remained in Washington's army. They believed the war was almost over. Howe was certain he could finish off Washington's army in the spring, so he did not pursue them into Pennsylvania.

Thomas Paine once again rallied people to the cause with his writing. In a series of pamphlets called ***The American Crisis***, he urged the soldiers to keep fighting, even though the situation looked bleak.

PRIMARY SOURCE

These are the times that try men's souls. The summer soldier and the sunshine patriot will in this crisis, shrink from the service of his country; but he that stands now deserves the love and thanks of man and woman. . . . What we obtain too cheap, we esteem too lightly; it is dearness only that gives everything its value.

Thomas Paine, *The American Crisis, No. 1*

Reading History

A. Recognizing Propaganda How does this passage promote the American cause?

Washington hoped a victory would encourage his weary soldiers. He also knew that they must attack the British forces soon because most of his men would leave when their enlistment was over on December 31.

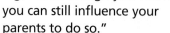

CITIZENSHIP ✦ IN ACTION

Exercising Free Speech

The British could have charged Thomas Paine with a crime for writing *The American Crisis*. The crime was sedition, or stirring up rebellion. By saying what he thought, Paine risked going to prison. Today U.S. citizens have the right to speak freely without fear of jail.

Like Thomas Paine, some students have used free speech to urge people to take action. For example, the Sidney Lanier Middle School in Houston, Texas, has published its school newspaper on the Internet. In October 1996, one writer urged other students to get involved in that year's election, saying, "Even though you will not be able to vote yet, you can still influence your parents to do so."

How Do You Exercise Free Speech?

1. Working in a small group, choose an issue that you care about. Look through newsmagazines for ideas.
2. Use a cluster diagram to record your feelings and opinions about the issue.
3. As a group, decide what action you think people should take on the issue.
4. Write an article expressing the group's opinion. Each member should read the article and suggest changes. Revise the article.
5. Send the revised article to the editorial page of your school or local newspaper.

For more about free speech . . .

RESEARCH LINKS
CLASSZONE.COM

Washington Crosses the Delaware On Christmas night 1776, Washington and his men crossed back over the Delaware River into New Jersey. At daybreak, they entered the city of Trenton and surprised the Hessian troops there. The Hessians did not fare well. Their gunpowder was damp from the weather, and their commander was killed. They surrendered. Washington's army took their supplies. The victory encouraged the soldiers and attracted more recruits to the Continental Army.

War at Sea

Not all of the fighting during the Revolution took place on land. More than 400 British ships sailed along the coast from Massachusetts to Georgia. Many small battles took place at sea.

At the beginning of the war, Americans allowed private ships to hunt down British supply ships. These ships were the beginning of the Continental Navy. Some people said these ships were no better than pirates because they stole all of the merchandise on the ships that they attacked. The Continental Navy had grown to about a dozen warships. Some states had their own navies.

John Paul Jones became the first American naval hero with his victory over the British navy off the British coast on September 23, 1779. In the midst of the battle, the confident British commander offered to allow Jones to surrender. Jones replied, "I have not yet begun to fight!" His success against the best navy in the world shocked the British and elated the Americans.

European Allies for the Patriots

Jones completed another important mission that helped the American cause. In 1777, he went to France to deliver the message that American troops had won some important battles against England.

France had been helping the colonies secretly for more than two years. With Jones's news, France joined openly with the Americans. France gave money, troops, and its support to the American cause. The **Marquis de Lafayette** was a young French noble who volunteered to serve in Washington's army. He persuaded the French king to send a

CONNECTIONS to Literature

Phyllis Wheatley

Phyllis Wheatley was America's first important African-American poet. She was born in Africa about 1753 and sold into slavery as a child. She was a household servant for the Wheatley family of Boston but was raised and educated as a family member.

Some of Wheatley's poems were about the Patriot cause. Of George Washington, she wrote:

Proceed, great chief, with virtue on thy side,

Thy evr'y action let the goddess guide.

A crown, a mansion, and a throne that shine,

With gold unfading, Washington! be thine.

In other poems, Wheatley connected America's fight against British oppression with the struggle for freedom of enslaved African Americans.

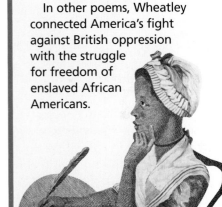

6,000-man army. He became a hero in both France and the United States. Later he took part in the French Revolution as well.

Another European leader who assisted in the American Revolution was Count Casimir Pulaski of Poland. General Washington requested that Pulaski be commissioned as an army officer because of his experience in fighting wars for independence in other countries. Pulaski was mortally wounded at the battle of Savannah on October 9, 1779. Fort Pulaski outside Savannah and Pulaski County were named for him.

War in the South

In 1778, the war had been going on for three years. Although the Americans had lost more battles than they had won, they refused to give up. Hoping to end the war, the British tried another plan. They began to fight in the South.

Reading History

B. Making Inferences Why would the British hope that fighting in the South would bring an end to the war?

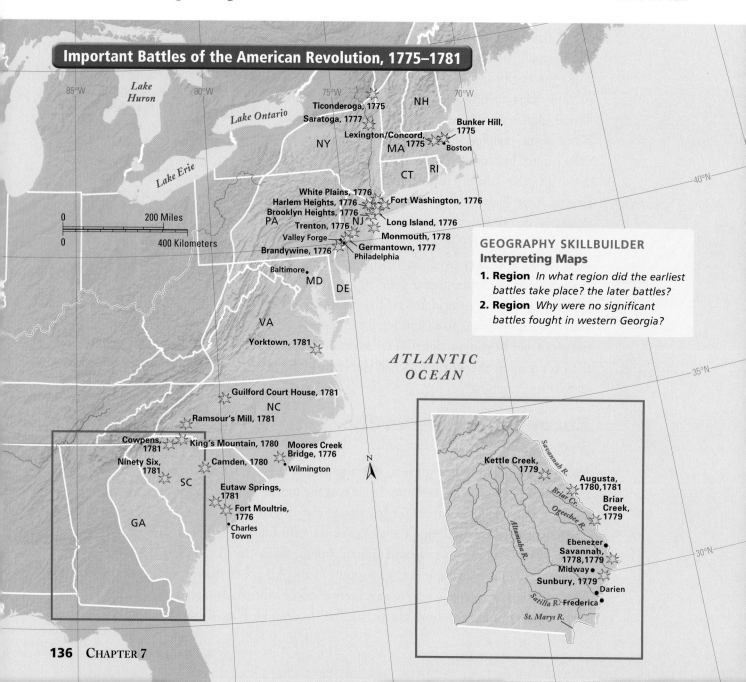

Important Battles of the American Revolution, 1775–1781

Lake Huron

Lake Ontario

Lake Erie

Ticonderoga, 1775
Saratoga, 1777
Lexington/Concord, 1775
NH
Bunker Hill, 1775
NY
MA
Boston
CT
RI

0   200 Miles
0   400 Kilometers

White Plains, 1776
Harlem Heights, 1776
Brooklyn Heights, 1776
PA
Trenton, 1776   NJ
Valley Forge
Brandywine, 1776
Germantown, 1777
Philadelphia

Fort Washington, 1776
Long Island, 1776
Monmouth, 1778

Baltimore
MD
DE

VA

Yorktown, 1781

GEOGRAPHY SKILLBUILDER
Interpreting Maps

1. **Region** In what region did the earliest battles take place? the later battles?
2. **Region** Why were no significant battles fought in western Georgia?

ATLANTIC OCEAN

Guilford Court House, 1781
NC
Ramsour's Mill, 1781
Cowpens, 1781   King's Mountain, 1780   Moores Creek Bridge, 1776
Ninety Six, 1781   Camden, 1780   Wilmington
SC
Eutaw Springs, 1781
Fort Moultrie, 1776
GA
Charles Town

N

Savannah R.
Kettle Creek, 1779
Augusta, 1780,1781
Briar Cr.
Briar Creek, 1779
Ogeechee R.
Altamaha R.
Ebenezer
Savannah 1778,1779
Midway
Sunbury, 1779   Darien
Satilla R.   Frederica
St. Marys R.

War in Georgia The British captured Savannah in December 1778. Then they worked their way south along the Georgia coast. They captured Sunbury and Midway. In each conflict, British troops greatly outnumbered local militia. They captured Augusta in January 1779. With help from the Creek, the British now controlled most of Georgia.

Fighting Comes to the Backcountry The British had not counted on the determination of the American colonists. Patriots in Georgia, as elsewhere, continued to fight against the British. When the British tried to take the Backcountry, Georgians, with the help of some South Carolinians, resisted.

The **Battle of Kettle Creek** is one example of Georgia resolve. In February 1779, Patriot forces led by Colonels Elijah Clarke and John Dooly attacked the Loyalist militia near Augusta. They were joined by South Carolina troops commanded by Andrew Pickens of South Carolina. The Loyalists were defeated. Only 9 Patriots were killed, but about 70 Loyalists were killed, and another 70 were captured.

The British Try to Take the South **General Cornwallis** was responsible for taking the colonies of North Carolina and Virginia. Yet he decided to wait to make his move. The British were not used to the hot, humid summers of the South.

Cornwallis's delay gave the North Carolina militia time to plan how to slow down the British. Battles in North Carolina and South Carolina moved the British farther and farther from their supplies on the coast.

▼ The 3,300 British troops led by Lt. General Archibald Campbell captured Savannah easily in December 1778. This drawing shows Patriot soldiers disabling their cannons before surrendering the town.

PATRIOT NANCY HART

A favorite story of the Revolutionary War in Georgia centers around Nancy Hart, for whom Hart County was named. While there are no contemporary accounts of the event, there are records to show that Nancy Hart was a real person. This story started circulating in 1849.

Legend has it that the Milledgeville *Southern Recorder* reported the story of Nancy Hart in 1825.

"One day, six Tories paid Nancy a call and demanded a meal. She soon spread before them smoking venison, hoe-cakes, and fresh honeycomb. Having stacked their arms, they seated themselves, and started to eat, when Nancy, quick as a flash, seized one of the guns, cocked it, and with a blazing oath declared she would blow out the brains of the first mortal that offered to rise or taste a mouthful! She sent one of her sons to inform the Whigs of her prisoners. Whether uncertain because of her cross-eyes which one she was aiming at, or transfixed by her ferocity, they remained quiet. The Whigs soon arrived and dealt with the Tories according to the rules of the times."

The legend goes on to say that in 1912, a newspaper reported that workers for the Elberton and Eastern Railroad found a grave. It contained six human skeletons and was on land that had been owned by Nancy Hart.

When they were forced to retreat in order to retrieve their supplies, they left most of Georgia and the Carolinas in American hands.

The End of the War

In 1781, most of the fighting occurred in Virginia. General Cornwallis set up his base at Yorktown in July. Yorktown is on a peninsula in the Chesapeake Bay. There his army could receive supplies by ship from New York.

Washington saw an opportunity to cut off the British supplies. In August, a large French fleet arrived from the West Indies. They blocked the Chesapeake Bay and trapped the British troops on the peninsula.

Washington, with the help of French forces, moved south. When British ships tried to reach Cornwallis, French ships drove them back. In the **Battle of Yorktown,** American and French troops attacked Yorktown with cannons. Cornwallis had no way out. On October 19, 1781, he surrendered. Although some fighting continued elsewhere, this was the last major battle of the war.

> **Reading History**
>
> **C. Making Inferences** How did the geography of Yorktown help Washington defeat Cornwallis?

The War Ends in Georgia   In June 1781, Colonel Clarke led Georgia and South Carolina troops in a successful attempt to take Augusta back from the British forces. This victory left Georgia's Backcountry free of British rule.

For most Georgians, the war ended when the British finally left Savannah in July 1782. The years after the war became a time of rapid growth in population, wealth, and production.

The Treaty of Paris   The war was not officially over until the Treaty of Paris in 1783. The Americans were able to control the negotiations. Terms of the treaty included recognition of the United States as a separate country and boundaries of the new nation.

From Colonies to States

Americans entered the Revolution because they wanted to control their own affairs. Through the war, they had learned that together, the colonies had a far greater strength than they had individually. After the war, the Articles of Confederation held 13 separate states together.

The new country had much work to do after the war. Within a few years, the country had grown beyond the Articles of Confederation. Leaders began to see the need for a more firmly united nation. Revising the Articles of Confederation led to the birth of the United States Constitution, as you will read in the next chapter.

Section Assessment

1. TERMS & NAMES

Explain the significance of:

a. *The American Crisis*

b. Marquis de Lafayette

c. Battle of Kettle Creek

d. General Cornwallis

e. Battle of Yorktown

2. TAKING NOTES

Use a chart like the one below to name the locations of battles in Georgia. Place a check mark noting whether the victory was for the Loyalists or Patriots.

Georgia Battle	Loyalist Victory	Patriot Victory

3. MAIN IDEAS

a. What was the significance of the Battle of Saratoga?

b. How did the physical geography of Yorktown assist the Patriot victory?

c. How did the Revolutionary War affect the growth of Georgia?

4. CRITICAL THINKING

Analyzing Causes

How did each of the following help bring about the British defeat at Yorktown?

Think About

• the location chosen by Cornwallis

• the French fleet and troops

• Washington's planning

   Technology/Music Research one of the battles that took place in Georgia. Commemorate the event by designing a **Web page** or writing a **song** celebrating the victory.

VISUAL SUMMARY

People and Events of the American Revolution

MILITARY

- George Washington commanded the Continental Army.
- Colonel William Prescott led Americans in the Battle of Bunker Hill.
- Marquis de Lafayette was a French nobleman who fought for the Americans.
- John Paul Jones won a major American naval victory.
- George Rogers Clark helped hold the Western frontier for America
- General Cornwallis surrendered at Yorktown, ending the war.

CIVILIAN

- Nobel W. Jones and Joseph Habersham led first open act of rebellion in Georgia.
- Thomas Paine shaped American public opinion with Common Sense.
- John Dickinson wrote the Olive Branch Petition.
- Thomas Jefferson wrote the Declaration of Independence.
- Nancy Hart defended her Georgia home against Loyalist raiders.
- Button Gwinnett, George Walton, and Lyman Hall were Georgia delegates to the Continental Congress.

TERMS & NAMES

Briefly explain the significance of the following.

1. Second Continental Congress
2. George Washington
3. Battle of Bunker Hill
4. *Common Sense*
5. Declaration of Independence
6. Thomas Jefferson
7. Marquis de Lafayette
8. Battle of Kettle Creek
9. General Cornwallis
10. Battle of Yorktown

REVIEW QUESTIONS

Moving Toward Independence (pages 125–129)

1. What factors led Georgia to support the Congressional resolutions?
2. Why was the Battle of Bunker Hill important?
3. What was the significance of the Battle of the Rice Boats?

Declaring Independence (pages 130–132)

4. Why was Jefferson chosen to write the Declaration?
5. What changes were made in the Declaration before it was accepted by Congress?
6. Who was first to sign the Declaration?

Fighting for Independence (pages 133–139)

7. What American victory was the turning point of the war?
8. What ally supported the American battle for independence?
9. How did Washington defeat the British at Yorktown?

CRITICAL THINKING

1. USING YOUR NOTES: TAKING NOTES

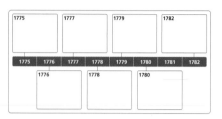

Using your completed chart, answer the questions below.

a. Which battles happened before the signing of the Declaration?
b. What key events took place in 1776?

2. ANALYZING LEADERSHIP

What qualities do you think George Washington had that made him such a respected leader?

3. APPLYING CITIZENSHIP SKILLS

What important roles did civilians play in the success of the war? Give a specific example from your reading.

4. THEME: CITIZENSHIP

Which revolutionary leaders displayed civic virtue by putting the good of the nation ahead of their own interests? Give a specific example from your reading.

5. SOLVING PROBLEMS

How did Washington lead a small, inexperienced force against a large professional army?

INTERACT *with* HISTORY

What sacrifices are worth making for freedom? Would you have made the sacrifices made by so many colonists?

Use the graph below and your knowledge of early American history to answer questions 1 through 3.

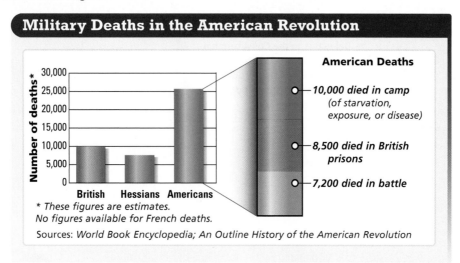

Military Deaths in the American Revolution

* These figures are estimates.
No figures available for French deaths.

Sources: *World Book Encyclopedia; An Outline History of the American Revolution*

American Deaths

10,000 died in camp (of starvation, exposure, or disease)

8,500 died in British prisons

7,200 died in battle

1. How many Americans died of starvation, exposure, or disease in camp?

   A. 25,000   C. 8,500
   B. 10,000   D. 7,200

2. How many British troops died in the war?

   A. 25,000   C. 8,500
   B. 7,500   D. 10,000

3. About how many more deaths did the Americans suffer than the British?

   A. 20,000   C. 10,000
   B. 15,000   D. 5,000

TEST PRACTICE
CLASSZONE.COM

ALTERNATIVE ASSESSMENT

1. CREATING A POSTER

Two of the diseases that killed American soldiers in camp were typhoid fever and smallpox. Do research to learn the following about one of these diseases: its cause, its symptoms, its treatment, and how common it is today. Use the information to create a public health poster to inform people about the disease.

2. COOPERATIVE LEARNING

The delegates of the Continental Congress debated the issue of slavery. Some wanted to keep Jefferson's slavery clause. Some wanted to delete it. Play the roles of those for and against the clause. Study the delegates' arguments. Then break into teams and debate the issue.

INTEGRATED TECHNOLOGY ACTIVITY

CREATING A MULTIMEDIA PRESENTATION

Use the Internet, your library, and a computer to prepare an electronic presentation on one of the major battles of the Revolutionary War. Try to include the following items in your presentation.

- Paintings of the conflict
- Photographs of artifacts
- Quotations from participants and witnesses
- Music of the period
- Recorded sound effects
- Graphs showing battle statistics

Show your presentation to the class.

RESEARCH LINKS
CLASSZONE.COM

Building a New Nation and State 1777–1830

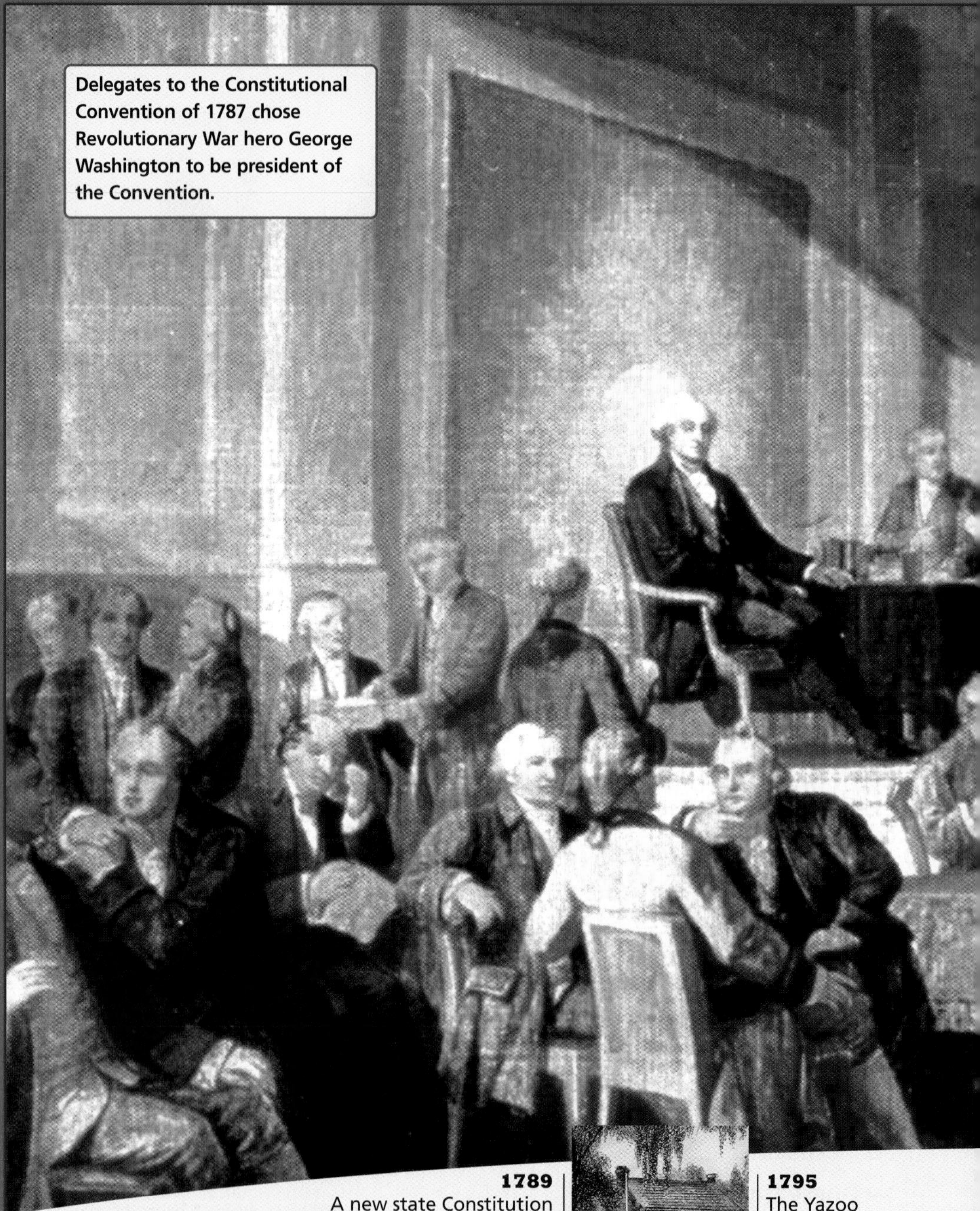

Delegates to the Constitutional Convention of 1787 chose Revolutionary War hero George Washington to be president of the Convention.

1777
First Georgia
Constitution is adopted.

1783
The Treaty
of Augusta
is negotiated.

1789
A new state Constitution
is adopted.

1790
The Treaty of New
York is negotiated.

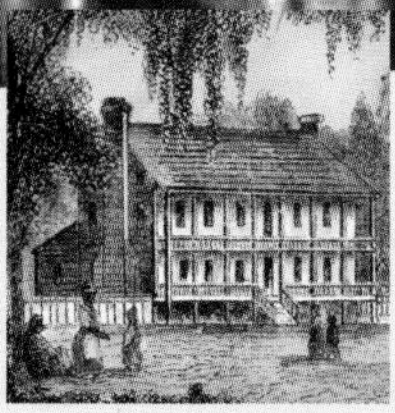

1795
The Yazoo
Act is passed.

1796
The Yazoo
Act is repealed.

GEORGIA
USA

1775

1781
The Articles of
Confederation
go into effect.

1783
Treaty of
Paris formally
ends the
Revolutionary War.

1788
U.S.
Constitution
is ratified.

The year is 1787, and your young country needs to reform its government. Now everyone is wondering what the new government will be like. You have been called to a convention to decide how the new government should be organized.

How do you form a government?

WHAT DO YOU THINK?

- What will be your main goal in creating a new government?

- How will you get the people at the convention to agree on important issues?

- What do you think your biggest challenges will be?

For more information on this chapter, visit . . .
RESEARCH LINKS
CLASSZONE.COM

1802
The Compact of 1802 is agreed to.
1803
The land lottery system is adopted.

1814
Battle of Horseshoe Bend. The Treaty of Fort Jackson is negotiated.

1828
Gold discovered in Dahlonega.

1800

1825

1803
Louisiana Purchase is made.
1804
Lewis and Clark expedition begins.

1812
War of 1812 begins.

1814
War of 1812 ends.

1828
Andrew Jackson is elected president.

1830
Indian Removal Act is passed.

Reading Strategy: Solving Problems

What Do You Know?

What do you think of when people talk about the U.S. government? Why do nations have governments? What does the U.S. government do?

THINK ABOUT

- what you've learned about the U.S. government from the news or your teachers
- what the purpose of a government is
- how the government affects your everyday life

What Do You Want to Know?

What questions do you have about the creation of the U.S. Constitution? Write those questions in your notebook before you read the chapter.

Solving Problems

When you read history, look for how people solved problems they faced in the past. Copy the chart below in your notebook. Use it to identify the methods that Americans used to solve the problems faced by the nation after declaring its independence.

 See Skillbuilder Handbook, page 553.

Taking Notes

Problems	Solutions
Western Lands	
Postwar Depression	
Representation in the New Government	
Slavery	

Creating a New Government

MAIN IDEA	WHY IT MATTERS NOW	TERMS & NAMES
The Founding Fathers created the document that established the framework for the new country. The document still guides our government today.	Even though the Constitution can be amended, its basic ideas still serve as the supreme law of our land.	Founding Fathers Articles of Confederation Constitutional Convention democratic republic checks and balances federalism Bill of Rights

SETTING THE STAGE

Creating a new country required the ideas and hard work of many people. The men who wrote the documents that declared our independence and framed our government were different in many ways, but they all agreed on one thing. They wanted a free country that was founded on reason. In the Declaration of Independence, they outlined the truths in which they believed.

But many practical questions remained. Could the new states work together to solve these problems, yet keep their own identities?

▲ Some of the most respected men in the nation served as delegates to the Constitutional Convention. Georgia was represented by Abraham Baldwin and William Few.

Taking Notes

Use your chart to identify the methods Americans used to solve problems in creating a new government.

Problems	Solutions
Western Lands	

Founding Fathers

The people who made the greatest contributions to the establishment of our country are often called the **Founding Fathers.** Those who wrote the Constitution are often referred to as the "framers" of the Constitution.

Some of the Founding Fathers served several roles. Here are some of the names that come to mind when we speak of Founding Fathers: George Washington, Thomas Jefferson, James Madison, John Adams, Benjamin Franklin, and Alexander Hamilton. Others who were influential include Patrick Henry and Thomas Paine. Remember that in the 1700s, white men were the only ones who participated publicly in politics.

Of course, many other people influenced the founding of our country. One of those was Abigail Adams, the wife of John Adams. She wrote many letters to her husband while he was away. She asked questions and offered opinions to him. Abigail became a trusted adviser to her husband. She was ahead of her time in thinking about the ways women should be treated.

The Articles of Confederation

The **Articles of Confederation** were the first form of a constitution for the new country. They were written at the same time the Declaration of Independence was written. Button Gwinnett of Georgia was part of the committee that wrote the Articles of Confederation.

The Articles of Confederation set up a system of government that divided power between the national government and the individual state governments. Congress was the national body of government. Congress could declare war, sign treaties, deliver the mail, and create money. But states had the most power. Each state could collect its own taxes, issue its own money, and support its own militia. Every state had one vote in Congress, no matter how large or small it was.

Congress passed the Articles in November 1777. Then the states voted on whether to accept the Articles. By 1778, eight states had ratified the Articles, but some small states that did not have land west of the Appalachian Mountains refused to sign. They wanted the states that did have this land to give it to the federal government. By 1781, all states had agreed to give up their Western lands and all 13 states accepted the Articles of Confederation. Georgia gave up the southern part of its western lands in 1778, but it did not actually give up the northern part until 1802.

The Northwest Ordinance

Congress surveyed the western lands and divided them for settlement. They called these lands the Northwest Territory. They eventually became the states of Ohio, Indiana, Michigan, Illinois, Wisconsin, and part of Minnesota. In 1787, Congress passed the Northwest Ordinance. This described how a territory would set

U.S. Government, 1776–1787

Successes of the Continental Congress

- Governed the nation during the Revolutionary War
- Negotiated the Treaty of Paris at the end of the war
- Passed the Land Ordinance of 1785
- Passed the Northwest Ordinance (1787)

- Lacked power to enforce laws
- Lacked power to levy taxes
- Lacked power to regulate trade among the states
- Required all 13 states to approve changes in the Articles

Weaknesses of the Articles of Confederation

SKILLBUILDER Interpreting Charts

1. *What do you think was the greatest success of the Continental Congress?*
2. *What do you think was the greatest weakness of the Articles of Confederation?*

up a government and become a state. It established laws such as freedom of religion and trial by jury. It also outlawed slavery. As new territories became part of the United States, they followed the pattern the Northwest Ordinance established.

Weaknesses of the Articles

The Articles of Confederation had some problems. Congress could not impose taxes, so it could not repay the massive debts left from fighting the war. It could not control trade or enforce laws, so it could not resolve trade disputes between the states. Some political leaders wanted to revise the Articles of Confederation.

Money Problems in the New Country   After the war, the country owed $42 million in war debts, much of it to soldiers who had fought in the war. There had been no money to pay them during the war. Unfortunately, there was no money after the war, either. Many soldiers received land in the Northwest Territory instead of money.

Congress was not alone in facing economic problems. Taxes were high in most states. Many people could not pay their taxes. In Massachusetts, the economy was so bad some citizens rebelled against the government.

Background

In 1788, Daniel Shays was pardoned for his actions.

Shays's Rebellion   Daniel Shays was a farmer in Massachusetts who had served in the Continental Army. Like many other farmers, he was unable to pay his taxes and was about to lose his property. In January 1787, Shays led a group of angry farmers to seize guns being

▼ Shays's rebels take over a Massachusetts courthouse.

stored in Springfield that belonged to the government. The governor of Massachusetts sent troops to stop them.

Shays's Rebellion did not last long, but it alarmed people everywhere. Massachusetts asked Congress for help, but Congress did not have the power or resources to help. Congress called a meeting to begin in May to revise the Articles of Confederation.

The Constitutional Convention of 1787

By May 25, 1787, all states except Rhode Island had sent representatives to Pennsylvania. Abraham Baldwin and William Few represented Georgia. They met at Independence Hall for what came to be known as the **Constitutional Convention**. Some came thinking they were simply revising the existing articles. Others came with the idea of designing a new government. No one knew quite what to expect.

Delegates to the Convention Some of America's most famous men were at the Convention. Many of the delegates to the Convention had also served in the Continental Congress. They had worked in their states' legislatures and helped write their constitutions.

These men had a very difficult job. They had to create a government that was strong enough to protect people's rights. But they had to make sure that the government itself did not have too much power.

The proof that they did their job well is that the United States Constitution is still the supreme law of the land. It outlines the form of government and defines the powers given to each branch of government.

Framing the Constitution

The first thing the delegates did was to elect George Washington as president of the Convention. One rule was to keep the discussions secret. They wanted everyone to be free to speak his mind or change it. They posted guards at the doors. They closed the windows, even though it was very hot. The delegates worked closely through the long, hot summer. Sometimes the debates were equally hot.

A Democratic Republic The delegates decided first that the new government should remain a **democratic republic.** A republic is a government in which people choose representatives to govern for

JAMES MADISON
1751–1836

James Madison may have made the greatest contribution of any of the Founders at the Constitutional Convention. He took thorough notes during the convention. His notes are the most detailed picture we have of the debates and drama of the convention.

To prepare for the meeting, Madison had spent months studying other countries' governments and had read more than a hundred books on government. Madison was so important that he earned the title "Father of the Constitution."

Reading History

A. Making Decisions Do you agree with the Founders' decision to keep the convention secret? Why or why not?

them. "Democratic" means that the republic reflects the will of the people.

Compromises Resolve Disputes   One of the greatest arguments during the Convention was the balance of power between large states and smaller states. Eventually, they reached a compromise that satisfied both the smaller and the larger states.

Under the Articles of Confederation, Congress was unicameral, meaning it had only one house. Under the new Constitution, it would be bicameral, or have two houses: the Senate and the House of Representatives. In the Senate, each state would have the same number of votes. In the House of Representatives, the number of votes would be based on a state's population. This was called the Great Compromise.

The Three-Fifths Compromise   This solution, however, created another problem. States strongly disagreed over how to count people. This affected two issues: how many delegates a state would have in the House of Representatives and taxes. There were many more slaves in Southern states. These states wanted to count slaves to decide representation, but they did not want to be taxed on them. Northern states felt that slaves should not be counted for representation but should be counted for taxation.

Reading History

B. Forming and Supporting Opinions   Did the delegates do the right thing in agreeing to the Three-Fifths Compromise? Explain.

The delegates agreed on another compromise to resolve this issue, called the Three-Fifths Compromise. They decided that every five slaves would count as three people. This applied to both Congressional representation and taxation.

Slavery sparked another heated debate. The Northern states had already outlawed slavery and importing slaves. They wanted to include this ban on slavery and the slave trade in the Constitution. The Southern states, particularly South Carolina and Georgia, would not agree to this. If necessary, they would reject the Constitution. Another compromise, the slave trade compromise, saved the situation. The delegates agreed that Congress could not ban the importation of slaves until 1808.

The Commerce Clause was the fourth compromise. It gave the national government the power to collect taxes and regulate trade between the states.

CONNECTIONS to Science

Preserving the Constitution

The National Archives is responsible for preserving the 200-year-old sheets of parchment on which the original Constitution was first written.

In 1995, scientists used fiber-optic light sources and computer-guided electronic cameras designed for space exploration to examine the pages. They discovered that, while the documents were unharmed, the glass of the airtight display case was deteriorating.

While new encasements of solid titanium were built, scientists had the first opportunity in 50 years to view the documents outside their glass enclosure. The Archives reopened in September 2003.

Checks and Balances

EXECUTIVE BRANCH

The President

- May pardon people convicted of federal crimes
- Appoints federal judges
- May veto laws passed by Congress
- May call special session of Congress

JUDICIAL BRANCH

The Supreme Court Other Federal Courts

- May declare president's actions unconstitutional
- May declare laws unconstitutional

LEGISLATIVE BRANCH

Senate and House of Representatives

- May override president's veto
- May refuse to approve treaty written by president
- May refuse to approve president's appointments
- May remove a president from office if he or she is found guilty of wrongdoing

- May overrule decisions of the courts by proposing constitutional amendments
- May remove federal judge if he or she is found guilty of wrongdoing

SKILLBUILDER

Interpreting Diagrams

This diagram shows how one branch of government checks the power of the other two branches.

1. *How does the executive branch check Congress and the Supreme Court?*
2. *How does Congress check the president and the judicial branch?*
3. *How does the judicial branch check the president and Congress?*

Division of Powers   They also agreed to divide power in the national government into three branches. The legislative branch would make the laws. The judicial branch would interpret the laws. And the executive branch would enforce the laws. Each branch would have the power to check, or control, the actions of the other two branches. This is called a system of **checks and balances.**

The Electoral College   Another important question was how to choose a president. The delegates agreed that voters in each state would elect representatives called electors. The number of electors for each state would equal the number of its senators and representatives. The electors would vote for the president. This system is called the Electoral College.

Delegates Approve the Constitution   After almost four months of debating these and other important questions, the delegates approved and signed the Constitution. Before it could become law, nine of the thirteen states had to approve or "ratify" the Constitution. Each state would hold a convention to decide whether to accept this new plan of government.

The States Debate the Constitution

Even before states held their conventions, people debated the new Constitution. Federalists were those people who strongly supported the Constitution. In the system of government called **federalism,** the

Background

The Role of the Press   The press played an important role in the debate over the Constitution. Most newspapers supported the Constitution. They gave the Federalists more publicity than the Antifederalists.

national government and the states share power. People who opposed the Constitution were called Antifederalists. They believed the Constitution took too much power away from the states. They were also concerned that there was no bill of rights. A bill of rights is a set of rules that defines people's rights.

Reading History

C. Drawing Conclusions
How did the lack of a bill of rights endanger the Constitution?

The Federalist **Papers**   Antifederalists published their views in newspapers and pamphlets. They tried to persuade people to vote against the Constitution. The Federalists published their own essays to answer the critics. James Madison, Alexander Hamilton, and John Jay wrote these essays. Their essays became known as *The Federalist* papers. They were later published in a book called *The Federalist*.

> **PRIMARY SOURCE**
>
> Yes, my countrymen, . . . I am clearly of the opinion it is in your best interest to adopt it [the Constitution]. I am convinced that this is the safest course for your liberty, your dignity, and your happiness.
>
> Alexander Hamilton, Federalist No. 1, October 27, 1787

The States Decide

Background

Rhode Island did not send delegates because it feared that a strong national government would force people to repay the war debts on difficult terms.

By early 1788, Delaware, New Jersey, Pennsylvania, Georgia, and Connecticut had voted for the Constitution. By late June, nine states had approved it. It was now officially ratified, but New York and Virginia had not yet made a decision. To be effective, these large and important states had to accept the Constitution.

With the promise that Congress would add a bill of rights, Virginia and New York ratified the Constitution. Rhode Island and North Carolina decided to remain independent of the United States. However, by 1790 both states had approved the Constitution and joined the country.

▼ The *Massachusetts Centinel* published this cartoon on August 2, 1788, in an effort to convince North Carolina and Rhode Island to approve the Constitution.

REDEUNT SATURNIA REGNA.

On the erection of the Eleventh PILLAR of the great National DOME, we beg leave most sincerely to felicitate "OUR DEAR COUNTRY."

Rise it will.

The foundation good—it may yet be SAVED.

The FEDERAL EDIFICE.

The Bill of Rights

Those who supported a bill of rights believed it would protect all Americans against the power of government. James Madison wrote the **Bill of Rights.** Passing the Bill of Rights was one of the first acts of the new federal government. These rights became the first ten amendments, or additions, to the Constitution.

The Bill of Rights guarantees such rights as freedom of speech, freedom of press, and freedom of religion. It gives people the right to speak out about their beliefs, to worship in their own way, and to be tried by a jury. Congress knew that no document could list every right of the people. The Ninth Amendment states that the Bill of Rights does not limit rights that are not specifically mentioned in the Constitution.

With the Bill of Rights, the people of the United States had truly won the rights they had fought for during the American Revolution. The Constitution and the Bill of Rights created a government based on law, with "the consent of the govern'd." The Bill of Rights was one of the first acts of the new government.

The Constitution established a new way to govern all the states and guaranteed all citizens the same basic rights. But within that framework, it was up to the individual states to decide how to govern themselves. In the next section, you will learn how Georgia developed its state government and wrestled to secure the rights for which its citizens had fought.

Section Assessment

1. TERMS & NAMES

Explain the significance of:

a. Founding Fathers

b. Articles of Confederation

c. Constitutional Convention

d. democratic republic

e. checks and balances

f. federalism

g. Bill of Rights

2. TAKING NOTES

Use a diagram like the one below to note the terms of four Constitutional compromises.

Compromise	Effect
Great Compromise	
Three-Fifths Compromise	
Slave Trade Compromise	
Commerce Clause	

3. MAIN IDEAS

a. What were some of the weaknesses of the Articles of Confederation?

b. What is the difference between a unicameral and a bicameral Congress? Which allows the people a greater voice?

c. What is another name for the Bill of Rights?

4. CRITICAL THINKING

Forming and Supporting Opinions

Which side would you have supported during Shays's Rebellion—the farmers or the officials who called out the militia? Why?

Think About
- the farmers' problems
- the government's situation

Technology/Art Make an **audio recording** of a speech or draw a **political cartoon** that expresses your views on the issue of the Three-Fifths Compromise.

Georgia as a State

MAIN IDEA	WHY IT MATTERS NOW	TERMS & NAMES
Georgia had to establish its own state government and make plans for a large portion of the state that was still frontier.	Georgia's decision about its government and land settlement still impacts Georgians today.	headright Alexander McGillivray Yazoo Land Fraud Compact of 1802 land lottery

SETTING THE STAGE

Georgia was the youngest colony when the country fought the war for independence. It was less settled and had fewer resources than other states. Georgia's political leaders had to write a constitution so that its government would provide for its citizens. Most of Georgia's territory was unsettled frontier. They needed citizens there who would support the growth of the state.

Much of the state was occupied by Creek and Cherokee. White settlers wanted their land for farming. How would ownership of land be determined? How would the state and its citizens be governed? Georgia's leaders had little experience in leading the state, and they had a big job ahead of them.

The State Constitution

By the time the Declaration of Independence was completed, Georgia had a temporary government in place, led by Archibald Bulloch. The government began writing a state constitution, which was finished in 1777. It set up a unicameral, or one-house, legislature. The legislature elected the governor and other state officials. John Treutlen was the first governor under the new constitution.

In 1789, Georgia adopted a state constitution that resembled the new U.S. Constitution. It called for a bicameral, or two-house, legislature and three branches of government: legislative, judicial, and executive.

The constitution also included plans for local governments. Counties were set up as local units of the state. They were responsible for keeping records and establishing a system of law. Each county seat was the center of local government. The courthouse and jail were located there. Counties were supposed to be small enough so that citizens could make the trip to the county seat and back home in one day by horse and buggy. As counties grew, they were divided and new seats were chosen.

▲ Georgia acquired more territory to the west. To encourage settlement of the Backcountry, Georgia gave free land to white settlers there.

Taking Notes

Use your chart to identify the methods Georgians used to solve problems in establishing their state.

Problems	Solutions
Western Lands	

Early Amendments

Legislators added important amendments to the Georgia constitution in 1795. One amendment changed the way of electing the governor. In future elections, both houses of the legislature would elect the governor. They also agreed that the legislature would meet in January, a practice that continues. Further, they established Louisville in present-day Jefferson County as the new state capital.

The Need to Settle the Land

Georgia's land claims stretched from the Atlantic Ocean and Savannah River on the east to the Mississippi River on the west. That vast stretch of land was Georgia's main concern in the 50 years following the Revolutionary War. About 95 percent of it was rough frontier. Settlers wanted to transform that wilderness into farms and communities.

At the end of the Revolutionary War, England had returned the colonies of East and West Florida to Spain. So once again, Georgia shared a southern border with Spain. Spain remained friendly with the Native Americans and supplied them with guns, ammunition, and other goods. Spain hoped the Native Americans would help block American expansion across the Southeast.

More Land for Settlement   In 1773, the British had negotiated a treaty for land with the Native Americans. Native Americans hoped to increase their trade by giving up the land. The Creek ceded a large portion of eastern middle Georgia, and the Cherokee ceded Piedmont land in northeast Georgia. In 1777, Georgia opened this area for settlement. Settlers from Georgia, Virginia, and the Carolinas rushed in.

Later, after the War, Georgia took property from Loyalist settlers as punishment and to help pay expenses from the war. Georgians also believed that Native Americans who had fought on the side of the British should help pay for the war by giving up more of their land. Georgians wanted the fertile land of the Piedmont.

The Headright Land Grant System   Since the early colonial times, Georgia leaders had given land away in order to attract settlers to the state. Free land attracted men who could serve in the state militia.

▼ Some Native Americans had gone heavily into debt to white traders. In 1773, the Creek and Cherokee agreed to give up more than 2 million acres, in part to satisfy those debts.

Reading History

A. Making Inferences
Why would the headright system ensure land was given to people who would farm it?

Georgia called the system used to distribute land a **headright** system because every "head" of household had a "right" to land. A head of household, usually a white man, declared his honesty and integrity and paid a small filing fee. Georgia wanted to give land to people who would build homes and farms on the land.

In 1782, each head of a family was entitled to 200 acres of land, with another 50 acres of land for each member of his family, including slaves, up to 1,000 acres. The government gave war veterans larger claims in payment for their military service. From the late 1780s through the 1790s, the government raised the 1,000-acre limit several times.

Conflict Over Native American Territory

After the Revolutionary War, the U.S. government felt it was important to restore peace with the Native Americans. Until that time, Georgia had made its own treaties with its Native American neighbors. Now the United States would make the treaties.

In 1783, the Cherokee gave up more than one million acres to the state in a treaty signed at Augusta. Settlers quickly filled the land. The Creek were less willing to give up their land. Under the 1783 treaty, a small group of Lower Creek gave up land east of the Oconee River. (See the map on page 157.) When the Upper Creek leader **Alexander McGillivray** heard this news, he said that giving up this land was not part of the treaty. But white settlers had already started moving into the territory.

The Oconee War McGillivray and the Upper Creek attacked the Backcountry settlers, hoping to make them leave. From 1787 to 1789, the Creek Indians and Georgians fought. The Creek killed 82 frontier settlers and wounded 29. They burned many houses and settlements. They took 140 settlers as prisoners, along with herds of stolen horses and cattle. Georgians responded by invading Creek country, killing residents and burning villages and crops. Chief McGillivray said that the Creek were not at war with the "whole American States," only with the Georgians who had taken their hunting grounds.

Native Americans and white settlers differed in their beliefs over land ownership. Native Americans believed that humans simply used the land and took care of it. They did not have "ownership." White settlers believed that when they bought land, it became theirs.

▼ Alexander McGillivray and the Upper Creek did not recognize the treaty giving up land east of the Oconee River and fought the settlers there.

Buckskins

In return for deerskins (buckskins), Native Americans could get the white man's tools. That is how the word "buck" came to stand for a dollar. They used buckskins as money. Here are some of the things Native Americans could get from the white settlers and the amount of buckskins it would take: a gun for 30 buckskins; an axe for 4; a hatchet for 2; three strings of beads for 1; and a bottle of rum for 1.

The Treaty of New York

The United States took action to stop the war. In the 1790 Treaty of New York, the United States government sided with the Creek claim to lands west of the Oconee River. (See the map on page 157.) The government said that white settlers who had moved onto the land would be removed from the land.

Georgians couldn't believe that the government had sided with the Creek. Therefore, many ignored the Treaty of New York, and the raids and massacres continued for the next several years.

Another provision of the Treaty of New York dealt with the way the Native Americans lived. The United States decided the Creek should live more like the white settlers. They wanted the Creek to change from a hunting way of life to one of farming and herding.

Many Georgians began to distrust and dislike the government. The Georgia pioneers knew the dangers of the frontier. They did not rely on the government to protect them and their families. Georgia pioneers began to build small forts in the frontier. Sometimes the forts became permanent homes. The women and children would spend all their time there. The men would work the countryside during the day and go to the fort for protection at night.

An Agent for Peace In 1796, the United States government selected an ex-senator from Georgia, Colonel Benjamin Hawkins, as an Agent to the Creek Nation. Hawkins was sent to a trading post on the St. Marys River. He negotiated a peace treaty with the Creek Indians. The treaty set up a system of trading posts in Native American territory that would be run by the government, in the belief that fair prices and trading practices might lessen conflict with the Native Americans. This worked for a number of years.

The number of white settlers continued to grow. The Native Americans still distrusted them, but the advantages of trade were greater than their distrust.

The Yazoo Land Fraud

When Native Americans surrendered their rights to the land, the state government could give the land to its citizens. The headright system worked well when Georgia was small and had a central government. As the state grew, the counties took over the job of granting land in their districts. Problems arose as some dishonest county leaders began selling land that was not suitable for farming. Worse yet, some sold land that

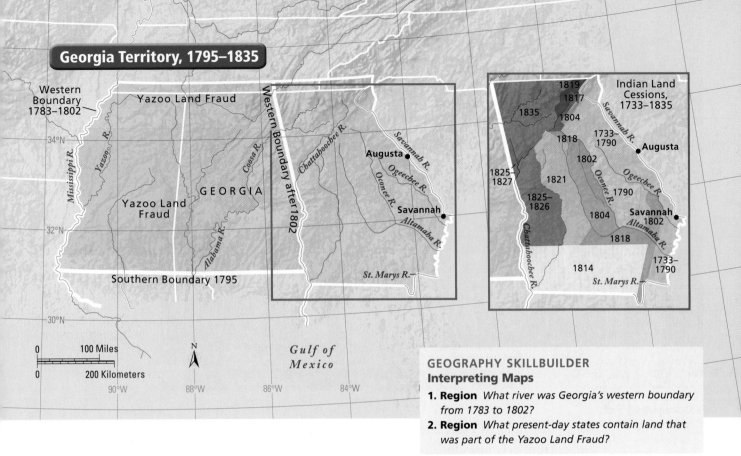

Georgia Territory, 1795–1835

Western Boundary 1783–1802

Yazoo Land Fraud

Western Boundary after 1802

34°N

Mississippi R.

Yazoo R.

Coosa R.

Chattahoochee R.

GEORGIA

Yazoo Land Fraud

Alabama R.

32°N

Southern Boundary 1795

30°N

Gulf of Mexico

Savannah R.

Augusta

Ogeechee R.

Oconee R.

Savannah

Altamaha R.

St. Marys R.

0   100 Miles
0   200 Kilometers

N

90°W   88°W   86°W   84°W

Indian Land Cessions, 1733–1835

1819
1817
1835
1804
1818
1733–1790
1802
1825–1827
1821
1790
1825–1826
1804
1818
1814
1733–1790

Savannah R.
Augusta
Oconee R.
Ogeechee R.
Savannah
1802
Altamaha R.
Chattahoochee R.
St. Marys R.

GEOGRAPHY SKILLBUILDER
Interpreting Maps

1. **Region** What river was Georgia's western boundary from 1783 to 1802?
2. **Region** What present-day states contain land that was part of the Yazoo Land Fraud?

did not exist. In Montgomery County, for example, 2,664,000 acres were granted, but the county only had 407,680 acres.

The most widely known land fraud in U.S. history was the **Yazoo Land Fraud** in 1795. It involved land in the western part of Georgia that now forms the states of Alabama and Mississippi.

Land companies formed to buy large pieces of land in western Georgia and Alabama along the Yazoo River. The companies would make money by selling the land in smaller portions to individuals. If the Native Americans could be moved off the western lands, land that had been purchased at a low cost would suddenly become very valuable.

The Yazoo Act   These land companies persuaded the Georgia legislature to pass the Yazoo Act in early 1795. This act allowed Georgia to sell large areas of its western lands to the private companies. Dishonest legislators were bribed to vote for the Yazoo Act with gifts of stock in the land companies and the promise of large profits.

The people of Georgia were very upset because the large companies bought most of the land, and then sold it to them for much higher prices. In the next election, Georgians voted most of the bill's supporters out of office. The government reversed the Yazoo Act on February 18, 1796. All records of the bill and the resulting land sales were taken out and publicly burned. As each document was handed to the clerk, he read its title. Then he cried out, "God save the State, and long preserve

Reading History

B. Summarizing
Why was the Yazoo Act a fraud?

▲ A magnifying glass was used to focus the sun's rays and start the fire to burn the Yazoo Land Act papers.

her rights, and may every attempt to injure them perish, as these wicked and corrupt acts now do!"

The Compact of 1802

Many important changes came after the Yazoo Land Fraud. In the **Compact of 1802,** Georgia gave up all of its land involved in the Yazoo Land Fraud to the United States. Georgia's boundaries became essentially the state's current boundaries. In return, the national government gave Georgia $1,250,000 and promised to remove all Native Americans from Georgia "as soon as it should become practicable."

In other words, Georgia gave up all the land from its new western boundary to the Mississippi River that King George II had given Oglethorpe and the trustees. In exchange, the state of Georgia received a clear title to all the land in Georgia. The United States agreed that northern Georgia belonged to the State of Georgia, not to the Cherokee. Georgians demanded that Cherokee land be given to white settlers.

The Land Lottery System

After the land fraud, people were suspicious of the headright system. They wanted a new system of land grants to distribute the newly acquired Native American lands. In 1803, the Georgia Legislature passed a Land Act that established a **land lottery** system.

Between 1805 and 1832, Georgia used the lottery system seven times to distribute land acquired from the Creek and the Cherokee. Most of the land east of the Oconee River was headright land. The western three-fifths of the state was "Land Lottery Georgia."

Reading History

C. Summarizing
What were two major results of the Yazoo Land Fraud?

When the state acquired land from Native Americans, it performed a survey of the new territory. The surveyors marked off the land into square farm-sized units. The land lots were 202.5 acres. Along the Coastal Plain where the soil was poor, lots were 490 acres.

After the state surveyed the lots, citizens registered to take part in the lottery. Applicants could be white males over 18, orphans, or widows. They paid a fee that covered the cost of running the lottery.

It held the lottery in Milledgeville. Tickets were numbered for each of the farm-sized square lots and placed in one drum. Another drum contained tickets with the names of people who registered for the lottery. A ticket was drawn from each drum and matched together. The named person won that piece of land. There were more people than units of land, so there were blank tickets mixed in with the numbered ones. The unlucky person who was matched with a blank ticket was said to have "drawn a blank." We still use that phrase today when we can't remember something.

▲ Headright lots were often oddly shaped because settlers could pick the location and shape of their lots. Under the lottery system, surveyors laid out square lots.

By 1802, Georgia had established its borders. In the next section you will learn how the rest of the United States expanded during this period.

Section **2** Assessment

1. TERMS & NAMES

Explain the significance of:

a. headright

b. Alexander McGillivray

c. Yazoo Land Fraud

d. Compact of 1802

e. land lottery

2. TAKING NOTES

Create a diagram like the one below. In each of the surrounding circles, write an advantage Georgians saw in settling its western territory.

Settling Georgia's Western Territory

3. MAIN IDEAS

a. Why were Georgia's Native Americans willing to open their land to white settlers?

b. Why were Georgia's leaders anxious to get most of the land settled?

c. Explain why the Compact of 1802 was bad news for Georgia's Native Americans.

4. CRITICAL THINKING

Evaluating

Why did the land lottery system replace the headright system?

Think About

• settlers' desire for new land

• the Yazoo Land Fraud

• Georgia's westward expansion

Language Arts/Art Write a **campaign brochure** promoting one of Georgia's early governors or draw a **political cartoon** about the Yazoo Land Fraud.

3

Land Expansion

MAIN IDEA	WHY IT MATTERS NOW	TERMS & NAMES
The new states were anxious for more land. The United States made treaties and adopted policies that made new land available.	The government created many of the most populous states and cities today from land that it acquired in the early to mid-1800s.	Louisiana Purchase Lewis and Clark expedition War of 1812 Creek War Andrew Jackson Battle of Horseshoe Bend Manifest Destiny

SETTING THE STAGE

In 1790, most people lived along the East Coast. But the population began growing very rapidly. Immigrants flocked to the new country in hopes of a new life and the opportunity to own their own land. Also, because living conditions were better, the birth rate was higher than it had been in previous years. Young Americans were eager to establish new homes.

By 1800, thousands of settlers were moving to the "West"—which to them meant the area between the Appalachian Mountains and the Mississippi River, the western border of the United States. Further west, France and Spain were negotiating for ownership of the Louisiana Territory—the vast region between the Mississippi River and the Rocky Mountains.

How could state and national leaders provide the land needed for so many young families anxious to settle the new country? And how would this growing population change the political face of the country?

▲ Settlers on the frontier learned to be self-reliant. Each family member contributed to the family's survival.

Pioneers Settle the West

As Georgia expanded, so did the United States. Some Americans had moved west before the American Revolution. After the war, thousands of settlers again began to cross the Appalachian Mountains in search of land and new opportunities.

The rich farmlands west of the Appalachians allowed pioneers to raise enough cattle, hogs, tobacco, and corn to sell to other colonies and overseas. The problem was getting these goods to market. Overland routes were long and difficult. Farmers began shipping their goods downstream on flatboats on the Ohio and Mississippi Rivers. The goods were loaded onto ships in the port city of New Orleans. These

Taking Notes

Use your chart to identify methods used by the United States to solve the problems of expansion.

Problems	Solutions
Western Lands	

farmers were concerned, however, because New Orleans belonged to Spain. Spanish officials made it difficult for Americans to unload and store goods at New Orleans.

The Louisiana Purchase

In 1800, Spain ruled New Orleans and a vast tract of land in the middle of the country. Its land included what is now southern Georgia, as well as Florida. In a secret treaty with France, Spain gave New Orleans and this tract of land to the French. In 1803, President Thomas Jefferson learned about the treaty. Jefferson came up with a plan to protect the United States and to help western farmers. He appointed two men to buy New Orleans and, if necessary, some of the nearby land.

At first, the French leader Napoleon Bonaparte refused the American offer. Pressed for money to continue his war against England, Napoleon changed his mind and offered to sell not only New Orleans but all French lands west of the Mississippi.

Jefferson's men acted quickly. They offered $15 million for the land. They did not have the authority to make this purchase, but they made the sale anyway and Congress later approved it. The **Louisiana Purchase** doubled the size of the United States.

Reading History

A. Making Inferences Why did Jefferson purchase Louisiana even though the Constitution said nothing about the president's right to buy land?

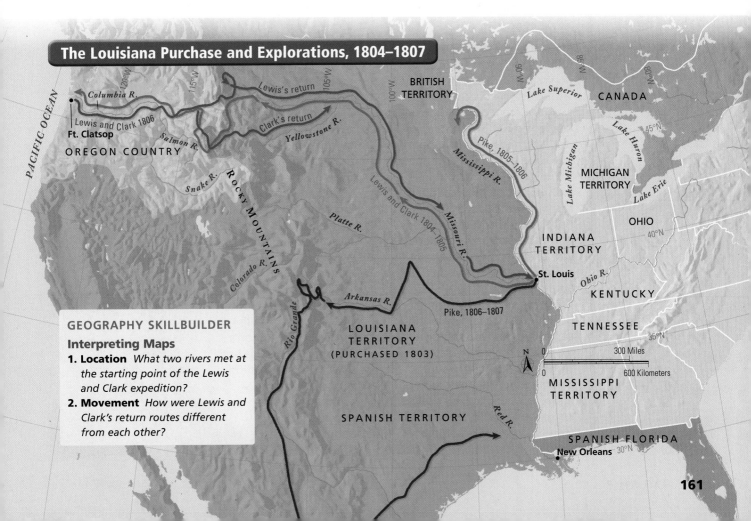

The Louisiana Purchase and Explorations, 1804–1807

GEOGRAPHY SKILLBUILDER
Interpreting Maps
1. **Location** What two rivers met at the starting point of the Lewis and Clark expedition?
2. **Movement** How were Lewis and Clark's return routes different from each other?

161

Exploring the Louisiana Purchase

President Jefferson sent explorers to find out about the new land. The explorers were to study the landforms, plants, animals, and natural resources. Jefferson also wanted to know about the Native Americans who lived in the new land.

Expeditions to the West Between 1804 and 1806, the **Lewis and Clark expedition** traveled through the northern part of the Louisiana Purchase. Led by Meriwether Lewis and William Clark, the Corps of Discovery traveled from St. Louis to the coast of Oregon. As they traveled west, they kept detailed journals and made maps of the land.

Two months before Lewis and Clark returned, a U.S. military officer and explorer named Zebulon Pike set out across the southern part of the Louisiana Purchase. He led his group west across the Great Plains into Colorado and as far south as the Rio Grande.

Vocabulary

corps (kor): a number of people acting together for a similar purpose

HISTORY MAKERS

MERIWETHER LEWIS
1774–1809

Meriwether Lewis was well qualified for the first overland expedition to the Pacific Northwest. In Virginia, he had become an expert hunter. From 1801 to 1803, he worked for President Jefferson, who had him study geography, mineralogy, and astronomy.

The expedition set out in the summer of 1803 and spent the winter in St. Louis. They traveled up the Missouri River to North Dakota and wintered with the friendly Mandan. In November 1805, they spied the Pacific Ocean.

The journals Lewis kept tell what the West was like in the early 1800s and are still exciting to read. In one entry, dated September 17, 1804, Lewis describes the "immense herds of Buffaloe, deer Elk and Antelopes which we saw in every direction feeding on the hills and plains."

WILLIAM CLARK
1770–1838

William Clark was an army friend of Meriwether Lewis. Lewis personally chose him to be co-captain of the Corps of Discovery.

Clark's experience in his state militia and the U.S. Army had taught him how to build forts, draw maps, and lead expeditions through enemy territory.

He had less formal training than Lewis, but with his six feet of height and muscular build, he was a more rugged explorer.

Clark's leadership skills smoothed disputes. Also, his artistic skills made the expedition's maps and drawings both accurate and beautiful. His maps and journal provided priceless information about the West.

These expeditions helped Americans know what the new land was like. Lewis and Clark brought back maps of the region and exciting stories of the things they had seen. Others became interested in going there to see the strange plants and animals. Before long, steamboats began sailing up the Missouri River as far as present-day North Dakota. The steamboats brought supplies to the settlements along the river.

The War of 1812

In Europe, France and England were again at war. The United States tried to stay out of the conflict. But in 1805, Britain began to prevent the United States from trading with France by seizing American ships. They also kidnapped American sailors to work on British ships.

Georgians were concerned about these actions, but British and Spanish influence over local Native Americans was even more alarming. Georgians suspected Britain of giving weapons to the Creek Indians so they would attack frontier settlements in Georgia.

By 1812, the United States could no longer ignore the growing threat. Congress declared war on Great Britain. This conflict was known as the **War of 1812**. Georgia and other Southern states called it the **Creek War**.

The Creek Join the War The Lower Creek Indians remained allies of the United States. But some Upper Creek joined the British. They thought if they won, they could reclaim their land in Georgia. These Creek were called Red Sticks. The Red Sticks fought the Lower Creek and then

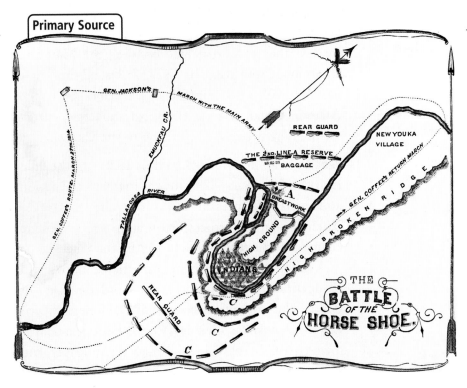

Primary Source

◀ The Battle of Horseshoe Bend was the final, decisive conflict of the Creek War. After their defeat, the Creek gave up all their land in southern Georgia.

attacked whites on the frontier. When the Red Sticks killed hundreds at Fort Mims in Alabama in March 1813, the military responded.

Several fights followed between the military and the Red Sticks, but in March 1814, **Andrew Jackson** defeated them at the **Battle of Horseshoe Bend** in eastern Alabama. As a result of this victory, Jackson became a general in the U.S. Army. After the battle, the Creek signed the Treaty of Fort Jackson. This treaty forced all Creek, both allies and enemies, to give up all their lands in southern Georgia and eastern Alabama.

The War of 1812 Ends   With neither side winning, the two countries signed a treaty ending the war on December 25, 1814. While the United States did not win, the country proved it could defend itself against the mightiest military power of the time.

Riches in Georgia Attract More Settlers

White settlers continued to pour into northern Georgia. They were attracted to the rich land, which was full of timber and other natural resources. Georgia leaders pressured the federal government to remove all Native Americans from the state, according to the Compact of 1802. The government negotiated treaties to obtain land for white settlers. It promised free land in the West to Native Americans who left Georgia.

Treaties in 1817, 1818, and 1819 added more land and pushed the border farther west. In the Indian Springs Treaty of 1821, the Creek gave up land between the Ocmulgee and Flint Rivers. In later treaties, they ceded the land between the Flint and Chattahoochee Rivers. By 1827, almost all the Creek had left. Georgia controlled the land from the Atlantic Ocean west to the Chattahoochee, except for the northwest area belonging to the Cherokee.

Gold   The discovery of gold in 1828 and the gold rush that began in 1829 brought many to the region and increased pressure to move the remaining Cherokee out of northern Georgia. In 1830, the state claimed all the territory occupied by the Cherokee.

A town called Auraria became the center of gold production. Auraria is the Latin word for "City of Gold." The town was just south of Dahlonega, which was then known as Licklog. Auraria became a boomtown overnight, with a major road, a newspaper, and a post office. In 1838, the federal government opened

Reading History

B. Drawing Conclusions
Why do you think the rich farm land would cause conflicts between Native Americans and white settlers?

STRANGE BUT TRUE

Georgia's Gold

The first U.S. gold rush took place in Georgia in 1829 near Dahlonega, which means "yellow" in the Cherokee language. A U.S. mint operated in the region for about 23 years before gold production slowed and the gold rush in California lured miners and investors away.

In those 23 years, the mint produced about 6 million dollars in gold coins. There was enough naturally occurring gold in the region that when the mint was closed down shortly before the Civil War, the bricks of the building were crushed to extract the gold.

If you could find one for sale today, a Dahlonega Mint one-dollar gold coin would sell for $75,000 or more.

a mint in Dahlonega to make gold coins, which are highly prized by collectors today.

Manifest Destiny and Andrew Jackson

Americans began to feel that it was their destiny to spread "from sea to shining sea." A newspaper editor named John O'Sullivan gave a name to this belief: Manifest Destiny. He used the word *manifest* to mean clear or obvious. The word *destiny* means events sure to happen. Therefore, **Manifest Destiny** suggested that expansion was not only good but bound to happen. Even if it meant pushing Mexicans and Native Americans out of the way.

▲ As early as the Spanish explorations, there were reports of gold in north Georgia. The promise of quick wealth brought many to the region.

In 1828, Andrew Jackson was elected president of the United States. Jackson, who was from Tennessee, was the first president from west of the Appalachian Mountains. Jackson represented the "common man." Other presidents had been from wealthy Virginia and Massachusetts families. Jackson selected "ordinary" men to serve with him in his government.

President Jackson was willing to help move the Native Americans off the land the settlers wanted. In the next chapter, you will learn more about the removal of Native Americans from Georgia.

Section Assessment

1. TERMS & NAMES

Explain the significance of:

a. Louisiana Purchase

b. Lewis and Clark expedition

c. War of 1812

d. Creek War

e. Andrew Jackson

f. Battle of Horseshoe Bend

g. Manifest Destiny

2. TAKING NOTES

Use a chart like the one below to record the events that led to the Louisiana Purchase.

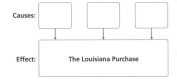

3. MAIN IDEAS

a. How did the Lewis and Clark expedition affect settlement of the American West?

b. What was the outcome of the Battle of Horseshoe Bend?

c. How did the discovery of gold affect the development of northern Georgia?

4. CRITICAL THINKING

Recognizing Effects

What were some of the effects of the explorations of the West after the American Revolution?

Think About
• the economic effects
• the cultural effects
• further land acquisitions

 World History/Geography Make an illustrated **time line** of the French, Spanish, and U.S. control of New Orleans or create a **map** of the bodies of water that affect the port.

VISUAL SUMMARY

Confederation to Constitution

1777
Continental Congress passes the Articles of Confederation.

1777
First Georgia state constitution is completed.

1777–1781
States debate ratification of the Articles of Confederation.

1786–1787
Shays's Rebellion occurs.

1787
Constitutional Convention is held in Philadelphia.

1788
U.S. Constitution is ratified.

1789
Government created by the new Constitution takes power.

New Georgia state constitution is completed.

1791
Bill of Rights is added to the U.S. Constitution.

TERMS & NAMES

Briefly explain the significance of the following.

1. Articles of Confederation
2. democratic republic
3. checks and balances
4. federalism
5. Bill of Rights
6. headright
7. Yazoo Land Fraud
8. land lottery
9. Louisiana Purchase
10. Lewis and Clark expedition

REVIEW QUESTIONS

Creating a New Government (pages 145–152)

1. Who had the most power under the Articles of Confederation?
2. What factors led to the Constitutional Convention?
3. How did the delegates to the Constitutional Convention balance the power of state and national governments?
4. What are *The Federalist* papers?

Georgia as a State (pages 153–159)

5. Who was the first governor of Georgia under the new state constitution?
6. What was the cause of the Oconee War?
7. What were the results of the Treaty of New York?

Land Expansion (pages 160–165)

8. Why did Jefferson appoint men to buy New Orleans?
9. What riches did people find in north Georgia?

CRITICAL THINKING

1. USING YOUR NOTES: SOLVING PROBLEMS

Problems	Solutions
Western Lands	
Postwar Depression	
Representation in the New Government	
Slavery	

Using your completed chart, answer the questions below.

a. How did the Constitutional Convention help solve the postwar economic problems in the country?
b. How did the Louisiana Purchase help solve the problems created by the western lands?

2. ANALYZING LEADERSHIP

What qualities do you think earned James Madison the title of "Father of the Constitution"?

3. APPLYING CITIZENSHIP SKILLS

Do you think the Founders were right to make the compromises they did? Why or why not?

4. THEME: DEMOCRATIC IDEALS

How do the Articles of Confederation and the Constitution each carry out democratic ideals?

5. RECOGNIZING EFFECTS

How might U.S. history be different if Virginia or New York had refused to ratify the Constitution?

INTERACT *with* HISTORY

Having read about the establishment of the new American government, would you have agreed with the decisions made? Why or why not?

Use the map and your knowledge of Georgia history to answer questions 1 through 3.

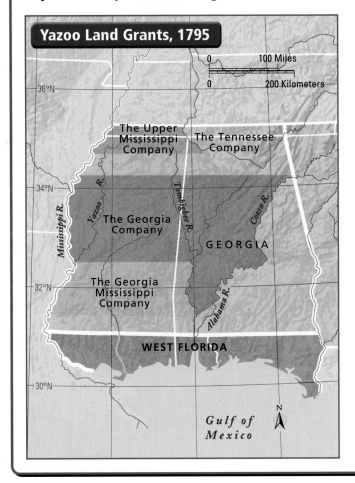

Yazoo Land Grants, 1795

1. Which land company owned the smallest area of land?

   A. Upper Mississippi Company
   B. The Georgia Company
   C. The Tennessee Company
   D. The Georgia Mississippi Company

2. The Yazoo River flowed through which two land companies?

   A. The Georgia Company and the Georgia Mississippi Company
   B. The Georgia Mississippi Company and the Upper Mississippi Company
   C. The Georgia Company and the Tennessee Company
   D. The Georgia Company and the Upper Mississippi Company

3. Which company owned land bordered by the Coosa and Mississippi Rivers?

   A. Upper Mississippi Company
   B. The Georgia Company
   C. The Tennessee Company
   D. The Georgia Mississippi Company

TEST PRACTICE
CLASSZONE.COM

ALTERNATIVE ASSESSMENT

1. MAKING A CHART

Do research to learn how the U.S. Constitution has been used as a model by other nations. Make a chart to summarize the information you find about one specific nation. Include the country, the date the country's constitution was ratified, and two ways in which that nation's constitution is similar to and different from the U.S. Constitution.

2. COOPERATIVE LEARNING

Do research to learn more about Lewis and Clark's Corps of Discovery. Read excerpts from their journals and other historical accounts. Then create a video documentary of their expedition.

INTEGRATED TECHNOLOGY ACTIVITY

CREATING A MULTIMEDIA MUSEUM EXHIBIT

The creation of the U.S. Constitution was one of the most important events in the nation's history. Use the Internet, your library, and a computer to prepare a multimedia museum exhibit on the Constitution. Diagram the layout for the exhibit, and write accompanying text or narrative. Consider the following as you prepare.

- Biographies, portraits, and primary sources

- Photographs or facsimiles of the documents

- Dramatic re-creations of the debates

RESEARCH LINKS
CLASSZONE.COM

Constitution HANDBOOK

Seven Principles of the Constitution

The Framers of the Constitution constructed a new system of government. Seven principles supported their efforts. To picture how these principles work, imagine seven building blocks. Together they form the foundation of the United States Constitution. The definitions and main ideas of the principles are shown in the graphics below.

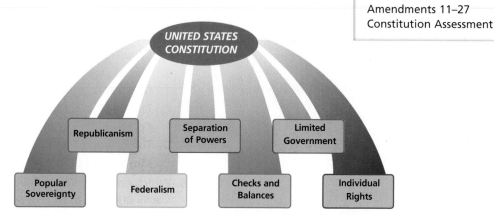

UNITED STATES CONSTITUTION

Republicanism · Separation of Powers · Limited Government

Popular Sovereignty · Federalism · Checks and Balances · Individual Rights

1 Popular Sovereignty
Who Gives the Government Its Power?

"We the people of the United States . . . establish this Constitution for the United States of America." These words from the Preamble, or introduction, to the Constitution clearly spell out the source of the government's power. The Constitution rests on the idea of **popular sovereignty**—a government in which the people rule.

2 Republicanism
How Are People's Views Represented in Government?

The Framers of the Constitution wanted the people to have a voice in government. Yet the Framers also feared that public opinion might stand in the way of sound decision making. To solve this problem, they looked to republicanism as a model of government. **Republicanism** is based on this belief: The people exercise their power by voting for their political representatives.

3 Federalism
How Is Power Shared?

The Framers wanted the states and the nation to become partners in governing. To build cooperation, the Framers turned to federalism. **Federalism** is a system of government in which power is divided between a central government and smaller political units, such as states.

The Framers used federalism to structure the Constitution. The Constitution assigns certain powers to the national government. These are *delegated powers*. Powers kept by the states are *reserved powers*. Powers shared or exercised by national and state governments are known as *concurrent powers*.

Federalism

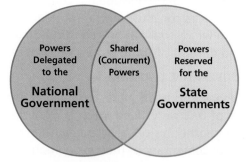

Powers Delegated to the **National Government**

Shared (Concurrent) Powers

Powers Reserved for the **State Governments**

The overlapping spheres of power bind the American people together.

4 Separation of Powers
How Is Power Divided?

Concerned that too much power might fall into the hands of a single group, the Framers built the idea of **separation of powers** into the Constitution. This principle means basic government roles are divided into branches. No one branch is given all the power. Articles 1, 2, and 3 of the Constitution detail how powers are split among the three branches.

5 Checks and Balances
How Is Power Evenly Distributed?

The Framers included a system of **checks and balances** in the Constitution to help make sure that the branches work together fairly.

Each branch of government can exercise checks, or controls, over the other branches. Though the branches of government are separate, they rely on one another to perform the work of government.

6 Limited Government
How Is Abuse of Power Prevented?

The principle of **limited government** is also closely related to the "rule of law": In the American government everyone, citizens and powerful leaders alike, must obey the law. Individuals or groups cannot twist or bypass the law to serve their own interests.

7 Individual Rights
How Are Personal Freedoms Protected?

The first ten amendments to the Constitution shield people from an overly powerful government. These amendments are called the Bill of Rights. The Bill of Rights guarantees certain **individual rights**. For example, government cannot control what people write or say. People also have the right to meet peacefully and to ask the government to correct a problem. Later amendments to the Constitution also advanced the cause of individual rights.

Separation of Powers

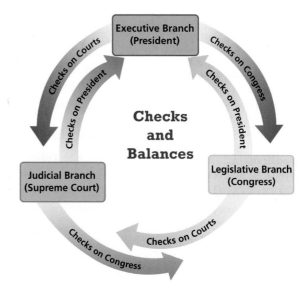

UNITED STATES CONSTITUTION

| **Article 1** Legislative Branch Congress makes the laws. | **Article 2** Executive Branch President enforces the laws. | **Article 3** Judicial Branch Supreme Court interprets the law. |

Checks and Balances

Executive Branch (President)

Checks on Courts · Checks on President · Checks on Congress · Checks on President · Judicial Branch (Supreme Court) · Legislative Branch (Congress) · Checks on Courts · Checks on Congress

HOW TO READ THE CONSTITUTION

The complete text of the Constitution of the United States begins on page 170. The main column has the actual text. Some of the spellings and punctuation have been updated for easier reading. Headings and subheadings have been added to the Constitution to help you find specific topics. Those parts of the Constitution that are no longer in use have been crossed out. "A Closer Look" notes and charts will help you understand issues related to the Constitution.

Assessment: Principles of the Constitution

1. MAIN IDEAS

a. What are the seven principles of government?

b. How does the Constitution reflect the principle of separation of powers?

c. Why did the Framers include a system of checks and balances in the Constitution?

2. CRITICAL THINKING

Forming Opinions How do the rights and responsibilities of U.S. citizenship reflect American national identity?

Think About
- what it means to be an American
- the rights and responsibilities of U.S. citizens

The Constitution of the United States

Preamble

We the people of the United States, in order to form a more perfect Union, establish justice, insure domestic tranquility, provide for the common defense, promote the general welfare, and secure the blessings of liberty to ourselves and our posterity, do ordain and establish this Constitution for the United States of America.

Article 1. *The Legislature*

Section 1. Congress All legislative powers herein granted shall be vested in a Congress of the United States, which shall consist of a Senate and House of Representatives.

Section 2. The House of Representatives

1. Elections The House of Representatives shall be composed of members chosen every second year by the people of the several states, and the **electors** in each state shall have the qualifications requisite for electors of the most numerous branch of the state legislature.

2. Qualifications No person shall be a Representative who shall not have attained to the age of twenty-five years, and been seven years a citizen of the United States, and who shall not, when elected, be an inhabitant of that state in which he shall be chosen.

3. Number of Representatives Representatives and direct taxes shall be apportioned among the several states which may be included within this Union, according to their respective numbers, which shall be determined by adding to the whole number of free persons, including those bound to service for a term of years, and excluding Indians not taxed, three-fifths of all other Persons. The actual **enumeration** shall be made within three years after the first meeting of the Congress of the United States, and within every subsequent term of ten years, in such manner as they shall by law direct. The number of Representatives shall not exceed one for every thirty thousand, but each state shall have at least one Representative; and until such enumeration shall be made, the state of New Hampshire shall be entitled to choose three, Massachusetts eight, Rhode Island and Providence Plantations one, Connecticut five, New York six, New Jersey four, Pennsylvania eight, Delaware one, Maryland six, Virginia ten, North Carolina five, South Carolina five, and Georgia three.

4. Vacancies When vacancies happen in the representation from any state, the executive authority thereof shall issue writs of election to fill such vacancies.

5. Officers and Impeachment The House of Representatives shall choose their Speaker and other officers; and shall have the sole power of **impeachment**.

Section 3. The Senate

1. Numbers The Senate of the United States shall be composed of two Senators from each state, ~~chosen by the legislature thereof,~~ for six years; and each Senator shall have one vote.

2. Classifying Terms Immediately after they shall be assembled in consequence of the first election, they shall be divided as equally as may be into three classes. The seats of the Senators of the first class shall be vacated at the expiration of the second year, of the second class at the expiration of the fourth year, and of the third class at the expiration of the sixth year, so that one-third may be chosen every second year; ~~and if vacancies happen by resignation, or otherwise, during the recess of the legislature of any state, the executive thereof may make temporary appointments until the next meeting of the legislature, which shall then fill such vacancies.~~

3. Qualifications No person shall be a Senator who shall not have attained to the age of thirty years, and been nine years a citizen of the United States, and who shall not, when elected, be an inhabitant of that state for which he shall be chosen.

4. Role of Vice-President The Vice-President of the United States shall be President of the Senate, but shall have no vote, unless they be equally divided.

5. Officers The Senate shall choose their other officers, and also a President **pro tempore,** in the absence of the Vice-President, or when he shall exercise the office of President of the United States.

6. Impeachment Trials The Senate shall have the sole power to try all impeachments. When sitting for that purpose, they shall be on oath or affirmation. When the President of the United States is tried, the Chief Justice shall preside: and no person shall be convicted without the concurrence of two-thirds of the members present.

7. Punishment for Impeachment Judgment in cases of impeachment shall not extend further than to removal from office, and disqualification to hold and enjoy any office of honor, trust or profit under the United States; but the party convicted shall nevertheless be liable and subject to **indictment,** trial, judgment and punishment, according to law.

Section 4. Congressional Elections

1. Regulations The times, places and manner of holding elections for Senators and Representatives shall be prescribed in each state by the legislature thereof; but the Congress may at any time by law make or alter such regulations, except as to the places of choosing Senators.

2. Sessions The Congress shall assemble at least once in every year, ~~and such meeting shall be on the first Monday in December, unless they shall by law appoint a different day.~~

Section 5. Rules and Procedures

1. Quorum Each house shall be the judge of the elections, returns and qualifications of its own members, and a majority of each shall constitute a **quorum** to do business; but a smaller number may adjourn from day to day, and may be authorized to compel the attendance of absent members, in such manner, and under such penalties as each house may provide.

2. Rules and Conduct Each house may determine the rules of its proceedings, punish its members for disorderly behavior, and, with the concurrence of two-thirds, expel a member.

A CLOSER LOOK

IMPEACHMENT

The House brings charges against the president. The Senate acts as the jury. The Chief Justice of the Supreme Court presides over the hearings.

2. How many presidents have been impeached?

A CLOSER LOOK

ELECTIONS

Representatives are elected every two years. There are no limits on the number of terms a person can serve.

3. What do you think are the advantages of holding frequent elections of representatives?

A CLOSER LOOK

SENATE RULES

Senate rules allow for debate on the floor. Using a tactic called filibustering, senators give long speeches to block the passage of a bill. The late Senator Strom Thurmond holds the filibustering record—24 hours, 18 minutes.

4. Why might a senator choose filibustering as a tactic to block a bill?

3. Congressional Records Each house shall keep a journal of its proceedings, and from time to time publish the same, excepting such parts as may in their judgment require secrecy; and the yeas and nays of the members of either house on any question shall, at the desire of one-fifth of those present, be entered on the journal.

4. Adjournment Neither house, during the session of Congress, shall, without the consent of the other, adjourn for more than three days, nor to any other place than that in which the two houses shall be sitting.

Section 6. Payment and Privileges

1. Salary The Senators and Representatives shall receive a compensation for their services, to be ascertained by law, and paid out of the treasury of the United States. They shall in all cases, except treason, felony and breach of the peace, be privileged from arrest during their attendance at the session of their respective houses, and in going to and returning from the same; and for any speech or debate in either house, they shall not be questioned in any other place.

2. Restrictions No Senator or Representative shall, during the time for which he was elected, be appointed to any civil office under the authority of the United States, which shall have been created, or the emoluments whereof shall have been increased during such time; and no person holding any office under the United States, shall be a member of either house during his continuance in office.

Section 7. How a Bill Becomes a Law

1. Tax Bills All bills for raising **revenue** shall originate in the House of Representatives; but the Senate may propose or concur with amendments as on other Bills.

2. Lawmaking Process Every bill which shall have passed the House of Representatives and the Senate, shall, before it become a law, be presented to the President of the United States; if he approves he shall sign it, but if not he shall return it, with his objections to that house in which it shall have originated, who shall enter the objections at large on their journal, and proceed to reconsider it. If after such reconsideration two-thirds of that house shall agree

A CLOSER LOOK   How a Bill Becomes a Law

Introduction

The House introduces a bill and refers it to a committee.

The Senate introduces a bill and refers it to a committee.

Committee Action

The House committee may approve, rewrite, or kill the bill.

The Senate committee may approve, rewrite, or kill the bill.

Floor Action

The House debates and votes on its version of the bill.

The Senate debates and votes on its version of the bill.

House and Senate committee members work out the differences between the two versions.

to pass the bill, it shall be sent, together with the objections, to the other house, by which it shall likewise be reconsidered, and if approved by two-thirds of that house, it shall become a law. But in all such cases the votes of both houses shall be determined by yeas and nays, and the names of the persons voting for and against the bill shall be entered on the journal of each house respectively. If any bill shall not be returned by the President within ten days (Sundays excepted) after it shall have been presented to him, the same shall be a law, in like manner as if he had signed it, unless the Congress by their adjournment prevent its return, in which case it shall not be a law.

3. Role of the President Every order, resolution, or vote to which the concurrence of the Senate and House of Representatives may be necessary (except on a question of adjournment) shall be presented to the President of the United States; and before the same shall take effect, shall be approved by him, or being disapproved by him, shall be repassed by two-thirds of the Senate and House of Representatives, according to the rules and limitations prescribed in the case of a bill.

Section 8. Powers Granted to Congress

1. Taxation The Congress shall have power to lay and collect taxes, duties, imposts and excises, to pay the debts and provide for the common defense and general welfare of the United States; but all duties, imposts and excises shall be uniform throughout the United States;

2. Credit To borrow money on the credit of the United States;

3. Commerce To regulate commerce with foreign nations, and among the several states, and with the Indian tribes;

4. Naturalization, Bankruptcy To establish a uniform rule of **naturalization,** and uniform laws on the subject of bankruptcies throughout the United States;

5. Money To coin money, regulate the value thereof, and of foreign coin, and fix the standard of weights and measures;

6. Counterfeiting To provide for the punishment of counterfeiting the securities and current coin of the United States;

A CLOSER LOOK

REGULATING COMMERCE
Commerce can also apply to travelers crossing state lines. Congress's power to regulate the movement of people from state to state paved the way for the Civil Rights Act of 1964. This act included fair treatment of interstate travelers. People of all races can use public places, such as hotels and bus stations.

6. To what other areas might the commerce clause apply?

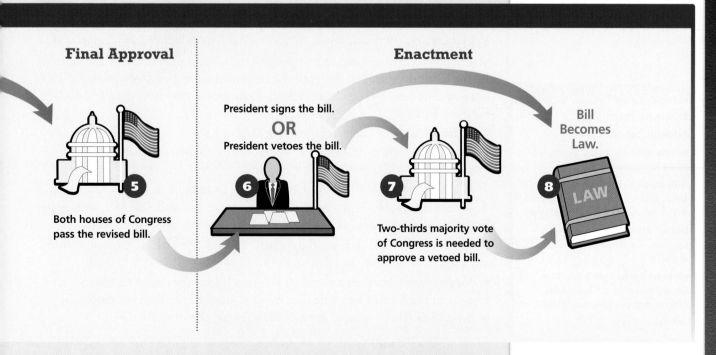

Final Approval   **Enactment**

President signs the bill.
OR
President vetoes the bill.

Bill Becomes Law.

5 — Both houses of Congress pass the revised bill.

6

7 — Two-thirds majority vote of Congress is needed to approve a vetoed bill.

8 — LAW

7. Post Office To establish post offices and post roads;

8. Patents, Copyrights To promote the progress of science and useful arts, by securing for limited times to authors and inventors the exclusive right to their respective writings and discoveries;

9. Federal Courts To constitute **tribunals** inferior to the Supreme Court;

10. International Law To define and punish piracies and **felonies** committed on the high seas, and offenses against the law of nations;

11. War To declare war, grant letters of marque and reprisal, and make rules concerning captures on land and water;

12. Army To raise and support armies, but no **appropriation** of money to that use shall be for a longer term than two years;

13. Navy To provide and maintain a navy;

14. Regulation of Armed Forces To make rules for the government and regulation of the land and naval forces;

15. Militia To provide for calling forth the **militia** to execute the laws of the Union, suppress insurrections and repel invasions;

16. Regulations for Militia To provide for organizing, arming, and disciplining the militia, and for governing such part of them as may be employed in the service of the United States, reserving to the states respectively the appointment of the officers, and the authority of training the militia according to the discipline prescribed by Congress;

17. District of Columbia To exercise exclusive legislation in all cases whatsoever, over such district (not exceeding ten miles square) as may, by cession of particular states, and the acceptance of Congress, become the seat of the government of the United States, and to exercise like authority over all places purchased by the consent of the legislature of the state in which the same shall be, for the erection of forts, magazines, arsenals, dockyards, and other needful buildings;—and

18. Elastic Clause To make all laws which shall be necessary and proper for carrying into execution the foregoing powers, and all other powers vested by this Constitution in the government of the United States, or in any department or officer thereof.

Section 9. Powers Denied Congress

1. Slave Trade ~~The migration or importation of such persons as any of the states now existing shall think proper to admit, shall not be prohibited by the Congress prior to the year one thousand eight hundred and eight, but a tax or duty may be imposed on such importation, not exceeding ten dollars for each person.~~

2. Habeas Corpus The privilege of the writ of habeas corpus shall not be suspended, unless when in cases of rebellion or invasion the public safety may require it.

3. Illegal Punishment No **bill of attainder** or **ex post facto law** shall be passed.

4. Direct Taxes No capitation, ~~or other direct,~~ tax shall be laid, ~~unless in proportion to the census or enumeration herein before directed to be taken.~~

5. Export Taxes No tax or duty shall be laid on articles exported from any state.

6. No Favorites No preference shall be given by any regulation of commerce or revenue to the ports of one state over those of another: nor shall vessels bound to, or from, one state be obliged to enter, clear, or pay duties in another.

7. Public Money No money shall be drawn from the treasury, but in consequence of appropriations made by law; and a regular statement and account of the receipts and expenditures of all public money shall be published from time to time.

8. Titles of Nobility No title of nobility shall be granted by the United States: and no person holding any office of profit or trust under them shall, without the consent of the Congress, accept of any present, emolument, office, or title, of any kind whatever, from any king, prince, or foreign state.

Section 10. Powers Denied the States

1. Restrictions No state shall enter into any treaty, alliance, or confederation; grant letters of marque and reprisal; coin money; emit bills of credit; make anything but gold and silver coin a **tender** in payment of debts; pass any bill of attainder, ex post facto law, or law impairing the obligation of contracts, or grant any title of nobility.

2. Import and Export Taxes No state shall, without the consent of the Congress, lay any imposts or duties on imports or exports, except what may be absolutely necessary for executing its inspection laws; and the net produce of all duties and imposts, laid by any state on imports or exports, shall be for the use of the treasury of the United States; and all such laws shall be subject to the revision and control of the Congress.

3. Peacetime and War Restraints No state shall, without the consent of Congress, lay any duty of tonnage, keep troops or ships of war in time of peace, enter into any agreement or compact with another state, or with a foreign power, or engage in war, unless actually invaded, or in such imminent danger as will not admit of delay.

A CLOSER LOOK

TITLES OF NOBILITY

The Framers disapproved of titles of nobility. The list of grievances in the Declaration of Independence included numerous examples of King George III's abuses of power. Symbols of these abuses included English titles of nobility, such as "king," "queen," and "duke." The Framers said clearly that there would be no such titles in the new republic.

8. How do TV news reporters address members of Congress and the president?

Article 1 Assessment

1. MAIN IDEAS

a. What is the main job of the legislative branch?

b. What role does the vice-president of the United States play in the Senate?

c. Why are there more members in the House of Representatives than the Senate?

d. What is one of the powers denied to Congress?

2. CRITICAL THINKING

Drawing Conclusions How does Article 1 show that the Constitution is a clearly defined yet flexible document?

Think About
• the powers of Congress
• the "elastic clause"

MAIN IDEA
The president and vice-president are the leaders of the executive branch. Their main role is to enforce the laws. The president commands the military and makes foreign treaties with the Senate's approval.

WHY IT MATTERS NOW
As the United States has become a world power, the authority of the president has also expanded.

Article 2. *The Executive*

Section 1. The Presidency

1. Terms of Office The executive power shall be vested in a President of the United States of America. He shall hold his office during the term of four years, and, together with the Vice-President, chosen for the same term, be elected, as follows:

2. Electoral College Each state shall appoint, in such manner as the Legislature thereof may direct, a number of electors, equal to the whole number of Senators and Representatives to which the State may be entitled in the Congress; but no Senator or Representative, or person holding an office of trust or profit under the United States, shall be appointed an elector.

A CLOSER LOOK Electoral College *(based on 2000 Census)*

American voters do not choose their president directly. Members of a group called the electoral college actually elect the president. Each state has electors. Together they form the electoral college. In most states, the winner takes all. Except for Maine and Nebraska, all the electoral votes of a state go to one set of candidates.

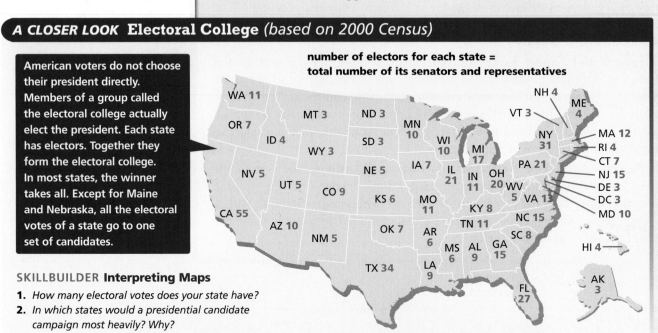

**number of electors for each state =
total number of its senators and representatives**

WA 11, OR 7, MT 3, ND 3, MN 10, NH 4, VT 3, ME 4, NY 31, MA 12, RI 4, ID 4, WY 3, SD 3, WI 10, MI 17, CT 7, NV 5, UT 5, NE 5, IA 7, IL 21, IN 11, OH 20, PA 21, NJ 15, DE 3, WV 5, VA 13, DC 3, CA 55, CO 9, KS 6, MO 11, KY 8, NC 15, MD 10, AZ 10, NM 5, OK 7, AR 6, TN 11, SC 8, HI 4, MS 6, AL 9, GA 15, TX 34, LA 9, FL 27, AK 3

SKILLBUILDER Interpreting Maps

1. *How many electoral votes does your state have?*
2. *In which states would a presidential candidate campaign most heavily? Why?*

3. Former Method of Electing President The electors shall meet in their respective states, and vote by ballot for two persons, of whom one at least shall not be an inhabitant of the same state with themselves. And they shall make a list of all the persons voted for, and of the number of votes for each; which list they shall sign and certify, and transmit sealed to the seat of the government of the United States, directed to the President of the Senate. The President of the Senate shall, in the presence of the Senate and House of Representatives, open all the certificates, and the votes shall then be counted. The person having the greatest number of votes shall be the President, if such number be a majority of the whole number of electors appointed; and if there be more than one who have such majority, and have an equal number of votes, then the House of Representatives shall immediately choose by ballot one of them for President; and if no person have a majority, then from the five highest on the list the said House shall in like manner choose the President. But in choosing the President, the votes shall be taken by States, the representation from each state having one vote; a quorum for this purpose shall consist of a member or members from two-thirds of the states, and a majority of all the states shall be necessary to a choice. In every case, after the choice of the President, the person having the greatest number of votes of the electors shall be the Vice-President.

VOCABULARY

natural-born citizen a citizen born in the United States or a U.S. commonwealth, or to parents who are U.S. citizens living outside the country

affirmation a statement declaring that something is true

reprieves delays or cancellations of punishment

But if there should remain two or more who have equal votes, the Senate shall choose from them by ballot the Vice-President.

4. Election Day The Congress may determine the time of choosing the electors, and the day on which they shall give their votes, which day shall be the same throughout the United States.

5. Qualifications No person except a **natural-born citizen,** or a citizen of the United States at the time of the adoption of this Constitution, shall be eligible to the office of President; neither shall any person be eligible to that office

A CLOSER LOOK Federal Office Terms and Requirements

POSITION	TERM	MINIMUM AGE	RESIDENCY	CITIZENSHIP
Representative	2 years	25	state in which elected	7 years
Senator	6 years	30	state in which elected	9 years
President	4 years	35	14 years in the U.S.	natural-born
Supreme Court Justice	unlimited	none	none	none

SKILLBUILDER Interpreting Charts
Why do you think the qualifications for a president are more demanding than for a senator or representative?

who shall not have attained to the age of thirty-five years, and been fourteen years a resident within the United States.

6. Succession In case of the removal of the President from office, or of his death, resignation, or inability to discharge the powers and duties of the said office, the same shall devolve on the Vice-President, and the Congress may by law provide for the case of removal, death, resignation or inability, both of the President and Vice-President, declaring what officer shall then act as President, and such officer shall act accordingly, until the disability be removed, or a President shall be elected.

7. Salary The President shall, at stated times, receive for his services, a compensation, which shall neither be increased nor diminished during the period for which he shall have been elected, and he shall not receive within that period any other emolument from the United States, or any of them.

8. Oath of Office Before he enter on the execution of his office, he shall take the following oath or **affirmation:**—"I do solemnly swear (or affirm) that I will faithfully execute the office of President of the United States, and will to the best of my ability, preserve, protect and defend the Constitution of the United States."

A CLOSER LOOK

Vice-President Lyndon Johnson, next in line of succession, takes the oath of office after the assassination of President John F. Kennedy in 1963. Johnson, like every U.S. president, promises to uphold the Constitution. The Twenty-Fifth Amendment sets up clearer procedures for presidential succession.

Section 2. Powers of the President

1. Military Powers The President shall be commander in chief of the Army and Navy of the United States, and of the militia of the several states, when called into the actual service of the United States; he may require the opinion, in writing, of the principal officer in each of the executive departments, upon any subject relating to the duties of their respective offices, and he shall have power to grant **reprieves** and pardons for offenses against the United States, except in cases of impeachment.

2. Treaties, Appointments He shall have power, by and with the advice and consent of the Senate, to make treaties, provided two-thirds of the Senators present concur; and he shall nominate, and by and with the advice and consent of the Senate, shall appoint ambassadors, other public ministers and consuls, judges of the Supreme Court, and all other officers of the United States, whose appointments are not herein otherwise provided for, and which shall be established by law; but the Congress may by law vest the appointment of such inferior officers, as they think proper, in the President alone, in the courts of law, or in the heads of departments.

3. Vacancies The President shall have power to fill up all vacancies that may happen during the recess of the Senate, by granting commissions which shall expire at the end of their next session.

Section 3. Presidential Duties
He shall from time to time give to the Congress information of the State of the Union, and recommend to their consideration such measures as he shall judge necessary and expedient; he may, on extraordinary occasions, **convene** both houses, or either of them, and in case of disagreement between them, with respect to the time of adjournment, he may adjourn them to such time as he shall think proper; he shall receive ambassadors and other public ministers; he shall take care that the laws be faithfully executed, and shall commission all the officers of the United States.

Section 4. Impeachment
The President, Vice-President and all civil officers of the United States shall be removed from office on impeachment for, and conviction of, treason, bribery, or other high crimes and **misdemeanors**.

A CLOSER LOOK

SUPREME COURT APPOINTMENTS

Recent presidents have used their power of appointment to add minorities and women to the Supreme Court. In 1967, President Lyndon Johnson appointed the first African-American justice, Thurgood Marshall. In 1981, President Ronald Reagan appointed the first woman, Sandra Day O'Connor.

9. What do you think influences a president's choice for a Supreme Court justice?

A CLOSER LOOK

STATE OF THE UNION

Major TV networks broadcast the State of the Union address to the whole nation. In this yearly message, the president urges Congress to achieve certain law-making goals. The president's speech also must gain the attention of TV viewers.

10. Why is the president's power to persuade an important political skill?

VOCABULARY

convene call together

misdemeanors violations of the law

Article 2 Assessment

1. MAIN IDEAS

a. What is the chief purpose of the executive branch?

b. What are the requirements for becoming president?

c. How does the Constitution limit the president's power to make appointments and treaties?

2. CRITICAL THINKING

Analyzing Issues Why do you think the Constitution states that the president must seek approval from the Senate for most political appointments and treaties?

Think About
• the abuse of power
• the will of the voters

Article 3. *The Judiciary*

Section 1. Federal Courts and Judges

The judicial power of the United States shall be vested in one Supreme Court, and in such **inferior courts** as the Congress may from time to time ordain and establish. The judges, both of the Supreme and inferior courts, shall hold their offices during good behavior, and shall, at stated times, receive for their services a compensation, which shall not be diminished during their continuance in office.

Section 2. The Courts' Authority

1. General Authority The judicial power shall extend to all cases, in law and equity, arising under this Constitution, the laws of the United States, and treaties made, or which shall be made, under their authority;—to all cases affecting ambassadors, other public ministers and consuls;—to all cases of admiralty and maritime jurisdiction;—to controversies to which the United States shall be a party;—to controversies between two or more states;— ~~between a state and citizens of another state;~~—between citizens of different states;—between citizens of the same state claiming lands under grants of different states, ~~and between a state, or the citizens thereof, and foreign states, citizens or subjects.~~

2. Supreme Court In all cases affecting ambassadors, other public ministers and consuls, and those in which a state shall be party, the Supreme Court shall have original jurisdiction. In all the other cases before mentioned, the Supreme Court shall have **appellate** jurisdiction, both as to law and fact, with such exceptions, and under such regulations, as the Congress shall make.

3. Trial by Jury The trial of all crimes, except in cases of impeachment, shall be by jury; and such trial shall be held in the state where the said crimes shall have been committed; but when not committed within any state, the trial shall be at such place or places as the Congress may by law have directed.

Section 3. Treason

1. Definition Treason against the United States shall consist only in levying war against them, or in adhering to their enemies, giving them aid and comfort. No person shall be convicted of treason unless on the testimony of two witnesses to the same overt act, or on confession in open court.

2. Punishment The Congress shall have power to declare the punishment of treason, but no attainder of treason shall work corruption of blood, or forfeiture except during the life of the person attained.

MAIN IDEA
The judicial branch interprets the laws. This branch includes the Supreme Court, the highest court in the nation, and other federal courts.

WHY IT MATTERS NOW
Supreme Court rulings can shape government policies on hotly debated issues.

VOCABULARY

inferior courts courts with less authority than the Supreme Court

appellate having power to review court decisions

A CLOSER LOOK

ORGANIZING FEDERAL COURTS
The Judiciary Act of 1789, passed by the First Congress, included establishing a Supreme Court with a chief justice and five associate justices and other lower federal courts.

11. How many Supreme Court justices are there today?

Article 3 Assessment

1. MAIN IDEAS

a. What is the main purpose of the judicial branch?

b. What is judicial review?

c. What are two kinds of cases that can begin in the Supreme Court?

2. CRITICAL THINKING

Drawing Conclusions Why might the Supreme Court feel less political pressure than Congress in making judgments about the Constitution?

Think About

• the appointment of Supreme Court justices

• Congress members' obligation to voters

MAIN IDEA
States must honor one another's laws, records, and court rulings.

WHY IT MATTERS NOW
Article 4 promotes cooperation, equality, and fair treatment of citizens from all the states.

A CLOSER LOOK

EXTRADITION

Persons charged with serious crimes cannot escape punishment by fleeing to another state. They must be returned to the first state and stand trial there.

12. Why do you think the Framers included the power of extradition?

MAIN IDEA
The Constitution can be amended, or formally changed.

WHY IT MATTERS NOW
The amendment process allows the Constitution to adapt to modern times.

Article 4. *Relations Among States*

Section 1. State Acts and Records
Full faith and credit shall be given in each state to the public acts, records, and judicial proceedings of every other state. And the Congress may by general laws prescribe the manner in which such acts, records and proceedings shall be proved, and the effect thereof.

Section 2. Rights of Citizens
1. Citizenship The citizens of each state shall be entitled to all privileges and **immunities** of citizens in the several states.

2. Extradition A person charged in any state with treason, felony, or other crime, who shall flee from justice, and be found in another state, shall on demand of the executive authority of the state from which he fled, be delivered up, to be removed to the state having jurisdiction of the crime.

3. Fugitive Slaves No person held to service or labor in one state, under the laws thereof, escaping into another, shall, in consequence of any law or regulation therein, be discharged from such service or labor, but shall be delivered up on claim of the party to whom such service or labor may be due.

Section 3. New States
1. Admission New states may be admitted by the Congress into this Union; but no new state shall be formed or erected within the jurisdiction of any other state; nor any state be formed by the junction of two or more states, or parts of states, without the consent of the legislatures of the states concerned as well as of the Congress.

2. Congressional Authority The Congress shall have power to dispose of and make all needful rules and regulations respecting the territory or other property belonging to the United States; and nothing in this Constitution shall be so construed as to prejudice any claims of the United States, or of any particular state.

Section 4. Guarantees to the States
The United States shall guarantee to every state in this Union a republican form of government, and shall protect each of them against invasion; and on application of the legislature, or of the executive (when the legislature cannot be convened) against domestic violence.

Article 5. *Amending the Constitution*

The Congress, whenever two-thirds of both houses shall deem it necessary, shall propose amendments to this Constitution, or, on the application of the legislatures of two-thirds of the several states, shall call a convention for proposing amendments, which, in either case, shall be valid to all intents and purposes, as part of this Constitution, when ratified by the legislatures of three-fourths of the several states, or by conventions in three-fourths thereof, as the one or the other mode of ratification may be proposed by the Congress; provided that no amendment which may be made prior to the year one thousand eight hundred and eight shall in any manner affect the first and fourth clauses in the ninth section of the first article; and that no state, without its consent, shall be deprived of its equal **suffrage** in the Senate.

Article 6. *Supremacy of the National Government*

Section 1. Valid Debts
All debts contracted and engagements entered into, before the adoption of this Constitution, shall be as valid against the United States under this Constitution, as under the Confederation.

Section 2. Supreme Law
This Constitution, and the laws of the United States which shall be made in pursuance thereof; and all treaties made, or which shall be made, under the authority of the United States, shall be the supreme law of the land; and the judges in every state shall be bound thereby, anything in the constitution or laws of any state to the contrary notwithstanding.

Section 3. Loyalty to Constitution
The Senators and Representatives before mentioned, and the members of the several state legislatures, and all executive and judicial officers, both of the United States and of the several states, shall be bound by oath or affirmation to support this Constitution; but no religious test shall ever be required as a qualification to any office or public trust under the United States.

MAIN IDEA
The Constitution, national laws, and treaties are the supreme, or highest, law of the land. All government officials must promise to support the Constitution.

WHY IT MATTERS NOW
The authority of federal laws over state laws helps keep the nation unified.

Article 7. *Ratification*

The **ratification** of the conventions of nine states shall be sufficient for the establishment of this Constitution between the states so ratifying the same. Done in convention by the **unanimous consent** of the states present, the seventeenth day of September in the year of our Lord one thousand seven hundred and eighty-seven and of the independence of the United States of America the twelfth. In witness whereof we have hereunto subscribed our names.

MAIN IDEA
Nine of the 13 states had to ratify, or approve, the Constitution before it could go into effect.

WHY IT MATTERS NOW
The approval of the Constitution launched a new plan of government still followed today.

George Washington—President and deputy from Virginia

New Hampshire: *John Langdon, Nicholas Gilman*

Massachusetts: *Nathaniel Gorham, Rufus King*

Connecticut: *William Samuel Johnson, Roger Sherman*

New York: *Alexander Hamilton*

New Jersey: *William Livingston, David Brearley, William Paterson, Jonathan Dayton*

Pennsylvania: *Benjamin Franklin, Thomas Mifflin, Robert Morris, George Clymer, Thomas FitzSimons, Jared Ingersoll, James Wilson, Gouverneur Morris*

Delaware: *George Read, Gunning Bedford, Jr., John Dickinson, Richard Bassett, Jacob Broom*

Maryland: *James McHenry, Dan of St. Thomas Jenifer, Daniel Carroll*

Virginia: *John Blair, James Madison, Jr.*

North Carolina: *William Blount, Richard Dobbs Spaight, Hugh Williamson*

South Carolina: *John Rutledge, Charles Cotesworth Pinckney, Charles Pinckney, Pierce Butler*

Georgia: *William Few, Abraham Baldwin*

Articles 4–7 Assessment

1. MAIN IDEAS

a. What rights does Article 4 guarantee to citizens if they go to other states in the nation?

b. What are two ways of proposing an amendment to the Constitution?

c. What makes up "the supreme law of the land"?

2. CRITICAL THINKING

Forming and Supporting Opinions Should the Framers of the Constitution have allowed the people to vote directly for ratification of the Constitution? Why or why not?

Think About
• the idea that the government belongs to the people
• the public's ability to make sound political decisions

The Bill of Rights

Several states approved the Constitution only if a list of guaranteed freedoms was added. While serving in the nation's first Congress, James Madison helped draft the Bill of Rights. In 1791, these first ten amendments became part of the Constitution.

AMENDMENTS 1–10. *The Bill of Rights*

AMENDMENT 1. Religious and Political Freedom (1791)

Congress shall make no law respecting an establishment of religion, or prohibiting the free exercise thereof; or **abridging** the freedom of speech, or of the press; or the right of the people peaceably to assemble, and to petition the Government for a redress of grievances.

A CLOSER LOOK The Five Freedoms

Freedom of Religion
Right to worship

Freedom of Speech
Right to state ideas

Freedom of the Press
Right to publish ideas

Freedom of Assembly
Right to meet peacefully in groups

Freedom to Petition
Right to protest the government

SKILLBUILDER Interpreting Charts
1. *Why is freedom of speech and the press important in a democratic society?*
2. *What impact has religious freedom had on the American way of life?*

AMENDMENT 2. Right to Bear Arms (1791)
A well-regulated militia, being necessary to the security of a free state, the right of the people to keep and bear arms, shall not be infringed.

AMENDMENT 3. Quartering Troops (1791)
No soldier shall, in time of peace be **quartered** in any house, without the consent of the owner, nor in time of war, but in a manner to be prescribed by law.

AMENDMENT 4. Search and Seizure (1791)
The right of the people to be secure in their persons, houses, papers, and effects, against unreasonable searches and seizures, shall not be violated, and no warrants shall issue, but upon probable cause, supported by oath or affirmation, and particularly describing the place to be searched, and the persons or things to be seized.

AMENDMENT 5. Rights of Accused Persons (1791)
No person shall be held to answer for a capital, or otherwise infamous crime, unless on a presentment or indictment of a Grand Jury, except in cases arising in the land or naval forces, or in the militia, when in actual service in time of war or public danger; nor shall any person be subject for the same offense to be twice

put in jeopardy of life or limb; nor shall be compelled in any criminal case to be a witness against himself, nor be deprived of life, liberty, or property, without **due process of law;** nor shall private property be taken for public use, without just compensation.

AMENDMENT 6. Right to a Speedy, Public Trial (1791)
In all criminal prosecutions, the accused shall enjoy the right to a speedy and public trial, by an impartial jury of the State and district wherein the crime shall have been committed, which district shall have been previously ascertained by law, and to be informed of the nature and cause of the accusation; to be confronted with the witnesses against him; to have **compulsory process** for obtaining witnesses in his favor, and to have the assistance of **counsel** for his defense.

AMENDMENT 7. Trial by Jury in Civil Cases (1791)
In suits at **common law,** where the value in controversy shall exceed twenty dollars, the right of trial by jury shall be preserved, and no fact tried by a jury, shall be otherwise reexamined in any court of the United States, than according to the rules of the common law.

AMENDMENT 8. Limits of Fines and Punishments (1791)
Excessive **bail** shall not be required, nor excessive fines imposed, nor cruel and unusual punishments inflicted.

AMENDMENT 9. Rights of People (1791)
The enumeration in the Constitution of certain rights shall not be construed to deny or disparage others retained by the people.

AMENDMENT 10. Powers of States and People (1791)
The powers not delegated to the United States by the Constitution, nor prohibited by it to the States, are reserved to the States respectively, or to the people.

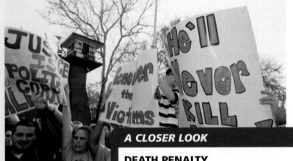

A CLOSER LOOK

DEATH PENALTY
Protesters claim that the death penalty violates the Eighth Amendment, which protects people against "cruel and unusual punishment." Supporters (above) believe that the death penalty is a justly deserved punishment.

Bill of Rights Assessment

1. MAIN IDEAS
a. Which amendment protects your privacy?
b. Which amendments guarantee fair legal treatment?
c. Which amendment prevents the federal government from taking powers away from the states and the people?

2. CRITICAL THINKING
Forming and Supporting Opinions The Fourth, Fifth, Sixth, Seventh, and Eighth Amendments protect innocent people accused of crimes. Do you think these five amendments also favor the rights of actual criminals? Explain.

Think About
- criminals who go free if valuable evidence is found after their trials
- criminals released on bail

Amendments 11–27

AMENDMENT 11. Lawsuits Against States (1798)

The Judicial power of the United States shall not be construed to extend to any suit in law or **equity**, commenced or prosecuted against one of the United States by citizens of another state, or by citizens or subjects of any foreign state.

AMENDMENT 12. Election of Executives (1804)

The electors shall meet in their respective states and vote by ballot for President and Vice-President, one of whom, at least, shall not be an inhabitant of the same state with themselves; they shall name in their ballots the person voted for as President, and in distinct ballots the person voted for as Vice-President, and they shall make distinct lists of all persons voted for as President, and of all persons voted for as Vice-President, and of the number of votes for each, which lists they shall sign and certify, and transmit sealed to the seat of the government of the United States, directed to the President of the Senate;—the President of the Senate shall, in the presence of the Senate and House of Representatives, open all the certificates and the votes shall then be counted;—the person having the greatest number of votes for President, shall be the President, if such number be a majority of the whole number of electors appointed; and if no person have such majority, then from the persons having the highest numbers not exceeding three on the list of those voted for as President, the House of Representatives shall choose immediately, by ballot, the President. But in choosing the President, the votes shall be taken by states, the representation from each state having one vote; a quorum for this purpose shall consist of a member or members from two-thirds of the states, and a majority of all the states shall be necessary to a choice. And if the House of Representatives shall not choose a President whenever the right of choice shall devolve upon them, before the fourth day of March next following, then the Vice-President shall act as President, as in the case of the death or other constitutional disability of the President. The person having the greatest number of votes as Vice-President, shall be the Vice-President, if such number be a majority of the whole number of Electors appointed, and if no person have a majority, then from the two highest numbers on the list, the Senate shall choose the Vice-President; a quorum for the purpose shall consist of two-thirds of the whole number of Senators, and a majority of the whole number shall be necessary to a choice. But no person constitutionally ineligible to the office of President shall be eligible to that of Vice-President of the United States.

AMENDMENT 13. Slavery Abolished (1865)

Section 1. Neither slavery nor involuntary **servitude**, except as a punishment for crime whereof the party shall have been duly convicted, shall exist within the United States, or any place subject to their jurisdiction.

Section 2. Congress shall have power to enforce this article by appropriate legislation.

A CLOSER LOOK

SEPARATE BALLOTS

The presidential election of 1800 ended in a tie between Thomas Jefferson and Aaron Burr. At this time, the candidate with the most votes became president. The runner-up became vice-president. The Twelfth Amendment calls for separate ballots for the president and vice-president. The vice-president is specifically elected to the office, rather than being the presidential candidate with the second-most votes.

13. Why do you think it is important for a presidential election to result in a clear-cut winner?

VOCABULARY

equity a system of justice not covered under common law

servitude being under the authority of an owner or master

naturalized granted nationality

insurrection revolt against authority

bounties rewards

AMENDMENT 14. Civil Rights (1868)

Section 1. All persons born or <u>naturalized</u> in the United States, and subject to the jurisdiction thereof, are citizens of the United States and of the state wherein they reside. No state shall make or enforce any law which shall abridge the privileges or immunities of citizens of the United States; nor shall any state deprive any person of life, liberty, or property, without due process of law; nor deny to any person within its jurisdiction the equal protection of the laws.

Section 2. Representatives shall be apportioned among the several states according to their respective numbers, counting the whole number of persons in each state, excluding Indians not taxed. But when the right to vote at any election for the choice of electors for President and Vice-President of the United States, Representatives in Congress, the executive and judicial officers of a state, or the members of the legislature thereof, is denied to any of the male inhabitants of such state, being twenty-one years of age, and citizens of the United States, or in any way abridged, except for participation in rebellion, or other crime, the basis of representation therein shall be reduced in the proportion which the number of such male citizens shall bear to the whole number of male citizens twenty-one years of age in such state.

Section 3. No person shall be a Senator or Representative in Congress, or elector of President and Vice-President, or hold any office, civil or military, under the United States, or under any state, who, having previously taken an oath, as a member of Congress, or as an officer of the United States, or as a member of any state legislature, or as an executive or judicial officer of any state, to support the Constitution of the United States, shall have engaged in <u>insurrection</u> or rebellion against the same, or given aid or comfort to the enemies thereof. But Congress may, by a vote of two-thirds of each house, remove such disability.

Section 4. The validity of the public debt of the United States, authorized by law, including debts incurred for payment of pensions and <u>bounties</u> for services in suppressing insurrection or rebellion, shall not be questioned. But neither the United States nor any state shall assume or pay any debt or obligation incurred in aid of insurrection or rebellion against the United States, or any claim for the loss or emancipation of any slave; but all such debts, obligations and claims shall be held illegal and void.

Section 5. The Congress shall have power to enforce, by appropriate legislation, the provisions of this article.

AMENDMENT 15. Right to Vote (1870)

Section 1. The right of citizens of the United States to vote shall not be denied or abridged by the United States or by any state on account of race, color, or previous condition of servitude.

Section 2. The Congress shall have power to enforce this article by appropriate legislation.

A CLOSER LOOK Reconstruction Amendments

The Thirteenth, Fourteenth, and Fifteenth Amendments are often called the Reconstruction Amendments. They were passed after the Civil War during the government's attempt to rebuild the Union and to grant rights to recently freed African Americans.

Amendment 13	Amendment 14	Amendment 15

1865	1868	1870
• Ended slavery in the United States	• Defined national and state citizenship • Protected citizens' rights • Promised "equal protection of the laws"	• Designed to protect African Americans' voting rights

SKILLBUILDER Interpreting Charts
What problems did these amendments try to solve?

AMENDMENT 16. Income Tax (1913)

The Congress shall have power to lay and collect taxes on incomes, from whatever source derived, without apportionment among the several states, and without regard to any census or enumeration.

AMENDMENT 17. Direct Election of Senators (1913)

Section 1. The Senate of the United States shall be composed of two Senators from each state, elected by the people thereof, for six years; and each Senator shall have one vote. The electors in each state shall have the qualifications requisite for electors of the most numerous branch of the state legislatures.

Section 2. When vacancies happen in the representation of any state in the Senate, the executive authority of such state shall issue writs of election to fill such vacancies: Provided, that the legislature of any state may empower the executive thereof to make temporary appointments until the people fill the vacancies by election as the legislature may direct.

A CLOSER LOOK

THE EQUAL RIGHTS AMENDMENT

Above, marchers campaign for woman suffrage. In 1920, the Nineteenth Amendment took effect, guaranteeing women the right to vote. Since then, women have slowly gained political power. Nevertheless, many women have continued to face discrimination in the United States. In 1923, The National Women's Party supported the passage of an equal rights amendment to protect women. Congress did not pass such an amendment until 1972. In 1982, however, the amendment died after it failed to be ratified by enough states to be added to the Constitution. Despite this setback, women such as the Congress members who belong to the Congressional Caucus for Women's Issues, pictured above, continue to press for economic, political, and social equality for women.

17. Why do you think the Nineteenth Amendment failed to create equality for women?

Section 3. This amendment shall not be so construed as to affect the election or term of any Senator chosen before it becomes valid as part of the Constitution.

AMENDMENT 18. Prohibition (1919)

~~**Section 1.** After one year from the ratification of this article the manufacture, sale, or transportation of intoxicating liquors within, the importation thereof into, or the exportation thereof from the United States and all territory subject to the jurisdiction thereof for beverage purposes is hereby prohibited.~~

~~**Section 2.** The Congress and the several states shall have concurrent power to enforce this article by appropriate legislation.~~

~~**Section 3.** This article shall be inoperative unless it shall have been ratified as an amendment to the Constitution by the legislatures of the several states, as provided in the Constitution, within seven years from the date of the submission hereof to the states by the Congress.~~

AMENDMENT 19. Woman Suffrage (1920)

Section 1. The right of citizens of the United States to vote shall not be denied or abridged by the United States or by any state on account of sex.

Section 2. Congress shall have power to enforce this article by appropriate legislation.

AMENDMENT 20. "Lame Duck" Sessions (1933)

Section 1. The terms of the President and Vice-President shall end at noon on the 20th day of January, and the terms of Senators and Representatives at noon on the 3rd day of January, of the years in which such terms would have ended if this article had not been ratified; and the terms of their successors shall then begin.

Section 2. The Congress shall assemble at least once in every year, and such meeting shall begin at noon on the 3rd day of January, unless they shall by law appoint a different day.

Section 3. If, at the time fixed for the beginning of the term of the President, the President elect shall have died, the Vice-President elect shall become President. If a President shall not have been chosen before the time fixed for the beginning of his term, or if the President elect shall have failed to qualify, then the Vice-President elect shall act as President until a President shall have qualified; and the Congress may by law provide for the case wherein neither a President elect nor a Vice-President elect shall have qualified, declaring who shall then act as President, or the manner in which one who is to act shall be selected, and such person shall act accordingly until a President or Vice-President shall have qualified.

Section 4. The Congress may by law provide for the case of the death of any of the persons from whom the House of Representatives may choose a President whenever the right of choice shall have devolved upon them, and for the case of the death of any of the persons from whom the Senate may choose a Vice-President whenever the right of choice shall have devolved upon them.

Section 5. Sections 1 and 2 shall take effect on the 15th day of October following the ratification of this article.

Section 6. This article shall be **inoperative** unless it shall have been ratified as an amendment to the Constitution by the legislatures of three-fourths of the several states within seven years from the date of its submission.

AMENDMENT 21. Repeal of Prohibition (1933)

Section 1. The eighteenth article of amendment to the Constitution of the United States is hereby repealed.

Section 2. The transportation or importation into any state, territory, or possession of the United States for delivery or use therein of intoxicating liquors, in violation of the laws thereof, is hereby prohibited.

Section 3. This article shall be inoperative unless it shall have been ratified as an amendment to the Constitution by conventions in the several states, as provided in the Constitution, within seven years from the date of the submission hereof to the states by the Congress.

AMENDMENT 22. Limit on Presidential Terms (1951)

Section 1. No person shall be elected to the office of the President more than twice, and no person who has held the office of President, or acted as President, for more than two years of a term to which some other person was elected President shall be elected to the office of the President more than once. ~~But this article shall not apply to any person holding the office of President when this article was proposed by the Congress, and shall not prevent any person who may be holding the office of President, or acting as President, during the term within which this article becomes operative from holding the office of President or acting as President during the remainder of such term.~~

Section 2. This article shall be inoperative unless it shall have been ratified as an amendment to the Constitution by the legislatures of three-fourths of the several states within seven years from the date of its submission to the states by the Congress.

AMENDMENT 23. Voting in District of Columbia (1961)

Section 1. The district constituting the seat of government of the United States shall appoint in such manner as Congress may direct: a number of electors of President and Vice-President equal to the whole number of Senators and Representatives in Congress to which the district would be entitled if it were a state, but in no event more than the least populous state; they shall be in addition to those appointed by the states, but they shall be considered, for the purposes of the election of President and Vice-President, to be electors appointed by a state; and they shall meet in the district and perform such duties as provided by the twelfth article of amendment.

Section 2. The Congress shall have power to enforce this article by appropriate legislation.

AMENDMENT 24. Abolition of Poll Taxes (1964)

Section 1. The right of citizens of the United States to vote in any **primary** or other election for President or Vice-President, for electors for President or Vice-President, or for Senator or Representative in Congress, shall not be denied or abridged by the United States or any state by reason of failure to pay any poll tax or other tax.

Section 2. The Congress shall have power to enforce this article by appropriate legislation.

PRESIDENTIAL DISABILITY

President John F. Kennedy's death in 1963 signaled the need for the Twenty-Fifth Amendment. The Constitution did not explain what to do in the case of a disabled president. The Twenty-Fifth Amendment provides for an orderly transfer of power.

19. What do you think can happen in a country where the rules for succession are not clear?

SUCCESSION

Who takes over if a president dies in office or is unable to serve? The top five in the line of succession follow:

- vice-president
- speaker of the house
- president pro tempore of the Senate
- secretary of state
- secretary of the treasury

20. Why should voters know the views of the vice-president?

AMENDMENT 25. Presidential Disability, Succession (1967)

Section 1. In case of the removal of the President from office or of his death or resignation, the Vice-President shall become President.

Section 2. Whenever there is a vacancy in the office of the Vice-President, the President shall nominate a Vice-President who shall take office upon confirmation by a majority vote of both houses of Congress.

Section 3. Whenever the President transmits to the President pro tempore of the Senate and the Speaker of the House of Representatives his written declaration that he is unable to discharge the powers and duties of his office, and until he transmits to them a written declaration to the contrary, such powers and duties shall be discharged by the Vice-President as Acting President.

Section 4. Whenever the Vice-President and a majority of either the principal officers of the executive departments or of such other body as Congress may by law provide, transmit to the President pro tempore of the Senate and the Speaker of the House of Representatives their written declaration that the President is unable to discharge the powers and duties of his office, the Vice-President shall immediately assume the powers and duties of the office as Acting President. Thereafter, when the President transmits to the President pro tempore of the Senate and the Speaker of the House of Representatives his written declaration that no inability exists, he shall resume the powers and duties of his office unless the Vice-President and a majority of either the principal officers of the executive department[s] or of such other body as Congress may by law provide, transmit within four days to the President pro tempore of the Senate and the Speaker of the House of Representatives their written declaration that the President is unable to discharge the powers and duties of his office. Thereupon Congress shall decide the issue, assembling within forty-eight hours for that purpose if not in session. If the Congress, within twenty-one days after receipt of the latter written declaration, or, if Congress is not in

A CLOSER LOOK Amendments Time Line *1791–1992*

Use the key below to help you categorize the amendments.

- ■ **Voting Rights**
- ■ **Social Changes**
- ■ **Overturned Supreme Court Decisions**
- ■ **Election Procedures and Conditions of Office**

Bill of Rights Amendments 1–10 1791

1790

Amendment 11 1798
Protects state from lawsuits filed by citizens of other states or countries.

Amendment 12 1804
Requires separate electoral ballots for president and vice-president.

Amendment 14 1868
Defines American citizenship and citizens' rights.

Amendment 13 1865
Bans slavery.

Amendment 15 1870
Stops national and state governments from denying the vote based on race.

session, within twenty-one days after Congress is required to assemble, determines by two thirds vote of both houses that the President is unable to discharge the powers and duties of his office, the Vice-President shall continue to discharge the same as Acting President; otherwise, the President shall resume the powers and duties of his office.

AMENDMENT 26. 18-year-old Vote (1971)

Section 1. The right of citizens of the United States, who are eighteen years of age or older, to vote shall not be denied or abridged by the United States or by any state on account of age.

Section 2. The Congress shall have power to enforce this article by appropriate legislation.

AMENDMENT 27. Congressional Pay (1992)

No law, varying the compensation for the services of the Senators and Representatives, shall take effect, until an election of Representatives shall have intervened.

A CLOSER LOOK

RIGHT TO VOTE

Members of the recording industry founded Rock the Vote. They urge young people to vote in elections.

Amendments 11–27 Assessment

1. MAIN IDEAS

a. Which amendments affected the office of president?

b. Which pair of amendments shows the failure of laws to solve a social problem?

c. Which amendments corrected unfair treatment toward African Americans and women?

2. CRITICAL THINKING

Summarizing What is the purpose of amending the Constitution?

Think About

• the purpose of the Constitution

• problems and issues that Americans have faced throughout U.S. history

---

Amendment 23
1961
Gives citizens of Washington, D.C., right to vote in presidential elections.

Amendment 19
1920
Extends the vote to women.

Amendment 24
1964
Bans poll taxes.

Amendment 18
1919
Prohibits making, selling, and shipping alcoholic beverages.

Amendment 21
1933
Repeals Amendment 18.

Amendment 26
1971
Gives 18-year-olds right to vote in federal and state elections.

2000

Amendment 16
1913
Allows Congress to tax incomes.

Amendment 20
1933
Changes date for starting new Congress and inaugurating new president.

Amendment 25
1967
Sets procedures for presidential succession.

Amendment 27
1992
Limits ability of Congress to increase its pay.

Amendment 17
1913
Establishes direct election of U.S. senators.

Amendment 22
1951
Limits terms president can serve to two.

VISUAL SUMMARY

The Constitution of the United States

WE THE PEOPLE

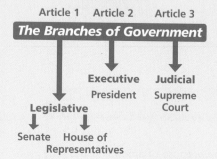

Article 1   Article 2   Article 3

The Branches of Government

Executive
President

Judicial
Supreme Court

Legislative

Senate   House of Representatives

Article 4   Article 6

The Federal System

Powers of the State

Powers of the National Government

"Supreme law of the land"

Article 5

Amending the Constitution

Making Changes

Bill of Rights

Amendments 1–10

Personal Freedoms

Personal Security

Rights of the Accused

Amendments 11–27

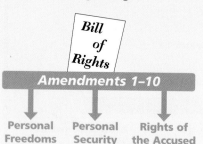

The living Constitution changes with the times.

VOCABULARY

Briefly explain the significance of each of the following.

1. electors
2. impeachment
3. naturalization
4. felonies
5. bill of attainder
6. ex post facto law
7. suffrage
8. due process of law
9. servitude
10. primary

SEVEN PRINCIPLES OF THE CONSTITUTION

Make a chart like the one shown. Then fill it in with a definition of each principle and an example from the Constitution.

Principle	Definition	Example
1. popular sovereignty		
2. republicanism		
3. federalism		
4. separation of powers		
5. checks and balances		
6. limited government		
7. individual rights		

REVIEW QUESTIONS

Article 1 (pages 170–175)

1. What are the requirements for becoming a member of the House of Representatives and the Senate?
2. What are two military powers granted to Congress?

Article 2 (pages 176–178)

3. How does the electoral college choose the president?
4. What are three powers of the president?

Article 3 (page 179)

5. What are the two most important powers of the federal courts?

Articles 4–7 (pages 180–181)

6. How can the Constitution be changed?
7. If a state law and a federal law conflict, which law must be obeyed? Why?
8. How was the Constitution ratified?

Bill of Rights and Amendments 11–27 (pages 182–191)

9. What five freedoms are guaranteed in the First Amendment?
10. Which amendments extend voting rights to a broader range of Americans?

CRITICAL THINKING

1. DRAWING CONCLUSIONS

In a two-column chart, summarize the processes for changing the Constitution. Then use your completed chart to answer the questions below.

Proposing Amendments	Ratifying Amendments
1.	1.
2.	2.

a. What role can citizens play in proposing amendments?

b. What do you think are the main reasons for changing the Constitution?

2. MAKING INFERENCES

Explain how the "elastic clause" in Article 1 gives Congress the authority to take action on other issues unknown to the Framers of the Constitution.

3. ANALYZING LEADERSHIP

Think about the president's roles described in the Constitution. What qualities does a president need to succeed as a leader in so many different areas?

4. RECOGNIZING EFFECTS

How would you describe the impact of the Fourteenth, Fifteenth, and Sixteenth Amendments on life in the United States?

5. APPLYING CITIZENSHIP

Suppose you and your family go on a road trip across several states. According to Article 4 of the Constitution, what citizens' rights do you have in the states you are visiting?

ALTERNATIVE ASSESSMENT

1. COOPERATIVE LEARNING ACTIVITY

Imagine you are asked to write a constitution for a newly formed country. Working with a group, use the outline below to organize and write your constitution.

I. Purpose of the Constitution (Preamble)

II. Making Laws (Legislative Branch)

III. Carrying Out the Laws (Executive Branch)

IV. Making Laws Fair (Judicial Branch)

V. Choosing Leaders

VI. Citizens' Rights (Bill of Rights)

INTERNET TECHNOLOGY ACTIVITY

2. MAKING A LEARNING CENTER

Creating the U.S. Constitution was one of the most important events in the nation's history. Use the Internet and the library to collect information for a learning center featuring the suggestions below.

- Find biographies and portraits of the Framers.
- Collect important primary sources such as James Madison's notes and *The Federalist* papers.
- Gather recent pictures and news articles about the Congress, the president, the Supreme Court, and the Bill of Rights.

STANDARDS-BASED ASSESSMENT

In 1937, President Franklin D. Roosevelt used interesting comparisons to explain how the government works.

I described the American form of government as a three-horse team provided by the Constitution to the American people so that their field might be plowed. The three horses are, of course, the three branches of government—the Congress, the Executive, and the Courts. . . . It is the American people themselves who are in the driver's seat. It is the American people themselves who want the furrow plowed.

Franklin D. Roosevelt, Radio Address

1. Which of the following best describes Roosevelt's view of popular sovereignty?

   A. American citizens do all the work of government.

   B. American citizens hold no power.

   C. American citizens hold ultimate power.

   D. American citizens set the agenda for government.

2. How does Roosevelt describe the separation of power?

   A. as a three-horse team

   B. as a field

   C. as a driver's seat

   D. as a furrow to be plowed

The Cherokee Nation and Removal 1800–1840

Section 1
The Cherokee

Section 2
Indian Removal

Contemporary Cherokee artist Talmadge Davis shows the influential Nanye-hi, a Cherokee Beloved Woman also known as Nancy Ward. As a Beloved Woman, she voted in the Nation's General Council, negotiated peace treaties, and could spare the lives of condemned war captives.

1812
Cherokee fight war with Jackson against Creek.

1819
Cherokee National Council decides to cede no more land.

GEORGIA USA

1800   1810   1820

1802
U.S. makes compact with Georgia to remove Native Americans.

1816
James Monroe is elected president.

INTERACT with HISTORY

It is 1830. The government has given your tribe a choice: move west to a reservation and keep your traditional way of life, or stay and adapt. Most of your tribal land has been sold or taken. The remaining land is isolated and not very good for farming.

Would you stay or would you leave?

WHAT DO YOU THINK?

- How would your life change if you stayed in Georgia?

- How would your life change if you moved west?

For more information on this chapter, visit . . .

RESEARCH LINKS
CLASSZONE.COM

1822
Cherokee establish a supreme court.

1827
John Ross becomes principal chief of Cherokee.

1832
Georgia loses Supreme Court decision in *Worcester* v. *Georgia*.

1838
Cherokee travel the Trail of Tears.

1830

1840

1828
Andrew Jackson is elected president.

1830
Indian Removal Act is passed by Congress.

1836
Martin Van Buren is elected president.

1838
Federal troops put Cherokee in stockades.

Reading Strategy:
Analyzing Points of View

What Do You Know?

What do you already know about the Cherokee culture? How has the Cherokee culture influenced the state of Georgia?

THINK ABOUT
- how Native Americans have been portrayed in movies, television, and historical fiction
- historical accounts you've read or documentaries you've seen about Native Americans

What Do You Want to Know?

What questions do you have about the Cherokee who settled in Georgia? About their removal from the state? Record those questions in your notebook before you read the chapter.

Analyzing Points of View

The people of Georgia and the Cherokee had very different views of land and their rights to claim it. Looking closely at their arguments can help you understand the reasons behind their points of view. Use the chart below to analyze the views of Georgians and of the Cherokee. Then write a summary that explains why different people took different positions.

S *See Skillbuilder Handbook, page 551.*

Taking Notes

Views of Georgians

Views of Cherokee

Summary Statement

The Cherokee

The Cherokee established a culture that was much like the white settlers' culture in order to live peacefully.

Part of the Cherokee heritage remains in Georgia, particularly in northern areas of the state.

New Echota
Sequoyah
Cherokee Phoenix
Elias Boudinot
Light Horse Guard
Cherokee Constitution
Major Ridge
John Ross

SETTING THE STAGE

The harmonious way of life of the Cherokee was disrupted by the arrival of English colonists. The settlers wanted the land the Native Americans lived on. Diseases brought by Europeans caused the Cherokee population to decrease from 30,000 to 16,000 by 1700. And yet they persevered.

In the French and Indian War, the Cherokee had fought on the side of the French. They were defeated. In the American Revolution, the Cherokee fought on the side of the British. They were defeated again. The Cherokee lost much of their land in trying to make peace with the settlers that remained. The Cherokee land was in jeopardy, land they had fought hard to keep. How would the Cherokee Nation continue? Would they become a part of the United States? Or would they be allowed to rule themselves? Would they be allowed to keep the land they loved so much?

▲ Creek houses were typically made of logs. As the Cherokee moved into northern Georgia, they forced the Creek out.

Settling the River Valleys

The Cherokee settled in the river valleys of the southern Appalachian Mountains. Their original territory included what is now northern Georgia, Alabama, and Mississippi. The Choctaw gave the Cherokee their name, which means "people of the cave country." The Cherokee called themselves *Ani'–Yun'wiya*, which means "the principal people."

The mountains in northern Georgia were well suited to the Cherokee. They were full of wildlife such as deer, elk, bears, turkeys, and small game. There were many fish in the streams, and hardwood trees bore nuts. For all of these reasons, northern Georgia was a good place for the Cherokee to live.

Taking Notes

Use your chart to analyze the view of Georgians and of the Cherokee as they shared the land of Georgia.

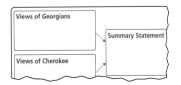

Cherokee Drive Out the Creek The Cherokee tried to farm, but plants would not grow well in the mountains. Favorite crops such as corn, beans, and squash needed the rich soil of the river valleys. But another tribe, the Creek, lived in these flatlands. The Creek and Cherokee fought over this fertile land. After many battles, the Cherokee finally forced the Creek out of northern Georgia.

The Cherokee took over the land and established permanent settlements there. Chota, along with settlements in the Sautee Valley, were the best known of these. The largest Cherokee population was in what is now White County. Many counties, rivers, and cities in Georgia today have Cherokee and Creek names: Chattahoochee, Chestatee, Etowah, Coosa, and Oconee.

The Colonists and the Cherokee

The British had one of the longest relationships with the Cherokee. But it wasn't always an easy association. After the French and Indian War, the British and the Cherokee developed a relationship that benefited both. The Cherokee provided two products the British wanted. The first was deerskin, which was used to make leather items. The second was war captives, who became slaves either in the colonies or in the West Indies. The Cherokee traded these for important supplies from the British, such as guns and ammunition, work tools, fabric, and kitchen utensils.

The Cherokee Adapt to Changes The Cherokee, like many other Native American tribes, had traditionally used a council to make decisions affecting the tribe. They worked hard to reach agreements on issues. This meant their government was democratic, much like our government today. The Cherokee system of government worked well because it used this council. It had also been successful because the Cherokee had chosen leaders who were inspiring.

As the colonies became established, however, the Cherokee changed the way they governed themselves. Europeans didn't want to deal with a council that might take a long time to make decisions. So the Cherokee abandoned their council form of government and let their

Reading History

A. Analyzing Points of View
Why did the Cherokee abandon their decision-making council?

warriors make decisions. This change meant giving up some of their freedom. The Cherokee hoped that if they adopted a lifestyle like that of white Americans, the new government would let the tribe continue to live on their land in peace.

The Cherokee situation changed again after the American Revolution. In the Treaty of Paris in 1783, Britain recognized the independence of the United States. It gave up all British rights and claims on the land. Now there was a new challenge. How would the United States deal with Native American tribes, such as the Cherokee, who had fought against them in the Revolution?

The United States and the Cherokee Nation

Reading History

B. Summarizing
Why did the U.S. government want to remove the Cherokee from their land?

Congress treated the Cherokee as conquered enemies—like people from a foreign land that they had captured. They wanted to move the Native Americans for two reasons. First, they wanted to see the end of Cherokee warfare. Second, the government wanted to obtain Cherokee land for settlers to farm.

The new government relocated, or moved, the Cherokee to a smaller tract of land and taught them different farming techniques. This new Cherokee Nation covered what is now northern Georgia, western North Carolina, eastern Tennessee, and northwestern Alabama. The U.S. government also sent agents to live with the Cherokee. The agents gave animals to herd, plows, and other farm tools to the men. They gave spinning wheels and looms to the women so they could learn to weave cloth.

"Civilizing" the Cherokee   For some settlers, it wasn't enough to relocate the Cherokee or teach them new ways of farming. They wanted to "civilize" the Cherokee by teaching them to dress like white people, follow a written code of law, read and write English, and follow the Christian faith. With the goal of "civilizing" the Cherokee in all of these ways, many missionaries went to live and work among the tribe.

▼ This Cherokee farmhouse is in Echota, Georgia.

The Cherokee resisted converting to Christianity. But they welcomed the education, tools, and training that the missionaries offered them. The Cherokee realized that their economy had depended too much on deerskin trading with white settlers. They knew they needed to find new ways of doing business.

Talking Leaves: A Written Language for the Cherokee

Sequoyah came up with the idea for a written language for the Cherokee when, as a young silversmith, he wanted to sign his work. He created 86 characters, one symbol for each syllable in the spoken Cherokee language. This system is called a "syllabary." The English alphabet is based on sounds instead of syllables.

The name the Cherokee gave to the language, Talking Leaves, made fun of whites. The Cherokee felt that when the written words no longer suited them, the white man's words dried up and blew away like leaves.

Sequoyah and the *Cherokee Phoenix*

The Cherokee Nation supported the civilization program because they believed it was the best way to survive. If they adopted the ways of the white settlers, they hoped they would be left alone to live in peace. It would be necessary to change their lifestyle in both big and small ways. They bought a printing press that had both the English alphabet and the alphabet that was invented by a Cherokee named Sequoyah. The press was located in the new Cherokee capital of **New Echota,** near what is today Calhoun, Georgia.

Sequoyah was born around 1770. Some say that his father may have been white, but Sequoyah was raised as a Cherokee. Sequoyah saw that the Europeans had an advantage because they could transmit their ideas through a written language. In the early 1800s, he began to develop a Cherokee alphabet. By 1821, he had produced a system with 86 symbols that represented Cherokee syllables. The system was so simple that anyone who spoke Cherokee could learn it in a few days.

Sequoyah's alphabet was the first step toward the Cherokee people learning to read. In 1828, they started their own newspaper, the ***Cherokee Phoenix,*** which was printed in both English and Cherokee. **Elias Boudinot** became the editor. Boudinot was a young Cherokee who had been educated in mission schools. He printed the nation's laws, local and world news, human interest stories, Bible passages, editorials, and advertisements in the paper.

Reading History

C. Making Inferences Why would having a written language give the Cherokee an advantage?

Primary Source

Changes in Lifestyle

Soon, Cherokee Indians were imitating the whites in other ways besides reading and writing. Many Cherokee became wealthy and built stylish houses, decorated with fine furniture and china. Some ran stores, mills, ferries, and taverns. Others became successful planters who raised and sold crops such as cotton. They even had enslaved Africans as workers. These Cherokee planters became an elite group that began to take over Cherokee politics.

A Government and Written Law

Politics was another area in which changes were taking place. In 1817, the Cherokee divided their territory into eight districts. Each district sent representatives to the national Cherokee Council. This national Cherokee government protected individual and common property. It also had the power to decide guilt or innocence in criminal cases. In 1819, the Cherokee National Council told the United States that the Cherokee would cede no more land. In 1822, the Cherokee established a supreme court to hear appeals from the district courts.

The Cherokee decided to compose a written code of law. Tribal laws had always been informal, but the Cherokee people were becoming more and more worried about their property rights. They thought a written code would help protect these rights. The first law that the Cherokee wrote, in 1808, created a national police force called the **Light Horse Guard.** These new laws were quite different from the old Cherokee traditions. In the past, a man's property had gone to his sister and his children upon his death. Under the new laws, his wife would inherit his property and possessions.

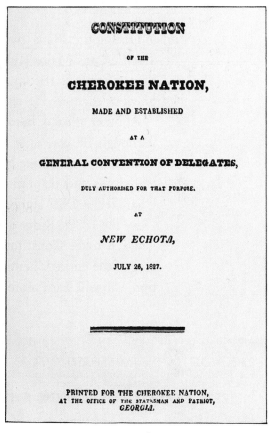

▲ The Constitution of the Cherokee Nation was written in 1827.

The Cherokee Constitution   In 1827, the Cherokee wrote the **Cherokee Constitution.** This document was similar to the U.S. Constitution because it established a legislature, a chief executive, and a judicial system. In addition, the Constitution defined the territory of the Cherokee Nation and declared that the Cherokee land belonged to the nation as a whole, not to individual people. Therefore, decisions about the land had to be made by the entire tribe.

Reading History

D. Finding Main Ideas How did the Cherokee Constitution resemble the U.S. Constitution?

Respected Cherokee Leaders

Thomas Jefferson observed that Native Americans tended to follow only leaders they respected. At times that meant that different family groups followed different leaders.

> **PRIMARY SOURCE**
>
> Their leaders conduct them by the influence of their character only. . . . Hence the origin of the parties [family groups] among them adhering to different leaders, and governed by their advice, not by their command.
>
> Thomas Jefferson in an 1816 letter to Francis Walker Gilmer

During the 1820s, two men rose to the top of the Cherokee Nation. The first was **Major Ridge.** He was respected for two reasons. He had been a leader in the Creek War of 1813, which you read about in the previous chapter. He was also a successful planter and businessman.

Another great Cherokee leader during this time was **John Ross.** Although he was only one-eighth Cherokee, he identified with the Cherokee people. Like Ridge, Ross was very successful. He owned several stores and plantations. John Ross became principal chief of the Cherokee in 1827 and served until 1866.

By the 1830s, Ridge and Ross would come in direct conflict, and the new Cherokee Constitution would be challenged. The continued success of the entire Cherokee Nation would be at stake. In the next section, you will learn more about how they faced these difficulties.

Background

The Cherokee had matrilineal clans. That is, they traced their family relationships through their mothers.

Section Assessment

1. TERMS & NAMES

Explain the significance of:

a. New Echota

b. Sequoyah

c. *Cherokee Phoenix*

d. Elias Boudinot

e. Light Horse Guard

f. Cherokee Constitution

g. Major Ridge

h. John Ross

2. TAKING NOTES

Use a chart like the one below to note the changes the Cherokee made after the 1700s in their lifestyle and political systems.

Changes for the Cherokee after 1700s	
Political	Lifestyle

3. MAIN IDEAS

a. How did the U.S. government plan to "civilize" the Cherokee?

b. Why were the Cherokee of New Echota willing to accept the white man's ways?

c. What political structures of the Cherokee Nation closely resembled the U.S. government?

4. CRITICAL THINKING

Supporting Opinions

Did the Cherokee gain any advantages in adapting to the civilization program of the white settlers? Explain.

Think About
• land use
• new laws
• the Cherokee Nation

Language Arts/Art Research the changes in Cherokee communities in this section. Write a **newspaper article** or design a **poster** that dramatizes these changes.

Indian Removal

MAIN IDEA	WHY IT MATTERS NOW	TERMS & NAMES
White settlers were determined to have all of the Southeastern land occupied by the Cherokee. They eventually succeeded.	Cherokee land became present-day Georgia counties that carried many reminders of the Cherokee heritage.	Indian Removal Act *Cherokee Nation* v. *Georgia* *Worcester* v. *Georgia* Treaty Party Treaty of New Echota Trail of Tears

SETTING THE STAGE

The Cherokee abandoned years of tradition to try to adapt to white settlers. They changed their lifestyle and their form of government in order to get along with the new federal government. Some Cherokee resisted the government's efforts and left Georgia, but most remained.

The citizens of Georgia were unhappy because they wanted the fertile Cherokee land that was good for growing cotton, logging timber, and mining gold. Would white settlers and the federal government let the Cherokee govern themselves? Would they leave the Cherokee and their land alone? Would there be another war? How long could the Cherokee resist?

▲ If the Cherokee were not allowed to remain on their tribal lands, they would have to find somewhere else to live.

Early Removal of Creek and Cherokee

The removal of Native Americans from Georgia started with the Compact of 1802. In that agreement, Georgia sold most of its land—from west of the Chattahoochee to the Mississippi River—to the United States. This area is now Alabama and Mississippi. In exchange, the federal government paid Georgia almost 1.25 million dollars and agreed to remove all Native Americans from Georgia territory.

Promises of Land to the West   The government promised to give land in present-day Arkansas and Oklahoma to Native Americans who left Georgia. The Creek tribe agreed to leave. In an 1821 treaty, the Creek gave up land between the Ocmulgee and Flint Rivers. Later, they surrendered land as far as the Chattahoochee River. By 1827, almost all

Taking Notes

Use your chart to analyze the views of Georgians and of the Cherokee as the Cherokee are removed from Georgia.

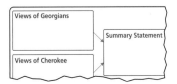

The Cherokee Nation and Removal   **203**

Creek were gone from Georgia. Most had relocated and resettled in present-day Oklahoma.

While he was president, Thomas Jefferson proposed that Native Americans who did not want to join white society could go to the new Louisiana Territory. Many tribes accepted this offer, including some Cherokee. The United States gave those who chose to go west some form of payment. Wealthy Cherokee were paid the full value of their houses, barns, fences, and orchards. Poor Cherokee each received a rifle, ammunition, a blanket, and a brass kettle or a beaver trap.

The Cherokee Refuse to Leave

When the federal government had made the Compact of 1802, officials thought that the Native Americans would give up all of their land through treaties. The Cherokee Nation did give up some land in 1819. After that, however, the Cherokee said they would surrender no more of their land. This meant the federal government could not fulfill the terms of the compact. White Georgians were furious.

In response, Georgia ordered all missionaries to leave the land. The state government pressured the Cherokee by removing their supporters.

▼ John Ross was unable to convince President Monroe to repeal the Compact of 1802.

It created the Georgia Guard, a special police force to enforce the laws against the Cherokee. The Georgia legislature then complained that with their 1827 constitution, the Cherokee Nation had developed a state within a state. This went against federal law. The state used this to challenge the Cherokee people's right to the land. It urged the federal government to remove the Cherokee from Georgia.

The Cherokee National Council sent John Ross, Major Ridge, and others to Washington, D.C., to persuade President James Monroe to repeal the Compact of 1802. The president held fast and refused to change the legislation. As stubborn as the federal government was, however, the Cherokee were even more determined that they would not leave their land.

Reading History

A. Summarizing What was the purpose of the Georgia Guard?

Reading History

B. Finding Main Ideas According to the Georgia legislature, how was the Cherokee Nation illegal?

The Cherokee Turn to the Supreme Court

Even though the Cherokee had fought with Andrew Jackson against the Creek in the War of 1812, Jackson had no sympathy for the Cherokee when he became president in 1828. Jackson was determined to open the Cherokee land to white settlers. In 1830, Jackson persuaded the United States Congress to pass the **Indian Removal Act**. This legislation gave the Cherokee a clear choice. They could live within the

Background

Gold was discovered on Cherokee land in 1828. The arrival of thousands of miners and the increasing value of the land made Georgians even more determined to remove the Cherokee.

laws of the Georgia government, however unfair they thought they were, or they could move west of the Mississippi River.

The Cherokee did not accept this. They were so determined to stay on their land that they took two important cases to the United States Supreme Court.

The Cherokee Sue Georgia In 1831, in **_Cherokee Nation_ v. _Georgia_,** the Cherokee sued Georgia over Georgia's involvement in a matter that the Cherokee felt should have been left to the tribe. The Georgia Guard had arrested a Cherokee man who had murdered another member of the Cherokee Nation. A Georgia court tried and convicted the suspect of violating Georgia law. The Cherokee argued that Georgia laws should not apply to the Cherokee Nation. The Supreme Court declared that the Cherokee Nation was a "domestic dependent nation" and had no right to sue.

There was a different outcome in the next case the Cherokee brought before the Supreme Court. Earlier, the state of Georgia had enacted a law requiring all missionaries to the Cherokee to swear an oath of allegiance to the state of Georgia and obtain a permit to live in the Cherokee territory. In the spring of 1831, the government ordered the Georgia Guard to arrest several missionaries who had refused to swear the oath or refused to leave. The missionaries were sentenced to four years in prison. One of the missionaries, Samuel Worcester, was named in the lawsuit. The result was the case known as **_Worcester_ v. _Georgia_.** In its decision, the Supreme Court sided with the Cherokee. Chief Justice Marshall ruled in 1832 that the Cherokee Nation was a distinct nation with its own laws, and that Georgia law was not valid within it.

THE CASE

OF

THE CHEROKEE NATION

against

THE STATE OF GEORGIA:

ARGUED AND DETERMINED AT

THE SUPREME COURT OF THE UNITED STATES,

JANUARY TERM 1831.

WITH

AN APPENDIX,

Containing the Opinion of Chancellor Kent on the Case ; the Treaties between the United States and the Cherokee Indians ; the Act of Congress of 1802, entitled ' An Act to regulate intercourse with the Indian tribes, &c.'; and the Laws of Georgia relative to the country occupied by the Cherokee Indians, within the boundary of that State.

BY RICHARD PETERS,

COUNSELLOR AT LAW.

Philadelphia:

JOHN GRIGG, 9 NORTH FOURTH STREET.

1831.

▲ When the Cherokee Nation sued Georgia in 1831, they hoped the Supreme Court would rule that they were a separate nation.

Georgia Defies Court Ruling Although *Worcester* v. *Georgia* was a triumph for the Cherokee, the Georgia government refused to accept the decision. Instead, Georgia established a land lottery that gave Cherokee land to Georgia citizens. Thousands of Georgians moved into Cherokee country. Despite the court ruling, the federal government did not support the Cherokee in the *Worcester* case. As President Jackson pointed out, the Supreme Court had no power to enforce its ruling. Jackson certainly had no intention of enforcing it. In fact, he encouraged Georgians to ignore the Supreme Court decision. The Cherokee were at a crossroads. What more could they do?

Reading History

C. Analyzing Points of View How did Georgians respond to *Worcester* v. *Georgia*?

Negotiating with the Federal Government

The two most respected Cherokee leaders, Major Ridge and John Ross, disagreed over how to proceed. Major Ridge, his son John Ridge, and his nephew Elias Boudinot said that the Cherokee had no choice but to negotiate with the United States. But John Ross and his supporters felt the Cherokee should continue to fight.

The Treaty Party   Major Ridge, John Ridge, and Elias Boudinot formed the **Treaty Party** to try to negotiate with the federal government. In December of 1835, approximately 100 Treaty Party members signed the **Treaty of New Echota.** This agreement gave up all Cherokee land in the Southeast. In exchange, the Cherokee received land in what is now northeastern Oklahoma.

Most Cherokee did not support the Treaty Party and its ideas. Under the leadership of John Ross, approximately 15,000 Cherokee signed a petition that said that the Treaty Party did not represent them. However, the federal government did not listen. The U.S. Senate ratified the Treaty of New Echota and gave the Cherokee two years to leave their land and move west.

Opposition to the Treaty   Ross would not give up. He opposed the Treaty of New Echota because he was afraid that in a few years, the government would demand that the Cherokee move farther west. Already, Cherokee who had moved west earlier had been forced to give up their land and move once again. Ross proposed several alternatives,

Reading History

D. Recognizing Effects   What did Ross believe would be the effect of accepting the Treaty of New Echota?

▼ Cherokee families gathered as many belongings as they could take with them on their long journey from Georgia to their new lands west of the Mississippi River.

but none were accepted. The Cherokee hoped that things would change when President Jackson left office in 1837. They decided to wait and did not move.

The Trail of Tears

Tensions between the settlers and the Cherokee continued to mount. Some government leaders seemed to fear that if the Cherokee remained in Georgia, they would be killed by white settlers. The government did not think that white settlers would move west of the Mississippi River. Therefore, they claimed that they wanted to protect the Cherokee by moving them west.

In the summer of 1838, federal troops were ordered to round up the Cherokee and put them in stockades, large enclosures for prisoners. To prevent the Cherokee from escaping and returning home, the troops burned the tribe's houses and crops.

Living conditions in the stockades were terrible. There was not enough food or water. Chief Ross watched hundreds of Cherokee die. Chief Ross asked the new president, Martin Van Buren, who had been elected in 1837, to let the Cherokee handle their own relocation. In the winter of 1838-39, the Cherokee Nation headed west, escorted by federal troops. The movement west was filled with hardships. The

Reading History

E. Summarizing
How did federal troops prevent the Cherokee from returning to their homes?

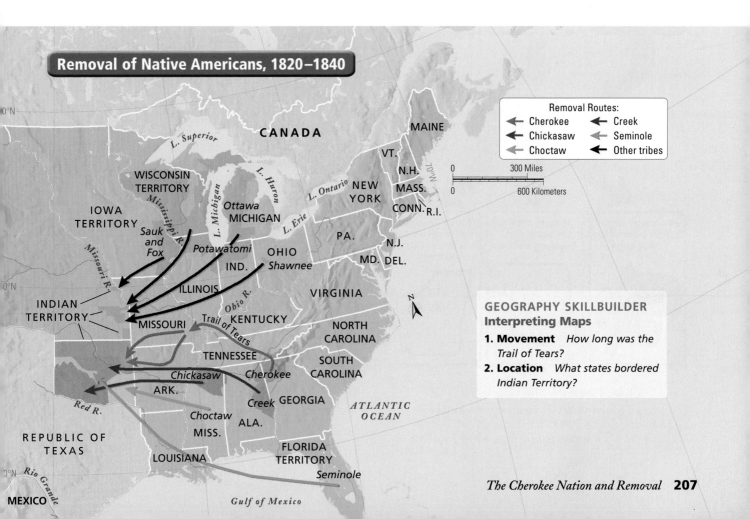

Removal of Native Americans, 1820–1840

Removal Routes:
← Cherokee   ← Creek
← Chickasaw   ← Seminole
← Choctaw   ← Other tribes

GEOGRAPHY SKILLBUILDER
Interpreting Maps

1. **Movement** How long was the Trail of Tears?
2. **Location** What states bordered Indian Territory?

Cherokee called it *Nunna-da-ul-tsun-yi* or "trail where they cried." It has become known as the **Trail of Tears**.

Many Cherokee died on the way to Oklahoma. One of them was John Ross's wife. When the surviving Cherokee reached what is present-day Oklahoma, they re-elected John Ross as their principal chief. They built schools, set up a newspaper, and created a new Cherokee capital. They began again.

Evaluating Indian Removal

In the end, both sides thought they were right. Georgians did not like the fact that the Cherokee had sided with the British in the War of 1812. This made the Cherokee foreign enemies in the eyes of Georgians.

The Cherokee thought they were being unfairly forced off land that had been theirs for generations. When they negotiated treaties, the terms were ignored within several years. When they won court decisions, the federal government did not enforce the rulings. They felt they had done their part by adapting to the white settlers' way of life. They thought they had proven that they deserved to rule themselves in their own nation.

Breaking Promises The federal government made the mistake of underestimating the Cherokee. The United States leadership did not understand the fierce loyalty that the Cherokee felt to their homeland. They did not understand how traumatic relocation would be for the Cherokee. Instead, they thought that trading Georgia land for land west of the Mississippi River would not matter to the Cherokee.

The federal government made promises it could not keep without resorting to force. The Compact of 1802 and Indian Removal Act in 1830 promised Cherokee land to white settlers. How would the history of Georgia

Reading History

F. Evaluating
How did establishing themselves as a nation affect the Cherokee?

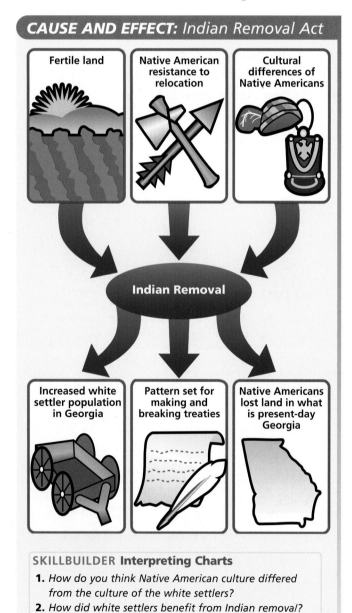

CAUSE AND EFFECT: *Indian Removal Act*

Fertile land

Native American resistance to relocation

Cultural differences of Native Americans

Indian Removal

Increased white settler population in Georgia

Pattern set for making and breaking treaties

Native Americans lost land in what is present-day Georgia

SKILLBUILDER Interpreting Charts

1. *How do you think Native American culture differed from the culture of the white settlers?*
2. *How did white settlers benefit from Indian removal?*

have been different if the United States leadership had taken the time to understand the Cherokee perspective?

The Cost of Removal There are different accounts of the number of Native Americans who died on the Trail of Tears. Government records taken at the time record the number of Cherokee deaths at only 500. Records of missionaries who accompanied the Cherokee put the number at close to 4,000. This figure is generally accepted as accurate.

The cost was high for the Cherokee, and their removal is one of the most tragic chapters in Georgia and American history. The Cherokee removal was part of a larger pattern of moving Native Americans from their homelands to locations farther west where it was assumed white settlers would not go. The Indian Removal Act of 1830 made specific promises that the land given to the Native Americans west of the Mississippi would be theirs forever.

> **PRIMARY SOURCE**
>
> . . . it shall be lawful for the President solemnly to assure the tribe or nation. . . . that the United States will forever secure and guaranty to them, . . . the country so exchanged with them, ...
>
> Indian Removal Act of 1830, Chap. CXLVIII, Sec. 3

As you will learn in the next chapter, white settlers continued their push west. As a result, the pattern of promises made and promises broken would force Native Americans to move farther west, often onto reservations.

Section 2 Assessment

1. TERMS & NAMES

Explain the significance of:

a. Indian Removal Act

b. *Cherokee Nation* v. *Georgia*

c. *Worcester* v. *Georgia*

d. Treaty Party

e. Treaty of New Echota

f. Trail of Tears

2. TAKING NOTES

Use a chart like the one below to note reasons Georgians believed the Native Americans should leave, and why the Cherokee believed they were entitled to stay on their land.

Georgia's Reasons
1.
2.
Cherokee Reasons
1.
2.

3. MAIN IDEAS

a. What was President Jefferson's plan for Native American removal?

b. Why did Georgians claim the Cherokee Nation was unconstitutional?

c. Why didn't the Cherokee leave Georgia as soon as the Indian Removal Act was passed?

4. CRITICAL THINKING

Recognizing Effects

What were some economic effects of the Indian Removal Act on Native Americans? On whites?

Think About

• what the Native Americans lost

• what the white settlers gained

Geography/Math Draw a **map** of the Trail of Tears or create a **chart** with statistics on the distance and the survival rates of the Cherokee people.

The Cherokee Nation

First Cherokee law and Light Horse Guard are established.
1808

1819
National Council tells the United States that the Cherokee will cede no more land.

1821
Sequoyah produces Cherokee alphabet.

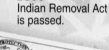

1822
Cherokee establish a supreme court.

1827
Cherokee Nation writes a constitution defining boundaries of the nation. John Ross becomes principal chief.

1828
Cherokee Phoenix is published. Gold is discovered in Georgia mountains. Andrew Jackson is elected president.

1830
Indian Removal Act is passed.

1831
Supreme Court rules in *Cherokee Nation* v. *Georgia*.

1832
Supreme Court rules in *Worcester* v. *Georgia*.

1835
Treaty Party negotiates Treaty of New Echota.

Cherokee travel the Trail of Tears.
1838–1839

TERMS & NAMES

Briefly explain the significance of the following.

1. Sequoyah
2. *Cherokee Phoenix*
3. New Echota
4. Elias Boudinot
5. Light Horse Guard
6. John Ross
7. Indian Removal Act
8. *Cherokee Nation* v. *Georgia*
9. Treaty Party
10. Trail of Tears

REVIEW QUESTIONS

The Cherokee (pages 197–202)

1. Why did the Cherokee originally settle in northern Georgia?
2. Why did the Cherokee abandon their ruling council?
3. Why did the U.S. government try to civilize the Cherokee?
4. According to the government, what did it mean to "civilize" the Cherokee?
5. What was the role of Indian agents?

Indian Removal (pages 203–209)

6. How did Georgians respond to the creation of the Cherokee Nation and their constitution?
7. What was the Treaty of New Echota?
8. How did most Cherokee respond to the Treaty of New Echota?
9. What mistakes did the federal government make in dealing with the Cherokee?

CRITICAL THINKING

1. USING YOUR NOTES: ANALYZING POINTS OF VIEW

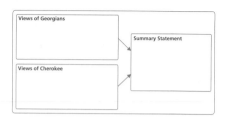

Using your completed chart, answer the questions below.

a. What laws, acts, and rulings supported the Georgians' view of the land?
b. What steps did the Cherokee take to establish their own nation?

2. ANALYZING LEADERSHIP

Evaluate the leadership of Andrew Jackson as it relates to the Cherokee. Was he a good leader for the country? Why or why not?

3. APPLYING CITIZENSHIP SKILLS

In what ways did the Cherokee laws and government mirror the United States government?

4. THEME: ECONOMICS

What role did economics play in the removal of the Cherokee?

5. IDENTIFYING AND SOLVING PROBLEMS

Evaluate Georgia's solution to the problem of land ownership. Would another solution have been better? Support your answer.

INTERACT with HISTORY

Having read about the Cherokee Nation, would you have supported the views of most Georgians? Why or why not?

Use the graph and your knowledge of American history to answer questions 1 through 3.

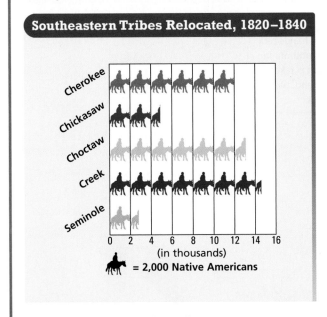

Southeastern Tribes Relocated, 1820–1840

Cherokee

Chickasaw

Choctaw

Creek

Seminole

0 2 4 6 8 10 12 14 16

(in thousands)

 = 2,000 Native Americans

1. What does the horse and rider image represent?

   A. Cherokee
   B. Chickasaw
   C. Creek
   D. 2,000 Native Americans

2. How many Cherokee people were relocated?

   A. 6,000
   B. 12,000
   C. 14,000
   D. 2,500

3. About how many Creek people were relocated?

   A. 7,000
   B. 8,000
   C. 12,000
   D. 14,500

TEST PRACTICE
CLASSZONE.COM

ALTERNATIVE ASSESSMENT

1. PREPARING A PROPOSAL

Plan and write a proposal outlining a solution to the problems between white settlers and Native Americans in Georgia in the 1800s. Brainstorm ideas. Then, identify the positives and negatives of each idea. Create your outline; write, revise, and make a final copy of your proposal. Present your proposal to the class and defend it.

2. COOPERATIVE LEARNING

Research the lives of the Cherokee in Georgia in the 1800s. Then work with your group to create an edition of the *Cherokee Phoenix.* Assign topics for articles based on your research. Remember what the newspaper featured.

- Laws of the nation
- Local and world news
- Human interest stories
- Bible passages
- Editorials and advertisements

Create graphics and design your pages. Publish the paper for your class.

INTEGRATED TECHNOLOGY ACTIVITY

PREPARE AN ELECTRONIC PRESENTATION

Use the Internet, your library, and a computer to prepare an electronic presentation that depicts the hardships of the Trail of Tears. Look for historical accounts, art, and articles that reveal what the journey was like for the Cherokee. Consider including the following items in your presentation.

- Maps of the trail
- Portraits
- Accounts of the journey
- Quotes from Jackson and other leaders

RESEARCH LINKS
CLASSZONE.COM

UNIT 3
CHAPTER
10

Antebellum Society 1800–1860

Section 1
Southern Culture

Section 2
Antebellum Society in Georgia

While overseers look on, field hands pick cotton on this antebellum plantation. In the background, picked cotton is taken to the cotton gin. In the foreground, baled cotton will be taken to market.

1793
Eli Whitney invents the cotton gin.

1801
Georgia's first university, Franklin College, is built.

1817
Georgia's legislature creates the poor school system.

GEORGIA
USA

1790

1808
Congress bans the African slave trade.

1812
War of 1812 disrupts U.S. shipping.

1820
Missouri Compromise balances the number of slave and free states.

It is 1825, and the Georgia economy is growing. Farmers are settling the western frontier. Cotton plantations are spreading. Textile mills are starting up. You are part of a commission determining what kinds of transportation Georgia should have as it grows.

How would you promote progress in Georgia?

WHAT DO YOU THINK?

- Would you recommend building canals and steamboats?

- Would you recommend building railroads?

For more information on this chapter, visit . . .

RESEARCH LINKS
CLASSZONE.COM

1837
First stake of the Western & Atlantic Railroad is driven.

1847
Atlanta, Georgia is incorporated.

1825

1860

1831
Nat Turner leads slave rebellion in Virginia.

1849
California gold rush begins.

1860
Abraham Lincoln is elected president.

CHAPTER 10

Reading Strategy: Taking Notes

What Do You Know?

What do you know about life in Georgia before the Civil War? What connects you to someone else who lives in Georgia?

THINK ABOUT

• what you've learned about life in the South before the Civil War from books, movies, historical fiction, or other classes

• how the economy and industry affect life in Georgia today

What Do You Want to Know?

What questions do you have about life in Georgia and the South before the Civil War? Record those questions in your notebook before you read the chapter.

Taking Notes

Writing down important ideas, names, dates, and events can help you remember more of what you read. A chart or an outline can help you organize your notes so you can use them to study in the future. Write notes from your reading related to the dates listed in the chart below.

S *See Skillbuilder Handbook, page 549.*

Taking Notes

Topic	Notes
Economy	
Transportation	
Education	
Society	

Southern Culture

MAIN IDEA	WHY IT MATTERS NOW	TERMS & NAMES

MAIN IDEA

The South had become a distinct region that was quite different from other regions in the United States by the 1850s.

WHY IT MATTERS NOW

The distinct culture that developed in the South during the early years of the 19th century still influences Southern life today.

TERMS & NAMES

antebellum
cotton gin
Terminus
poor school system

SETTING THE STAGE

As the United States grew, three distinct regions developed: the North, the South, and the West. They developed different economies, cultures, and even different patterns of speaking.

From the colony's founding in 1732 until the Civil War, Georgians focused on expanding their colony and becoming prosperous. They acquired land from the Native Americans and worked the land, often with enslaved people from Africa. **Antebellum** means "before the war." Antebellum society describes the culture that developed in the South before the Civil War, a society and culture that differed from other regions of the United States.

The antebellum society was based on cotton. Southern culture became very different from that of other regions. Would those differences prove to be helpful or harmful?

▲ In the Southern antebellum economy, cotton growers could sell as much as they could grow.

"Cotton Is King"

Georgia farms and plantations grew many crops, but "Cotton is King" was a popular phrase. English textile mills created a huge demand for Southern cotton. In the late 1700s, farmers grew Sea Island cotton on the islands off the coast of Georgia and South Carolina. Most Georgia farmers, however, grew short-staple cotton. Short-staple cotton was easier to grow, but it had a sticky, green seed that was difficult to remove.

In 1793, Eli Whitney designed a machine that would change that— the **cotton gin.** Whitney was working for Mrs. Catherine Greene, widow of Revolutionary War general Nathaniel Greene. Mrs. Greene was struggling to make her plantation profitable. Cleaning the cotton, or removing the seed, was a lengthy process. A worker could clean just one pound of this cotton in a day. Using a cotton gin, a worker could

Taking Notes

Use your chart to make notes about the growth of the Southern culture.

Topic	Notes
Economy	

In Whitney's cotton gin, cotton was fed through a row of saw blades. The saw's teeth pulled the cotton—but not the seeds—through a metal grill. Brushes removed clean cotton fiber caught on the saw's teeth.

clean as much as 50 pounds of cotton a day. As a result, many more planters began growing cotton.

The Cotton Boom

The cotton gin and the resulting cotton boom led the South to focus on agriculture. This focus set it on a different path from the industrial growth of the North and affected Southern life in several important ways.

Cotton was a valuable crop because it was easy to sell and commanded high prices. Since demand was high, planters could sell as much as they raised. Planters began to grow more cotton than other crops. Cotton exports increased, and the South's dependence on cotton began.

As cotton became easier and more profitable to grow, cotton farming moved away from the coastal regions. Georgia farmers demanded that the state and federal governments follow through on their promises to acquire land belonging to the Creek and Cherokee in western Georgia. This forced more Native Americans off their land.

Growing cotton required a large work force, so slavery continued to be an important source of labor in the South. As farmers planted more fields with cotton, they needed more slaves to work them. Many slaves were sold south and west to the newly established cotton plantations.

Slavery Expands   Cotton production rose steeply from 1790 to 1860. The number of enslaved people in the South also increased. In 1820, the South earned $22 million from cotton exports. By the late 1830s, earnings from cotton exports were nearly ten times greater, close to $200 million.

As cotton earnings rose, so did the price of slaves. A male field hand sold for $300 in the 1790s. By the late 1830s, the price had jumped to $1,000. After 1808, when it became illegal to import Africans for use as slaves, the trading of slaves already in the country increased.

Difficulties with Farming

Many Georgia farmers did not use the mechanical inventions available for farming. Part of the reason was that they had no money to invest in equipment. The primary piece of farm equipment was the hoe used to thin the cotton plants and cut the weeds from among the cotton plants. The one-mule cottonseed planter was about the only improvement to their equipment.

Reading History

A. Recognizing Effects What impact did the cotton gin have on the South?

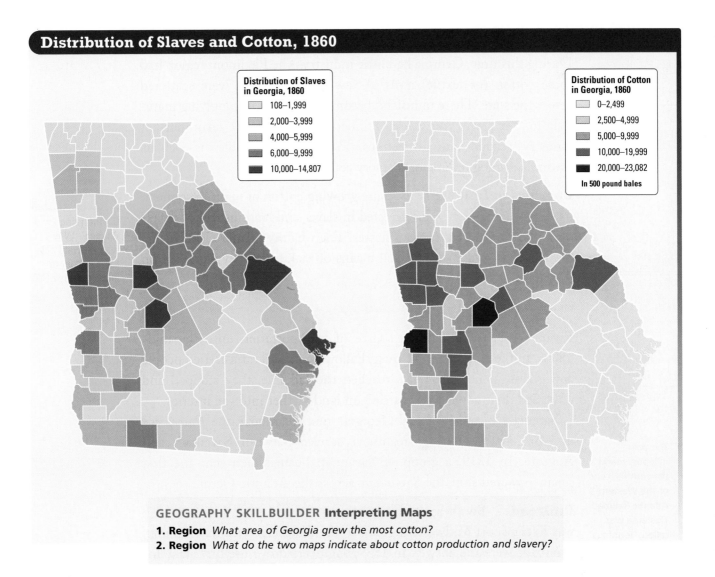

Distribution of Slaves in Georgia, 1860

- 108–1,999
- 2,000–3,999
- 4,000–5,999
- 6,000–9,999
- 10,000–14,807

Distribution of Cotton in Georgia, 1860

- 0–2,499
- 2,500–4,999
- 5,000–9,999
- 10,000–19,999
- 20,000–23,082

In 500 pound bales

GEOGRAPHY SKILLBUILDER Interpreting Maps

1. **Region** *What area of Georgia grew the most cotton?*
2. **Region** *What do the two maps indicate about cotton production and slavery?*

Soil Exhaustion Georgia farmers also dealt with the problem of soil exhaustion. They planted the same crop year after year, which took important nutrients for growing plants out of the soil. Farmers referred to this soil as "exhausted" because it could no longer grow crops. To find fresh soil, planters established plantations farther and farther west. Cotton production gradually shifted west into Alabama, Louisiana, and Texas. By the 1850s, some of the wealthier farmers had started using bird droppings known as guano, imported from South America, as a fertilizer. But this was too expensive for most small farmers to use.

Crop Failures Georgians soon relied too much on cotton. When they made money on cotton, they used it to buy more land to grow cotton and more slaves to work the land. They did not borrow money to expand their farming operations. When their crops failed, they had no credit record. They could not prove that they could repay a loan. So when crops failed, so did many of Georgia's farms. In 1828, the state established the Central Bank of Georgia to loan money to smaller farmers.

Industry in Georgia

During this time, Georgia had little industry. The Piedmont region had some cotton (or textile) mills. A few iron industries were scattered across the state. These industries became important in supplying materials for the Civil War cause. Timber continued to be an important industry, second only to textiles. Flour and gristmills, as well as sawmills, sprang up in almost every county.

Barriers to Industry   Because growing cotton brought in so much money, wealthy Georgians invested in slaves and land instead of developing new industries and businesses. The wealthy planter class had no need to change their traditional means of making money while cotton growing was still profitable.

Reading History

B. Analyzing Causes   Why was growing cotton a barrier to industrial growth?

Transportation in Georgia

Rivers were Georgia's main source of transportation until the mid-1800s. In the state's early history, shallow boats and rafts carried people and goods. When the boats reached the fall line, they stopped and unloaded their goods to be carried on land farther into the interior.

Samuel Howard launched Georgia's first steamboat, the *Enterprise*, in April 1816, offering steamboat service between Savannah and Augusta. In 1819, a group of Savannah businessmen sent the first steam-powered ship, the *Savannah*, across the Atlantic Ocean.

Railroads   Southern business owners realized that they needed a way to transport Midwestern goods to the Southern coast for shipping. Railroads were the answer. In 1837, engineers drove the first stake for the Western and Atlantic Railroad (W&A). They placed a stake on a ridge about seven miles east of the Chattahoochee River. That point, called **Terminus,** was the beginning of modern-day Atlanta. By 1860, all but two of the South's major railroads passed through Atlanta. As a result, Atlanta was called "the Gate City."

Education in Georgia

The Georgia legislature authorized charters for some private academies of learning as early as 1783. Wealthy families would send their children to these academies to learn English, math, science, and Latin.

Public School Systems   Despite a national public education movement in the mid-1800s, Georgia did not develop a strong public school system until later. Most Georgians felt it was the family's responsibility to educate children. In 1817, the Georgia legislature created the **poor school system** to educate needy children, mainly boys. Poor schools taught three years of basic reading, writing, and math.

▼ The zero milepost marks the southern end of the Western & Atlantic Railroad. This area was called "Terminus" and was renamed Atlanta in 1845. The milepost is now in Underground Atlanta.

Many Georgians, however, were too embarrassed to send their children to a state-funded poor school. If they were able, they preferred to pay tuition to send them to old field schools in the community. These schools also offered a very basic education, but only for a few months of the year when children were not needed on the farm.

Higher Education The state's first public university, Franklin College in Athens, now the University of Georgia, was chartered in 1785. It was the first state university in the nation. John Milledge donated 633 acres of land as a site for the campus, which opened in 1801. Women were first permitted to enroll in 1918.

Formal training for medical doctors was new in America in the 1800s. Augusta established the Medical College of Georgia in 1828.

The first women's college in the nation was Georgia Female College, later called Wesleyan Female College. It was one of many colleges at the time that were supported by a religious organization, in this case the Georgia Conference of the Methodist Episcopal Church. The school first opened its doors in Macon in 1839 to 90 students, most of whom took courses in the sciences—very progressive for the 1800s.

Religion

The South was swept up in a religious movement known as the Great Revival in its antebellum years. Church membership across the country was higher than ever before. Camp meetings attracted and converted thousands of people, black and white, who spent days listening to the fiery sermons of Protestant ministers.

Most enslaved workers were forced to adopt the Christian religion when they arrived in America. Slaveholders believed that religion helped them to control their slaves. But it served a different role for the enslaved people. They identified with the Bible story of the children of Israel who were held in bondage by Egypt's king and who were eventually led to freedom.

Reform in Georgia

The spirit of the times across the nation called for improvements in the welfare of its citizens. Georgia also enacted reforms that improved the lives of criminals, the mentally ill and physically challenged, as well as children who were blind or deaf.

In 1816, Georgia passed laws to improve the treatment of criminals. Georgia's county jails were required for the first time to provide clothing, blankets, heat, and medical attention to their inmates.

Prior to this time of reform, mentally ill people, as well as those challenged by Down's syndrome and those who had epileptic seizures, were subject to sometimes-brutal treatment, including imprisonment. In 1842, Georgia built a more humane "insane" asylum in Milledgeville to house its mentally ill. It was the largest facility of its kind in the world.

Cave Springs, Georgia, became the site of a school for deaf persons in 1847. In 1852, the state built the Georgia Academy for the Blind in Macon. Both schools remain in operation today.

Reading History

C. Recognizing Effects How did reformers change the treatment of prisoners, the disabled, and the mentally ill?

Georgia's Cities

In 1860, Savannah was the largest Georgia city with 22,000 people. Augusta was the next largest with about 12,500 people. Columbus, Macon, and Atlanta had populations under 10,000. Over 90 percent of Georgia's people lived in rural areas or in small towns. In the next section, you will learn more about the kinds of people who lived in Georgia.

Section 1 Assessment

1. TERMS & NAMES

Explain the significance of:

a. antebellum

b. cotton gin

c. Terminus

d. poor school system

2. TAKING NOTES

Use a diagram like the one shown below to note the difficulties faced by Georgia farmers and one effect each difficulty had on efficient cotton production.

Difficulty	Effect on Production

3. MAIN IDEAS

a. What is one reason that Georgia was behind other states in establishing public education?

b. How did the invention of the cotton gin affect Georgia?

c. Why was the development of a railroad important to all regions of the United States?

4. CRITICAL THINKING

Forming and Supporting Opinions

What made the South's antebellum society a distinct culture, different from the rest of the United States?

Think About

• profits and demands of growing cotton

• rural populations

• lack of industry and education

Math/Technology Create a **graph** of cotton production or make a **storyboard** for a video on the problems of antebellum Georgia farmers' overdependence on cotton.

Antebellum Society in Georgia

MAIN IDEA	WHY IT MATTERS NOW	TERMS & NAMES

MAIN IDEA

Antebellum Georgia developed distinct social classes based largely on race and partly on economic opportunity.

WHY IT MATTERS NOW

We can use the experiences of 1850 Georgia to make sure that we do not repeat the same social and economic mistakes of that period.

TERMS & NAMES

planter
plantation
overseer

yeoman farmer
field hand
house slave

SETTING THE STAGE

While the South had become a distinct region by 1850, there were differences within the South and within Georgia. Whites and African Americans lived differently from each other. In addition, wealthy white planters lived differently from white yeoman farmers. There was very little mixing among the social classes.

Racism is the belief by some that people of one race are superior to those of another. This belief had crept into colonial America along with the first Africans forcibly carried to its shores.

The system of slavery changed the economy of the South. It changed the people who lived within it even more. How would social classes affect the development of the state? How would they affect the people within each class?

▲ The cotton gin made growing cotton more profitable.

The Old South

Georgia, like other Southern states, was divided into different social classes. Race was the most critical factor. No matter how poor or how uneducated white Georgians might be, they saw themselves as having higher social status than African Americans—whether free or enslaved. Even when African Americans became free or gained wealth, they were not considered to have the social status of whites.

Only about one fourth of the South's white population owned slaves. Most slave owners had one to ten slaves. A very small percentage of whites held most of the slave population. Owning slaves was a sign of wealth and political power.

Taking Notes

Use your chart to make notes about antebellum society in Georgia.

Topic	Notes
Economy	

Planters

Georgia's wealthy elite were called **planters**. Planters were those who owned 20 or more slaves to work on plantations. **Plantations** were large farms that extended over hundreds of acres. However, in 1860 fewer than 3,000 of Georgia's 600,000 white citizens could be called planters.

Most planters lived a comfortable life, although most of their money was in land and slaves. The typical plantation owner's house was more modest than the ornate mansions so often associated with the antebellum South. A planter's home was usually plain, unpainted, and simply furnished. The wealthiest planters built what was known as the "big house" decorated with furnishings imported from Europe.

Plantations were actually small communities. They included cotton gins, barns, equipment sheds, blacksmith shops, and various other buildings. Housing for the laborers sat in one section of the plantation. The plantation was usually equipped to take care of most of the people who lived on it.

▼ The "big house" of a wealthy planter such as this house in Macon (top) was usually situated on a prime spot on the plantation. The house of a yeoman farmer (bottom) was usually made of logs.

Plantation owners frequently employed an **overseer,** who took charge of the farming operation. The owners lived in the towns and cities so their families could enjoy better social lives and education for their children. This practice was true especially in the coastal regions, where the plantation owners had an additional reason to live in the cities: to avoid the disease-carrying insects that were close to the swamps.

Planters were often well educated and involved in society. Many planters were community leaders and held positions in state or national government. They sent their children to private academies and then on to college with the expectation that they would become community leaders themselves.

Yeoman Farmers

Most whites in Georgia were yeoman farmers. A **yeoman farmer** is one who owns a few acres of land and grows crops on them. These farmers lived in the pine barrens of the Coastal Plain and the Piedmont regions of the state. Some owned a few slaves, some did not own any, and others rented their farms from larger landowners. Eventually a few became wealthy enough to become a part of the planter class. But most just hoped to own enough land and property to provide a good life for their families.

Reading History

A. Drawing Conclusions
Why did yeoman farmers have to be resourceful?

Yeoman farmers had to be very resourceful. A family would hunt, trap, own livestock, and grow food as well as cash crops in order to survive. Most practiced free-range herding. This meant that they marked their cattle and then let them roam the open range to find food.

They often cleared spots in the forests to grow corn. The corn provided food for the families and fodder for the livestock. In some case, they distilled the corn into liquor for another source of income. Livestock and corn provided the basis for the life and culture of those who lived on the frontier.

Georgia's small farmers lived in rural neighborhoods called settlements. Many times families stayed close together. They built split-rail fences, barns, smokehouses, and chicken pens. Settlements usually appeared at a crossroads area. Mills, stores, and churches also appeared at the crossroads. In many cases, the county seat was located there. People would come there to conduct their legal business as well as shop, trade, vote, and visit.

Poor Whites   Poor whites did not own land and often hired themselves out to landowners and business owners. They lived at the subsistence level, barely getting by in terms of food, clothing, and shelter. By 1860, many of them had moved to towns to work in textile mills.

Vocabulary

subsistence: the lowest level of survival

DAILY LIFE

Backcountry Speech
The people who lived in frontier regions maintained a different speech from those in other regions. They kept many of the patterns of their ancestors from the Highlands of Scotland.

They might speak of "biling" (boiling) a pot of water, hearing a "sarment" (sermon) on Sunday, looking out the "winder" (window), wearing a "yaller" (yellow) dress, or using "pizen" (poison) to kill insects.

They also attached different meanings to some words, such as "fixin' to" for "getting ready to." Their speech included use of double negatives: "I don't have no meat."

Free African Americans

Reading History

B. Forming and Supporting Opinions Why would free African Americans remain in Georgia?

About 3,500 free African Americans lived in Georgia in 1850. Slaveholders freed many of them or they had purchased their freedom. They lived mainly in the towns where they could find work. In many places, they had to register, even though they were free. In some cases, free African Americans were kidnapped and returned to slavery.

Enslaved Africans

Enslaved Africans' lives depended on who they worked for and what they did. Slaveholders regarded slaves as property. Some slaveholders were cruel to their slaves; others tried to be kind.

Different Roles on a Plantation On a plantation, **field hands** plowed, hoed, and harvested the crops. They worked under a driver, another African American who was responsible for maintaining discipline among the workers.

On large cotton plantations, planters used the gang labor system. Under this system, slaves worked in a field together from sunup to sundown. Coastal rice plantations and tobacco plantations used the task system, in which slaves had specific jobs to do. After tasks were finished, they could turn to other activities, such as tending their own garden plots.

Enslaved African Americans with special skills worked as carpenters and blacksmiths. Sometimes slaveholders might hire them out to do work on other plantations. Occasionally a skilled worker would be allowed to keep part of the money earned. White laborers were resentful when planters hired slaves because that took jobs away from them.

Planters also used enslaved workers as **house slaves.** They cooked, cleaned, wove cloth, sewed clothing, made the goods the plantation needed, and cared for the plantation owner's children.

Life Under Slavery Most enslaved workers lived in the slave quarters, but some lived in servants' quarters in the planters' houses. They

Reading History

C. Compare and Contrast What were the differences between labor systems on cotton plantations and those on rice and tobacco plantations?

▼ A group of slaves gathers outside their quarters on a plantation on Cockspur Island, east of Savannah.

received rations of food and clothing from the storehouse on the plantation. Many enslaved families were allowed to have their own garden plots to grow food to feed themselves. Sometimes they were allowed to sell any surplus food and keep part of the money.

Teaching slaves to read and write was illegal, although some were taught and passed the knowledge on to others. These skills allowed them to help with the paperwork of the plantation and read the Bible.

Slaves could not legally marry, but many owners would recognize an informal marriage. This would not keep a couple together, however, since an owner could sell a slave at any time. The children of slaves were slaves as well. Husbands, wives, parents, and children were sold and separated throughout the South.

Resistance   Enslaved African Americans developed ways to protest their conditions. Some escaped to the North, which was very difficult to do. If they were caught, they would be severely punished to keep others from following. The most common way to protest was to work slowly, which also was punishable if the overseer or planter suspected.

The cotton boom changed the economy of the South. But slavery affected all the people who lived there. While they needed more enslaved African Americans to work on the plantations, many white Georgians grew afraid of slave revolts. They enacted harsh slave codes to control slaves. In the next chapter, you will read more about how the issue of slavery created problems between the North and the South.

Section 2 Assessment

1. TERMS & NAMES
Explain the significance of:

a. planters

b. plantations

c. overseer

d. yeoman farmers

e. field hands

f. house slaves

2. TAKING NOTES
Create a chart like this one. Then fill in a key fact about Georgia's yeoman farmers under each category.

Yeoman Farmers	
Location	
Ancestry	
Economy	
Community	

3. MAIN IDEAS

a. Describe the three main classes of white society in 1850s Georgia.

b. Describe the hierarchy of importance within the slave community.

c. Describe some methods slaveowners used to control slaves.

4. CRITICAL THINKING
Solving Problems

How did slavery divide Georgia in the 1850s?

Think About
• economic opportunities
• social opportunities

 Language Arts/Speech   Write a **newspaper editorial** or give a **speech** that warns antebellum Georgians that their economic decisions will have long-lasting effects.

VISUAL SUMMARY

The Southern Economy, 1800 to 1860

CAUSES
- English textile mills generate demand for cotton.
- Cotton gin increases productivity.

EFFECT/CAUSE
Cotton Boom

EFFECTS
- Dependence on cotton
- Westward movement
- Native Americans forced off land
- Dependence on slavery
- Soil exhaustion
- Distinct social classes
- Little industry

TERMS & NAMES

Briefly explain the significance of the following.

1. antebellum
2. cotton gin
3. poor school system
4. old field schools
5. planters
6. plantations
7. overseer
8. yeoman farmers
9. field hands
10. house slaves

REVIEW QUESTIONS

Southern Culture (pages 215–220)

1. What role did Eli Whitney play in the cotton boom?
2. What difficulties did Georgia farmers face?
3. How did the cotton boom affect industry in Georgia?
4. What was Terminus?
5. Why did slaves identify with the children of Israel?
6. What were Georgia's five major cities in 1860?

Antebellum Society in Georgia (pages 221–225)

7. What social classes were present in the South?
8. What factor was most critical in determining social class?
9. Where did most plantation owners live? Why?
10. What was free-range herding?

CRITICAL THINKING

1. USING YOUR NOTES: TAKING NOTES

Topic	Notes
Economy	
Transportation	
Education	
Society	

Using your completed chart, answer the questions below.

a. What were two primary sources of transportation in Georgia at this time?

b. Was education a high priority in Georgia at this time? Why or why not?

2. ANALYZING LEADERSHIP

Planters held the leading role in Southern society. Do you think they exercised their role responsibly? Why or why not?

3. APPLYING CITIZENSHIP SKILLS

What was the relationship between social class and citizenship in the South?

4. THEME: SCIENCE AND TECHNOLOGY

How did the invention of the cotton gin shape Southern society?

5. FORMING AND SUPPORTING OPINIONS

Did the cotton gin make a positive contribution to Southern life? Why or why not?

INTERACT *with* HISTORY

If you had lived in antebellum Georgia, how would you have worked to promote progress in the state?

Use the chart and your knowledge of American history to answer questions 1 through 3.

Cotton Production, 1800–1860

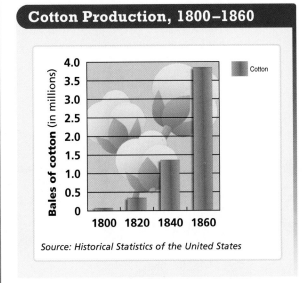

Source: Historical Statistics of the United States

1. How much cotton was produced in 1860?
   - A. 375,000 pounds
   - B. 375,000 bales
   - C. 3.75 tons
   - D. 3.75 million bales

2. How did cotton production change between 1840 and 1860?
   - A. It increased 3.5%
   - B. It increased 3.5 million bales
   - C. It increased ten times
   - D. It increased 2.5 million bales

3. How did cotton production change between 1820 and 1840?
   - A. It increased 50%
   - B. It increased 1.0%
   - C. It increased 1.0 million bales
   - D. It increased 1.0 tons

TEST PRACTICE
CLASSZONE.COM

ALTERNATIVE ASSESSMENT

1. DIAGRAMMING A PROCESS

Research the process of producing a new cotton sweater. Include these phases: farming the cotton, processing the cotton, and weaving the fabric. Diagram the complete process, and present the process to the class.

2. COOPERATIVE LEARNING

As a team, develop a series of monologues on antebellum life from the perspective of people from different Southern social classes. Research the lives of people who lived during the period. Then assign the parts, develop your characters, and write first-person narratives. Present your monologues to the class.

INTEGRATED TECHNOLOGY ACTIVITY

PREPARING AN ELECTRONIC EXHIBIT

Use the Internet, your library, and a computer to prepare an electronic exhibit to show what slavery was like on cotton plantations. Research different topics, including the items listed below.

- What people wore
- What their houses were like
- What rules they lived under
- What stories they told
- What songs they sang

Part of your exhibit might be a virtual model of a plantation or recordings of slave narratives.

RESEARCH LINKS
CLASSZONE.COM

The Road to Disunion 1780s–1860

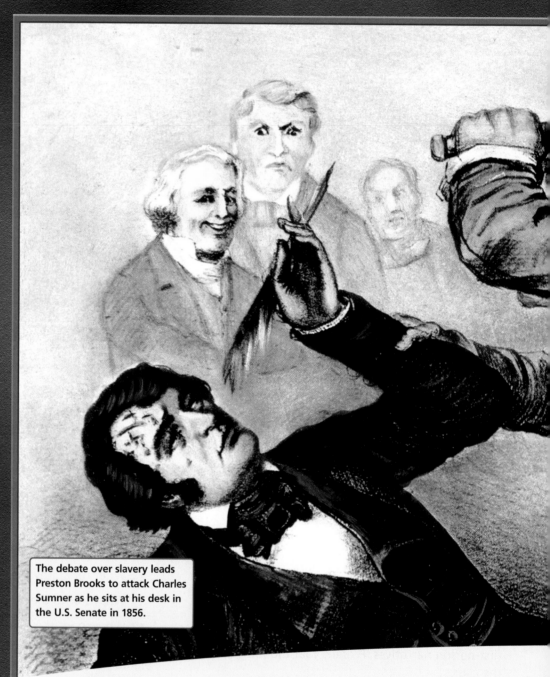

The debate over slavery leads Preston Brooks to attack Charles Sumner as he sits at his desk in the U.S. Senate in 1856.

1788
Georgia becomes the fourth state to ratify the U.S. Constitution

1817
First Seminole war begins.

GEORGIA USA 1780

1800

1820

1783
The American Revolution ends

1808
Congress bans the slave trade.

1820
Missouri Compromise balances number of slave and free states.

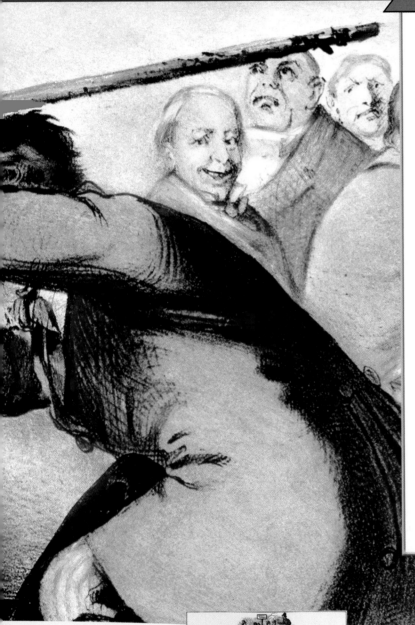

You are a member of Congress in the 1850s. Tensions are running high over the issue of slavery. People are turning to violence, unable to discuss their differences reasonably. Violence has broken out in a few states and even in the halls of Congress. You worry that soon violence will spread across the country.

How would you keep the nation together?

WHAT DO YOU THINK?

- Why did people feel so strongly about slavery?

- Do you think debates, such as those between Lincoln and Douglas, can settle emotional issues without leading to violence?

For more information on this chapter, visit . . .

RESEARCH LINKS
CLASSZONE.COM

1831
William Lloyd Garrison begins publishing *The Liberator*.

1860
The state of Georgia calls for a convention to discuss a Southern Confederacy.

1861
Georgia seizes Fort Pulaski.

1840

1860

1828
Tariff of Abominations signed into law. Andrew Jackson elected president.

1846
Wilmot Proviso is introduced.

1854
Congress passes the Kansas-Nebraska Act.

1861
The Confederate States of America is formed.

CHAPTER 11

Reading Strategy: Summarizing

What Do You Know?

What do you think about when you hear the terms *slavery* and *abolition*? Why do you think the issue of slavery caused so much anger and resentment?

THINK ABOUT

• what you've learned about the differences between the North and the South from books, travel, television, or movies

• reasons people have violent conflicts today

What Do You Want to Know?

What questions do you have about the causes of the Civil War? Record those questions in your notebook before you read the chapter.

Summarizing

Using your own words to write main ideas and important details as you read can help you remember more of what you read. To summarize, restate each main idea you find, along with any important supporting details or facts. In the diagram below, summarize the main ideas and facts related to each issue.

 See Skillbuilder Handbook, page 549.

Taking Notes

Main Ideas	Facts
Tariff of Abominations	
Northwest Ordinance of 1787	
Missouri Compromise	
Wilmot Proviso	
Compromise of 1850	
Kansas-Nebraska Act	

Growing Sectional Differences

There was a difference of opinion about the role of the federal government in the affairs of each state.

Americans still disagree today about the role of the federal government in state affairs.

sectionalism
Tariff of Abominations
secede

nullify
states' rights

SETTING THE STAGE

In the first half of the 19th century, the Northern and Southern parts of the new nation were growing apart. They differed in the ways they made a living. They differed socially. And they differed in their political views.

Southerners were concerned about the federal government trying to tell individual states what to do. Could the federal government force states to obey federal laws? Did the federal government have the right to decide how the territories would be governed? Did each state have the right to determine which federal laws to obey and which to ignore?

▲ As the North and South grew apart, the future of the nation began to look uncertain. These differences would eventually lead to the South breaking from the Union.

States' Rights

While nationalism united the country, sectionalism threatened to drive it apart. **Sectionalism** is loyalty to the concerns of your own region or section of the country, rather than to the nation as a whole. One issue that ignited strong feelings of sectionalism was tariffs. Tariffs are taxes on items coming from other countries.

Tariff of Abominations   In 1828, Northern manufacturers asked Congress for help. They could not compete against British factory owners who sold their products for less than the Americans. Congress helped by passing a tariff. This tariff helped the North but hurt the South. People in the South bought many goods from other countries. The tariff raised prices on many of the items they bought. Southern cotton growers feared that the British might respond by buying cotton elsewhere. Opponents called it the **Tariff of Abominations.** An abomination is something that is greatly disliked or horrible.

Taking Notes

Use your diagram to summarize the main ideas and facts related to the Tariff of Abominations.

Main Ideas	Facts
Tariff of Abominations	

Nullification Crisis Leaders in South Carolina were especially unhappy with the Tariff of Abominations. Their economy was in a slump, and the new tariff made it even worse. They threatened to **secede,** or leave the Union. John C. Calhoun from South Carolina was Andrew Jackson's vice-president. Calhoun did not want South Carolina to secede. He believed that a state had the right to **nullify,** or reject, a federal law.

Certain privileges that states possess to govern themselves without interference from the federal government are called **states' rights.** Calhoun believed that Congress had no right to impose a tariff that favored one section of the country over another.

Reading History

A. Identifying Problems What problems was the federal government trying to solve by charging tariffs on some goods?

ECONOMICS *in* HISTORY

How Tariffs Work

Tariffs are taxes added to the cost of goods imported from another country. There are two kinds of tariffs—revenue tariffs and protective tariffs. **Revenue tariffs** are used to raise money for the government, like the sales taxes that states add to what we buy today. These tariffs tend to be fairly low. **Protective tariffs** are usually much higher. They have another goal: to persuade consumers to buy goods made in their own country instead of purchasing foreign-made products. Congress passed a protective tariff in 1828 to help companies.

The illustration shows how a protective tariff works. A British-made teapot sells for $3.50, and a similar teapot made in the United States sells for $4.00. Most shoppers will buy the British teapot and save 50 cents. But when the government adds a 40% tariff to British goods, the price of the British teapot soars to $4.90. The result: consumers buy the now-cheaper American teapots.

CONNECT TO HISTORY
1. **Recognizing Effects** What problems did the tariffs cause for Southerners?

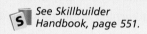 *See Skillbuilder Handbook, page 551.*

CONNECT TO TODAY
2. **Making Inferences** Today, many leaders around the world promote the idea of "free trade." What do you think "free trade" means?

For more about tariffs . . .

 **RESEARCH LINKS** CLASSZONE.COM

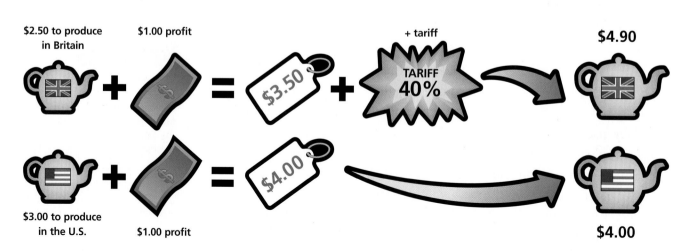

$2.50 to produce in Britain $1.00 profit   + tariff $4.90

TARIFF 40%

$3.00 to produce in the U.S. $1.00 profit $4.00

Reading History

B. Summarizing
How did the issue of tariffs threaten to tear the Union apart?

President Jackson opposed nullification, but he did not want South Carolina to leave the Union. Other Southern states disliked the tariff, but they did not support nullification, either. The Georgia legislature sent a message with their stand on nullification.

> **PRIMARY SOURCE**
>
> We abhor the doctrine of Nullification as neither a peaceful, nor a constitutional remedy, but, on the contrary, as tending to civil commotion and disunion.
>
> quoted in *The Development of Southern Sectionalism*, by Charles Sydnor

Other Southern states refused to support South Carolina's threats.

President Jackson was angry. He declared that South Carolina's threat to nullify the tariffs was against the law. Jackson threatened to use force to make sure federal laws were obeyed and the Union held together.

Henry Clay of Kentucky found a solution. He convinced Congress to enact a new tariff called the Tariff of 1833. It imposed a lower tariff over a ten-year period. South Carolina withdrew its threat of nullification. The issue of states' rights had pushed the nation close to a crisis, but for the moment, cooler heads prevailed. In the next section, you will read about another, ultimately more divisive issue—slavery.

▲ **People sewed the palmetto emblem to their clothing to show their support for nullification. The palmetto is a South Carolina symbol.**

Section 1 Assessment

1. TERMS & NAMES
Explain the significance of:

a. sectionalism

b. Tariff of Abominations

c. secede

d. nullify

e. states' rights

2. TAKING NOTES

Use a diagram like the one below to note the arguments used against the Tariff of Abominations.

Tariff Opponents' Arguments
1.
2.

3. MAIN IDEAS

a. Why was a tariff harder on Southern states than on Northern states?

b. Explain what the concept of states' rights includes.

c. What convinced South Carolina to withdraw its threat to secede from the Union?

4. CRITICAL THINKING
Recognizing Effects

How would the doctrine of nullification make it difficult for the federal government to operate?

Think About
- its effect on the enforcement of laws
- its effect on the power of the federal government

ACTIVITY -OPTIONS-   **Language Arts/Speech**   Write a one-page **position paper** on the pros and cons of a tariff that is in effect today, or hold a **press conference** about the issue.

2

The Issue of Slavery

MAIN IDEA	WHY IT MATTERS NOW	TERMS & NAMES
The government allowed slavery in more areas of the nation.	The issue over the expansion of slavery caused bitter disputes between the North and South.	Missouri Compromise Wilmot Proviso abolition California gold rush

SETTING THE STAGE

The United States greatly expanded its territory westward during the first half of the 1800s. Slavery was an issue whenever the government added a new territory. It emerged when a territory applied for statehood. Would the territory be brought into the Union as a slave state or a free state?

Upsetting the balance of slave states and free states in Congress would give one side or the other a political advantage. Free states would lose power in Congress if a slave state were added. If a free state were added, slave states would lose power. The nation needed to find a solution.

▲ After the Louisiana Purchase in 1803, Americans began to move west. With each new territory, the balance between slave and free states was threatened.

Early Compromises over Slavery

In the 1770s and early 1780s, Northern states started to pass laws ending slavery. Vermont, Massachusetts, and Connecticut, for example, passed laws that abolished slavery or provided for the gradual emancipation of slaves who resided in those states. As a result, there was a growing division between Northern and Southern states about slavery.

Compromises in the Constitution The framers of the Constitution included several compromises over the issue in 1787. They did not use the term "slaves" in the Constitution. Instead, they used the phrase "other persons."

One compromise occurred when Georgia and South Carolina refused to join the Union until it was agreed that Congress would not end the slave trade until 1808. Another compromise, the Three-Fifths Compromise, gave the South greater representation in Congress by agreeing to count slaves as part of the population. The Constitution also dealt with the issue of slaves who escaped. A clause in the Constitution

Taking Notes

Use your diagram to summarize the main ideas and facts related to the Northwest Ordinance, Missouri Compromise, and the Wilmot Proviso.

Main Ideas	Facts
Tariff of Abominations	

required that states had to return runaway slaves to the state where they escaped.

Slavery in New Territories   Slavery became an issue whenever a new territory was added to the United States. The Northwest Ordinance of 1787 outlined how the Northwest Territory would be managed. Slavery was not allowed in this area, which included the current states of Ohio, Indiana, Illinois, Wisconsin, and part of Minnesota.

In 1790, another compromise, the Southwest Ordinance, allowed slavery in new territories south of the Ohio River. The ordinance established how the territory south of the Ohio River and between the Mississippi River and the Appalachian Mountains would be organized. This area later became the states of Kentucky, Tennessee, and Alabama.

The Missouri Compromise

In 1808, the federal law came into effect that ended the foreign slave trade. Many people believed that without a steady flow of Africans coming into the country, slavery would eventually die out. However, no one could predict that British textile mills would need a tremendous amount of cotton from the South. Slaveholders from Southern states moved west looking for new land to grow more cotton. They needed slave labor to do that.

In 1819, residents of the Missouri territory asked to enter the Union as a slave state. If Missouri was admitted as a slave state, it would upset the balance in Congress and make the South stronger politically. At the time, the nation had 11 slave states and 11 free states. Missouri, as a slave state, would give the pro-slavery forces an advantage in Congress. Northern congressmen tried to block Missouri's admission. Southern congressmen argued that Congress had no power to prevent it from entering the Union.

In 1820, Henry Clay of Kentucky proposed a two-part solution called the **Missouri Compromise.** First, Maine was admitted as a free state and Missouri was admitted as a slave state. Second, slavery was prohibited in the Louisiana territory north of the 36°30' line of latitude. Only a small portion of land was south of that line. Much more land was north of the line, and this land could be divided into free states. This part of the Missouri Compromise created problems later.

Reading History

A. Finding Main Ideas Why did the institution of slavery continue to grow after the law forbade any further importation of slaves?

Reading History

B. Summarizing What were the terms of the Missouri Compromise?

NOW & THEN

Liberia

In 1817, the American Colonization Society formed to promote the idea of returning slaves to Africa. William H. Crawford of Georgia, James Madison, and President James Monroe helped organize the society. The society established a colony on the coast of Africa and named it Liberia.

One Liberian village was named New Georgia. About 1,200 Georgia slaves were freed and sent to Liberia. A descendant of a former Georgia slave became president of the Republic of Liberia in the 1940s.

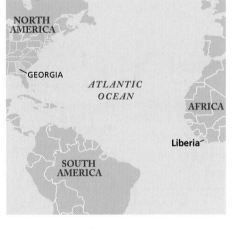

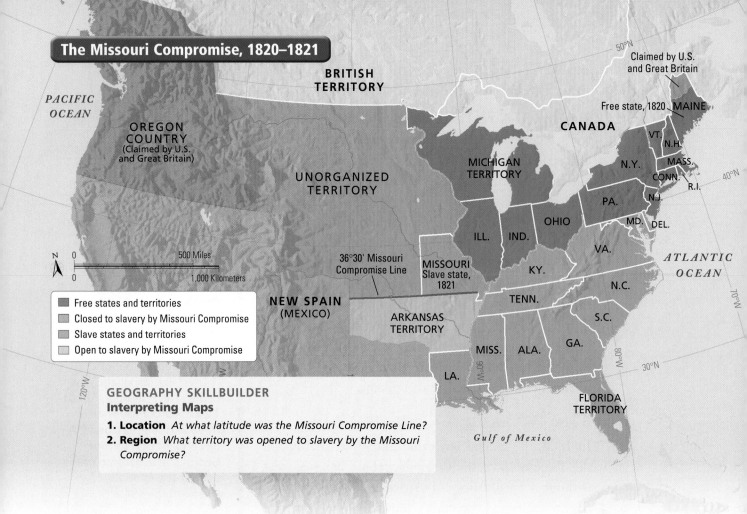

The Missouri Compromise, 1820–1821

BRITISH TERRITORY

Claimed by U.S. and Great Britain

PACIFIC OCEAN

OREGON COUNTRY
(Claimed by U.S. and Great Britain)

UNORGANIZED TERRITORY

Free state, 1820 MAINE

CANADA

MICHIGAN TERRITORY

VT.
N.H.
N.Y.
MASS.
CONN.
R.I.
PA.
N.J.
OHIO
MD.
DEL.
ILL. IND.
VA.

36°30' Missouri Compromise Line

MISSOURI
Slave state, 1821

KY.

ATLANTIC OCEAN

NEW SPAIN (MEXICO)

ARKANSAS TERRITORY

TENN.

N.C.

S.C.

N

0   500 Miles
0   1,000 Kilometers

Free states and territories
Closed to slavery by Missouri Compromise
Slave states and territories
Open to slavery by Missouri Compromise

MISS. ALA. GA.

LA.

FLORIDA TERRITORY

Gulf of Mexico

GEOGRAPHY SKILLBUILDER
Interpreting Maps

1. **Location** At what latitude was the Missouri Compromise Line?
2. **Region** What territory was opened to slavery by the Missouri Compromise?

Not everyone was convinced that the issue of slavery had been settled. One Georgia legislator warned, "We have kindled a fire which all the waters of the ocean cannot put out, which seas of blood can only extinguish." For the moment, however, both sides agreed to the compromise.

Critics of Slavery

One of the most important reform movements at this time was **abolition**. People who supported abolition, or abolitionists, demanded an end to slavery. In the 1830s, many antislavery groups formed. The most important was the American Anti-Slavery Society (AASS). This group demanded immediate emancipation of slaves. It also campaigned for equal rights for free African Americans. Southern slaveholders saw these groups as real threats.

There were many critics of slavery. Frederick Douglass had been enslaved. His persuasive writing and speaking skills won people over to the abolition movement. William Lloyd Garrison started his antislavery newspaper *The Liberator* in 1831. He also helped organize abolition groups like the AASS.

Reading History

C. Analyzing Points of View How would the Grimké sisters' background help them as abolitionist speakers?

Vocabulary

morality: standards of good or right behavior

Reading History

D. Summarizing What were some reasons Southerners used to defend slavery?

Some Southerners did not support slavery. Sarah and Angelina Grimké were sisters from South Carolina who were important leaders in the abolition movement. Hinton Rowan Helper was another Southerner who did not like slavery. He was less concerned about the morality of slavery. He believed that slavery was harmful to the Southern economy.

Defenders of Slavery

Southern slaveholders defended the institution of slavery, saying it was necessary to their economy. They also believed that slaves were nothing more than property. Some claimed that since the Bible did not condemn slavery, it was not immoral.

By the 1850s, arguments for slavery were changing. Some claimed that people of African descent could not care for themselves in the modern world and needed slaveholders to protect and guide them. Georgian Thomas R. R. Cobb wrote a book in 1858 that defended slavery.

Another Southerner, George Fitzhugh, wrote a book arguing that the system of free labor in the North was a complete failure. He claimed that people working for wages in Northern factories were worse off than slaves living on the plantations. Fitzhugh believed slavery was a much better system.

HISTORY MAKERS

SARAH AND ANGELINA GRIMKÉ

Sarah Grimké (1792–1873) and her sister Angelina (1805–1879), were among the most influential abolitionists in the United States. The Grimké sisters were from a wealthy Southern aristocratic family, the daughters of a slaveholding judge in Charleston, South Carolina.

The Grimkés wrote numerous pamphlets and newspaper articles and spoke extensively throughout New England on the evils of slavery. Their pamphlets were publicly burned in South Carolina. There was a storm of protest at their "improper behavior," and the sisters were warned that they would be arrested if they ever returned home.

Westward Expansion and Slavery

As the United States grew westward, the conflict over slavery became even more divisive. Southern states became less agreeable to compromise.

War with Mexico   In 1845, the Republic of Texas asked to join the Union. The United States accepted. Mexico felt this was an act of aggression. War broke out between Mexico and the United States in April 1846. By 1848, the United States had defeated Mexico, which turned over a large area of land to the United States. Nine states later came from this territory: Arizona, California, Nevada, New Mexico, Utah, and portions of Colorado, Kansas, Oklahoma, and Wyoming.

Wilmot Proviso   In the early 1840s, the major political issues were banking, tariffs, roads, and land. After the United States had gone to war against Mexico, slavery became the issue again. Representative David Wilmot of Pennsylvania proposed the **Wilmot Proviso.** This law would forbid slavery in any territory acquired during the War with Mexico.

The Wilmot Proviso did not pass. But it did cause greater conflict over slavery. Many in the North believed that the South had supported the war to acquire new territory for the expansion of slavery. John C. Calhoun argued that allowing slavery in the new territories was a Constitutional right. Robert Toombs of Georgia warned Northern politicians that if they blocked the spread of slavery into new territories, he would support "disunion."

Reading History

E. Forming and Supporting Opinions Did the South support the War with Mexico to gain more slave territory?

The California Gold Rush   In early 1848, John A. Sutter discovered gold on his property in the California territory. This started the **California gold rush.** Within a year, thousands of people traveled to California to seek their fortunes in gold mining. Southern slaveholders arrived with their slaves to mine for gold. Most Californians did not want to compete for gold against slave labor.

California asked to be admitted to the Union as a free state. In 1849, there were 15 slave and 15 free states. Admitting California would put that balance of power at risk. Slavery as a political and moral issue was still a major problem, as you will read in the next section.

Section 2 Assessment

1. TERMS & NAMES

Explain the significance of:

a. Missouri Compromise

b. abolition

c. Wilmot Proviso

d. California gold rush

2. TAKING NOTES

Use a chart like the one below to note the effect of different political solutions on the distribution of slavery in the United States.

Slavery Territory Legislation	Date Enacted	Effect
Northwest Ordinance	1787	
Southwest Ordinance	1790	
Missouri Compromise	1820	
Wilmot Proviso	1846 (proposed)	

3. MAIN IDEAS

a. How did the framers of the Constitution handle the slavery issue?

b. What kept slavery strong after the 1808 law forbidding the importation of slaves?

c. How did westward expansion affect the conflict over slavery?

4. CRITICAL THINKING

Comparing and Contrasting

How was the Missouri Compromise similar to and different from the ordinances of 1787 and 1790?

Think About

• the regional tensions at the time the compromises were proposed

• the provisions of the compromises

Language Arts/Art   Research one of the abolitionist leaders or organizations. Write a short **biography** of that leader or design a **poster** for that organization.

3

The Southern States Secede

MAIN IDEA	WHY IT MATTERS NOW	TERMS & NAMES
Events in the 1850s led the Southern states, including Georgia, to secede.	This was the only time in U.S. history that states seceded from the Union.	Compromise of 1850 *Dred Scott* v. *Sandford* Underground Railroad Harpers Ferry popular sovereignty Abraham Lincoln Milledgeville Jefferson Davis

SETTING THE STAGE

By 1850, slavery was the most important issue in national politics. The debate grew louder and stronger throughout the decade. Supporters of slavery were convinced that the antislavery forces were winning.

Then Abraham Lincoln was elected president. Lincoln's election convinced many Southerners that compromise was no longer possible. Many Southern slaveholders and political leaders thought the only solution was to leave the Union. Was this the only solution? Could they reach a compromise? What would happen if some states left the Union?

The Compromise of 1850

Southerners were afraid that they were losing power and that the North was becoming more dominant. If California was admitted as a free state, it would throw off the balance of free and slave states in Congress.

Again, Henry Clay found a solution. It was called the **Compromise of 1850.** The compromise did these things:

- admitted California as a free state
- abolished slavery in the District of Columbia
- created a stronger fugitive slave law
- let the territories of New Mexico and Utah make their own decisions about slavery

John C. Calhoun of South Carolina criticized the Compromise of 1850. He insisted that the agricultural economy of the South was being neglected in favor of the more industrial and commercial interests of the Northern economy. Calhoun warned that the final result would be the end of the Union if a better solution could not be found.

▲ In his first inaugural address, Lincoln argued passionately for the North and the South to preserve the Union.

Taking Notes

Use your diagram to summarize the main ideas and facts related to the Compromise of 1850 and the Kansas-Nebraska Act.

Main Ideas	Facts
Tariff of Abominations	

The Georgia Platform   That year, Georgians held a convention to discuss the Compromise of 1850. They decided that secession was not the best way to preserve slavery and protect the state's rights at that time. The "Georgia Platform" outlined their support for the compromise and their concerns for the future. Delegates wanted to "preserve that Union which has extended the sway of republican government over a vast wilderness to another ocean, and proportionally advanced their civilization and national greatness." But secession remained a topic in Southern politics.

Fugitive Slave Act   Part of the Compromise of 1850 was the enactment of this federal law, which required the return of escaped slaves, no matter where they were captured. Under the Fugitive Slave Act, slaves could not free themselves by escaping to a territory or state where slavery was illegal. Any law enforcement official who did not arrest an escaped slave faced prosecution. Anyone who helped a slave to escape faced fines and imprisonment.

The provision requiring Northerners to help recapture slaves caused great anger. Outrage at this act caused Harriet Beecher Stowe to write *Uncle Tom's Cabin,* a novel that portrayed slavery as brutal and immoral. The book was wildly popular in the North. But white Southerners believed the book falsely criticized the South and slavery.

The Underground Railroad   Antislavery forces in the North collected money to help slaves make their way to freedom. They also set up a network of safe houses and hiding places. This network

◀ Harriet Tubman (above), an escaped slave, was a well-known guide on the Underground Railroad. Most slaves who escaped came from states bordering free states.

was called the **Underground Railroad.** Even though people could be jailed for helping slaves escape, many people volunteered to help. Harriet Tubman, a former slave, helped over 300 people escape to freedom.

Slaves from Georgia and other Southern states made their way to the Northern states. From there they could go to Canada and avoid capture. Some headed for Florida and hid in the swamps with groups of Seminole Indians.

The Kansas-Nebraska Act

Congress approved the Kansas-Nebraska Act on May 30, 1854. This act allowed the Kansas and Nebraska territories to vote on whether they wanted to be free or slave territories. Those territories included five present-day states: Kansas, Nebraska, Montana, South Dakota, and North Dakota. Allowing residents to decide for themselves was called **popular sovereignty.** The old Missouri Compromise line (36°30') was no longer used to determine where slavery was allowed.

Vocabulary

sovereignty: supreme and self-governing authority

Those for and against slavery quickly moved into the Kansas territory so they could vote on the issue of slavery. Proslavery forces won the election. Antislavery forces claimed proslavery settlers had cheated. Antislavery settlers held another election, but proslavery settlers refused to participate. Two separate legislatures were formed. One was proslavery; the other was antislavery. Violence broke out. Newspapers referred to this mini-civil war as "Bleeding Kansas." President Franklin Pierce ordered federal troops to end the violence.

The Dred Scott Case

Dred Scott, a slave, filed a lawsuit in the Missouri courts, **_Dred Scott v. Sandford._** Scott wanted freedom for himself, his wife, and two daughters. He believed that since they had lived for a short time in a free territory (Minnesota), they were free citizens. The Missouri courts ruled against him.

The case went to the Supreme Court in 1856. In 1857, the Supreme Court ruled against Scott. Chief Justice Roger B. Taney [TAW nee] said that Scott was not a U.S. citizen. Therefore, he could not sue in U.S. courts. Taney said that slaves "are not included, and were not intended to be included, under the word 'citizens' in the Constitution." Southern slaveholders believed it was an important victory.

▲ Dred Scott first sued for his freedom in 1846. The Supreme Court, led by Chief Justice Taney, did not rule on the case until 1857.

John Brown's Raid on Harpers Ferry

John Brown lived in the Kansas territory, and he opposed slavery. In the winter of 1857–1858 he led raids on slaveholders. With the help of his sons and other volunteers, he freed slaves and threatened slaveholders in the Kansas territory.

▲ Many Southerners believed that John Brown's raid was part of a larger plot by abolitionists and Republicans to destroy slavery.

On the evening of October 16, 1859, Brown led an attack on the federal arsenal at **Harpers Ferry**, Virginia. Brown and 21 followers overpowered the guards at the arsenal. Brown hoped that news of his actions would lead slaves to gather at Harpers Ferry. There, Brown would give them weapons and urge them to go and free other slaves. It did not work out that way.

News of the attack reached the governor of Virginia. He ordered the Virginia state militia to report to Harpers Ferry. In addition, President James Buchanan sent federal marines to take back the arsenal and arrest Brown and his followers. Ten of Brown's followers were killed, and Brown was wounded in the assault on the arsenal. Virginia tried, convicted, and hanged Brown for treason. His raids and execution pushed the North and South much closer to war.

Vocabulary

arsenal: space to store guns and ammunition

The Republican Party

In 1854, a group of Northern Democrats had become unhappy with their party because the Southern members of the party supported slavery in the new territories. They had formed a new political organization—the Republican Party. The Republican Party believed that slavery should not be allowed in the new territories.

Lincoln-Douglas Debates In 1858, Republican Abraham Lincoln and Democrat Stephen A. Douglas ran in the Illinois Senate race. Lincoln criticized Douglas for not condemning slavery. At a debate, Lincoln told the audience, "this government cannot endure permanently half slave and half free."

Douglas believed in popular sovereignty, that people of a territory or state should decide the question of slavery for themselves. He claimed that Lincoln was a radical abolitionist and said that Lincoln would work to free all of the slaves. Douglas won the election. But Lincoln's speeches against slavery made him a national figure.

The 1860 Election

As the nation headed toward the election of 1860, the issue of slavery raised tensions to the breaking point. Political parties disagreed strongly over the issue. Even within the same party, Northerners and Southerners could not agree on a platform or a candidate.

In 1860, more than 400,000 slaves lived in Georgia. Most slaves lived in the Piedmont region and along coastal Georgia. Many enslaved and free African Americans lived in Georgia's largest cities—Savannah, Augusta, Columbus, and Macon. Slaveholders wanted a president who would promise not to attack the institution of slavery, which supported the Southern economy.

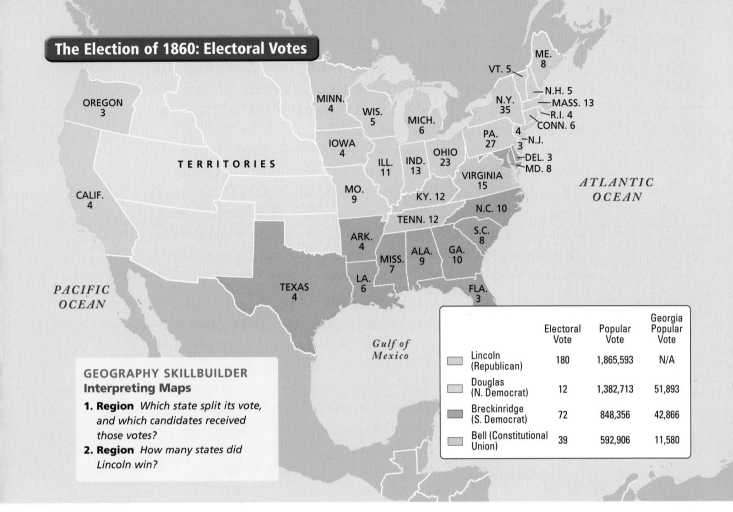

The Election of 1860: Electoral Votes

OREGON 3

MINN. 4

WIS. 5

MICH. 6

IOWA 4

ME. 8

VT. 5

N.H. 5

N.Y. 35

MASS. 13

R.I. 4

CONN. 6

PA. 27

N.J. 4 3

DEL. 3

MD. 8

TERRITORIES

CALIF. 4

ILL. 11

IND. 13

OHIO 23

VIRGINIA 15

ATLANTIC OCEAN

MO. 9

KY. 12

N.C. 10

TENN. 12

ARK. 4

S.C. 8

PACIFIC OCEAN

MISS. 7

ALA. 9

GA. 10

TEXAS 4

LA. 6

FLA. 3

Gulf of Mexico

		Electoral Vote	Popular Vote	Georgia Popular Vote
	Lincoln (Republican)	180	1,865,593	N/A
	Douglas (N. Democrat)	12	1,382,713	51,893
	Breckinridge (S. Democrat)	72	848,356	42,866
	Bell (Constitutional Union)	39	592,906	11,580

GEOGRAPHY SKILLBUILDER
Interpreting Maps
1. **Region** Which state split its vote, and which candidates received those votes?
2. **Region** How many states did Lincoln win?

The Republicans selected **Abraham Lincoln** as their candidate for the 1860 presidential election. Part of their platform was to prevent slavery in the territories.

Democrats could not agree on the issue of slavery. Within the Democratic Party, Democrats from the North wanted popular sovereignty for the territories. Democrats from the South did not. As a result, the Southern delegates walked out of the convention.

Northern Democrats selected Stephen A. Douglas as their presidential candidate. They tried to win Southern voters by choosing Herschel V. Johnson of Georgia for the vice-presidential candidate. The Southern Democrats rejected Douglas and Johnson. They selected John Breckinridge of Kentucky as their candidate.

John Bell of Tennessee was the candidate of the Constitutional Union Party. Its goal was to preserve the Union.

Lincoln was elected president with 40 percent of the popular vote and 59 percent of the electoral vote. His name was not even on the ballot in the Southern states. Lincoln's election convinced many Southerners that they should leave the Union. They believed that Lincoln would lead the federal government to abolish slavery.

Reading History

A. Recognizing Effects How did slavery affect U.S. political parties in 1860?

Southern States Secede

Lincoln would not take office until March 4, 1861. James Buchanan was still president when South Carolina became the first state to secede from the Union. Just days after Lincoln was elected, the South Carolina legislature voted 169 to 0 to leave the Union.

Some Southerners, however, wanted to remain in the Union if a compromise over slavery could be reached. Senator John J. Crittenden of Kentucky proposed that amendments be added to the Constitution. These amendments, called the Crittenden Plan, would protect slavery in the Southern states. Further, the federal government would never be allowed to change the amendments. But this plan was not acceptable to Southern states or Northern Republicans.

▲ The Governor's Mansion in Milledgeville was occupied from 1807 when Milledgeville became the state capital until 1868.

Georgia Secedes After receiving news of the presidential election, Georgia's political leaders gathered in the state capital of **Milledgeville.** They called for immediate secession. However, not all Georgians were willing to act so quickly. Three men, Alexander H. Stephens, Benjamin H. Hill, and Herschel V. Johnson, argued for a compromise between the North and South. But they also supported Georgia's right to secede. These people were known as cooperationists.

The Georgia government held a convention beginning January 16, 1861, in Milledgeville to discuss secession. Every county sent delegates. Most favored secession. Some opposed immediate action. On January 29, after days of heated discussion, the vote was 208 to 89 for immediate secession. Even those who had not voted for secession pledged their "lives, our fortunes, and our sacred honor to the defense of Georgia." Georgia was now the free and independent "Republic of Georgia."

Disagreements over Secession A number of Georgians did not want to secede from the Union. These people were called Unionists. Most of the Unionists lived in the northern hill counties and the southern pine barren counties. These people thought secession was unpatriotic. They did not have large numbers of slaves, so they were less concerned about the slavery issue.

The plantation areas that relied on slave labor and people living in towns and cities generally supported secession. But even in those places, some people would have preferred to remain in the Union. Georgia and the South were never unanimously behind the idea of leaving the Union.

Before Lincoln took the oath of office, Mississippi, Florida, Alabama, Georgia, Louisiana, and Texas had joined South Carolina in

Reading History

B. Compare and Contrast What were the differences and/or similarities between those in favor of secession, cooperationists, and Unionists?

leaving the Union. Virginia, Arkansas, North Carolina, and Tennessee seceded soon afterward.

Georgia Joins the Confederacy

On February 4, 1861, representatives from the seceding states met in Montgomery, Alabama, to start a new nation. T. R. R. Cobb and Robert Toombs from Georgia served on the committee assigned to write a new constitution. By the end of the meeting, a new constitution was in place. It was much like the U.S. Constitution. The biggest difference was that the Confederate Constitution specifically allowed slavery.

Background

Before becoming president of the Confederacy, Davis had been a hero during the War with Mexico and a U.S. senator.

The group also selected **Jefferson Davis** from Mississippi as president of the Confederate States of America. Alexander H. Stephens from Crawfordville, Georgia, became vice president. President Davis appointed Robert Toombs of Washington, Georgia, as the new nation's secretary of state. At his inauguration, Davis urged the remaining slaveholding states still in the Union to join the new nation.

A convention of Georgia representatives ratified the Confederate Constitution on March 16, 1861. Then they amended the Georgia constitution to show their new allegiance. Georgia was now one of the Confederate States of America. In the next chapter, you will learn about the outcome of this rebellion.

▲ As president of the Confederate States of America, Jefferson Davis had to immediately form a national government and prepare for war at the same time.

Section 3 Assessment

1. TERMS & NAMES

Explain the significance of:

a. Compromise of 1850

b. *Scott* v. *Sandford*

c. Harpers Ferry

d. Abraham Lincoln

e. Milledgeville

f. Jefferson Davis

2. TAKING NOTES

Use a spider map like the one below to show four causes of secession.

3. MAIN IDEAS

a. What was the primary economic difference between the North and South?

b. Describe Georgia's vote for secession in terms of where people lived.

c. What was the major difference between the U.S. Constitution and the Confederate Constitution?

4. CRITICAL THINKING

Comparing

How was the South's situation before the Civil War similar to the Patriots' situation before declaring independence in 1776? How was it different?

Think About
• their dependence on others
• their opponents' strengths

Speech/Technology Make a **speech** or design a **Web site** about the life and accomplishments of one of the political leaders in Georgia at the time of the vote for secession.

VISUAL SUMMARY

A Nation Breaks Apart

SLAVERY

1846
Wilmot Proviso

Compromise of **1850**

1854
Kansas Nebraska Act

1855
"Bleeding Kansas"

1857
Dred Scott v. *Sandford*

1859
Attack on Harpers Ferry

Election of **1860**

1861
Georgia Secedes, Confederate Constitution Ratified

SECESSION

TERMS & NAMES

Briefly explain the significance of the following.

1. Tariff of Abominations
2. secede
3. states' rights
4. Missouri Compromise
5. Wilmot Proviso
6. Compromise of 1850
7. *Dred Scott* v. *Sandford*
8. Harpers Ferry

REVIEW QUESTIONS

Growing Sectional Differences (pages 231–233)

1. Why did the Tariff of Abominations result in sectionalism?
2. What caused South Carolina to withdraw its threat of nullification in 1833?

The Issue of Slavery (pages 234–238)

3. How did Congress attempt to settle the question of slavery in new territories?
4. What was the American Colonization Society?
5. What group demanded the immediate emancipation of slaves and equal rights for free blacks?
6. What two key events led to westward expansion and raised the question of slavery in the west?

The Southern States Secede (pages 239–245)

7. What was the Georgia Platform?
8. What result did the Kansas-Nebraska Act have in the territory of Kansas?
9. How did Georgia respond to Lincoln's election?

CRITICAL THINKING

1. USING YOUR NOTES: SUMMARIZING

Main Ideas	Facts
Tariff of Abominations	
Northwest Ordinance of 1787	
Missouri Compromise	
Wilmot Proviso	
Compromise of 1850	
Kansas-Nebraska Act	

Using your completed chart, answer the questions below.

a. Which act admitted Maine as a free state?
b. Which law was proposed in response to the War with Mexico?

2. ANALYZING LEADERSHIP

What qualities of leadership do you see in the life of Henry Clay? Do you believe he was a good leader? Why or why not?

3. APPLYING CITIZENSHIP SKILLS

How did leaders of the abolitionist movement exercise their rights as citizens?

4. THEME: DIVERSITY AND UNITY

What could have been done in the 1850s to prevent the Southern states from seceding? What did Americans have in common that could have overcome their differences?

5. ANALYZING POINTS OF VIEW

How did Georgians differ in their views of secession? What led to these differences?

INTERACT *with* HISTORY

What solution might you have offered to address the issues faced by slave and free states? After reading this chapter, do you think your solution would have worked? Why or why not?

Use the map and your knowledge of American history to answer questions 1 through 3.

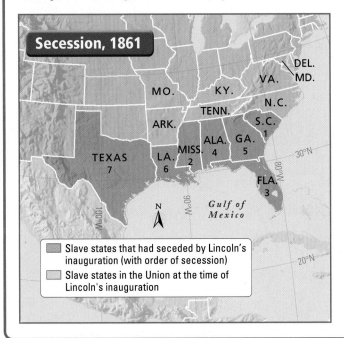

Secession, 1861

MO.   KY.   VA.   DEL. MD.

TENN.   N.C.

ARK.   S.C. 1

TEXAS 7   LA. 6   MISS. 2   ALA. 4   GA. 5

30°N

80°W

FLA. 3

90°W

100°W

20°N

Gulf of Mexico

N

 Slave states that had seceded by Lincoln's inauguration (with order of secession)

Slave states in the Union at the time of Lincoln's inauguration

1. The first two states to secede were:
   - **A.** South Carolina and Georgia
   - **B.** South Carolina and Mississippi
   - **C.** North Carolina and South Carolina
   - **D.** Virginia and Kentucky

2. When did Georgia secede?
   - **A.** After Alabama
   - **B.** After Lincoln's inauguration
   - **C.** After 1861
   - **D.** After Texas

3. Slave states in the Union at the time of Lincoln's inauguration included:
   - **A.** Arkansas and Texas
   - **B.** Ohio and Virginia
   - **C.** South Carolina and North Carolina
   - **D.** Virginia and North Carolina

TEST PRACTICE
CLASSZONE.COM

ALTERNATIVE ASSESSMENT

1. MAKING AN ANNOTATED MAP

Create an annotated map of the Underground Railroad. Research to find the main routes, and place them on a map. Then add notations using some of the following suggestions.

- Do research to find stories of slaves who escaped along the Underground Railroad.

- Put brief, typed summaries of a few stories on the map, with arrows connecting them to the right route.

- Draw illustrations of escape narratives and put them on the map.

- Research to discover appropriate songs. Then create a recording that can play as people view the map.

2. COOPERATIVE LEARNING

Working in small groups, do research on the Dred Scott case. Present a mock trial of the case. Research the roles of the major participants. Have the class render a verdict at the end of the trial. How does your verdict compare with history?

INTEGRATED TECHNOLOGY ACTIVITIES

1. USING THE INTERNET

Use the Internet to research Georgia history in the 1840s and 1850s. Write a brief report on a specific person or event that influenced the state in this period. Create a bibliography, being careful to cite all of your sources correctly.

2. MAKING A CLASS PRESENTATION

In both the North and the South, opinion was divided about the necessity or wisdom of going to war. Using the Internet or library, read primary sources about the events preceding the Civil War. Use presentation software to share reasons why some individuals were in favor and some were opposed to the Civil War.

 **RESEARCH LINKS**
CLASSZONE.COM

The Civil War 1861–1865

SCOTT'S GREAT SNAKE.

GEORGIA USA

1860   1861   1862

January 1861
Georgia votes to secede from the Union.

February 1861
Georgia joins the Confederacy.

April 1862
Union spies board the train in Marietta, Georgia.

1860
Abraham Lincoln is elected president.

April 1861
Fort Sumter is taken by Confederate forces.

1862
Battle of Shiloh

In the Battle of Kennesaw Mountain, Confederate artillery and rifle fire inflicted heavy Union losses, repulsed the attack, and won the battle.

It is June 1864. For several weeks, Union troops have advanced through Georgia. Confederate General Joseph E. Johnston's soldiers have dug in at Kennesaw Mountain, waiting for the assault. By the end of the day, 3,000 Union troops and 1,000 Confederate troops will lie dead.

How might a civil war be worse than other wars?

WHAT DO YOU THINK?

- What sort of physical destruction might take place in a civil war?

- What social, political, and economic trouble might be likely to occur in a civil war?

For more information on this chapter, visit . . .

RESEARCH LINKS
CLASSZONE.COM

September 1863
Battle of Chickamauga

September 1864
Atlanta falls to Sherman.

December 1864
Savannah is occupied.

1865 President Davis is captured.

1863

1864

1865

1863
Emancipation Proclamation is issued.

1863 Confederate forces are defeated at Gettysburg and Vicksburg.

1864 Lincoln is reelected.

April 1865
Union takes Richmond. Lee surrenders. Lincoln is assassinated.

Reading Strategy:
Comparing and Contrasting

What Do You Know?

What do you think of when you hear the phrase *civil war?* What would it be like to fight in a war of brother against brother? Where and how did the Civil War begin?

THINK ABOUT

• what a civil war is

• what you've learned about the Civil War from movies, television, and books

• reasons that countries threaten to break apart in today's world

What Do You Want to Know?

What details do you need to help you understand what happened in the Civil War? Make a list of those details in your notebook before you read the chapter.

Comparing and Contrasting

When you compare, you look for similarities between two or more objects, ideas, events, or people. When you contrast, you look for differences. Comparing and contrasting can be a useful strategy for studying the two sides in a war. Use the chart shown here to compare and contrast the impact of the Civil War on the North and the South.

 See Skillbuilder Handbook, page 551.

 Taking Notes

	North	South
Reasons for Fighting		
Advantages		
Disadvantages		
Military Strategy		
Battle Victories		

The Fighting Begins

MAIN IDEA

The availability of men and material was a major factor in the outcome of the war.

WHY IT MATTERS NOW

The South's inability to provide for itself during the war affected economic decisions after the war that still impact Georgians today.

TERMS & NAMES

Anaconda Plan
King Cotton diplomacy
Fort Sumter
Battle of Bull Run
Fort Pulaski

SETTING THE STAGE

What caused the nation to split apart? Why did it lead to a war between the North and South? The North could have allowed the Southern states to leave without a fight. But President Abraham Lincoln refused to let the nation be destroyed, so he used force to bring it back together.

Once the war began, what resources were available to both sides? How did each side plan to fight? Both sides were confident that they would win. Northern leaders believed they could quickly return the Southern states to the Union. Southerners were convinced they could defend their region against a Northern invasion.

Causes of the Civil War

Slavery was a main reason for the Civil War, but there were other important factors. Different lifestyles and attitudes also played a part.

How the Regions Viewed One Another Southerners believed that Northerners were bad mannered and greedy. Northerners thought Southerners were backwards and unsophisticated. This regional stereotyping led to fear and hatred of each side for the other.

Loss of Control Many Southerners believed in states' rights. They argued that the federal government did not have the right to tell individual states what to do. When Northern Republicans gained control of Congress and Abraham Lincoln was elected president, many Southerners believed that they had lost control of their destiny.

Economic Differences The South remained mostly agricultural. The North began to develop industries, while maintaining its agriculture. Large cities developed in the North, but few cities developed in the South. There were not many wage earners (people who are paid for

THE HERCULES OF THE UNION, SLAYING THE GREAT DRAGON OF SECESSION.

▲ This political cartoon shows Union General Winfield Scott slaying the dragon of secession.

Taking Notes

Use your chart to compare and contrast the impact made on the North and South as fighting begins.

	North	South
Reasons for Fighting		
Advantages		

The Civil War **251**

Resources, 1860

The pie charts show the relative strengths of the Union and the Confederacy in population and industry.

Total U.S. Population

29% 71%

Total U.S. Railroad Mileage

29% 71%

Total U.S. Manufacturing Plants

15% 85%

Total U.S. Industrial Workers

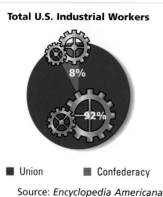

8% 92%

■ Union   ■ Confederacy

Source: *Encyclopedia Americana*

SKILLBUILDER
Interpreting Charts

1. *Which side had more resources?*
2. *How might the North's railways and factories have helped its armies?*

doing a job) in the South because the plantation economy depended on slave labor. In the North, slavery had all but disappeared, replaced by wage labor.

The differences made it difficult to reach a compromise. Some believed that the two regions had distinct cultures. They even disagreed over what to call the conflict. Southerners referred to the Civil War as the "War of Northern Aggression." Many Northerners called the conflict the "War of the Rebellion."

Resources of the North and South

The North had significant advantages over the South in the areas of economic and human resources. About 85 percent of the nation's factories and over twice the amount of railroad lines were located in the North.

Economic Resources Northern industry produced almost all the firearms, cloth, iron, ships, boats, and shoes in the country. The South, on the other hand, produced mostly agricultural products such as cotton, corn, wheat, and livestock. Because many Southern farmers grew mostly cotton, the South had a hard time growing enough food for both the military and civilians. The North also had a system of banks and controlled most of the nation's wealth. The South relied mainly on Northern banks and invested most of its wealth in slaves.

Human Resources Over 22 million people lived in the North, while the South had a population of 9 million, including 3.5 million slaves. About 92 percent of the nation's industrial work force lived in the North. In a military conflict, the South's smaller population was at a great disadvantage.

Military Forces and Leaders The Northern or Union army had about 16,000 soldiers, mostly stationed at frontier outposts in the West. The Southern states had no standing army. They turned to state militias for their first troops. In Georgia, local militias filled the initial ranks of the Southern or Confederate Army. Militia units supplied most of their own equipment. Georgia units were among the best equipped in the Confederate Army.

Reading History

A. Making Generalizations How did the economies of the North and the South differ?

▶ Although Confederate General James Longstreet often disagreed with Robert E. Lee's tactics, he is considered one of the foremost generals of the Civil War.

◀ Confederate General James "Jeb" Stuart led the cavalry of the Army of Northern Virginia in many significant battles during the war.

The South did have strong military leaders. Many officers resigned from the United States Army and joined the Confederate Army. Some officers trained at West Point. Others trained at Southern military academies such as The Citadel.

The Confederacy could never provide its soldiers with enough supplies such as uniforms, tents, wagons, weapons, or food. But Southern troops looked for supplies in the countryside and on the battlefield to make up for the shortages. Somehow, Confederate forces never lost a battle because they lacked supplies.

Georgia's Resources

Georgia was an important source of military goods, food supplies, and other items for the Confederacy. Atlanta was smaller than other Georgia cities at the time, but it was a major transportation center. Its factories produced both military and nonmilitary goods. It had a large mill that made cannons, rails for railroads, and pistols. A large arsenal that made bullets, saddles, and other military supplies was also located in Atlanta.

Industry One of Georgia's largest industries was milling grain into flour and meal. Another large industry was textiles. At the start of the Civil War, Georgia had 33 cotton mills. Georgia had more textile manufacturing than any other Southern state.

Agriculture At the beginning of the war, the state and Confederate governments encouraged farmers to reduce cotton production. They needed farmers to increase food crops, especially corn to feed the soldiers.

Railroads In 1860, Georgia had over 1,400 miles of railroads, more than any other Southern state. These major Southern railroads ran through Atlanta.

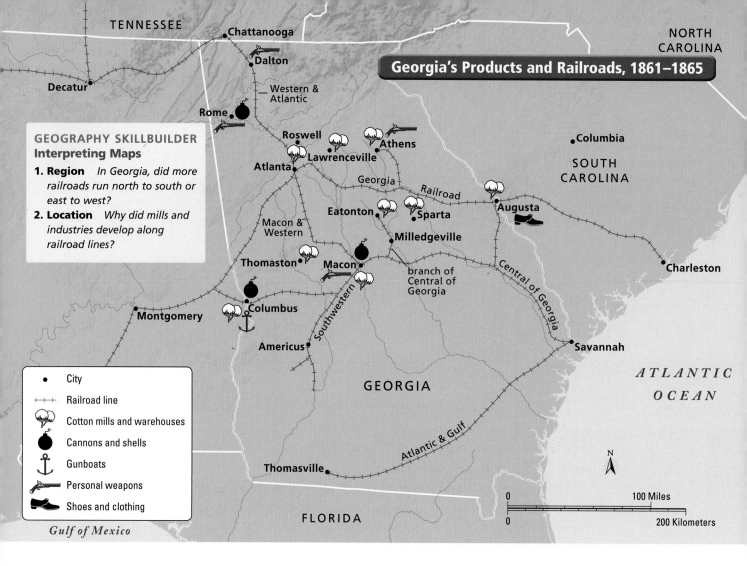

Georgia's Products and Railroads, 1861–1865

TENNESSEE

NORTH CAROLINA

Chattanooga
Dalton
Decatur
Western & Atlantic
Rome
Roswell
Athens
Columbia
SOUTH CAROLINA
Lawrenceville
Atlanta
Georgia Railroad
Augusta
Macon & Western
Eatonton
Sparta
Charleston
Milledgeville
Thomaston
Macon
branch of Central of Georgia
Central of Georgia
Montgomery
Columbus
Southwestern
Savannah
Americus
ATLANTIC OCEAN
GEORGIA
Atlantic & Gulf
N
Thomasville
FLORIDA
Gulf of Mexico

GEOGRAPHY SKILLBUILDER
Interpreting Maps
1. **Region** In Georgia, did more railroads run north to south or east to west?
2. **Location** Why did mills and industries develop along railroad lines?

- • City
- ┼┼┼ Railroad line
- Cotton mills and warehouses
- Cannons and shells
- Gunboats
- Personal weapons
- Shoes and clothing

0   100 Miles
0   200 Kilometers

Military Strategies of the North and South

Northern leaders thought that the conflict would not last long. Their initial strategy was to fight a limited war that did not require a lot of fighting. General Winfield Scott established a blockade of Northern ships around the Southern states' coastline, particularly at the mouth of the Mississippi River. The blockade prevented the South from exporting cotton and receiving supplies. This plan was called the **Anaconda Plan** after the large snake that strangles its prey.

Many Northerners opposed this plan. The Northern public wanted a quick end to the "rebellion." Lincoln agreed that the federal government had to force the Southern states back into the Union instead of waiting for them to surrender. That meant sending Union troops into the Southern states to defeat the Confederate Army. Because Richmond, Virginia, was the Confederate capital, Lincoln ordered federal troops into Virginia in the summer of 1861.

King Cotton Diplomacy Confederate leaders hoped the North would tire of war and accept Southern independence. The South hoped to break the Union blockade with the help of European countries.

Reading History

B. Supporting Opinions At the beginning of the Civil War, which side would you have predicted to win?

Countries such as England and France needed cotton from the South. The South believed this need for their product would win foreign support. This policy was known as **King Cotton diplomacy**. However, European countries found other sources of cotton during the war.

The South used ships known as blockade runners to break through or avoid the naval blockade. Georgia's famous poet Sidney Lanier served as a signal officer on a blockade runner. Merchants smuggled cotton out of Georgia by sending it down the Apalachicola River to the Gulf Coast. A small fleet of boats known as the "Mosquito Fleet" helped blockade runners get into Savannah harbor. Josiah Tatnall commanded the Mosquito Fleet. But as the war progressed, the North's blockade became more effective.

▲ Sidney Lanier commanded the blockade runner *Lucy* during the Civil War.

Fighting Begins

Confederate soldiers fired the first shots of the war at **Fort Sumter**. This fort sat on an island in the middle of the Charleston, South Carolina, harbor. Major Robert Anderson commanded the Union forces. Confederate forces stopped supplies from reaching the fort. Without supplies, Anderson would eventually have to surrender. Lincoln ordered the fort resupplied. But before the supply ship could arrive, General P. G. T. Beauregard ordered Confederate forces to open fire on the fort. The bombardment began on the morning of April 12, 1861. After 33 hours, Anderson surrendered. The Civil War had begun.

First Bull Run The first major battle between the North and South occurred on July 21, 1861, at a railway center near Bull Run River in Manassas, Virginia. The Union called it the **Battle of Bull Run**. The Confederates called it the Battle of Manassas. The battle took place not far from Washington, D.C. As news of the coming battle spread, citizens of Washington flocked to the site to watch the battle. They expected the Union forces to easily defeat the Confederate troops. Union forces attacked and slowly pushed the Confederates back.

At one point in the battle, a Southern officer fired up his troops by pointing to Confederate General Thomas J. Jackson. The officer shouted, "There is Jackson standing like a stone wall! Rally behind the Virginians!" This incident won Jackson the nickname "Stonewall" Jackson. His men held fast against the Union assault.

The Confederates launched a successful counterattack and broke the ranks of the Union troops. Union soldiers and spectators fled. The Confederate Army had won a major victory. When T. R. R. Cobb of Georgia heard the outcome of the battle, he declared the Southern victory "one of the decisive battles of the world." He was wrong. Other battles during the Civil War had far greater consequences.

Background

In most cases, the South named a battle after a nearby town. The North used a landmark near the fighting, usually a stream.

▲ *The General* is in the collection of the Southern Museum of Civil War and Locomotive History in Cobb County.

Georgia at the Beginning of the War

Reading History

C. Recognizing Effects How did the outbreak of the war affect Georgians?

Before the war began, Governor Joe Brown ordered the First Regiment of Georgia Volunteers to hold **Fort Pulaski.** Located at the mouth of the Savannah River, it guarded the city of Savannah. In April 1862, Union troops shelled the fort. Confederate forces surrendered, and federal troops occupied it, making the port of Savannah unusable to Confederate fleets.

Union forces also conducted raids against the railroads in northern Georgia. They wanted to stop supplies going from Atlanta to the Confederate troops in Tennessee. In April, about 20 Union soldiers dressed as civilians boarded a locomotive named *The General* in Marietta. They planned to destroy the railroad tracks, bridges, and telegraph wires as they headed to the safety of the federal lines. But Confederate forces captured the raiders. Some were hanged and the rest were sent to Confederate prisons.

As Northern and Southern political and military leaders prepared for further fighting, soldiers and those at home faced challenges of their own. In the next section, you will learn what life was like for those in the ranks and those left behind.

Section 1 Assessment

1. TERMS & NAMES
Explain the significance of:

a. Anaconda Plan

b. King Cotton diplomacy

c. Fort Sumter

d. Battle of Bull Run

e. Fort Pulaski

2. TAKING NOTES
Use a chart similar to the one below to compare the resources of the North and the South at the start of the Civil War.

	North	South
Population		
Money		
Roads and Railroads		
Military Leaders		

3. MAIN IDEAS

a. Explain why the "Anaconda Plan" was a good name for this Union strategy.

b. What was the outcome of the Battle of Bull Run (Manassas)?

c. Why was it important for the North to control Fort Pulaski?

4. CRITICAL THINKING
Comparing

How was the South's situation in the Civil War similar to the situation of the Patriots in the Revolutionary War?

Think About

• the soldiers' reasons for fighting

• the strengths of the opponents

• location of the fighting

Language Arts/Music Create a **political cartoon** or write a **song** that expresses Northern or Southern attitudes at the beginning of the Civil War.

Life on the Front Lines and at Home

MAIN IDEA

As the war intensified, life on the battlefield and at home became far worse than ever imagined.

WHY IT MATTERS NOW

The difficulties that Southerners endured during the Civil War helped forge a regional identity that is still a part of United States culture.

TERMS & NAMES

draft
20-slave exemption
food riot
54th Massachusetts Colored
  Volunteers

SETTING THE STAGE

Early battles between Northern and Southern troops were minor compared with what was to come. Many soldiers writing to family and friends back home began ending their letters, "I remain yours, until death."

People at home also suffered hardships. Women whose husbands had gone to war found it difficult to provide for their families. Farmers who remained at home to grow crops and raise livestock faced shortages of seed and feed. Life in small Georgia towns such as Milledgeville, Athens, and Washington changed as the shortages began to take their toll. Everyone eagerly waited to hear news about the fighting in faraway places. Sometimes there was news of victory, sometimes defeat.

▲ No battles took place in Georgia during the first two years of the war. But the war did affect Georgians at home. High prices and severe shortages of food and goods made life difficult for all.

Those Who Fought

Most Civil War soldiers were between the ages of 18 and 30. Many came from rural areas and had never traveled far from home. Most did not fully understand all of the reasons for the war.

Northern recruits believed that they were fighting to preserve the Union. Southern recruits thought that they were fighting to guarantee the rights of the states to govern themselves. When asked why he was fighting against the North, one Confederate soldier replied, "Because you're down here." Before the end of the war, almost all of the soldiers were fighting just to stay alive and to return home.

Volunteers and Recruits in the South On March 6, 1861, the Confederate government authorized an army of 100,000 to serve for 12

Taking Notes

Use your chart to compare and contrast the impact of war on the North and South—on the front lines and at home.

	North	South
Reasons for Fighting		
Advantages		

months. Militia units from the seceding states made up the new Confederate Army. Georgia Governor Joseph E. Brown did not want all of the Georgia troops to be assigned to the Confederate Army, so he created state militias that remained in Georgia to defend the state. Overall, about 120,000 Georgians served in the Confederate Army or state militias.

At the beginning of the war, the new Confederate Army was overwhelmed by volunteers. Men from all walks of life volunteered, even political leaders such as Robert Toombs and Howell Cobb. Sometimes wealthy men formed companies from their area and paid for the company's uniforms and weapons. The Confederate government turned away some 200,000 volunteers because there were not enough weapons or supplies.

By the spring of 1862, it was difficult for the South to find volunteers. Soldiers wrote back to brothers and cousins warning them to stay out of the military. Hubert Dent, a member of the Eufala Rifles from Georgia, told his wife that "many of our officers are resigning since the fight . . . they have had enough of battles."

▲ Recruiting posters encouraged men to enlist in the army.

The Confederate Draft The Confederate government passed a Conscription Act or **draft** in April 1862, requiring citizens to serve in the military. This was the first draft in American history. White men from 18 to 35 years old were required to serve a minimum of 3 years. Later, the draft included those 17 to 50 years of age.

Anyone who was drafted could pay a fee and hire a substitute to take his place. Men in some professions and government employees did not have to serve. Railroad employees; telegraph operators; workers in cotton mills, mines, or foundries; and shoemakers were also exempted. It was important to keep transportation and industry going to supply the army.

One exemption was known as the **20-slave exemption.** For every 20 slaves on a plantation, 1 white man was exempted. Some Southerners saw it as a way for the wealthy to avoid military service. Some believed that the Civil War had become "a rich man's war and a poor man's fight."

Volunteers and Recruits in the North At the start of the Civil War, the federal government asked for 500,000 volunteers to enlist in the military. Many men rushed to join, but after much of the excitement and patriotic spirit began to fade, the number of volunteers slowed. The U.S. Congress passed a draft on March 3, 1863.

There were exemptions to the Union draft. Men could be exempted if they were ill or the only person caring for a widow, a child, or other dependent. A man could avoid service by providing a substitute or paying a fee of $300. Over half of those drafted chose one of those options.

Reading History

A. Drawing Conclusions Why were many soldiers dissatisfied with the draft laws?

Draft Riots   Many people believed that this was unfair. In the summer of 1863, a riot broke out in New York City. The mob demonstrated against unfair practices used in the draft. The mob shouted "down with the rich" and also assaulted African Americans (who were not citizens and so were exempt from the draft). The increasingly violent mob was eventually controlled by soldiers brought in from the battlefields.

A Soldier's Life

At the start of the war, volunteers poured into recruiting stations. Soldiers marched off to battle with full stomachs, great expectations, plenty of ammunition and weapons, camping gear, and new uniforms. Many did not realize the dangers that they would face on the battlefield or the boredom they would experience in the camps. A soldier's life was monotonous. Soldiers often had to wait in camp for the next battle, which could be weeks or months away. They could march for days and even weeks before reaching their next encounter. Battles could last one, two, or three days. Then, the soldiers would pack up and march on to the next camp.

Food   Both sides tried to provide enough food for their soldiers. However, this was not always possible. Rations included flour, salted or pickled beef and pork, rice, dried peas, goober peas (peanuts), cornbread, and dried fruit. Often, green vegetables and fresh fruit were scarce. Soldiers foraged or looked for food to add to their diets. Southern soldiers sometimes ate wild onions and sassafras buds to prevent a disease called scurvy.

Soldiers hunted, fished, and sometimes stole farm animals for an evening meal. Some Georgia troops stationed along the Florida coast tried eating alligator and thought it tasted "a good deal like catfish."

Reading History

B. Making Inferences What changes could have helped slow down the spread of disease among soldiers?

Health   Fighting was dangerous, but more men died off the battlefield than on. Wounded soldiers' chances for recovery in field hospitals were not good. Doctors and surgeons had little or no battlefield medical experience. Surgeons performed operations without sterilized instruments.

STRANGE BUT TRUE

Deadlier Than Bullets

"Look at our company—21 have died of disease, 18 have become so unhealthy as to be discharged, and only four have been killed in battle." So a Louisiana officer explained the high death rate in the Civil War.

More than twice as many men died of disease as died of battle wounds. Intestinal disorders, including typhoid fever, diarrhea, and dysentery, killed the most. Pneumonia, tuberculosis, and malaria killed many others.

Bad water and food, poor diet, exposure to cold and rain, unsanitary conditions, and disease-carrying insects all contributed to the high rate of disease.

Clothing   Early in the war, uniforms were provided by states, towns, or wealthy individuals who formed their own companies. This resulted in a wide variety of colors and styles. Gradually, blue became the official uniform color for the North and gray became the official uniform of the South. At first, Northern manufacturers provided shoddy (poorly made) uniforms to the troops. Later, they provided better-made uniforms in different sizes. This was the first time that men's clothing was made in sizes. Most uniforms were made of wool, which was very uncomfortable in the warm climate of the South.

The official Confederate uniform was a long, gray, double-breasted coat with sky-blue trousers. Different colors trimmed the uniforms: red for artillery, blue for infantry, and yellow for cavalry. However, uniforms were scarce. Militias supplied their own and often selected different styles and colors. Soldiers also wore homemade clothes. It was difficult to tell friend from foe on the battlefield. There was a standard cap, but many Southern soldiers preferred a floppy, wide-brimmed hat.

One of the most troublesome shortages was shoes. Northern troops had a good supply of shoes. Some Confederate troops did not have shoes. They wrapped burlap or cloth around their feet. After battles, Southern troops gathered up much-needed supplies such as shoes, blankets, and clothing from dead Union and Confederate soldiers.

A Soldier's Equipment

Union troops were better equipped than Confederate troops. If a soldier lost or used up his equipment, he could get replacements from his quartermaster.

Most Confederate soldiers received a rifle and bayonet, cartridge box, tin cup, and blanket.

Life at Home

Northerners and Southerners were eager to hear the status of the war and the fate of their family and friends. News of a soldier's death came to his loved ones either from his commanding officer or as part of the lists of dead, wounded, captured, or missing in action in the local newspaper. Maxcy Boston, who was attached to the Oglethorpe Light Infantry of the 8th Georgia Regiment, died at the Second Battle of Manassas in August 1863. Maxcy's father learned of his son's death in a letter.

PRIMARY SOURCE

Dear Sir—It is with feelings of the deepest regret that I have to inform you of the death of your son. He was killed yesterday while nobly contending for our freedom in the front ranks of his company.

quoted in *Confederate Reminiscences and Letters, 1861–1865*

Supplies As supplies became scarcer, some Southern women started rioting. They were angry because of high prices for basic items such as flour or bacon. In more than a dozen cities and towns across the South, women staged **food riots,** demanding better rations and prices. If they didn't riot, they often just took what they needed. President Jefferson Davis finally intervened to restore order.

Soldiers did not always have access to clean water. A lack of soap, particularly in the Southern ranks, and poor hygiene resulted in unhealthy conditions that affected the soldiers' ability to fight.

To make up for shortages, Southern soldiers took weapons from the dead on the battlefield.

CLARA BARTON
1821–1912

Trained as a schoolteacher, Clara Barton was working for the government when the Civil War began. She organized a relief agency to help with the war effort. "While our soldiers stand and fight," she said, "I can stand and feed and nurse them."

She also made food for soldiers in camp and tended to the wounded and dying on the battlefield. At Antietam, she held a doctor's operating table steady as cannon balls burst all around them. The doctor called her "the angel of the battlefield." After the war, Barton founded the American Red Cross.

At the beginning of the war, the Confederate government planned to pay for anything they took from civilians. After a few years, however, soaring inflation made Confederate money worthless. People were less willing to give up property such as crops and livestock, clothing, horses, and wagons. They needed those items for themselves.

Then, the Confederate government ordered the impressment of goods. This meant it could take what was needed, even if the owner was unwilling. In turn, the government gave owners receipts called promissory notes for their goods.

Women's Roles   In the South, women took on new roles that many had believed they could not perform. Before the war, women were generally responsible for cooking, cleaning, and raising children.

With the men off to war, wives of plantation owners were sometimes left in charge of large-scale agricultural businesses. Wives and daughters of small-scale farmers were responsible for all the farm duties as well as the household tasks. Life could be extremely difficult for these women, running the farms and taking care of the children by themselves.

In addition, women made uniforms, tents, socks, blankets, and coats for men in the military. One group of Georgia women raised money for an ironclad ship for use in coastal defense. Women also worked in factories such as the one in Rossville, Georgia, that made cloth for the military.

Northern and Southern women played other important roles in the Civil War, as well. They served as spies and informants. Some even disguised themselves as men and enlisted to fight. Many worked as nurses. Clara Barton from Massachusetts worked on the battlefield, tending the wounded and dying. Dorothea Dix and about 3,000 other women worked as nurses and volunteers for the North. Southern women volunteered and worked in military hospitals of the Confederacy. The largest Civil War hospital was located in Richmond, Virginia.

African-American Soldiers

Slaves had found ways to escape from the South for many years. In Georgia during the war, one of the best escape routes was to the Sea Islands. Union troops held these islands. Soldiers took escaped slaves to settlements such as those on St. Simons Island and St. Catherines Island.

Vocabulary

inflation: an increase in the price of goods and services and a decrease in the value of money

Reading History

C. Summarizing How did women participate in the Civil War?

Background

The Ladies Gunboat Association raised $115,000 to convert a blockade runner into an ironclad known as the *CSS Atlanta.*

When the Union army began to recruit freedmen in the South, a number of volunteers came from the Sea Islands. Georgia freedmen were added to new companies such as the 1st through 5th South Carolina Volunteers. These companies formed the 21st United States Colored Troops.

African-American troops were part of the federal forces stationed on St. Simons Island. The African-American troops were part of the **54th Massachusetts Colored Volunteers** and the 2nd South Carolina Colored Volunteers. The 54th Massachusetts Regiment was one of the first African-American regiments organized in the North. Their success and bravery led to increased African-American enlistment.

About 200,000 African Americans fought for the Union. By the end of the Civil War, over 10 percent of Union forces were African American. More than 37,000 African-American soldiers died fighting for the Union.

The soldiers of the 54th Massachusetts and other African-American regiments faced grave danger if captured. Rather than take African Americans as prisoners, Confederate soldiers often shot them or returned them to slavery.

In 1864, the Confederate government dismissed the idea of drafting slaves to fight for the Confederacy. But by early 1865, Southern forces needed help keeping Union troops from sweeping through the South. The Confederate Congress approved drafting slaves in March, but none were actually called to serve as combat soldiers.

The hardships intensified as the war continued. In the next section, you will learn about the major battles of the Civil War.

Reading History

D. Making Inferences
Why would African Americans want to fight for the Union Army?

Section 2 Assessment

1. TERMS & NAMES
Explain the significance of:

a. draft

b. 20-slave exemption

c. food riots

d. 54th Massachusetts Colored Volunteers

2. TAKING NOTES
Use the following diagram to identify the basic living conditions of soldiers.

Food	
Health	
Clothing	
Equipment	

3. MAIN IDEAS

a. What factors, other than the battlefield, contributed to the deaths and poor health of soldiers?

b. How did the Confederate soldiers' "uniforms" cause problems for them?

c. What hardships did women and men who stayed at home face?

4. CRITICAL THINKING
Forming and Supporting Opinions

What were the motives that led individual soldiers to fight in the Civil War?

Think About
- white Union soldiers
- African-American Union soldiers
- white Confederate soldiers

Language Arts/Art Reread the section about a soldier's life. Then write a **diary entry** or draw a **picture** of your camp as though you were a Confederate soldier.

3

The War Continues

MAIN IDEA	WHY IT MATTERS NOW	TERMS & NAMES
In 1863, the tide of the war turned. The Emancipation Proclamation in January and the Battle of Gettysburg in July changed the course of the war.	If the Union had lost this important battle, the United States might look very different now.	Battle of Shiloh Ulysses S. Grant William Tecumseh Sherman Robert E. Lee Battle of Antietam Emancipation Proclamation Battle of Gettysburg

SETTING THE STAGE

After almost a year of fighting, neither side could claim a decisive victory. In the East, Union General George McClellan drilled his troops relentlessly, but seemed reluctant to confront Confederate forces. In the West, however, Union General Ulysses S. Grant showed great skill on the battlefield. Victories in Tennessee had forced Confederate troops to retreat. Grant followed them.

The commander of the Confederate forces in the area, General Albert Sidney Johnston, ordered his troops to Corinth, Mississippi. Corinth was an important Confederate railroad center. The Confederacy had lost river access to Union forces. Johnston was determined to protect its railroad supply lines.

▲ A veteran of the War with Mexico, Albert Sidney Johnston resigned his U.S. Army commission in 1861 and was appointed a general by Confederate President Davis.

Shiloh and Antietam

The **Battle of Shiloh** was the first conflict between the North and South that showed how fierce and horrible later battles would be. Shiloh is near the Tennessee River, just north of the Mississippi-Tennessee border. (See map on page 266.) Early in the morning of April 6, 1862, General Albert Sidney Johnston joined forces with General P. G. T. Beauregard about 20 miles from the Union forces at Shiloh Church. With over 40,000 troops, Johnston decided to attack before more troops could arrive.

Johnston surprised the Union troops commanded by General Henry W. Halleck. The fighting lasted over 12 hours that first day. It appeared to be a Confederate victory, but the fighting was not over. That night rain fell, soaking the soldiers. Tired, hungry, and wet, they waited for the next day's fighting to begin.

Taking Notes

Use your chart to compare and contrast the impact on the North and South as the war continues.

	North	South
Reasons for Fighting		
Advantages		

HISTORY MAKERS

ULYSSES S. GRANT
1822–1885

General Ulysses S. Grant was an unlikely war hero. Although educated at West Point Military Academy, he was a poor student and showed little interest in an army career. With his quiet manner and rumpled uniform, he did not impress his fellow officers.

Yet on the battlefield, Grant proved to be a brilliant general. Focused and cool under fire, he won the first major Union victories of the war.

Grant was willing to fight Lee—even if the costs were high. He told his generals, "Wherever Lee goes, there you will go also."

ROBERT E. LEE
1807–1870

Robert E. Lee seemed destined for greatness. In his crisp uniform and trim white beard, Lee was a dashing figure on the battlefield.

Born to a leading Virginia family, Lee was a top student at West Point and won praise for his actions in the War with Mexico. General Winfield Scott called him "the very best soldier I have ever seen in the field."

Lee did not want to fight the Union, but he felt he had to stand by Virginia. "I did only what my duty demanded," Lee said. "I could have taken no other course without dishonor."

Background

The South called this conflict the Battle of Pittsburg Landing.

During the night, Union General **Ulysses S. Grant** moved up fresh soldiers. The next day he staged a surprise attack and overwhelmed the Confederate Army. Over 100,000 soldiers were involved in the battle. The North had more than 13,000 casualties (1,754 killed). The South suffered about 10,700 casualties with 1,728 soldiers killed. Union General **William Tecumseh Sherman** recalled that there were "piles of dead soldiers' mangled bodies . . . without heads and legs. . . . The scenes on this field would have cured anybody of war." Neither side had a system for gathering the dead. Grant said, "A person can walk in any given direction without stepping on ground." The battle convinced Northern military leaders that the war was going to last a long time.

Reading History

A. Forming and Supporting Opinions How did the difficult decisions made by Lee and Grant affect the war?

Later in the summer of 1862, the Confederate army had a series of victories against Union forces. In June, General **Robert E. Lee** and the Army of Northern Virginia defeated a Union army led by General George McClellan. McClellan was trying to capture the Confederate capital of Richmond, Virginia. The battle became known as the Seven Days' Battles. Fighting was fierce.

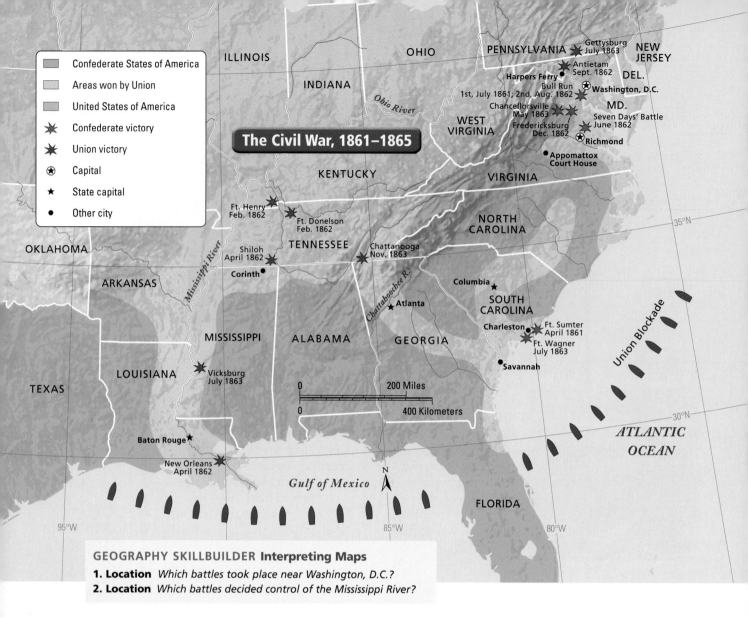

ILLINOIS OHIO PENNSYLVANIA Gettysburg NEW
July 1863 JERSEY

INDIANA Antietam
Sept. 1862 DEL.
Harpers Ferry
Bull Run Washington, D.C.
Ohio River 1st, July 1861; 2nd, Aug. 1862
Chancellorsville MD.
WEST May 1863 Seven Days' Battle
The Civil War, 1861–1865 VIRGINIA Fredericksburg June 1862
Dec. 1862 Richmond

KENTUCKY VIRGINIA Appomattox
Court House

35°N
NORTH
CAROLINA
Ft. Henry
Feb. 1862 Ft. Donelson
Feb. 1862
OKLAHOMA TENNESSEE Chattanooga
Shiloh Nov. 1863
ARKANSAS April 1862 Columbia
Corinth SOUTH
CAROLINA
Atlanta Charleston Ft. Sumter
April 1861
MISSISSIPPI ALABAMA GEORGIA Ft. Wagner
July 1863

Union Blockade
Vicksburg Savannah
LOUISIANA July 1863
0 200 Miles
TEXAS 0 400 Kilometers
30°N
Baton Rouge ATLANTIC
OCEAN
New Orleans N
April 1862 *Gulf of Mexico*
FLORIDA
95°W 85°W 80°W

Legend:
- Confederate States of America
- Areas won by Union
- United States of America
- ✴ Confederate victory
- ✴ Union victory
- ⊛ Capital
- ★ State capital
- • Other city

GEOGRAPHY SKILLBUILDER Interpreting Maps
1. Location *Which battles took place near Washington, D.C.?*
2. Location *Which battles decided control of the Mississippi River?*

Riding a wave of victories, General Lee believed that it was time to invade the North. Lee's 50,000 troops crossed the Potomac into Maryland on September 5, 1862. As soldiers reached the northern shore, they shouted and started singing. Confidence was high.

A Union soldier found a copy of Lee's battle plans carelessly left in an abandoned camp by a Confederate officer. McClellan used the information to attack Lee's Confederate lines at Sharpsburg, Maryland, on September 16, 1862. The **Battle of Antietam** (an TEE tuhm) had begun. After two days, Lee retreated to Virginia. When it was over, 23,000 Union and Confederate soldiers had been killed or wounded.

The Emancipation Proclamation

When Lee was defeated at Antietam, Lincoln felt that the time was right for a major announcement. He signed the **Emancipation Proclamation,** which made all slaves in the rebellious states "forever free." The proclamation did not apply to slaveholding states that were still a part of the Union. The proclamation went into effect January 1, 1863.

Reading History

B. Drawing Conclusions Why did Lee decide to invade the North at this time?

Background

The South called this the Battle of Sharpsburg.

Background

News of the proclamation did not reach the slaves of Galveston, Texas, until June 19, 1865. The celebration of "Juneteenth" marks that day.

Political opponents in the North criticized Lincoln. Some said the proclamation went too far and would make the rebellious states even more rebellious. It might even cause slaveholding states such as Kentucky and Maryland to leave the Union and join the Confederacy.

Others said it did not go far enough because it did not free all slaves. Lincoln knew he did not have the power under the Constitution to free the slaves in areas within the Union. But the president had special wartime powers that gave him the right to seize enemy property. Since the Confederacy was at war with the Union, and slaves were the property of the enemy, the president could free them.

Now the war had a special moral purpose—freedom for all people. Many Europeans supported the Emancipation Proclamation because they strongly opposed slavery. The South wanted England to recognize the Confederacy as a nation and perhaps offer help and foreign aid. The Emancipation Proclamation ended those attempts. Now, it was a clear choice for many in Europe. They could side with the North and the ideals of freedom. Or they could side with the South, and the "peculiar institution" of slavery.

Gettysburg

Reading History

C. Making Inferences Why do you think a Southern victory on Northern soil would have been significant?

Lee won the Battle of Chancellorsville, Virginia, in May 1863. He decided to take the war into the North again, hoping that a Confederate victory in Union territory would convince Northerners to call for an end to the fighting.

Lee's troops made camp about 45 miles from Harrisburg, Pennsylvania. Confederate troops went to the town of Gettysburg to seize a supply of shoes at a shoe factory. The troops met the forward cavalry troops of the Union Army of the Potomac. The **Battle of Gettysburg** began the next day.

In the first two days of battle, Confederate forces seemed to be winning. The third day, Lee attacked the center of the Union forces. The primary fighting occurred in the late afternoon at Cemetery Ridge. Lee ordered General George Pickett and his forces to charge, but Union forces were ready. Within a few minutes, almost half of Pickett's 13,000 troops lay dead or wounded. Sick at heart, Lee retreated, leading his troops

▼ Gettysburg was the largest battle of the Civil War. More than 7,000 soldiers died. Another 44,000 were wounded or missing.

The Gettysburg Address

President Abraham Lincoln's speech, given on November 19, 1863, at the dedication of a cemetery for soldiers killed in the Battle of Gettysburg, is considered one of the greatest speeches of all time.

Four score and seven years ago, our fathers brought forth on this continent a new nation, conceived in liberty, and dedicated to the proposition that all men are created equal.

Now we are engaged in a great civil war, testing whether that nation or any nation so conceived and so dedicated, can long endure. We are met on a great battlefield of that war. We have come to dedicate a portion of that field, as a final resting place for those who here gave their lives that that nation might live. It is altogether fitting and proper that we should do this.

But, in a larger sense, we cannot dedicate—we cannot consecrate—we cannot hallow—this ground. The brave men, living and dead, who struggled here, have consecrated it, far above our poor power to add or detract. The world will little note, nor long remember what we say here, but it can never forget what they did here. It is for us the living, rather, to be dedicated here to the unfinished work which they who fought here have thus far so nobly advanced. It is rather for us to be here dedicated to the great task remaining before us—that from these honored dead we take increased devotion to that cause for which they gave the last full measure of devotion—that we here highly resolve that these dead shall not have died in vain—that this nation, under God, shall have a new birth of freedom—and that government of the people, by the people, for the people, shall not perish from the earth.

THINKING CRITICALLY

1. **Making Inferences** What cause does Lincoln refer to in his address?
2. **Analyzing Points of View** How does Lincoln justify continuing the war despite the large number of soldiers killed at Gettysburg?
3. **Drawing Conclusions** Why has Lincoln's speech become famous?

For more about the Gettysburg Address . . .

RESEARCH LINKS
CLASSZONE.COM

▲ After three days of fighting, 51,000 Union and Confederate soldiers lay dead or wounded on the battlefield.

back to Virginia. Over one third of Lee's army, or 28,000 men, were injured or dead. Union forces lost about 23,000 men.

Lincoln was deeply moved by the losses suffered at Gettysburg. He traveled to the battle site for the dedication of a cemetery. Lincoln's speech lasted only two minutes and was ten sentences long. He believed that what he said there would not be remembered. He was wrong.

Chickamauga and Chattanooga

In September 1863, Confederate General Braxton Bragg defeated Union forces at Chickamauga in northern Georgia. However, instead of chasing the retreating Union forces after his victory, Bragg trapped them in Chattanooga, Tennessee. He placed cannons on Lookout Mountain to the south of the city, and then he stationed infantry on

Vocabulary

Chickamauga: "river of death" in the Cherokee language

Missionary Ridge to the east and on roads leading into Chattanooga from the west.

Grant understood the serious situation that faced the Union army in Chattanooga. He went to Chattanooga to direct the campaign personally. Sherman brought reinforcements from Mississippi.

On November 24, the stronger Union army attacked the Confederates on Lookout Mountain. This attack was called the "Battle Above the Clouds" because 10,000 Union troops charged up the mountain in a heavy fog. They drove the 2,000 Confederate defenders off the mountain.

Bragg quickly reassembled over half of his remaining force at Missionary Ridge to prepare for the next assault. The 23,000 Union troops attacked the Confederates the next day and drove Bragg's forces out. The Confederate troops retreated 30 miles southward before stopping to regroup.

The Confederate troops set up winter camp at Dalton, Georgia. That winter, there were a few small fights with Union troops but no major battles. It was very cold, and rations were meager.

In March 1864, Lincoln named Grant commander of all the Union armies. Grant developed a plan to defeat the Confederacy. He would pursue Lee's army in Virginia, while Sherman and his troops pushed the war into the Deep South. In the next section, you will learn how Sherman brought the war to Georgia.

Reading History

D. Making Inferences How did the strategy of Grant differ from the strategy of McClellan?

Section 3 Assessment

1. TERMS & NAMES

Explain the significance of:

a. Battle of Shiloh

b. Ulysses S. Grant

c. William T. Sherman

d. Robert E. Lee

e. Battle of Antietam

f. Emancipation Proclamation

g. Battle of Gettysburg

2. TAKING NOTES

Review the section and find six key events to place on a time line like the one shown below.

3. MAIN IDEAS

a. What were the terms of the Emancipation Proclamation?

b. Why was the immediate impact of the Emancipation Proclamation limited?

c. How did events at Chickamauga and Chattanooga affect Georgians?

4. CRITICAL THINKING

Making Predictions

Do you think the war would have ended differently if the South had won at Gettysburg?

Think About
• Northern resources
• Southern strategy

Language Arts/Technology Create a **historical marker** on posterboard or design a **Web page** about a battle or leader of the Civil War.

4

War Comes to Georgia

MAIN IDEA	WHY IT MATTERS NOW	TERMS & NAMES
Through 1863, almost all of the fighting of the war occurred outside Georgia. But in 1864, Union strategy focused on destroying Georgia's resources and its people's will to fight.	Sherman's march through Georgia devastated the land and people for years to come. Recovery was slow.	March to the Sea Field Order No. 120 Andersonville Field Order No. 15

SETTING THE STAGE

With the Union victories at Gettysburg and Vicksburg, the tide of the war began to turn. After Chickamauga and Chattanooga, Union troops were poised on Georgia's northern border.

Grant left to take command of Union forces fighting Lee's army in Virginia. He left Sherman in command of about 100,000 troops. Confederate President Jefferson Davis replaced Bragg with Confederate General Joseph E. Johnston. Johnston commanded a force of about 53,000 men. Both sides set up winter camp and waited for spring. By April, Sherman was ready to move.

▲ Union and Confederate troops spent an uncomfortable winter camped in barracks such as these. The winter of 1864 was cold and the rations were meager.

The Georgia Campaign

Sherman's plan was to march through Georgia, take Atlanta, and then proceed to Savannah. Then his army would turn north through South Carolina and North Carolina. Sherman wrote about his plan to keep Johnston's and Lee's troops from joining forces.

> **PRIMARY SOURCE**
>
> I was required to follow it [Johnston's army] up closely and persistently, so that in no event could any part be detached to assist General Lee in Virginia; General Grant undertaking in like manner to keep Lee so busy that he could not respond to any calls of help by Johnston.
>
> from the memoirs of General W. T. Sherman

Johnston's orders were to stop Sherman's advance through Georgia. But often Sherman simply moved around Johnston's army and continued southward. President Davis disliked Johnston's tactics. He wanted Johnston to take an offensive stance against Sherman.

Taking Notes

Use your chart to note the impact on Georgia as Union forces move in.

	North	South
Reasons for Fighting		
Advantages		

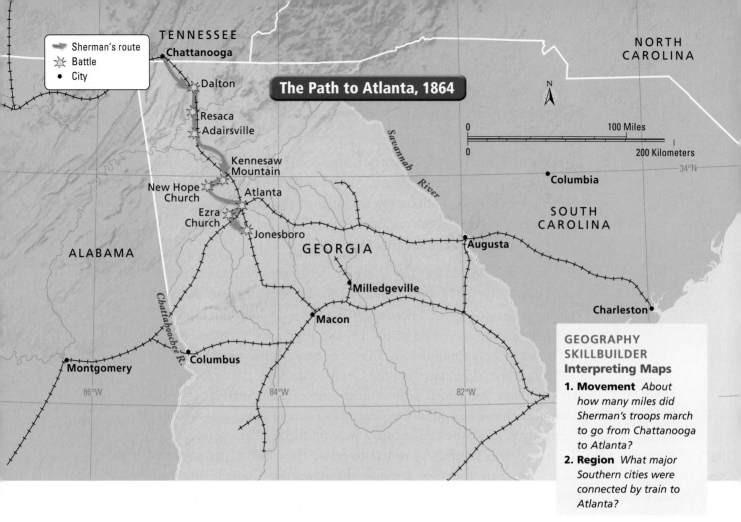

The Path to Atlanta, 1864

GEOGRAPHY
SKILLBUILDER
Interpreting Maps
1. **Movement** About
   how many miles did
   Sherman's troops march
   to go from Chattanooga
   to Atlanta?
2. **Region** What major
   Southern cities were
   connected by train to
   Atlanta?

The Path to Atlanta

Small battles occurred in Georgia, all along the path to Atlanta.
Sherman referred to this part of his campaign as "one grand skirmish."
This was a different type of war for the soldiers on both sides. They
were used to fighting a big battle and moving on to wait, sometimes for
months, for the next encounter.

Confederate troops fought, retreated, and fought again. One soldier
with Co. H 63 Ga. [Infantry] Regiment, Mercers Brigade, wrote to his
wife about the running battle.

PRIMARY SOURCE

We have had nothing but fighting. . . . The first battle we had above Dalton
at Rockface Mountain & we have been falling back ever since. . . . The
second battle we had at Resaca, the third at Calhoun, the fourth below
Calhoun, the fifth at [Adairsville], the sixth at [Cassville]. . . . Where the next
will be I cannot tell, but think we will drop back to Atlanta & there will be a
heavy battle.

John M. McNell, quoted in *Confederate Reminiscences and Letters, 1861–1865*

Dalton Union forces met heavier resistance around the town of
Dalton, where most of the Confederate forces had spent the winter.
There was fighting along the bluffs in an area called "Buzzard's Roost"
and Dug Gap. At Dug Gap, the Confederates rolled large boulders

down on the Union troops charging up the hill. Although the Union army outnumbered the Confederate forces, Sherman could not take the Confederate positions. So he simply went around them in a maneuver called "flanking."

Resaca to New Hope Church Union forces met strong resistance at Resaca a few days later. Again, Sherman decided to circle around Johnston's army and continue toward Atlanta. He used the same plan again over the next month at Adairsville, Cassville, and New Hope Church to continue marching toward Atlanta.

Kennesaw Mountain The Battle of Kennesaw Mountain was the first major battle on Georgia soil. After weeks of small skirmishes and skirting Johnston's forces, Sherman decided to meet Johnston head-on. The weather was hot—almost 100°F—and very rainy.

The battle began on June 27, 1864. Sherman's forces were unable to take Kennesaw Mountain from the Confederate army. Again, Sherman went around Johnston, who quickly retreated south across the Chattahoochee River. Johnston prepared to defend the city of Atlanta.

By July 9, 1864, the Union forces were on the northern banks of the Chattahoochee, waiting for orders to cross. They had to use pontoon bridges to cross the river because the retreating Confederates had burned all the bridges.

> **Vocabulary**
>
> **pontoon bridge:** a temporary bridge resting on portable floats across a body of water

▼ Johnston's troops burned the bridges behind them to hinder the Union troops. Sherman's troops constructed pontoon bridges such as these to cross the Chattahoochee.

The Atlanta Campaign

Unhappy with Johnston's retreat, President Davis replaced him with General John B. Hood. Davis wanted Hood not only to defend the city but also to attack Union forces. On July 20, Hood attacked Union forces along Peachtree Creek, north of Atlanta. A Union private described the front line when the Confederates attacked.

PRIMARY SOURCE

Then the Rebs came toward us. . . . the firing really began. The gunfire exceeded anything that I had ever heard before. . . . The Rebs came to within 10 paces of us, at which time our musket balls became too thick for them. . . . The entire field was scattered with dead, wounded, and dying.

Frederick Charles Buerstatte, July 20, 1864, diary entry

Vocabulary

siege: the surrounding of a city, town, or fortress by an army trying to capture it

The Siege of Atlanta The Confederates eventually retreated to fortifications protecting the city of Atlanta. Sherman shelled the city for almost 40 days. Although homes and buildings were severely damaged, most of the civilians and soldiers survived. Many spent most of their time in makeshift shelters called bomb proofs.

Ezra Church and Jonesboro After several weeks of fighting, Sherman shifted his forces west of Atlanta. General Hood attacked Sherman at Ezra Church on July 28. Hood's attack failed, and he retreated. On August 31, Hood tried to surprise Union troops at Jonesboro. After losing there, Hood realized that he could no longer

▶ Sherman's march brought the Civil War into Georgians' homes. Atlanta's industry and railroads made it an important military target.

protect Atlanta. He ordered all military and railroad equipment destroyed. Hood's troops left the city on September 1.

Sherman Enters Atlanta   On September 2, Union forces marched into Atlanta. About 32,000 Union soldiers and 35,000 Confederate troops were killed, wounded, or captured. Sherman had taken Atlanta at a high cost to both sides. Some leaders criticized Sherman for being too heavy-handed in his siege of Atlanta. Sherman responded, "I will answer that war is war, and not popularity seeking."

Sherman decided that the 1,600 men, women, and children remaining in Atlanta had to leave. The mayor of Atlanta, James Calhoun, and General Hood complained that this was cruel. Sherman disagreed but opened a camp south of the city. It was located at the railroad station known as Rough and Ready. Atlanta citizens could stay at the camp if they had nowhere else to go. Both Union and Confederate soldiers worked at the camp. Prisoners of war were exchanged there as well.

Sherman's triumph in conquering Atlanta encouraged Northerners that victory was possible. But the war was not yet over.

▲ Before the war, Sherman served as president of the Louisiana Military Academy (which became Louisiana State University).

Sherman's March to the Sea

After securing Atlanta, Sherman wanted to take his army through the middle of Georgia, all the way to Savannah. This meant marching without a line of supplies. At first, President Lincoln and Grant did not like the plan. They worried that without a supply line, Sherman's army would get into trouble. But Sherman insisted that it was possible.

> *PRIMARY SOURCE*
>
> If we can march a well-appointed army right through [Confederate] territory, it is a demonstration to the world, foreign and domestic, that we have a power which Davis cannot resist. . . . I can make the march, and make Georgia howl!
>
> W. T. Sherman, quoted in *Battle Cry of Freedom* by James McPherson

Sherman remained in Atlanta for over two months. His troops rested and restocked their supplies. Sherman was ready to move at the beginning of November. He ordered all major buildings in Atlanta destroyed.

Field Order No. 120   Sherman issued special marching orders for the **March to the Sea,** the final phase of his march through Georgia. **Field Order No. 120** ordered soldiers to live off the land. They would gather food from fields and drive off livestock. Soldiers who had the duty of collecting food, horses and mules, and other supplies were called "bummers." Soldiers were forbidden to enter the homes of civilians and steal their property. They were supposed to leave enough food behind for the people. But many Northern soldiers ignored these orders.

Reading History

B. Making Inferences How did Field Order No. 120 affect civilians in Georgia?

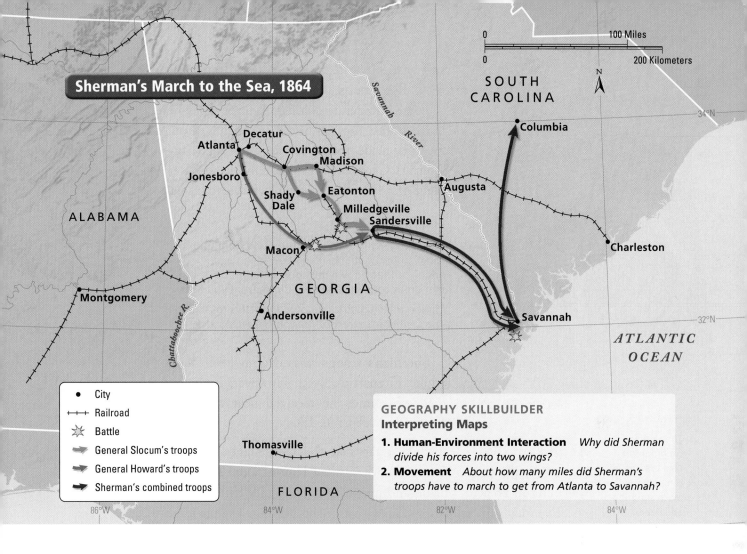

Sherman's March to the Sea, 1864

Legend:
- City
- Railroad
- Battle
- General Slocum's troops
- General Howard's troops
- Sherman's combined troops

GEOGRAPHY SKILLBUILDER
Interpreting Maps
1. **Human-Environment Interaction** *Why did Sherman divide his forces into two wings?*
2. **Movement** *About how many miles did Sherman's troops have to march to get from Atlanta to Savannah?*

Sherman waged total war: a war not only against enemy troops, but against everything that supported the enemy. His troops tore up rail lines and destroyed crops. Officers were instructed not to destroy homes and buildings in "districts and neighborhoods where the army is unmolested." However, if they encountered resistance, they were to burn homes and businesses.

The only opposition Sherman's troops faced in their journey from Atlanta to the coast was the state militia, 3,500 Confederate cavalry commanded by General Joseph Wheeler and a handful of volunteers.

Sherman divided his army into two wings. General O. O. Howard commanded the right wing. General H. W. Slocum commanded the left wing. Sherman traveled with the left wing. On November 21, Sherman rested at a plantation. When he realized that it belonged to Howell Cobb, a Confederate army general, he confiscated the crops and ordered that nothing be spared.

Reactions to Sherman's March Freed slaves heartily welcomed the Union troops. Some white civilians feared their coming. Some expressed amazement at the kindness and respect displayed by the Union forces. Others complained bitterly about having their property seized and homes burned to the ground. The few Confederate forces

Background

Sherman's soldiers crippled Georgia's railroads by tying "Sherman's neckties." They would heat the tracks over a bonfire until they were red-hot, then twist and bend them around nearby trees and telegraph poles.

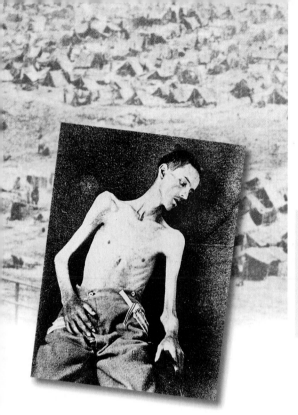

still in the area made small guerrilla attacks on the Union troops.

For Confederate soldiers fighting elsewhere in the South, news of Sherman's march through Georgia made them fear for their loved ones' safety. A Georgian with the 45th Georgia Regiment near Petersburg, Virginia, wrote to his wife.

PRIMARY SOURCE

I have eagerly gathered all the news from Ga I could to find out Sherman's course . . . and I hope . . . that he will pass our section . . . But I will feel great concern till I hear direct from you again.

Marion Hill Fitzpatrick, quoted in *Letters to Amanda: The Civil War Letters of Marion Hill Fitzpatrick*

Sherman's troops missed Crawford County where Fitzpatrick lived. However, Fitzpatrick died of wounds he received near Petersburg, Virginia, on April 6, 1865.

Andersonville Meanwhile, guards at the Confederate prison at **Andersonville** prepared to defend it against Union raids. The prison was built on 26 acres of land and meant to hold 10,000 Union prisoners. Eventually it held over 33,000 prisoners. Almost 13,000 Union prisoners died from disease, starvation, and horrible living conditions before the end of the war.

▲ The terrible conditions at Civil War prison camps caused much suffering and death.

Reading History

C. Making Inferences Why were the death rates so high at many Civil War prison camps?

From the State Capital to Savannah

As Union forces approached the state capital of Milledgeville, the Georgia government left. This included the Georgia legislature, the Georgia State Supreme Court, and Governor Brown. As Governor Brown retreated, he appealed to the people of Georgia to resist the invading forces. But when the first of the Union forces arrived on November 22, 1864, the town was undefended. The penitentiary and factories were burned. Some businesses and homes were looted. Sherman arrived at Milledgeville the next day. He spent the night in the governor's mansion. The next day, the march continued eastward.

The Battle at the Oconee River Bridge Confederate troops confronted Sherman's forces south of Milledgeville at a railroad bridge crossing the Oconee River on November 24. The Confederate force, about 400 men, were an odd mix of infantry and cavalry, prisoners from the penitentiary, and young cadets from the Georgia Military Institute. Some cadets were only 14 years old. Despite valiant efforts in which many lost their lives, the Confederate troops could not slow down Sherman's march.

The two wings of Sherman's army met at Sandersville, and then moved eastward toward the Georgia coast.

Sherman Advances   News of Sherman's arrival in the coastal area of Georgia worried many plantation owners there. In Liberty County, the daughter of a plantation owner recalled that time.

> **PRIMARY SOURCE**
>
> Rumors came that Sherman's army was coming through Georgia burning and devastating the country. Rumors of horrible treatment of old men and ladies. . . . A rough crowd poured through the house going through the rooms, searching every bureau, wardrobe, closets, and trunks. They took all silverware and jewelry.
>
> Cornelia Jones Pond, *Life on a Liberty County Plantation*

Fall of Savannah   Throughout the war, Union forces had not been able to take Savannah by sea. The city was well defended by Fort Jackson, a squadron of small Confederate ships, underwater mines, earthen fortifications, and obstructions in the river. Yet the city was not prepared for an invasion by land.

On December 13, 1864, Sherman's forces reached the mouth of the Ogeechee River. South of Savannah, the Union army captured Fort McAllister after a very brief fight. With its earthen walls, the fort had withstood Union naval attacks during the war, but it could not defend against a land attack.

With the fall of Fort McAllister, Confederate General William J. Hardee decided it was impossible to defend the city. Hardee and his men escaped across the Savannah River on a makeshift pontoon bridge during the night of December 20. They joined other Confederate forces that fought Sherman's forces all the way into North Carolina.

▼ When Savannah was captured, Sherman sent word to President Lincoln. "I beg to present to you as a Christmas gift, the city of Savannah."

277

On December 21, Union troops marched into Savannah and took the city. There was very little looting. Many Savannah residents were relieved that Sherman did not inflict the kind of damage upon their city that Atlanta had experienced. After taking Savannah, Sherman's troops turned north into South Carolina. The devastation intensified, as many Union soldiers believed South Carolina had started the Civil War.

Freedmen   From the beginning of Sherman's march into Georgia, former slaves flocked to the Union troops. The problem of feeding and caring for the growing number posed a problem for Sherman. They also slowed down his march. Sherman turned to Secretary of War Edwin Stanton for a solution.

Field Order No. 15   Stanton met with some of the freedmen in Savannah and asked what they wanted. They wanted land to grow crops and care for their families. Sherman issued **Field Order No. 15** on January 16, 1865. This gave each head of household 40 acres of land. The land was along the coast from Charleston, South Carolina, to Jacksonville, Florida.

Almost 40,000 freedmen lived on their 40 acres of land. But they had no clear ownership. The land was later returned to the former owners. For a short time, freedmen had the resources to provide for themselves.

Sherman's march through Georgia and the Carolinas took a heavy physical and emotional toll on the South. Prospects for a Confederate victory looked bleak. In the next section, you will learn about the fall of the Confederacy and the end of the Civil War.

Section 4 Assessment

1. TERMS & NAMES

Explain the significance of:

a. March to the Sea

b. Field Order No. 120

c. Andersonville

d. Field Order No. 15

2. TAKING NOTES

Use a diagram such as the one below to list the purpose of Sherman's march and its effects.

Purpose

↓

Sherman's March

↓

Effects

3. MAIN IDEAS

a. How did Sherman's march practice "total war"?

b. Why did Sherman burn Atlanta?

c. How did Sherman's march help secure a Union victory?

4. CRITICAL THINKING

Recognizing Effects

Why did Sherman march his army through Georgia?

Think About

• the effect on Southern resources and morale

• the effect on Northern resources and morale

• the effect on Georgia soldiers

ACTIVITY -OPTIONS-   **Language Arts/Geography** Write a **newspaper account** or draw a **map** of Sherman's march through Georgia as if you were an eyewitness to the event.

5

The War's End

MAIN IDEA	WHY IT MATTERS NOW	TERMS & NAMES
With the capture of the Confederate capital at Richmond and Lee's surrender, the war drew to a close.	With the end of the Civil War, the Union was reunited once again. The Union grew into the United States we have today.	Appomattox Court House John Wilkes Booth

▲ After four long years, the Civil War was coming to a close. Union and Confederate soldiers were weary of fighting.

SETTING THE STAGE

After years of fighting, Southern troops were tired, disillusioned, hungry, and outnumbered. In Virginia, Grant was wearing down Lee's troops. Sherman had swept through Georgia, had turned north, and was marching through the Carolinas.

The war was coming to a close. Some Southerners were ready to end the conflict. But some wanted to carry on the fighting, even if the odds were against their side.

Surrender at Appomattox

On April 1, 1865, Lee sent word to President Jefferson Davis that he could not stop Union troops from taking Richmond. Davis and the remaining government officials quickly left the city. Union troops entered Richmond the next day. President Lincoln went to Richmond. As he walked the streets of the city, freed slaves and Union troops cheered.

PRIMARY SOURCE

Thank God I have lived to see this. It seems to me that I have been dreaming a horrid dream for four years, and now the nightmare is gone. I want to see Richmond.
Abraham Lincoln, quoted by James McPherson in *Battle Cry of Freedom*

Lee wanted to continue the fight. But he did not get the chance. His army was short of supplies, outnumbered, weary from years of fighting, and cut off from other troops. General Lee knew that it was time to end the fighting.

Lee met with Grant at **Appomattox Court House,** Virginia, on April 9, 1865. They agreed on the terms of surrender. Three days later, about 25,000 Confederate troops surrendered their weapons and were allowed to go home. They would not be tried for treason.

Taking Notes

Use your chart to compare and contrast the impact on the North and South as the war ends.

	North	South
Reasons for Fighting		
Advantages		

Confederate forces across the South continued fighting for a few weeks longer. Many supporters of the Confederate cause received the news of Lee's surrender with disbelief and great sadness.

The Assassination of Lincoln

People celebrated in the streets of Washington, D.C., when the news of Lee's surrender reached them. President Lincoln gave a speech from the balcony of the White House. He talked about his plans to reunite the Union. He said that freed slaves and those citizens who had remained loyal to the Union would be involved in the process. In the crowd was a Confederate sympathizer—**John Wilkes Booth.** He decided to assassinate President Lincoln.

As Lincoln and his wife attended a play at Ford's Theater a few nights later, on April 14, 1865, Booth entered the private box and shot Lincoln in the head. The president died the next day. Booth escaped the theater but was later cornered and shot while trying to escape.

The Confederacy Finally Falls

Union cavalry moved into western Georgia from Alabama a few days after Lee's surrender. They captured the city of Columbus. Then they left for Macon.

General Howell Cobb commanded the troops defending Macon. Outnumbered 13,000 to 3,000, Cobb surrendered. A few weeks later, Governor Brown formally surrendered the Georgia Militia and all of its weapons. Union troops arrested Georgia's political leaders, Brown, Cobb, Alexander Stephens, and Benjamin H. Hill. Robert Toombs escaped capture and went to Europe. Major Henry Wirz, commander

Background

Thousands of mourners stood beside the tracks as Lincoln's body was taken by train to Springfield, Illinois.

Costs of the Civil War

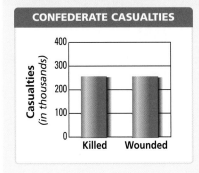

CONFEDERATE CASUALTIES

Casualties (in thousands)

400
300
200
100
0

Killed   Wounded

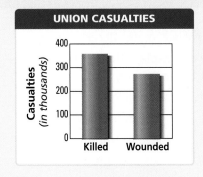

UNION CASUALTIES

Casualties (in thousands)

400
300
200
100
0

Killed   Wounded

SKILLBUILDER

Interpreting Graphs

1. *About how many Confederate soldiers were killed in the Civil War?*

2. *Approximately how many soldiers were wounded in the war?*

Sources: *World Book; Historical Statistics of the United States; The United States Civil War Center*

of Andersonville Prison, was arrested, tried, found guilty, and executed for war crimes.

President Davis fled Richmond in early April 1865. In May, Davis met with his cabinet in Washington, Georgia, and temporarily dissolved the Confederate government. But Davis was not ready to give up. He hoped the North would tire of fighting and allow the Southern states to remain independent. However, Davis and his family were captured near Irwinville, Georgia, on May 10. The Civil War was over.

Many Southerners could not accept the fact that they had lost. For years after the war ended, Southerners struggled with the outcome. In the next chapter, you will read about the challenges that faced them as the South re-entered the Union.

Reading History

A. Making Inferences How did the idea of states' rights affect the Confederacy's ability to fight effectively against the Union army?

Section Assessment

1. TERMS & NAMES

Explain the significance of:

a. Appomattox Court House

b. John Wilkes Booth

2. TAKING NOTES

Use a diagram such as the one below to review the events of this section that led to the fall of the Confederacy. Which seems more important, and why?

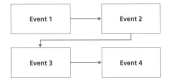

Event 1 → Event 2

Event 3 → Event 4

3. MAIN IDEAS

a. What were Lincoln's plans to restore the Union?

b. Why did Davis continue fighting after Lee surrendered?

4. CRITICAL THINKING

Making Inferences

How do you think the assassination of President Lincoln affected the nation?

Think About

• the reaction of ordinary citizens

• its impact on government

ACTIVITY -OPTIONS-   **Language Arts/Music** Write a **two-page report** or write a **song** about one of the regiments that fought in the Civil War.

The Civil War **281**

VISUAL SUMMARY

The Civil War 1861–1865

1860
• Abraham Lincoln elected president.

1861
• Georgia votes to secede from the Union.
• Georgia joins the confederacy.
• Fort Sumter is taken by Confederate forces.

1862
• Union spies board train in Marietta, Georgia.
• Battle of Shiloh
• Fort Pulaski surrenders to Union forces.

1863
• Emancipation Proclamation is issued.
• Confederate forces defeated at Gettysburg and Vicksburg.
• Battle of Chickamauga

1864
• Atlanta falls to Sherman.
• Lincoln is reelected.
• Savannah is occupied.

1865
• President Davis captured.
• Union takes Richmond. Lee surrenders. Lincoln is assassinated.

TERMS & NAMES

Briefly explain the significance of the following.

1. Anaconda Plan
2. King Cotton diplomacy
3. 20-slave exemption
4. Ulysses S. Grant
5. Robert E. Lee
6. Emancipation Proclamation
7. March to the Sea
8. Andersonville
9. Appomattox Court House
10. John Wilkes Booth

REVIEW QUESTIONS

The Fighting Begins (pages 251–256)

1. Why did Union troops conduct raids in northern Georgia in the spring of 1862?
2. What resources did Georgia supply to the Confederacy?

Life on the Front Lines and at Home (pages 257–263)

3. How did the Civil War affect farm production?
4. How did Georgia freedmen respond to the Civil War?

The War Continues (pages 264–269)

5. What wartime power allowed Lincoln to free the slaves?
6. Why did the Union defeat Bragg at Chattanooga?

War Comes to Georgia (pages 270–278)

7. Why were the battles of the March to the Sea different?
8. What was the first major battle on Georgia soil?

The War's End (pages 279–281)

9. Where were the terms of surrender worked out?
10. What event signaled the end of the Confederacy?

CRITICAL THINKING

1. USING YOUR NOTES: COMPARING AND CONTRASTING

	North	South
Reasons for Fighting		
Advantages		
Disadvantages		
Military Strategy		
Battle Victories		

Using your completed chart, answer the questions below.

a. How did white and black Southerners react to the Emancipation Proclamation?
b. How did inflation affect the North and the South?

2. ANALYZING LEADERSHIP

Why might people have been surprised at Grant's success as a general?

3. APPLYING CITIZENSHIP SKILLS

How might the war have changed the commonly held view of women's role as citizens?

4. THEME: CITIZENSHIP

How could people on both sides of the Civil War believe that they were being good citizens by fighting?

5. MAKING INFERENCES

Why did so many people volunteer to fight in the Civil War?

6. DRAWING CONCLUSIONS

How might the common experience of West Point training be both an advantage and a disadvantage to Lee and Grant?

INTERACT *with* HISTORY

Having read about the battles during the Civil War, do you think you would have wanted to keep fighting? Why or why not?

Use the map and your knowledge of Georgia history to answer questions 1 through 3.

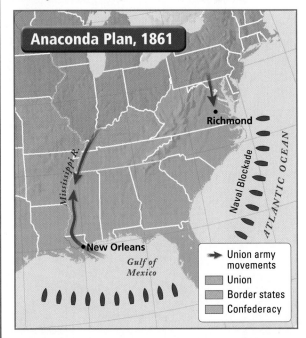

Anaconda Plan, 1861

Richmond

Mississippi R.

Naval Blockade

ATLANTIC OCEAN

New Orleans

Gulf of Mexico

→ Union army movements

Union

Border states

Confederacy

1. What do the arrows indicate?

   A. Civilians trying to avoid war zones
   B. Major battlefields
   C. The movements of the Union Army
   D. The movements of the Confederate Army

2. What major area(s) did the blockade cover?

   A. Atlantic Ocean coastline
   B. The Atlantic Ocean and Great Lakes
   C. Gulf of Mexico and Mississippi River
   D. Gulf coast, Mississippi River, Eastern coastline

3. What area is targeted by Union troops?

   A. Border states
   B. The Confederacy
   C. The Gulf of Mexico
   D. The Mississippi

TEST PRACTICE
CLASSZONE.COM

ALTERNATIVE ASSESSMENT

1. GIVING A MOTIVATIONAL SPEECH

In the days leading up to the war and in the early months of the war, feelings ran high on both sides. While there were plenty of people who were firm in their support of either the Union or the Confederacy, there were many others who were unsure of where their loyalty should lie. Choose a side and write a speech in which you try to motivate others to join you in supporting either the Union or the Confederacy. Your speech should be based on facts. Present your speech to your class.

2. COOPERATIVE LEARNING

Participate in a panel discussion about Lincoln's decision to go to war to save the Union. Was there an alternative?

INTEGRATED TECHNOLOGY ACTIVITY

PREPARING AN ELECTRONIC PRESENTATION

Use the Internet, your library, and a computer to prepare an electronic presentation that depicts the hardship of life in the military training camps during the Civil War. Look for diaries, letters, photos, art, and newspaper articles that reveal what life was like for the soldiers. Try to include the following items in your presentation.

- Mealtimes
- Sleeping conditions
- Uniforms
- Loneliness
- Health care
- Boredom/recreation

RESEARCH LINKS
CLASSZONE.COM

Reconstruction of Georgia and the South 1863-1877

These freedmen in Macon, like other African Americans across the country, registered to vote for the first time in 1867.

1865
Constitutional Convention

1867
John Pope becomes commander of Georgia military district.

1868
African-American legislators removed from office.

GEORGIA
USA   1863

1865
Andrew Johnson becomes president. Congress creates Freedmen's Bureau.

1867
Military Reconstruction Acts passed.

1868
Fourteenth Amendment extends full citizenship to African Americans.

The Civil War has just ended, and the Southern economy is in ruins. Slavery has been abolished. Northerners and Southerners feel deep anger toward one another. As a member of Congress, you must help rebuild the nation.

How would you rebuild the Union?

WHAT DO YOU THINK?

- What problems would you face in rebuilding the nation?

- How would you ease tensions between the North and South?

- How would you help freed African Americans?

For more information on this chapter, visit . . .

RESEARCH LINKS
CLASSZONE.COM

1871
Georgia represented in both houses of Congress for first time since Civil War.

1874
Georgia forms nation's first state department of agriculture.

 1870

1877

1870
Fifteenth Amendment guarantees voting rights to African Americans.

1872
Grant is reelected president.

1877
Rutherford B. Hayes inaugurated as president and ends Reconstruction.

Reading Strategy: Evaluating

What Do You Know?

What do you think it means to reconstruct something? What kinds of things did the U.S. government need to reconstruct after the Civil War? Which of these issues do you think was most important?

THINK ABOUT
• what you've learned about the Civil War in the last two chapters
• what you've learned about civil rights in the United States from television, movies, and books

What Do You Want to Know?

What questions do you have about Reconstruction? Record those questions in your notebook before you read the chapter.

Evaluating

What were the positive and negative effects of the plans for Reconstruction? Overall, were the plans successful? When you make a judgment about Reconstruction or any other period in history, you evaluate it. As you evaluate, think about what the government wanted to accomplish. Then look for both positive and negative results. Based on these results, use the chart below to write your overall evaluation.

S *See Skillbuilder Handbook, page 553.*

 Taking Notes

Reconstruction

Positive Results:

Evaluation:

Negative Results:

Reconstruction of the South Begins

MAIN IDEA	WHY IT MATTERS NOW	TERMS & NAMES

The process of reuniting the nation was a difficult one.	Reconstruction shaped the South's economy and political structure well into the 20th century.	freedman sharecropping
		Thirteenth black code
		  Amendment Fourteenth
		Freedmen's Amendment
		  Bureau

SETTING THE STAGE

After the fighting ended, the next step was putting the country back together. How was it going to happen? President Abraham Lincoln wanted the nation reunited and did not think that the Southern states should be harshly punished. When Lincoln was assassinated, it was a blow to the South.

There were, however, Northern Republicans in Congress who wanted the South to suffer for trying to destroy the Union. Before Congress could write guidelines for bringing Southern states back into the Union, Lincoln's successor implemented his own plans.

Conditions after the War

When the Civil War ended, the South was an economic, political, and social wreck. Most of the region's railroads were either damaged or had been destroyed. Cities and towns like Atlanta, Georgia; Richmond, Virginia; and Columbia, South Carolina, were in ruins.

Both whites and African Americans were mainly concerned with surviving in the months after the war. There were food shortages across the South. Many people were unable to get shelter and clothing. State and local governments were disorganized and not much help. Life for **freedmen,** or former slaves, and Southern whites was very unstable.

Southern whites understood that the South had been defeated. But many remained defiant and angry. Eliza Frances Andrews of Washington, Georgia, made her feelings about the North clear.

PRIMARY SOURCE

If all the words of hatred in every language . . . were lumped together . . . they could not tell how I hate Yankees.

Eliza Andrews, in *Wartime Journal of a Georgia Girl*

▲ The Freedmen's Bureau worked to help freedmen and poor whites find food, shelter, and clothing. The Bureau supervised the hiring and management of freedmen who worked on plantations and farms.

Taking Notes

Use your chart to evaluate Reconstruction efforts in the South.

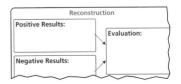

Reconstruction

Positive Results:

Evaluation:

Negative Results:

▲ Freedmen gather on this Hilton Head, South Carolina, plantation during the Union occupation of the property.

Freedmen were getting used to their freedom. They did things that had been prohibited under slavery—held religious services without white supervision, bought guns, were not courteous to whites, and even changed their names.

Many freedmen wanted to distance themselves from whites, who had been their oppressors. Freedmen also wanted to find relatives and close friends who had been sold to other slave owners. Some traveled for months and over hundreds of miles trying to find their husband or wife, parent or child. Freedmen also migrated to the North and West, and to Southern towns and cities, looking for better opportunities and a safer environment in which to pursue their lives.

Reading History

A. Analyzing Causes For what reasons did former slaves move?

Presidential Reconstruction

Attempts to put the Union back together began as early as 1863. In December 1863, President Lincoln issued the Proclamation of Amnesty and Reconstruction. This was a plan to rebuild or "reconstruct" the social, political, and economic structures of the Southern states before allowing them back into the Union. White male voters of a Southern state could take an oath of loyalty to the Union. Only high-ranking Confederate military leaders and officers were prohibited from taking the oath. After 10 percent of the state's white male voters took the oath, they could write a new constitution that included a clause making slavery illegal. Representatives could then be seated in Congress. This was known as the Ten Percent Plan.

The Radical Republicans Radical Republicans were Republicans in Congress who wanted the federal government to remake Southern politics and society. They thought Lincoln was too lenient and Congress should take the lead in reconstructing the Union. Lincoln rejected their plan. When he was assassinated in April 1865, there was not a clear program in place to reconstruct the nation.

When Lincoln died, Vice-President Andrew Johnson became president. His ideas for Reconstruction were similar to Lincoln's. But he set higher demands for Southerners to return to the Union. First, he excluded any Southerner who had owned more than $20,000 in property from taking the oath of loyalty. Most people that wealthy had owned slaves. They could, however, appeal directly to President Johnson for permission to take the oath.

President Johnson had additional requirements for Southern states.

- ratify the **Thirteenth Amendment,** which outlawed slavery
- annul (cancel) the Ordinance of Secession
- cancel all wartime debts
- write a new constitution that included a provision abolishing slavery

Radical Republicans were not happy with Johnson's Reconstruction program. They felt the political and military leaders of the South needed to be punished more and that the pardons were too easy to obtain. In addition, the Radicals believed that Johnson did not have the authority to make policy without approval from Congress.

The Bureau for Refugees, Freedmen, and Abandoned Lands
Congress created the **Freedmen's Bureau** on March 3, 1865. It was one

▶ Members of the U.S. House of Representatives celebrate the enactment of the Thirteenth Amendment, ending slavery.

of the few things that the president and Congress agreed was needed. The primary purpose of the Freedmen's Bureau was to help the freedmen and poor whites obtain food, shelter, and clothing.

The Bureau also established schools for the freedmen. Religious organizations also created schools. The American Baptist Home Missionary Society started the Augusta Baptist Institute, which later became Morehouse College. In 1872, the American Missionary Association opened the school that became Atlanta University.

Southern Labor

After the Civil War, whites still held most of the land. Some African Americans had received land along the coast but were required to return it when President Johnson pardoned the original owners. Proposals to distribute land to freedmen did not pass in Congress.

Without property of their own, former slaves returned to working on plantations. They returned not as slaves, but as wage earners. One Freedmen's Bureau official noted that white landowners found it difficult to change their relationship with freedmen.

Background

Civil War deaths and the departure of slaves from plantations created a labor shortage in the South.

PRIMARY SOURCE

Some think . . . that the only difference between freedom and slavery is that then the negroes were obliged to work for nothing; now they have to pay for what they used to have for nothing.

quoted in *Reconstruction,* by Eric Foner

▼ Gang labor is one system of work that developed. Here a group of workers plow and hoe cotton in a field on a plantation in Columbus.

Plantation owners desperately needed workers to cultivate and harvest crops, particularly cotton. Several different systems of work developed.

Gang Labor   At first, some landowners tried to re-create the system of slavery by using groups of workers under the supervision of a white overseer. Workers could be fined for not working hard. They could be whipped for not obeying orders. This was too much like slavery. Freedmen preferred working in small groups with supervision from someone of their choosing. Often, entire families made up one of these squads of workers.

Wage Labor   Most landowners wanted to pay workers in cash, but they had very little money. Workers agreed to be paid when the crops were harvested. At harvest time, landowners sold their crop and paid workers in cash (called standing wages) or gave workers a portion of the harvested crop (called share wages).

Contract System   Workers signed a contract that explained the arrangement between the worker and landowner. Having enough workers one year did not mean that there would be enough for the next year. If a landowner was abusive or unfair, the freedmen could find other work the next year. Georgian Howell Cobb discovered that he could not find enough workers to harvest his crops in 1867 because the workers (many of whom were his former slaves) had found work elsewhere. They did not like the way they had been treated. "They feel no gratitude towards us," Cobb complained.

▲ Before the Civil War, Howell Cobb was a U.S. congressman and Speaker of the House, as well as governor of Georgia from 1851 to 1853.

Reading History

B. Analyzing Causes Why did freedmen and poor whites turn to sharecropping?

Landowners who needed workers but did not have much money felt the wage labor system was too costly. Freedmen were also unhappy with the wage labor system. Landowners frequently cheated their workers out of their wages and still treated them as slaves. Freedmen, and poor whites too, turned to sharecropping.

Sharecropping   Under the **sharecropping** system, a freedman or poor white contracted to work a plot of land for the landowner. The landowner decided what crops to grow (most often cotton). The sharecropper received a portion of the crop at harvest time, usually half of the crop. White farmers as well as African-American farmers became sharecroppers. By 1880, one third of the white farmers in the Deep South were working someone else's land.

The landowner provided the sharecroppers with a place to live, or a simple shack, as well as seed for planting, farm tools, and even food on credit. The landowner deducted the cost of these items from the money sharecroppers earned from their portion of the crop. The landowner always handled the sale of the crop and kept the accounts of the sharecroppers.

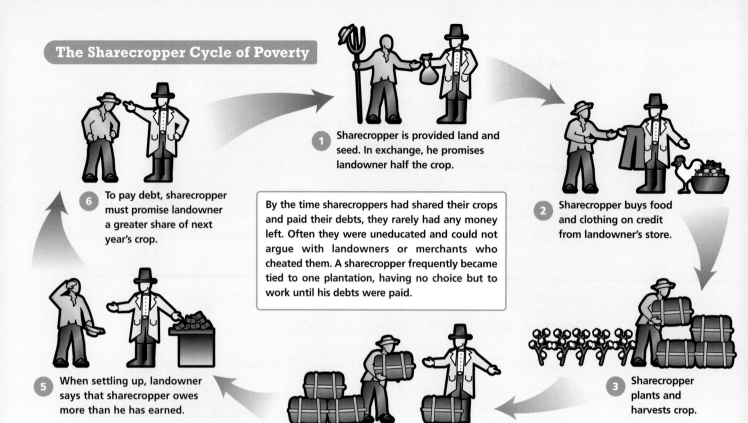

The Sharecropper Cycle of Poverty

1 Sharecropper is provided land and seed. In exchange, he promises landowner half the crop.

2 Sharecropper buys food and clothing on credit from landowner's store.

3 Sharecropper plants and harvests crop.

4 Sharecropper gives landowner crop to sell. Sharecropper will get half the earnings, minus the cost of his purchases for the year.

5 When settling up, landowner says that sharecropper owes more than he has earned.

6 To pay debt, sharecropper must promise landowner a greater share of next year's crop.

By the time sharecroppers had shared their crops and paid their debts, they rarely had any money left. Often they were uneducated and could not argue with landowners or merchants who cheated them. A sharecropper frequently became tied to one plantation, having no choice but to work until his debts were paid.

The system gave people without land a place to live and gave landowners cheap labor. But sharecroppers were at the mercy of the landowners and local merchants, who often charged high interest rates on goods sold on credit. Landowners sometimes cheated sharecroppers by underpaying them for their share of the crop. There were also years when cotton prices were so low that it was impossible to make a profit. Sometimes, bad weather destroyed part, or all, of the crop.

Debt Peonage Sharecroppers often found that at the end of the year they were in debt. They had no way to pay off the debt; so, landowners carried the debt over to the next year. Sharecroppers who remained with the same landowner went further into debt each year. They had a legal obligation to pay the debt. Laws were passed throughout the South that kept sharecroppers from moving if they owed a landowner money. This was known as debt peonage.

Georgia's Reconstruction

In June 1865, President Johnson appointed James Johnson from Columbus, Georgia, as the state's provisional governor. Governor Johnson called for a convention to be held in late October.

The Constitutional Convention of 1865 All the delegates to Georgia's convention were white men. Most had opposed secession, but wanted to preserve white supremacy, or the control of the political system by whites. The convention reluctantly went along with the requirements President Johnson had set for Southerners to rejoin the Union.

In November, statewide elections were held. Charles J. Jenkins became the first governor elected after the war. Jenkins was a former Georgia state attorney general, senator, and Supreme Court judge from Augusta who authored the Georgia Platform of 1850.

Freedmen in Georgia knew that once a new state government was in place, federal troops would leave Georgia. Freedmen would be defenseless against a government headed by the white males who had run the government before the war. Only federal troops could guarantee their safety.

The newly elected legislature met in Milledgeville in December and ratified the Thirteenth Amendment banning slavery. The legislature also elected Alexander Stephens and Herschel V. Johnson as the state's two senators to Congress.

Mistreatment of Freedmen

Georgia had met all of President Johnson's requirements for returning to the Union. But Radical and Moderate Republicans still refused to let the Southern representatives into Congress because they disapproved of how Southern states were treating African Americans. Although slavery was now illegal, Southern whites found other ways to control former slaves.

HISTORY MAKERS

HERSCHEL V. JOHNSON 1812–1880
Although he was a plantation owner, Herschel V. Johnson devoted most of his career to politics. He served as governor of Georgia, U.S. senator, vice-presidential candidate on the Douglas ticket, and senator in the Confederate Congress.

Although he was a strong supporter of states' rights, he argued for preserving the Union at the Georgia secession convention. During the war, he voiced his dissatisfaction with President Jefferson Davis.

Even though he had not supported secession, his prominent position in the Confederacy made him a controversial choice to represent Georgia in the U.S. Congress.

Black Codes During Reconstruction, Southern whites had passed a variety of new laws called **black codes,** which restricted freedmen's rights. The codes created racial segregation, prohibited interracial marriage, blocked African Americans from serving on juries, and prevented them from testifying against whites. African Americans who were disorderly or could not prove that they had a job could be arrested. They were forced to work on road crews or farms. Often, landowners paid their fines and required them to work off the debt.

Reading History

C. Analyzing Causes What was the main reason Southern states passed black codes?

The state of Georgia enacted laws that allowed whipping as a punishment for minor crimes and permitted imprisonment for not having a job. Other laws regulated the hours and duties of workers in labor contracts and allowed employers to fire workers without paying any wages that were owed.

Radical and Moderate Republicans in Congress were angry about the mistreatment of the freedmen in the South. They threatened to stop Southern states' return to the Union.

Congress Responds

In December 1865, a Congressional committee began investigating conditions in the South. The Joint Committee on Reconstruction reported that the Southern state and local governments were not functioning properly, and they were not protecting the rights of the freedmen. The committee advised against allowing Southern representatives to take their seats in Congress. That meant the Southern states could not rejoin the Union.

Civil Rights Act of 1866 Northern Republicans were outraged at the South's attempts to deny freedmen their rights. The Civil Rights Act of 1866 guaranteed the rights of freedmen and blocked the South's black codes. The Freedmen's Bureau, which was scheduled to end soon, was extended. Congress passed both measures over a veto by President Johnson. It decided to add these guarantees to the Constitution. Congress passed the **Fourteenth Amendment** in June 1866, which guaranteed citizenship and equal rights to all persons born in the United States, except Native Americans.

Congress required the Southern states to ratify the Fourteenth Amendment before readmission to the Union. President Johnson told the Southern states to reject the amendment. Georgia's legislature soundly rejected adoption of the Fourteenth Amendment. When the U.S. Congress reconvened later in the year, it was not happy with Georgia and the South. You will learn in the next section how Congress replaced Presidential Reconstruction with Radical Reconstruction.

Reading History

D. Making Inferences Why did President Johnson reject the Civil Rights Act and the Fourteenth Amendment?

Section 1 Assessment

1. TERMS & NAMES

Explain the significance of:

a. freedman

b. Thirteenth Amendment

c. Freedmen's Bureau

d. sharecropping

e. black code

f. Fourteenth Amendment

2. TAKING NOTES

Use a diagram like the one below to review details about sharecropping for sharecroppers and landowners.

Sharecropping
Sharecroppers — Landowners

3. MAIN IDEAS

a. Why did landowners want freedmen to remain in the same area?

b. What was the difference between Presidential and Congressional Reconstruction?

c. What did Georgia and other states try to do to limit freedmen's rights?

4. CRITICAL THINKING

Evaluating

Do you think Congress was justified in not readmitting Georgia to the Union?

Think About

• President Johnson's requirements for reinstatement

• the Civil Rights Act of 1866

• the Fourteenth Amendment

Speech/Art Make a **speech** to President Johnson or design a **mural** explaining why land should be given to newly freed African Americans.

Radical Reconstruction

SETTING THE STAGE

Radical Republicans in Congress refused to let President Johnson make Reconstruction policy. Johnson's actions angered both the Moderate and Radical Republicans in Congress.

Congress was also disturbed about how Southern states treated freedmen. They passed laws that prevented Southern states from abusing the rights of freedmen.

In Georgia, whites struggled with the political and economic changes. Many whites refused to accept a Georgia government in which both freedmen and whites participated. Eventually, white Georgians regained control of the political system. How would this affect the future of Georgia?

▲ Under Radical Reconstruction, Congress required the Southern states to hold new conventions to rewrite the state constitutions.

Congressional Reconstruction

In March of 1867, Congress passed the **Military Reconstruction Acts.** This was the beginning of Congressional Reconstruction (also known as Radical Reconstruction). President Johnson vetoed the bill, but Congress once again overrode his veto. Congress divided the 10 unreconstructed states into 5 military districts. Georgia was in the 3rd district with Florida and Alabama.

Now, to be eligible to become part of the Union, states had to write new constitutions, guarantee African-American males over the age of 21 the right to vote, and approve the Fourteenth Amendment guaranteeing constitutional rights. In addition, former Confederate officeholders were not allowed to vote or run for office.

Use your chart to evaluate Radical Reconstruction results.

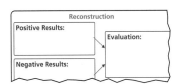

Impeachment In February 1868, Republicans in Congress decided to impeach President Johnson. Impeach means "to charge someone with wrongdoing." If found guilty, Johnson could be removed from office. Johnson had clashed with the Republicans and Congress over Reconstruction policies. He had even campaigned against Republican Congressional candidates in the election of 1866. The Senate failed to remove Johnson from office by one vote. Johnson remained president, but he had lost any power to control Reconstruction policy.

Reconstruction in Georgia

Major General John Pope was the first commander of the 3rd military district. His headquarters were in Atlanta. In April of 1867, he registered 102,411 whites and 98,507 blacks to vote. In November, Georgians voted to hold a constitutional convention. This was the first time African Americans voted in Georgia. Many whites boycotted the vote, and the measure passed 102,283 for a convention to 4,127 against.

The convention opened in Atlanta on December 9, 1867. It was supposed to be held in the state capital of Milledgeville. But hotel owners

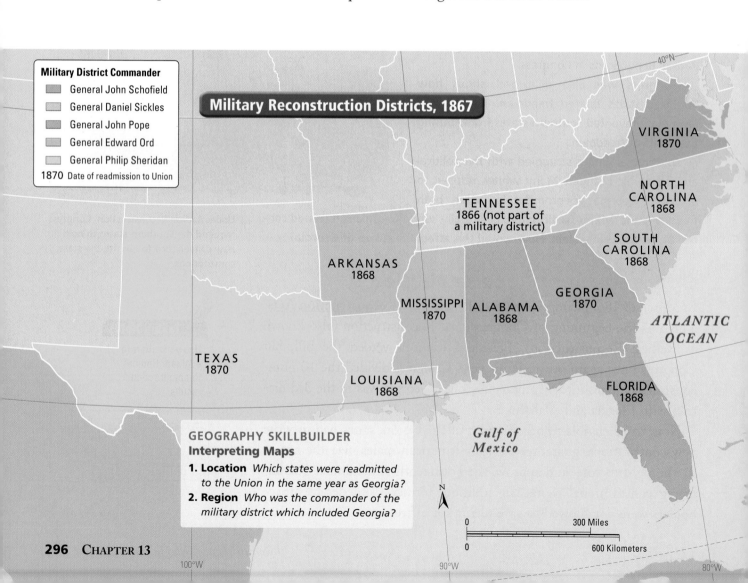

Military District Commander
- General John Schofield
- General Daniel Sickles
- General John Pope
- General Edward Ord
- General Philip Sheridan
- 1870 Date of readmission to Union

Military Reconstruction Districts, 1867

VIRGINIA 1870

NORTH CAROLINA 1868

TENNESSEE 1866 (not part of a military district)

SOUTH CAROLINA 1868

ARKANSAS 1868

MISSISSIPPI 1870

ALABAMA 1868

GEORGIA 1870

ATLANTIC OCEAN

TEXAS 1870

LOUISIANA 1868

FLORIDA 1868

Gulf of Mexico

GEOGRAPHY SKILLBUILDER
Interpreting Maps
1. **Location** Which states were readmitted to the Union in the same year as Georgia?
2. **Region** Who was the commander of the military district which included Georgia?

N

0 | 300 Miles
0 | 600 Kilometers

refused to reserve rooms for the African-American delegates. Whites complained that the delegates were carpetbaggers and scalawags. **Carpetbagger** was an insulting term used to describe a Northerner who moved to the South after the Civil War. Some came to work with the Reconstruction governments. Others came because they saw a money-making opportunity. **Scalawags** were white Southerners who worked with the Republican party and the Reconstruction governments, much to the disgust of fellow Southerners.

John Emory Bryant was a carpetbagger who settled in Augusta after the Civil War. As a newspaper editor and Freedmen's Bureau worker, he campaigned for the rights of freedmen. Many white Augustans disliked him. Former Governor Joe Brown was labeled a scalawag. Originally a Democrat, he became a Republican after the war. Many Georgians thought this was a sign that he was against Georgia and white supremacy.

The 1868 Constitution The delegates to the convention worked for three months to write a new state constitution. The 1868 constitution included several provisions.

- voting rights for all adult males
- a prohibition on slavery
- support of free public education
- whipping abolished as a form of punishment
- a poll tax
- capitol moved from Milledgeville to Atlanta

Rufus B. Bullock was elected governor over a Democratic candidate, former Confederate General John B. Gordon. Twenty-nine African Americans were elected to the House and three to the Senate. Georgia ratified the Fourteenth Amendment on July 21 and sent representatives to Washington, D.C., seeking readmission to the Union. Congress had adjourned for the summer, so Georgia was not readmitted, but federal troops were withdrawn from the state.

African Americans Removed from Office In September 1868, white Democrats in the legislature removed the African-American members. The Democrats said that nothing in the Georgia constitution gave African Americans the right to hold office, even if they could vote. They were replaced with the runners-up in their elections—all white Democrats. The Republicans fought back. But the Democrats had more

Reading History

A. Drawing Conclusions Why was former governor Joe Brown considered a scalawag?

NOW & THEN

African Americans in Congress

Between 1870 and 1877, 16 African Americans served in Congress. Seven are shown in the picture below, including Representative Jefferson Franklin Long of Georgia, standing, on the right. Two were senators: Hiram R. Revels and Blanche K. Bruce, both of whom were from Mississippi.

In 2004, 39 African Americans were in Congress. The longest-serving member was John Conyers, a representative from Michigan elected in 1964. Only two African-American senators were elected in the 20th century. Massachusetts senator Edward W. Brooke served from 1967 to 1979. Illinois senator Carol Moseley-Braun served from 1993 to 1999.

economic power, were better organized, and used violence to control politics and government.

African Americans in Politics

Throughout the South, African Americans formed **Union Leagues** and Equal Rights Associations. These organizations worked to protect African Americans' rights to vote and run for office. They also worked to obtain the same rights as whites, especially the right to earn a living. Georgia's freedmen were very active in creating Union Leagues.

African-American Politicians in Georgia In late 1865, freedmen held political meetings in Augusta, Macon, Savannah, and Columbus to discuss problems they were facing. Fair pay, the right to vote, jury duty, access to public accommodations, and education were some of the problems they talked about.

Aaron A. Bradley was a slave who escaped to the North before the Civil War started. He became a lawyer; when the war ended, he moved to Savannah. As a leader of the Chatham County Union League, he promoted land ownership and spoke out on voting rights for freedmen.

Tunis G. Campbell, Sr., was a Northern abolitionist who became the military governor of the Georgia sea islands of St. Catherines, Ossabaw, and Sapelo. Later, Campbell served in the Georgia Senate. Like Aaron Bradley, he was outspoken in his defense of freedmen's rights. He criticized white efforts to prevent freedmen from voting and owning land. His son, Tunis, Jr., was elected a state legislator from McIntosh County.

▼ Jefferson Franklin Long was the first African American to make a speech in the U.S. House of Representatives.

Elected Officials Jefferson Franklin Long was born into slavery in Crawford County, Georgia. After being freed, he became a tailor in Macon. In 1870, Long was elected to the House of Representatives of the U.S. Congress. Long spoke out for a bill that would make it more difficult for former Confederate officers to hold public office. Long served only a few months because the election was to fill a vacancy, and he chose not to run a second time. He returned to his business in Macon.

Henry McNeal Turner was elected state senator from Bibb County in 1868. He had been raised in the South as a free African American. He was a licensed preacher in the African Methodist Episcopal Church. He served in the Union army and was later assigned to the Freedmen's Bureau in Macon. Like other African-American politicians and activists in Georgia, Turner promoted land ownership, education, and voting rights for the state's African-American population. Many white Georgians disliked him for his radical positions.

Violence and Return to Military Rule

Southern whites soon realized that freedmen were determined to participate in the political system and society. Secret organizations of whites formed to terrorize the freedmen and their supporters. Often, white Democrats used these organizations as tools to keep freedmen from running for office or voting.

Reading History

B. Finding Main Ideas What were the goals of the Ku Klux Klan?

The Ku Klux Klan The most dangerous secret society to African Americans was the **Ku Klux Klan.** The Klan was started in Tennessee in 1866 by Confederate war veterans. Other Klan groups quickly formed throughout the South. They used terror and violence to keep freedmen from voting, holding office, and exercising their rights. Lynchings and other attacks on freedmen were common in Georgia and throughout the South.

On September 19, 1868, violence broke out in Camilla, Georgia, when 200 to 400 African-American Republicans arrived for a rally. Many of them carried sticks and guns for protection. Before they reached the town, the county sheriff warned them not to enter Camilla with their weapons. They ignored his warning. When they entered town, a fight broke out. The African Americans fled. For the next few

◄ This political cartoon shows the impact of violence and intimidation on African-American families in the South.

days, local whites and sheriff's deputies hunted them down. As many as 30 African Americans were killed or wounded.

Threats Against Voters Another example of violence during this period occurred in Savannah during the November 1868 elections. The Chatham County Union League, headed by Aaron A. Bradley, warned the local Klan that African-American voters would not be scared away from the polls. On election day, a fight broke out at the polls. Two African Americans and a white policeman were killed. The African Americans were driven from the polls, but tried to return later in the day to vote. Armed with weapons, the voters clashed with a white mob.

After Congressional hearings on violence in the South, especially in Georgia, Congress ordered federal troops back into the South. In December 1869, federal troops returned to Georgia. General Alfred H. Terry was appointed military governor. One of his first acts was to reinstate the African-American representatives in the Georgia legislature. White Georgians referred to this as Terry's Purge.

Georgia and the South's Final Reconstruction

On February 2, 1870, Congress passed another measure—the **Fifteenth Amendment,** which guaranteed all male citizens the right to vote regardless of "race, color, or previous condition of servitude." This law did not apply only to the South. At the time the Fifteenth Amendment was passed, 16 states still prohibited African-American men from voting. Georgia, Mississippi, Virginia, and Texas were required to ratify the Fifteenth Amendment before being readmitted to the Union.

Vocabulary

purge: to remove impurities or undesirable elements by cleansing

Civil Rights Amendments and Laws, 1865–1875	
Thirteenth Amendment (1865)	• Granted full emancipation (freedom) to slaves • Ratified by a majority of states in December 1865
Civil Rights Act of 1866	• Granted citizenship and equal rights to all persons born in the United States (except Native Americans)
Fourteenth Amendment (1868)	• Granted citizenship and equal protection of the law to all persons born in the United States (except Native Americans)
Fifteenth Amendment (1870)	• Protected the voting rights of African Americans
Civil Rights Act of 1875	• Outlawed racial segregation in public services • Ensured the right of African Americans to serve as jurors

SKILLBUILDER Interpreting Charts

1. *Which amendment and law are most similar?*

2. *Which amendment specifically protects voting rights?*

Reading History

C. Comparing
How was the Fifteenth Amendment a step beyond the Fourteenth Amendment?

Vocabulary

redeem: to save or restore honor

Georgia Readmitted to Union   The Georgia legislature ratified the Fifteenth Amendment, and Congress officially readmitted Georgia to the Union on July 15, 1870. Later that year, Georgia held elections. The Democrats gained control of the state legislature.

The Democrats accused Governor Rufus Bullock of corruption. He resigned and left Georgia. He would be the last Republican governor in Georgia until Sonny Perdue took office in 2003.

Democrat James M. Smith of Columbus was elected governor in January 1872. Federal troops left Georgia. Federally supervised Reconstruction in Georgia ended. The state was considered "redeemed," and the whites who took control were referred to as the **Redeemers.**

Congressional Reconstruction policies remained in effect until 1876. The final outcome of the presidential election of 1876 was the key to ending Reconstruction. Republican Rutherford B. Hayes and Democrat Samuel J. Tilden had the same number of electoral votes. Hayes made a deal with Southern Democrats in Florida, South Carolina, and Louisiana. If they gave him their electoral votes, he would withdraw the Union troops stationed in the South. This was called the Compromise of 1877.

Northerners were becoming less interested in protecting the rights of African Americans in the South. The economy in the North needed attention. Southerners, too, turned their attention to the growth of their economy. You will learn about the shift from agriculture to industry in the South in the next chapter.

Section 2 Assessment

1. TERMS & NAMES

Explain the significance of:

a. Military Reconstruction Acts

b. carpetbagger and scalawag

c. Rufus B. Bullock

d. Union League

e. Ku Klux Klan

f. Fifteenth Amendment

g. Redeemer

2. TAKING NOTES

Use a diagram like the one below to organize your notes on the following politicians: Aaron A. Bradley, Tunis G. Campbell, Sr., and Henry McNeal Turner.

3. MAIN IDEAS

a. How did the Military Reconstruction Acts divide the South?

b. What new laws did the Constitution of 1868 include? Are any of those laws still in place today?

c. What was the relation between white Democrats in Georgia and the South with the Ku Klux Klan?

4. CRITICAL THINKING

Drawing Conclusions

Why do you think the Republicans were willing to agree to the Compromise of 1877 and end Reconstruction?

Think About
• the election of 1877
• the Fifteenth Amendment

 Language Arts/Civics   Research Ku Klux Klan activities barring African Americans from voting. Write an **editorial** or write a **law** that would protect voting rights.

VISUAL SUMMARY

Reconstruction

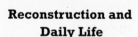

Rebuilding the Union

During Reconstruction, Congress decided how the Southern states would be readmitted to the Union and passed laws to improve conditions for freed people.

★

Reconstruction and Daily Life

After slavery ended, freed African Americans reunited their families, attended school, and began working for pay. Racist violence and lack of landslowed their progress.

★

End of Reconstruction

In the 1870's hostile Supreme Court decisions, the Southern Democrats' return to power, and the withdrawal of federal troops from the South ended Reconstruction.

TERMS & NAMES

Briefly explain the significance of the following.

1. Andrew Johnson
2. Freedmen's Bureau
3. black codes
4. Military Reconstruction Acts
5. carpetbagger
6. Union League
7. Fifteenth Amendment
8. Redeemer

REVIEW QUESTIONS

Reconstruction of the South Begins (pages 287–294)

1. What was President Lincoln's plan for Reconstruction?
2. What was President Johnson's plan for Reconstruction?
3. Why were Radical Republicans unhappy with President Johnson?
4. What new systems of labor developed in the South?
5. What actions did Republicans take to protect the rights of freedmen?

Radical Reconstruction (pages 295–301)

6. What was Congress's plan for Radical Reconstruction?
7. How did Georgia respond to Radical Reconstruction?
8. What were Equal Rights Associations?
9. How did Southern whites respond to the new rights of freedmen?
10. What was the result of the Compromise of 1877?

CRITICAL THINKING

1. USING YOUR NOTES: EVALUATING

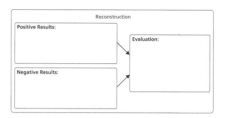

Using your completed chart, answer the questions below.

a. What is the most significant result of Congressional Reconstruction?
b. Was the Congressional plan for Reconstruction effective? Support your answer.

2. ANALYZING LEADERSHIP

Why might Reconstruction be considered a time in which the presidency was weak?

3. APPLYING CITIZENSHIP SKILLS

How were citizenship skills reflected by prominent African Americans during Reconstruction?

4. THEME: DEMOCRATIC IDEALS

How did the Fourteenth and Fifteenth Amendments promote greater equality for African Americans?

5. MAKING DECISIONS

Identify a decision made by Georgia in the period of Reconstruction. What were the reasons for the decision? What were the results?

INTERACT with HISTORY

Having read about the plans for Reconstruction, do you think life in the South might have been better if Lincoln had lived? Why or why not?

Use the map and your knowledge of American history to answer questions 1 through 3.

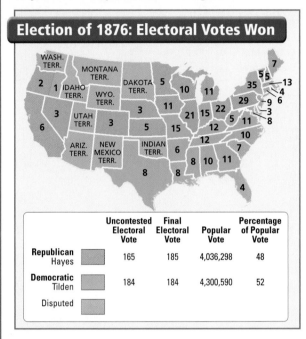

Election of 1876: Electoral Votes Won

		Uncontested Electoral Vote	Final Electoral Vote	Popular Vote	Percentage of Popular Vote
Republican Hayes		165	185	4,036,298	48
Democratic Tilden		184	184	4,300,590	52
Disputed					

1. What do the red states indicate?
   A. States won by Hayes
   B. States won by Tilden
   C. States that were disputed
   D. Territories

2. How many states were disputed in the election?
   A. Three
   B. Four
   C. Five
   D. None

3. What was the final electoral vote count for Hayes?
   A. 165
   B. 184
   C. 185
   D. 48

TEST PRACTICE
CLASSZONE.COM

ALTERNATIVE ASSESSMENT

1. WRITING LETTERS

Write letters you imagine that the following people would write about Reconstruction.

a. a member of the old Southern upper class

b. a newly freed African American

c. a white Northern carpetbagger

Be sure to use standard grammar, spelling, sentence structure, and punctuation in your letters.

2. COOPERATIVE LEARNING

The impeachment trial of Andrew Johnson was a dramatic and colorful event. Many officials pleaded their case, whether for or against the president. Working in a small group, research the trial using resources such as diaries, journals, autobiographies, letters, and books. Each group member should choose an official who spoke at the trial and collect some of his quotes. The group should then reenact the trial in front of the class.

INTEGRATED TECHNOLOGY ACTIVITY

PREPARING AN ELECTRONIC PRESENTATION

Use the Internet and your library to research the life of a Georgia leader for African-American rights during the Reconstruction era. Find images, diaries, memoirs, biographies, news articles, and other resources that tell the story of that person's life. Use presentation software to share your information with the class. Consider the following suggestions to get started.

- Photographs or paintings of the individual

- A timeline of important events in that person's life

- Excerpts from primary sources that discuss the individual

- Web pages with further information

RESEARCH LINKS
CLASSZONE.COM

A New South and a New Georgia 1877–1900

Women sew bags for agricultural and industrial products at the Fulton Cotton Mill in Atlanta. Factory work was one of the few opportunities for women to earn cash wages.

1865
Constitutional Convention

1867
Atlanta University is chartered. Augusta Institute (to become Morehouse College) is founded.

GEORGIA
USA 1860   1870

1863
Two companies begin to build transcontinental railroad.

INTERACT with HISTORY

The year is 1898. You work in a cotton mill that is hot and badly lit. The machine that you operate is dangerous. The economy is doing poorly, so the factory has cut your wages. Some of your coworkers have gone out on strike. They want better pay and working conditions.

How would you try to change conditions?

WHAT DO YOU THINK?

- What might you risk if you were to join the strike?

- What might you gain if you were to take part?

- What other methods might you use to persuade your employer to meet your demands?

For more information on this chapter, visit . . .
RESEARCH LINKS
CLASSZONE.COM

1877
State capital is moved from Milledgeville to Atlanta.

1881
International Cotton Exposition in Atlanta

1886
First Coca-Cola is served in Jacob's Pharmacy, Atlanta.

1889
Henry W. Grady dies. First electric streetcar in Atlanta.

1880

1890

1876
Alexander Graham Bell patents the telephone.

1882
Thomas Edison installs electric lights in New York City.

1894
Pullman strike halts rail traffic across the nation.

CHAPTER 14

Reading Strategy:
Analyzing Causes and Recognizing Effects

What Do You Know?

Do you know of any businesses that started back in the 1800s? How do businesses grow?

THINK ABOUT

• businesses that you see in your community
• businesses that are advertised on television, in magazines or newspapers, or on the Internet

What Do You Want to Know?

What questions do you have about how businesses grew in the North and South after the Civil War? About how the South evolved from a plantation economy? Record those questions in your notebook before you read the chapter.

Analyzing Causes and Recognizing Effects

The actions or conditions that lead to a historical event are its causes. The consequences of an event are its effects. As you read the chapter, look for the causes and effects of industrial growth in the North and South. Causes include geographical factors and actions by individuals and the government. Effects include both benefits and problems. Use the diagram below to record the causes and effects.

S See Skillbuilder Handbook, page 551.

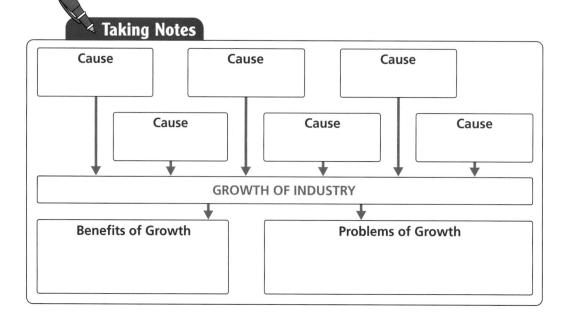

Taking Notes

Cause	Cause	Cause

| Cause | Cause | Cause |

GROWTH OF INDUSTRY

| **Benefits of Growth** | **Problems of Growth** |

American Modernization

MAIN IDEA	WHY IT MATTERS NOW	TERMS & NAMES
The United States experienced tremendous growth and change in the late 1800s.	The growth of the late 1800s shaped the economy and society that we have today.	monopoly laissez-faire Sherman Antitrust Act immigrant

SETTING THE STAGE

After the Civil War, the nation began returning to peacetime activities. In the North, the Industrial Revolution was well under way. Factories were producing greater numbers of goods. Industrialists were building great fortunes. Millions of people worked in the nation's new industries.

New towns appeared. Old towns and cities grew—some were among the largest in the world. Immigrants from overseas and people from America's rural areas flocked to cities like Chicago, New York, Philadelphia, and Atlanta looking for work and a new life. How would the new towns change life in America?

▲ The Mountain City Glass Works opened in Tallapoosa, Georgia, in 1889. Tallapoosa attracted many Northern investors and tourists.

Industrialization

In the 1870s and 1880s, plenty of natural resources, labor, new markets, money, and new inventions helped business and industry grow tremendously. Machine-made goods quickly replaced goods made by hand. Many believed that the larger the business, the better it operated. A large business could charge the consumer less for its product.

Robber Barons and Monopolies   Some companies grew so large that they had a **monopoly,** or complete control of the business in their fields. Once they controlled most of the business, they could charge as much as they liked for their products. Owners of these big businesses became very wealthy. In the late 1800s, they were called "robber barons." Andrew Carnegie, who owned Carnegie Steel, and John D. Rockefeller, who owned Standard Oil Company, were two of the most important industrialists of this era. Monopolies developed in the following industries: steel; railroads; telephone and telegraph; farm equipment; and even sugar, fruit, and vegetables.

Use your diagram to record the causes and effects of American modernization.

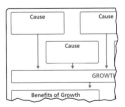

A New South and a New Georgia   **307**

T. A. EDISON.
Electric-Lamp.

Thomas A. Edison

Imagine life without being able to burn lights 24 hours a day. Or without movies and recorded music. Edison invented not only the light bulb, but also the phonograph and a moving-picture viewer.

A. G. BELL.
TELEGRAPHY.

No. 174,465.   Patented March 7, 1876.

Alexander Graham Bell

As a teacher of the deaf, Bell experimented to learn how vowel sounds are produced. This led to his interest in the electrical transmission of speech.

Labor Unions   During this period of rapid growth, companies grew more powerful. Workers wanted a way to bargain—or make deals with—the business owners. Workers organized into labor unions such as the Knights of Labor and the American Federation of Labor. Unions tried to help workers settle disputes and negotiate wages, working hours, and working conditions with employers.

Sometimes, instead of talking to their employers, workers would leave their jobs to go out on strike. They believed they could get employers to accept their demands that way. Employers often responded to a strike by hiring replacement workers called "scabs," or by shutting down the business until workers gave up and returned to work.

The Problems of Industrialization   There was a negative side to industrialization in America. Workers were often mistreated and forced to work long hours. Critics of industrialization complained that a few men became very wealthy, while most remained quite poor. Poverty increased. Up to this time, government had had a **laissez-faire** attitude toward big business, which means "leave it alone."

Americans began to demand that the federal government and Congress do something to curb the problems caused by big business and industrialization. In 1890, Congress passed the **Sherman Antitrust Act.** It outlawed any attempts to create a monopoly. The Sherman Antitrust Act couldn't solve all of the problems created by industrialization, but it is still used today to prevent monopolies.

Modernization

Many new inventions and methods of doing things better improved life during this time. Thomas Edison found a way to provide electricity to a wide area. In 1882, he opened a power plant in New York City's financial district. Electricity was used to light city streets and business signs.

Electricity also changed transportation in American cities. Electric streetcars, such as those introduced in Richmond, Virginia, in 1888,

Reading History

A. Making Inferences Why would outlawing monopolies solve the problems created by big business and industrialization?

made it possible to travel greater distances from the center of the city. City borders expanded as people commuted farther to do business.

Urbanization

America's towns and cities grew rapidly in the period from the end of the Civil War to 1900. Businesses built factories and offices, and banking services developed in cities. Most large cities were in the Northeast, with some in the West and Midwest. Cities like New York, San Francisco, Chicago, and Boston became important regional urban centers.

Reading History

B. Drawing Conclusions
Why did so few immigrants settle in the South?

From the 1860s to the end of the century, millions of European **immigrants** came to the United States. They settled in the towns and cities of the Northeast and Midwest. Communities of immigrants such as Little Italy in New York and Greektown in Detroit developed within cities. Very few immigrants settled in the South.

Suburbs As cities grew, many people wanted to get away from the growing problems of urban America—poverty, filth, disease, overcrowding, and noise. People with money could afford to move to areas outside the city limits—the suburbs. One of Atlanta's first suburbs, Inman Park, was created in the late 1880s. Suburbs were advertised as perfect places for building new homes, where residents could enjoy the trees, rolling hills, and fresh air.

In the next section, you will learn about the transformation of the South in the new industrial era. The Old South made way for the New South.

Section 1 Assessment

1. TERMS & NAMES

Explain the significance of:

a. monopoly

b. laissez-faire

c. Sherman Antitrust Act

d. immigrant

2. TAKING NOTES

Use a diagram like the one below to note some of the positive and negative effects of the explosive growth in America during this time.

3. MAIN IDEAS

a. What was the purpose of labor unions?

b. How did electricity contribute to the changes in urban America?

c. Why did people move to the suburbs?

4. CRITICAL THINKING

Forming and Supporting Opinions

Do you think that monopolies are always bad for the country? Explain your opinion.

Think About

• how a business may become a monopoly

• how a monopoly affects competition

• how a monopoly affects consumers

Language Arts/Art Decide whether unions should be encouraged. Write an **editorial** or create a **poster** expressing your opinion.

The New South

SETTING THE STAGE

Before the Civil War, the South did not have much industry compared to the North. Most Southern industry was focused on agriculture—cotton, tobacco, and sugar. Many said that the South did not need a lot of factories.

The Civil War changed Southern industry. Factories opened to make military supplies and other goods for the South. Although Southern manufacturing increased during the war, the South had not been able to supply enough materials.

After the war, some Southerners realized the advantages of industry and manufacturing. The Old South was gone. How would they build a "New South"?

▲ The presence of a cotton mill, such as this one in Columbus, symbolized growth and progress. However, some complained that the South needed more than textiles to have a strong industrial economy.

The New South Movement

From 1877 to the 1910s, the South focused on rebuilding its economic, social, and political structures, which had been badly damaged during the Civil War. A group of leaders, including several from Georgia, wanted to build a "New South." They believed that a **New South** needed to make these changes in order to prosper:

- expand its industries
- rely less on a few cash crops such as cotton
- grow more food crops

Adding industry and new crops to the Southern economy was called "diversification."

During and after Reconstruction, few Southerners had enough money to start new industries. Northern banks and businessmen, however, did have money to invest. They saw great potential in the South's abundant natural resources and raw materials, including timber, coal, iron ore, and cotton. The South also had cheap labor and a good year-round climate.

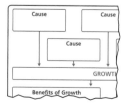

Taking Notes

Use your diagram to record the causes and effects of growth in the New South.

Reading History

A. Finding Main Ideas Why did Northern businessmen see potential in the South?

The supporters of the New South movement accepted and encouraged Northern investment in machinery and factories in the South. But at the same time, they worried that their economic survival depended too much on the North. They saw the North profiting from the South's vast supply of raw materials. If Southerners could build more factories and grow more crops themselves, they would not need to rely on the North for help.

Advocates and Critics

Henry W. Grady, editor of the *Atlanta Constitution* in 1880, was a leading supporter of the New South movement. He popularized the term "New South."

> **PRIMARY SOURCE**
>
> We have sowed towns and cities in the place of theories, and put business above politics. We have challenged your spinners in Massachusetts and your iron-makers in Pennsylvania. . . . We have fallen in love with your work.
>
> Henry Grady, "The New South," speech delivered December 22, 1886

The New South in Georgia   Three major Georgia politicians promoted the idea of a New South in Georgia: John B. Gordon, Joseph Brown, and Alfred Colquitt. In the late 1880s, these men held Georgia's governor's office and the two U.S. Senate seats. These New South promoters wanted economic change. But they insisted that whites should continue to be at the top of the social order.

▲ Henry Grady promoted the New South in editorials and articles in the *Atlanta Constitution* and gave speeches throughout the country.

Reading History

B. Analyzing Points of View Why did some Georgians want to keep their state rural and their economy agricultural?

Not everyone in Georgia was happy with the promise of a New South. Those who opposed the New South did not care for large cities, capitalism, mass production, or anything to do with modernizing the South. They wanted to keep Georgia rural and agricultural.

The Lost Cause Movement   The South had lost the Civil War. The Old South no longer existed. But some people could not accept that the old way of life would not return. Their belief was called the **Lost Cause.** Many Confederate veterans and Southerners wanted nothing to do with the North. For them, changing the Southern economy to be more like that of the North, even if it was for the better, was not acceptable. The New South movement's connection with the North turned them against Grady and others who wanted change.

But even those who rejected the New South movement eventually saw the benefits of industry and diversification for the South. They liked the idea of a healthy economy, even though they held on to the memory of the past.

Much of the concern was about control. Would new industries and factories draw too many workers away from farms? Who would control

Detecting Bias in the Media

Unbiased reporting is one of the responsibilities of a free press. It allows citizens to weigh the facts and come to their own understanding of issues and events. In the 1890s, however, journalists were not always concerned with bias.

Newspaper and magazine editors and reporters led the way in promoting the New South ideals. Henry Grady and Joel Chandler Harris, who worked at the *Atlanta Constitution,* wrote articles about attracting new industry and businesses. Other Southern newspapers also promoted the need for Southerners to become more "Yankee-like."

Can You Find Bias in the Media?

1. With a small group, collect news stories from different sources that cover the same issue or event.
2. Record any differences in the way a specific issue or event is covered by the oral, written, or visual sources you have selected.
3. Review the differences and decide whether any of the authors showed bias in their coverage.
4. Write a report that describes any bias you might detect. Explain why the biased source might have reported the story that way.

For more about free speech . . .

RESEARCH LINKS
CLASSZONE.COM

the politics of a New South? Who would pay the taxes needed to make improvements such as better roads?

Southern Business and Industry

Many businesses began to grow and develop after Reconstruction. The number of Southerners working in manufacturing increased dramatically during this time.

Cotton Mills   From the 1880s to the 1920s, many new cotton textile mills opened in the South. White farmers and people in the Piedmont were drawn to jobs in the mills. Often, entire families worked long, hard days in the mill. Mill workers were called **lintheads** because of the cotton lint that stuck to their hair and clothes.

Mill owners provided not only jobs but also places to live. Sometimes mill villages contained the factory, workers' houses, churches, stores, and even schools. They were often separate from the town, and local townspeople looked down on mill workers. But a textile mill meant growth, and many small towns encouraged business owners to bring mills to their area.

Reading History

C. Drawing Conclusions
Why did townspeople look down on mill workers?

▶ Mill workers faced uncomfortable and even dangerous working conditions. The mill was hot, and the work was boring. Lint hung in the air, landing on their heads, on their clothes, and in their lungs.

Other Industries Some complained that the South needed more than just cotton mills to create a strong industrial economy. Other industries developed also. The tobacco industry became a major force in North Carolina. The steel industry grew rapidly in Alabama. Timber, coal, oil, and cottonseed processing also were major industries by 1900.

Southern Agriculture

Reading History

D. Making Inferences How would small farms contribute to the South relying less on the North?

Supporters of the New South hoped that small, self-sufficient farms would replace large plantations. This would strengthen the region's agricultural economy and allow more farmers to make a living. Supporters also wanted farmers to grow more food crops instead of relying heavily on cash crops such as cotton. These changes would help the South become more self-reliant.

The system of sharecropping that had grown after the war prevented this from happening. After the war, most plantations still belonged to individual landowners. They rented parcels of land out to farmers. By the 1880s, sharecroppers cultivated most farmland in the South. They had to grow cash crops, especially cotton, that could be sold easily in order to pay their debts. Because they relied on cotton and tobacco, they could not grow food crops. They were forced to buy the other supplies they needed, such as food, from their share of the crops. In that way sharecroppers remained in debt to landowners and the local merchants. Large plantations continued to make a few men wealthy while workers remained poor.

Other Growth Factors

If the South's economy was to grow, a steady supply of labor and better transportation was needed. People were needed to work in the fields and in the new factories. And, more railroads were needed to move goods across the South and into other areas of the country.

Railroads　The South's railroads were largely damaged or destroyed during the Civil War. But by 1870, the South had built more than 10,000 miles of railroad line. By 1890, this had increased to almost 40,000 miles. By 1900, most Southerners lived near a railroad. It brought many Southerners into a larger world—connecting them with regional and even national markets.

Labor　Despite the low wages and poor working conditions, labor unions were not very successful in the South. Trade unions did appear in larger towns like Atlanta in the 1860s and 1870s. One of the first unions in Atlanta was the Workingmen's Union Number One, formed in 1869. The Knights of Labor appeared in Rome, Atlanta, and Augusta in the 1870s. But membership was never very high.

Convict Labor　Because of the need for workers, Southern legislatures passed laws that made it possible for landowners to "lease" convicts (prisoners). Businessmen put them to work building railroads and roads, and growing and harvesting crops.

Businesses treated convict labor poorly. Most convicts were African American. They were beaten, underfed, and forced to perform dangerous work. Often convicts worked on chain gangs. These were groups of workers joined together with chains so they could not escape. Chain gangs worked on farms, in mines, and on railroads.

◀ This handbill from 1870 announced a meeting to protest chain gangs in Georgia, particularly the use of African-American children.

A NEW SYSTEM OF **CHAIN-GANG SLAVERY IN GEORGIA.**

Little girls and boys under ten years of age are sent to chain-gangs for three potatoes or singing Shoo-fly, with great locks and chains around their necks; colored bogusly-convicted women and men are let out for ten cents per day to do out-doors work that

Reading History

E. Analyzing Causes　What caused Southern businesses to hire convicts?

Southern Cities and Towns

In 1860, only about 7 percent of Southerners lived in urban areas (2,500 or more people). After the war, however, Southern cities and towns grew rapidly. By 1900, over 15 percent of Southerners lived in urban areas. Southern cities such as Atlanta, Nashville, Richmond, and Birmingham grew significantly. The improved regional economy created the means to develop more businesses and industry. Many African Americans, young white single men and women, and widows moved to cities looking for jobs and better opportunities.

Market Towns When the economy of an area began to grow, **market towns** sprang up. Hundreds of towns with populations of 5,000 to 10,000 appeared during this period. Usually these towns had a cotton gin and a handful of stores that sold goods to local farmers. They grew larger if they had a rail depot. Area farmers would travel to these market towns to ship their crops to other regions.

▲ Sleepy villages or crossroads could become a market town, a local center of trade.

Southern cities and towns boasted of hotels, opera houses, colleges, railroad stations, and grand homes. **Boosters** promoted the growth of their towns and were ambitious in their goals to make their towns even bigger. They boasted of conveniences such as mail delivery, fire departments, electricity, street railways, telephone service, and public schools and colleges.

The New South was enjoying, and suffering the pains of, a growing economy. In the next section you will learn more about how Georgia's urban and rural areas grew and changed.

Reading History

F. Forming and Supporting Opinions What did boosters gain in promoting the growth of their towns or cities?

Section 2 Assessment

1. TERMS & NAMES

Explain the significance of:

a. New South

b. Henry W. Grady

c. Lost Cause

d. linthead

e. market town

f. booster

2. TAKING NOTES

Use a diagram like the one below to list the major changes the supporters of the New South wanted to see.

1.
2.
3.
4.

3. MAIN IDEAS

a. What was so new about the New South?

b. What attracted Northern investors and businessmen to the South?

c. Why did some people not accept the idea of a New South?

4. CRITICAL THINKING

Analyzing Effects

How did railroads aid industrial growth? Who benefited most from the growth of industry? Explain.

Think About
• market towns
• urban and suburban growth
• expanding market

Math/Speech Research how your community or city grew over the last century. Create a **graph** of its growth cycle or prepare an **oral report** on growth trends.

3

Urban and Rural Worlds of Georgia

MAIN IDEA

Georgia was changing. Some areas remained rural, while others became more urban.

WHY IT MATTERS NOW

Georgia is still a mix of rural and urban areas today.

TERMS & NAMES

crop lien
Alonzo F. Herndon

SETTING THE STAGE

Before the war, Georgia had been largely rural and agricultural, but this was changing. Georgians had to rebuild towns and cities after years of neglect or destruction from the war. They needed to make decisions about creating a new way of life. Landowners needed to decide what to grow and how they would find workers. Merchants and businessmen were deciding what new industries were needed to strengthen the state's economy.

In creating new ways of life, how would Georgians combine their former agricultural ways with the industrial plans of the New South?

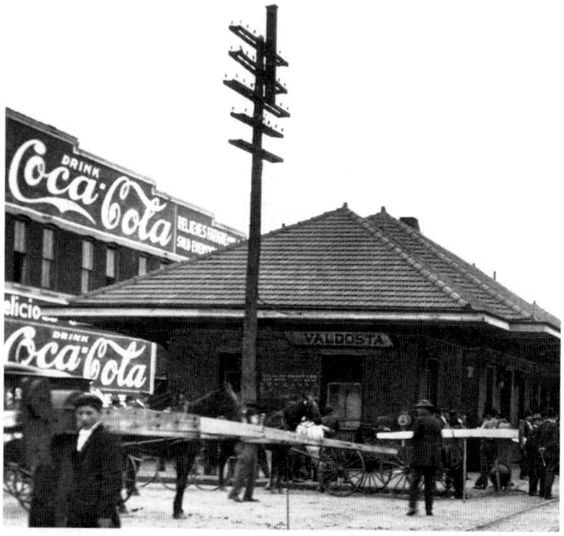

▲ In Georgia in the late 1800s, a location on a rail line was critical to a town's progress. The town of Valdosta began in 1860, along an extension of the Atlantic and Gulf Railroad.

Georgia Agriculture

About 70 percent of farmers in Georgia grew mostly cotton. When farmers grew more cotton, they planted fewer food crops such as sweet potatoes, peas, and corn. They raised less livestock.

Cotton and Other Cash Crops One Georgian declared that cotton "is the best friend the Southern farmer has got now." Why were farmers so enthusiastic about cotton? Because it was a cash crop. Cotton and tobacco were crops that could be sold easily and would bring in the most money.

In addition, merchants wanted to be paid in cotton because it was easy to sell. Farmers needed to pay their debts, and cash crops such as cotton were the best way to do it. In 1900, Georgia was second in cotton production in the South.

Some farmers grew tobacco, but tobacco took a lot of work. Most tobacco in Georgia and the Carolinas was grown in small plots of 2 to 4 acres. Corn was the second most grown crop in Georgia before and after the Civil War.

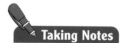

Taking Notes

Use your diagram to record causes and effects of the growth of urban and rural Georgia.

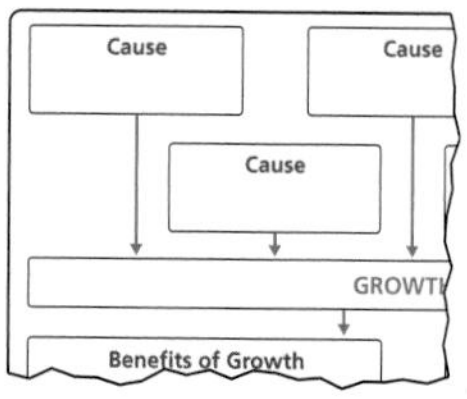

Food Crops The price of cotton was not always reliable. When too many farmers grew cotton, the price fell. Some farmers had to look for other profitable crops, such as peanuts and pecans. Other farmers decided to raise vegetables and fruits, such as sweet potatoes, white potatoes, and watermelons. Georgians grew over 100,000 acres of watermelons in 1900.

Peaches were so successful that Georgia became known as the Peach State. The area south of Macon became the center of the Georgia peach industry. Shipments of peaches to locations outside the region began in the 1870s, and by 1900, merchants sent over 3,000 train cars of peaches all over the nation every year.

Dairy cows were also profitable. Middle and south Georgia had good weather and plentiful feed for dairy cows. People in towns such as Atlanta and Augusta bought the milk, buttermilk, cream, and butter from Georgia dairy farmers.

▲ Farmers in Macon County developed several popular varieties of peaches in the 1870s and 1880s—the Elberta, the Georgia Belle, and the Hiley Belle.

Life on the Farm

In many ways, life on a farm after the war was not much different than before the war. Families worked together to survive. Men worked in the fields while women tended children and the household chores. But women and children also helped with farm chores, such as tilling the soil, planting seeds, weeding, and harvesting.

Most Georgia farmers were either sharecroppers or tenant farmers. The landowner usually determined what was to be grown by sharecroppers. Local merchants also influenced what farmers grew. State laws gave merchants and landowners legal rights to a tenant's crops. These were called **crop liens**.

If a family owned land, it was usually a small piece. The main crop was usually cotton. Small farmers might also grow some corn or other food crops to feed the family or to sell at market. The only way to make more money was to use fertilizers to enrich the soil. But most farmers did not have the money for that. Most of the farmers who owned small tracts of land were white. Most African-American farmers were either tenants or sharecroppers.

Georgia's Towns and Cities

The Civil War and lack of money during the Reconstruction years had resulted in the destruction or decay of many of Georgia's towns and cities. Slowly, Georgia began to rebuild.

Atlanta   Atlanta had suffered almost total destruction during the war. Sherman had ordered all the public buildings, railroad property, factories, and warehouses to be destroyed. Some private homes, churches, and other buildings had also been burned. As many as 5,000 buildings had been destroyed. Only about 400 buildings remained standing, mostly private homes.

But by the end of 1865, Atlanta was hard at work rebuilding the city. Railroad lines were repaired and running, and the population was growing (over 20,000 by 1870). Banks, shops, mills, and other businesses opened and were doing a brisk business. In 1867, Atlanta became the state capital and grew quickly. Henry Grady gave a speech in New York about the changes in the South. In attendance was General William Tecumseh Sherman, the man who had destroyed Atlanta during the war. Grady proudly spoke of the new Atlanta.

Reading History

A. Making Inferences Why did Henry Grady address Sherman in his speech?

PRIMARY SOURCE

I want to say to General Sherman . . . . that from the ashes he left us in 1864 we have raised a brave and beautiful city. . . . The New South is enamored of her new work. Her soul is stirred with the breath of a new life. . . . She is thrilling with the consciousness of growing power and prosperity.

Henry Grady, "The New South," speech delivered December 22, 1886

By 1890, the population of Atlanta had grown to more than 65,000. In 1892, the eight-story Equitable Building became the South's first skyscraper. New railroad lines such as the Georgia, Carolina & Northern made Atlanta a bigger player in the region's economy, and its population reached almost 155,000 by 1910. Atlanta became a leader of the economic future of the state and the region.

▼ A scene on Broughton Street in Savannah in 1900.

Savannah   Not long after General Sherman's troops left Savannah, the effort to rebuild had begun. Savannah had not suffered much physical damage during the war. But there was a lot to be done to get the city back on its feet. The city appointed a Board of Public Education to create and manage a new school system.

Before the war, cotton and lumber exports had been an important part of the city's economy. After the war, cotton remained the primary export. But by 1870, naval stores (turpentine, rosin, pitch, and pine tar) were also an important industry. By 1900, Savannah's population reached 55,000. The port shipped naval stores and cotton around the world. The city also had a number of factories—a knitting mill, cottonseed oil mills, a canning factory, a foundry, machine shops, and carriage makers. It was also the home office for a number of ocean and river shipping lines.

Macon   After the war Macon also began to rebuild. By 1866, the Central Railroad connecting Macon to Savannah reopened. The city paved Cherry Street, opened a city hospital for the poor, and dedicated a new courthouse in 1870. New businesses such as the Central Bank of Georgia opened their doors. By 1900, Macon was one of the more prosperous cities in the state. It had cotton mills, foundries, furniture factories, railroad shops, brick and tile makers, carriage and wagon builders, and machine shops. New railroad lines brought even more business.

> ### PRIMARY SOURCE
>
> The position of Macon in the heart of middle Georgia, where all the railways—north, south, east and west—converge as to a common center, renders it probably the most important and most promising inland town of this state.
>
> quoted in *Georgia: History Written by Those Who Lived It,* edited by Robert Somers

Georgia Business and Industry

By 1900, Georgia had 15 large industrial companies (11 cotton mills and 4 railroad shops) that employed over 500 workers each. The state had numerous smaller industries, such as buggy and wagon makers, small cotton mills, cottonseed oil mills, lumber mills, coal mines, and brick factories. Some of these businesses and industries went on to become a major part

Georgia Industries in 1900

COTTON

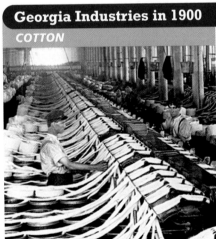

Textile mills were the biggest industry in the state. In 1900 about 75 mills operated in 47 towns. Many more were under construction. Most were located in cities.

TIMBER

Dr. Charles Holmes Herty invented new processes for extracting resin and later developed a method for using Southern pine trees to make newsprint and paper. That process created a new pulpwood industry for Georgia and the South.

SOFT DRINK

Coca-Cola was invented in 1885 by Atlanta pharmacist Dr. John Pemberton as a headache remedy. He mixed oils, cola nuts, coca leaves, and caffeine to create a special syrup. He added seltzer water and called it Coca-Cola.

CATHERINE EVANS WHITENER
1880–1964

Catherine Evans Whitener's career began in 1892 when she was 12 and admired an old tufted bedspread. She made one for herself using an almost totally lost technique called "candle wicking."

Family, friends, and then department stores asked her to make more. As the business grew, she taught others. Their bedspreads were often their families' only source of income when crops failed.

By 1941, America's bedspread industry, centered in Dalton, Georgia, employed 10,000 workers with sales of over 25 million dollars.

of Georgia's economy. The early local bedspread industry developed into a booming carpet and textile industry. Today, the area around Dalton in northwest Georgia is referred to as the carpet capital of the world. It is the home of major companies such as Shaw Industries, Cabin Crafts, and Mohawk Carpets.

Cotton States Exposition   The Expo opened in Atlanta, mirroring an exposition held in Chicago two years earlier. Businessmen showcased their industries to show that the South was an equal player in the national economy. A large Harris-Corlis steam engine was demonstrated to the crowds. Over 800,000 people visited the three-month-long exposition with its exhibits about modern equipment and cotton.

African Americans in Georgia's Cities

As segregation practices increased in the 1880s and 1890s, many African Americans created their own neighborhoods in Georgia's cities. By the 1890s, 15 percent of the African Americans in the South lived in towns and cities.

At the end of the Civil War, many skilled and semi-skilled African Americans lived in Georgia. They were trained in carpentry, blacksmithing, barbering, bricklaying, and other fields. Slowly they were pushed aside by poor whites seeking these higher paying jobs.

Emerging African-American Businessmen
As the trades and services came under white control, a problem arose. Whites would not work or provide services for African Americans. When that happened, African-American businessmen stepped in. Herman E. Perry started a construction business and opened the Standard Life Insurance Company. **Alonzo F. Herndon** owned the Crystal Palace Barber Shop on Peachtree Street. The shop catered to whites and the business was a great success. In 1905, Herndon created the Atlanta Mutual Insurance Association, which sold policies to African Americans. This company became the Atlanta Life Insurance Company, which today is the largest African-American-owned stockholder insurance company in the United States.

As African-American businesses grew, black business and entertainment districts emerged. In Augusta, it was Gwinnett Street; in Atlanta, it was Auburn Avenue.

◄ Alonzo Herndon was born a slave, but through hard work and investing, he became a prosperous property owner by the early 1900s.

African-American lawyers, doctors, and other professionals located their offices in these districts. They founded and managed their own hospitals and schools and opened savings banks and insurance companies. A black elite began to form. African Americans formed clubs and fraternal organizations like the Knights of Pythias. They created an environment separate from the white-dominated community, one in which African Americans did not have to face discrimination.

As whites and African Americans began to take part in Georgia's economic rebirth, they also wanted to participate in the politics of their state. In the next chapter you will learn about these efforts.

Section ③ Assessment

1. TERMS & NAMES

Explain the significance of:

a. crop lien

b. Alonzo F. Herndon

2. TAKING NOTES

Use a diagram like the one below to note how each city accomplished rebuilding.

City	Rebuilding
Atlanta	
Macon	
Savannah	

3. MAIN IDEAS

a. Summarize the ways in which farmers diversified their crops.

b. Discuss the importance of the carpet, cotton, and timber industries to the economy of Georgia.

c. Why did African Americans create their own neighborhoods?

4. CRITICAL THINKING

Evaluating

What were some of the advantages and disadvantages of growing cotton on a small farm?

Think About
• cash crops
• labor
• food crops

ACTIVITY -OPTIONS- **Language Arts/Technology** Write a **script** for a 10-minute documentary or design a **Web page** about an industry leader from this time period.

VISUAL SUMMARY

Changes in American Life

Northern Cities Grow and Change

Industrialization caused Northern cities to grow.

Modernization

New inventions improve life.

Immigration

Millions of Europeans settle in the Northeast and Midwest.

American Life Around 1900

New South Emerges

The South builds new political, economic, and social structures.

Segregation

Racial and ethnic minorities face discrimination across the country.

WHITES ONLY

Georgia Cities and Towns Grow

Atlanta, Macon, and Savannah rebuild and grow.

TERMS & NAMES

Briefly explain the significance of the following.

1. monopoly
2. laissez-faire
3. Sherman Antitrust Act
4. New South
5. Henry W. Grady
6. Lost Cause
7. market towns
8. booster
9. crop lien
10. Alonzo F. Herndon

REVIEW QUESTIONS

American Modernization (pages 307–309)

1. Why did business and industry grow in the 1870s and 1880s?
2. What is a robber baron?
3. Why did labor unions appear at this point in history?

The New South (pages 310–315)

4. Why did some Southerners have trouble accepting the New South?
5. Which Georgia politicians promoted a New South?
6. What new industries appeared in the New South?

Urban and Rural Worlds of Georgia (pages 316–321)

7. Why was cotton "the best friend the Southern farmer has got now"?
8. What was life like for most Georgia farmers?
9. What industries became a major part of Georgia's economy?
10. How did segregation lead to a black elite?

CRITICAL THINKING

1. USING YOUR NOTES: ANALYZING CAUSES AND EFFECTS

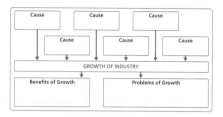

Using your completed chart, answer the questions below.

a. How did the growth of railroads act as a cause of industrial growth?

b. Who do you think benefited most from the growth of industry? Explain.

2. ANALYZING LEADERSHIP

How did men like Herman E. Perry and Alonzo F. Herndon lead in their communities?

3. APPLYING CITIZENSHIP SKILLS

How did the labor movement work to address the problems of industrialization?

4. THEME: ECONOMICS IN HISTORY

Why was diversification necessary for the growth of the Southern economy?

5. FORMING AND SUPPORTING OPINIONS

If the South had diversified sooner, do you think the Civil War would still have happened?

INTERACT *with* HISTORY

Having read about the urban and rural worlds in Georgia, would you have chosen farm life or city life? Why?

Use the graph and your knowledge of Georgia history to answer questions 1 and 2.

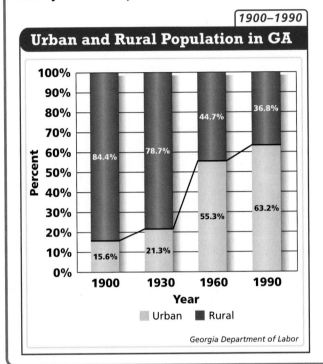

1900–1990

Urban and Rural Population in GA

Percent (y-axis)

Year (x-axis): 1900, 1930, 1960, 1990

84.4%, 78.7%, 44.7%, 36.8%

15.6%, 21.3%, 55.3%, 63.2%

☐ Urban ■ Rural

Georgia Department of Labor

1. What percentage of Georgians lived in urban areas in 1990?

   A. 84.4%
   B. 15.6%
   C. 21.3%
   D. 63.2%

2. During which years did Georgia's urban population increase the most?

   A. 1900–1930
   B. 1930–1960
   C. 1960–1990
   D. 1870–1900

3. By what percentage did the urban population grow between 1900 and 1990?

   A. 42%
   B. 36.8%
   C. 84.4%
   D. 47.6%

TEST PRACTICE
CLASSZONE.COM

ALTERNATIVE ASSESSMENT

1. MAKING A GRAPH

Do research to determine the number of immigrants who came from various countries between 1880 and 1900. Find out where immigrants come from today. Make a graph that displays your findings. Explain your graph to the class.

2. COOPERATIVE LEARNING

With a group from your class, research life in a Georgia market town or city during the late 1800s. Look at maps and historical records. Then create a model market town or city. Include labels and notes on your model to identify important landmarks and areas. Present your model to the class.

INTEGRATED TECHNOLOGY ACTIVITY

USING THE INTERNET

Use the Internet and your library to research the life of a Georgia business or political leader from this chapter. Prepare a monologue based on the life of this person. Include the person's background, accomplishments, and life experiences. Prepare an outline of your monologue and a bibliography of your sources for your teacher. Present your monologue to the class in costume.

RESEARCH LINKS
CLASSZONE.COM

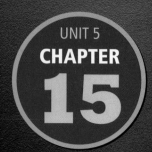

CHAPTER

15

Responding to Changes 1869–1917

The successful Cotton States Exposition hosted by Atlanta in 1895 showed the country how Georgia and the South were changing.

1877
Alfred Colquitt is elected governor. Constitution is rewritten to include county-unit system.

1872
John B. Gordon is elected to U.S. Senate. Gustavus J. Orr becomes state school commissioner.

1855
Joseph E. Brown is elected governor.

**GEORGIA
USA**

1850

1859
Gold is discovered in Rocky Mountains.

1867
The Grange is founded.

1869
First transcontinental railroad is built.

INTERACT
with HISTORY

It is 1890. You are a Georgia farmer and a member of the Southern Farmers' Alliance. Georgia's textile industry has grown and demand for cotton is high again. But you and your fellow farmers are discouraged by the lack of government support for the issues you face.

How will changes and reforms in national politics change your state?

WHAT DO YOU THINK?

- How can farmers effect change in government?

- How can forming alliances with other farmers benefit everyone?

- How might you persuade your fellow Georgians that change is needed?

For more information on this chapter, visit . . .

RESEARCH LINKS
CLASSZONE.COM

1906
John Hope becomes first black president of Atlanta Baptist College (Morehouse).

1907
Convict lease system is abolished.

1912
Juliette Gordon Low starts Girl Scouts.

1885

1920

1890
Wounded Knee massacre

1892
Populist Party's first national convention

1909
NAACP is founded in New York.

1920
19th Amendment (women's vote)

CHAPTER 15

Reading Strategy:
Identifying and Solving Problems

What Do You Know?
What do you know about life in the United States at the turn of the last century? What do you know about life in Georgia at that time?

THINK ABOUT
- what you've learned about problems created by westward expansion and the growth of cities
- what you know about racism and segregation in the South

What Do You Want to Know?
What questions do you have about life at the turn of the last century? About how Americans worked to solve their problems? Record those questions in your notebook before you read the chapter.

Identifying and Solving Problems
This chapter focuses on the problems that Americans faced at the turn of the last century and how they worked to solve those problems. A graphic organizer can help you keep track of problems and solutions. Major problems faced by the nation at the turn of the century are listed in the first column of the chart below. As you read, record solutions for these problems in the second column of the chart.

 See Skillbuilder Handbook, page 553.

 Taking Notes

Problems	Solutions
Political: One-party control in the South; disfranchisement; Jim Crow laws	
Social: Increasing poverty; lack of education; lack of civil rights for African Americans and women	
Environmental: Lack of adequate sewer systems; impure water and food	

America Expands Westward

MAIN IDEA	WHY IT MATTERS NOW	TERMS & NAMES

MAIN IDEA

The United States reunited after the Civil War and expanded westward.

WHY IT MATTERS NOW

Westward settlement expanded the mainland United States from coast to coast to the size it is today.

TERMS & NAMES

reservation
Wounded Knee
transcontinental railroad
Homestead Act of 1862
Exoduster

SETTING THE STAGE

The land west of the Mississippi River held vast resources. From the end of the Civil War to the beginning of the twentieth century, American settlers flooded into this territory.

> *PRIMARY SOURCE*
>
> Go West, young man.
> Horace Greeley, editor of the *New York Tribune*

From 1865 to 1900, more and more white settlers and business owners demanded access to the land the federal government had given to the Native Americans. The government responded by breaking up the land. Many Americans believed it was the fate of their country to spread "from sea to shining sea." This belief, known as Manifest Destiny, required that the entire West be settled. But how do you develop such a vast territory? What do you need to create businesses, farms, towns, and cities?

▲ Although the West was peopled with many Native Americans, such as Buffalo Bird Woman (above), and Mexicans, white settlers wanted the land for themselves.

Native Americans and Expansion

In the 1820s and 1830s, the federal government forced the Creek and Cherokee from Georgia to move to present-day Oklahoma. They also moved other tribes from the East to this area. The federal government believed that American settlers would never want the land.

Several tribes already lived in the West. The Sioux and other smaller tribes lived in the Northern Plains. The Cheyenne and Arapaho tribes lived in the Central Plains. The Navaho, Apache, Pueblo, Hopi, and Ute tribes lived in the Southwest. The Chinook and Tillamook lived in the Northwest. Their land, and the buffalo that roamed free and provided the tribes with food and skins, were in the way of the coming railroad.

Taking Notes

Use your chart to record solutions to major problems as America expands westward.

Problems	Solutions
Political: One-party control in the South; disfranchisement; Jim Crow laws	
Social: Increasing poverty; lack of education; lack of civil rights for African Americans and women	

Some tribes agreed to move to **reservations**—much smaller areas of land that the federal government had set aside. Reservation land was often so poor that growing crops or hunting did not provide enough food.

The federal government created the Bureau of Indian Affairs (BIA) to manage the reservations and provide for the people who lived on them. But many of the BIA officials were corrupt and did not work for the best interests of the Native Americans.

Some Native Americans refused to leave their land. They fought white settlers and federal troops. But it was not enough. Although fighting continued, the tribes in the West were waging a losing battle. In 1890, federal troops massacred over 200 Sioux men, women, and children at **Wounded Knee** in South Dakota. That massacre ended Native American armed resistance to relocating on the reservations.

Reading History

A. Making Inferences Why did some tribes agree to move to reservations?

Reading History

B. Recognizing Effects What were the results of the Wounded Knee massacre?

The Transcontinental Railroad

Railroads provided transportation into the unsettled areas of the West. They also provided a way to send livestock, crops, and minerals to market.

On May 10, 1869, the Union Pacific Railroad and the Central Pacific Railroad—built using immigrant and Native American laborers—connected at Promontory Point, Utah. This was the first **transcontinental railroad**. It connected the East Coast of the United States with the West Coast. Other railroad lines soon followed, bringing many white settlers.

▲ This golden spike united the Union Pacific and Central Pacific Railroads.

Agriculture and Business

As the federal government pushed Native Americans onto smaller and smaller regions of the West, white settlers moved onto their lands. The **Homestead Act of 1862** gave citizens 160 acres of land if they promised to live on the land for 5 years. That land was used in several ways.

Farmers from Many Places   Some farmers were Americans who migrated from the Eastern United States. Others were immigrants who came directly from Europe to the West. African Americans, calling themselves **Exodusters,** left the South and moved to the Midwest to get away from discrimination, violence, and poverty. The name referred to the biblical story of the exodus out of Egypt.

Cattle Ranching   Cattle ranching was one of the first large-scale uses of land in the West. In 1867, Joseph McCoy opened a stockyard in Abilene, Kansas, where the Kansas Pacific Railroad line ended. Soon, Texans were driving Texas Longhorns to Abilene along the Chisholm Trail. Other cow towns sprang up along railroad lines at the end of the cattle trails.

The people who drove the herds to market were known as cowboys. Many cowboys were African Americans or Mexicans. The era of the cattle drive was short. By 1900, so many railroads served the Midwest and

Vocabulary

stockyard: a large enclosed yard where cattle or pigs are kept until slaughtered, sold, or shipped elsewhere

West that the cattle drive was no longer necessary.

Cattle ranching spread across the West—to Kansas, Colorado, Montana, and other places that had plenty of grassy plains. Many ranchers did not own the land that the cattle grazed on. This was known as open-range or free-range ranching. Eventually, this ended as more and more public land was purchased and fenced off.

Reading History

C. Analyzing Causes What caused the decline of cattle ranching on the open range?

▲ About 50,000 African Americans settled in Kansas, Missouri, Indiana, and Illinois.

Mining The discovery of mineral deposits such as gold, silver, copper, and lead in the western territories contributed to the rush to settle the region. Gold was first discovered in 1848 in California. Further discoveries of gold, silver, and copper in Nevada, the Black Hills of the Dakotas, Colorado, Idaho, and Montana attracted great numbers of people to the West, hoping to make their fortunes.

As other Americans focused on settling the West, Southerners worked to put their own region in order, as you will read about in the next section.

Section 1 Assessment

1. TERMS & NAMES

Explain the significance of:

a. Transcontinental railroad

b. reservation

c. Wounded Knee

d. Homestead Act of 1862

e. Exoduster

2. TAKING NOTES

Use a chart like the one below to note the impact the transcontinental railroad had on Native Americans, Western settlers, cowboys, and immigrants.

People	How Affected by the Railroad
Native Americans	
Western Settlers	
Cowboys	
Immigrants	

3. MAIN IDEAS

a. How did the transcontinental railroad contribute to westward expansion?

b. How did the federal government attempt to manage reservations?

c. What role did cattle ranching play in the development of the West?

4. CRITICAL THINKING

Evaluating

Why did Native Americans resist reservations so violently, then cease resisting?

Think About
• ancestral homelands
• living conditions
• government support

Language Arts/Art Imagine you have just moved to a homestead in the West. Write a **letter** to friends back home or draw a **picture** that describes your new way of life.

Democrats Control Georgia Politics

MAIN IDEA	WHY IT MATTERS NOW	TERMS & NAMES
Georgia was led by one political party from the 1870s well into the twentieth century.	One-party rule ended as Georgia became more connected to the rest of the nation. Today, there are several political parties in the state.	Bourbon Triumvirate county unit system Dr. William H. Felton Southern Farmers' Alliance Colored Farmers' Alliance Populist Party

SETTING THE STAGE

When Reconstruction ended, white Southerners began rebuilding the South in the way they wanted. Using one-party rule and the call for white unity, Georgia's political leaders made sure they kept control of the state.

Poor white and black farmers faced constant debt, but the political leaders seemed uninterested in their problems. Some people challenged the leadership of the Democratic Party. They formed new political organizations and won elections. Could they take political power away from the Bourbon Democrats, who had led since the end of Reconstruction? Could they make changes that would ease the burdens of Georgia's small farmers?

▲ Farmers such as this Gwinnett County, Georgia, family often felt their problems were ignored by state officials.

The Bourbon Triumvirate

The governor's race in 1872 proved that the Democratic Party was in full control of Georgia politics. The Republican candidate for governor lost by a wide margin to Democratic Governor James M. Smith. In the 1876 governor's election, Democrat Alfred Colquitt beat the Republican candidate 111,297 to 33,433 votes.

Three men—John B. Gordon, Alfred Holt Colquitt, and Joseph E. Brown—controlled the Democratic Party in Georgia from the 1870s to the 1890s. They became known as the **Bourbon Triumvirate** (a triumvirate is a ruling group of three people). Radical Republicans gave them the name "Bourbon" for a line of French kings who were said to have "learned nothing and forgotten nothing."

The Triumvirate showed special favor for Atlanta. They supported the growth of industry and modernization but did not like raising taxes

Taking Notes

Use your chart to record solutions to problems Georgians faced under one-party rule.

Problems	Solutions
Political: One-party control in the South; disfranchisement; Jim Crow laws	
Social: Increasing poverty; lack of education; lack of civil rights for African Americans and women	

The Bourbon Triumvirate

In 1872, the Georgia Assembly elected John B. Gordon to the U.S. Senate. He was elected governor twice in the 1880s.

Joseph E. Brown was governor of Georgia for four terms from 1855 to 1865. After Reconstruction, Brown served as a U.S. senator.

Alfred Holt Colquitt was governor of Georgia from 1877 to 1882 and was a U.S. senator from 1883 to 1894.

Reading History

A. Analyzing Points of View How would the Bourbon Triumvirate profit from supporting the New South movement?

to pay for the changes. That caused some conflict within the party. The Triumvirate appeared to be devoted to the Lost Cause. But at the same time, they supported the New South movement, especially where they could profit from it.

Georgia Constitution of 1877   In 1877, legislators rewrote the state constitution. One measure of the new constitution gave rural counties an advantage in elections to the state legislature. The **county unit system** assigned the 6 counties with the greatest population 3 representatives each to the legislature, the next 26 counties had 2 representatives each, and the last 105 counties had 1 representative each in the lower House. A representative had two votes.

This ensured that the counties with the greatest population would not control the legislature. Small rural counties possessed much greater power than their population might have given them. The county unit system continued until 1963.

Voices of Change

Democratic leaders were supported by white landowners and successful businessmen who wanted to keep control of the state's economy and political system. With an ineffective Republican Party and a Democratic Party controlled by only a few leaders, there was not much dissent or compromise. Many people felt they were not well represented. Small farmers, sharecroppers and tenants, blacks, and poor whites had no way to voice their concerns. Some found their voice in the Independent movement of the 1870s.

Independent Movement   In 1874, an Independent candidate, **Dr. William H. Felton,** from Cartersville, won a seat in the U.S. Congress and served three terms. Felton supported the rights of Georgia's small farmers against the interests of big landowners and businessmen.

In 1878, two other Independent candidates were elected to the U.S. Congress. The Independents thought they had a chance to take control away from the Democrats if they won the governor's race of 1880, but they failed to do so. Dr. Felton was not re-elected to Congress. By 1882, the Independent movement had died out.

The Grange   Southern sharecroppers, tenant farmers, and farmers with small plots of land faced growing debts. They could not adequately feed, clothe, and house their families. They could not pay their debts to the merchants and landowners. Small farmers and sharecroppers in the Midwest and West also faced the same problems.

Southern landowners joined a new organization called the National Grange of the Patrons of Husbandry. It was also known as the Grange. The Grange began as a social group. Local Granges held dances and other activities for the farmers. Eventually, they took on political and economic issues. They established Grange-owned stores and cotton gins to reduce costs for the farmers. While the Grange was not able to accomplish much, farmers began to express a desire to improve their lives.

Southern Farmers' Alliance   A new organization, called the **Southern Farmers' Alliance,** formed in Texas in the late 1870s to help the Southern farmer. In the late 1880s, the Alliance opened cooperative stores where members could buy goods at reasonable prices and on credit. Alliance members also combined their cotton crops to get a better price at market.

Vocabulary

Independent: not committed to a particular political party

Reading History

B. Analyzing Causes How did the Grange inspire farmers to make changes in their lives?

▼ The Grange and the Southern Farmers' Alliance tried to help small farmers and tenant farmers, such as this Carroll County family.

In 1890, William Northern, a member of the Alliance, became governor of Georgia. Most of the state legislators supported the Alliance platform. There were about 2,000 Alliance clubs with over 100,000 members in Georgia and 1 million members nationwide. A Georgia Alliance member wrote, "We are going to get out of debt and be free and independent people once more."

Colored Farmers' Alliance   African Americans were not admitted into the Southern Farmers' Alliance. So they created their own group, the **Colored Farmers' Alliance.** It included more tenants, sharecroppers, and farm workers than the white Southern Alliance. The Colored Farmers' Alliance tried to force landowners to pay its members more money for picking cotton, but it was unsuccessful.

> **PRIMARY SOURCE**
>
> A Negro county alliance convention met at Monroe, in this state, on Saturday last and adopted resolutions in effect as follows: They pledge themselves not to pick . . . a lock of cotton . . . for less than seventy-five cents per hundred . . . that they will work for no person for less than $1 per day in the winter and $1.25 in the summer, and to work only eight hours per day.
>
> *Atlanta Constitution,* September 11, 1889

The Populist Movement

Despite the Southern Farmers' Alliance's growth in Georgia, it began to lose momentum nationally in 1890. But farmers in Georgia and throughout the nation still faced the same problems. Farming costs were increasing, the railroads were charging unfair rates, and more and more people were losing their farms. Farmers realized they needed political representation. In 1890, Northern and Southern farmers created their own political party to represent their concerns.

▼ As a Populist candidate, Tom Watson campaigned for equality. Later in life, however, he turned and became angry and spiteful.

The Populist Party   The **Populist Party** supported the following reforms and programs to help farmers and the working class. The Populist programs included several critical reforms, such as:

- an income tax
- the vote for women
- government control of railroads
- programs to provide credit to farmers
- direct election of U.S. senators by popular vote

Populist Party candidates in Texas and Georgia also appealed to African-American voters. In Georgia, Thomas Edward Watson began his career as an Alliance supporter. He

ran for the Georgia legislature. Watson argued that the industrialization of the New South did little to help Georgia's small farmers. He asked black and white owners of small farms to elect him because he understood their problems. He won the election.

The Populist Party held its first national convention in Omaha, Nebraska, in the summer of 1892. They nominated James B. Weaver as their candidate for president.

The Populist Party Threatens Democrats Many former Southern Farmers' Alliance members joined the Populist Party. This concerned the Democrats. They wanted to keep the Democratic Party dominant and did not like the idea of African Americans and whites joining together. Weaver placed third in the election.

Tom Watson ran as the Populist Party's vice-presidential candidate in 1896 and presidential candidate in 1904 but was defeated. In 1920, he ran against Hoke Smith for the U.S. Senate—and won. At that time, Watson no longer wanted the black vote. In fact, he became very hostile to African Americans, Jews, and Catholics. It seemed that during his political career he had wanted the black vote only when he needed it to win.

Politicians in power throughout the South and conservative white voters had become even more concerned about the outcome of elections. In the next section, you will read more about their attempts to control those outcomes.

Reading History

C. Making Inferences Why did Democrats want to keep African Americans and whites from joining together?

Section 2 Assessment

1. TERMS & NAMES

Explain the significance of:

a. Bourbon Triumvirate

b. county unit system

c. Dr. William H. Felton

d. Southern Farmers' Alliance

e. Colored Farmers' Alliance

f. Populist Party

2. TAKING NOTES

Use a diagram like the one below to take notes on the political movements discussed in this section. Write the name of the movement and one fact about it in each circle.

Political Movement Name: / Fact: (×3)

3. MAIN IDEAS

a. How did the county unit system give rural counties more power?

b. Why couldn't the Democratic Party keep whites from joining other political groups?

c. What were the goals of the Grange and, later, the Southern Farmers' Alliance? Did they succeed?

4. CRITICAL THINKING

Drawing Conclusions

Why did the Populist Party favor government regulation of the railroads?

Think About

• powers of monopolies
• importance of railroads to farmers

ACTIVITY -OPTIONS- **Technology/Speech** Plan an informational **Web page** or deliver a political **campaign speech** to potential voters about a political movement or alliance discussed in this section.

Segregation and Discrimination

MAIN IDEA	WHY IT MATTERS NOW	TERMS & NAMES
Southern whites passed laws and sometimes used violence to prevent African Americans from enjoying their rights.	The right to vote and equal rights took decades for African Americans to achieve.	disfranchisement poll tax white primary Jim Crow laws *Plessy* v. *Ferguson* lynching Booker T. Washington W. E. B. DuBois

SETTING THE STAGE

Democrats controlled the South's political system in the 1880s and 1890s. They had successfully dealt with challenges from the Independent and Populist movements. But they still worried about their ability to maintain power.

One concern they had was the vote. If enough people did not like the government, they could vote for change. What if African Americans and poor whites combined their votes to defeat Democrats? What could Democrats do to maintain power in the hands of a few white men? The answer many came up with was to restrict who could vote.

▲ Southern Democrats used several different methods to prevent African Americans from voting.

Guarantees of Political Equality

The Fourteenth Amendment to the Constitution declared that all persons born in the United States were citizens, except for Native Americans. It further declared that no state could make laws that took away privileges of United States citizens. The Fifteenth Amendment of the Constitution said that the right to vote could not be denied to any United States citizen on account of race, color, or previous servitude (meaning slavery). In other words, African Americans had gained the legal right to participate in Southern political society. But most white Southerners could not accept this.

White Southerners wanted to weaken any claims African Americans made for political rights. Politicians warned white voters that unless they kept a strong Democratic Party in place, African Americans would come to rule Georgia's politics and try to claim social equality as well.

Taking Notes

Use your chart to record solutions to problems created by segregation and discrimination.

Problems	Solutions
Political: One-party control in the South; disfranchisement; Jim Crow laws	
Social: Increasing poverty; lack of education; lack of civil rights for African Americans and women	

Preventing the Right to Vote

Reading History

A. Finding Main Ideas Why did Georgia enact laws that disfranchised African Americans?

<u>**Disfranchisement**</u> means depriving a person of one of the rights of citizenship, such as the right to vote. Southern Democrats increased their chance of remaining in office by enacting laws that prevented people from voting. By 1908, all Southern states had enacted laws that disfranchised most African Americans. Georgia added a poll tax, a literacy test, an understanding clause, and a grandfather clause.

Poll Tax   A <u>**poll tax**</u> was a fee that had to be paid before a person could vote. It was the most effective means of preventing poor whites and African Americans from voting. Every Southern state enacted a poll tax. The tax accumulated with each election, and a voter had to pay the tax for every election, whether he voted or not. For example, if a man had not voted for 10 elections, he would have to pay the tax for those 10 before he could vote in the next election.

Literacy Test and Understanding Clause   A literacy test and an understanding clause determined if people could read and understand the Constitution. Inevitably, the official giving the test failed African Americans or other "undesirable" voters.

Grandfather Clause   Grandfather clauses blocked African Americans from registering to vote, but not poor whites. If a man's father

CITIZENSHIP IN ACTION

Exercising the Vote

The Fifteenth Amendment guaranteed the right to vote. The Nineteenth Amendment gave women the vote. The Twenty-Sixth Amendment lowered the voting age from 21 to 18. Today's elections are open to all citizens aged 18 years and older.

Future voters can practice casting their votes in mock, or pretend, elections. The National Student/Parent Mock Election teaches students to be informed voters. Mock presidential elections attract coverage by the media. Television stations may even broadcast live from schools, interviewing student voters.

In November 2003, Coastal Middle School in Savannah held a forum for the city's mayoral candidates. Students served as commentators and interviewed candidates with questions prepared in advance. They questioned the candidates on topics such as crime reduction, bringing more business to Savannah, improving public schools, and the candidates' goals for improving life in Savannah. Local television stations covered the event.

How Do You Set Up a Mock Election?

1. Choose issues and candidates and then set up a mock election in your classroom. (You could focus on the national, state, or local level.)
2. Create the materials of an election, such as the polling place, ballots, and posters.
3. Campaign for the candidates or the issues you support.
4. Conduct the voting.
5. Prepare mock media reports on the election's outcome. You may want to interview voters.

For more about citizenship and voting . . .

RESEARCH LINKS CLASSZONE.COM

or grandfather had voted in a state election before 1867, the man could register to vote. This barred African Americans from voting since they had not been allowed to vote in Georgia and the South before 1867.

Reading History

B. Summarizing
How did white primaries keep African Americans from voting?

White Primary Another way to disfranchise African Americans was the **white primary**. The Fifteenth Amendment guaranteed the right to vote in an election. Democrats argued that primaries to select candidates were private votes among party members in a private organization, and the Fifteenth Amendment did not apply. However, in most cases there was only one candidate in the general election—a white Democrat. The primary effectively was the election.

Segregation and Jim Crow

Before the Civil War, the system of slavery had effectively separated the races. After the war, Southern states passed laws to keep them separated. These were called **Jim Crow laws.**

In 1883, the Supreme Court ruled that the Fourteenth Amendment applied only to governments and not private citizens. The Court said the Constitution allowed segregation of public places such as restaurants, trains, waiting rooms, and even drinking fountains. Georgia was the first state to pass Jim Crow laws for streetcars. What had been an accepted social practice was now legalized.

Even though African-American children learned about the Jim Crow laws, many did not understand discrimination until they were older. One woman described living under segregation laws.

> **PRIMARY SOURCE**
> Naturally, you would ask, "Why?" The question would always come back that we were living in a country that had segregated laws. . . . You were not looked upon as having full rights that all other citizens should have. . . . You have to watch your behavior.
> Lillian Smith quoted in *Remembering Jim Crow* by William Chafe

NOW & THEN

Jim Crow and Segregation

In *Plessy* v. *Ferguson* (1896), the Supreme Court upheld a Jim Crow law, ruling that "separate but equal" rail cars for African Americans and whites were constitutional.

In the early 1950s, African Americans sued to end segregation and to integrate the public schools. In 1954, the Supreme Court heard these cases, bound together by a case brought by an African American named Oliver Brown who sued the Topeka School Board for preventing his daughter from attending the neighborhood elementary school. The Supreme Court ruled that if schools are separate, they are naturally unequal. That is, segregation was unconstitutional.

African Americans and their supporters thought that Jim Crow laws were unconstitutional. They took their complaints to the courts.

In 1896, the Supreme Court ruled in ***Plessy v. Ferguson*** that "separate but equal" facilities were not unconstitutional. It was not until 1954 that the courts threw out the idea of "separate but equal" as the law of the land.

Racial Violence

From Reconstruction to the 1950s, some white Southerners used lynching to control African Americans. Most **lynchings** involved shooting or hanging individuals—mostly black men—during this time.

Sometimes, a mob would take African Americans, arrested on suspicion of committing a crime, from jail and lynch them. Other times, rumors were enough to send a community into a frenzy. Mobs roamed the streets looking for the guilty. Frequently, mobs grabbed the first available African American and took their anger out on that person. From the 1880s to the 1950s, almost 5,000 people were lynched in the United States, most of them in the South.

Atlanta Race Riot of 1906 In the governor's race of 1906, the two major candidates, Hoke Smith and Clark Howell, campaigned on a platform to take the vote away from African-American Georgians. They used their newspapers, the *Atlanta Journal* and the *Atlanta Constitution*, to promote disfranchisement.

In September, the Atlanta newspapers reported numerous attacks on white women. These reports set off a riot. A white mob descended on the African-American neighborhoods of Atlanta, attacking people and destroying homes and businesses. African Americans fought back. But they were outnumbered, and the Atlanta police gave little assistance.

The rioting ended a few days later. Hundreds had been injured. It was reported that 15 to 30 African Americans had been killed and thousands of African Americans had left the city for the safety of the countryside.

African-American Reactions

African Americans often disagreed about their role in Southern society. Of course, all were completely opposed to violence against them. But there was a difference of opinion about how they should react. Should they accept discrimination and segregation? Or should they fight for their rights under the Constitution?

In 1895, **Booker T. Washington,** a teacher and early leader for racial equality, made a speech in which he said African Americans should focus on learning skills and gaining economic strength. He believed that they had to earn the respect and the right to demand equality. Washington told his mainly white audience that he supported the efforts of African Americans to work their way up to full participation in society.

Reading History

C. Forming and Supporting Opinions Why did whites use violence, or the threat of violence, to control African Americans?

▼ Booker T. Washington's speech at the Cotton States Exposition of 1895 became known as the "Atlanta Compromise."

To gain white support for his educational work, Washington described his vision of equality.

PRIMARY SOURCE

In purely social matters [whites and blacks] can be as separate as the fingers, yet one as the hand in all things essential to mutual progress.

Booker T. Washington, speaking at the 1895 Cotton States Exposition

Washington also reminded white Southerners that the African-American workforce had created the wealth of the South. He feared that African Americans would be cast aside and immigrants used in their place for labor.

W. E. B. DuBois   Not everyone agreed with Washington. One man who strongly disagreed with Washington's strategy was <u>**W. E. B. DuBois**</u> [doo BOYS]. DuBois was a highly respected sociology professor at Atlanta University. He believed that African Americans deserved equal access to the political, social, and economic worlds of the South.

Like John Hope of Atlanta, DuBois believed that African Americans should receive the same education as whites. At this time, most whites believed that the only education that poor whites and African Americans needed was technical training. DuBois and Washington represented two extremes in the African-American community.

Reading History

D. Analyzing Points of View
How did Washington and DuBois differ on how African Americans should react to discrimination?

John and Lugenia Burns Hope: Reform and Education for African Americans

John Hope was born in Augusta, Georgia, in 1868. He earned a degree at Brown University in Rhode Island. Hope returned to Georgia to promote liberal education for black Americans. He believed in total equality with whites. Hope was a friend of Booker T. Washington but strongly disagreed with him.

In 1906, Hope became the first black president of Atlanta Baptist College, now called Morehouse College. He was responsible for creating the Atlanta University Center—Clark Atlanta University, Morehouse College, and Spelman College. Hope was also involved in many local and national civic organizations. One of the most important was the Committee on Interracial Cooperation (CIC). Hope was the CIC's first president.

Lugenia Burns was from Chicago. She was involved in many progressive programs in Chicago to improve the lives of African Americans. She married Hope in 1896 and continued her work in Atlanta. She created the Neighborhood Union, an organization that worked to improve the living conditions of African Americans. She was active in many other groups, such as the Association of Southern Women for the Prevention of Lynching.

National Association for the Advancement of Colored People (NAACP) The National Association for the Advancement of Colored People (NAACP) was founded in 1909 in New York by African Americans and whites concerned about the treatment of African Americans. The NAACP worked to end discrimination and to gain equal rights for black Americans.

W. E. B. DuBois was one of the founding members. One of the NAACP's goals was to stop the lynchings in the South. The NAACP reported incidents of lynching to the national press and African-American newspapers. This was effective in publicizing the violent side of Southern culture.

Ida B. Wells, another founding member of the NAACP, was an African-American teacher from Memphis. She became a journalist after the lynching of three of her friends. Her blistering articles called for an end to lynching and other racially motivated crimes. Threats to her life forced her to leave Memphis and move to Chicago where she continued her crusade for racial and gender equality.

Other nation-wide movements and organizations were also working to reform society. American life was changing very rapidly and boundaries were expanding. In the next section, you will learn more about the efforts many Americans made to move society forward, and solve problems along the way.

Section 3 Assessment

1. TERMS & NAMES

Explain the significance of:

a. disfranchisement

b. poll tax

c. white primary

d. Jim Crow laws

e. *Plessy* v. *Ferguson*

f. lynching

g. Booker T. Washington

h. W. E. B. DuBois

2. TAKING NOTES

Use a diagram like the one below to compare and contrast the ideas of Booker T. Washington and W. E. B. DuBois.

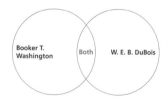

Booker T. Washington | Both | W. E. B. DuBois

3. MAIN IDEAS

a. What were the methods used to keep African Americans from voting?

b. Why did whites want Southern society to remain segregated?

c. What does "separate but equal" mean? Was it a good description of segregated facilities in the South? Why or why not?

4. CRITICAL THINKING

Solving Problems

What could have ended discrimination against African Americans in the U.S. at the turn of the last century?

Think About

• attitudes of whites about nonwhites

• the efforts of African Americans to find jobs and security

• competition for jobs

ACTIVITY -OPTIONS- **Speech/Art** Write a **speech** or design a **brochure** to convince people to bring an end to Jim Crow laws or violence against African Americans in the late 1800s.

The Progressive Movement

SETTING THE STAGE

The Industrial Revolution in America created great wealth. Many Americans welcomed industrialization. It led to higher income and living standards. During what is called the Progressive Era, many people began to recognize that industrialization also created problems. They wanted to find solutions to these problems.

Local, state, and federal governments had not been involved in the lives of citizens or the workings of the economy. During this time, however, people began to think the government could help fix some of the problems Americans were experiencing.

▲ Gustavus Orr served as state school commissioner for 16 years and gained a national reputation for his progressive views on education.

The Progressive Movement Begins

By the 1890s, many Americans were aware of growing problems in society. Poverty was rising and becoming more concentrated in the nation's cities. Politics and government were more corrupt. American cities could not provide adequate services, such as sewer systems and fresh water, to all of its citizens. There was an increasing division between the wealthy and the poor. And the federal government did not control or monitor powerful big business.

The **Progressive Movement** was not a single organization or group of people. It was many groups trying to improve society. People who campaigned to make changes and correct the problems in society were known as progressives.

When voluntary methods were not enough, progressives turned to government—local, state, and federal—for assistance. They also used newspapers and magazines to expose the unfair practices of big business, the corruption of elected officials, and the horrid living conditions of

Taking Notes

Use your chart to record solutions to problems that surfaced as a result of the Industrial Revolution.

Problems	Solutions
Political: One-party control in the South; disfranchisement; Jim Crow laws	
Social: Increasing poverty; lack of education; lack of civil rights for African Americans and women	

America's poor. Writers and newspaper reporters who wrote about these issues were called muckrakers. These journalists created a public demand for reform. Muckraker Ida Tarbell, for instance, accused Standard Oil of using unfair business practices to drive small competing companies out of business. Jacob Riis, a Danish immigrant, wrote and photographed living conditions of immigrants in the slums of New York. He published *How the Other Half Lives* to spur legislation that improved living conditions.

The progressive reformers shared at least one of the following three goals: first, to reform government and expand democracy; second, to promote social welfare; and third, to establish economic reform.

Progressives in Georgia

In Georgia and the South, progressive reform benefited mainly whites. But people of both races worked to help Southern blacks also. Progressives focused on several issues.

Education In the 1870s and 1880s, the state provided money only for elementary schools. Many Georgians were not willing to pay higher taxes to support the state's public school system. Many children did not attend school regularly because their families needed them on the farm, especially at planting and harvest time. Lower-income families relied on everyone working to help the family survive.

Gustavus James Orr is considered the "father of the common school movement" in Georgia. He became the state's school commissioner in 1872 and pushed for a school to train teachers. He also supported education for African Americans. Orr strongly supported vocational training—learning a useful skill—as the best form of education for Georgia's citizens.

Reading History

A. Summarizing
What were the issues that Southern progressives focused on?

Local city and county governments were responsible for high schools. Most chose to spend very little or no money on them. But in 1912, progressives worked for the passage of a constitutional amendment that would include high schools in state funding. A few years later, the state passed a mandatory school attendance law.

Railroad Regulation Farmers complained that railroads charged unfair rates to the small farm owners. Progressives such as Governor

Hoke Smith and Senator Tom Watson worked to regulate the railroads and make them treat all customers fairly.

City Management   Many city officials were not experienced in managing the rapid growth of the South's towns and cities. The Better Government Movement pushed for more efficient city management.

Disease Control   Great progress was made in preventing and treating many diseases like hookworm and pellegra. Georgia and other Southern states started programs to promote cleanliness, sanitary toilets, clean drinking water, and inspection of meat and dairy products.

New Farming Techniques   Southern farmers were taught new, more productive ways to grow crops. Women learned how to better preserve foods. That helped feed the family throughout the year.

Settlement Houses   The **settlement house** idea began in Chicago but quickly spread. Charlotte, Knoxville, New Orleans, and Atlanta all had settlement houses. Settlement houses offered help to immigrants and people living in poverty. Services such as free kindergarten, laundry, legal aid, and health care were offered so poor people could improve their lives.

Women's Rights   In Georgia, **Rebecca Latimer Felton,** wife of Independent candidate Dr. William Felton, actively campaigned for many causes. She supported antilynching, prohibition, and antismoking, and she condemned the drinking of Coca-Cola (along with groups such as the Georgia Baptist Association). In the early days, one of the ingredients of the soft drink was the addictive plant coca. Felton also promoted child care, compulsory school attendance, and admission of women to the University of Georgia.

▼ In 1922, Rebecca Latimer Felton became the first woman to serve in the U.S. Senate. She filled a vacancy for one day.

Rebecca Felton argued for equal status for women—something that was seen as too progressive for the South and most of the nation. She did not accept the belief that the proper role of the woman was only as a wife, mother, and housekeeper. Felton was the first woman to serve in the U.S. Senate. For one day in November 1922, Governor Thomas Hardwick appointed her to fill the seat left vacant by the death of Senator Tom Watson. Although she was very progressive in many things, Felton still defended white supremacy.

**JULIETTE GORDON LOW
1860–1927**

Juliette Gordon Low was from the upper class of Savannah. While in England, she met Sir Robert Baden-Powell, founder of the Boy Scouts. Low wanted young women to have a similar organization. With her own money, she started the Girl Scouts of America in the United States in 1912.

Early Girl Scout troops helped with the war effort during World War I. When Low died in 1927, more than 160,000 girls had become Girl Scouts.

Although women in the South—and the nation—during this time could not participate fully in society, they got involved by joining church groups, social clubs, and temperance leagues (promoting abstinence from drinking). Clubs such as the Atlanta Woman's Club, the Civic Improvement League in Augusta, and the Georgia Federation of Women gave women a presence in society. Women also found new jobs as teachers, sales clerks, and journalists.

Women's Suffrage Women like Rebecca Felton and Frances Smith Whiteside pushed for women's right to vote in Georgia. But Georgia's political leaders were not interested in this progressive reform. Georgia eventually had to allow women to vote when the Nineteenth Amendment to the U.S. Constitution became law in 1920.

Prohibition Georgia moved toward outlawing the possession or consumption of alcohol well before the national ban in 1919. Governor Hoke Smith, the editor of the *Atlanta Journal,* campaigned for prohibition. The Women's Christian Temperance Union, the Anti-Saloon League, and many different women's social and religious groups joined. Individual counties in Georgia voted to prohibit alcohol. In 1907, it was the first Southern state to enact laws outlawing the sale of alcohol.

Child Labor Laws were in place in Georgia by 1916 to prevent textile mills and other businesses from hiring young children. Factory owners ignored the laws and continued to use children as young as ten years old. In fact, Georgia led the nation in employing children between the ages of 10 and 15. These children worked long hours in dangerous conditions for as little as 4 cents a day.

Convict Lease System The convict lease system was abolished in 1908 after the state's leading newspapers, farm and labor groups, and religious leaders led an intense campaign against the practice. Since the 1870s, prisoners had worked in coal mines and on railroads. There were many abuses of the system, and prisoners received horrible treatment. In response to such a public outcry, led in part by Rebecca Latimer Felton, Georgia's General Assembly established a new system, where children and adult convicts were kept separate. State prison farms housed prisoners, who were put to work on public roads.

Reading History

B. Finding Main Ideas How did women participate in society before they achieved the vote?

The Nation Comes Together

Slowly, the nation was coming together. White Southerners had regained control of their politics and economy after Reconstruction. Northern businessmen invested greater amounts of money in the South.

In the 1890s, Americans expanded their influence across the globe. Most sought business opportunities in far-off places such as China. Americans were concerned about the influence of European nations on areas such as Latin America. They wanted free access to do business anywhere in the world.

The Spanish-American War, which was fought in 1898, seemed to reunite white Southerners and Northerners under the same cause—fighting Spanish imperialism in American waters. Many said that the Mason-Dixon Line, the line dividing the South and the North, would disappear. Everyone would become Americans first.

Not all Southerners or Northerners were that optimistic. Some did not support the Spanish-American War. Many did not think that it could wash away the bitterness still held in the hearts of Civil War veterans.

Americans became even more concerned when a war broke out in Europe. Would Americans be drawn into the conflict? In the next chapter, you will learn more about the social, political, and economic effects of America's involvement in World War I.

Reading History

C. Forming and Supporting Opinions Do you think that fighting a war against a common enemy helped end the bitterness of the Civil War?

Section 4 Assessment

1. TERMS & NAMES
Explain the significance of:

a. Progressive Movement

b. Gustavus James Orr

c. settlement house

d. Rebecca Latimer Felton

2. TAKING NOTES
Use a diagram like the one below to list some of the main issues during the Southern Progressive movement.

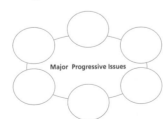

Major Progressive Issues

3. MAIN IDEAS
a. What was the Progressive Movement? Who were its members?

b. How did women play a greater role in society during this time?

c. Why did some people think that the Spanish-American War brought Southerners and Northerners closer?

4. CRITICAL THINKING
Forming and Supporting Opinions

How did muckrakers contribute to the reform of society?

Think About
• public opinion
• politicians' reputations
• the spirit of reform

ACTIVITY -OPTIONS- **Language Arts/Technology** Write a short **biography** of one of the women reformers discussed in this section, or create an illustrated **time line** of that person's life and work.

VISUAL SUMMARY

The Country Responds to Change 1869 to 1917s

WESTWARD EXPANSION
- Bureau of Indian Affairs
- Homestead Act of 1862
- Wounded Knee

ONE PARTY CONTROL IN GEORGIA
- Georgia Constitution of 1877
- Independent Party
- Populist Party
- Southern Farmers' and Colored Farmers' Alliances

AFRICAN AMERICAN CIVIL RIGHTS
- Disfranchisement
- Jim Crow laws
- *Plessy v. Ferguson*
- NAACP

INDUSTRIAL REVOLUTION
- The Progressive Movement
- Education and city management reforms
- Railroad regulation
- Women's rights
- Child labor laws

TERMS & NAMES

Briefly explain the significance of the following.

1. transcontinental railroad
2. Wounded Knee
3. Homestead Act of 1862
4. Bourbon Triumvirate
5. Southern Farmers' Alliance
6. Colored Farmers' Alliance
7. disfranchisement
8. poll tax
9. *Plessy v. Ferguson*
10. Progressive Movement

REVIEW QUESTIONS

America Expands Westward (pages 327–329)

1. How did the transcontinental railroad affect life in the West?
2. What was the role of the Bureau of Indian Affairs?

Democrats Control Georgia Politics (pages 330–334)

3. Who was Dr. William H. Felton?
4. What reforms and programs were supported by the Populist Party?

Segregation and Discrimination (pages 335–340)

5. How did Southerners prevent African Americans from voting?
6. How did W. E. B. DuBois and Booker T. Washington disagree on equal rights for African Americans?

The Progressive Movement (pages 341–345)

7. What problems in American society led to the Progressive Movement?
8. What issues were the focus of Georgia Progressives?

CRITICAL THINKING

1. USING YOUR NOTES: IDENTIFYING AND SOLVING PROBLEMS

Problems	Solutions
Political: One-party control in the South; disfranchisement; Jim Crow laws	
Social: Increasing poverty; lack of education; lack of civil rights for African Americans and women	
Environmental: Lack of adequate sewer systems; impure water and food	

Using your completed chart, answer the questions below.

a. Which solution was most effective? Why?
b. Which solution was least effective and why?

2. ANALYZING LEADERSHIP

Think about the actions of Booker T. Washington and W. E. B. DuBois. Whose approach to discrimination was the most likely to be effective? Why?

3. APPLYING CITIZENSHIP SKILLS

What group or individual worked most effectively to promote equal rights? Explain your answer.

4. THEME: IMPACT OF THE INDIVIDUAL

How did individuals affect the life of the country during the Progressive Era?

5. DRAWING CONCLUSIONS

Why did the Populist Party favor the direct election of U.S. senators by popular vote?

INTERACT *with* HISTORY

Having read about the issues faced by Americans at the turn of the century, do you think you would have been a progressive? If so, what causes would you have worked to support?

Use the map and your knowledge of American history to answer questions 1 through 3.

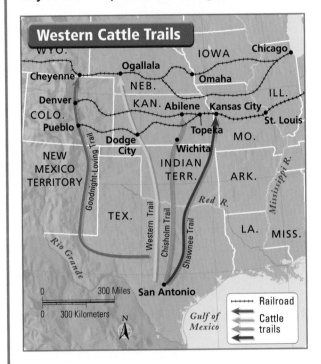

Western Cattle Trails

1. Where did the cattle trails begin?

   A. San Antonio
   B. Kansas
   C. Cheyenne
   D. Texas

2. What is the longest cattle trail?

   A. Goodnight-Loving Trail
   B. Western Trail
   C. Chisholm Trail
   D. Shawnee Trail

3. Which cattle trails supplied Chicago?

   A. Shawnee and Chisholm Trails
   B. Shawnee and Western Trails
   C. Western and Goodnight-Loving Trails
   D. Chisholm and Western Trails

TEST PRACTICE
CLASSZONE.COM

ALTERNATIVE ASSESSMENT

1. WRITING A PROPOSAL

Progressives worked to solve many problems in their society. Now it's your turn to be a progressive. Identify a problem in your school or community. Conduct interviews and research the problem to determine the best possible solution. Then write a proposal outlining your solution for the school board or for community leaders. Present your proposal to your class.

2. COOPERATIVE LEARNING

The Populist Movement developed a platform (or a statement of principles) to help farmers and working-class Americans. With a team, research the platforms of historical and contemporary political parties. Now place yourself in the years 1869 to 1917, and create your own political party. Pick a name for your party, design your own symbol, and write your own platform—the principles of your party. What issues will you address? What will you stand for? Present your new party to the class.

INTEGRATED TECHNOLOGY ACTIVITY

PREPARING AN ELECTRONIC PRESENTATION

Racial discrimination has been a sad feature of Georgia history. Use your library and the Internet to research racism, segregation, and civil rights in Georgia. Then create a multimedia presentation on this topic using the questions below as guides.

- What groups faced discrimination?

- How were racism and segregation evident in Georgia?

- Which civil rights leaders had connections with Georgia?

- How were civil rights leaders active in Georgia?

- Which newspaper articles, biographies, or autobiographies cover these events?

RESEARCH LINKS
CLASSZONE.COM

World War I and the 1920s 1914–1930

These soldiers trained at Camp Wheeler before sailing to France to fight in World War I.

1915
Leo Frank is lynched by Georgia mob.
Rebirth of Ku Klux Klan

1918
Georgia ratifies the
18th Amendment
(bans alcohol)

GEORGIA
USA

1910

1914
U.S.-built Panama
Canal opens

1917
Wilson asks Congress to
declare war on Germany.

1918
World
War I ends.

The year is 1917, and the United States has been drawn into World War I. Each citizen is called upon to help the war effort. Some will join the American armed forces and go to fight in Europe. Others will work in factories at home, producing weapons and supplies. Even children will do their part.

How will you support the war effort?

WHAT DO YOU THINK?

- How can Americans at home help win the war?

- What might U.S. soldiers experience in Europe?

- How might being at war affect the country?

For more information on this chapter, visit . . .

RESEARCH LINKS
CLASSZONE.COM

1922
Rebecca Latimer Felton becomes the first woman to serve in the U. S. Senate.

1923
Dial telephone service begins in Atlanta.

1925
Coca-Cola magnate Asa Candler gives Candler Field to Atlanta for an airport.

1920

1930

1920
Warren G. Harding is elected president.

1923
Calvin Coolidge becomes president.

1929
U.S. stock market crashes. Great Depression begins.

Reading Strategy: Finding Main Ideas

What Do You Know?

What do you already know about World War I and the Roaring Twenties? What caused the war? How did the war influence the 1920s?

THINK ABOUT

- documentaries and books you've read about wars
- how you've seen the 1920s portrayed in movies, television, and historical fiction
- what happens to a country when rapid changes take place

I WANT YOU FOR U.S. ARMY
NEAREST RECRUITING STATION

What Do You Want to Know?

What questions do you have about the causes and effects of World War I? About life during the 1920s? Record those questions in your notebook before you read the chapter.

Finding Main Ideas

To understand what you read, learn to find the main idea of each paragraph, topic heading, and section. Remember that the supporting details help to explain the main idea. On the chart below, write down the main idea presented in this chapter for each category of American life.

S *See Skillbuilder Handbook, page 549.*

Taking Notes

Categories	Main Ideas
Government and Politics	
Business	
Agriculture	
Technology	
Society	

America and Georgia Go to War

MAIN IDEA

Americans became involved in World War I even though they did not think it was their fight.

WHY IT MATTERS NOW

American participation in World War I changed the way Americans viewed the world. World War I led to greater U.S. involvement in the world than ever before.

TERMS & NAMES

Allied Powers
Central Powers
Woodrow Wilson
Selective Service Act
Spanish influenza epidemic

SETTING THE STAGE

When war broke out in Europe in August 1914, Americans were more concerned with their own problems. They believed that the war in Europe was a European problem. But the United States was eventually drawn into the war.

American businesses exported many goods to Europe on merchant ships. And American citizens traveled on passenger vessels owned by European countries at war. Those ships entered dangerous waters off the coast of Europe. Merchant ships and passenger vessels were sunk. Americans were killed.

The war in Europe had a tremendous impact on the United States. On the battlefield and on the homefront, the war brought about many changes. It was a war that would shape the direction of the twentieth century.

▲ Life in the trenches alternated between boredom and intense activity. Perhaps one third of all casualties on the Western Front were killed or wounded in the trenches.

The War Begins

World War I began as a conflict between the countries of Austria-Hungary and Serbia. On June 28, 1914, a young Serbian man shot and killed Archduke Franz Ferdinand, who was the heir to the throne of Austria-Hungary. Austria-Hungary declared war on Serbia.

Three main systems of beliefs contributed to World War I: imperialism, nationalism, and militarism. Tensions were high because of them.

Imperialism   European countries were competing for colonies in Africa and Asia. The colonies provided important resources to the countries that claimed them. Germany had fewer colonies than Britain and France. German leaders thought they deserved more.

Nationalism   Citizens of European countries felt a strong sense of nationalism, or pride and loyalty for their own countries. The strong spirit of nationalism caused tensions, especially between ethnic groups.

Taking Notes

Use your chart to capture the main ideas regarding America's experience in the war.

Categories	Main Ideas
Government and Politics	
Business	

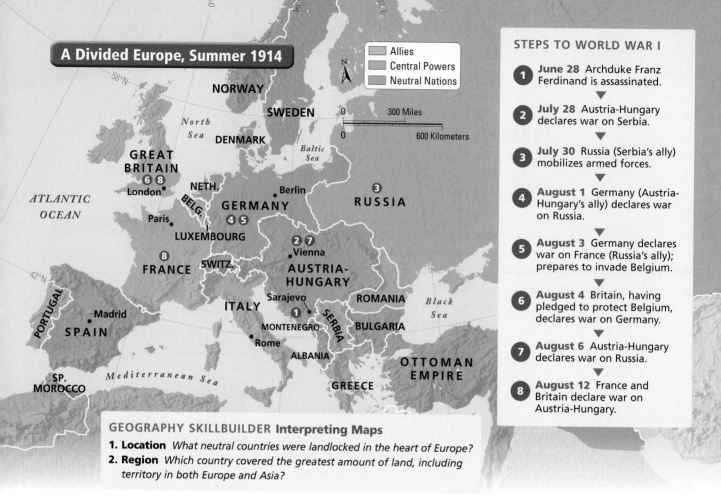

A Divided Europe, Summer 1914

Allies
Central Powers
Neutral Nations

NORWAY
SWEDEN
North Sea
DENMARK
Baltic Sea
GREAT BRITAIN ⑥⑧
London
NETH.
Berlin
GERMANY
RUSSIA ③
ATLANTIC OCEAN
BELG.
Paris
④⑤
LUXEMBOURG
SWITZ.
⑧
FRANCE
Vienna ②⑦
AUSTRIA-HUNGARY
ITALY
Sarajevo
①
ROMANIA
Black Sea
Madrid
MONTENEGRO
SERBIA
BULGARIA
PORTUGAL
SPAIN
Rome
ALBANIA
OTTOMAN EMPIRE
SP. MOROCCO
Mediterranean Sea
GREECE

0   300 Miles
0   600 Kilometers

STEPS TO WORLD WAR I

① **June 28** Archduke Franz Ferdinand is assassinated.

② **July 28** Austria-Hungary declares war on Serbia.

③ **July 30** Russia (Serbia's ally) mobilizes armed forces.

④ **August 1** Germany (Austria-Hungary's ally) declares war on Russia.

⑤ **August 3** Germany declares war on France (Russia's ally); prepares to invade Belgium.

⑥ **August 4** Britain, having pledged to protect Belgium, declares war on Germany.

⑦ **August 6** Austria-Hungary declares war on Russia.

⑧ **August 12** France and Britain declare war on Austria-Hungary.

GEOGRAPHY SKILLBUILDER Interpreting Maps
1. **Location** What neutral countries were landlocked in the heart of Europe?
2. **Region** Which country covered the greatest amount of land, including territory in both Europe and Asia?

Militarism   European countries believed they needed a large military force to protect their land and people. The major powers in Europe had built up their armies and navies.

The conflict between Austria-Hungary and Serbia eventually involved 32 countries. Many countries joined the conflict because they had agreements to come to each other's defense if they were attacked. The countries at war were divided into two groups—the Allied Powers and the Central Powers.

The **Allied Powers** consisted of 28 countries, including Great Britain, France, Russia, Italy, Belgium, Greece, Albania, Portugal, Japan, and eventually the United States. They opposed the **Central Powers,** including Germany, Austria-Hungary, the Ottoman Empire, and Bulgaria. Neutral countries in Europe, such as Spain and Switzerland, refused to take sides.

America's Position   When the conflict started, the United States was not interested in joining the fighting in Europe. President **Woodrow Wilson** promised Americans that he would keep them out of the fight. For a time, the country remained neutral.

Eventually, the United States was drawn into the conflict. In the fall of 1914, the British blockaded German ports and seized all goods bound for Germany. In response, German submarines sank Allied merchant ships off the British coast. In May 1915, a German submarine, called a U-boat, fired a torpedo on the British passenger ship *Lusitania* and killed 1,198 people. Of those passengers, 128 were Americans.

In 1917, German U-boats sank American-owned merchant ships. Americans were angered and demanded revenge. On April 2, 1917, Wilson asked the U.S. Congress to declare war against Germany and the Central Powers. What Americans had seen as a European war was now their war, and the world's.

Reading History

A. Making Inferences Why did the sinking of the *Lusitania* turn Americans against Germany?

Background

U-boat was short for "undersea boat."

> **PRIMARY SOURCE**
>
> [W]e shall fight for the things which we have always carried nearest our hearts—for democracy, for the right . . . [of all people] to have a voice in their own governments, for the rights and liberties of small nations, [to] bring peace and safety to all nations and make the world itself at last free.
>
> Woodrow Wilson, Message to Congress, April 2, 1917

▲ In the 1916 election, the Democratic Party's slogan in support of Wilson was, "He kept us out of war." Wilson was re-elected.

War in Europe

Congress passed the **Selective Service Act** requiring all men between the ages of 21 and 31 to register. The government then selected the ones to be drafted into the military from that pool of men.

Many Georgia politicians such as Tom Watson believed the federal government did not have the right to draft Georgia citizens or, for that matter, any U.S citizen. Even so, Congress passed the law establishing the draft.

The American Expeditionary Force, led by General John J. Pershing, arrived in Europe in June 1917. It joined the French and British along a defense line known as the Western Front. This line between the Allies and German armies stretched across Belgium and Eastern France all the way to the Swiss border.

More than 100,000 Georgians served in the military during World War I, and Georgia was a major location for military training facilities during the war. In early 1917, the federal government sent General Leonard L. Wood to Georgia to establish training facilities. There were already several federal government sites in Georgia: the Augusta Arsenal, Fort Screven on the Savannah River, Fort Oglethorpe south of Chattanooga, and Fort McPherson near Atlanta.

The turning point of the war came in the summer of 1918. With American help, the Allies pushed the Germans back from the Western Front. By early September, the Allies had taken back all of the territory that the Germans had taken. By November, the Germans realized that they could not win.

Georgia's Military Training Facilities, 1918

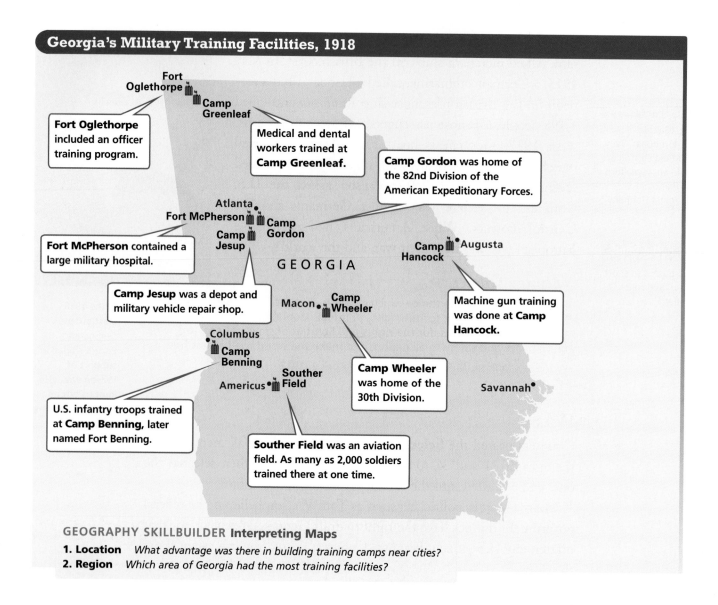

Fort Oglethorpe included an officer training program.

Fort Oglethorpe

Camp Greenleaf

Medical and dental workers trained at **Camp Greenleaf.**

Camp Gordon was home of the 82nd Division of the American Expeditionary Forces.

Atlanta
Fort McPherson
Camp Gordon
Camp Jesup

Fort McPherson contained a large military hospital.

GEORGIA

Camp Hancock · Augusta

Camp Jesup was a depot and military vehicle repair shop.

Macon · Camp Wheeler

Machine gun training was done at **Camp Hancock.**

Columbus
Camp Benning

Americus · Souther Field

Camp Wheeler was home of the 30th Division.

Savannah

U.S. infantry troops trained at Camp Benning, later named Fort Benning.

Souther Field was an aviation field. As many as 2,000 soldiers trained there at one time.

GEOGRAPHY SKILLBUILDER Interpreting Maps

1. **Location**   *What advantage was there in building training camps near cities?*
2. **Region**   *Which area of Georgia had the most training facilities?*

The End of the War   On November 11, 1918, the Allied and Central Powers signed an armistice (an agreement to end the fighting). More than 100,000 American soldiers had died in the war. The death toll of World War I reached 15 million people—civilians and soldiers. People across the U.S. celebrated as news reached their towns. The war was over, and Americans wanted to get back to a normal life.

Impact of World War I on the South

American troops needed supplies and materials for the war effort: wagons, carts, chemicals for explosives, coal, iron, steel, timber, and cotton. They needed personal items such as uniforms, food, and cigarettes. Georgians provided many of these items. The demand for Georgia's products improved the state's economy. When American textile mills started making uniforms and other war supplies, cotton prices went up. Landowners, and even sharecroppers, earned more money for their efforts. Many paid off their debts for the first time in many years.

Georgians Cope with War   Georgians at home dealt with problems caused by the war. Meat and gasoline were in short supply. Families waited nervously to hear from loved ones serving on the front lines. People worried about spies sneaking into the United States. They were afraid there might be attacks on training camps and places that made war supplies. Congress passed laws that made it illegal for people to talk against the president, the war, the draft, the flag, and even the Boy Scouts. Freedom of speech was restricted for the sake of national security.

People on the home front contributed to the war effort in different ways. Citizens bought Liberty Bonds to help pay for the war. Others gave patriotic speeches. Some people helped by providing entertainment and comfort to American soldiers.

Reading History

B. Finding Main Ideas   How did civilians contribute to the war effort?

Women Contribute to the War Effort   Women worked in the Red Cross canteens providing food and beverages to soldiers in training camps or at railroad stations where trains carried them off to war. Women came together in homes and churches to knit socks and sweaters and sew hospital gowns for soldiers overseas. Some joined organizations such as the Women's Council of National Defense and the National League for Women's Services. These groups organized collections of food and scrap metal for the war effort.

American women helped in Europe as well. Many became Red Cross volunteers and nurses' aides. Some volunteered to work in hospitals near the front lines or drive ambulances. One woman from Georgia wrote home about her experience in the midst of battle.

PRIMARY SOURCE

I will be glad . . . when peace does come. It is midnight now . . . and I can hear the big guns shooting and growling as our boys drive the Germans toward their home, but, oh the poor tired wounded ones that will be here in the morning.

quoted in *Georgia and the Great War* by Todd Womack

▼ An old postcard shows women of the Savannah chapter of the American Red Cross preparing to distribute food and drinks to soldiers heading to war.

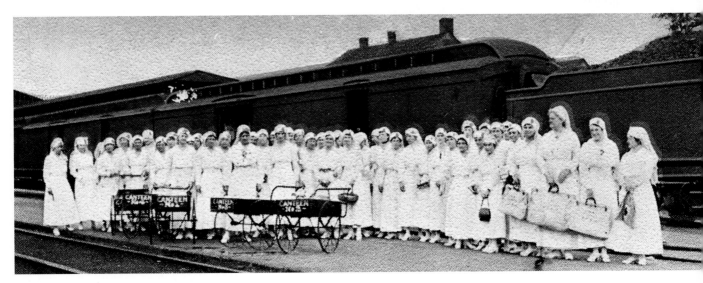

Killer Viruses

Severe acute respiratory syndrome, or SARS, bears an eerie resemblance to the Spanish flu epidemic of 1918–1919: In November 2002, a deadly new virus surfaced in China. In 2003, the SARS virus spread to more than 20 countries, infecting more than 8,000 people worldwide and killing more than 700.

In 1918, many flu victims came down with pneumonia and died within a week. Before the year was out, the flu epidemic had killed more American people than all the wars of this century combined.

Spanish Influenza Epidemic

In 1918, Georgians had to fight another battle at home—the **Spanish influenza epidemic**. Soldiers fighting in World War I spread the flu around the world. The epidemic came to the United States in the fall of 1918 and to Georgia in October of that year.

The flu was first reported at Camp Hancock near Augusta. Over 2,000 cases of the Spanish flu were reported in Georgia in a short time. As a precaution, public places such as schools and churches were closed until the epidemic ended. In Athens, the University of Georgia closed.

The epidemic in Georgia ended just weeks after it had begun. When it was over, more than 675,000 Americans had died of complications caused by the Spanish flu. Worldwide, it is estimated that over 25 million people died.

Americans who had fought in Europe brought more home with them than the Spanish influenza, however. They brought home new ideas and ways of thinking about the world around them. In the next section, you will learn more about how Georgia changed as a result of these new influences.

> **Vocabulary**
>
> **epidemic:** an outbreak of a contagious disease that spreads rapidly and widely

---

Section 1 Assessment

1. TERMS & NAMES

Explain the significance of:

a. Allied Powers

b. Central Powers

c. Woodrow Wilson

d. Selective Service Act

e. Spanish influenza epidemic

2. TAKING NOTES

Use a diagram like the one below to show how American groups or individuals helped fight the war.

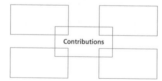

3. MAIN IDEAS

a. What were the conditions in Europe that eventually led to World War I?

b. What was Woodrow Wilson's position on the war in Europe when it started in 1914?

c. How did women support the war effort?

4. CRITICAL THINKING

Analyzing Causes

How did imperialism, nationalism, and militarism work to reinforce each other?

Think About
- the goals of each
- how nationalism might have encouraged military buildup
- how nationalism contributed to the race for colonies

 Art/Language Arts Design a **poster** to encourage Americans at home to support the war effort or write a **letter** in the voice of a soldier in the war.

The Roaring Twenties and a New Generation

MAIN IDEA	WHY IT MATTERS NOW	TERMS & NAMES

MAIN IDEA

The 1920s were a time of dramatic change in how people lived.

WHY IT MATTERS NOW

Changes in attitudes, beliefs, and economic practices that began in the 1920s are still influencing Americans today.

TERMS & NAMES

Prohibition
Nineteenth Amendment
Great Migration
Henry Ford
Dixie Highway

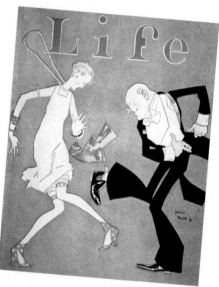

▲ For many, the Twenties were a time to kick up their heels.

SETTING THE STAGE

After the war ended, people in the United States turned their attention to life back home. In the 1920s, the nation's economy grew dramatically. More people were able to buy more things. Life appeared to be getting better. The youth of America experimented with fun, freedom, and fashion. Automobiles made it easier for people to go longer distances in a shorter amount of time.

There were still major problems in America. Racism was still strong. Many Americans feared any people who were not "like them." The threats of Communism, immorality, and a growing presence of immigrants concerned Americans who believed that their society was perfect. Anything different or representing radical change was suspect.

Americans wanted to protect their world—to keep it the way it was. But there were major flaws in the nation's economy. Those flaws would bring the economy and the nation crashing down in just a few years.

Social Changes

The 1920s are probably best noted for changes in attitudes and fashions. When someone says "The Roaring Twenties," the first image that comes to mind is that of a "flapper." A "flapper" was a young woman with short hair, a short skirt, and a carefree attitude. She represented the "new woman," willing to try things women had not been allowed to do before.

Not all women became flappers. But many were intrigued by the apparent personal freedom of the flapper. They started cutting their hair shorter and wearing makeup and shorter skirts.

These personal freedoms gave way to more liberal ideas about women working outside the home. They worked in business offices, retail stores, and factories. Those with a college education became teachers, nurses, librarians, social workers, and bankers. Attitudes toward

Taking Notes

Use your chart to capture the main ideas regarding the Roaring Twenties.

Categories	Main Ideas
Government and Politics	
Business	

marriage began to change. Laborsaving appliances such as electric refrigerators and vacuum cleaners, and convenience foods made life easier.

The Eighteenth Amendment Some people had been working for years to make alcohol illegal in the United States. In 1920, the Eighteenth Amendment—Prohibition of Intoxicating Liquors—became part of the Constitution. Under **Prohibition,** people were not allowed to make, sell, or transport any alcoholic beverages. This remained the law until 1933.

Vocabulary

prohibition: a law that forbids or prevents the use or manufacture of something

The Nineteenth Amendment The **Nineteenth Amendment** giving women the right to vote was passed in 1920. Some women even ran for political office. Voters elected Bessie Kempton and Viola Ross Napier to the Georgia legislature in 1922.

Changes for African Americans

Many African Americans had held good-paying jobs in the wartime industries. These jobs raised their expectations for a better life. In the years immediately after World War I, 1.5 million African Americans

moved to cities in the North. This was called the **Great Migration**. Over 100,000 African-American Georgians left the state between 1900 and 1920. They gained some economic power in the North, but they still faced discrimination in jobs and housing. Tensions between blacks and whites in Northern cities led to race riots.

▲ *The Migration of the Negro,* Panel No. 1 (1940–1941), by Jacob Lawrence, shows three of the most common destinations for African Americans leaving the South.

The National Association for the Advancement of Colored People (NAACP) worked to protect the rights of African Americans. It also worked to make people aware of crimes against African Americans but was not able to persuade Congress to pass laws that would end discrimination.

Marcus Garvey led a Back-to-Africa movement in the 1920s. He had some of the same ideas for establishing a separate nation that the American Colonization Society had proposed back in 1817. He said, "If Europe is for the Europeans, then Africa shall be for the black peoples of the world." Few African Americans migrated to Africa, but Garvey set an example for future black political movements.

Reading History

A. Analyzing Points of View What action did Marcus Garvey believe would improve the life of African Americans?

Resistance to Change

Naturally, not all people agreed with the personal freedoms of the Roaring Twenties. The period could best be described as a time of cultural clashes. On one side were those who believed individuals should be able to express themselves. On the other side were those who still held traditional economic and moral values.

The Leo Frank Case in Atlanta   In 1913, Mary Phagan, a 13-year-old worker at the National Pencil Factory in Atlanta, was found dead in the factory. The factory's manager, Leo Frank, a Jewish man from New York, was accused of the crime. He was found guilty and sentenced to death.

Two years later, the governor changed his sentence to life in prison. At that, a group of men from Mary's hometown, Marietta, drove to the state prison and kidnapped Frank. They took him back to Marietta and lynched him while a mob of people watched.

In 1982, Alonzo Mann, who had worked at the factory with Mary, stepped forward. He said that he had seen a sweeper at the factory, Jim Conley, with Mary's body. Conley had threatened to hurt or kill him if he told. In failing health, Mann felt he finally had to tell the truth. The Georgia Board of Pardons issued a pardon to Leo Frank in 1986, seventy years after his brutal death.

Revival of the KKK   The Leo Frank case was one event that led to a revival of the Ku Klux Klan (KKK). Public opinion in that event seemed to support the hatred and racism KKK members felt toward minorities. In addition, the 1915 motion picture *Birth of a Nation* showed the KKK in a positive light. African Americans, scalawags, and carpetbaggers were portrayed as evil forces that had ruined the South.

▼ More than 40,000 KKK members march in Washington, D.C., in 1925 to show their growing numbers.

Why did the Klan become so popular? Many people were afraid of the changes occurring around them—new people, new environments, rapid growth, changing morals, and new social habits. Instead of accepting the new things in American society, many people lashed out, hoping they could prevent their world from changing.

The Klan claimed that they could help return things to the way they used to be. During Reconstruction, the KKK had attacked African Americans. After a KKK rebirth in the 1910s and revival in the 1920s, the KKK focused their hatred on anyone who was not like them—primarily African Americans, Jews, and Catholics. The KKK was not limited to the Southern states. Membership increased across the nation, especially in Indiana, Alabama, Georgia, and Louisiana.

The Automobile Changes Georgia

In 1900, there were only a few automobiles in the United States. Early automobiles were expensive and fragile. Historians credit **Henry Ford** with changing the automobile from a toy of the wealthy to a necessity for everyone. In 1903, he founded the Ford Motor Company. By 1913, Ford was using interchangeable parts and an assembly line to build cars. With Ford's method, a cheaper, more durable car could be assembled in 93 minutes instead of several hours.

Reading History

B. Recognizing Effects What effect did the assembly line have on the price of cars?

Other manufacturers in the United States and the world copied Ford's process. The number of cars produced rose from 570,000 in 1914 to 1,600,000 in 1919. By the end of the 1920s, more than 27 million automobiles were on America's roads. A new culture changed the nation—the car culture. The automobile became more important to Southerners, both rich and poor, than almost any other possession.

In the South, most people who owned automobiles lived in towns and cities. In Fulton County (where Atlanta is located), about 6,000 cars were registered in 1916. By the mid-1920s, Atlantans owned more than 45,000 cars. A growing number of highways connected Atlanta to the other major cities in Georgia.

Building Automobiles in Georgia   From 1900 to 1920, many small companies started manufacturing automobiles. All but a handful

Georgia's Autos and Where They Were Made

Many small automobile manufacturing companies started up during this time. The cars shown in the table were built in Georgia. Shown in the picture are the White Star Automobile Company workers with two of the Georgia company's first models.

MODEL	BUILT IN	MODEL	BUILT IN
Athens	Athens	Howard	Macon
New South	Augusta	Nor-X	Norcross
Dublin	Dublin	Batchelor	Savannah
Ridley	LaGrange	Hicks	Waycross

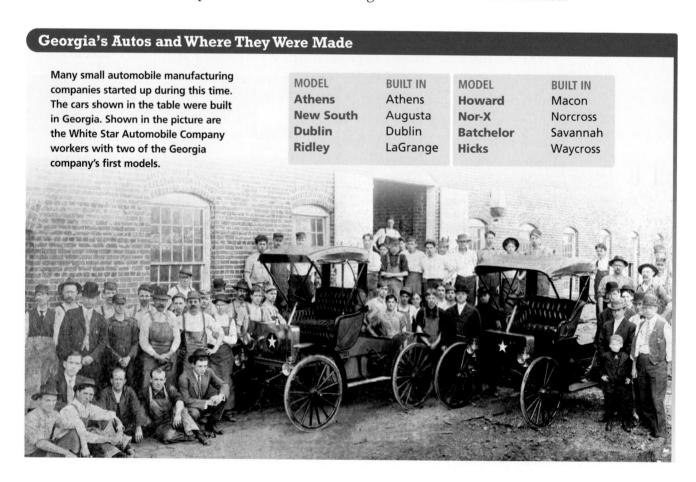

of them quickly failed. The Hanson Motor Company was the most successful Georgia manufacturer. It opened in Atlanta in 1917 and was in business until 1925. It built about 1,800 automobiles.

Good Roads Movement With more automobiles there was a need for more improved roads. The "Good Roads Movement" promoted the need for better roads throughout the South.

The Federal Aid Road Act of 1916 helped Georgia and other states. Under the act, federal and state governments worked together to fund and build good roads.

One major highway ran through Georgia—the **Dixie Highway**. Completed in 1927, it stretched 5,700 miles from the Great Lakes to the Florida Keys. It passed through Atlanta, Marietta, Smyrna, and Jonesboro. It brought tourists through Georgia and gave Georgians better access to Northern states.

Modernization and Change

Across the United States, the economy was strong. Construction was booming. Factories switched from producing war materials to producing consumer products. Between 1919 and 1929, industrial production nearly doubled in the United States.

National retail chains, such as A&P and Woolworth's, spread across the country. One could go to an A&P grocery store in Atlanta or Los Angeles and find the same brand-name products.

Regional chains also developed. Piggly Wiggly grocery stores opened in Memphis, Tennessee, in 1916 and changed the way people shopped. Until that time, a clerk would get items for shoppers. At Piggly Wiggly, people steered their carts through the aisles and picked out their items. This was one of the first self-service grocery stores in America.

▲ The Savannah Races were run from 1908 to 1911. Thousands lined the course to watch the race.

World War I and the 1920s

▲ Shoppers pose for a picture at this opening of a new Piggly Wiggly in 1920.

Factory jobs provided steady work, and wages reached an all-time high. Most Americans bought more goods and enjoyed a higher standard of living than they ever had before.

Credit Many people thought the good times of the 1920s would never end. Thus, another business practice found its way onto the American scene. Credit—or the installment plan—allowed consumers to buy items with a small down payment now and the balance due in regular payments in the future. This helped people buy the things they wanted even when they did not have the cash to pay for them.

In the next section, you will learn more about how Georgia's economy changed during the 1920s.

Reading History

C. Summarizing
How did advances in technology change the lives of Americans?

Section 2 Assessment

1. TERMS & NAMES

Explain the significance of:

a. Prohibition

b. Nineteenth Amendment

c. Great Migration

d. Henry Ford

e. Dixie Highway

2. TAKING NOTES

Use a cluster diagram to review the social changes of the Roaring Twenties. Which has had lasting influence?

Social Changes

3. MAIN IDEAS

a. Summarize why groups such as the KKK and those who lynched Leo Frank were able to survive in the 1920s.

b. In what way did automobiles change the American landscape?

c. How did buying on credit change American lifestyles?

4. CRITICAL THINKING

Drawing Conclusions

How did the growth and changes in the 1920s affect race relations?

Think About
• economic opportunities
• new social settings
• conflicts between groups

ACTIVITY -OPTIONS-

Art/Music Draw a **poster** with an image that represents the Roaring Twenties or write a **song** that captures the spirit of the times.

Georgia's Economy in the 1920s

SETTING THE STAGE

The 1920s was a decade of prosperity. People were buying more things, and that strengthened the economy. Factory jobs meant steady work and higher wages. People had more money to spend on expensive items such as automobiles, houses, and new appliances. Companies grew in size and wealth.

The nation was changing dramatically. How was Georgia changing? Its cities had grown as the demands of the war industry had grown. Its farms had prospered as well. But the economy changed again with the end of the war. How did those changes affect the way Georgians lived?

▲ The kaolin industry still plays a major role in Georgia's economy.

Georgia's Economy Grows

Industry continued expanding in the 1920s. More textile mills opened in Georgia. The Coca-Cola Company expanded its market to include most of the South.

Industries that relied on the natural resources of the state flourished. Deposits of the mineral bauxite found in Georgia were used to make aluminum. Timber was still in demand. Cotton and cottonseed were still needed to make clothing and oil. The **kaolin** (KAY-uh-lihn) industry grew dramatically in the early 1920s. Kaolin is a white clay that is used in making plastics, toothpaste, medicine, porcelain, paint, and coating for paper. Kaolin is found along the fall line from Macon to Wrens in about 13 counties.

Georgia's Cities

The 1920 U.S. Census revealed that, for the first time, more people lived in towns and cities than in the countryside. The growing population in cities led to changes in lifestyle and culture.

Promoting Georgia's Cities Towns and cities of all sizes campaigned to attract people and businesses. Atlanta, Macon, Augusta, and

Taking Notes

Use your chart to capture the main ideas about Georgia's economy in the 1920s.

Categories	Main Ideas
Government and Politics	
Business	

▲ The economy and population of Atlanta grew steadily through the "Atlanta Forward" campaign.

Savannah all had special programs to promote their towns. Dalton advertised its low taxes on factories. Gainesville offered businesses free land and tax exemptions. The competition was intense. Every town wanted to attract the most people.

One of the most successful campaigns was in Atlanta. The Atlanta Chamber of Commerce, along with businessmen like Ivan Allen, Sr., started a national advertising campaign called "**Atlanta Forward**." From 1925 to 1930, over 700 new businesses moved to Atlanta. Along with the new businesses came thousands of new jobs and millions of dollars in wages.

The Arrival of the Airplane   One sign of a modern city was the opening of an airport. Inventors had been perfecting airplanes when World War I began. The need for faster and better airplanes pushed the development of the airplane forward.

In the 1920s, Alderman **William B. Hartsfield** convinced Atlanta's mayor to invest in the future of airplanes. Hartsfield believed they would become the newest form of transportation for people, mail, and goods. Hartsfield insisted that if Atlanta was to be an important city, it had to have an airport. In 1925, Atlanta acquired the 287-acre Atlanta Speedway site for a new airfield—Candler Field.

In 1928, Atlanta became a stop on the route for federal airmail to New York. Pitcairn Aviation ran mail between Atlanta and New York. Delta Air Lines moved to Atlanta in 1941 and is still one of the area's largest employers.

Georgia's Agriculture in the 1920s

In 1920, the United States economy went through a short, but severe, downturn called a recession. Cotton prices dropped from 35 cents during the war to below 10 cents a pound. Farmers could not make a profit at that price. And then another problem plagued Georgia's cotton farmers.

Boll Weevils   In addition to the economic recession after the war, Georgia farmers faced the invasion of the **boll weevil** beetle. Boll weevils had been sighted in Georgia in 1913 but did not become a real problem until 1918.

Reading History

A. Analyzing Points of View Why did Hartsfield believe that Atlanta could not be an important city without an airport?

Reading History

B. Making Inferences What could have contributed to the recession in 1920?

The boll weevil lays its eggs in the cotton pod or boll. The newly hatched larvae eat the cotton boll. From 1918 to 1923, the cotton crop in Georgia dropped by almost 75 percent because of these beetles.

Many farmers, tenants, and sharecroppers gave up on farming. Some moved to nearby towns to work in textile mills or other jobs that paid cash wages. Others left for the industrial cities of the North. One former farm wife described her family's move.

PRIMARY SOURCE

We was farmers and the boll weevils got there and you couldn't make anything. So my husband come up here and went to work at the Atlanta Paper Company. And he sent back for me and I come up here.

Lula Daugherty, quoted in *Living Atlanta: An Oral History of the City, 1914–1948*, edited by Clifford M. Kuhn

▲ The invasion of the boll weevil, a recession in 1920, and a drought in 1925 drove many cotton growers to give up farming altogether.

By 1930, almost 60 percent of Georgia's farmers were sharecroppers or tenants. Most could not afford the modern conveniences of the consumer revolution of the 1920s. Most Georgia farmers did not own a tractor. Many did not have electricity, running water, or indoor plumbing. Georgia's farmers had been left out of the excess and prosperity of the Roaring Twenties. Things would only get worse in the 1930s, as you will learn in the next chapter.

Section 3 Assessment

1. TERMS & NAMES

Explain the significance of:

a. kaolin

b. "Atlanta Forward" campaign

c. William B. Hartsfield

d. boll weevil

2. TAKING NOTES

Use a table like the one below to note how Georgia's cities grew in this period.

Georgia's Cities Grow in the 1920s
1.
2.
3.

3. MAIN IDEAS

a. With all the new industry in Georgia in the 1920s, why was the state's economy still weak?

b. How did Georgia's towns attract new businesses and new people?

c. How did Atlanta get its first airport, Candler Field?

4. CRITICAL THINKING

Analyzing Causes

Which developments in Georgia added to the state's prosperity?

Think About

• the state's natural resources
• big business
• new industry

Language Arts/Art Write a **newspaper advertisement** to attract new businesses to your area or design a **poster** that can be distributed around the state.

VISUAL SUMMARY

The Roaring Twenties

POLITICS
- WWI ends in 1918, launching America into a period of economic growth and prosperity.
- The Nineteenth Amendment gives women the right to vote.

ECONOMICS
- Business prospers in the 1920s.
- Some groups, including Georgia farmers, face hardships.

TECHNOLOGY
- Technological developments, such as the assembly line, power new prosperity.
- The growing importance of flight and airports enables Atlanta to become a major economic center.

SOCIETY AND CULTURE
- Changes in society bring new attitudes and lifestyles, especially for young people and women.
- Social changes meet with resistance. It is a time of cultural clashes.

TERMS & NAMES

Briefly explain the significance of the following.

1. Allied and Central Powers
2. Woodrow Wilson
3. Spanish influenza epidemic
4. Henry Ford
5. Dixie Highway
6. Nineteenth Amendment
7. kaolin
8. Atlanta Forward
9. William B. Hartsfield
10. boll weevil

REVIEW QUESTIONS

America and Georgia Go to War (pages 351–356)

1. What event started World War I?
2. What were the three main causes of World War I?
3. What event brought America into the war?
4. What impact did the war have on Georgia?

The Roaring Twenties and a New Generation (pages 357–362)

5. How did the changes of the 1920s affect minorities?
6. What was the effect of the new car culture in the South?
7. What changes resulted from the strong 1920s economy?

Georgia's Economy in the 1920s (pages 363–365)

8. What industries grew in Georgia in the 1920s?
9. What factors contributed to Atlanta's growth in the 1920s?
10. By 1930, most of Georgia's farmers were sharecroppers or tenants. Why?

CRITICAL THINKING

1. USING YOUR NOTES: SEQUENCING EVENTS

Categories	Main Ideas
Government and Politics	
Business	
Agriculture	
Technology	
Society	

Using your completed chart, answer the questions below.

a. What group of people didn't prosper in the 1920s?
b. What factors contributed to the growth of the economy?

2. ANALYZING LEADERSHIP

Good leaders have a vision for the future. What leader from this chapter influenced life in the 1920s with his vision?

3. APPLYING CITIZENSHIP SKILLS

Are limitations on freedom of speech justified by war? Explain your opinion.

4. THEME: SCIENCE AND TECHNOLOGY

What advances in technology contributed to the prosperity of the 1920s?

5. MAKING GENERALIZATIONS

How did the social and economic changes of the 1920s affect Americans?

INTERACT with HISTORY

In your opinion, which changes in American life discussed in this chapter would have affected you the most?

Use the chart and your knowledge of American history to answer questions 1 through 3.

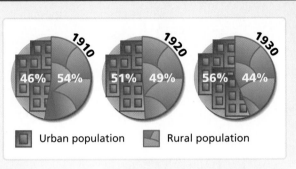

Urbanization of America, 1910–1930

1910: 46% / 54%
1920: 51% / 49%
1930: 56% / 44%

☐ Urban population   ◩ Rural population

1. What was the total percentage increase in the urban population from 1910 to 1930?

   A. 5%   **C.** 46%
   B. 10%   **D.** 56%

2. During which 10-year period did the United States become more urban than rural?

   A. 1910s   **C.** 1930s
   B. 1920s   **D.** 1940s

3. What percentage of the population was rural in 1930?

   A. 54%   **C.** 56%
   B. 49%   **D.** 44%

TEST PRACTICE
CLASSZONE.COM

ALTERNATIVE ASSESSMENT

1. ANALYZING MUSIC OF THE WAR YEARS

During World War I, songs such as "Johnny, I Hardly Knew Ye" protested the war, while "Over There" and "Pack Up Your Troubles" cheered the troops. Analyze the lyrics of a wartime song, examining its attitude toward the war.

2. COOPERATIVE LEARNING

National advertising became an important way to promote new products to the public during the 1920s. Working in a small group, write a radio ad or draw a magazine ad for a product that made life easier during the 1920s, such as a car, refrigerator, toaster, vacuum cleaner, sewing machine, fan, or washer. Make sure your advertisement covers the following topics.

a. Do research on the product. Describe the product in the 1920s.

b. How will the product improve life for Americans?

c. How much does the product cost?

INTEGRATED TECHNOLOGY ACTIVITY

PLANNING A WEB PAGE ON THE ROARING TWENTIES

The 1920s were years of great creativity. American popular culture was being spread throughout the nation and abroad by radio and movies. Use the library or search the Internet for information about the music, fashions, fads, and celebrities of the period. Create a Roaring Twenties Web page by following the suggestions below.

- Select appropriate images of personalities, fashions, and fads.

- Include biographical information and quotations.

- Choose music that captures the spirit of the era.

- Decide which Web sites would be good links for visitors to your page.

RESEARCH LINKS
CLASSZONE.COM

The Great Depression and the New Deal 1928–1940

Section 1
The Great Depression

Section 2
The New Deal in the South

Section 3
Life During the Depression

During the 1920s and 1930s, it was hard for farmers, such as this Monroe County family, to make enough money to survive.

1931
Reorganization Act of 1931 drastically reduces number of state agencies.

1932
Herndon is convicted of insurrection. Eugene Talmadge is elected governor.

GEORGIA USA   1928

1928
Herbert Hoover is elected president.

1929
U.S. stock market crashes. Great Depression begins.

1932
Franklin D. Roosevelt is elected president.

1933
Tennessee Valley Authority is created.

It's 1932. The economy is bad, and millions of people are out of work. Some are starving. Two men are running for president. One says the government should give money to the poor. The other says this will make people stop looking for jobs. He wants charity groups to help people in need.

Who do you think should help the poor?

WHAT DO YOU THINK?

- Is the government responsible for everyone's well-being?

- What responsibility do individuals have to help others?

- What is the best way to help people out of poverty?

For more information on this chapter, visit . . .

RESEARCH LINKS
CLASSZONE.COM

1934
The Masters golf tournament begins.

1936
Eurith D. Rivers is elected governor. "Little New Deal" programs in Georgia

1939
Gone With the Wind premieres in Atlanta.

1934

1940

1935
Congress passes
Social Security Act.

1939
John Steinbeck publishes *The Grapes of Wrath* about migrant workers.

Reading Strategy: Evaluating

What Do You Know?

What do people do to get by when they are unable to find work? Where can they turn for help?

THINK ABOUT
- stories you've heard or read about the Great Depression
- photographs or documentaries you've seen about the Great Depression
- movies and books about people with economic struggles

What Do You Want to Know?

What questions do you have about how the Great Depression affected Americans? What facts and details would you like to learn about government actions during that period? Record those questions in your notebook before you read the chapter.

Evaluating

To evaluate is to make a judgment about something. As you read this chapter, look for details about how President Hoover and President Roosevelt responded to the Great Depression. Record those details in a chart like the one below. Then evaluate how effective those responses were at making the situation better.

 See Skillbuilder Handbook, page 553.

 **Taking Notes**

GREAT DEPRESSION

President Hoover's Responses	President Roosevelt's Responses
Effectiveness	**Effectiveness**

The Great Depression

The American economy in the late 1920s had weaknesses.

Government involvement in the economy today is a direct result of the response to the economic problems of the 1920s and 1930s.

Black Tuesday
Great Depression
Franklin D. Roosevelt
Brain Trust

SETTING THE STAGE

In 1928, Herbert Hoover, the Republican candidate, was elected president. The nation was happy with the two previous Republican presidential administrations and they expected to be happy with Hoover. They were also happy with the way the U.S. economy was strong and growing.

A few months after Hoover was sworn in, however, it became clear that the economy was not as sound as people had thought. What had happened? What would President Hoover do in response? How did the ever-worsening economy affect Georgians? And to whom would Americans turn for help?

▲ Many people believed Hoover when he predicted continuing prosperity. He was elected president in 1928 by a landslide.

The Crash of 1929 and the Great Depression

Herbert Hoover's election in 1928 reflected Americans' belief that all was well. Hoover believed that government should not interfere with how business worked. He wanted business owners to decide what was fair in their businesses, rather than have the government dictate to them. Hoover had been Secretary of Commerce under President Calvin Coolidge, who had also believed that business should be left alone.

In the 1920s, more people invested in the stock market than ever before. Some used their life savings to buy shares of stock in companies that appeared to be growing and becoming more valuable every year. It seemed to be a sure thing. In September of 1929, the stock market began losing ground. People assumed that it was a temporary trend and the stock market would bounce back in a few weeks.

On October 29, 1929, later called **Black Tuesday,** the New York Stock Exchange had one of the worst days of its history. In one day, over 16 million shares of stock were traded as prices fell and people sold their stock in fear that prices would drop even further. Most stocks sold for

Taking Notes

Use your chart to record details and evaluate the presidents' responses to the Depression.

Weather: ...

The Atlanta Journal. **FINAL HOME EDITION**

VOL. XLVII. NO. 244 — ... — ATLANTA, GA., TUESDAY EVENING, OCTOBER 29, 1929 — ... — PRICE FIVE CENTS

STOCKS TURN UPWARD LATE AFTER ALL-DAY ROUT

Dr. John Roach Straton, Noted Fundamentalist, Dies

FLIERS SEEKING AIRLINER LOST WITH 5 ABOARD

Mountainous Region on New Mexico-Arizona Border Is Combed

STRUCK BAD STORM

Disaster Similar to That Suffered by T. A. T. Ship Feared

Four Are Rescued From Blazing Home

NEW IMPETUS IS GIVEN DRIVE FOR THE CHEST

CLEAN-UP IS PUSHED

Second Appeal Broadcast Over WSB Brings in $800 More

Hector Roll of Business Concerns Lists Generous Contributors

Football Star to Marry Daughter of Chrysler and Heiress to His Fortune

HEART ATTACK PROVES FATAL TO DR. STRATON

Fundamental Leader Dies at New York Sanitarium

ILL MANY MONTHS

Baptist Pastor Gained National Prominence as Foe of Evolution

CLIFTON SPRINGS, N. Y., Oct. 29

Dr. Straton Dies

STRONG RALLY HALTS ROUT OF STOCK PRICES

Leaders Turn Upward in Afternoon—Board Refuses to Close Exchange

DELIVERY EXTENDED

Big Bankers Reduce Their Margin Requirements to Relieve Credit

Al Smith Wondering

▲ The *Atlanta Journal Constitution* reported the ominous news from New York.

less money than they had originally been purchased. Some investors lost millions. Many companies and banks went broke. Stockholders no longer thought the declining market was temporary.

Black Tuesday signaled the end of the Roaring Twenties. It was also the beginning of the **Great Depression,** a long period of economic problems for the nation that lasted throughout the 1930s.

Causes of the Depression

The stock market crash was not the cause of the Great Depression. The crash and the Depression were the result of a number of related problems of the American economy in the late 1920s.

- A few people held most of the wealth, so fewer people had money to buy things.
- Manufacturers and businesses produced too many items. American consumers were not buying enough to keep up with production.
- Prices for some items were too high. People did not want to pay those prices.
- Farmers were producing more than consumers were buying. Prices for agricultural goods fell, making it even harder for farmers to make a living.
- The coal industry, textile industry, and railroads were in financial trouble because of competition and falling demand.
- There was too much debt. Too many companies and people owed more than they could pay back.
- Many banks were in trouble because of poor management and the lack of an agency to watch their practices.
- The federal government did not have any ways to monitor the activity of businesses, the stock market, and banks. The government also failed to provide a steady and even flow of money into the economy.

Background

This pattern of selling stocks and withdrawing deposits out of fear is the reason that depressions of the 1800s are also called panics.

Reading History

A. Making Inferences Why were industry and agriculture producing more than Americans could buy in this era?

Impact of the Crash on Georgians

After decades of rebuilding after the Civil War, Georgia was still struggling to make economic progress around the turn of the century. With an economy based largely on one crop and smaller industries, Georgia was vulnerable to economic disruption from the stock market crash and the Depression.

Agriculture   By the 1930s, Georgia farmers were in serious financial trouble. Invasion by the boll weevil had devastated the cotton crop in the early 1920s. From 1920 to 1925, farmers abandoned over 3 million acres of land in Georgia that had been devoted to growing cotton. Then the price of cotton began to fall as textile mills closed for lack of sales.

As a result, landowners could not make payments on their land or farm equipment, and many lost their farms. Landowners kicked sharecroppers and tenants off the land because they could not sell the crops. Many families became homeless and had nowhere to go.

Industry and Business   Some industries had developed in Georgia and other Southern states in the 1920s. In Georgia, textile mills, cottonseed oil mills, and the kaolin industry had all grown. But all the economic

ECONOMICS *in* HISTORY

Recession and Depression

Many people hoped the economy would fix itself because they believed depressions were a natural part of the business cycle (shown below). Economies go through ups and downs. The period when an economy is at its worst is a trough. There are two kinds of troughs—recessions and depressions. A depression is more severe.

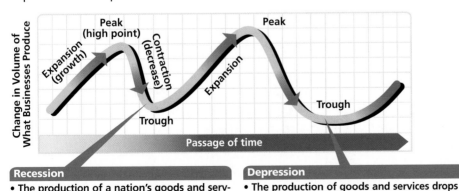

Recession
- The production of a nation's goods and services goes down each month for six months.
- Business owners produce less and invest less in new equipment and facilities. They also lay off workers.
- Consumers buy fewer goods.

Depression
- The production of goods and services drops lower than in a recession.
- The period of no economic growth is longer than in a recession. Unemployment is higher.
- The slowdown may spread to other countries; international trade declines dramatically.

CONNECT TO HISTORY
1. **Evaluating** Why were the hard times of the 1930s a depression, not a recession?

 See Skillbuilder Handbook, page 553.

CONNECT TO TODAY
2. **Making Inferences** How would today's world be affected differently by a depression in the United States than by one in Holland? Explain.

For more about economics . . .

RESEARCH LINKS
CLASSZONE.COM

gains of the 1920s were lost in the Depression. Many Georgians lost their jobs.

Small business owners were hit especially hard. Mrs. Inex Dennis owned a coal supply company in Augusta. The Depression took her completely by surprise.

PRIMARY SOURCE

I lost a lot of money on coal that had already been delivered on credit. . . . I didn't realize that the trouble was here to stay and kept on selling on credit. . . . I mortgaged my home to keep my boys in school and to buy coal and wood. . . . I couldn't refuse [to extend credit] when folks would tell me they had sickness or that their little children were cold.

Mrs. Inex Dennis of Augusta, Georgia, quoted in *American Life Histories: Manuscripts from the Federal Writers' Project, 1936–1940*

Vocabulary

credit: an agreement to pay over time, instead of all at once

Unemployment At the height of the Depression, 25 percent of working-age Americans were unemployed. In urban areas, the unemployment rate was as high as 70 percent. In Atlanta, unemployment reached 75 percent in some African-American neighborhoods. In 1932, if a person still had a job, she or he faced as much as a 50-percent drop in pay. People relied on the kindness of churches and community organizations for food.

Many people lived in makeshift homes made out of cardboard, discarded wood, and anything that could help keep the weather off them. People built these homes along railroad lines, on the edge of town, and even in city parks. The communities of shacks were called "Hoovervilles"

▼ This 1938 photograph shows shacks on Fraser Street in Atlanta, near the state capitol building.

374

because people blamed President Hoover for the unemployment and homelessness of so many Americans.

Banks   Thousands of banks in Georgia and across the nation simply closed their doors. People who had money in a bank were scared that they would lose everything. They rushed to the banks and demanded their money. The banks did not have enough money to give everyone, and they closed. Many banks had invested in the stock market. Using money deposited by their customers, they bought stock in companies that went broke at the start of the Depression.

Hoover Reacts Conservatively

Reading History

B. Finding Main Ideas What were Hoover's solutions to the problems caused by the Depression, and did they succeed?

As the Depression deepened in 1930 and 1931, people wondered what the federal government was going to do. President Hoover fought the Depression by trying to balance the federal budget. He cut back on government spending and raised taxes. But these actions pulled money out of the economy and, in the opinion of most economists, made the slump worse. Hoover believed that volunteer efforts could assist people in need. Churches and charities such as the Salvation Army and the Red Cross helped some needy Americans, but they weren't able to help everyone who needed it.

By 1932, Hoover realized that the federal government had to take more direct steps to improve the economy. He set up an agency to lend money to states, cities, and towns. The money would be used for public works projects, such as building roads and dams. The new projects would also create jobs for the unemployed.

▼ This soup kitchen in Chicago served up to 3,500 unemployed men daily, at a cost of $300 a day.

Time for Revolution?   The Communist Party in the United States was a small political party. It thought that the severe economic problems, high unemployment, homelessness, and hunger across the nation created the opportunity for revolt.

In 1932, Angelo Herndon, a young African-American Communist organizer, arrived in Atlanta. Herndon gathered almost 1,000 people to march to City Hall and demand help. It was effective. The city increased its funding for emergency relief. But Herndon was arrested and charged with insurrection—trying to overthrow the government. Herndon was convicted and sentenced to 20 years on a Georgia chain gang. The U.S. Supreme Court eventually overturned the sentence, but Herndon spent 5 years in prison before he was released.

The Great Depression and the New Deal   **375**

Mar. 4. 1933 THE NEW YORKER Price 15 cents

The 1932 Presidential Election: "Try Something"

Hoover had not responded quickly enough to the growing crisis. He expected the economy to fix itself without interference from the federal government. By July 1932, the economy was at its lowest point since the Crash of 1929. People in the United States were looking for an immediate solution.

In the 1932 presidential election, the Republican Hoover ran against the Democrat **Franklin D. Roosevelt.** Roosevelt promised the voters that he would "do something" about the economy. It was not clear exactly what he would do, but he would try.

▲ This cartoon shows a beaming Franklin Roosevelt riding to his inauguration with a dejected Herbert Hoover.

PRIMARY SOURCE

The country needs and, unless I mistake its temper, the country demands bold, persistent experimentation. It is common sense to take a method and try it: If it fails, admit it frankly and try another. But above all, try something.

Franklin D. Roosevelt, in a speech at Oglethorpe University, May 22, 1932

Roosevelt was elected. In the months leading up to taking office in March 1933, he assembled a group of experts that became known as the **Brain Trust.** They came up with different programs and plans to fight the Depression. In the next section, you will read about their plans.

Section 1 Assessment

1. TERMS & NAMES

Explain the significance of:

a. Black Tuesday

b. Great Depression

c. Franklin D. Roosevelt

d. Brain Trust

2. TAKING NOTES

Use a chart like the one below to note the impact the Depression had on the different parts of Georgia's economy.

Economy:	Impact:
Agriculture	
Industry	
Employment	
Banks	

3. MAIN IDEAS

a. What were the causes of the Depression? Which cause had the most impact? Why?

b. Why was Angelo Herndon arrested, convicted, and sentenced to jail? What does his story represent?

c. What was Hoover's plan for stopping the Depression? Why didn't it work?

4. CRITICAL THINKING

Contrasting

How did Hoover and most Americans differ in their view of the role of the federal government?

Think About

• Hoover's attitude about federal relief

• what Americans might have expected from Hoover

ACTIVITY -OPTIONS- **Math/Speech** Create a **graph** or record a series of **radio news bulletins** about the changes in stock market value from September through October 1929.

The New Deal in the South

SETTING THE STAGE

Roosevelt put federal programs and agencies in place to create jobs and give money. Individual states had only to ask for help from the federal government.

In the Southern states, there was a long-held belief that states—and individuals—should take care of themselves. Would they be willing to accept "hand outs" from the federal government? How would the Southern states recover if they didn't accept the federal help? Would the programs work?

▲ The Farm Security Administration established the rural rehabilitation program. It offered loans and other assistance to clients such as this Greene County man who had been hit hard by the Depression.

"A New Deal for the American People"

When Franklin Delano Roosevelt, often called FDR, took office on March 4, 1933, he immediately set his programs in motion. These programs were part of his **New Deal** program to fight the Depression.

One of the first things Roosevelt did was to declare a "bank holiday" and ordered all banks closed temporarily to stop people from taking out their money. When a bank could prove that it had enough money to operate, the government allowed it to reopen.

The Hundred Days In the session of Congress that began March 9, 1933, Roosevelt proposed to Congress dozens of laws creating numerous federal agencies. During what came to be called the **Hundred Days,** he introduced legislation to accomplish three goals, known as the "three Rs."

1. **relief** for jobless and homeless people
2. **recovery** for agriculture and industry
3. **reforms** to change how the economy worked

Taking Notes

Use your chart to record details and evaluate the effectiveness of Roosevelt's New Deal.

GREAT DEPRESSION	
President Hoover's Responses	Presiden
Effectiveness	

New Deal programs dealt with every aspect of the Depression: unemployment, poverty, poor housing, labor disputes, preservation of natural resources, development of energy sources, such as electricity, and aid to the nation's farmers. The chart on page 381 lists several major New Deal programs and explains what those programs accomplished. People called them "alphabet soup" programs because they were known by their initials.

Roosevelt and his advisors hoped that with these New Deal programs and agencies the federal government could provide relief from the Depression, rebuild the damaged economy, and enact economic reforms to prevent any further depressions.

Talmadge Resists the New Deal

In 1932, **Eugene Talmadge** was elected governor of Georgia. Talmadge did not like the New Deal programs. He resisted the federal jobs programs. Talmadge believed that if people were paid more to work on federal programs, they would be unwilling to work on farms. The federal government listened to Talmadge's concerns and kept federal wages similar to local rates. At harvest time, federal projects stopped so that there would be more people available to pick cotton.

In 1934, Talmadge won re-election by a landslide. Small farmers and wage earners of the state supported him. Talmadge won because he convinced voters that he was the person to take care of them.

Talmadge restricted many programs in the early days of the New Deal, but he could not keep them out of the state. He also misjudged

Reading History

A. Drawing Conclusions How did Talmadge convince voters he would take care of them?

▶ Eugene Talmadge was especially critical of the Agricultural Adjustment Act, a federal program that limited the amount of crops farmers could grow.

the Georgia voters. They wanted help from the government. In the state elections of 1936, the voters turned to a group of politicians that opposed Talmadge's ideas. Led by new Governor **Eurith D. Rivers,** these politicians brought more New Deal assistance to the state. Governor Rivers's administration was called the "Little New Deal." Georgia became one of the first states to have a federally operated relief program.

New Deal Programs in Georgia

The programs of the New Deal were national and affected Americans across the country. Georgia and Georgians were affected by many of the programs and participated in the national recovery.

Agricultural Adjustment Administration (AAA)   The AAA provided cash payments to farmers who reduced the number of acres they planted or the size of their herds. In 1933, the AAA paid Southern cotton farmers to destroy almost 10 million acres of cotton. This reduced the supply and raised cotton prices. It also reduced the need for many sharecroppers and tenant farmers. Landowners benefited from the federal program, but poor whites and African Americans were hurt by it.

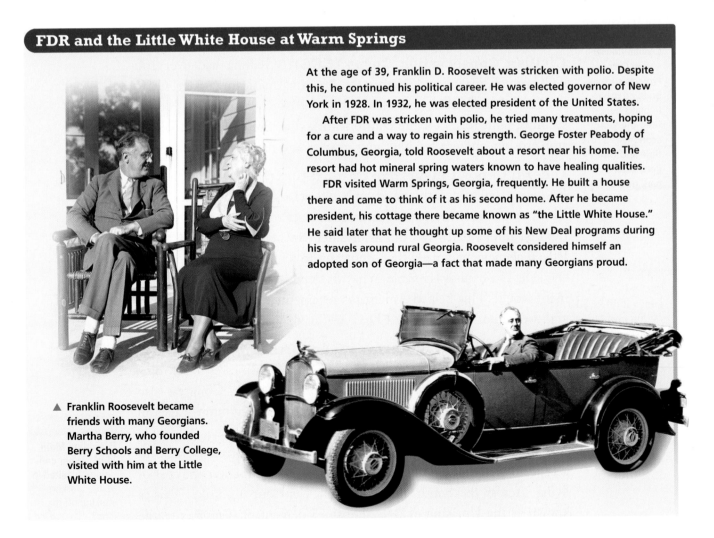

FDR and the Little White House at Warm Springs

At the age of 39, Franklin D. Roosevelt was stricken with polio. Despite this, he continued his political career. He was elected governor of New York in 1928. In 1932, he was elected president of the United States.

After FDR was stricken with polio, he tried many treatments, hoping for a cure and a way to regain his strength. George Foster Peabody of Columbus, Georgia, told Roosevelt about a resort near his home. The resort had hot mineral spring waters known to have healing qualities.

FDR visited Warm Springs, Georgia, frequently. He built a house there and came to think of it as his second home. After he became president, his cottage there became known as "the Little White House." He said later that he thought up some of his New Deal programs during his travels around rural Georgia. Roosevelt considered himself an adopted son of Georgia—a fact that made many Georgians proud.

▲ Franklin Roosevelt became friends with many Georgians. Martha Berry, who founded Berry Schools and Berry College, visited with him at the Little White House.

▲ Workers enlisted in Roosevelt's Civilian Conservation Corps. Projects such as building cabins in parks benefited the local economies at the time and future generations of park goers.

Civilian Conservation Corps (CCC)   Georgia had over 100 CCC camps, including 15 camps for African American workers. CCC workers planted trees, restocked lakes and rivers with fish, drained swamps, built roads for fire control, worked as firefighters, worked to stop erosion, and erected buildings in state and national parks.

Federal Deposit Insurance Corporation (FDIC)   By the time Roosevelt took office, thousands of banks across the nation had closed. Most people lost their money and became afraid to use banks. One of the first things that FDR did as president was create the FDIC. This federal agency guaranteed that money up to $5,000 deposited in banks was safe. If a bank was unable to pay its depositors, the federal government would. This helped Americans regain their confidence in banks and the economy. Today, the FDIC insures deposits up to $100,000.

National Industrial Recovery Act (NIRA)   This act gave workers the right to join unions and encouraged businesses to set minimum wages and maximum hours of work per week. Congress also passed laws that limited work hours, guaranteed minimum wages in certain jobs, and provided for better working conditions.

Textile mill owners followed the guidelines but forced workers to accept heavier workloads at a rate of pay that did not cover the cost of living. Across the South, textile workers went out on strike. This is known as the **Uprising of '34**. Almost 75 percent of Georgia's textile

Reading History

B. Finding Main Ideas What conditions resulted in textile workers walking off their jobs?

workers walked off their jobs. Within months, over 230,000 mill workers joined the United Textile Workers of America. The strike ended in Georgia after Governor Talmadge ordered the National Guard to arrest thousands of strikers and their leaders.

Tennessee Valley Authority (TVA)   The TVA built almost 20 dams in the Tennessee River Valley to generate electricity. The TVA brought electricity to the rural areas of the seven-state region. It is still a major provider of electricity and jobs in the region today.

Rural Electrification Administration (REA)   In the 1930s, most people living in urban areas of the country had access to electricity. But only about ten percent of the people living in the countryside had electricity. Private power companies did not want to supply power to the people scattered about the countryside because it would cost too

Major Programs of the New Deal

	PROGRAMS	ACCOMPLISHMENTS
Hundred Days, 1933	**FERA** (Federal Emergency Relief Administration)	Provided federal money for relief projects to the roughly 13 million unemployed
	PWA (Public Works Administration)	Created jobs by having people build highways, bridges, and other public works
	AAA (Agricultural Adjustment Administration)	Regulated farm production and promoted soil conservation
	TVA (Tennessee Valley Authority)	Planned development of the Tennessee Valley region
	CCC (Civilian Conservation Corps)	Hired young men to plant trees, build dams, and work on other conservation projects
	FDIC (Federal Deposit Insurance Corporation)	Protected the money of depositors in insured banks
	NRA (National Recovery Administration)	Regulated industry and raised wages and prices
Second New Deal, 1935	**WPA** (Works Progress Administration)	Established large-scale national works programs to create jobs
	REA (Rural Electrification Administration)	Brought electricity to rural areas
	NYA (National Youth Administration)	Set up job programs for young people and helped them continue their education
	Wagner Act	Protected labor's right to form unions and set up a board to hear labor disputes
	Social Security Act	Provided workers with unemployment insurance and retirement benefits

SKILLBUILDER Interpreting Charts
1. *How did the PWA and the CCC help both those who were hired and the nation as a whole?*
2. *How did the Second New Deal help both young and old workers?*

much to run lines to them. The REA brought electricity to almost 300,000 families in rural areas of Tennessee, Alabama, Georgia, and North Carolina.

African Americans and the New Deal   African Americans in Georgia felt the blow of the Depression especially hard. African Americans did not benefit as much from New Deal programs. They encountered either exclusion or segregation at every turn. In one incident, whites paraded in Atlanta demanding that African Americans be fired from their jobs and replaced by white workers. In 1935, the average amount of relief for whites in Atlanta was $32.66 per month. For African Americans it was $19.29.

Although African Americans received only a small portion of the federal benefits, they overwhelmingly supported Roosevelt and the New Deal. These programs convinced many African Americans to vote Democrat. Roosevelt named a number of African Americans to government positions that administered the New Deal programs.

Women in the New Deal   The first lady, Eleanor Roosevelt, was a champion of African Americans, women, and children. She actively worked on social reforms. Because her husband had a disability, Mrs. Roosevelt acted as his "eyes and ears." She toured the country, visiting coal mines, work camps, and hospitals to find out how New Deal programs were working. Then she told the president what she learned and made suggestions.

In 1933, Eleanor Roosevelt began to hold regular press conferences for women reporters. At these, the first lady introduced the women who ran New Deal programs. During Roosevelt's presidency, more women held positions with the government than ever before. Frances Perkins served as secretary of labor, making her the first female cabinet officer. She supported laws granting a minimum wage, a limit on child employment, and unemployment compensation.

The Second New Deal

In 1935, the Supreme Court declared a number of New Deal programs and legislation unconstitutional. The Court ruled that the federal government had gone beyond the powers granted to it under the Constitution. Roosevelt and his advisors went to work to replace the cancelled programs with new programs, called the Second New Deal.

NOW & THEN

Social Security

Today, many young people worry that the Social Security trust fund won't have enough money for their pensions. For one thing, people live longer now than they did in the 1930s. Also, the percentage of people receiving benefits keeps increasing compared to the number paying into the system. Last, Social Security benefits have been expanded since the 1930s.

Reading History

C. Making Inferences Why do you think Eleanor Roosevelt publicized the women who worked in government?

In August 1935, Congress passed one of the most important bills of the century—the Social Security Act. Under this act, workers and employers made payments into a special fund. When they retired, they would draw a pension from this fund. The act also helped laid-off workers, disabled workers, and needy families with dependent children.

The Second New Deal in Georgia The **Works Progress Administration** (WPA) created the Federal Writers Project. Painters, architects, writers, and actors produced public art projects. Artists painted murals that were placed in post offices in many Georgia towns. The WPA also collected information on the history and culture of every state in the Union. In Georgia, Gay B. Shepperson served as the WPA's Relief Administrator. She was the only woman to serve as a state administrator.

Before the New Deal programs, 5 million acres of land in Georgia alone had lost its topsoil and the ability to grow crops. The Soil Conservation Service taught Southern farmers how to preserve their land by using crop rotation and other forms of conservation. The federal government paid farmers subsidies to use these measures. They also introduced plants to control erosion. Kudzu was one plant used to control erosion. It later became one of the South's agricultural problems.

The New Deal addressed many of the difficulties Americans experienced during the Great Depression. Despite these efforts, Americans continued to suffer from harsh economic conditions, as you will read in the next section.

Section 2 Assessment

1. TERMS & NAMES

Explain the significance of:

a. New Deal

b. Hundred Days

c. Eugene Talmadge

d. Eurith D. Rivers

e. Uprising of '34

f. Works Progress Administration

2. TAKING NOTES

Create a chart like this one to define the goal and give examples of each of the "three R's" of the New Deal.

Relief	Recovery	Reforms
Goal:	Goal:	Goal:
Examples:	Examples:	Examples:
1.	1.	1.
2.	2.	2.
3.	3.	3.

3. MAIN IDEAS

a. Why did Roosevelt declare a bank holiday as one of his first acts as president?

b. Why did Governor Talmadge oppose New Deal programs?

c. What did owners do to push textile workers into going out on strike in 1934?

4. CRITICAL THINKING

Drawing Conclusions

Of the following New Deal programs, which one do you think affects your life the most? Explain.

Think About
• Social Security
• AAA
• TVA
• FDIC
• WPA

ACTIVITY -OPTIONS- **Art/Technology** Choose one aspect of the New Deal that you have an opinion about. Create a **political cartoon** or design a **Web page** expressing your opinion.

Life During the Depression

<table>
<tr><td>

MAIN IDEA

During the Depression, people suffered great hardships but found ways to survive.

</td><td>

WHY IT MATTERS NOW

Because of this, a generation was scarred by suffering in ways that later generations were not.

</td><td>

TERMS & NAMES

Erskine Caldwell

Public Works Administration (PWA)

Techwood Homes

University Homes

</td></tr>
</table>

SETTING THE STAGE

By the late 1930s, the Southern states were considered to be in the worst economic shape of the entire nation. "The Nation's Number One Economic Problem" was the phrase used in a report on the economic conditions of the South.

How did people in the South and the rest of the country deal with the Depression? How could they support their families? Were people miserable all the time? Or did they find ways to forget about their troubles?

▲ Children, such as these in Kingsland, Georgia, had to grow up fast in the Depression. Many took jobs after school or dropped out to work or help take care of their families.

Living with the Depression

Even with the economic recovery measures of the New Deal programs, unemployment remained high. In 1936, for example, 9 million people across the nation had no jobs.

Jobs Across Georgia, landowners hired fewer laborers and share-croppers. People wandered about looking for a place to live and a small plot of land to grow enough crops to provide for their families.

In 1932, Georgia writer **Erskine Caldwell** wrote *Tobacco Road*, a popular novel about Georgia's white sharecroppers that later became a movie. His portrayal of rural Georgia was not very positive. But there was some truth in the hopelessness he wrote about.

Many people relied on programs such as the PWA and WPA for work. Often, for a family to survive, both the husband and wife and even the children worked. Some businesses laid off men and hired women because women worked for less money. Men were still considered the "bread winners," but women were entering the workplace in increasing numbers. Without work, many families could not pay their mortgages and lost their homes.

Taking Notes

Use your chart to record details and evaluate the presidents' responses to people's needs during the Depression.

GREAT DEPRESSION

President Hoover's Responses	Presiden
Effectiveness	

▲ Eleanor Roosevelt (standing, right) tours a WPA building site on a trip to Georgia.

Vocabulary

slum: a neighborhood with overcrowded and dangerous housing

Reading History

A. Drawing Conclusions Why were so many people living in city slums during this time?

Background

Oliver Hardy was from Milledgeville, Georgia.

Places to Live   The number and size of Hoovervilles across the nation were increasing. In cities, more people were living in slums. The New Deal attempted to improve living conditions for the nation's poor and to provide housing for the homeless.

A 1934 federal study revealed that many homes in Atlanta had no running water, indoor toilets, or baths. As much as 39 percent of Atlanta's population lived in substandard housing. Most were African Americans with little hope that the city government would help them.

The **Public Works Administration** (PWA) had the job of cleaning up the nation's slums. It was also responsible for building public housing. In Atlanta, it built **Techwood Homes**, which was for white tenants and opened in 1935. **University Homes**, which was for black tenants, opened in early 1937.

Entertainment During the Depression

During the 1930s, people found ways to forget their troubles for a short time. Spectator sports were popular. Going to the movies became a favorite pastime for Americans. At first, the Depression caused attendance to decline. But audiences soon grew. Hard times made people eager for entertainment. Inside the movie theater, viewers could forget their troubles while watching comedians like the Marx Brothers or Laurel and Hardy. Or they followed a young girl with curly locks—Shirley Temple.

When people did not have money for luxury items or entertainment, they found inexpensive ways to enjoy themselves. People played cards, went window shopping, fished, or played neighborhood sports and other games.

One game that became popular during the Depression was Monopoly. Charles Darrow, an unemployed salesman, created the game as an inexpensive activity for his friends. They liked the game so much, they asked him to make more copies. Eventually, Darrow sold the game to Parker Brothers, and retired a millionaire.

Reading History

B. Finding Main Ideas What forms of entertainment were popular and affordable during the Depression?

Gone With the Wind Georgians participated in the new Hollywood movie craze with the Atlanta premiere of *Gone With the Wind*. The movie was adapted from the popular book by Margaret Mitchell, which had sold over two million copies. The movie premiered at the Loew's Grand Theater in Atlanta on December 15, 1939. Two thousand people paid ten dollars each to attend the premier. Outside the theater a large crowd gathered to catch a glimpse of the stars and dignitaries—Vivian Leigh, Clark Gable and his wife Carol Lombard, Mayor William B. Hartsfield, and Margaret Mitchell.

▲ The premiere of *Gone With the Wind* was a whirlwind event. The mayor of Atlanta even closed public schools and gave city employees the day off.

Radio Many people gathered around the radio, much like people watch television today. *Mercury Theatre* and *Campbell Playhouse* presented dramas, comedies, mysteries, and serials. People listened to shows such as *Abbott & Costello, Jack Benny, Superman,* and *The Lone Ranger*.

Attendance at organized sports such as baseball dropped during the 1930s. Many people could not afford to buy tickets, but listened to the games on the radio.

Seeking a Better Life

New Deal programs did not make life better for everyone. They could not solve longstanding problems overnight. Farmers and sharecroppers still had to deal with poor soil. Many did not have the money to buy fertilizers or expensive tractors to work the land. And, there was still the problem of crop prices that were too low to make a profit.

Some Georgians chose to leave and make a new life elsewhere. Many took to the open road. They hitchhiked or jumped on a train passing through town. President Jimmy Carter remembered the Depression years when people had passed by his home in South Georgia.

PRIMARY SOURCE

During some of the worst years of the Depression, the most frequent travelers we saw in front of our house were tramps. . . . They were usually men traveling alone or in small groups. Every now and then an entire family would go by. . . . When Mama was home we never turned away anyone who came to our back door asking for food or a drink of water. Those who showed up were invariably polite, and most of them offered to cut wood or do other yard work in return for a sandwich.

President Jimmy Carter

▲ This Carroll County family was photographed in 1941 by Jack Delano for the Farm Security Administration.

The Depression and New Deal had a tremendous impact on Georgia and its citizens. Even more changes were on the way. In 1939 and 1940, the federal government began to buy land in Georgia and build military training facilities. Although the United States was not yet directly involved in the war in Europe, many American leaders knew it soon would be. In the next chapter, you will learn about the important role Georgia played at home and on the battlefields as America prepared for war.

Section 3 Assessment

1. TERMS & NAMES

Explain the significance of:

a. Erskine Caldwell

b. Public Works Administration

c. Techwood Homes

d. University Homes

2. TAKING NOTES

Use a cluster diagram like the one below to record details from this section on how people coped during the Depression.

Coping During the Depression

3. MAIN IDEAS

a. How did families survive during the Depression?

b. What did the New Deal do to improve living conditions in slum areas of large cities like Atlanta?

c. What did families do for entertainment during the Great Depression?

4. CRITICAL THINKING

Analyzing Causes

Why do you think the South was considered the "Nation's Number One Economic Problem"?

Think About
• the South's agricultural economy
• the South's rural population
• the South's urban conditions

ACTIVITY -OPTIONS- **Language Arts/Technology** Ask older relatives what they know of the Depression and New Deal. Capture their responses in a **written interview** or an **audio recording**.

VISUAL SUMMARY

The Great Depression and New Deal

CAUSES

- Problems in agriculture and some industries
- Unequal income distribution
- Too much inventory
- Too much debt
- Stock market speculation
- Lack of government involvement in business

October 29, 1929

*** THE URBAN DAILY ***
YOUR COMPLETE NEWS

WALL STREET IN PANIC AS STOCKS CRASH

EFFECT: DEPRESSION

- Stock market crash
- Bank and business failures
- High unemployment
- Hunger and homelessness

EFFECT: NEW DEAL

- Government takes a large role in relief for the hungry and homeless
- Aid for agriculture and industry
- Economic reforms

SWEEPING

THE DEPRESSION OUT

TERMS & NAMES

Briefly explain the significance of the following.

1. Black Tuesday
2. Great Depression
3. Franklin Delano Roosevelt
4. Brain Trust
5. New Deal
6. Eugene Talmadge
7. Uprising of '34
8. PWA
9. Techwood Homes and University Homes

REVIEW QUESTIONS

The Great Depression (pages 371–376)

1. Why did stock prices fall so quickly during the stock market crash?
2. What were the problems in Georgia that contributed to the Depression?
3. Who did President Hoover think should help the needy?
4. Why was Roosevelt such an appealing candidate?

The New Deal in the South (pages 377–383)

5. What were Roosevelt's three R's?
6. Which New Deal programs most affected Georgia?
7. How did the New Deal affect most African Americans?
8. What was the Second New Deal?

Life During the Depression (pages 384–387)

9. What was life like in the South during the Great Depression?

CRITICAL THINKING

1. USING YOUR NOTES: EVALUATING

GREAT DEPRESSION	
President Hoover's Responses	President Roosevelt's Responses
Effectiveness	Effectiveness

Using your completed chart, answer the questions below.

a. What do you think was Hoover's most successful response to the Depression?

b. How would you evaluate FDR's presidency? Was he a great president? Why or why not?

2. ANALYZING LEADERSHIP

Contrast the leadership of Presidents Hoover and Roosevelt. Who was the best leader? Why?

3. APPLYING CITIZENSHIP SKILLS

How were the following citizenship skills important during the Depression: staying informed about issues and voting?

4. THEME: ECONOMICS IN HISTORY

What reforms did FDR make to strengthen the economy?

5. ANALYZING CAUSES

Review the economic problems leading to the Depression. What similar problems exist in the economy today?

INTERACT with HISTORY

Now that you've read about the Depression, who do you think should help the poor? Why?

STANDARDS-BASED ASSESSMENT

Use the graph and your knowledge of American history to answer questions 1 through 3.

Unemployment Rate, 1929–1941

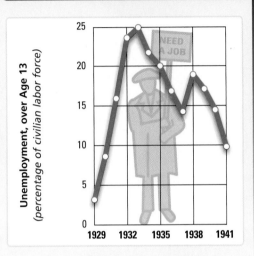

Unemployment, over Age 13
(percentage of civilian labor force)

25

20

15

10

5

0

1929 1932 1935 1938 1941

1. What does the vertical axis represent?

   A. Unemployment rate

   B. Percentage of unemployed over age 13

   C. Number of unemployed over age 13

   D. The year

2. What happened to unemployment between the years 1929 and 1932?

   A. It rose about 20%

   B. It rose about 25%

   C. It rose by about 20 million

   D. It rose by about 25 million

3. What happened to unemployment between the years 1935 and 1938?

   A. It fell about 15%

   B. It fell to about 10%

   C. It fell more than 5%, then rose again

   D. It fell to about 15 million

TEST PRACTICE
CLASSZONE.COM

ALTERNATIVE ASSESSMENT

1. ANALYZING PRIMARY SOURCES

During the Depression, Americans turned to popular entertainment to escape their troubles. View or listen to songs and radio shows from the period. Select one to analyze. What does it reflect about the time? Share your analysis with the class.

2. COOPERATIVE LEARNING

Work in teams to debate the following question: Should the government go into debt to help the poor? Decide on your position as a team. Then select and research leaders of the Depression era who represent your view. Use your leaders as resources for your debate.

INTEGRATED TECHNOLOGY ACTIVITY

PREPARING A MULTIMEDIA PRESENTATION

Choose an aspect of the Great Depression in the South that you would like to learn more about. Use books, the Internet, and software to research your topic. Then prepare a multimedia presentation for your class. Consider including the following resources.

- Oral histories

- Quotations from speeches

- Photographs and art

- Excerpts from literature

- Videotaped interviews with older people who lived around that time

RESEARCH LINKS
CLASSZONE.COM

America and Georgia in World War II 1938–1945

Soldiers train for battle at Fort Stewart in 1941.

1939
Georgia ratifies the Bill of Rights.

1942
Liberty Ships are built in Brunswick and Savannah. Air Force base in Macon trains soldiers.

GEORGIA USA   1938

1940
Selective Training and Service Act is signed into law.

1941
Congress passes Lend-Lease Act. Japan bombs American naval base at Pearl Harbor, Hawaii.

The year is 1943. The United States and its Allies are fighting in Europe, the Pacific, and North Africa. Many young men have joined the military. Many young women have joined the effort as well, in organizations such as the WAC and the Red Cross. Even those at home are contributing, with victory gardens and scrap metal drives.

What can you do to help the war effort?

WHAT DO YOU THINK?

- What sacrifices do soldiers and other volunteers make?

- How can people at home contribute during wartime?

For more information on this chapter, visit . . .

RESEARCH LINKS
CLASSZONE.COM

1943
First B-29 bombers are built in Marietta. WAVES train at Georgia State College for Women.

1945

1944
U.S. and Allies invade Europe at Normandy.

1945
Roosevelt dies at Warm Springs. Germany surrenders. U.S. drops atomic bombs on Hiroshima and Nagasaki. Japan surrenders.

America and Georgia in World War II **391**

Reading Strategy: Sequencing Events

What Do You Know?

What do you think of when you hear the word "dictator" and the phrase "World War II"? Where did the fighting take place in this war?

THINK ABOUT

• what you have learned about dictators from the news, teachers, parents, or older persons
• what you have learned about World War II from books, movies, or television

What Do You Want to Know?

What questions do you have about World War II? Record those questions in your notebook before you read the chapter.

Sequencing Events

Sequencing means putting events in the order in which they happen in time. In learning about World War II, you'll find it helpful to list important events in order. For example, you might record important battles and their dates in a graphic organizer such as the one below. Copy this organizer into your notebook and fill it in as you read the chapter.

S See Skillbuilder Handbook, page 549.

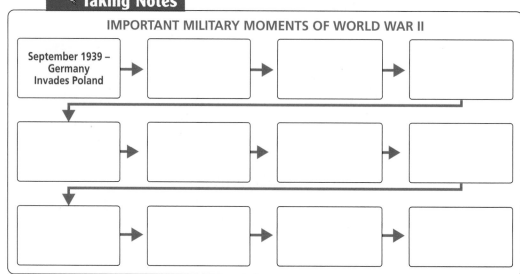

Taking Notes

IMPORTANT MILITARY MOMENTS OF WORLD WAR II

September 1939 – Germany Invades Poland

The War Begins

1

MAIN IDEA	WHY IT MATTERS NOW	TERMS & NAMES
In 1941, the United States was drawn into another world war.	Since World War II, the United States has been greatly involved in world affairs.	Benito Mussolini fascism Adolf Hitler Nazi Party	Hideki Tojo Axis Powers Allied Powers Lend-Lease Act Pearl Harbor

SETTING THE STAGE

The United States was not the only country in the 1930s that experienced a severe economic depression. European countries devastated by World War I faced tough times as well. Europeans wanted leaders who could restore order. Germans and Italians turned to men who used military power and a strong sense of nationalism to achieve their goals.

At the same time, Japanese leaders wanted to expand into Asia. Japan occupied parts of China and planned to take more. Japanese leaders saw the United States as an unwelcome presence in the Pacific. Would they do something about it?

▲ Adolf Hitler, leader of Germany, and Benito Mussolini, prime minister of Italy, were powerful fascist leaders.

The Rise of Dictators

After World War I, new leaders emerged in Italy and Germany who promised to fix their countries' problems. They appealed to people's strong sense of loyalty to their countries. These leaders claimed that they could return Italy and Germany to their former glory and power.

Italy   In 1922, **Benito Mussolini** became the prime minister of Italy, promising to turn the economy around. He started the political movement called **fascism** (FASH-iz-uhm). Fascists believed that the government should control everything in society. Their extreme nationalism, or belief in the superiority of their own country's heritage, often led to racism. They oppressed people who did not share their views.

Fascism emphasized a supreme ruler and the use of military power to further the nation's interests. Mussolini established himself as dictator in 1925. To increase Italy's power, he invaded Libya and attacked Ethiopia in 1935.

Taking Notes

Use your graphic organizer to put events in order as World War II begins.

September 1939 – Germany Invades Poland →   →

CONNECTIONS Science to

German Scientists

Many scientists left Germany or gave up their German citizenship after the Nazis took power. The most famous German scientist to do so was the physicist Albert Einstein.

Einstein, a German Jew, was visiting the United States when Hitler took control of Germany in 1933. Einstein announced he would not return home. "I shall live only in a country where civil liberty, tolerance and equality of all citizens before the law prevail," he said.

Einstein played a key role in convincing President Roosevelt to support research that would lead to the development of nuclear weapons.

Germany In 1933, another fascist leader, **Adolf Hitler,** came to power in Germany. Hitler and his fascist political organization, the **Nazi Party,** took control. He declared himself the *Führer* (total ruler) of Germany and said that a 1,000-year *reich* (empire) had begun.

Hitler promised to strengthen the nation's economy and its military. At the end of World War I, the Allied Powers had ordered Germany to pay money for war damages. These payments kept Germany's economy very weak. Hitler stopped all payments to the Allies, increased the size of the military, and purchased more weapons.

In 1935, Hitler invaded an area called the Rhineland between France and Germany. He claimed that this territory belonged to Germany. France and the other former allies did nothing to stop him.

Japan Japan had occupied Manchuria, a large section of China, in 1931. The United States condemned Japan's actions. The United States was concerned that Japan was trying to take control of East Asia, including colonies belonging to France, Britain, and the United States. Like Italy and Germany, Japanese military and political leaders wanted to make Japan more powerful.

When Japan entered into an alliance with Germany and Italy in 1940, the United States blocked steel shipments to Japan and froze the assets of Japanese companies. The Japanese prime minister, **Hideki Tojo,** was determined to use the power of the Japanese military to drive the Americans out of the Pacific. The United States had a major naval base at Pearl Harbor in Hawaii.

Opposing Forces Germany, Italy, and Japan formed an alliance to strengthen each country's own desire for more power and control. These three countries were known as the **Axis Powers.** They were opposed by the old alliance of Great Britain and France known as the **Allied Powers.**

War Begins in Europe

The Allied Powers did not want to use force to stop Hitler. They used diplomacy—asking Hitler to stop taking any more territory. He promised the British prime minister, Neville Chamberlain, that he would not attack any more European countries. Hitler lied. In September 1939, Hitler staged a *blitzkrieg* ("lightning war") against Poland.

Reading History

A. Finding Main Ideas What factors led to the rise of dictators and facism after World War I?

The Allies Join the War   Great Britain and France had promised Poland that they would come to its defense if it was attacked. They declared war on Germany. World War II had started.

Reading History

B. Making Inferences Why do you think Stalin made an agreement with Hitler?

Britain and France assumed that Josef Stalin, leader of the Soviet Union, would be an ally. But Stalin and Hitler had made a secret agreement in August 1939. The two agreed to divide Poland between their countries. Stalin was just as eager to conquer new territory as Hitler.

In April 1940, Hitler conquered Denmark and Norway. In May, the German military launched a *blitzkrieg* against Belgium, Luxembourg, and the Netherlands. In June 1940, Germany invaded France. Within two weeks, the Germans had reached Paris. The country surrendered soon after.

The Battle of Britain   After taking France, Hitler turned his attention to Great Britain. In what became known as the Battle of Britain, the German air force tried to defeat Great Britain by bombing it. On June 18, 1940, Britain's new prime minister, Winston Churchill, spoke to his fellow citizens.

PRIMARY SOURCE

The Battle of Britain is about to begin. . . . If we can stand up to [Hitler], all Europe may be free. . . . But if we fail, then the whole world . . . will sink into the abyss of a new Dark Age. . . . Let us therefore brace ourselves to our duties, and so bear ourselves that, if the British Empire and its Commonwealth last for a thousand years, men will still say, "This was their finest hour."

Winston Churchill to the House of Commons, June 18, 1940

Great Britain withstood the constant bombing. But supplies, military equipment, and pilots to fly British fighter planes were becoming scarce. Great Britain needed aid from its allies if it was to continue fighting.

◀ A British family sits among the devastation caused by German bombs.

Germany Invades the Soviet Union In June 1941, Hitler launched a surprise invasion on his ally, the Soviet Union. Then, using the *blitzkrieg* tactics that had worked so well in Western Europe, Hitler tried to capture the cities of Leningrad and Moscow. In December 1941, the Soviet army drove the Germans back from Moscow during the harshest winter Russia had experienced in decades. It defended Leningrad for almost two and a half years before finally driving the Germans back. By January 1944, the Soviets had suffered more than one million deaths, mostly civilians who died of starvation. The Soviet Union would fight the rest of the war on the side of the Allied forces.

The United States Reacts

Many Americans believed that U.S. involvement in World War I had been a mistake. Others believed that war was not the way for countries to solve their problems with one another.

Isolationism Most Americans favored a policy of isolationism. They felt the country should stay out of the affairs of European countries and let them settle their differences any way they wanted. Besides, the United States was still fighting a war—against the Great Depression.

Reading History

C. Making Inferences Why did Hitler attack Stalin after making him an ally only months earlier?

World War II in Europe, 1939–1945

Neutral nations
Area held by Allies
Axis powers
Germany's maximum expansion

GEOGRAPHY SKILLBUILDER
Interpreting Maps

1. **Place** Which European nations were neutral?
2. **Region** Which countries were allied with Great Britain?

President Roosevelt and Congress passed a series of laws from 1935 to 1937 called Neutrality Acts, designed to prevent the United States from getting involved in the European war. Americans were not allowed to ride on ships that belonged to warring nations. United States banks could not lend money or give credit to European countries at war.

Lend-Lease Act   By the late 1930s, the American people began to realize the threat that Hitler posed to Europe and to freedom everywhere. Roosevelt and his advisors knew that it was only a matter of time before the United States would join the war in Europe. It could not remain neutral.

Congress passed the **Lend-Lease Act** in early 1941. It gave Roosevelt the power to lend or rent military goods (airplanes, tanks, bullets, and equipment, for example) to any country he thought was important to U.S. interests. By the end of the war, the Lend-Lease program had supplied the Allies with over 50 billion dollars in material.

Great Britain's superior navy escorted American merchant ships filled with goods across the Atlantic. However, the Germans had U-boats (submarines) that sank many merchant ships. When it became clear that the Germans were willing to sink American ships, Roosevelt issued a "shoot on sight" order. Unofficially, the United States was at war with Germany. But it was another event that pushed them into the war officially.

Attack on Pearl Harbor   In the early morning hours of December 7, 1941, Japanese warplanes staged a surprise attack on the U.S. Pacific

◀ Disaster struck the U.S. Armed Services (or Forces) when Japanese planes bombed ships anchored in Pearl Harbor. This surprise attack marked the beginning of World War II for the United States.

Fleet stationed at **Pearl Harbor,** Hawaii. They killed over 2,300 military personnel and civilians, and destroyed 19 ships. It was a major blow to the United States. Major damage to the ships and warplanes of the Pacific Fleet meant that the United States could not adequately protect American interests in the Pacific.

A Declaration of War   The day after the attack on Pearl Harbor, Roosevelt asked Congress for a declaration of war against Japan. He called the attack on Pearl Harbor a "date which will live in infamy." The only member of Congress to vote against the declaration was Jeannette Rankin of Montana. Rankin said, "As a woman I can't go to war, and I refuse to send anyone else." She had also been one of the members of Congress to vote against entering World War I. Rankin had lived in Bogart, Georgia, in the 1920s and 1930s before returning to Montana to run for Congress.

Americans were eager to respond to the attack. They supported going to war against Japan. They also supported going to war against Germany. The American people were ready to fight.

Because both Germany and Italy had an alliance with Japan, they declared war on the United States on December 11. The stage was set for a world war. The only questions to be answered were when, and where, would the United States enter the war? You will learn how the United States responded to the declaration of war in the next section.

▲ Unlike most Americans, Jeannette Rankin did not support the declaration of war.

Reading History

D. Analyzing Causes What was the main source of the conflict between Japan and the United States?

Section 1 Assessment

1. TERMS & NAMES

Explain the significance of:

a. Benito Mussolini

b. fascism

c. Adolf Hitler

d. Nazi Party

e. Hideki Tojo

f. Axis Powers

g. Allied Powers

h. Lend-Lease Act

i. Pearl Harbor

2. TAKING NOTES

Use a chart like the one below to organize information about each Axis leader and what he wanted to achieve for his country.

Axis Leader	Country	Political Intentions

3. MAIN IDEAS

a. Why did fascism gain a hold in Europe in the 1920s and early 1930s?

b. What was so important about the outcome of the Battle of Britain?

c. What was America's reaction to the Japanese attack on Pearl Harbor?

4. CRITICAL THINKING

Supporting Opinions

Why did Americans want to remain neutral during World War II? Should the United States have joined the Allies before the bombing of Pearl Harbor?

Think About

• the Depression
• the U.S. role in World War I
• the Lend-Lease Act

Language Arts/Geography   Imagine that your country has been invaded by Germany. Write a **journal entry** describing the invasion or draw a **map** of the invasion route.

Fighting the War

SETTING THE STAGE

The United States went from being a neutral nation to one that was fighting very powerful enemies in two different parts of the world. The nation would need to prepare. Military and consumer industries across Georgia and the United States began to gear up to outfit the military with the supplies it needed to fight.

President Roosevelt and his military advisors also had to decide how and where to fight. Where would they start? There were two areas, or theaters, of military activity during World War II—the European Theater and the Pacific Theater.

▲ A flood of government orders brings the depressed textile mills in Greene County, Georgia, back to life.

The United States Prepares for War

The American military was quite small at the start of 1942 and was not prepared to fight a world war. It would take a great effort to mobilize and equip a fighting force—especially one fighting in two different places on the globe. American industry needed to produce a large amount of equipment for the hundreds of thousands of troops training for war. President Roosevelt asked U.S. business leaders to set aside making other products to make the tanks, antiaircraft guns, planes, ships, ammunition, and vast amounts of other military equipment.

The United States had to decide where to begin the fight. The German air force was slowly destroying Great Britain's ability to fight. Constant bombing reduced the country's resources and weakened the will of its citizens. In the Pacific, the U.S. Navy was all but destroyed. It would be months before enough ships were built to move troops into position to attack Japanese forces.

If Great Britain surrendered to Hitler, the United States would face the almost impossible task of gaining a foothold in Europe. As a result, U.S. leaders decided to enter the fight in Europe before they entered the

Taking Notes

Use your graphic organizer to put events in order as the United States is drawn into the fighting.

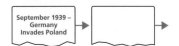

September 1939 – Germany Invades Poland → ☐ →

fight in the Pacific. The United States would begin the offensive in the Pacific Theater when they had rebuilt their naval forces.

The European Theater

The United States did not want to risk an invasion of Europe so early in the war. American and British officials convinced the Allies to invade an area of North Africa held by the Germans. In November 1942, U.S. troops landed in North Africa. There they fought both the Italian and German armies. The Allies defeated the Axis Powers and drove them out of North Africa. Then they prepared to launch an attack on Italy.

Allied forces invaded Italy in July 1943. The Italian government quickly surrendered, but German troops in Italy continued fighting for months. From their position in Italy, Allied planes attacked German railroads, factories, military installations, and oil reserves. As Allied forces bombed targets in Germany and Central Europe, they prepared for a major invasion in another area of Europe.

D-Day   On June 6, 1944, code-named **<u>D-Day</u>,** the largest armada in history approached the coast of occupied France. More than 600 ships carrying 175,000 Allied soldiers, equipment, supplies, tanks, and other vehicles landed on Omaha Beach in Normandy on the northwest coast of France. They unloaded their cargo onto the beach using special landing craft. The Allies used over 11,000 airplanes in the assault, parachuting tens of thousands of soldiers further inland. The soldiers met great resistance and many soldiers died.

Allied soldiers moved inland through France. They liberated the city of Paris on August 25. German troops resisted the Allied advance. On December 16, the Germans launched a massive attack on Allied forces. In the Battle of the Bulge, the Germans pushed the Allied lines back, but only for a few short weeks. By late February 1945, Allied troops were pushing the German army back into Germany.

The goal was to reach Berlin, the capital. Allied forces moved through Germany

Reading History

A. Making Decisions Why did the allies decide to attack the Axis Powers in North Africa before invading Europe?

▼ American troops storm Omaha Beach in Normandy in northern France on June 6, 1944.

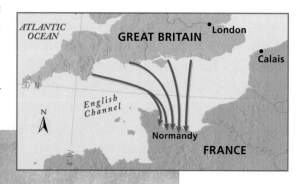

from the west while Soviet Allied forces advanced from the east. The Allies allowed the Soviet army to enter the city of Berlin first.

On April 12, 1945, Franklin Delano Roosevelt died of a brain hemorrhage at his vacation home in Warm Springs, Georgia. Vice-President Harry S Truman became president of the United States. By then, Allied troops were within reach of Hitler, but to avoid capture, he killed himself on April 30, 1945.

On May 8, 1945, Germany surrendered. This was called **V-E Day,** for Victory in Europe. Truman and his advisors then turned their attention to ending the war in the Pacific.

Liberating the Concentration Camps

As Allied forces moved further into Germany and German-occupied territory, they found a ghastly secret. Part of Hitler's plan was to "purify" the German race by removing all Jews from Europe. Hitler also wanted to eliminate homosexuals, gypsies, and people with physical abnormalities or mental conditions. His method—"The Final Solution"—was to imprison them in **concentration camps** and then kill them.

Allied forces liberated a number of concentration camps. Buchenwald, Dachau, and Auschwitz were some of the more infamous camps. By the end of the war, over 6 million Jews had died in the Nazi concentration camps. It is estimated that a total of 11 million people were killed or died from starvation and mistreatment in the camps over approximately 6 years. This atrocity has become known as the Holocaust.

▼ Young prisoners interned at the concentration camp at Dachau cheer their liberators, the 42nd Division of the U.S. Army.

The Pacific Theater

The strategy for fighting the Japanese in the Pacific was simple. U.S. forces would retake the islands in the Pacific, "**island hopping**" from one island to another toward Japan. They would either force the Japanese military to surrender or invade Japan. From May 1942 to June 1945, U.S. forces island hopped toward the Philippines and Japan. The United States also bombed cities, factories, and military facilities in Japan.

In June 1945, the United States was in position to invade the main islands of Japan. It would take hundreds of thousands of troops and massive amounts of equipment and supplies. Allied military leaders wondered if an invasion would succeed. The U.S. considered using a new kind of bomb to end the war with Japan. President Truman warned Japan to surrender or face destruction.

Reading History

B. Summarizing What was the Allies' strategy in the Pacific?

The Atomic Bomb On August 6, 1945, the B-29 bomber *Enola Gay* dropped a single **atomic bomb** (code-named "Little Boy") on the Japanese city of Hiroshima. President Truman announced the Hiroshima bombing in a radio broadcast. He demanded Japan's surrender and warned all Japanese civilians to leave their industrial cities because the United States was prepared to drop a second bomb. Japan's leaders refused to surrender. So, just three days after the first, another atomic bomb (code-named "Fat Man") was dropped on Nagasaki.

Reading History

C. Finding Main Ideas Why did the United States decide to use the atomic bomb?

The second bombing ended the war almost immediately. But it came with a great loss of life to the Japanese people. Over 110,000 people were killed immediately by the bomb blasts and more than 100,000 others died within a few months or years from radiation exposure.

▼ The intense blast of the atomic bomb dropped on Nagasaki emitted a "mushroom cloud."

The War Ends

On August 14, 1945, a few days after the second bomb was dropped, the Japanese government stopped fighting. The Allies called this **V-J Day,** for Victory in Japan. On September 2, 1945, the Japanese government officially surrendered. The war was finally over.

The war had a tremendous effect on the soldiers and civilians who were in the war zone. No war had ever claimed as many lives or caused as much destruction. Approximately 20 million soldiers were killed; 400,000 of those killed were Americans. Civilian casualties also numbered in the millions. Both Allied and Axis powers bombed cities, destroyed villages, and brought much destruction to civilian life. Nearly 21 million orphans, prisoners of war, survivors of Nazi concentration camps, and refugees from war-torn areas were left to try to put their lives back together after the war in Europe and Asia.

Even though no battles of World War II took place in the continental United States, the war had a tremendous impact on Americans at home. Georgians contributed to the war effort in many important ways, as you will read in the next section.

World War II Military Casualties, 1939–1945		
NATION	DEAD	WOUNDED
Soviet Union	7,500,000	5,000,000
Germany	3,500,000	7,250,000
China	2,200,000	1,762,000
Japan	1,219,000	295,247
United States	405,399	671,278
Great Britain	329,208	348,403
France	210,671	390,000
Italy	77,494	120,000

Source: *World Book*

SKILLBUILDER Interpreting Charts

1. *Which two nations suffered the most casualties in World War II?*
2. *Which of the major combatants suffered the fewest casualties?*

Reading History

D. Recognizing Effects How did the war affect civilians in the war zone?

Section 2 Assessment

1. TERMS & NAMES
Explain the significance of:

a. D-Day

b. V-E Day

c. concentration camp

d. island hopping

e. atomic bomb

f. V-J Day

2. TAKING NOTES
Use a diagram like the one shown below to identify the key events that led to the Allies' victory in Europe.

3. MAIN IDEAS
a. Why was U.S. industrial power so important for winning World War II?

b. Why did the U.S. enter the war in Europe right away and not fight in the Pacific until later?

c. Why did the U.S. decide to use the atomic bomb against Japan?

4. CRITICAL THINKING
Forming Opinions

What might be the arguments for and against using the atomic bomb on Japan?

Think About
• consequences of invading Japan
• the bomb's destructive power

ACTIVITY -OPTIONS-

Art/Geography Research German concentration camps. Build a **collage** of photos or create a **map** depicting the location of Nazi concentration camps in Europe.

Georgia's Contribution to the War

MAIN IDEA	WHY IT MATTERS NOW	TERMS & NAMES
Georgia played a crucial role in preparing the United States military for war.	Many of the World War II military facilities remain, and are still in use, in Georgia.	B-29 Liberty Ship Camp Stewart Fort Benning WAVES

SETTING THE STAGE

At the start of World War II, the United States needed to build up its military resources to fight a global war. Farmers grew more crops. Factories converted to manufacturing weapons and other wartime items. The United States needed its industrial might to fight, and win, the war. Georgia farmers and factories joined the war effort.

The army needed many soldiers. Americans from all walks of life joined or were called up to serve. Women were also an important part of the military. Georgians served in many different ways during the war.

At home, the new soldiers needed training and places to train. Military camps were built in Georgia because it had lots of open land, good year-round climate, and easy access to transportation.

▲ Men at Fort Benning prepare for a jump as a part of their paratrooper training.

The Nation and Georgia Mobilize

Even before the United States entered World War II, Americans had supported increasing the size of the military. The events in Europe, and Japan's efforts to control all of East Asia, were evidence that the world was a dangerous place.

National Mobilization The Selective Training and Service Act was signed into law in 1940. From November 1941 to the end of the war, the government called more than 10 million Americans to service. Another 5 million Americans volunteered. Over 300,000 Georgia men and women served in the military during World War II. Almost 7,000 died. They came from all across the state and from all backgrounds.

Women also played an important role in the military. While they did not serve in combat, women did serve in support positions, such as nurses, clerks, and pilots who transported planes. Their divisions were

Use your graphic organizer to put events in order as Georgia contributes to the war effort.

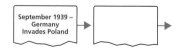

September 1939 – Germany Invades Poland

Reading History

A. Finding Main Ideas What roles did American women serve in the war effort?

known as the Women's Army Corps (WAC), the Women's Air Force Service Pilots (WASP), and the Navy's Women Appointed for Voluntary Emergency Service (WAVES), among others.

Airplanes One of the weapons that the United States needed was the airplane. Fighters, bombers, and transport planes had to be quickly built. Airplane factories sprang up in Georgia, California, Michigan, and other locations across the country.

In Georgia, Bell Aircraft built a factory in Marietta to assemble the **B-29** Superfortress bomber. The thousands of new jobs and millions of dollars in wages had a dramatic effect on the quiet little town. The first B-29s rolled off the assembly line in December 1943. At the height of production, almost 28,000 people worked at the 2-million-square-foot factory. More than 6,000 women had the opportunity to work at these higher-paying factory jobs.

Shipbuilding At the start of the war, the United States did not have enough ships to transport cargo to war zones. Many cargo ships had been sunk by German U-boats. The federal government called for the construction of hundreds of new ships.

In Georgia, the ports of Savannah and Brunswick had large shipbuilding operations that built 447-foot-long **Liberty Ships.** These ships carried soldiers and supplies to Europe and the Pacific. They were given names like the USS *Charles H. Herty,* USS *Clark Howell,* USS *Robert Toombs,* USS *Juliette Low,* USS *Henry W. Grady,* USS *John B. Gordon,* and USS *Martha Berry.* Georgia's famous citizens were well represented on the oceans of the world.

Almost 200 ships were built in Brunswick and Savannah between 1942 and the end of the war. Many workers came from Georgia farms to

▲ The B-29 was built in Marietta. Liberty Ships were built in Savannah and Brunswick.

work in the shipyards. The Southeastern Shipbuilding Corporation in Savannah hired over 800 new workers. In Brunswick, almost 16,000 men and women worked around the clock to build the ships that helped liberate the world from tyranny.

Agriculture   The federal government encouraged Georgia farmers to grow crops other than cotton. Food crops, dairy products, and meat to feed soldiers at home and overseas were in great demand. Peanuts were also an important crop used for oil.

Training Allied Troops in Georgia

At the beginning of World War II, the United States needed training bases. The Southern states offered plenty of land in areas with small numbers of people. Georgia and Texas had more training facilities than any other states in the nation.

Camp Stewart   Military leaders began to recognize that whoever controlled the skies had an advantage on the battlefield. Antiaircraft guns provided some protection to the troops from air raids. The federal government trained over 600,000 troops to serve in antiaircraft squads.

To train these troops, the military needed a new facility—one with a great deal of land because soldiers used live ammunition during practice. **Camp Stewart,** near Savannah, was selected. It covered 280,000 acres and spread over parts of 5 counties. By 1943, the camp had as many as 50,000 military personnel.

Camp Gordon and Fort Benning   Another military facility created during the war was Camp Gordon (now known as Fort Gordon). The military used it for infantry and tank training. It was also a camp for German and Italian POWs (prisoners of war). During World War II, **Fort Benning** in Columbus became the home of the First Infantry Division, Airborne Training, and Officer Candidate School for the Army. The fort sits on 180,000 acres.

Warner Robins Air Force Base   In August 1942, Warner Robins Air Force Base in Macon opened to train soldiers in airplane maintenance and other support jobs. Military planes were also serviced and maintained at the base.

French and British troops also used some Georgia training camps. British antiaircraft personnel trained at Camp Stewart near Savannah.

> **Reading History**
>
> **B. Finding Main Ideas**   What role did Georgia play in training Allied troops?

The British Royal Air Force (RAF) used the flight training schools at Cochran Field in Macon, Moody Field in Valdosta, and Turner Field in Albany to train RAF pilots. Although the climate was a little hot for most of the British, one trainee fondly remembered the friendliness he was shown by the people of Georgia.

PRIMARY SOURCE

The many invitations to Sunday dinner, which by now has almost become an institution, afforded to most of us our first experience of that most delectable dish of all—Fried Chicken. Memories of chicken served with corn on the cob and hot biscuits will live in our minds when the sordid aspects of this war have vanished.

quoted in James C. Mesco, Masters Thesis, Georgia College & State University

In addition to training facilities, many of these military bases served as POW camps. During the war, Georgia had 14 German and Italian POW camps. The largest was located at Camp Gordon. Prisoners received good treatment at the camps but were required to work. Many worked on farms harvesting cotton and peanuts. Others worked in lumber mills and at turpentine stills. They were a welcome sight to farmers who had problems finding workers.

Reading History

C. Summarizing
What kinds of training did the camps, bases, and colleges offer?

College Campuses In addition to camps that trained fighting soldiers, many college campuses served as training facilities. Soldiers learned all sorts of skills, such as nursing, handling supplies, planning, and flight training.

▼ Americans rallied behind the war effort. Women enlisted in the Armed Forces and served as pilots.

Colleges Used as Training Facilities With so many Americans involved in the war effort, fewer young people were going to college. The military paid to use their facilities. This meant that colleges and universities could remain open and pay their faculty.

Georgia Tech housed Marine Corps students, and offered Navy training classes and Army specialty training programs. University of Georgia students signed up for cadet training. The university also hosted a naval preflight program and an Army Specialized Training Program. In 1943, the university did not have enough civilian students left to field a football team and cancelled the season. More than 200 University of Georgia students lost their lives fighting in the war.

Women in the Military Many female military personnel were based in Georgia. Women pilots worked as test pilots and instrument observers. They also towed targets for antiaircraft training and shuttled planes and combat pilots between bases.

Women also trained at Georgia State College for Women (now Georgia College & State University) in Milledgeville. In 1943, the campus became a naval training school for **WAVES,** or Women Appointed for Volunteer Emergency Service. During the remaining two years of the war, over 15,000 women trained at the school. Women learned naval procedures and clerical work, freeing men for combat duty.

Georgians served in many ways in the military. In the next section, you will learn how Georgia civilians also made sacrifices and contributions to the war effort.

> **Reading History**
>
> **D. Drawing Conclusions**
> Why were women pilots and WAVES trained and employed in large numbers?

Section ③ Assessment

1. TERMS & NAMES

Explain the significance of:

a. B-29

b. Liberty Ship

c. Camp Stewart

d. Fort Benning

e. WAVES

2. TAKING NOTES

Use a cluster diagram like the one below to review the ways in which American women contributed to the war effort.

3. MAIN IDEAS

a. What role did Georgia play in the training of Allied troops?

b. What roles did women play in the military during World War II?

c. How did Georgia's industries contribute to the war effort?

d. In what way did college campuses aid the war effort?

4. CRITICAL THINKING

Analyzing Causes

Why was Georgia a good location for military training facilities?

Think About
• large spaces of open land
• small populations in rural areas
• accessible coastline

Language Arts/Technology Write a **diary entry** as if you are a Navy WAVES describing your life during training or make an **audio recording** of a radio interview.

The Impact of the War at Home

SETTING THE STAGE

Apart from the attack on Pearl Harbor and islands in the Pacific, no fighting took place in the United States. The impact of the war, however, was felt throughout American society. There were major changes in the social and economic fabric of America.

When the war in Europe and the Pacific ended, all Americans celebrated. They believed that World War II had been a "good war" because the United States and its allies had defeated a dangerous enemy—one intent on destroying democratic nations around the world.

Social and Economic Impact of the War

Although the actual fighting was far away, there were sober reminders of the conflict along the eastern shore of the United States. In the first half of 1942, German U-boats operated off the coast, looking for merchant ships to sink.

On April 8, 1942, the German U-boat 123 sank two oil tankers off the coast of Georgia near St. Simons Island. People there heard a tremendous explosion when a German torpedo hit the first ship, the SS *Oklahoma*. Local residents rescued some crew members, but 19 were killed.

The incident frightened people and made them realize how dangerous war could be even at home. After the war, a German U-boat commander told how he watched people playing on the beaches during the day and saw the lights of homes and businesses at night.

Life in Georgia   Georgians, and all Americans, supported the U.S. involvement in the war. People at home found ways to help the war effort. They collected and donated scrap metal, rubber, newspaper, and even cooking oil to be used to make weapons and other military equipment. They planted **victory gardens** to feed their own families so farmers' produce could be sent to the troops overseas.

▲ A private of the 24th Infantry stationed at Fort Benning tests a new piece of communication equipment.

 **Taking Notes**

Use your graphic organizer to put events in order as the impact of war is felt in Georgia.

September 1939 – Germany Invades Poland ➡ ➡

FALL 1943

Hastings'

Seeds · Plants · Bulbs

▲ Georgians ordered supplies for their victory gardens from Hasting's Seed Company in Atlanta. Ration books and coupons bought groceries they could not grow.

The war demanded major changes in the way people lived. "Use it up, wear it out, make it do, or do without" was a popular motto. To save resources for the troops, the federal government rationed items like gas, rubber tires, and food, especially meat and sugar.

Every month, families received **ration cards,** or coupon books that they used to get what they needed. When they had used up their limit they could not get any more until the next month. Gasoline and tires were in very short supply. One Atlanta teacher remembered that she took the bus because she did not have enough gas each month to drive to work.

> **PRIMARY SOURCE**
>
> I couldn't get gas. Teaching either was deemed not essential, or they thought that I could ride the bus.
>
> quoted in *Living Atlanta,* edited by Clifford Kuhn

Racial Tensions Changes in American society caused by the war sometimes caused friction. Much of the conflict happened when people traveled to areas of the country that had different social habits or ways of life. Some whites and most African-American soldiers from the North who found themselves in the South were puzzled by the system of segregation.

In Georgia, people sometimes refused to follow the segregation laws. African-American soldiers refused to give up their seats on buses. Others refused to accept insults and racial slurs thrown at them. Even some local African Americans found ways to protest segregation. For example, in 1944, a group of students from Savannah State College refused to give up their seats on a bus to white passengers.

These clashes were not happening only in the South. Conflicts among racial and ethnic groups occurred across the nation. In the summer of 1943, African Americans and whites clashed in New York, Detroit, Mobile, and other cities across the country. A riot broke out in Los Angeles between white soldiers and Latinos.

> **Reading History**
>
> **A. Finding Causes** What caused increasing racial tensions during the war?

There was also a growing friction between the races on military bases—especially in the Southern states. Soldiers arriving for training at Camp Gordon or Fort Benning were segregated by race. Outside the training camps, African-American troops were expected to follow the local customs, which included segregation. Sometimes, white Southern officers were assigned to all-black platoons or regiments. This created tense situations that often led to mistreatment of black troops or even outbreaks of violence.

Camp Stewart Riot In June 1943, a rumor spread through the African-American barracks at Camp Stewart that white military policemen had beaten a black woman to death. African-American soldiers had complained for months about mistreatment and disrespect from white officers. That feeling, combined with the rumor of violence, triggered the start of a riot.

Some African-American soldiers armed themselves and started toward the front gates of the camp. They encountered some white military police and opened fire. After both sides fired thousands of rounds of ammunition, one military police officer lay dead, another fatally wounded. The base commander convinced the African-American soldiers to lay down their arms. A major catastrophe had been avoided.

▲ Although both African Americans and whites fought in World War II, units were segregated. This military police officer was stationed at Fort Benning.

Georgia's Wartime Economy

Reading History

B. Finding Main Ideas How did war affect Georgia's economy?

Georgia's economy was still firmly rooted in agriculture during the war. Demand for food at the state's military training facilities increased Georgia farmers' profits.

Throughout the 1940s and into the 1950s, textiles remained the largest form of manufacturing in the state. Other types of industry, such as food processing and lumber, increased in importance. One Georgia company that benefited significantly from the war was Coca-Cola. The company won a government contract with the military to supply soldiers with the soft drink. Bottling factories were set up in Europe and in the Pacific. Having a Coca-Cola reminded soldiers of home.

Overall, the population of the South decreased in the first years of the war. Many left the countryside for high-paying jobs in defense industries in the North and West. Some Georgia towns and cities grew in population because they had new wartime factories. Savannah's population increased almost 30 percent—largely the result of shipbuilding.

The new factories and federal installations in Georgia meant that more people were earning a living from working in a factory or business. Georgia Representative Carl Vinson and Senator Richard B. Russell helped attract defense contracts and military facilities to the state. After the war, the number of factory jobs dropped. However, the war industries began a trend toward more industry in Georgia—and better opportunities to earn a living for Georgians.

The War Ends

In May 1945, Americans celebrated the end of the war in Europe. A few months later, people across the nation again poured into the streets to celebrate. In Atlanta, thousands of Georgians celebrated V-J Day, or Victory in Japan Day, on Peachtree Street.

Georgians Resume Their Lives Many young couples in America had been separated by the war. In early 1941 Barbara Woodall Taylor from Fairborn, Georgia, had met her future husband, Charles Taylor. Taylor had been in training at Camp Wheeler in

▼ Peachtree Street in Atlanta was the scene for celebrations such as V-E Day and V-J Day.

Macon. They dated for eight months before getting married. The army and the war kept them apart for the first years of their marriage. This was something that many couples endured throughout the war. Like many couples who were separated by war, Barbara and Charles kept in touch by writing letters. The letters often took weeks to be delivered.

PRIMARY SOURCE

Sometimes I wonder how I stand this, but every day I go right on with my working, eating, and sleeping, and then another day is gone and I love you twice as much as I did the day before. . . .

quoted in *Miss You: The World War II Letters of Barbara Wooddall Taylor and Charles E. Taylor*

Hoping for a Brighter Future   Happily, the Taylors were reunited at the end of the war. They and tens of thousands of young couples could now begin building their futures. Quite often, women decided to pursue the roles of wives and mothers full time at home after having worked in factories or other defense industries during the war. Many young men had interrupted their educations and wanted to return to school. Others took advantage of government programs for soldiers to start their college education.

Many things in Georgia, in the United States, and in the world changed dramatically after the war. In the next chapter, you will learn how those changes affected our state and our country.

Section 4 Assessment

1. TERMS & NAMES

Explain the significance of:

a. victory gardens

b. ration card

2. TAKING NOTES

Use a cluster diagram like the one shown below to review the ways Georgians at home contributed to the war effort.

Effort on the Home Front

3. MAIN IDEAS

a. How did World War II affect people in Georgia?

b. What caused racial tensions to increase during the war?

c. How did the war affect the economy of Georgia?

d. What contributions did Georgians make to the war effort?

4. CRITICAL THINKING

Analyzing Causes

Why did Georgia's economy improve during the war?

Think About
• the geographic location of Georgia
• the industry already established in Georgia
• Georgia's agricultural products

 ACTIVITY -OPTIONS-   **Art/Language Arts**   Design a **poster** or write a **newspaper advertisement** that encourages recycling, rationing, and collecting supplies to contribute to the war effort.

VISUAL SUMMARY

World War II

1936
Germany and Italy form Axis.

- Japan enters alliance with Germany and Italy.
- Germany invades France.
- Battle of Britain.
1940

1939
Germany invades Poland.

1941
- Hitler invades Soviet Union.
- Japan attacks Pearl Harbor.

1942
Allies invade North Africa.

1943
Allies invade Italy.

- Allies invade Europe at Normandy.
- Liberation of Paris.
- Battle of the Bulge.
1945

- Germany surrenders.
- United States drops atomic bombs in Japan.
- Japan surrenders.
1945

TERMS & NAMES

Briefly explain the significance of the following.

1. fascism
2. Adolf Hitler
3. Pearl Harbor
4. D-Day
5. V-E Day
6. concentration camp
7. V-J Day
8. Camp Stewart
9. WAVES
10. ration card

REVIEW QUESTIONS

The War Begins (pages 393–398)

1. What factors led to the rise of Mussolini and Hitler?
2. Why did Japan enter an alliance with Germany?
3. What did the Lend-Lease Act allow?

Fighting the War (pages 399–403)

4. What was D-Day and why was it significant?
5. What was the strategy of island hopping?
6. Why did Truman drop the atomic bombs on Japan?

Georgia's Contribution to the War (pages 404–408)

7. How did Georgia contribute to the war effort?
8. How did the B-29 bomber affect Georgia?

The Impact of the War at Home (pages 409–413)

9. How did the war affect Georgia's economy?
10. How did the war lead to racial tensions?

CRITICAL THINKING

1. USING YOUR NOTES: SEQUENCING EVENTS

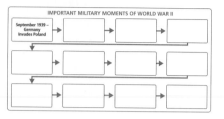

Using your completed chart, answer the questions below.

a. What is the first event to directly involve the United States?
b. Which event was most important and why?

2. ANALYZING LEADERSHIP

Do you agree or disagree with Truman's decision to drop the atomic bombs? Why?

3. APPLYING CITIZENSHIP SKILLS

How did citizens play a role in supporting the war effort?

4. THEME: AMERICA IN THE WORLD

Do you think the policy of isolationism was good or bad for America? Why?

5. DRAWING CONCLUSIONS

How did the war years affect women's roles in society?

INTERACT with HISTORY

Would you be willing to risk your life to protect people in another country? Why or why not?

Use the map and your knowledge of world history to answer questions 1 through 3.

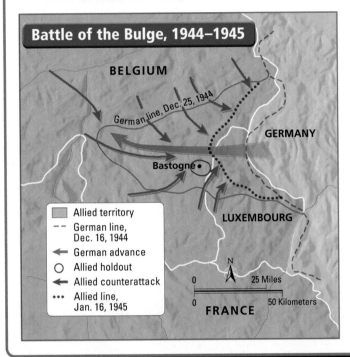

Battle of the Bulge, 1944–1945

BELGIUM

German line, Dec. 25, 1944

GERMANY

Bastogne•

LUXEMBOURG

N

0   25 Miles

0   50 Kilometers

FRANCE

Allied territory
- - German line, Dec. 16, 1944
← German advance
○ Allied holdout
← Allied counterattack
••• Allied line, Jan. 16, 1945

1. About how many miles westward had the Germans advanced by Christmas 1944?

   A. 25 miles
   B. 50 miles
   C. 75 miles
   D. 100 miles

2. When did the battle end?

   A. December 16, 1944
   B. December 25, 1944
   C. January 16, 1945
   D. Can't tell from the map

3. In which countries was the battle fought?

   A. Germany and Belgium
   B. France and Belgium
   C. Belgium and Luxembourg
   D. Germany and Luxembourg

TEST PRACTICE
CLASSZONE.COM

ALTERNATIVE ASSESSMENT

1. WRITING A DIARY

Imagine you are a woman who has found a job in Georgia in an aircraft factory or a shipyard during the war. Write a diary entry describing the changes the war has brought to your life.

2. COOPERATIVE LEARNING

Work with a team to create a news show about the experiences of Georgians at home or abroad during World War II. Choose a specific year between 1941 and 1945 and a specific location, such as a hospital, factory, or battle front.

- In your team, divide up the roles of anchor, reporter, and interviewees.
- Write a script for your role.
- Conduct your "broadcast" in front of the class.

INTEGRATED TECHNOLOGY ACTIVITY

1. PREPARING AN ELECTRONIC PRESENTATION

Use the Internet, your library, and a computer to research the Holocaust and prepare your own virtual Holocaust museum. To create your museum, you might do the following.

- Examine more in depth one of the Nazi concentration camps in Europe.
- Research individual experiences of the Holocaust by reading accounts of Elie Wiesel, Anne Frank, or Gerda Weissman Klein.
- Use photographs and other visuals, including captions.
- Create a map depicting the locations of the concentration camps.
- Examine the U.S. response to the Holocaust.

RESEARCH LINKS
CLASSZONE.COM

Changes in Georgia and America 1945–1963

As soldiers returned from World War II, housing was in short supply. Developments such as Atlanta's Fairview Terrace were built quickly.

1941
Governor Eugene Talmadge's segregation practices create controversy.

1945
Flannery O'Connor graduates from Georgia State College for Women.

1947
Helen Douglas Mankin is first woman elected to Congress from Georgia.

GEORGIA
USA

1945

1944
G.I. Bill is enacted.

1945
United Nations is established.

1948
Harry S Truman is elected president.

In the 1950s, American technology produced a flood of consumer goods. These included cars and houses in new suburbs across the country. You and your family have moved to a new house in a growing suburb—which some people think of as the American Dream.

What do you think is the American Dream?

WHAT DO YOU THINK?

- How might the American Dream be connected to prosperity?

- How might the American Dream involve helping others?

- How might the American Dream be connected to freedom? democracy? justice?

For more information on this chapter, visit . . .

RESEARCH LINKS
CLASSZONE.COM

1953
Delta Air Lines merges with Chicago and Southern Air Lines.

1956
Lake Sidney Lanier is finished.

1962
Federal court rules county-unit system unconstitutional.

1954

1963

1952
Dwight D. Eisenhower is elected president.

1954
Congress investigates McCarthy's charge of communism in the U.S. Army.

1960
John F. Kennedy is elected president.

1962
Kennedy demands Soviet Union remove weapons in Cuba.

Reading Strategy:
Analyzing Causes and Recognizing Effects

What Do You Know?

What comes to mind when you think about the fifties? What do you know about how life in America and Georgia changed following World War II?

THINK ABOUT
• what you've learned about the 1950s from movies, television, or books you've read
• the effects of nuclear weapons and communism in the world today

What Do You Want to Know?

What questions do you have about American culture and politics in the Cold War years? Record those questions in your notebook before you read the chapter.

Analyzing Causes and Recognizing Effects

A single event in history can have many causes. And one action or cause may result in many effects. Analyzing cause-and-effect relationships can help you understand more of what you read about history. Use the chart below to list the effects of the end of World War II in America and in Georgia.

 See Skillbuilder Handbook, page 551.

Taking Notes

	Effects in America	Effects in Georgia
End of World War II		

Postwar America

MAIN IDEA	WHY IT MATTERS NOW	TERMS & NAMES
The years after World War II were a time of rapid change in American society.	The patterns of how we live today can be traced back to this period.	G.I. Bill baby boomer suburb Flannery O'Connor Carson McCullers

SETTING THE STAGE

The Great Depression and World War II had a tremendous impact on the United States. From October 1929, when the American economy crashed, to August 1945, when World War II ended, Americans endured almost 16 years of economic troubles and warfare. They wanted to pick up where they had left off and get on with their lives.

That was not always possible. Many things had changed. People faced a new world with new ways of living and working. Americans were generally optimistic about the future. They were eager to enjoy the economic prosperity of the late 1940s and 1950s.

▲ From 1945 to the mid-1950s, America needed 16 million new homes. Building many houses with the same floor plan made construction faster and cheaper.

The Baby Boom Generation

In June 1945, the population of the United States was approximately 140,000,000. More than 12 million Americans served in the military at that time. Among them were 320,000 Georgians. Most would be returning to the United States and civilian life in a short time.

These men and women would want to find nice places to live and good jobs. Many would want to return to school and finish out their education. Like soldiers across the country, many took advantage of the Serviceman's Readjustment Act of 1944. Also known as the **G.I. Bill,** it provided veterans with free education, assistance with mortgages for homes, and help starting small businesses.

Almost eight million veterans went to school on the G.I. Bill. Most went to technical schools and learned a trade. More than two million chose to attend colleges and universities. By 1949, 40 percent of all college

Taking Notes

Use your chart to list the effects of the end of World War II on American and Georgian society.

	Effects in America	Effects in Georgia
End of World War II		

students were war veterans. Schools had a difficult time providing housing and even teachers to cover the huge increases in enrollment.

Educating the Baby Boom Generation The U.S. birth rate increased dramatically when military personnel returned to civilian life. Americans born between 1946 and 1964 are called **baby boomers.**

The jump in the number of children created a new problem—how to educate them. The country had too few schools and too few teachers.

Then, in 1957, the Soviet Union launched the first space satellite, called Sputnik. It convinced Americans that the Soviet Union had an education advantage over the United States, especially in science and mathematics.

The country had to catch up and pull ahead—it was a matter of national security. Congress enacted legislation offering low-cost college loans to students who wanted to become teachers. It also gave federal funds to public schools for new laboratories and textbooks to aid in teaching the sciences and mathematics.

Housing the Baby Boomers The G.I. Bill also provided for low-cost federal loans for new homes. Many of these homes were located in the **suburbs,** outside the city center. The number of people living in the suburbs grew by 46 percent in the 1950s.

The Consumer Nation of the 1950s and 1960s

Automobiles
During the Great Depression and World War II, most Americans were unable to buy a new car. After the war, they made up for that. In the 1930s, most families had one car. By the 1950s, many families had two. Automobiles were big and powerful. There was little concern about gas mileage—the emphasis was on power. Most automobiles were equipped with large V-8 engines. Automobile safety was not a major concern. Chevrolets, Fords, Pontiacs, and Cadillacs were the American automobiles of choice. There were very few foreign-made vehicles.

Television
In the late 1940s, a new form of communication was introduced to Americans. By the mid-1950s, television was the major form of communication and entertainment in America. In 1950, only about 9 percent of homes had televisions. By 1960, almost 90 percent of households had at least one television.

Reading History

A. Summarizing
How did the growth of suburbs contribute to segregation?

Although the suburbs represented the growing prosperity of the middle class, they also represented the segregation of American society. By 1960, over 37 million people lived in the suburbs, but very few minorities lived there.

Many African Americans could not afford to live in the suburbs. And African Americans faced the problem of racism. People in the suburbs often refused to sell their homes to African Americans and other racial and ethnic groups.

Popular Culture in the 1950s

The American economy was booming. Families had more leisure time. By the mid-1950s, entertainment was becoming big business.

Music   In the 1950s, many teenagers rejected the music of their parents. They embraced a new type of music that combined rhythm and blues with mainstream white music. The new form of music came to be known as rock 'n' roll. Artists like Elvis Presley, Fats Domino, Little Richard, Chuck Berry, and Jerry Lee Lewis were popular.

Jazz was also prevalent in the urban areas of America. The crooning sounds of Perry Como, Frank Sinatra, Nat King Cole, and Rosemary Clooney represented other forms of popular music of the era.

Convenience Products
Americans in the 1950s wanted things that were convenient—that would save them time and effort. Products like TV dinners and fast food restaurants such as McDonald's, Kentucky Fried Chicken, and Burger King became popular.

Clothing
People wore clothes made from new manufactured materials like rayon and nylon. Most people dressed conservatively. College students dressed for class, men in coats and ties and women in dresses. Blue jeans became an important part of Americans' leisure wear and came to represent a youthful rebellion against the more formal fashions of the period.

Sports
Many Americans were earning more money. They also had more leisure time. As a result, spectator sports increased in popularity during the 1950s and 1960s. Americans crowded into stadiums to watch baseball and football. Basketball was becoming a popular sport. Increasingly, television brought these sports into more people's lives.

▲ Georgians such as Otis Redding
(left) and Ray Charles (right) gained
a national audience for their music.

Georgia Musicians   Many Georgians contributed to the musical scene in the 1950s and 1960s. Ray Charles was born in Albany, Georgia, in 1930. One of his most famous songs is "Georgia on My Mind." Brenda Lee was born in Atlanta. She signed her first recording contract when she was only 11 years old. Gladys Knight, also from Atlanta, headed a group called Gladys Knight and the Pips. Otis Redding, of Dawson, toured with a backup group called Booker T. and the MGs through the 1960s. His most famous song, "Sittin' on the Dock of the Bay," was released shortly after his death in 1967.

Little Richard grew up in the poor section of Macon. He got his big break with the release of his song "Tutti Frutti." He was inducted into the Rock and Roll Hall of Fame in 1986. James Brown, raised in Augusta, often referred to himself as the "Hardest Working Man in Show Business" and is also known as the "Godfather of Soul."

The Role of Women   As more people moved to the suburbs, women's roles in the family began to change. Many Americans believed that a woman's natural role was that of mother, devoted wife, and keeper of the house. While many women accepted this idea, roles began to change. More women went to college. More women were working outside the home, although the idea of a woman having a long-term career was still rare.

Literature   In the years after the war, many Americans believed their society and country were the best in the world. But some writers saw problems in American society. Their writing reflected their concerns.

Ernest Hemingway, J. D. Salinger, and John Steinbeck were well-known American writers during this time. Many of them wrote about the difficulties people faced in a fast-paced, quickly changing America.

Reading History

B. Drawing Conclusions
Why were novels about difficulties faced in a fast-paced world so popular?

Georgia Writers   A number of Georgians contributed to the American literary scene. **Flannery O'Connor** is perhaps the best-known writer from Georgia. O'Connor was born in Savannah. She graduated from Georgia State College for Women (now Georgia College & State University) in 1945. She died of lupus in 1964, but during her short life, she wrote 2 novels and 31 short stories.

Carson McCullers was born and raised in Columbus, Georgia. At the age of 23, she published her first novel, *The Heart Is a Lonely Hunter*. It was made into a movie, as was her second novel. McCullers' stories are set in the South, full of tragedy and danger, which fascinated Americans of this time. The style became known as Southern Gothic.

America was changing. The world was changing as well. As Americans went about their daily lives and recovered from World War II, they did not feel completely secure. You will learn more about the United States' focus on issues of national security in the next section.

▲ Flannery O'Connor and Carson McCullers wrote about people in the small towns of the South.

Section 1 Assessment

1. TERMS & NAMES
Explain the significance of:

a. G.I. Bill

b. baby boomer

c. suburb

d. Flannery O'Connor

e. Carson McCullers

2. TAKING NOTES
Create a web like the one below to examine the way life was changing for the baby boom generation.

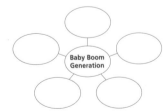

Baby Boom Generation

3. MAIN IDEAS
a. How did the G.I. Bill help veterans when they returned home?

b. What was different about the music of the 1950s?

c. What was it like to be a consumer in the late 1940s and 1950s?

4. CRITICAL THINKING
Contrasting

Do you think the American lifestyle has changed significantly since the 1950s? Explain.

Think About
• expectations about suburban/urban living
• changes in transportation and workplace

ACTIVITY -OPTIONS-

Technology/Music   Research one aspect of music in the 1950s, and either plan a **Web page** to share your information, or write your own **song** that fits this time period.

2

Cold War America

MAIN IDEA	WHY IT MATTERS NOW	TERMS & NAMES
Americans believed that new enemies, especially the Soviet Union, threatened their existence.	The United States and its allies won the Cold War between communism and democratic nations in 1989 when the Soviet Union collapsed.	Cold War nuclear arms race iron curtain containment Joseph R. McCarthy Cuban missile crisis

SETTING THE STAGE

In World War II the United States and its allies had defeated an enemy that threatened the entire world. But there was still concern about the security of America. Many people believed communism posed a great threat. The Soviet Union, China, and their friends became America's newest enemies. The hostile relationships and fierce competition between communist countries and the United States was referred to as the **Cold War**.

When American leaders realized the tremendous power of the atomic bomb, they wanted to keep it out of the hands of their enemies. They failed. Americans worried about the potential for "total annihilation"—an atomic war that would destroy the entire planet. While Americans were enjoying prosperity, they worried about the threat of atomic destruction.

▲ The balance of power in the world changed as other countries learned how to make atomic bombs.

The Atomic Bomb

The United States did not want to share the knowledge of how to make atomic bombs with other countries, including its allies. President Truman and his advisors created a government agency, the Atomic Energy Commission, to protect the secrets of building nuclear weapons.

Despite these efforts, other countries learned how to build atomic bombs. In 1949, the Soviet Union detonated a nuclear bomb. Now the country's newest enemy also had the most destructive weapon in the history of humanity.

The competition for atomic weapons between the Soviet Union and the United States called the **nuclear arms race** had begun. Americans became concerned that a nuclear war would devastate the entire world. Both sides would be destroyed—there would be no winner in a nuclear war.

Taking Notes

Use your chart to list the effects World War II had on Cold War America.

	Effects in America	Effects in Georgia
End of World War II		

▲ Families prepared for the possibility of a nuclear bomb. Some built shelters and stocked them with enough supplies for a few days.

Civil Defense   Americans prepared defenses against nuclear attack as well as they could. Children practiced nuclear attack drills in school. For example, they were taught to "duck and cover" under their desks if an atomic explosion occurred. People built fallout shelters in their backyards. Life continued as normal, but the possibility of nuclear attack was in the back of the minds of most Americans.

Fighting a Hot and Cold War

The United States was the greatest military power in the world. But the nation was faced with what many believed was a new enemy—communism. Fighting this new enemy was not only a physical war. It was also a psychological and diplomatic war.

Postwar Japan   The United States was successful in helping rebuild its former enemies, particularly Japan and Germany. As military governor of Japan, General Douglas MacArthur implemented programs and reforms that not only rebuilt Japan but also changed its economic, political, and governmental systems. Japan was now a democracy.

The United States trained the Japanese in methods used in American industry. Japanese companies eagerly adopted these new ideas and techniques. Within a couple of decades, some of Japan's industries, such as automobile manufacturing, became successful worldwide.

The Iron Curtain   The Allied Powers—the United States, France, England, and the Soviet Union—occupied Germany after the war. The Soviet Union controlled about half of Germany and half of the city of Berlin. It was unwilling to give up control over this territory. The Soviet Union also tried to control other countries in central and eastern Europe and in the Middle East.

In 1946, Soviet leader Joseph Stalin announced that he was no longer willing to cooperate with the Allied Powers. He wanted to concentrate on building the power and influence of the Soviet Union. The Soviet Union refused to communicate with its former allies. Former Prime Minister Winston Churchill declared that Stalin had erected an **iron curtain,** shutting off the Soviet Union from the rest of the world.

Marshall Plan   The United States believed it was critical to get European countries back on their feet economically. American leaders believed that the Great Depression of the 1930s had been one of the causes of World War II.

Secretary of State George Marshall introduced the Marshall Plan to rebuild Europe. The plan included 17 western European nations and the Soviet Union. But the Soviets were against the idea of rebuilding Germany and did not want to participate. When the United States began sending aid to Germany, the Soviets blocked access to the western half of Berlin.

Containment   To maintain security after the war, the United States created NATO (North Atlantic Treaty Organization) in 1949. This was an alliance of 11 European countries and the United States that promised to help each other in case of an invasion by the Soviet Union. NATO was a major part of the plan to contain, or stop, the spread of

Reading History

B. Finding Main Ideas How did the relationship between the United States and the Soviet Union change after World War II?

Europe after World War II, 1955

Member of NATO, 1955
Member of Warsaw Pact, 1955

GEOGRAPHY SKILLBUILDER Interpreting Maps
1. **Location** *What westernmost country in Europe was a member of NATO?*
2. **Region** *Which NATO members directly bordered the Warsaw Pact countries?*

communism. **Containment** became the foreign policy of the United States for the next 40 years.

The Soviet Union and other Communist Eastern European countries began to feel threatened by the United States and NATO Alliance. In 1955, these countries signed the Warsaw Pact. In this treaty, they promised to defend each other if they were attacked. Although NATO still exists, the Warsaw Pact was dissolved in 1991.

Threats From Within

Reading History

C. Drawing Conclusions
Why was communism regarded as a threat by the United States?

As early as 1940, the federal government was concerned about the internal threat from communism. The House Un-American Activities Committee (HUAC) investigated charges that communists were influencing all aspects of society—unions, government, even the movies.

▼ Joseph McCarthy (standing) conducts hearings of the House Un-American Activities Committee.

Joseph R. McCarthy In the 1950s, the effort to find communists in the United States continued. The most famous public official to speak against communism was the Republican Senator **Joseph R. McCarthy** of Wisconsin. McCarthy conducted hearings to expose communists in the government. Often, though, McCarthy had no evidence to support his charges. He ruined many people's lives and careers. McCarthy's accusations went on for almost four years.

In April 1954, Congress called a special hearing to investigate McCarthy's charges about communism in the Army. McCarthy could not support the accusations he had made. The hearings turned public opinion against McCarthy and ended his political career.

The Korean Conflict

In 1947, Mao Tse Tung, a communist, took control of China. The United States and her allies saw the spread of communism in Asia as a threat to democratic nations and freedom around the globe.

On June 24, 1950, Communist-controlled North Korea invaded South Korea. The United States, with the support of the United Nations, sent troops to stop the invasion. China entered the fighting because it believed that the United States was threatening its territory.

After three years of fighting, neither side had won. Since no formal declaration of war had been issued, it was considered a "conflict," not a war. On July 27, 1953, both sides signed a ceasefire that ended the fighting and established a new border between the two Koreas. Almost

▲ In 1960, at age 43, John F. Kennedy became the youngest U.S. president ever elected.

110,000 U.S. soldiers had been killed or wounded or were missing in action.

The Kennedy Years

In 1960, the national political scene changed. People looked to new leaders to take them into the future. The Democratic candidate for president was a young Senator from Massachusetts— John F. Kennedy. His opponent was Republican Vice-President Richard M. Nixon. Kennedy won the election.

As a candidate, Kennedy had promised to protect America from communism, keep the economy healthy, and support the rights of all Americans. He wanted to take Americans to a "New Frontier," in which America's social problems would be solved. But his efforts to fight communism around the world often prevented him from focusing on domestic social issues.

Bay of Pigs   The Communist regime of Fidel Castro on the island of Cuba, close to the United States, caused great concern. Soon after taking office, Kennedy gave his support to a group of Cuban nationals who wanted to overthrow Castro. The CIA (Central Intelligence Agency) supplied the anti-Castro forces with weapons and training. In April 1961, these forces landed in Cuba at a place called the Bay of Pigs. The Cuban nationals were captured and the invasion failed.

The Berlin Wall   The next crisis came in August 1961. The Soviet Union was concerned about the number of people leaving Soviet-held East Berlin by walking across to West Berlin. Although West Berlin was part of West Germany, the city of Berlin was surrounded by East Germany. (See the map on page 426.) Nikita Khrushchev, the new leader of the Soviet Union, ordered a wall built around the communist section of Berlin to keep its people from leaving. The wall divided Berlin.

Cuban Missile Crisis   The worst foreign diplomacy problem Kennedy faced was the **Cuban missile crisis.** In the autumn of 1962, American spy planes detected Soviet missiles in Cuba. From that location, missiles armed with nuclear weapons could easily strike a large portion of the United States.

Kennedy blocked Soviet ships from reaching Cuba. He then demanded that the Soviets remove all weapons in Cuba. The "missiles of October" caused great concern. Military troops at Fort Stewart in Georgia were sent to Florida to set up defenses against a possible attack from Cuba. For 13 days there was a real possibility of a nuclear war between the United

Reading History

D. Making Inferences Why did Kennedy offer weapons and training to Cuban nationals?

States and the Soviet Union. Khrushchev finally agreed to remove the weapons, but only if the United States promised not to invade Cuba.

Vietnam   The Kennedy administration also faced a difficult international situation in Vietnam. This country had been divided into North and South Vietnam. North Vietnam's leader was Ho Chi Minh. The United States considered him a communist threat to South Vietnam. America had been contributing money, weapons, and military advisors to South Vietnam's government to help defend the country.

Civil Rights   In 1954, the U.S. Supreme Court had ruled in *Brown* v. *Board of Education* that segregation in public schools was unconstitutional. States where segregation had been the law were ordered to open all public facilities to all people. But many Southern states refused to abide by the Supreme Court's ruling.

In 1957, the Little Rock, Arkansas, school board made plans to integrate. Nine African-American students were to enroll at Central High School. The governor used the National Guard to prevent them from entering the school. After three weeks, President Eisenhower ordered the 101st Airborne into Little Rock to keep the peace and protect the students as they entered the school.

Some Georgia politicians continued to fight desegregation. They argued that the federal government did not have the right to tell the state how to conduct its own affairs. This is known as the states' rights position. Political figures in Georgia, such as Lester Maddox, declared that desegregation, or integration, would never happen as long as they were in charge.

▼ Thurgood Marshall (center) sits with African-American students who integrated schools in Little Rock, Arkansas, in 1957.

However, an increasing number of whites recognized that desegregation was going to happen. They worked with African Americans to make sure that the transformation from a segregated society to an integrated society went smoothly. Many business owners, directors of large corporations, and progressive politicians in Georgia did not want to see any violence in the state. They realized that it would be bad for business.

▲ Kennedy's flag-draped casket is drawn through the streets of Washington, D.C., during the slain leader's funeral procession.

Reading History

E. Drawing Conclusions
How would violence be bad for business?

President Kennedy Is Assassinated   On November 22, 1963, President Kennedy was assassinated while riding through the streets of Dallas, Texas. News of his death shocked the nation. Even his political opponents were stunned that he had been killed.

The entire nation mourned Kennedy. He represented a new era in America—one filled with confidence, hope, and a commitment to changing things for the better. In his inauguration speech, Kennedy had challenged: Americans "ask not what your country can do for you, ask what you can do for your country." Kennedy gave his life for his country. His death made people realize that there was still much to do.

As the country strengthened its position in the world, the economy at home grew stronger also. The standard of living increased across the United States, as well as in Georgia, as you will read in the next section.

Background

The man accused of shooting Kennedy, Lee Harvey Oswald, was killed two days later by another assassin.

Section 2 Assessment

1. TERMS & NAMES

Explain the significance of:

a. Cold War

b. nuclear arms race

c. iron curtain

d. containment

e. Joseph R. McCarthy

f. Cuban missile crisis

2. TAKING NOTES

In a chart, explain the goals of the Cold War programs listed below.

Program	Goal
Containment Policy	
Marshall Plan	
NATO	

3. MAIN IDEAS

a. Why did the U.S. try to keep information about nuclear weapons to itself?

b. How did relations between the United States and the Soviet Union change after World War II?

c. How did HUAC represent the mood of the United States about communism?

4. CRITICAL THINKING

Forming Opinions

Do you think an exaggerated fear of communism could occur again? Explain.

Think About
• relations between the U.S. and Russia today
• U.S. attitudes toward opposing views
• beliefs about communism

 ACTIVITY -OPTIONS-   **Science/Art**   Research peacetime uses of nuclear energy. Prepare a **report** or draw a **poster** that argues for or against nuclear energy.

Georgia's Growing Economy

3

MAIN IDEA	WHY IT MATTERS NOW	TERMS & NAMES
Georgia's farms and cities went through significant changes from the 1940s through the 1960s.	The changes of the 1940s through the 1960s created the world that Georgians live in today.	Operation Dixie Lake Sidney Lanier

SETTING THE STAGE

World War II affected Georgia's economy tremendously. The population of the state also changed. Across the nation people moved about looking for better paying jobs. Some Georgians moved out of state, but people from nearby states began to move in to work in the defense industries and military bases.

World War II also changed where people lived in the state. Fewer workers were needed on the farms. As jobs in the rural areas decreased, people moved to towns and cities to find new jobs. And, people who lived in cities began to move to the suburbs.

Georgia's business and industry also began to change. More factories opened in urban areas. New methods of farming changed agriculture. Life in Georgia, and the nation, was permanently changed by the war.

▲ During the 1950s and 1960s, many people moved to the urban centers of Georgia. Five Points, in Atlanta, was a bustling business district.

Population Trends in Georgia

Over one million Georgians left the state during the 1940s. Many of those were young adults seeking new opportunities elsewhere. After the war, many people moved to Georgia.

Shifting Populations Large numbers of African-American and white farmers and sharecroppers moved to the cities between the 1930s and the 1960s. They could no longer make a living off the land or find work as farm laborers.

In the rural areas of Georgia, the population fell dramatically. In 1940, 1,368,000 people lived on 216,000 farms in the state. By 1970, only 228,000 people lived on fewer than 64,430 Georgia farms. In 1940, almost 60,000 African-American farmers lived in Georgia. By 1970, that number had fallen to 5,500.

Taking Notes

Use your chart to list the effects World War II had on Georgia's economy.

	Effects in America	Effects in Georgia
End of World War II		

Urban Growth   The loss of population was offset by people moving into Georgia from other states. Many came because of the high-paying jobs in defense industry factories. Others came to work in industries that serviced military bases and growing urban areas. Most settled in urban areas like Atlanta or at military facilities like Fort Stewart near Savannah. Many had high levels of skills and education that helped improve the Georgia economy.

As cities in Georgia grew, public agencies such as police, water, and health were strained. City governments could not keep up with the growth. They did not have the money to expand public services or build new schools or roads. Some urban residents began moving into the suburbs. Many were middle class or upper class people who thought that schools and other services would be better in the suburbs.

Reading History

A. Summarizing
How does urban growth lead to suburban growth?

Changes in Business and Industry

After the war, Georgia's economy expanded rapidly. Georgians were making more money than ever before. From 1940 to 1950, the average yearly income in Georgia rose from $350 to $1,000. The growth was largely due to an increase in the middle class in Georgia. However, most Georgia factory workers and farmers still earned less than the national average.

Managers, professionals, owners, and executives in wholesale and retail businesses, finance, insurance, real estate, and other services formed about 20 percent of Georgia's workforce in 1940. By 1960, their number had increased to about 33 percent.

▼ The Savannah Sugar Refining Corporation loads processed sugar onto boats waiting at its dock on the Savannah River.

Urban Centers Most of the prosperity in Georgia during this time was centered in and around the city of Atlanta. More than one third of the new factory jobs in the late 1940s and 1950s were concentrated in the three counties of metropolitan Atlanta: Cobb, DeKalb, and Fulton.

The port of Savannah was also an economic center. Savannah had been importing goods and exporting the natural resources of Georgia and the Southeastern United States since before the Civil War. It has continued to grow since World War II, and it is now one of the largest ports in the United States.

Federal spending also contributed to the state's economy. During the war, the state's 12 military bases were staffed with almost 80,000 military personnel and employed over 39,000 civilians.

Industry Manufacturing, especially automobile assembly and carpet production, remained an important economic force in the state. In the late 1940s, General Motors opened an assembly factory in Doraville, near Atlanta. Ford opened a new factory in Hapeville. Dalton became the center of Georgia's textile industry. Cabin Crafts and Shaw Industries produced rugs, robes, and bedspreads. In the 1950s, local industries began mass production of carpets. Other businesses, such as banking, transportation, public utilities, and real estate, grew in importance during this time.

Labor Unions Labor unions renewed their efforts to organize after World War II. **Operation Dixie** was the name given to the effort by the CIO (Congress of Industrial Organizations) to set up unions in the South. Operation Dixie's Southern headquarters was in Atlanta. Attempts to organize textile workers often met with violence and intimidation. Striking workers were beaten and organizers were run out of town. The Textile Workers' Union of America actually lost membership in the South during this time. Eventually, unions would become more common in Georgia as more manufacturing and industry moved in.

Reading History

B. Making Inferences Who was keeping labor unions out of the South?

NOW & THEN

Modern Benefits Won by Unions

Today, many Americans work 40 hours per week—perhaps 8–5, Monday through Friday. Contrast this situation with the 10- to 12-hour days of most 19th century workers. The 8-hour day was one benefit won by labor unions. Other benefits unions won include workers' compensation (insurance that pays for injuries received on the job), pensions, and paid vacation.

Unions continue to fight to improve the lives of working Americans. In recent years, they have tried to increase benefits for part-time and temporary workers. They have also fought for safety standards to prevent injuries, such as carpal tunnel syndrome, which affects many workers who use computers.

Changes in Agriculture

Rural Georgia changed dramatically after World War II. The prosperity during wartime that had meant greater profits and a higher standard of living for most Georgians, even sharecroppers, came to an end. People began leaving their small farms for work in towns and cities.

Mechanization   Farmers began to rely on tractors for their farm-work. In 1940, there were 10,000 tractors in Georgia. By 1960, there were almost 100,000 tractors—enough for at least one tractor for every farm in Georgia. With tractors to till the soil and harvesting machines to bring in the crops, landowners did not need as many sharecroppers to work their land. Many sharecroppers and renters were forced off the land by the increasing mechanization of farming. Those who stayed faced hard times. Most families on small farms earned much less than the average Georgia family.

Reading History

C. Recognizing Effects   How did the use of tractors affect sharecroppers negatively?

Dairy and Livestock   Before the war, raising dairy cattle had not been profitable in Georgia and the South. There was a lack of money to invest in the industry. There were also not enough refrigerated tanker trucks to transport the milk to urban areas for processing and sale. During the war, however, improvements in transportation and growing markets made raising cows a good way to earn a living. Local farmers supplied dairy and meat to nearby cities and military bases, as well as troops overseas.

Landowners and farmers in north Georgia turned to commercial poultry. In 1950, there were over 7,300 poultry farms in Georgia. By the late 1960s, Georgia poultry farms produced over 2 billion eggs and sold over 400 million chickens for processing each year. Today, the poultry industry is the largest part of the state's agricultural production.

Improved Farming Methods   New strains of more productive crops, new chemicals to control weeds and pests, and better organization of farms all contributed to improved farm production. Farmers produced greater amounts with less labor. But it also cost more to run

▼ Poultry farms such as this one in Talmo, Georgia, helped make Hall County the "Poultry Capital of the World."

Reading History

D. Summarizing
How did mechanization and improved farming methods drive small farms out of business?

a farm than it had before. Most sharecroppers and small farmers did not have the money to farm this way. Many small farmers sold their properties, which were merged into larger farming operations.

Crop Diversity Agriculture was becoming less important during this time. By 1970, it accounted for only about 3.5 percent of the state's gross product (the amount of value of all goods and services). In addition, what Georgians grew on their farms changed from 1950 to 1970, as the agricultural economy grew more diverse. Cotton became less important; by 1960, only 10 percent of Georgia's farmland was used to grow cotton. In 1970, peanuts brought in more money than cotton. By the 1980s, poultry farming and livestock would make up almost half of Georgia's farming. Peanuts, soybeans, and tobacco accounted for about 27 percent, and cotton—the former "king"—represented only 2.5 percent of Georgia's agricultural product. In spite of these changes, though, farmers and landowners still faced a difficult time making a living.

Changes in Urban Georgia

Atlanta, Savannah, Augusta, Macon, and Columbus were centers of economic growth from the late 1940s to the 1960s. As people and businesses moved into these metropolitan areas, more office buildings, warehouses, shopping centers, houses, and apartments were needed. There was also a growing demand for basic services like water, electricity, sewerage, medical care, education, and law enforcement.

Transportation The city of Atlanta had grown into the major hub for railroad lines in the southeast. It also became a major crossroads for the new Interstate highway system built by the federal government in the late 1950s and 1960s. I-75, I-20, and I-85 intersected in Atlanta—making it one of the most important ground transportation centers in the country.

Atlanta also had Hartsfield Airport. It was the home base for Delta Air Lines and a major hub for what was then Eastern Airlines and Southern Airways. The Metropolitan Atlanta Rapid Transit Authority (MARTA)

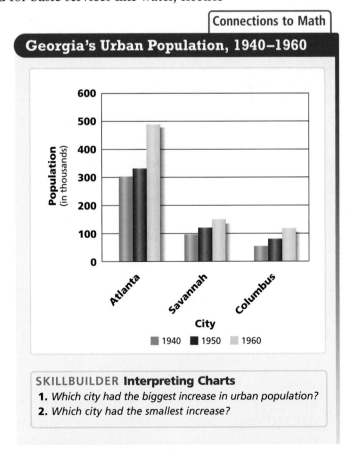

Connections to Math

Georgia's Urban Population, 1940–1960

SKILLBUILDER **Interpreting Charts**
1. *Which city had the biggest increase in urban population?*
2. *Which city had the smallest increase?*

▲ Buford Dam created Lake Sidney Lanier at the headwaters of the Chattahoochee River. Although the dam was completed in 1956, it took two years for the lake to fill up.

was created in the 1960s to develop a mass transit system. While the new system temporarily relieved the problem of traffic congestion, it did not solve it. As Atlanta grew, movement in and around the city became a major issue.

Lake Sidney Lanier As the Atlanta metropolitan area grew, the area needed more water. The Chattahoochee River provided most of the city's water. To grow, Atlanta would need an even larger source. In the 1950s, work began on a network of dams along the Chattahoochee. The goal was to create a lake large enough to supply the area's growing population. It would also help control flooding in the area. **Lake Sidney Lanier** was finished in 1956. The lake is named for Georgia's most famous poet, Sidney Clopton Lanier.

The growth of Georgia's economy increased pressure to make changes in its political systems, as you will read in the next section.

Section ③ Assessment

1. TERMS & NAMES
Explain the significance of:

a. Operation Dixie

b. Lake Sidney Lanier

2. TAKING NOTES
In a chart like the one below, explain the changes that occurred in Georgia from the 1940s to the 1960s in the following areas.

| Population |
| Business/Industry |
| Agriculture |

3. MAIN IDEAS

a. How did Georgia's population change from the 1930s to the 1960s?

b. What industries became important to Georgia's economy from the late 1940s to the 1960s?

c. How did Georgia farms change from the 1940s to the 1960s?

4. CRITICAL THINKING
Drawing Conclusions

How did the improvements in farming techniques lead to a decrease in the number of farmers?

Think About
- the use of tractors to till soil and harvest crops
- the cost of equipment and supplies

ACTIVITY -OPTIONS- **Science/Art** Find out what machines were available in post-World War II Georgia. Design an **exhibit** or create a **model** of one of the machines. Explain its date and function.

Political Changes in Georgia

4

SETTING THE STAGE

Georgia went through many changes from the 1930s through the 1960s. Some of Georgia's political leaders tried to prevent these changes. They refused help from the federal government. They tried to run the state using the power of their personalities and political connections.

Other politicians, though, supported change. They wanted to make things better for Georgians by enacting reforms of state government. They provided better services for Georgians and promoted the state as a modern and progressive place.

▲ Carl Sanders from Augusta was a progressive, pro-urban candidate for governor in 1962. His election signaled a change in Georgia politics.

Politics in World War II Georgia

Republican Eugene Talmadge became governor of Georgia in 1941 on a platform opposing New Deal programs. In 1941, Governor Talmadge turned his attention to the state's colleges. He wanted to rid Georgia's higher education of all "foreign" influences. By that he meant anyone not from Georgia or who did not agree with him—especially on the issue of segregated schools. The actions he took came to be called the **Board of Regents controversy**.

Talmadge accused two college educators of promoting desegregation in Georgia schools. He demanded that the Board of Regents fire both professors. When it did not, Talmadge forced two members of the board to resign and appointed new members. The new board did fire the two educators.

When Georgia's public schools lost the recognition of the Southern Association of Colleges and Secondary Schools, parents, students, and many citizens of Georgia became angry at Talmadge for causing this problem. The voters of Georgia turned against him in 1942 and elected someone who promised to fix the problem.

Taking Notes

Use your chart to list the effects World War II had on the political scene in Georgia.

	Effects in America	Effects in Georgia
End of World War II		

Governor Ellis Arnall Attorney General Ellis Arnall ran against Eugene Talmadge in 1942 and won. He disagreed with Talmadge's heavy-handed use of power. He promised to reform state government. Arnall made several changes that reduced the power of the governor's office. He established the Department of Corrections and abolished chain gangs and other severe punishments in prisons. He formed the Board of Pardons and Paroles that ended the practice of selling pardons.

Reading History

A. Finding Main Ideas How was Ellis Arnall able to defeat Talmadge?

Arnall supported a Georgia constitutional amendment in 1943 to change the voting age in the state from 21 to 18. The legislature passed the amendment and the voters approved it. Georgia was the first state to give 18-year-olds the vote.

By the 1940s, the Georgia Constitution of 1877 had been amended over 300 times. Arnall began the process of updating the state's constitution. The Constitution of 1945 was approved by the General Assembly and later by Georgia voters.

Atlanta's Political Leadership

William Berry Hartsfield was elected mayor of Atlanta in 1937. He held that office until 1962, except for 1940–1942. The city grew dramatically in size and population during his administration.

> *PRIMARY SOURCE*
>
> He's got a hot temper, a stinging tongue, a strong will, a quick wit, a kind heart, a sense of history, a sense of destiny, a sense of humor, a capacity for growth, and a built-in finely turned political radar set that seldom has failed him in his public life.
>
> quote about William Berry Hartsfield in *Atlanta Journal,* June 7, 1961.

Hartsfield was reelected so often because he was able to convince white and black leaders to act together for a common purpose. Atlanta was then seen as a Southern city that was focused on doing business. Hartsfield was a moderate progressive. He is best known for his efforts to start a municipal airport for Atlanta (while he was a councilman in the 1920s), his support of the Atlanta zoo (now ZooAtlanta), and his success at reforming the city's police and fire departments. He was also mayor during the integration of the public schools.

HISTORY MAKERS

WILLIAM HARTSFIELD 1890–1971

Atlanta's longest-serving mayor, William Berry Hartsfield, became known as Atlanta's "father of aviation." That's because, in the 1920s, Hartsfield saw the airport as the key to the city's economic prosperity long before passenger flights were a common way to travel.

During Hartsfield's tenure, the city purchased an old racetrack, Candler Field, and developed the Atlanta Municipal Airport. By 1957, it became the busiest airport in the country with more than two million passengers. Renamed William B. Hartsfield Atlanta Airport in 1971 and the Jackson-Hartsfield Atlanta International Airport in 2003, the airport now serves more than 78 million passengers annually.

Georgia Politics

Reforms in state and local politics, which began slowly before World War II, would eventually bring an end to segregation in Georgia and throughout the South. Georgia's political process started to include African Americans and women.

Gaining Political Power Through the Vote   In 1946, the Supreme Court ruled in *Chapman* v. *King* that Georgia's all-white primary was unconstitutional. African-American leaders John Wesley Dobbs and A. T. Walden founded the Atlanta Civil and Political League. They also initiated a campaign to register African Americans in Atlanta. They saw a chance to gain political power through the vote.

Reading History

B. Drawing Conclusions
How did the ruling in *Chapman* v. *King* result in the election of Georgia's first congresswoman?

The voter registration campaign was successful. African-American voters in Atlanta increased from 7,000 to around 24,000 in just two months. The African-American community now had the power to influence the outcome of city elections. The African-American voters endorsed the liberal candidate **Helen Douglas Mankin,** who was running in a special election.

Mankin won her first political race for a seat in the Georgia General Assembly in 1936. She ran for a seat in the Fifth Congressional District in 1947. Mankin was the first woman to represent Georgia in the U.S. Congress. Her victory represented a major change in Georgia politics— a coalition of white and black voters.

▲ A drive to register more African-American voters in 1946 helped the liberal Helen Douglas Mankin defeat her conservative opponent.

1946 Governor's Race   Eugene Talmadge decided to run for governor again in 1946. Talmadge was worried about the new political coalition of whites and blacks. So he campaigned on a platform of white supremacy. He blamed outside forces for the problems in Georgia. He promised to protect Georgia and Georgians from change. Talmadge's opponent received more popular votes but lost the election because Talmadge had more support in rural counties. But before he could take office, Eugene Talmadge died. This created much confusion over who would become the next governor. This confusion was called the **three governors controversy.**

Three Governors Controversy   Herman Talmadge, Eugene's son, claimed to be the rightful governor because he had received a number of write-in votes in the election. M. E. Thompson was elected Lieutenant

Three Governors Controversy

In 1946, three different men, Herman Talmadge, Ellis Arnall, and Melvin E. Thompson, declared themselves the governor of Georgia. Secretary of State Ben W. Fortson, Jr. refused to give up the official State Seal until the Georgia Supreme Court decided who was the actual governor.

The State Seal was used on all important documents. Without it, a governor could not do his job. Fortson hid the State Seal under the seat cushion of his wheelchair during the day. He took it home with him at night. When the Georgia Supreme Court declared Thompson to be the governor, Fortson gave him the State Seal.

Governor in the same election. He claimed that he should be the next governor. The sitting governor, Ellis Arnall, supported Thompson. Arnall refused to give up the governorship until the matter was settled in court.

Herman Talmadge's supporters broke into Governor Arnall's office. They changed the locks and declared Talmadge as governor. Arnall set up an office at the Capitol's information booth. Lieutenant Governor Thompson opened his governor's office in a nearby office building.

In 1947, the Georgia Supreme Court ruled that Thompson was the official governor until a special election could be held. In 1948, Herman Talmadge defeated Thompson. He promised Georgians that he would bring back the all-white primary, although that did not happen. Herman Talmadge served two terms as governor.

County Unit System Struck Down Despite the growth of the state's metropolitan counties, rural counties still controlled the state's political system. The county unit system guaranteed that these counties could control the state. It also helped to keep in place the system of segregation by giving rural counties, which were more conservative, more representation.

Reading History

C. Finding Main Ideas How did the county unit system support segregation?

Before Georgia politics could make any real reforms, the county-unit system had to change. In 1962, the federal courts ruled that the system was unconstitutional and Georgia adopted a "one man, one vote" system. This finally allowed a liberal candidate from urban Georgia to become governor.

<u>Carl Sanders</u> of Augusta promised to reform state government, bring new businesses and industry to the state, and improve education. He also promised to improve Georgia's national reputation. Governor Sanders' victory in 1962 over his better-known and better-connected opponent represented a change in Georgia's future by sending a message that the past was no longer the model to follow.

Georgia Politicians on the National Scene

Several Georgia politicians became influential in Washington. They represented Georgia's interests in Congress, and helped shape policies that affected all Americans.

Richard B. Russell, Jr. In 1920, at the age of 23, <u>Richard B. Russell, Jr.</u> won his first political race, a seat in the Georgia State

House. In 1930, he was elected governor and served one term. From 1933 to 1971, Russell served as Georgia's U.S. Senator. He was initially a strong supporter of President Roosevelt's New Deal programs, particularly those designed to help poor rural Americans. As the Depression wore on, however, he became less supportive. In the 1950s, Russell, along with other Southern politicians, opposed federal legislation to end segregation in the South. While he supported a strong defense for the nation, he opposed U.S. involvement in Vietnam. In 1969, he was elected president pro tem of the Senate.

Carl Vinson   Elected to the U.S. House of Representatives when he was 30 years old, **Carl Vinson** was the youngest member of Congress at that time. He served 50 years in the U.S. House of Representatives. He is best known for his support of the expansion of the U.S. military—naval and air power and is credited with creating the "two-ocean" navy. In 1964, President Johnson awarded him the Presidential Medal of Freedom with Special Distinction, the highest award a civilian can receive. In 1980, the nuclear-powered aircraft carrier USS *Carl Vinson* was named in his honor. He died the next year.

The period from the end of World War II to the 1960s was a time of prosperity and growth in America. But there were problems as well. There was growing poverty in America's cities for example. There was racism and discrimination in American society. In the next chapter you will read about the people committed to ending discrimination.

Section 4 Assessment

1. TERMS & NAMES

Explain the significance of:

a. Board of Regents controversy

b. Helen Douglas Mankin

c. three governors controversy

d. Carl Sanders

e. Richard B. Russell, Jr.

f. Carl Vinson

2. TAKING NOTES

Use a chart like the one shown to record important details about the year 1946 as covered in this section. Who participated and what historical significance did each event represent?

Event	Participant(s)	Significance

3. MAIN IDEAS

a. How did the ruling in *Chapman* v. *King* change Georgia's political system?

b. How was Arnall able to defeat Talmadge in the race for governor in 1942?

c. How would eliminating the county unit system allow state reforms to happen?

4. CRITICAL THINKING

Drawing Conclusions

How did William Berry Hartsfield's leadership contribute to the growth of Atlanta?

Think About
• the number of years he served as mayor
• his ability to create political coalitions
• his efforts to build an airport in Atlanta

Technology/Language Arts   Interview someone who remembers JFK's assassination. Create a **radio broadcast** of the interview or write it as a **magazine feature**.

VISUAL SUMMARY

The Cold War Years

1945
United Nations is established.

Stalin raises the iron curtain.
1946

1947
• Marshall Plan is established to rebuild Europe.
• U. S. joins NATO.
• Communists take control of China.

Soviets detonate a nuclear bomb, setting off the nuclear arms race.
1949

1950
• Communist-controlled North Korea invades South Korea.
• The U. S. and NATO defend South Korea.

1953
The Korean war ends.

1954
Joseph R. McCarthy conducts hearings to expose suspected Communists.

• Bay of Pigs invasion fails.
• The Soviet Union builds the Berlin Wall.
1961

President Kennedy ends the Cuban Missile Crisis.
1962

TERMS & NAMES

Briefly explain the significance of the following.

1. G.I. Bill
2. baby boomer
3. Cold War
4. iron curtain
5. containment
6. Operation Dixie
7. Lake Sidney Lanier
8. Board of Regents controversy
9. Helen Douglas Mankin
10. three governors controversy

REVIEW QUESTIONS

Postwar America (pages 419–423)

1. What problems resulted from the baby boom?
2. How did the increase in consumer goods affect American life?

Cold War America (pages 424–430)

3. What was the Marshall Plan?
4. How did the fear of communism affect Americans?

Georgia's Growing Economy (pages 431–436)

5. How did Georgia's economy develop in this period?
6. How did Georgia's agriculture change?

Political Changes in Georgia (pages 437–441)

7. What contributions did Ellis Arnall make to Georgia?
8. What was *Brown* v. *Board of Education*?

CRITICAL THINKING

1. USING YOUR NOTES: ANALYZING CAUSES AND RECOGNIZING EFFECTS

	Effects in America	Effects in Georgia
End of World War II		

Using your completed chart, answer the questions below.

a. How did the end of the war affect the American family?
b. What was the most significant change in Georgia following World War II?

2. ANALYZING LEADERSHIP

How was William Berry Hartsfield's leadership important to the growth of Atlanta?

3. APPLYING CITIZENSHIP SKILLS

Was McCarthyism or communism a greater threat to American life? Explain your answer.

4. THEME: ECONOMICS IN HISTORY

What economic factors impacted agriculture in Georgia?

5. IDENTIFYING AND SOLVING PROBLEMS

What problem was the policy of containment intended to solve? Was it an effective solution?

INTERACT with HISTORY

How are the American dreams and values you read about similar to your personal dreams? How are they different?

STANDARDS-BASED ASSESSMENT

Use the graph and your knowledge of American history to answer questions 1 through 3.

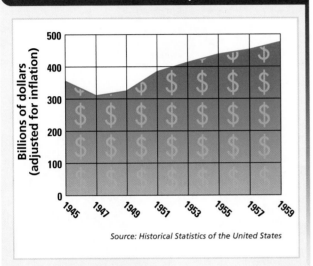

Gross National Product, 1945–1959

Source: Historical Statistics of the United States

1. In dollars, approximately how much did the GNP increase between 1945 and 1951?
   A. About $20 million
   B. About $20 billion
   C. About $50 million
   D. About $100 million

2. About how much did the GNP increase between 1951 and 1959?
   A. About $120 million
   B. About $120 billion
   C. About $100 billion
   D. About $50 million

3. Which two-year period showed the greatest increase in GNP?
   A. 1947–1949
   B. 1949–1951
   C. 1955–1957
   D. 1957–1959

TEST PRACTICE
CLASSZONE.COM

ALTERNATIVE ASSESSMENT

1. CREATING A COMMERCIAL

America's new consumer lifestyle brought many new items into the home. Choose an item for the home that was popular in the 1950s and make a commercial for it. First, consider the benefits of the products for the family. Then write your script and design your props. Use original art or packaging from the period if you can. Videotape your commercial or present it live to the class.

2. COOPERATIVE LEARNING

Examine images of life in Georgia in the 1950s. Working in groups, look at newspapers, magazines, documentaries, and books of the era. Present your findings as a short play about a family in Georgia in the 1950s. Prepare for the presentation using these suggestions.

- Make a list of the media images you want to use.
- Assign roles to other students as writers, actors, directors, and narrator.
- Identify props or costumes that you need.

INTEGRATED TECHNOLOGY ACTIVITY

PREPARING AN ELECTRONIC PRESENTATION

The Cold War years following World War II were years of great political change. Prepare an electronic presentation about one major event from the Cold War years. Use the library and the Internet to find books, articles, and documentaries on your topic. Research the key personalities and events involved. You might choose from the following list.

- Stalin and the iron curtain
- The history of NATO
- McCarthy and the HUAC
- The Korean conflict
- The Bay of Pigs
- The Berlin Wall
- The Cuban missile crisis

RESEARCH LINKS
CLASSZONE.COM

Civil Rights and Civil Wrongs 1930–1968

Ralph Abernathy (wearing a blue shirt and a cross) and others march arm in arm down an Atlanta street in 1970.

1933
Georgia ratifies Twentieth Amendment.

1942
NAACP chapter starts in Savannah.

GEORGIA
USA   1930

1933
Tennessee Valley Authority (TVA) is created.

1941
U.S. enters World War II.

1945
United Nations is established.

It is 1960, and you live in a larger Georgia city. For decades, African Americans across the South have endured racial segregation. Now they are protesting against it—in spite of the risk of being attacked. You must decide whether or not you will participate in the protests and, if you do, in what way.

How would you stop injustice in society?

WHAT DO YOU THINK?

- How far would you be willing to go to help the protesters?

- In what ways, besides protesting, could you help to end segregation?

For more information on this chapter, visit . . .

RESEARCH LINKS
CLASSZONE.COM

1951
Georgia ratifies the Twenty-second Amendment.

1957
SCLC is founded, with Martin Luther King, Jr., as its leader.

1960
Atlanta students begin sit-ins. SNCC is established.

1961
Albany Movement is launched.

1949

1968

1954
Public school segregation is ruled unconstitutional in *Brown* v. *Board of Education*.

1963
March on Washington takes place. Kennedy is assassinated.

1964
Congress passes Civil Rights Act.

1968
Martin Luther King, Jr., is assassinated.

Reading Strategy:
Comparing and Contrasting

What Do You Know?

What do you know about the civil rights movement in America? How did the South respond to the end of segregation?

THINK ABOUT

• what you have learned about the civil rights movement from books, television, and movies

• what you have read and seen about the struggle for civil rights in other countries around the world

What Do You Want to Know?

What questions do you have about the civil rights movement in America? What would you like to know about how desegregation affected Georgia? Record those questions in your notebook before you read the chapter.

Comparing and Contrasting

Comparing and contrasting the beliefs, strategies, and behaviors of people or groups can help you better understand their role in history. To compare, look at similarities and differences between two or more things. To contrast, look only at the differences. Use the diagram below to compare and contrast the views and approaches of the leaders and groups listed. How did each respond to the issue of civil rights?

 See Skillbuilder Handbook, page 551.

 **Taking Notes**

	Approach to Civil Rights
NAACP	
President Roosevelt	
President Truman	
Dr. Martin Luther King, Jr.	
President Eisenhower	
SCLC	
President Kennedy	
Malcolm X	
Black Panthers	

The Civil Rights Movement Begins

MAIN IDEA	WHY IT MATTERS NOW	TERMS & NAMES
African Americans struggled to overcome racism and discrimination in the United States.	The civil rights movement made American society more integrated and brought greater equality.	NAACP Executive Order 8802 Dixiecrat

SETTING THE STAGE

With the passage of the Fourteenth and Fifteenth Amendments after the Civil War, African Americans were guaranteed their rights under the Constitution. But they found that laws were not always obeyed. Racism remained a strong influence on American society, especially in the South.

African Americans endured constant discrimination and violence. They were prevented from enjoying the freedoms that belonged to all American citizens. They fought to overcome the wall of racism that surrounded the entire nation. There were some successes, but they came in small portions over a long period of time.

▲ A white man and a black man take drinks from segregated drinking fountains, which were common throughout the South.

Early Attempts to Gain Equal Rights

In 1896, the U.S. Supreme Court handed down a decision that "separate but equal" facilities for blacks and whites did not violate the Constitution. The case, *Plessy v. Ferguson*, made segregation legal in America for the first half of the twentieth century. But often these separate black and white schools and other public facilities were not of equal quality. Segregation only enforced the racist attitudes and practices of many Americans.

National Association for the Advancement of Colored People (NAACP)   Not all African Americans accepted this second-class status. The **NAACP** was founded in 1909 by a group of blacks and whites that included W. E. B. DuBois and Ida B. Wells. The NAACP worked to gain equal treatment for African-American citizens. The group told the public about the terror and violence that African Americans in the South experienced. They also worked through the courts to gain rights for African Americans.

Taking Notes

Use your chart to compare and contrast this section's groups and leaders as the civil rights movement begins.

	Approach to Civil Rights
NAACP	
President Roosevelt	

▲ The Savannah chapter of the NAACP set a goal of 5,000 new members for 1942, its first year.

In the 1930s, the NAACP attacked the idea of "separate but equal" by filing lawsuits to force Southern states to provide equal facilities. However, Southern states clearly failed to provide equal school facilities as required by the law. White schools had better buildings, books, and equipment than African-American schools.

Postwar Changes Strengthen Protests

During World War II, many African Americans served in the military. They distinguished themselves fighting to protect the United States, but when they returned home, they faced discrimination and even violence. Many African Americans became convinced that they had to stand up for their rights.

In 1942, Reverend Ralph Mark Gilbert started a new chapter of the NAACP in Savannah. The group worked to register African Americans to vote. By 1946, they had registered more than 22,000 African-American voters. The city's African-American community gained political power from the large voting bloc, or group.

White Primaries Are Struck Down During the 1920s and 1930s, the NAACP had tried to eliminate the Southern practice of allowing only whites to vote in political primaries. In 1944, the Supreme Court in *Smith* v. *Allwright* ruled that the primary was an important part of the election process. The court ruled that not allowing African Americans to participate violated their Fifteenth Amendment right to vote.

Georgia and other Southern states resisted the *Allwright* decision. In the summer of 1944, an African-American man named Primus King

Reading History

A. Making Inferences
Why were African Americans more determined to win equal rights after World War II?

Vocabulary

primary: a meeting of registered voters of a political party to nominate candidates for office

tried to vote in a local Democratic primary in Columbus. King was not allowed to vote because the Georgia Constitution held that the primary was open only to whites. He took his case to court and argued that Georgia's law that excluded African Americans from the primary violated his rights under the Fifteenth Amendment.

After two years in the courts, King won the right to vote in the primaries. The color barrier that prevented African Americans in Georgia from participating equally in the voting process had fallen. But it would take more than this to bring about equality in the South.

▲ Demonstrators in San Francisco march silently, carrying four symbolic coffins. They are protesting the 1946 lynching of four African Americans in Georgia.

Resistance and Decline   Some whites across the South feared the new social order in which African Americans refused to accept the discrimination and violence of a segregated society. In October 1945, the Ku Klux Klan burned a large cross on top of Stone Mountain. It was a reminder that intimidation and racial violence were still a part of Southern society.

By 1950, the progress made by NAACP chapters throughout Georgia had eroded. Pressure from the white community and threats of violence from the Klan after the war caused over half the chapters to close. Membership fell from 11,000 in 1946 to about 3,100 by 1950. Most remaining members lived in Atlanta or Savannah. It was in those cities that the civil rights movement reemerged in the late 1950s.

Federal Support for Civil Rights

In 1941, A. Philip Randolph began to organize a march on Washington. He wanted to publicize the fact that African Americans were excluded from most of the high-paying jobs in defense industries. Randolph told President Roosevelt that he would call off the march if Roosevelt promised to do something about the problem.

In response, President Roosevelt issued **Executive Order 8802**. It prohibited any "discrimination in the employment of workers in defense industries or government because of race, creed, color, or national origin. . . ." President Roosevelt also created the Fair Employment Practices Committee. This federal committee ensured that wartime industries followed the executive order.

An increasing number of African Americans in the postwar South became willing to demand their rights because of the newfound support

Reading History

B. Drawing Conclusions
Why was the federal government more supportive of civil rights?

from the federal government. It was more open to challenging the Southern states on issues of equality and protection of its citizens.

To Secure These Rights   President Roosevelt's successor, Harry S Truman, was an important supporter of African-American efforts to gain their rights. He clashed with his fellow Democrats in the South who did not support civil rights measures. Truman created the President's Commission on Civil Rights in 1947 to find ways to protect civil rights. Its report—*To Secure These Rights*—recommended ways to make sure all Americans had equal access to education, good housing, and jobs. The commission suggested new laws against lynching and making the Civil Rights Division of the Department of Justice more powerful.

Dixiecrats   At the 1948 Democratic Presidential Convention, many Southern Democrats didn't like the Democratic Party platform, which included measures supporting civil rights. During the convention, 35 Southern delegates walked out in protest.

These Southern Democrats formed their own party called the States' Rights Party, also known as the **Dixiecrat** Party. J. Strom Thurmond from South Carolina ran as their presidential candidate. He won in four Southern states and received over one million votes. Although the Dixiecrats did not win in the national election, they represented resistance by Southern whites to accept efforts to improve African-American lives. In spite of this, African Americans would continue their struggle for equal rights, as you will read in the next section.

Reading History

C. Finding Main Ideas   Why did Southern Democrats form their own party?

Section 1 Assessment

1. TERMS & NAMES
Explain the significance of:

a. NAACP

b. Executive Order 8802

d. Dixiecrat

2. TAKING NOTES
Use a chart like the one shown below to record the effects on civil rights of the following federal decisions or programs.

Causes	Effects
Plessy v. Ferguson	
Smith v. Allwright	
Roosevelt's New Deal	
Executive Order 8802	
President's Commission on Civil Rights	

3. MAIN IDEAS
a. What were some of the strategies used by the NAACP to gain rights for African Americans?

b. Why was it important to end the all-white Democratic primaries in the South?

c. How and why did the Dixiecrat Party come into existence?

4. CRITICAL THINKING
Analyzing Causes and Recognizing Effects

Why did membership in Georgia's NAACP chapters increase after the war and decrease by two thirds within the decade?

Think About
• soldiers bringing home new ideas
• the white majority's influence

Technology/Language Arts   Plan a **multimedia presentation** on one of the groups mentioned in this section or write a **pamphlet** explaining that group's goals.

The Movement Grows

2

MAIN IDEA

The civil rights movement made significant gains during the 1950s.

WHY IT MATTERS NOW

This was the beginning of the end of legalized segregation—the end of a dual society and the start of an equal society.

TERMS & NAMES

Brown v. *Board of Education*
Southern Manifesto
Montgomery bus boycott
Martin Luther King, Jr.
SCLC
SNCC

◀ In 1954, Thurgood Marshall persuaded the Supreme Court that racial segregation in schools was not constitutional.

SETTING THE STAGE

For years, African Americans were forced to accept the way things were in the South—racism, violence, and discrimination. It made them second-class citizens. They made some efforts to change their world, to gain access to their constitutional rights. But they had to be careful not to push too far. The result could be deadly.

In the 1950s, African Americans began to see the real possibility of gaining equal rights and equal access to public facilities. They used a tactic called nonviolent direct action to gain their rights. It was very effective.

Challenging Segregation in Education

In the early 1950s, civil rights activists continued to attack segregated education in the South through the courts. In ***Brown v. Board of Education,*** the U.S. Supreme Court took up the issue of separate educational facilities. The Court wondered whether there was the possibility of equality if schools were racially segregated. Were white-controlled school boards providing white children with better schools, teachers, books, and equipment?

PRIMARY SOURCE

Does segregation of the children in public schools solely on the basis of race, even though the physical facilities and other 'tangible' factors may be equal, deprive the children of the minority group of equal educational opportunities?

Chief Justice Earl Warren, *Brown* v. *Board of Education of Topeka*

On May 17, 1954, the Supreme Court declared that the doctrine of "separate but equal" educational facilities was not fair. The facilities were

✎ Taking Notes

Use your chart to compare and contrast this section's groups and leaders as the civil rights movement grows.

	Approach to Civil Rights
NAACP	
President Roosevelt	

▲ High school students in Atlanta gather to hear the announcement of the Supreme Court's decision in *Brown* v. *Board of Education*.

not equal, and would never be equal. This meant that the decades-old defense of segregation in schools was no longer legal.

Avoiding Compliance with the Law

Segregationists (those favoring segregation) referred to the date that the *Brown* v. *Board of Education* decision was handed down as "Black Monday." Their world of two separate societies—one white and one black—was under attack from outside forces. In response, they resisted.

Massive Resistance   What would Southern states do now that separate educational facilities were illegal under the Constitution? Segregationist politicians and officials decided the best course of action was to ignore the Supreme Court ruling. This strategy was called "massive resistance." If the white South put up enough of a fight against desegregation, maybe the federal government would back down.

The Southern Manifesto   In 1956, 100 Southern members of Congress signed a letter that became known as the **Southern Manifesto.** Georgia's entire congressional delegation signed, indicating their support for Southern states to resist "forced integration." They also promised to find a legal way to reverse the decision of the Supreme Court.

In Georgia, Governor Herman Talmadge promised to keep the races separate and maintain the segregated public school system. Numerous Georgia politicians agreed. Senator Richard B. Russell, Jr. called the Supreme Court's decision a "flagrant abuse of the judicial power."

Reading History

A. Making Inferences Why might the *Brown* ruling lead to the end of segregation in other public facilities?

Vocabulary

manifesto: an official declaration by a group or party about action they intend to take

Another way to resist desegregation was to shut down the schools. The Georgia General Assembly had passed a law in 1955 withholding state funds from any school system in Georgia that desegregated. Since most school systems that wanted to integrate could not operate without this money, they closed. This preserved segregation, but did not educate children.

Attacking Segregation of Public Facilities

In spite of white resistance, the civil rights movement continued to grow. On December 1, 1955, Rosa Parks refused to give up her seat to a white man on a Montgomery, Alabama, bus. A Montgomery city law required African Americans to obey bus drivers' directions on where to sit. Parks was arrested for breaking this law. When news of her arrest reached African-American religious and community leaders, they came together to organize the **Montgomery bus boycott**. They chose as their leader the Reverend Dr. **Martin Luther King, Jr.,** the new minister of the Dexter Avenue Baptist Church.

The boycott leaders identified several practices they wanted changed. They demanded that African Americans riding the buses be treated with respect. They wanted to end segregated seating and use a "first come, first served" policy. They also wanted the bus company to hire African Americans as drivers.

Almost all of the riders on the city buses were African Americans. During the boycott, most found other ways to get around town. Ridership fell dramatically. Pressure began to build on city officials to settle.

After one year, the city of Montgomery gave in to the demands and ended segregation on Montgomery buses. Reverend King, along with fellow boycott leaders E. D. Nixon and Ralph David Abernathy, boarded a bus on December 21, 1956. The boycott was over. And the civil rights movement had found an important new leader—Martin Luther King, Jr.

Little Rock, Arkansas   In 1957, the federal government acted to enforce a federal court order to integrate the public schools in Little Rock, Arkansas. The Governor of Arkansas, Orville Faubus, had called out the Arkansas National Guard to prevent nine African-American

Reading History

B. Summarizing What were the boycott leaders' demands?

DAILY LIFE

Bus Segregation

Before the Montgomery bus boycott put an end to them, the rules for segregation on buses were complicated. African Americans were required to pay their fares to the bus driver, then get off the bus and get back on through the rear door.

If the front of the bus was full and another white person entered, African Americans were required to give up their seats. They were forced to sit further back in the bus, not ever across the aisle from a white person.

Rosa Parks (below), an active NAACP member, challenged those laws simply by remaining seated when a white person boarded the bus.

**MARTIN LUTHER KING, JR.
1929–1968**

Martin Luther King, Jr.'s college entrance scores were so high he enrolled in Morehouse College in Atlanta at the age of 15. King went on to seminary and by the age of 19 was a minister at Ebenezer Baptist Church.

In 1964, at the age of 35, the Rev. Dr. Martin Luther King, Jr., became the youngest man to win the Nobel Peace Prize. As he accepted the prize, King spoke about his hopes for the future. "Granted that we face a world crisis which leaves us standing so often amid the surging murmur of life's restless sea. But every crisis has both its dangers and its opportunities. It can spell either salvation or doom. In a dark confused world the kingdom of God may yet reign in the hearts of men."

students from attending Central High School. He argued that he had done this to prevent an outbreak of violence.

President Dwight D. Eisenhower sent federal troops—the 101st Airborne—to make sure that the "new" students were allowed to attend Central High School. It sent a message that the federal government would not allow violence or allow a state to ignore federal law.

Organizing the Civil Rights Movement

The success of the Montgomery bus boycott led to other boycotts across the South. A group of African-American leaders decided that they needed to create an organization that would direct the movement for civil rights in the South.

Southern Christian Leadership Conference
On January 11, 1957, a group of ministers and civil rights leaders met in Atlanta and formed the Southern Christian Leadership Conference, or **SCLC**.

The SCLC managed the civil rights movement in the South. Reverend Dr. Martin Luther King, Jr., along with Ralph Abernathy, Sr., Jesse Jackson, Hosea Williams, John Lewis, and Andrew Young were important leaders in the organization. King served as president.

The SCLC advocated the philosophy of nonviolent protest. It believed that the success of the bus boycott proved that nonviolent action was the best way to confront racism and segregation in the South.

The Movement Gains Strength

Civil rights leaders and young people involved in the civil rights movement wanted to win their rights as citizens. They wanted those rights immediately—not gradually. They did not like the fact that many Southern states had either failed to desegregate public facilities, such as stores and restaurants, or had made little effort.

Greensboro   On February 1, 1960, four African-American college students from North Carolina A&T College sat down at the lunch counter at the F.W. Woolworth department store in Greensboro, North

Background

The nine African-American students chosen to integrate Central High School became known as the Little Rock Nine.

Reading History

C. Recognizing Effects   How did the success of the bus boycott convince the leaders of the SCLC that an organization was needed in the civil rights movement?

Reading History

D. Solving Problems How did African Americans end discrimination practices at the stores and lunch counters?

Carolina. The waitress refused to serve them. At that time, restaurants in the South were segregated—whites and blacks were not allowed to eat in the same restaurant. The students returned to the restaurant every day and refused to leave until they were served. The "sit-in," a form of nonviolent protest, lasted six months before the lunch counter was desegregated. Within days, other young African Americans across the South staged similar sit-ins.

Civil Rights Movement in Georgia

Sit-ins were held in Savannah, Rome, Macon, Augusta, and Atlanta. A group of students from local black colleges led a sit-in at the lunch counter in Rich's department store in downtown Atlanta. Martin Luther King, Jr., joined them. This started a boycott of downtown Atlanta stores.

The boycott lasted for three months. It ended when older African-American leaders in Atlanta accepted the white business community's promise to desegregate their stores. Many young activists did not like the settlement because there was no guarantee of ending the segregation and discrimination against African Americans. They challenged Martin Luther King, Sr., and other established black leaders' decision to end the boycott.

Martin Luther King, Jr., stepped in and brought the protesters together. A generation gap in the civil rights movement between the older leaders and the younger protesters was revealed. This breach would increase over the next few years and lead to a division in the civil rights movement.

Martin Luther King, Jr., and the Philosophy of Nonviolence

Martin Luther King, Jr., and other Southern black ministers founded the Southern Christian Leadership Conference (SCLC) in 1957. They hoped to make further gains in equal rights using boycotts and other nonviolent strategies after their successful cooperative stand against bus segregation. King was inspired by the changes brought about by the works of Jesus and by touring India to study the nonviolent strategies used by leaders such as Mohandas Gandhi.

In late 1967, King started a Poor People's Campaign to work on economic problems that had not been addressed by earlier civil rights reforms. King was in Memphis supporting striking sanitation workers when he delivered what became his final speech, "I've Been to the Mountaintop." The next day, April 4, 1968, King was assassinated.

The legacy of Martin Luther King, Jr., came from his belief that only love could convert people to the side of justice. He described the power of nonviolent resisters: "We will wear you down by our capacity to suffer. And in winning our freedom . . . we will win you in the process."

Student Non-Violent Coordinating Committee (SNCC)
Young African Americans in Atlanta who wanted to participate in the civil rights movement organized the Student Non-violent Coordinating Committee, or **SNCC** (pronounced SNICK). Julian Bond, John Lewis, and Lonnie King were leaders in the Atlanta-based organization. They worked very closely with the SCLC in the early years.

Desegregating Georgia's Schools

Desegregating Georgia's schools did *not* take place quickly. However, the process did take place without the violence that occurred in neighboring Southern states, including Arkansas.

▲ Charlayne Hunter (left) and Hamilton Holmes walk to the University of Georgia registrar's office.

Desegregating the University of Georgia   In 1959, two African-American students from Atlanta, Charlayne Hunter and Hamilton Holmes, attempted to enroll in the University of Georgia Law School. They were told that the school was already full for the fall quarter. Hunter and Hamilton did not believe that excuse. They sued the university and continued to apply for admission each quarter.

University and state officials hoped that if they stalled long enough, the two would give up their efforts to enroll. They did not. In December 1960, the court ordered the university to admit them. The two graduated from the University of Georgia in 1963.

Atlanta Public Schools   Business and political leaders in Atlanta were unwilling to close down the city's schools to prevent integration. They thought it would not be good for the local economy and Atlanta's reputation as a modern Southern city that was supposed to be "Too Busy to Hate."

Mayor William B. Hartsfield made sure that the integration of Atlanta's schools went smoothly. He did not want the kind of violence that had occurred a few years earlier when Little Rock, Arkansas, integrated its schools.

On August 30, 1961, nine African-American students began their first day in four different all-white high schools. The nine students arrived in unmarked police cars driven by plainclothes officers 10 minutes before school started. The students left 10 minutes before the final bell the same way.

Reading History

E. Summarizing
Why did Atlanta's leaders want their schools' integration to be managed carefully?

Many families kept their children home the first day, afraid that there might be trouble. But there was none. One African-American student, Willie Jean Black, said that the white students were "not overly friendly, but they were well mannered." President Kennedy praised the city of Atlanta.

PRIMARY SOURCE

I strongly urge the officials and citizens of all communities . . . to look closely at what Atlanta has done . . . with courage, tolerance and, above all, with respect for the law.

President John F. Kennedy, quoted in the *Atlanta Journal-Constitution,* August 31, 1961

▲ Atlanta's public schools desegregated peacefully. Within 30 days, downtown lunch counters also became integrated.

Attendance returned to normal levels by the end of the first week of school. The federal government was determined to desegregate public schools. The 1964 Civil Rights Act required schools to integrate or lose federal funding. In 1969, the federal government required that the Georgia State Board of Education withhold state funds from school systems that were not integrated. By 1971, all of Georgia's school systems were officially integrated. Those years saw battles for equality throughout Georgia, not just in its schools, as you will read in the next section.

Reading History

F. Compare and Contrast How did the Civil Rights Act of 1964 affect school boards' decisions to integrate?

Section 2 Assessment

1. TERMS & NAMES

Explain the significance of:

a. *Brown* v. *Board of Education*

b. Southern Manifesto

c. Montgomery bus boycott

d. Martin Luther King, Jr.

e. SCLC

f. SNCC

2. TAKING NOTES

Use a cluster diagram to record details about the early civil rights movement. Include federal government actions, individual state reactions, and African-American community reactions.

Early Civil Rights Movement

3. MAIN IDEAS

a. Why was "separate but equal" ruled unconstitutional?

b. Do you think advocates of massive resistance were breaking the law?

c. Why were boycotts and sit-ins so effective in ending segregation of public facilities?

4. CRITICAL THINKING

Recognizing Effects

What were the most important results of the Montgomery bus boycott?

Think About

• respect for African Americans

• the leadership of Martin Luther King, Jr.

Art/Technology Create a **wall of fame** or plan a **Web page** that pays tribute to several leaders of the civil rights movement.

Victories and Losses in the Movement

SETTING THE STAGE

In the early 1960s, African Americans challenged segregation in many aspects of Southern life. The slow process of going through the courts to win their civil rights was not enough. Nonviolent direct action proved to be quicker. The walls of segregation were falling.

But direct action was also more dangerous. The danger could be simply the humiliations suffered by demonstrators at sit-ins. Or, it could be as violent as turning police dogs loose on young children marching in demonstrations. It could even include death. But in the end, the struggle for freedom was successful—at a great cost.

▲ A young freedom marcher wears a helmet for protection as he walks along the route from Selma to Montgomery in 1965.

Freedom Summer, 1961

In May 1961, several buses carrying "freedom riders," African-American and white protesters, made their way from Washington, D.C., through the Southern states. Organized by CORE (the Congress on Racial Equality), the freedom riders wanted to show that despite federal law, facilities such as public transportation were still segregated in the South. The white protesters sat in the back and the African-American riders sat in the front of the buses.

In Alabama, segregationists firebombed one bus and destroyed it. An angry mob attacked another bus in Birmingham and severely beat the freedom riders, white and black. In Mississippi, authorities arrested freedom riders for using a "whites only" restroom and sentenced them to 60 days in jail.

The Albany Movement In the fall of 1961, SNCC decided to launch a voter registration drive in Albany, Georgia. SNCC organizers also wanted to protest all forms of segregation and racial inequality in

Taking Notes

Use your chart to compare and contrast this section's groups and leaders as the civil rights movement experiences victories and losses.

	Approach to Civil Rights
NAACP	
President Roosevelt	

▲ Freedom riders sit disconsolately outside their burned-out bus. It was burned by a mob who attacked them on the highway.

the town. It recruited African-American students from Albany State College to start a sit-in at the bus station. They planned to use all means of nonviolent resistance at once: sit-ins, boycotts, legal action, and mass demonstrations. Ministers and African-American leaders joined with SNCC to create the Albany Movement. They selected a new minister in town, Dr. William Anderson, as leader.

The demonstrations began in December 1961. A small group of freedom riders joined the demonstrators. Hundreds of freedom riders and local protesters were promptly arrested. Dr. Martin Luther King, Jr. joined the demonstrations and was arrested.

City officials promised to meet some of the demonstrators' demands and drop charges against them if the marches ended and King left town. After two days in jail, King and the demonstrators were released. The city did not keep its word. The Albany Movement failed to accomplish its goals. It was one of the few defeats for the civil rights movement in the early 1960s. But it taught the protest leaders a valuable lesson. They would not try to protest all forms of segregation simultaneously, but tackle one part of the big problem at a time, such as voting or schools.

Reading History

A. Forming Opinions Do you agree with King's assessment that the protesters had taken on too big of an issue?

1963—A Year of Victory and Tragedy

The civil rights movement had great successes in 1963. But it also experienced great tragedy.

Birmingham, 1963 Nonviolent activists had achieved a certain amount of success. They needed even more public attention if the hateful practice of discrimination was to be defeated. Civil rights activists turned their attention to Birmingham, Alabama. The city had shut down playgrounds and golf courses rather than integrate them. Reverend King led a series of demonstrations against segregated facilities in the city. He was arrested for not having a permit to demonstrate. While in jail, he wrote his "Letter from the Birmingham City Jail." The letter criticized white ministers in Birmingham for not doing more to help.

In May 1963, over 1,000 African-American protesters, many of them children, marched through the city demanding access to public facilities and an end to segregation. Birmingham police chief Eugene "Bull" Conner, who had a reputation for violence, ordered police dogs to be released on the marchers. The dogs bit a number of people. Police turned fire hoses on the marchers. The water pressure was so great that it knocked people down and pushed them along the ground. Television cameras captured all of this. That night, the entire nation watched in horror as the peaceful marchers were attacked.

Reading History

B. Drawing Conclusions Why did civil rights leaders choose to protest in cities where they were likely to face violence?

A Bombing Kills Four   Eventually, Birmingham's business owners agreed to desegregate public facilities. But the violence was not over. In September, the Sixteenth Street Baptist Church was bombed. The dynamite exploded during services on Sunday morning, killing four African-American girls. Equal rights came at a very high price. After more violence in that city, Birmingham was nicknamed "Bombing-ham." The brutality and violence stunned the country.

The March on Washington   The growing violence in the South concerned many civil rights leaders. They were disappointed with the lack of support from the Kennedy administration. The **March on Washington** for Jobs and Freedom was organized to push President Kennedy and Congress into helping the civil rights movement. On August 28, 1963, more than 250,000 people gathered at the Washington Monument to show their commitment to the civil rights movement and the tactic of non-violence. African Americans, whites, Native Americans, and Hispanics marched together.

Throughout the day, speakers talked about the rights of all Americans to be treated fairly.

▼ The 1963 March on Washington brought blacks and whites together in support for equal rights, jobs, and freedom.

▲ Although Dr. King's speech came at the end of a long, hot, August day, his words electrified the crowd.

The high point of the day came at the end. Dr. King's "I Have a Dream" speech is one of the most important speeches in American history. It was a statement of hopes and dreams that our society and our world would one day be based on equality.

President Kennedy Is Assassinated   On November 22, 1963, President Kennedy was assassinated as his motorcade made its way through downtown Dallas, Texas. The nation was shocked and deeply saddened. Kennedy had been an important friend and supporter of civil rights. Many people saw his death as a blow to the movement.

The Civil Rights Act of 1964

Before Kennedy was assassinated, he had sent a Civil Rights Bill to Congress. The bill was very controversial. Many were not sure that Congress would pass the bill. After his death, Kennedy's vice-president and successor, President Lyndon B. Johnson, used his skill as a politician to get the bill passed.

Reading History

C. Supporting Opinions Did Kennedy's death contribute to the passage of the Civil Rights Act of 1964?

The bill became the **Civil Rights Act of 1964.** It outlawed segregation in public facilities and discrimination in employment. It also created the Equal Employment Opportunity Commission (EEOC), a government agency to serve as a "watchdog" to stop discrimination in employment based on race, religion, or gender. Within weeks, segregated facilities across the South opened up to African Americans.

Not all business owners accepted the new federal law. In Atlanta, restaurant owner Lester Maddox publicly refused to serve African Americans. He later closed his restaurant rather than integrate.

The Struggle to Vote

The leaders of the civil rights movement were successful in desegregating public facilities. But they realized that they also needed political power. To do that, they needed to register African Americans to vote.

Freedom Summer of 1964   The Civil Rights Act of 1964 outlawed discrimination against any American citizen. But Southern states continued taking actions to prevent African Americans from voting. In the summer of 1964, thousands of volunteers recruited by SNCC started a voter registration drive in the Southern states. It was dangerous work. In Mississippi, three civil rights workers were murdered.

Selma, Alabama, 1965   Martin Luther King, Jr., organized a voter registration drive in Selma, Alabama, in 1965. Only one percent of eligible African Americans in Selma were registered to vote at that time. During the drive, hundreds of African Americans tried to register to vote. Many were arrested and jailed for parading without a permit. The protest lasted for weeks but without success. No additional African Americans were able to register to vote in Selma.

King then organized a march from Selma to the state capitol in Montgomery (50 miles away) to gain more attention and support for the voter registration campaign. On March 7, 1965, called "Bloody Sunday," hundreds of people began marching to Montgomery. As the marchers reached the Edmund Pettus Bridge, the Alabama State Police attacked. Police on horseback chased the marchers down. Other policemen armed with nightsticks and whips beat the peaceful marchers. The march was stopped that day.

Marchers took the matter to federal court, which ruled in their favor. The march resumed on March 21, but this time under the protection

Background

The route from Selma to Montgomery is now known as the Selma-to-Montgomery National Historic Trail.

▼ Hundreds of African Americans line up to register to vote in Americus, Georgia, in 1965.

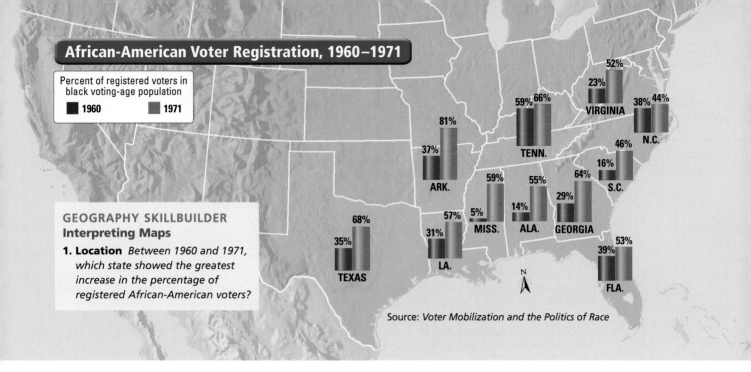

African-American Voter Registration, 1960–1971

Percent of registered voters in black voting-age population
■ 1960   ■ 1971

52%
23%
VIRGINIA
38% 44%
N.C.
59% 66%
TENN.
81%
37%
ARK.
46%
16%
S.C.
59%
5%
MISS.
55%
14%
ALA.
64%
29%
GEORGIA
68%
35%
TEXAS
57%
31%
LA.
53%
39%
FLA.

N

GEOGRAPHY SKILLBUILDER
Interpreting Maps
1. **Location** *Between 1960 and 1971, which state showed the greatest increase in the percentage of registered African-American voters?*

Source: *Voter Mobilization and the Politics of Race*

of federal officials. About 3,200 protesters walked 12 miles a day and slept by the side of the road at night. More people joined along the way. By the time the marchers arrived in Montgomery four days later, there were 25,000 people taking part. Their march attracted national attention to their campaign. President Johnson took notice.

Voting Rights Act of 1965 To restrict access to voting, Southern states had laws that required people to pass a test about the state and federal constitutions. Some states required a literacy test. Segregationists also used intimidation and violence to prevent African Americans from exercising their rights to vote.

Reading History

D. Summarizing
What was the result of the Voting Rights Act of 1965 in Georgia?

The massive voter registration campaigns throughout the South brought national attention to these obvious discrimination practices. In response, Congress passed the **Voting Rights Act of 1965**. This act made it illegal for states to use these tactics to prevent African Americans from voting. In 1964, only 23 percent of all African Americans of voting age in the United States were registered to vote. By 1969, 61 percent had registered.

In Georgia, thousands of African Americans registered to vote in 1965. The African-American community gained enough political power to elect its own representatives to office. Six African Americans were elected to the Georgia State House of Representatives, including **Grace Towns Hamilton,** the first African-American woman from the Deep South elected to a state legislature.

Changes in the Movement

The civil rights movement made some impressive gains in the early 1960s. But by the mid-1960s, the movement was experiencing internal conflicts. Not everyone involved with the movement was happy with the speed and direction it had taken.

Civil Rights Acts of the 1950s and 1960s

CIVIL RIGHTS ACT OF 1957

- Established federal Commission on Civil Rights
- Established a Civil Rights Division in the Justice Department to enforce civil rights laws
- Increased federal power to protect voting rights

CIVIL RIGHTS ACT OF 1964

- Banned most discrimination in employment and in public accommodations
- Increased federal power to protect voting rights and speed up school desegregation
- Established Equal Employment Opportunity Commission to ensure fair treatment in employment

VOTING RIGHTS ACT OF 1965

- Eliminated voter literacy tests
- Enabled federal examiners to register voters

CIVIL RIGHTS ACT OF 1968

- Prohibited discrimination in the sale or rental of most housing
- Strengthened antilynching laws
- Made it a crime to harm civil rights workers

SKILLBUILDER Interpreting Charts

1. Which law do you think benefited the most people? Explain your choice.

Some wanted to continue using the nonviolent tactics that had worked so well in the past. Others wanted to use more forceful measures to gain their rights. Many African Americans, in the South and across the nation, were becoming angry and frustrated with the slow progress and continued white resistance. The new, young civil rights leaders were not willing to wait for the rewards of their efforts. Many African Americans outside the South felt that the civil rights movement had ignored their problems.

Radical Resistance and Separatism African Americans in major cities, such as Los Angeles, Detroit, New York, and Chicago, organized against discrimination, racism, and poverty. Frustrations often led to angry resistance. In August 1965, the black Los Angeles neighborhood of Watts was the scene of six days of rioting. The riot began because African Americans believed that Los Angeles police had beaten a black suspect. The next year, more than 40 different cases of violence that were linked to racial situations broke out.

Groups like the Black Muslims believed that King was wrong to accept violence passively. **Malcolm X** and other black leaders advocated self-defense. The Black Panthers, including Huey Newton and Bobby Seale, preached the use of violence to achieve freedom and equality.

In the late 1960s, some civil rights groups adopted the idea of "separatism," believing that separation and economic independence from white society was the best answer. Black Muslims criticized the civil rights movement for its willingness to work with whites. Organizations such as SNCC and CORE became more radical and militant.

Reading History

E. Finding Main Ideas Why did the civil rights movement become divided over nonviolence?

Background

Malcolm X eventually changed his mind about using violence. When he was assassinated in February 1965, Black Muslims were accused of the crime.

Opposition to the War Even Dr. King changed focus somewhat. He had not wanted to jeopardize President Johnson's support of civil rights by criticizing U.S. involvement in Vietnam. But in 1967, this changed. King opposed the war on moral grounds and because it took money away from federal antipoverty programs in the United States. He also objected because the soldiers were mostly poor and African American.

Martin Luther King, Jr.'s Assassination In April 1968, King traveled to Memphis, Tennessee, to help a group of sanitation workers who were striking for better pay and working conditions. On April 4, 1968, King was killed by an assassin's bullet as he stood on the balcony of the Lorraine Motel. He was 39 years old. The nation mourned the loss of the great civil rights leader. The night before he was killed, King spoke to a large congregation.

> **PRIMARY SOURCE**
>
> We've got some difficult days ahead. But it really doesn't matter with me now, because I've been to the mountaintop and I don't mind. Like anybody, I would like to live a long life. Longevity has its place. But I'm not concerned about that now. I just want to do God's will, and He's allowed me to go up to the mountain. And I've looked over and I've seen the Promised Land.
>
> Martin Luther King, Jr., April 3, 1968, Memphis, Tennessee

The turbulent struggle for civil rights, and the future events in the United States and Georgia that you will learn about in the next chapter, helped make our country what it is today.

Section Assessment

1. TERMS & NAMES

Explain the significance of:

a. March on Washington

b. Civil Rights Act of 1964

c. Voting Rights Act of 1965

d. Grace Towns Hamilton

e. Malcolm X

2. TAKING NOTES

Use a time line like the one shown to record important events of the civil rights movement covered in this section.

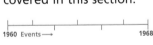

1960 Events → 1968

3. MAIN IDEAS

a. Why did civil rights leaders organize the August 1963 March on Washington?

b. What were the provisions of the Civil Rights Act of 1964?

c. Why did some African-American leaders move away from nonviolent direct action by the late 1960s?

4. CRITICAL THINKING

Making Inferences

Why do you think the right to vote was so important to African Americans?

Think About

• for whom they might vote

• for what they might vote

• what they were willing to endure to win voting rights

 Art/Speech Imagine that you are taking part in the March on Washington. Design a **poster** you might carry, or deliver a **speech** in favor of civil rights.

The Civil Rights Era

Executive
Order 8802
1942

1944
Smith v.
Allwright

1947
President's
Commission
on Civil Rights

Brown v. Board
of Education
1954

Montgomery
bus boycott
1955

1956
Southern
Manifesto

- Greensboro lunch
counter sit-in
- University of
Georgia admits
African American
students.
1960

1957
- Government
enforces
school
integration in
Little Rock.
- SCLC is
formed.

1961
Atlanta schools
begin integration.

1963
- Dr. King writes
"Letter from a
Birmingham Jail."
- March on
Washington
- President
Kennedy is
assassinated.

Civil Rights
Act of 1964
1964

1965
- March to
Montgomery
- Voting Rights
Act of 1965

1968
Dr. King is
assassinated.

TERMS & NAMES

Briefly explain the significance of the following.

1. NAACP
2. Executive Order 8802
3. Dixiecrat
4. Southern Manifesto
5. Montgomery bus boycott
6. Martin Luther King, Jr.
7. March on Washington
8. Civil Rights Act of 1964
9. Voting Rights Act of 1965
10. Malcolm X

REVIEW QUESTIONS

The Civil Rights Movement Begins (pages 447–450)

1. How did Southern whites respond to new African American rights?
2. Who was Primus King?
3. How did President Truman support civil rights?

The Movement Grows (pages 451–457)

4. Why did some call the date of the *Brown* v. *Board of Education* decision "Black Monday"?
5. What was the strategy of "massive resistance"?
6. What was the SCLC?
7. What strategies did civil rights protesters use?

Victories and Losses in the Movement (pages 458–465)

8. What events led to the March on Washington?
9. What were the results of African-American voter registration drives?
10. How did the strategies of Dr. King and Malcolm X differ?

CRITICAL THINKING

1. USING YOUR NOTES: COMPARING AND CONTRASTING

	Approach to Civil Rights
NAACP	
President Roosevelt	
President Truman	
Dr. Martin Luther King, Jr.	
President Eisenhower	
SCLC	
President Kennedy	
Malcolm X	
Black Panthers	

Using your completed chart, answer the questions below.

a. How did the NAACP and SCLC differ in their approach to civil rights?

b. How would you contrast the approaches of Dr. King, Malcolm X, and the Black Panthers?

2. ANALYZING LEADERSHIP

What qualities do you think made Martin Luther King, Jr., an effective leader?

3. APPLYING CITIZENSHIP SKILLS

How did the nonviolent methods used by protesters during the civil rights movement demonstrate good citizenship?

4. THEME: DEMOCRATIC IDEALS

How did the participants in the civil rights movement advance the democratic ideals of the United States?

5. MAKING GENERALIZATIONS

In what ways do you think the lives of Americans today differ from the lives of Americans who lived before the civil rights movement?

INTERACT *with* HISTORY

How has your study of the civil rights era influenced how you might act to change injustices in society?

Use the chart and your knowledge of American history to answer questions 1 through 3.

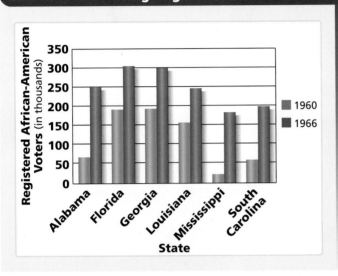

Effect of the Voting Rights Act of 1965

1. Which state had the lowest percentage of registered African-American voters in 1960?

   A. Mississippi

   B. Georgia

   C. Alabama

   D. South Carolina

2. Which state had the highest percentage of registered African-American voters in 1966?

   A. Florida

   B. Alabama

   C. Mississippi

   D. South Carolina

3. Which state had the biggest increase in registered African-American voters from 1960 to 1966?

   A. Alabama

   B. Mississippi

   C. Georgia

   D. Florida

TEST PRACTICE
CLASSZONE.COM

ALTERNATIVE ASSESSMENT

1. PERFORMING A DRAMATIC READING

Dr. Martin Luther King, Jr., and many others expressed their desires and dreams for change in American society through books, articles, speeches, poetry, and songs. Select one reading that you feel reflects the ideals of the civil rights movement, and present your reading to the class.

2. COOPERATIVE LEARNING

The March on Washington was a pivotal moment in the American movement for civil rights. Use the Internet, books, and other resources to create a special radio broadcast on the March on Washington. Consider including the following content.

- Descriptions of and sound bytes from the marchers
- The recollections of participants
- Recordings of speeches
- Different newspaper accounts of the march

INTEGRATED TECHNOLOGY ACTIVITY

DESIGNING A WEB SITE

Select an important civil rights leader or event from Georgia history. Then research that event or person using the library and the Internet. Use the following items to prepare a Web site telling the story of that event or person.

- Books
- Articles
- Photographs
- News stories
- Documentaries

What effect did that person or event have on Georgia? How does that affect you today?

RESEARCH LINKS
CLASSZONE.COM

A Time of Transition 1960–1976

Veterans in Atlanta study the "Moving Wall," a half-size replica of the Vietnam Veterans Memorial that travels the country.

1962
Hartsfield Airport is rebuilt to accommodate jet airplanes.

1966
Milwaukee Braves move to Atlanta and become the Atlanta Braves.

GEORGIA USA   1960   1968

1963
Lyndon B. Johnson becomes president.

1964
Gulf of Tonkin Resolution is passed.

1968
Richard M. Nixon is elected president.

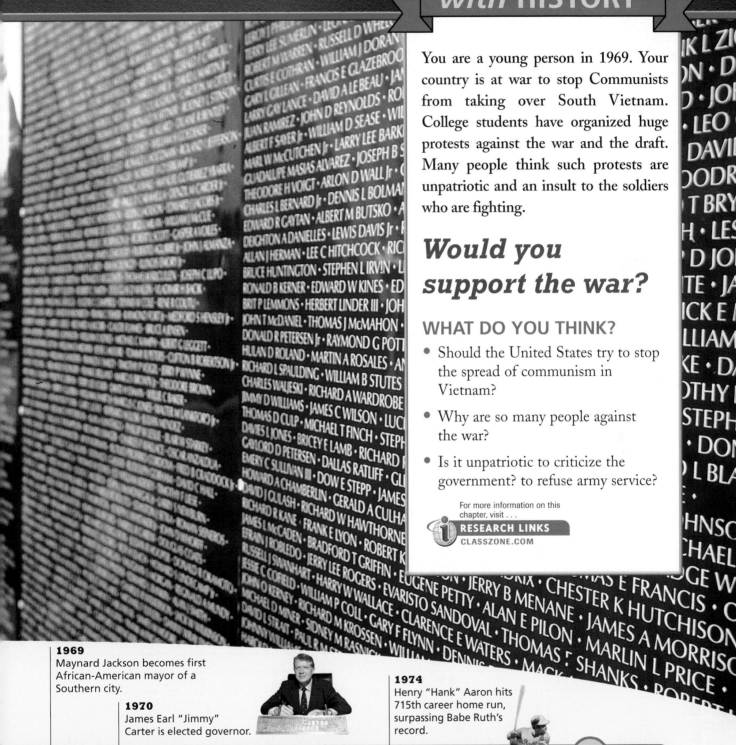

INTERACT with HISTORY

You are a young person in 1969. Your country is at war to stop Communists from taking over South Vietnam. College students have organized huge protests against the war and the draft. Many people think such protests are unpatriotic and an insult to the soldiers who are fighting.

Would you support the war?

WHAT DO YOU THINK?

- Should the United States try to stop the spread of communism in Vietnam?

- Why are so many people against the war?

- Is it unpatriotic to criticize the government? to refuse army service?

For more information on this chapter, visit . . .

 **RESEARCH LINKS** CLASSZONE.COM

1969
Maynard Jackson becomes first African-American mayor of a Southern city.

1970
James Earl "Jimmy" Carter is elected governor.

1974
Henry "Hank" Aaron hits 715th career home run, surpassing Babe Ruth's record.

1976

1970
Four students are killed during an antiwar protest at Kent State University.

1972
Watergate scandal begins.

1973
U.S. involvement in Vietnam War ends.

1976
U.S. celebrates its bicentennial.

A Time of Transition **469**

CHAPTER 21

Reading Strategy:
Categorizing Information

What Do You Know?

What do you know about the politics and protests of the Vietnam era? What other events of the 1960s contributed to changes in our society?

THINK ABOUT

• what you've seen in movies or read in books about the 1960s

• the effects of war on a country

What Do You Want to Know?

What questions do you have about the events of the 1960s? What would you like to know about the politics and social changes of that time? Record those questions in your notebook before you read the chapter.

Categorizing Information

Categorizing information as you read can help you identify and understand patterns and developments in historical events. When you categorize, you sort people, objects, ideas, or other information into groups. What information can you record about the political and social changes of the 1960s and 1970s as you read?

S *See Skillbuilder Handbook, page 550.*

Taking Notes

Political Changes	Social Changes

Effects	Effects

The Nation in Turmoil

MAIN IDEA	WHY IT MATTERS NOW	TERMS & NAMES
The social, political, economic, and technological changes of the 1960s and 1970s caused unrest and controversy throughout the nation.	Citizens learned the true meaning of democracy: that there is room for disagreement, but the country can still survive.	containment Gulf of Tonkin Resolution Tet Offensive Richard Nixon Twenty-Sixth Amendment Great Society Watergate

SETTING THE STAGE

The 1960s were a time of great social change in the United States. African Americans and whites challenged racial barriers. Women redefined what it meant to be female. People protested the Vietnam War in ways no other American war had been protested. Young people openly rebelled against established beliefs and practices. New technology changed lifestyles more rapidly than ever before.

Could a state and nation endure such rapid changes? Could people be strongly divided on important issues and still be united as a state and nation?

▲ "Hippies" and "flower children" rebelled against traditional values through different music, clothes, and lifestyles.

Vietnam

During the Cold War, the foreign policy of the United States was **containment,** or keeping communism from spreading around the world. Since 1950, the United States had sent money and military aid to those fighting communism in Vietnam, a small country in Southeast Asia that was divided politically into North Vietnam and South Vietnam.

The conflict between North and South Vietnam dragged on for many years, and American involvement increased steadily. By 1963, the United States had more than 16,000 military personnel there.

In 1964, President Lyndon Johnson asked Congress to pass the **Gulf of Tonkin Resolution,** giving him power to use military force in Vietnam. In March 1965, the United States began bombing North Vietnam and sent in ground troops. By the end of that year, 184,000 U.S. soldiers were stationed in Vietnam. By the end of 1968, more than 536,000 Americans were there.

Taking Notes

Use your chart to record the national political and social turmoil of the 1960s and 1970s.

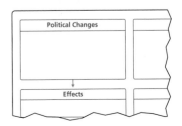

CONNECTIONS
Science to

Agent Orange

To give American soldiers a better chance against the Viet Cong, U.S. troops sprayed the jungle with the chemical Agent Orange, named for the orange bands that marked the drums in which it was stored. The chemical was a weed killer and helped destroy the hideouts and food supplies of the Viet Cong. But years later, people learned that Agent Orange may have harmed U.S. soldiers. Many who were exposed to the chemical became victims of skin diseases and cancers.

A Different Kind of War The fighting in Vietnam was different from what U.S. soldiers had faced in World War II or in the Korean War. There was no front line. That is, the enemy mixed in with the general population and fought everywhere—in the city streets, in the countryside, even recruiting boys to throw grenades into troop transports. The communist soldiers in South Vietnam, called Viet Cong, used guerrilla warfare. They would suddenly emerge from underground tunnels to fight. Then, they would disappear back into the tunnels.

Growing Unease with the War The Vietnam War was the first televised war. Americans were disturbed by the images of their "boys" wading through rice paddies and jungles surrounded by land mines and enemy fire. They also saw the devastation of villages in Vietnam. In January 1968, the Communists launched the **Tet Offensive.** They took over South Vietnamese cities, killing military personnel, government officials, and civilians. Americans were stunned. It made them question whether involvement in Vietnam was a wise idea. Hundreds of U.S. soldiers were dying every week. The cost of the war seemed too high.

As the war escalated, antiwar feelings grew at home. Religious leaders, civil rights activists, journalists, teachers, and students condemned the war. College campuses became centers for protests, which were seen on national television. In Georgia, the Board of Regents closed all of the colleges of the university system for a few days to protect their staff and students.

The U.S. Withdraws from Vietnam Americans began to realize that they were not winning the war. In March 1968, President Johnson announced that he would stop bombing most of North Vietnam. Instead, he would start bargaining for peace. Johnson decided not to run for re-election.

Richard Nixon, the Republican candidate, won the 1968 presidential election largely because he promised to bring "peace with honor." Finally, on January 27, 1973, the United States and South Vietnam signed a peace agreement with North Vietnam and the Viet Cong. The United States agreed to withdraw all its troops. North Vietnam agreed not to invade South Vietnam. On March 29, the last U.S. troops left Vietnam. In 1975, North Vietnam invaded South Vietnam and captured the capital, Saigon.

> **Background**
>
> Tet is the Vietnamese celebration of the lunar New Year.

> **Reading History**
>
> **A. Analyzing Causes** Why was the war so hard for the United States to win?

The Legacy of the War The impact of the Vietnam War on veterans and their families is still obvious. Many U.S. soldiers who fought in Vietnam were forever changed. Art Stiles, a teacher in Henry County, served for 19 months in Vietnam. He described his experience returning to the United States.

> **PRIMARY SOURCE**
>
> I left as a 20-year-old for Vietnam, ready to do battle for my country and our way of life. I got angry that others could not understand our noble cause. I had left our country thinking that the American people saw me as brave, heroic, or honorable. Little did I realize that I would come home to protestors who wanted to take their frustrations out on me.
>
> Sergeant Major (ret.) Art Stiles

The **Twenty-Sixth Amendment** in 1971 lowering the voting age from 21 to 18 is one of the most obvious political effects of the war. Supporters of the amendment argued that anyone old enough to be drafted should be allowed to vote. The military draft ended in 1973 because so many people opposed it. Georgia sent 228,000 soldiers to serve in Vietnam. Sadly, over 1,700 of them died in the conflict between 1955 and 1973.

Student Protests Against the War Many young people were not part of the hippie culture but did protest against the Vietnam War. College students became the largest, most vocal group of protesters and demonstrators. The biggest group of protesting college students was the Students for a Democratic Society, which led demonstrations across the country. They claimed that the United States was engaging them in an illegal political action; the war in Vietnam was a civil war and other countries should not be involved.

Reading History

B. Finding Main Ideas What role did the group Students for a Democratic Society play in the Vietnam era?

▼ Opinion was divided over the war. Supporters rallied in defense of the troops (left) and demonstrators protested U.S. involvement (right).

Belief in Social Progress

The 1960s began with a great deal of idealism. People felt they could make a difference. Many felt that the government should play a part in improving opportunities for all Americans.

The Great Society When Lyndon Johnson became president after Kennedy was assassinated, he inherited the Vietnam crisis. Johnson wanted to be remembered as a social reformer rather than as a war president. He created many domestic programs, including reforms in education, medical care for the elderly, aid to cities, and support for civil rights. He referred to his program as the **Great Society**. Many of these programs still exist today. Laws were also passed to protect the environment and provide federal money for education.

Crisis of Faith in Politics

Gradually, some of the idealism of the American people of the early 1960s began to wear away. Events of the early 1970s made some people unhappy with the government. They resented President Johnson's programs because they were funded by tax dollars. The extra expense caused deficit spending, which is spending more money than is available.

The Pentagon Papers Public anger and distrust of the federal government grew when people learned that leaders had not been truthful about the war. In 1971, Daniel Ellsberg released military documents known as the Pentagon Papers. They showed that the past four presidents, Eisenhower, Kennedy, Johnson, and Nixon, had not been honest with the public about U.S. involvement and goals in Vietnam.

Watergate The greatest blow to American confidence in its political leaders came in 1972 with the **Watergate** scandal. During the presidential campaign of 1972, some of Nixon's re-election campaign workers broke into the Democratic Party headquarters in the Watergate building in Washington, D.C. They wanted to steal information that could help Nixon get re-elected. Nixon may not have known about the break-in, but he participated in an attempt to cover it up. He illegally used the Central Intelligence Agency to stop a Federal Bureau of Investigation inquiry into Watergate. The Senate investigated the Watergate scandal. President Nixon resigned to avoid an impeachment. Vice President Gerald Ford was sworn in as president on August 9, 1974.

Reading History

C. Recognizing Effects How did Americans come to lose faith in politics?

Background

Eventually, 25 members of the Nixon administration were convicted and served prison terms for crimes connected to Watergate.

Unrest in Georgia

Georgia had its share of turmoil during the late 1960s. Many Georgians resisted changes that were taking place elsewhere in the nation. When news of Martin Luther King's assassination came in April 1968, riots occurred in Albany, Fort Valley, Macon, and Savannah. However, no riots occurred in Atlanta. Its leaders had learned how to handle crises in ways that avoided violence.

The battle to desegregate Georgia's schools continued into the 1970s. In February 1972, Richmond County received a court order for its schools to be integrated. Approximately 65 percent of white school children in Augusta and Richmond County boycotted classes. As far away as Savannah, half of the city's white students were kept at home in support of the boycott.

In the next section, you will learn more about the changes that came to Georgia during this time.

Reading History

D. Summarizing
Why did Georgia students boycott classes in 1972?

▲ The *Atlanta Constitution* broke the news of Nixon's resignation.

Section ① Assessment

1. TERMS & NAMES

Explain the significance of:

a. containment

b. Gulf of Tonkin Resolution

c. Tet Offensive

d. Richard Nixon

e. Twenty-Sixth Amendment

f. Great Society

g. Watergate

2. TAKING NOTES

Review the section and identify a key event for each date on the time line below.

March 1965   January 1968   March 1968   January 1973

3. MAIN IDEAS

a. How did television affect support for the Vietnam War?

b. Why was there a "crisis of faith" in politics during the war?

c. What role did Students for a Democratic Society play during the Vietnam War?

4. CRITICAL THINKING

Forming and Supporting Opinions

What is your opinion of the way the United States ended its involvement in the Vietnam War?

Think About
• what happened to South Vietnam
• the United States' options

Technology/Language Arts Interview someone who remembers Watergate. Create a **radio broadcast** of the interview or write a question-and-answer **magazine feature**.

Changes in Georgia

<table>
<tr><td></td></tr>
</table>

MAIN IDEA	**WHY IT MATTERS NOW**	**TERMS & NAMES**
Political changes in Georgia in the 1960s and 1970s affected opportunities for people and the way groups saw one another.	Georgians began to learn to tolerate differences and to accept social and political change.	one man, one vote Maynard Jackson Lester Maddox Jimmy Carter MARTA

SETTING THE STAGE

The turmoil of the 1960s and 1970s allowed groups that had historically been silent to begin raising their voices. African Americans began to take advantage of the opportunities made available to them by the civil rights acts.

Changes in Georgia's political system made it possible to elect African Americans to political office for the first time since Reconstruction. Some whites welcomed this. Others did not. But things could not continue the way they had. Change was inevitable. What did that mean for Georgians of both races?

▲ African Americans and whites wait in line together to vote.

Political Changes

Before 1962, Georgia used the county unit system of voting. Elections were not settled by popular vote. Instead, each of Georgia's 159 counties was assigned two, four, or six unit votes, depending on its population. The candidate who won the most votes in the county won the county's unit votes. This system gave unequal power to rural counties and helped maintain white control of Georgia politics.

A New Voting System   In April 1962, the U.S. Supreme Court ruled that state legislatures could not give more representation to one group over another in this way. They called it the **"one man, one vote"** decision. Because urban counties and rural counties often had different goals and voted differently on issues, Atlanta politicians welcomed this ruling. Many people lived in Fulton County, where Atlanta is located, but often lost out in political issues because smaller rural counties would outvote them.

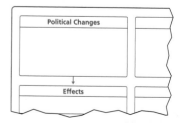

Use your chart to record Georgia's political and social turmoil of the 1960s and 1970s.

African-American Politicians Are Elected The Supreme Court decision meant that elections would be decided by the most *people* voting for a candidate—not the most *counties*. After the change in the voting system, Leroy Johnson was elected to the state senate from Atlanta's Fifth Congressional District. He was the first African American elected to the state legislature since Reconstruction.

Reading History

A. Finding Main Ideas Why were Johnson's, Jackson's, and Young's elections important events for African-American voters?

In 1969, **Maynard Jackson** ran for vice-mayor of Atlanta and won. In 1973, Jackson was elected mayor of Atlanta. He was the first African-American mayor of a major Southern city. Jackson won 25 percent of the white vote. In 1972, Andrew Young won Atlanta's Fifth District congressional seat. White voters helped him win the race.

Lester Maddox **Lester Maddox** was a controversial figure in Georgia politics. He strongly opposed integration and the gains of the civil rights movement. Maddox lost two campaigns for mayor of Atlanta and another for state lieutenant governor in the late 1950s and early 1960s.

Maddox was the Democratic candidate for governor in 1966. Republicans had voted for Maddox in the Democratic primary, thinking that he would be the easiest Democratic candidate to defeat. In the election, neither candidate received a majority. The General Assembly had to pick the winner. Democrats were in control of the assembly, and they chose Maddox.

Maddox surprised many Georgians when he denounced violence and vowed to uphold the authority of the federal government. Maddox established "Little People's Day" at the Capitol every other Wednesday. It was open to black and white visitors alike. Maddox appointed African Americans to local draft boards and the state patrol.

Reading History

B. Supporting Opinions What is your opinion of the concept of a "Little People's Day"?

Jimmy Carter In 1966, Lester Maddox was challenged in the Democratic primary by James Earl **"Jimmy" Carter.** At the time, Carter was a little-known state senator from south Georgia and he did not win. Carter campaigned again for governor in 1970. Carter promised to continue "Little People's Day." Maddox ran for lieutenant governor because he was not allowed by law to run for a second term as governor. Both men won their elections.

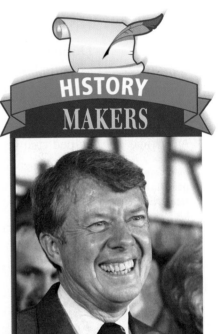

HISTORY MAKERS

JAMES EARL CARTER, JR.
1924–

James Earl (Jimmy) Carter was born and raised in Plains, Georgia. He served seven years as a naval officer on nuclear submarines and then returned to Plains to take over the Carter family farms. In 1962, he entered state politics as a senator, and eight years later he was elected governor of Georgia. He emphasized efficiency in government and the removal of racial barriers.

Carter said in his inaugural speech: "[T]he time for racial segregation is over. . . . No poor, rural, weak, or black person should ever have to bear the additional burden of being deprived of the opportunity of an education, a job, or simple justice."

Jimmy Carter and his wife, Rosalynn, had travelled throughout Georgia and listened to its people and their concerns. Carter wanted to improve Georgia's image, and he started by reorganizing the state government. Carter said that he would be a "New South" governor. He told his supporters, "I say to you quite frankly that the time for racial discrimination is over."

Social Changes

During the 1960s and 1970s, Georgia society was changing as much as its politics. People from all walks of life and various events contributed to the changing environment.

Hank Aaron   Outside of the political arena, a sports event in 1974 helped change the face of race relations. On April 8, 1974, an Atlanta Braves baseball player, Henry "Hank" Aaron, hit his 715th career home run. His record surpassed Babe Ruth's home run record.

President Nixon called to congratulate him. Clearly, Aaron had become a sports hero. What many people didn't know was that he had received many threats and hate mail. Some people did not want an African American to break Babe Ruth's record. Aaron had hired a bodyguard, moved to different housing, and used a false name when he registered in hotels. At the end of the game, Aaron said, "I just thank God it's all over."

Population and Housing   By 1960, Atlanta's population was 36 percent African American. By 1966, the city's population was 44 percent African American. Between 1960 and 1970, 70,000 blacks moved into Atlanta, while 60,000 whites moved out. Around 1963, Atlanta's business leaders formed an investment group to provide loans to develop new housing in the city.

During the same time, the metropolitan area added 160,000 new jobs. The possibility for access to more jobs and affordable public transportation was assured when **MARTA**—Metropolitan Atlanta

▼ An elaborate ceremony was held before the game in which Hank Aaron hit his famous record-breaking home run.

Reading History

C. Making Inferences How did Hank Aaron's record change the face of Georgia's race relations?

Rapid Transit Authority—was approved in 1971. The general assembly passed a one-cent local sales tax to help fund MARTA. For workers in downtown Atlanta, MARTA promised an affordable way to get to work and connected different parts of the metropolitan area.

Legislators from all across the state promoted the bill. Atlanta would be the first Southern city to have a rapid transit system. That would be good for the entire state because it would be a sign of progress and Georgia's commitment to be a state that is good for business.

▲ MARTA service began on June 30, 1979.

Reading History

D. Finding Main Ideas How did MARTA contribute to the growth of downtown Atlanta and improve conditions for workers?

More Choices for Georgians

As Atlanta grew, people began to see the city as the social and cultural capital of the state to a greater degree than they saw it as the political capital. More importantly, the image of Atlanta—and of Georgia—was changing. As people from all over the country made their way to the attractions of Atlanta, their image of "Georgia" was that of a new and exciting place. However, the growth of Atlanta did not necessarily contribute to the growth of the rest of the state, as you'll learn in the next section.

Section 2 Assessment

1. TERMS & NAMES

Explain the significance of:

a. one man, one vote

b. Maynard Jackson

c. Lester Maddox

d. Jimmy Carter

e. MARTA

2. TAKING NOTES

Use a spider diagram to describe how changes in Georgia politics affected African Americans.

Changes for African Americans

3. MAIN IDEAS

a. How was Maddox able to defeat Carter in the 1966 governor's race?

b. Why were the elections of Johnson, Jackson, and Young especially important to black voters?

c. How did MARTA help people who worked in downtown Atlanta?

4. CRITICAL THINKING

Evaluating

Why did the "one man, one vote" decision please Atlanta's politicians?

Think About

• the number of counties in Georgia

• the concentration of population in Georgia

Math/Language Arts Research Hank Aaron and create a **graph** of his baseball statistics, or prepare a one-page **report** of his life after retiring from baseball.

Two Georgias Take Shape

MAIN IDEA	WHY IT MATTERS NOW	TERMS & NAMES
Atlanta's rapid growth between 1960 and 1980 caused differences between the metropolitan region and the rest of the state.	Over half of Georgia's population lives in the metropolitan Atlanta region. Atlanta determines much of what happens in the state.	Hartsfield International Airport Two Georgias

SETTING THE STAGE

Before the 1960s, Georgia was primarily a rural state. During the 1960s, cities started trying to attract more businesses and to convince people to relocate there. Atlanta led the way in attracting large businesses. Why would a "charming Southern state" want to change its image? What would be the impact of millions of dollars in road construction? How would Georgia change with new businesses coming to the state?

▲ A regional plan laid out in 1946 paved the way for Atlanta to become not only a regional center but a leader in the Sunbelt states.

Atlanta, USA

Atlanta's business and political leaders worked hard to present Atlanta as a modern city. They wanted people to think of Atlanta as more than a city in the South, but as an international city—one that could compete with cities around the United States and around the world. These leaders wanted people outside of Atlanta to see the city as an exciting, dynamic place that would be a good location for businesses, events, and people. Many state advertising campaigns referred to the city as "Atlanta, USA."

The Role of Transportation   One of the most important factors in Atlanta's development was transportation. In the 19th century, Atlanta developed because of the many railroads that ran in and out of the city. In the twentieth century, the airport and interstate system spurred great growth. As early as 1946, Mayor Hartsfield had introduced plans for the "Downtown Connector." His plan brought major interstate highways through the heart of downtown Atlanta. They would connect the north side and the south side. With another interstate highway running east and west, Atlanta would become the crossroads of the South.

Taking Notes

Use your chart to record the political and social turmoil that shaped two Georgias.

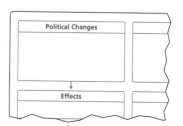

Political Changes

Effects

Reading History

A. Analyzing Causes, Recognizing Effects How did the growth of Atlanta's transportation system result in the growth of the city?

Mayor Hartsfield also wanted to make Atlanta a major air transportation center. In 1962, Hartsfield Airport was reconstructed so that jet airplanes could use the airport. With a good transportation system, people from all over the world could come to Atlanta. In 1971, Hartsfield Airport became **Hartsfield International Airport.**

The new transportation system brought large businesses to Atlanta. New businesses brought employees with them. The city became a center for conventions.

Atlanta's leaders worked to bring professional sports franchises to the city. The Atlanta Braves, a major league baseball team, began to play in the city in 1966. The same year, the Falcons, an NFL football team, took the field for the first time. The Atlanta Hawks, the professional basketball team, came a couple of years later.

Atlanta's leaders also focused on developing entertainment and cultural destinations. Six Flags Over Georgia came to Atlanta in the late 1960s, along with the Atlanta Civic Center, the Peachtree Center, and the Merchandise Mart. By the end of the decade, the World Congress Center was being developed. New choices for entertainment and cultural events were easily accessible to people all over Georgia and throughout the Southeast.

When people visited Atlanta, they decided it might be a nice place to live. In 1965, for the first time, Atlanta needed two phone directories because its population had grown so large. By the end of the 1970s, "metropolitan Atlanta" included 15 counties and 40 percent of the state's population. The counties surrounding Atlanta were a mixture of suburbs, office buildings, apartment complexes, and malls.

▲ In 1971, Hartsfield Airport became Hartsfield International Airport.

The Other Georgia

Rural Georgia in the 1970s looked very different from metropolitan Atlanta. Many rural counties still did not have enough doctors, dentists, and medical facilities. The infant death rate remained higher than the national average.

Many Georgians changed the way they earned their income. Many people stopped farming and began commuting to towns and cities to work in service industry jobs. For those who continued farming, their farms became larger, and the land became more valuable.

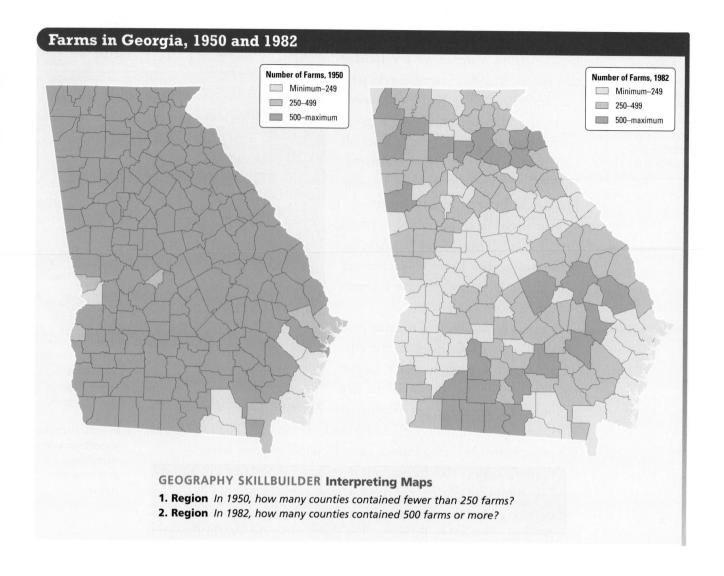

Number of Farms, 1950
- Minimum–249
- 250–499
- 500–maximum

Number of Farms, 1982
- Minimum–249
- 250–499
- 500–maximum

GEOGRAPHY SKILLBUILDER **Interpreting Maps**
1. **Region** *In 1950, how many counties contained fewer than 250 farms?*
2. **Region** *In 1982, how many counties contained 500 farms or more?*

Housing Housing improved for many Georgians. The "ranch" style became popular for new houses. The ranch style was a one-story house, typically with several bedrooms, a bathroom, a living room, a kitchen, and a den.

Televisions and air conditioners were popular appliances in Georgia in the 1960s. By the late 1960s, 94 percent of Georgia homes had television sets. By the 1970s, most homes had electricity, stoves, refrigerators, and telephones. Some had automatic washers and dryers.

The changes in housing and conveniences changed some social habits. Through Georgia's early years, families enjoyed sitting on their front porches in the evening. It was cooler outside than inside, and it gave them a chance to talk with each other or to visit with neighbors who were close by. But many ranch homes of the 1960s didn't include a large porch. The addition of air conditioning and television prompted many families to stay inside and gather in front of the TV where it was cool.

Other cities, particularly Savannah, tried to maintain the Old South charm that had made them popular with tourists. Savannah, Georgia's

Reading History

B. Supporting Opinions What aspects of Savannah would make it a popular tourist destination?

oldest city, continued its effort to restore and preserve its old homes and gardens. Civic leaders started developing the riverfront with hotels, shops, and restaurants.

Growth of Two Georgias

Transportation contributed to the development of Atlanta. Businesses wanted to locate in areas where they could be quickly connected to other business centers. People wanted to live where they had easy access to a good transportation system so they could get to work easily.

Towns grew along major highways. Towns farther away began to wither. People began to refer to **"Two Georgias."** Some used the term to mean that Atlanta was one kind of Georgia, and everything else was "the other Georgia." Others used "Two Georgias" to mean that some places were growing because of transportation and businesses, but in "the other Georgia," things were staying as they had been for decades.

Both meanings of "Two Georgias" describe the challenges facing Georgia even today. How do state leaders balance the needs of metropolitan residents with the needs of rural residents?

As the nation approached its bicentennial, many states struggled with similar issues. In the next chapter you will learn how one Georgian proposed to improve the economy and restore American confidence in its political system.

Section ③ Assessment

1. TERMS & NAMES

Explain the significance of:

a. Hartsfield International Airport

b. Two Georgias

2. TAKING NOTES

Use a diagram like the one below to identify the factors that contributed to the growth of Atlanta.

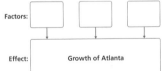

Factors:

Effect: Growth of Atlanta

3. MAIN IDEAS

a. Why did Atlanta's leaders advertise it as "Atlanta, USA"?

b. How did farms change in the 1960s and 1970s?

c. What happened to areas of Georgia that did not get major highway systems?

4. CRITICAL THINKING

Forming and Supporting Opinions

What political and economic issues face the "Two Georgias"?

Think About
- where business will grow
- where the state will spend money to make improvements
- where politicians will find the most voters

Speech/Technology Write and perform a television **commercial** or design a **Web site** that highlights both urban and rural Georgia lifestyles.

VISUAL SUMMARY

The Country Transitions, 1960 to 1976

1962
U.S. Supreme Court rules "one man, one vote."

1964
• Lyndon Johnson is elected President.
• Congress passes Gulf of Tonkin Resolution.

1965
U.S. begins bombing North Vietnam.

1966
Jimmy Carter becomes Georgia's governor.

1968
• Communists launch Tet Offensive.
• Richard Nixon is elected President.
• Dr. King is assassinated.

• Richmond County schools are ordered to integrate.
• Watergate scandal is revealed.
1972

• Peace agreement is signed.
• Maynard Jackson becomes first Southern African-American mayor.
1973

• President Nixon resigns.
• Gerald Ford becomes President.
• Hank Aaron hits 715th home run.
1974

TERMS & NAMES

Briefly explain the significance of the following.

1. containment
2. Gulf of Tonkin Resolution
3. Tet Offensive
4. Richard Nixon
5. Twenty-Sixth Amendment
6. Watergate
7. Maynard Jackson
8. Lester Maddox
9. Jimmy Carter
10. MARTA

REVIEW QUESTIONS

The Nation in Turmoil (pages 471–475)

1. What factors led to American antiwar feelings?
2. How did the war impact the United States?
3. What was the Great Society?
4. What factors led to unrest in Georgia in the late 1960s?

Changes in Georgia (pages 476–479)

5. How did the "one man, one vote" Supreme Court ruling affect Georgia?
6. How did Hank Aaron affect race relations in the South?
7. How did Atlanta change in the 1960s?

Two Georgias Take Shape (pages 480–483)

8. How did transportation impact Atlanta?
9. How did changes in housing and conveniences in the 1960s affect social habits?
10. What are the "Two Georgias"?

CRITICAL THINKING

1. USING YOUR NOTES:
CATEGORIZING INFORMATION

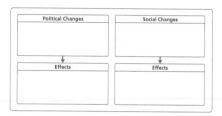

Using your completed chart, answer the questions below.

a. What factors led to a growing distrust of government?
b. What changes in this era most impacted African Americans?

2. ANALYZING LEADERSHIP

Evaluate the leadership of Lester Maddox. Why do you think he made such surprising decisions when elected to office?

3. APPLYING CITIZENSHIP SKILLS

During the Vietnam War, many Americans made the choice to avoid the draft and protest. Many broke the law to follow their conscience. Did they do the right thing? Why or why not?

4. THEME: DIVERSITY AND UNITY

How were civil rights for African Americans advanced in the 1960s?

5. MAKING DECISIONS

How would you evaluate President Johnson's leadership during the war and his decision not to seek a second term as president?

INTERACT with HISTORY

If you had lived during the Vietnam War, would you have supported or protested the war? Why?

Use the chart and your knowledge of American history to answer questions 1 through 3.

U.S. Deaths in Four Wars		
WAR	BATTLE DEATHS	OTHER DEATHS*
World War I	53,513	63,195
World War II	292,131	115,185
Korean War	33,629	20,617
Vietnam War	47,244	10,446

*accidents, diseases, etc.

Source: Harry G. Summers, Jr., *Vietnam War Almanac*

1. Which war or wars caused more battle deaths than the Vietnam War?
   A. World War I
   B. World War II
   C. World Wars I and II
   D. World War II and Korean War

2. Which war had the lowest ratio of non-battle deaths to battle deaths?
   A. World War I
   B. World War II
   C. Korean War
   D. Vietnam War

3. What does the third column represent?
   A. Wars
   B. Battle deaths
   C. Deaths from accidents, diseases, etc.
   D. U.S. deaths in Vietnam

TEST PRACTICE
CLASSZONE.COM

ALTERNATIVE ASSESSMENT

1. WRITING A LETTER

What political or social issue do you have a strong opinion about? Write a letter to a local, state, or national representative voicing your opinion. Be sure to support your opinion with facts. And be careful to use correct format, grammar, spelling, and punctuation.

2. COOPERATIVE LEARNING

The fall of President Richard Nixon was one of the most dramatic events of modern American history. Working in a small group, research Nixon's last two years in office. Pick one event from this time and write a one-act play about the incident. Use primary sources, such as diaries or tape transcripts, to create your dialogue. Present your play and ask for comments from your classmates.

INTEGRATED TECHNOLOGY ACTIVITY

PREPARING A WEB SITE

The cities in Georgia have changed dramatically in recent years. Pick a city (maybe yours) and design a Web site for attracting tourists. Plan the organization of the site. Then write your copy and collect photographs and images. Your site might include the following items.

- A history of your area
- A map of the area
- Biographies of important people
- Photographs of significant buildings and area attractions
- Information about area attractions and businesses
- Reviews of local restaurants

RESEARCH LINKS
CLASSZONE.COM

Problems and Prosperity 1976–1990

President Jimmy Carter sets the tone for a more informal presidency when he and his wife Rosalynn walk down Pennsylvania Avenue at his inauguration.

1976
Jimmy Carter becomes first Georgian elected president.

1979
"Georgia on My Mind" becomes state song.

1982
Diet Coke is introduced.

GEORGIA USA 1976

1978
Camp David Accords take place.

1979
Iran hostage crisis begins.

1980
Ronald Reagan is elected president.

It is 1976 and many Americans are struggling. Prices for food, housing, and health care are increasing at the same time a lot of people are unemployed. The resignation of the president two years earlier has left people disillusioned with government and what it can do to help their lives. A young Georgian, Jimmy Carter, has started campaigning for president. He promises to deal honestly with the people and work to improve the economy.

How would you win people's trust as leader?

WHAT DO YOU THINK?

- What leadership qualities are important during difficult times?

- What would you do to restore people's trust in government?

For more information on this chapter, visit . . .

RESEARCH LINKS
CLASSZONE.COM

1986
Carter Presidential Museum and Library is dedicated.

1988
Democratic Convention is held in Atlanta.

1990
Georgia's 24th Infant Division is involved ir Persian Gulf War.

1983

1990

1986
Space shuttle *Challenger* explodes, killing all seven astronauts.

1988
George H. W. Bush is elected president.

Reading Strategy: Summarizing

What Do You Know?

What do you know about the presidencies of Jimmy Carter and Ronald Reagan? What do you know about government today in Georgia?

THINK ABOUT

• what you have learned about recent presidencies and world events from news, books, or television

• what you have learned about Georgia government from television, newspapers, family, or friends

What Do You Want to Know?

What questions do you have about Presidents Carter and Reagan? What questions do you have about Georgia government? Record those questions in your notebook before you read the chapter.

Summarizing

Using your own words to write main ideas and important details as you read can help you remember more. To summarize, restate each main idea you find along with any important supporting details or facts. In the diagram below, summarize the key events of each presidency.

S *See Skillbuilder Handbook, page 549.*

Taking Notes

President Ford	
President Carter	
President Reagan	
President George H. W. Bush	

The Carter Years

MAIN IDEA	WHY IT MATTERS NOW	TERMS & NAMES
Jimmy Carter was president of the United States during some very difficult years for the country.	Even after he left the presidency, Carter continued to work as a diplomat for human rights.	OPEC Camp David Accords Iran hostage crisis

SETTING THE STAGE

After Watergate, confidence in the American presidency was at an all-time low. It would take someone very different in office to make the American people believe in the office again. No one expected a little-known Georgia governor to enter the presidential race of 1976. And, certainly, no one expected him to win! What could a president do to restore America's faith in the office? What did the people expect of him? Could any president provide all the answers needed to rebuild the economy and restore confidence?

▲ Jimmy Carter established a solid base of support in the South and among African Americans.

Gerald Ford

When Richard Nixon resigned because of the Watergate scandal in 1974, Gerald Ford became president. Ford did not want to see a former president put on trial, so he pardoned Nixon for any crimes committed during the Watergate scandal. Many people were angry because of the pardon.

During Ford's administration, the economy was in bad shape. Inflation was high, and people lost their jobs. Ford proposed a program to fight inflation, but it was largely unsuccessful.

Ford was the Republican candidate in the 1976 presidential election. But he lost the election to Democrat Jimmy Carter, the former governor of Georgia.

Jimmy Carter Is Elected

Jimmy Carter surprised friends and other politicians in Georgia when he decided not to run for re-election for Georgia governor in 1975. Instead, he would run for president of the United States. Most political commentators thought Carter had no chance. Few people outside of Georgia knew anything about him. One big obstacle that he would have to overcome was the image that Southerners were racist.

Taking Notes

Use your chart to summarize the key events of the Carter years.

President Ford	
President Carter	
President Reagan	

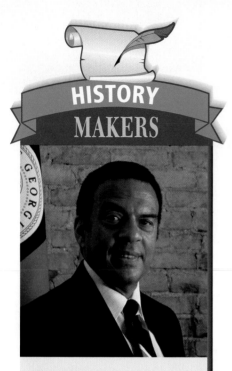
**ANDREW JACKSON
YOUNG, JR.
1932–**

As a young minister, Andrew Jackson Young, Jr., became interested in nonviolent resistance to achieve social change. During the civil rights movement of the late 1950s, Young registered African-American voters and organized peaceful protests, even in the face of death threats. Young worked closely with Dr. Martin Luther King, Jr., and was with him when he was shot in 1968.

In 1972, Young became Georgia's first African-American congressman since Reconstruction. President Carter appointed Young ambassador to the United Nations in 1976. Young was elected mayor of Atlanta in 1981 and again in 1985. Today, Young remains active in the struggle for human rights.

Help from Andrew Young   Andrew Young, one of Atlanta's black senators, helped campaign for Carter. They had worked together when Carter was governor. Young had seen how Carter interacted with African Americans and with whites. Young advised Governor Carter on a number of issues. When Carter ran for president, Young helped win the support of African-American leaders across the country. Because Young had been a leader in the civil rights movement and an aide to Martin Luther King, Jr., people listened to him.

An Honest Politician   In his campaign, Carter said he would never lie to the American people. He promised honesty in government and support for human rights throughout the world. He also ran as an "outsider"—someone who had conducted his political career outside Washington, D.C. The race was close. The states were almost evenly divided between Ford and Carter. In the end, Carter won. Carter became the first candidate from Georgia to be elected president, and the first presidential candidate from the Deep South to be elected since the Civil War.

Carter Takes Office

Americans hoped that Carter would bring fresh solutions to the country's economic problems and restore faith in American government. In his first speech as president, his inaugural address, Carter opened by saying, "This inauguration ceremony marks a new beginning, a new dedication within our Government, and a new spirit among us all." He continued the theme of working together.

> **PRIMARY SOURCE**
>
> Let us create together a new national spirit of unity and trust. Your strength can compensate for my weakness, and your wisdom can help to minimize my mistakes. . . . Let us learn together and laugh together and work together and pray together, confident that in the end we will triumph together in the right.
>
> President James Earl Carter, inaugural address, January 20, 1976

Reading History

A. Drawing Conclusions
Why were Carter's assurances of honesty important in his election campaign?

President Carter promised to remain "close" to the American people. After the speech, he and his wife walked from the Capitol building to the White House instead of taking the traditional limousine ride.

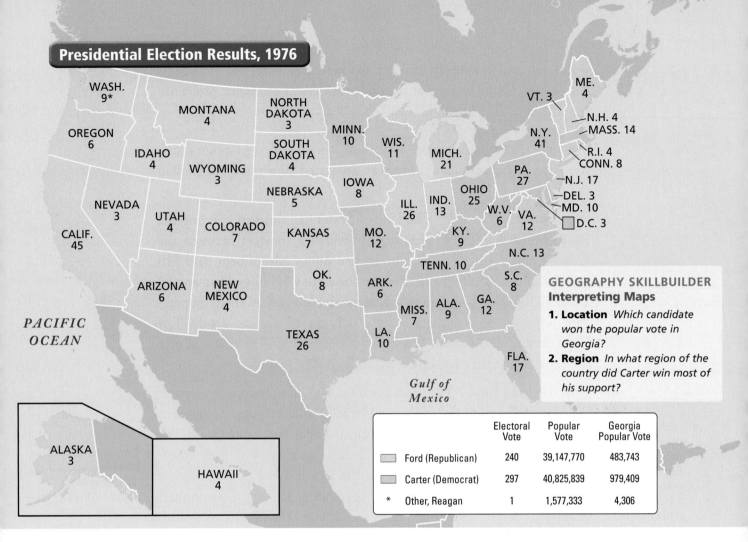

Presidential Election Results, 1976

WASH.
9*

OREGON
6

MONTANA
4

IDAHO
4

WYOMING
3

NEVADA
3

UTAH
4

CALIF.
45

ARIZONA
6

NORTH
DAKOTA
3

SOUTH
DAKOTA
4

NEBRASKA
5

COLORADO
7

NEW
MEXICO
4

MINN.
10

IOWA
8

KANSAS
7

OK.
8

TEXAS
26

WIS.
11

ILL.
26

MO.
12

ARK.
6

MISS.
7

LA.
10

MICH.
21

IND.
13

KY.
9

TENN. 10

ALA.
9

GA.
12

OHIO
25

W.V.
6

VA.
12

N.C. 13

S.C.
8

FLA.
17

PA.
27

N.Y.
41

VT. 3

ME.
4

N.H. 4

MASS. 14

R.I. 4

CONN. 8

N.J. 17

DEL. 3

MD. 10

D.C. 3

PACIFIC
OCEAN

Gulf of
Mexico

ALASKA
3

HAWAII
4

GEOGRAPHY SKILLBUILDER
Interpreting Maps

1. **Location** *Which candidate won the popular vote in Georgia?*
2. **Region** *In what region of the country did Carter win most of his support?*

		Electoral Vote	Popular Vote	Georgia Popular Vote
	Ford (Republican)	240	39,147,770	483,743
	Carter (Democrat)	297	40,825,839	979,409
*	Other, Reagan	1	1,577,333	4,306

Carter and Domestic Issues

The American people did elect an "outsider" as president, but long-time politicians in Washington did not like a newcomer in charge. Carter and Congress clashed many times.

Carter and the Energy Crisis One of the worst conflicts with Congress was over the energy crisis. Just after Carter took office in 1977, oil and natural gas shortages forced prices for gasoline and heating oil to rise rapidly. Carter asked Americans to do everything they could to conserve energy. He sent a national energy program to Congress for their approval. The program decreased oil imports, increased production of oil and natural gas at home, and promoted alternative energy sources such as coal, nuclear, and solar energy.

Congress passed some of Carter's proposals. However, **OPEC** (Organization of Petroleum Exporting Countries) raised its prices again, causing gasoline and oil prices to increase dramatically. OPEC is an organization of mainly Arab oil-producing nations. It raised its prices in protest of U.S. support of Israel in its war with neighboring Arab nations. The United States experienced inflation, which is a rise

Reading History

B. Summarizing
What was Carter's plan to reduce U.S. dependence on foreign supplies?

in prices of goods and a decrease in the value of money. The economy worsened, and businesses laid off workers. Like the two presidents before him, Carter was not able to solve America's economic problems.

Carter's Foreign Policy

President Carter faced several important issues involving foreign countries during his presidency. He was dedicated to a policy of human rights and high ideals.

The Panama Canal   The United States had finished building the Panama Canal in 1914. The canal provided a shortcut between the Atlantic and Pacific Oceans. The United States government paid $10 million for the right to the land where the canal was built and an annual fee of $250,000. Many Latin American people resented the U.S. presence. President Carter thought he should try to win the goodwill of Latin American countries. He signed a treaty in 1977 that would give the canal to Panama in the year 2000.

The Middle East   President Carter also tried to reduce tensions in the Middle East. In 1978, he invited Israeli Prime Minister Menachem Begin and Egyptian President Anwar al-Sadat to Camp David, the presidential retreat in Maryland, to discuss peace between their countries. In the **Camp David Accords,** the Israeli and Egyptian leaders agreed on how to end some of the long-standing disputes between their countries. Some historians think the Camp David Accords were Carter's most important achievement as President of the United States.

▼ Jimmy Carter's personal diplomacy led to a historic peace treaty signed by Menachem Begin of Israel (left) and Anwar al-Sadat of Egypt (right).

Reading History

C. Finding Main Ideas   What successes did Carter have in foreign policy?

Reading History

D. Making Inferences Why were Iranians angry with the U.S. for allowing the Shah to come to America?

The Hostage Crisis in Iran In November 1979, Muslim leaders in Iran overthrew the Shah (king) of Iran. Carter allowed the Shah to come to the United States for medical treatment. This made the Iranians angry. They struck back at the United States by taking over the American embassy in Iran. They took 52 Americans as hostages. This began the **Iran hostage crisis.**

The hostage crisis lasted for 444 days. As it dragged on, more Americans began to blame Carter.

Ronald Reagan, the former governor of California, was the Republican nominee for president. Reagan sounded very forceful in his campaign speeches when he spoke of using military force to bring the hostages home. Reagan's plans for dealing with the hostage crisis and the weak economy won the election for him.

Soon after the election, the Iranians began negotiating with the United States. On the day that Reagan took office, they agreed to release the hostages. On January 21, 1981, the day after the inauguration, former President Carter flew to West Germany to greet the freed hostages. Carter had pursued a policy of restraint, but Americans thought he was weak. In the next section, you will read how Reagan took the nation in a more conservative direction.

▲ Negotiations during Jimmy Carter's last month in office finally led to the release of the American hostages in Iran.

Section 1 Assessment

1. TERMS & NAMES

Explain the significance of:

a. OPEC

b. Camp David Accords

c. Iran hostage crisis

2. TAKING NOTES

Use a chart like the one below to list the high points and low points of the Carter presidency.

Carter's Presidency	
High Points	Low Points

3. MAIN IDEAS

a. Why did Carter win the 1976 election over Ford?

b. What were some problems related to energy use that occurred during Carter's term?

c. What successes did Carter have with foreign policy?

4. CRITICAL THINKING

Evaluating

Do you think Ford made a good decision in pardoning Nixon? Explain why or why not.

Think About

• the reputation of the presidential office

• the role of the president in upholding laws

• the political situation of the country

Math/Art Research inflation in the 1970s. Make a **graph** to show the annual rate change or create a **political cartoon** about how inflation affects people's lives.

The Reagan and Bush Years

MAIN IDEA	WHY IT MATTERS NOW	TERMS & NAMES

MAIN IDEA

Several changes in the 1980s made Georgia more widely known nationally and internationally.

WHY IT MATTERS NOW

The political and economic advances of the 1980s influenced the people, businesses, and ideas that are in Georgia today.

TERMS & NAMES

Ronald Reagan
supply-side economics
George H. W. Bush
Persian Gulf War
Andrew Young

SETTING THE STAGE

As president, Ronald Reagan worked to pull the country out of a recession and restore economic confidence. While he was doing that, Georgia's leaders were working to make Georgia better known to businesses throughout the world. Political and business leaders in Georgia advertised Georgia as a good place to visit, to work, and to live.

Could Georgia's leaders "sell" Georgia to the world? If they were successful, what would be the impact on Georgia? How would Georgia change?

Reagan's Domestic Policies

In his inaugural address, President **Ronald Reagan** said, "Government is not the solution to our problem. . . . It is time to check the growth of government." Reagan was a conservative who favored fewer government controls and more individual freedom in economic matters.

▲ Ronald Reagan promised voters he would "get government off our backs."

Lower Taxes   Reagan's administration followed the theory of **supply-side economics.** Simply put, this theory was that if taxes were lower, people would have more money to spend on products. Banks could loan money to businesses to improve productivity. The supply of goods would increase, and the prices of goods would go down. This was popularly known as the "trickle-down theory." President Reagan convinced Congress to lower income taxes by 25 percent over three years.

Government Is Less Involved   Reagan believed that business would grow more rapidly with less government interference. Therefore, he eased the restrictions on—or deregulated—many industries. For example, he deregulated the airline industry. Reagan also believed there should be less government spending on certain programs. He reduced or eliminated several government programs during his administration.

Taking Notes

Use your chart to summarize the key events of the Reagan and Bush presidencies.

President Ford	
President Carter	
President Reagan	

494   CHAPTER 22

Reagan Is Re-elected

After a recession in 1982, the American economy began to grow more rapidly than it had since the 1960s. By 1983, inflation had decreased and more people had jobs. Many people felt better about their jobs and their future. At the same time, President Reagan increased military spending and challenged the Soviet Union to give its citizens more freedoms.

The downside to Reagan's policies were that they caused large deficits in government spending. Deficits occur when one spends more money than is earned. Because tax rates were lower, the federal government had less money. While Reagan cut other programs, he increased spending on the military.

Reading History

A. Drawing Conclusions
Why did people give Reagan credit for the improved economy?

People credited Reagan for the improved economy. When he ran for re-election in 1984, he asked the question, "Are you better off now than you were four years ago?" Reagan won in a landslide victory over the Democratic candidate, Walter Mondale. Over 60 percent of Georgia voters chose Reagan.

A Changing World

Reagan's vice-president was **George H. W. Bush.** Because of the Twenty-Second Amendment, Reagan was not allowed to run for president for a third term. Bush ran for president in 1988. The Reagan presidency had been popular, so people voted for Bush, hoping he would continue Reagan's policies. Bush defeated the Democratic candidate, Michael Dukakis, winning the electoral votes of 41 states. Over 60 percent of Georgia voters chose Bush.

The Fall of the Soviet Union The world changed dramatically during President Bush's term. One of the biggest political events of the time was the end of the Soviet Union and communism in its territory in 1989. Several new European countries were formed from the former Soviet Union.

The Gulf War In August 1990, another crisis hit the Middle East. Iraq invaded a neighboring country, Kuwait. Kuwait was a major oil supplier to the United States. President Bush led a group of 39 nations in sending United Nations military forces to free Kuwait. The conflict was known as the **Persian Gulf War.** In less than one month, the U.N. forces drove the Iraqis out of Kuwait. The 24th Infantry Division from Fort

NOW & THEN

The Berlin Wall
Communists built the Berlin Wall in 1961 to separate Communist East Berlin from West Berlin. In November 1989, as communism began to fall, East Germans tore down the wall. The photograph below shows Germans celebrating the demolition of the wall. Andreas Ramos witnessed the event.

The final slab was moved away. A stream of East Germans began to pour through. . . . Looking around, I saw an indescribable joy in people's faces. It was the end of the government telling people what not to do, it was the end of the Wall, the war, the East, the West.

Stewart in Georgia played an important role in the conflict. President Bush visited Fort Stewart to welcome the troops home after the war.

Georgia on the Move

During the 1980s, Georgia was becoming more prominent in politics. In addition, its strong economy was attracting people from other parts of the country.

Andrew Young and Atlanta   In 1977, President Carter named **Andrew Young** ambassador to the United Nations. As Young visited countries of the world, he made connections that would later bring more international business and favorable attention to Georgia.

When Young returned to Atlanta in 1979, he ran for and was elected mayor. Under Young, Atlanta continued to grow. Much of this growth in the 1970s and early 1980s was in the metropolitan area—a large region of counties that extended well into north Georgia. "Edge cities" grew outside Atlanta as people left the inner city to find bigger houses, safer streets, and middle class neighborhoods. From 1982 to 1987, metropolitan Atlanta led the nation in job growth. People from other parts of Georgia and all over the world continued to flock to Atlanta.

The 1988 Democratic Convention   In 1988, the Democratic Party held its national convention in Atlanta. The delegates saw true Southern hospitality. The convention schedule kept them close to the

Reading History

B. Summarizing What contributions did Andrew Young make to Atlanta?

▼ During the 1980s, companies such as Coca-Cola, Delta, CNN, and SunTrust helped Atlanta lead the nation in job growth.

Omni Hotel and the World Congress Center where the convention was held. They saw the best of Atlanta. *National Geographic* wrote that Atlanta "prides itself on a degree of racial harmony and cooperation rare among large U.S. cities." The success of the Democratic Convention let others know that Atlanta and Georgia were capable of handling large crowds of people. It also made Georgia more familiar to people across the country.

▲ Televised coverage of the 1988 Democratic Convention put Georgia on the map for many Americans.

A Changing Population

At the end of the 1980s, approximately six million people were living in Georgia. Of those, two thirds had been born in the state; the other third had come from another state or another country. Through the 1980s, Georgia's population increased by 18.6 percent. Neighboring states averaged a growth of 17.4 percent during that time, and the national growth rate was only 9.8 percent.

As Abraham Lincoln stated in the Gettysburg Address, our government is "of the people, by the people, for the people." As the people of Georgia change, government must respond to their changing needs. In the next section, you will learn more about the structure of Georgia government.

Reading History

C. Analyzing Causes What caused Georgia's population growth to reach almost double the rate of the rest of the nation?

Section 2 Assessment

1. TERMS & NAMES

Explain the significance of:

a. Ronald Reagan

b. supply-side economics

c. George H. W. Bush

d. Persian Gulf War

e. Andrew Young

2. TAKING NOTES

Use a diagram like the one below to note the details of President Reagan's conservative policy goals.

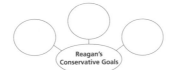

Reagan's Conservative Goals

3. MAIN IDEAS

a. What was Ronald Reagan's viewpoint on the role of government in business?

b. What dramatic world events occurred during George H. W. Bush's presidency?

c. How did Georgia's population change as businesses from other states and countries located in Georgia?

4. CRITICAL THINKING

Drawing Conclusions

What did President Reagan hope to accomplish with his economic policies? Was he successful?

Think About
• Ronald Reagan's continued popularity
• the rate of inflation
• deficit spending

ACTIVITY -OPTIONS- **Geography/Art** Create a **map** showing the republics that made up the Soviet Union and the independent nations they became, or make a **collage** of images of the times.

Modern State Government

MAIN IDEA	WHY IT MATTERS NOW	TERMS & NAMES
Georgia's state constitution outlines the framework for Georgia government.	All citizens of Georgia are under the laws and protection of the state constitution.	democratic republic executive branch legislative branch governor General Assembly judicial branch juvenile court system

SETTING THE STAGE

If you lived alone on an island, would you need government? Probably not. If you and only one other person lived on the island, would you need government? Probably so. It would not look like government as you know it in modern society, but the two of you would need some understanding of rules of behavior. That would be a very simple form of government.

Consider the six million people who live in Georgia. Who determines the rules for them? Who ensures the protection of their lives, property, and freedoms? Who pays for the public services they receive? What can each citizen do to participate in the state's government?

▲ Georgia's governor, the Senate and House of Representatives, and the Supreme Court are all located in the Capitol Building in Atlanta.

Three Levels of Government

The United States of America has three main levels of government: federal, or national; state; and local. Citizens receive services from each of the three levels. Citizens obey the laws at each level of government and pay the taxes imposed by each level. Each level of government has the power to make laws. If there is disagreement between the laws at different levels, the laws of the national government prevail.

A Democratic Republic Our system of government is a **democratic republic,** in which the supreme power lies in a body of citizens who choose representatives to govern them. The central government is called the federal government. Each state has a government. The state and national levels share certain powers. Each level also has powers granted only to its level.

Taking Notes

Use a diagram like the one below to make notes on the three branches of Georgia's state government.

Georgia's State Government

Branch   Branch   Branch
1.   1.   1.
2.   2.   2.

The State Constitution

Reading History

A. Supporting Opinions Why does government need written guidelines?

Government needs a written set of guidelines as a framework for how it conducts its job. That written document is a constitution. Georgia has had 10 state constitutions—the most recent one was adopted in 1983.

Georgia's constitutions have been based largely on the U.S. Constitution. Georgia's current constitution has a preamble and a bill of rights. It outlines the structure of governments, elections, the three branches of government, taxation, public education, and local government. It also details the process for amending the constitution.

Comparing Constitutions

United States Constitution	Georgia Constitution
PREAMBLE	
We the people of the United States, in order to form a more perfect Union, establish justice, insure domestic tranquility, provide for the common defense, promote the general welfare, and secure the blessings of liberty to ourselves and our posterity, do ordain and establish this Constitution.	To perpetuate the principles of free government, insure justice to all, preserve peace, promote the interest and happiness of the citizen and of the family, and transmit to posterity the enjoyment of liberty, we the people of Georgia, relying on the protection and guidance of almighty God, do ordain and establish this Constitution.
ARTICLES	
Article 1 — The Legislative Branch	Article 1 — The Bill of Rights
Article 2 — The Executive Branch	Article 2 — Voting and Elections
Article 3 — The Judicial Branch	Article 3 — Legislative Branch
Article 4 — Relations Among States	Article 4 — Constitutional Boards and Commissions
Article 5 — The Amending Process	Article 5 — Executive Branch
Article 6 — National Supremacy	Article 6 — Judicial Branch
Article 7 — Ratification Procedure	Article 7 — Taxations and Finance
Amendments 1–10 — The Bill of Rights	Article 8 — Education
Amendments 11–26 — Other Amendments	Article 9 — Counties and Municipal Corporations
	Article 10 — Amendments to the Constitution
	Article 11 — Miscellaneous Provisions
AMENDMENT PROCESS	
Amendments may be proposed by a vote of two-thirds of the members of both Houses of Congress or by a constitutional convention.	Amendments may be proposed by a vote of two-thirds of both Houses of the Georgia Legislature.
Amendments must be ratified by three-fourths of the state legislatures or by special state conventions.	Amendments must be ratified by a majority vote of the general electorate in a statewide referendum.

SKILLBUILDER Interpreting Charts

1. *What option is available in the amendment process of the U.S. Constitution that is not available in Georgia's process?*
2. *Which elements do the constitutions have in common?*

The Three Branches of Georgia Government

	Executive Branch	Legislative Branch	Judicial Branch
Primary Official or Group	Governor*	General Assembly	Supreme Court*
Primary Role	Enforce Laws	Make Laws	Interpret Laws
Support Organizations	Lieutenant Governor* State School Superintendent* Secretary of State* Attorney General* Commissioner of Agriculture* Commissioner of Insurance Commissioner of Labor*	Senate (up to 56 members)* House of Representatives (180 members or more)*	Court of Appeals* Superior Courts* State Courts Juvenile Courts Probate Courts Magistrate Courts

* Indicates elected official, or organization for which officials are elected in Georgia.

SKILLBUILDER Interpreting Charts

1. *What topic do all three branches of government address, each in a different way?*
2. *Which branch of government has one primary official?*

The Branches of Government

Georgia state government is divided into three branches. This helps ensure that one branch does not gain too much power.

The Legislative Branch

The **legislative branch** of state government is responsible for making the laws. In Georgia, the legislative branch is called the **General Assembly.** It is responsible for making the laws. The General Assembly has two houses, the House of Representatives and the Senate, that pass laws for Georgia. Voters elect the members of the legislative branch to two-year terms.

The Legislative Session The General Assembly meets for 40 days, beginning the second Monday in January. This session is one of the shortest among the state legislatures in the United States. During the session, many laws or bills are considered. They are either proposed, changed, or discarded. The proposals are usually for laws that (1) regulate people's behavior, (2) provide for local government, (3) allow the state to raise and spend money, or (4) provide for state services. Appropriations bills (bills that raise taxes or spend money) must come from the House of Representatives. The Senate is responsible for confirming the governor's choices for appointed positions.

Reading History

B. Summarizing What is the advantage of having three branches of government?

Georgia has the second largest state legislature in the country. The House of Representatives can have no fewer than 180 members. The Senate can have no more than 56 members. Congressional district boundaries usually cause much political debate. Boundaries are usually changed every 10 years when a new census is finished. The goal is to create congressional districts that ensure fair representation for all groups of people.

▲ Members applaud during a session of the Georgia House of Representatives.

Influencing the Legislature   Individual citizens can contact legislators to express their opinions. Lobbyists—professionals who are paid by groups or businesses to represent their ideas—also try to influence the vote of legislatures. Lobbyists may help legislators by providing them with information about issues before the General Assembly meets. But lobbyists also have access that ordinary citizens do not, because legislators tend to seek out the well-informed lobbyists for their opinions.

The Executive Branch

When the legislative branch passes laws, these laws must be enforced, or carried out. This is the duty of the **executive branch**. The executive branch is the largest branch of state government.

The chief officer of the executive branch is the **governor**. The powers of the governor include proposing the annual state budget, vetoing legislation, and appointing members of state boards. The governor represents Georgia to the federal government and to the governments of other states.

Reading History

C. Summarizing
What are constitutional officers?

The executive branch includes several constitutional officers who are heads of their departments. The constitutional officers are elected directly by the voters for four-year terms. They are called constitutional officers because their duties and authority are explained in the constitution. Constitutional officers include the governor, lieutenant governor, secretary of state, attorney general, commissioner of insurance, state school superintendent, commissioner of labor, and commissioner of agriculture.

The Judicial Branch

The **judicial branch** is made up of the different levels of courts. Courts apply and interpret the laws that have been made by the legislative branch. State courts handle two general classes of disputes: civil and criminal. In civil cases, the court must help settle disputes between two

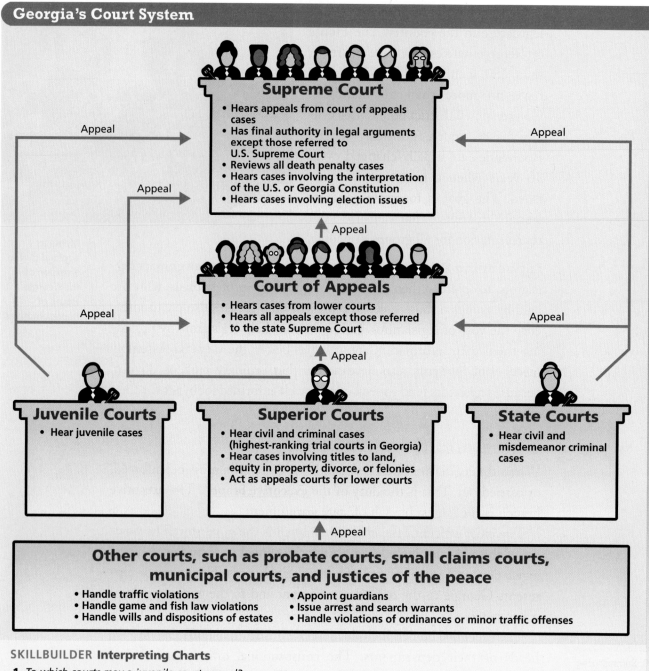

Supreme Court
- Hears appeals from court of appeals cases
- Has final authority in legal arguments except those referred to U.S. Supreme Court
- Reviews all death penalty cases
- Hears cases involving the interpretation of the U.S. or Georgia Constitution
- Hears cases involving election issues

Appeal

Appeal

Appeal

Appeal

Court of Appeals
- Hears cases from lower courts
- Hears all appeals except those referred to the state Supreme Court

Appeal

Appeal

Appeal

Appeal

Juvenile Courts
- Hear juvenile cases

Superior Courts
- Hear civil and criminal cases (highest-ranking trial courts in Georgia)
- Hear cases involving titles to land, equity in property, divorce, or felonies
- Act as appeals courts for lower courts

State Courts
- Hear civil and misdemeanor criminal cases

Appeal

Other courts, such as probate courts, small claims courts, municipal courts, and justices of the peace
- Handle traffic violations
- Handle game and fish law violations
- Handle wills and dispositions of estates
- Appoint guardians
- Issue arrest and search warrants
- Handle violations of ordinances or minor traffic offenses

SKILLBUILDER Interpreting Charts
1. *To which courts may a juvenile court appeal?*
2. *Which court would hear an appeal to a traffic violation case?*

or more parties. In criminal cases, the state takes legal action against someone who has been arrested for committing a crime (breaking the law). Different courts have different responsibilities.

The superior courts are trial courts that have the authority to hear cases involving state law. Two other types of trial courts are juvenile courts, for people under 17 years of age, and state courts.

The court of appeals and the Supreme Court do not hold trials. Instead, they review decisions made by the trial courts to determine

Reading History

D. Summarizing
Which courts do not hold trials?

whether the decisions were fair. The Georgia Supreme Court is the highest court in the state.

The Juvenile Court System

The **juvenile court system** was established to give special consideration to people under 17 years of age. The juvenile court system can be responsible for hearing cases of people who are up to 21 years of age if the offense is minor.

"Delinquent" is the word used to describe a juvenile who commits serious acts that would be considered criminal if an adult had committed them. If the parents cannot manage a young person whose actions would *not* be considered criminal if he or she were an adult, the youth is called an "unruly juvenile." A "deprived juvenile" is one who has been neglected or who needs special help from the court. The juvenile court hears cases for all three categories of juveniles.

Some counties have judges who hear only juvenile cases. In other counties, the superior court judge holds special sessions for juveniles or, appoints a referee to hear juvenile cases. If a juvenile commits a serious crime, such as murder, the juvenile may be tried as an adult. In that event, the superior court handles the case.

Juvenile Cases Children or youths under the age of 17 are usually tried in juvenile courts. Many people do not want juveniles to be treated in the same way as adult criminals.

▼ In a "mock court," young people learn the different roles that are involved in a trial, such as judge, jury, prosecutor, or defense attorney.

A delinquency trial for juveniles is almost the same as an adult criminal trial, except that many of the terms are changed to remind people that they are dealing with minors. The trial is known as an *adjudicatory hearing*. The sentencing is a *dispositional hearing*. Juveniles are not arrested; they are *detained*. Juveniles are not sentenced or imprisoned by the juvenile court. They are put into the *custody* of the juvenile or youth service agency of the state.

In recent years, there has been an increase in the number of violent crimes committed by juveniles. This has resulted in a larger number of juvenile offenders being treated as adults and tried in adult courts. After being convicted in an adult court, a juvenile is considered an adult for the rest of her or his life.

Plans for Positive Change Juvenile courts use skilled professionals to work out rehabilitation plans for juvenile delinquents to help them work through their problems and become law-abiding youths. After an agreement on a plan is reached, it is confirmed by a judicial order. The minor is responsible for following the plan. If he or she does not follow the plan, the juvenile is in contempt of court. In that case, a more serious or restrictive plan may be imposed.

The state court system is a service put in place by citizens for the protection of their fellow citizens. Local governments provide protections and services for citizens as well, as you will learn in the next section.

Vocabulary

minor: a person under legal age; not yet a legal adult

Reading History

E. Analyzing Causes Why is there a larger number of juvenile offenders being tried in adult court?

Section 3 Assessment

1. TERMS & NAMES

Explain the significance of:

a. democratic republic

b. legislative branch

c. General Assembly

d. executive branch

e. governor

f. judicial branch

g. juvenile court system

2. TAKING NOTES

Use a chart like the one below to note the different terms used to define juvenile and adult criminal cases.

Criminal Trials	
Juvenile	Adult

3. MAIN IDEAS

a. What role do lobbyists play?

b. What houses make up the General Assembly, and what is their role?

c. Why is there a separate judicial system for juveniles?

4. CRITICAL THINKING

Drawing Conclusions

Why does having three branches of government ensure that one authority cannot obtain too much power?

Think About

• representatives of the people at each level of government

• each level's responsibility to the people

ACTIVITY -OPTIONS- **Language Arts/Art** Write a **letter** to your state representative expressing an opinion about a state issue or create a **display** about the job of a state representative.

Georgia's Local Governments

4

MAIN IDEA
City and county governments provide many services to the people who live in them.

WHY IT MATTERS NOW
Many government services that benefit you are provided by local governments such as a county or city government.

TERMS & NAMES
property tax
usage fee
fourth branch

SETTING THE STAGE

Local governments supply a variety of government services. Georgia has 159 counties and 533 cities. Each county and city has a government. Cities range in size from Edgehill in Glascock County, which had 30 residents in the 2000 census, to Atlanta, with more than 400,000 residents. Voters elect the officials who run county and city governments. City and county school systems are special forms of governments that provide educational services.

▲ Registering to vote takes only a few minutes. After your county receives your completed form, it will send a card telling you where your voting location is.

City and County Government

Many of the day-to-day government services you use are provided by local governments. Police and fire protection come from local resources. Local governments maintain many of the roads you travel on, including the road signs and lights that keep those roads safe. They also supply building, plumbing, and electrical inspectors to make sure that new buildings are properly built.

County and city governments serve fewer people than the federal and state government. Focusing on the needs of local citizens, their services vary depending on funds available and the people's needs. For example, some local governments provide recycling services to residents, while others do not. Local governments are the levels of government closest to your community. Knowing more about how they operate makes you a better citizen—a citizen who participates and helps to get things done.

County Government The county that you live in has a county seat. It is often the oldest city in the county. Many of the county's government offices, including the county's courts, are in the county seat.

Taking Notes

Use a diagram like the one below to list important details and facts about Georgia's local governments.

County Government	City Government

Most funds that county governments need in order to operate come from one of two sources: funds from the federal and state governments and taxes and fees from local residents. Taxes include **property taxes** paid on the value of the land and buildings owned by people and businesses; local sales taxes, which are a small percentage added onto the state sales tax; and special purpose taxes, such as hotel-motel taxes, franchise taxes, etc. Fees include fines and penalties, such as traffic tickets, late charges, etc.; licenses and permits; and **usage fees,** such as small fees to visit and use a county park.

The forms of county government vary widely throughout Georgia. Each county has one or more full-time or part-time elected officials who oversee the government.

City Government   Cities in Georgia have one of three forms of government—weak mayor-council, strong mayor-council, and council-manager. Cities are chartered by the state. Each city charter describes its form of government. In all forms, voters elect the primary officials, who appoint others to oversee various departments of city government.

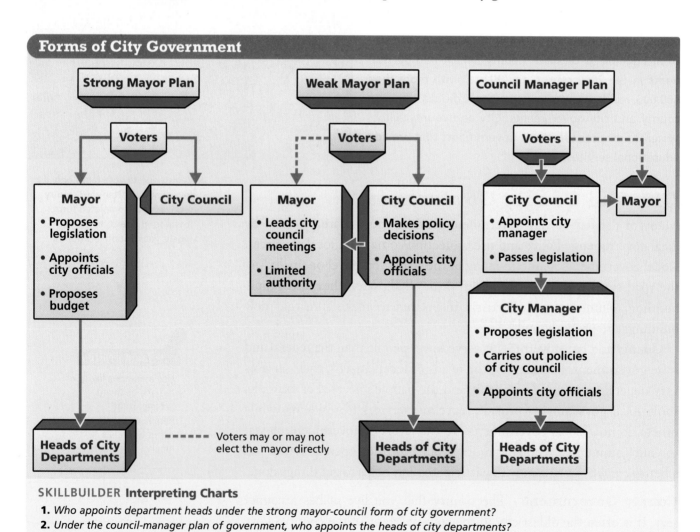

Forms of City Government

Strong Mayor Plan

Voters

Mayor
• Proposes legislation
• Appoints city officials
• Proposes budget

City Council

Heads of City Departments

Weak Mayor Plan

Voters

Mayor
• Leads city council meetings
• Limited authority

City Council
• Makes policy decisions
• Appoints city officials

Heads of City Departments

Council Manager Plan

Voters

City Council
• Appoints city manager
• Passes legislation

Mayor

City Manager
• Proposes legislation
• Carries out policies of city council
• Appoints city officials

Heads of City Departments

‑ ‑ ‑ ‑ ‑ Voters may or may not elect the mayor directly

SKILLBUILDER Interpreting Charts
1. *Who appoints department heads under the strong mayor-council form of city government?*
2. *Under the council-manager plan of government, who appoints the heads of city departments?*

Large cities like Atlanta have a strong mayor-council form. Medium-size and small cities usually use one of the other forms.

City services, like county services, vary. Most funds for city governments come from the same sources as county governments. The elected officials balance the needs of the city's residents against the funds available. They work to provide as many services as possible to the residents.

Citizenship

A citizen is a person who is granted services, protection, and rights by the city, county, state, or country in which he or she lives. In exchange, the citizen has certain duties. Citizens are the important **"fourth branch"** of government in a democratic republic.

Voting   Voting is one of the most important responsibilities and rights of a citizen. To be eligible to vote, a person must be a U.S. citizen, a legal resident of the state and county where he or she will be voting, and at least 18 years of age by the time of the next election.

Paying Taxes   All citizens receive government services. Citizens help pay for those services through different kinds of taxes.

Other Ways to Be Good Citizens   You do not have to wait until you are 18 years old to start being a good citizen. Citizens who volunteer work together to improve quality of life for other citizens. Volunteer agencies may be found at every level of government. Government can operate effectively only when citizens do their part.

Section 4 Assessment

1. TERMS & NAMES

Explain the significance of:

a. property tax

b. usage fee

c. "fourth branch"

2. TAKING NOTES

Use a diagram like the one shown below to note the important duties and rights of Georgia's citizens.

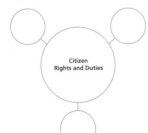

Citizen Rights and Duties

3. MAIN IDEAS

a. What sources of funding do local governments have?

b. What factors do county and city government leaders consider when deciding what services they should provide?

c. What are the requirements for voting eligibility in Georgia?

4. CRITICAL THINKING

Evaluating

Why is it important for citizens to participate in government by voting?

Think About

• the responsibilities of citizenship

• the need to make opinions known to elected officials

ACTIVITY -OPTIONS-   **Language Arts/Technology**   Research local volunteer opportunities for young people. Create a **bulletin board** or make a **Web site** listing groups that desire volunteer help.

VISUAL SUMMARY

VISUAL SUMMARY
Georgia Government Today

LEGISLATIVE BRANCH: THE GENERAL ASSEMBLY

- Consists of House of Representatives and Senate
- Passes laws for Georgia

EXECUTIVE BRANCH: THE GOVERNOR

- Proposes annual state budget
- Vetoes legislation
- Appoints members of state boards
- Represents state to federal government

JUDICIAL BRANCH: THE COURTS

- Applies and interprets laws
- Consists of superior court, juveniles courts, state courts, courts of appeals, Supreme Court, and other lower courts

TERMS & NAMES

Briefly explain the significance of the following.

1. OPEC
2. Camp David Accords
3. Iran hostage crisis
4. Ronald Reagan
5. George H. W. Bush
6. Persian Gulf War
7. Andrew Young
8. legislative branch
9. executive branch
10. property tax

REVIEW QUESTIONS

The Carter Years (pages 489–493)

1. Why was Carter's promise of honesty in government important to his election?
2. How did the Iran hostage crisis affect Carter's presidency?

The Reagan and Bush Years (pages 494–497)

3. How did Reagan attempt to check the growth of the federal government?
4. What contribution did Andrew Young make to Atlanta?

Modern State Government (pages 498–504)

5. What is the role of the legislative branch?
6. What are constitutional officers?

Georgia's Local Governments (pages 505–507)

7. What services do local governments provide?
8. What are the primary duties of a citizen?

CRITICAL THINKING

1. USING YOUR NOTES: SUMMARIZING

President Ford	
President Carter	
President Reagan	
President Bush	

Using your completed chart, answer the questions below.

a. Why was Carter able to defeat President Ford?

b. Why do you think President Reagan was able to win two terms in office while President Carter was elected for only one term?

2. ANALYZING LEADERSHIP

How has the leadership of Andrew Young impacted the state of Georgia?

3. APPLYING CITIZENSHIP SKILLS

How is responding to an energy crisis by conserving your own energy use a display of citizenship?

4. THEME: CITIZENSHIP

Which responsibility of citizenship do you think is the most important one? Why?

5. IDENTIFYING AND SOLVING PROBLEMS

What problems did the presidents covered in this chapter have to deal with? Which president do you think dealt with these issues most effectively? Why?

INTERACT with HISTORY

What can you personally do to contribute to the growth and prosperity of your community?

Use the graph and your knowledge of American history to answer questions 1 through 3.

Major Energy Sources, 1850–1980

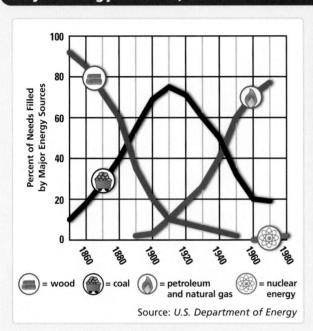

Percent of Needs Filled by Major Energy Sources

 = wood
= coal
= petroleum and natural gas
= nuclear energy

Source: *U.S. Department of Energy*

1. Which fuel supplied most of the nation's energy between 1850 and 1880?

   A. Wood
   B. Coal
   C. Petroleum and natural gas
   D. Nuclear energy

2. When did petroleum and natural gas begin to be used as fuel?

   A. 1850
   B. 1880
   C. 1890
   D. 1900

3. Which fuel supplied most of the nation's energy in 1970?

   A. Wood
   B. Coal
   C. Petroleum and natural gas
   D. Nuclear energy

 **TEST PRACTICE**
CLASSZONE.COM

ALTERNATIVE ASSESSMENT

1. MAKING A MAP

Research the territory that was the subject of the negotiations at Camp David in 1979. Make a three-dimensional map that shows the land, including its location relative to Egypt, Israel, and the other countries in the Middle East. Use your map to show the resources of the territory.

2. COOPERATIVE LEARNING

Volunteerism is an important part of citizenship. Find an opportunity to volunteer with a group in your community. Then create a video documentary showcasing your acts of service. Show your class what you did as a volunteer and reflect on your experiences. How does serving others change your outlook on life?

INTEGRATED TECHNOLOGY ACTIVITY

PREPARING AN ELECTRONIC PRESENTATION

Jimmy Carter served as our country's president and continues to serve as an international leader and humanitarian. Use your library and the Internet to research his accomplishments, focusing on his contributions as governor, as president, and as a private citizen. Then prepare an electronic presentation that depicts his life as a leader in Georgia and in the world community. Use newspaper articles, books, letters, photos, and your textbook as sources.

RESEARCH LINKS
CLASSZONE.COM

Georgia Enters the 21st Century 1990–present

Section 1
Georgia on the National and International Scene

Section 2
National Trends and Issues

Section 3
Georgia's Issues for the Future

Metropolitan Atlanta is entering its third consecutive decade of growth.

1987
Billy Payne organizes the Georgia Amateur Athletics Foundation.

1990
Atlanta is selected to host the 1996 Olympic Games.

1991
Zell Miller is elected governor and proposes HOPE scholarships.

GEORGIA
USA

1990

1990
Hubble Space Telescope is launched.

1992
William Clinton is elected president.

1993
Congress passes NAFTA.

→ INTERACT ←
with HISTORY

The time is four years from now, and you're about to finish high school. Your friends ask about your plans for the future. At graduation, the speaker urges your class not to focus just on earning money, but also to care about making the world a better place. How can you do that?

What can you contribute to the future?

WHAT DO YOU THINK?

- What are your talents, and how could you use them to benefit both yourself and society?

- What things do you really enjoy doing?

- What do you think the United States and the world need most from your generation?

For more information on this chapter, visit . . .

RESEARCH LINKS
CLASSZONE.COM

1995
Newt Gingrich is elected speaker of the House of Representatives.

1997
Turner Field becomes new home of the Atlanta Braves.

2002
Sonny Perdue becomes first Republican governor since Reconstruction.

present

1995
Murrah Building in Oklahoma City is bombed.

1998
Clinton is impeached.

2000
George W. Bush is elected president.

2001
World Trade Center and Pentagon are attacked by terrorists.

Reading Strategy:
Analyzing Causes and Recognizing Effects

What Do You Know?
What do you already know about how Atlanta and Georgia have grown and developed in recent years? What challenges are facing Georgia?

THINK ABOUT
- what you have read and seen in the news about trends in technology, globalization, and terrorism
- issues facing your community and your state

What Do You Want to Know?
What questions do you have about changes and challenges in your country? In your state? Record those questions in your notebook before you read the chapter.

Analyzing Causes and Recognizing Effects
A single event in history can have many causes. And one action or cause may result in many effects. Analyzing cause-and-effect relationships can help you understand more of what you read about history. Use the chart below to list and summarize the effects of Atlanta's growth in Georgia and the city of Atlanta.

 See Skillbuilder Handbook, page 551.

 Taking Notes

CAUSE: GROWTH OF GEORGIA AND ATLANTA					
Effect					
Summary of Effects					
Responses to Effects					

Georgia on the National and International Scene

MAIN IDEA	WHY IT MATTERS NOW	TERMS & NAMES
Georgia became recognized nationally and internationally during the 1990s.	Georgia's reputation among other states and countries affects its continued growth and opportunities for its citizens.	1996 Olympic Games Newt Gingrich Contract with America HOPE scholarships

SETTING THE STAGE

Georgia experienced rapid growth in the 1970s and 1980s, especially in Atlanta. For several years, Atlanta had tried to establish itself as an international city, to be seen in the same light as other world cities. Some people said that Atlanta didn't have what it takes to be like Paris, London, or Tokyo. What would it take for the world to see Atlanta as an international city?

Once Atlanta had won the right to host the Olympic Games, construction began on the many buildings that would be needed.

The 1996 Olympic Games

On September 18, 1990, the president of the International Olympic Committee made an announcement that would change the face of Atlanta and other cities in Georgia. "The International Olympic Committee has awarded the **1996 Olympic Games** to the city of—Atlanta!"

One Man's Dream The dream of bringing the international games to Georgia in 1996 began with Billy Payne. Payne began working on his plan in 1987. He organized a group called the Georgia Amateur Athletics Foundation and asked people to support the idea of Atlanta hosting the Olympic Games.

Mayor Andrew Young and other city and corporate leaders funded a presentation to be given by Payne and his committee to the U.S. Olympic Committee. In the spring of 1988, the U.S. Olympic Committee chose Atlanta to be the bid city from the United States.

For two years, Payne and his organizing committee prepared Atlanta's bid to host the 1996 Summer Games. Most of the venues and structures they promised were only dreams at the time. The stadiums,

Taking Notes

Use your chart to summarize the effects of Atlanta's growth on Georgia on the national and international scene.

CAUSE: GROWTH OF GEORGIA AND ATLANTA		
Effect		
Summary of Effects		

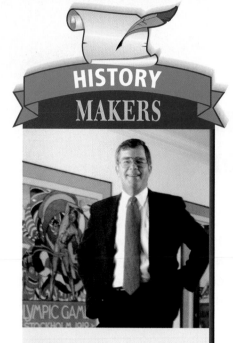

BILLY PAYNE
1947–

William Porter "Billy" Payne was born in Athens, Georgia, and has lived in Atlanta for over 40 years. It was Billy Payne's leadership that brought the 1996 Centennial Olympic Games to Atlanta. Payne was a leader during his years at the University of Georgia, too, as a star football player and an academic all-American. He went on to become a lawyer and the president of the Atlanta Committee for the Olympic Games. Under Payne's leadership, Atlanta staged the largest Olympics in history, with more athletes and more spectators than any previous Games.

aquatic centers, and Centennial Park would all need to be built for the Olympics. When Atlanta was awarded the bid, its residents celebrated and then began the hard work of preparing the city.

Reviving Atlanta   Atlanta had gone through some hard times in the late 1980s and early 1990s. Many downtown businesses had left for the suburbs. Rich's store in downtown Atlanta, a tradition since 1867, closed in 1991.

People began to see the Olympics as the spark that would bring new life to Atlanta. The booster spirit of Atlanta returned. Everyone began talking about getting things done "in time for the Olympics." Voters in Atlanta passed a referendum in 1994 for $150 million to repair streets and sewers. Atlanta was not the only city involved. Other sites in Georgia would host events, and they were making improvements also. They all prepared to entertain visitors and showcase their towns and cities. In each city, facilities were built that would remain long after the Olympic Games were over.

The Summer of 1996   On July 19, 1996, 100 days before the Games were to begin, not a single venue was completed. Crews worked around the clock to get everything in shape to receive visitors from around the world.

During the Games, the world learned that Atlanta had the transportation and facilities to host a world event. MARTA proved to be a capable transportation system, as did Hartsfield International Airport.

Terrorism Cannot Stop the Games   The Olympics were marred by a terrorist bombing at Centennial Park. Not even the bombing could keep the Games from going on. After the bombing, visitors united to prove that they would not give in to violence and terrorism. Some people carried signs that said, "The Games WILL go on!" As the Olympics closed, Georgians were proud of what they had accomplished.

Georgians in National Politics

In 1978, Republican **Newt Gingrich** was elected to the U.S. Congress. Before his election, he had been a history professor at West Georgia College. Gingrich worked to advance the platform of the Republican Party. He became a well-known face and voice for conservative policies. He helped other Republicans win congressional seats. In 1995, he was

Background

Jonesboro, Stone Mountain, Conyers, Columbus, Savannah, Augusta, and Athens all hosted events during the Olympics.

Reading History

A. Finding Main Ideas   How did hosting the Olympic Games benefit Atlanta?

▲ The Contract with America became the Republican Party's agenda for the first 100 days of the 105th Congress.

elected Speaker of the House of Representatives by the votes of the majority and the support of his Republican colleagues.

Gingrich developed a plan called the **Contract with America**. The Republican Party adopted it as its platform for the 1994 national elections. The contract generally wanted to restrict tax increases, find and eliminate wasteful spending, and make Congress more responsive to the public. Many Americans liked these ideas and voted for Republican candidates. Republicans gained control of both the House and the Senate for the first time in decades.

A Democratic President and a Republican Congress

Bill Clinton was elected president in 1992 and re-elected in 1996. With Republicans in control of Congress and a Democratic president, it was hard for one side or the other to win on issues. Americans grew angry when the president and Congress could not agree on a national budget. Most people grew impatient with Congress. This helped President Clinton win re-election in 1996.

During President Clinton's second term, he was accused of lying under oath about an improper relationship with a White House intern. Lying under oath is a crime, and the House of Representatives voted to impeach the president. During the trial in January 1999, the Senate acquitted President Clinton (found him "not guilty").

Georgia Continues to Grow

People and businesses continued to migrate to the edge cities outside of downtown Atlanta. By 2000, the population of Georgia was over eight million. Over half of the population lived in Atlanta and the Metropolitan

Reading History

B. Analyzing Causes Why would having a Republican-controlled Congress and a Democratic president—or vice versa—make it harder to pass legislation?

Vocabulary

impeach: to accuse a public official of wrongdoing

Statistical Area (MSA); 85 percent of those people lived in the 20 counties surrounding Atlanta.

Between the 1960s and the 1980s, when the city of Atlanta grew rapidly, the state legislature was usually willing to provide money to improve the infrastructure in Atlanta. The growth of Atlanta was good for the entire state. Georgia's political and business leaders continue to discuss the issue of whether it is fair for state money to support the city of Atlanta.

▲ Governor Zell Miller, a former teacher, emphasized education. He created the HOPE scholarship as well as the only free state-sponsored pre-kindergarten program in the nation.

New HOPE for Education

Zell Miller became Georgia's governor in 1991. He proposed a state-funded lottery, with the profits used to help deserving Georgia students acquire college scholarships. These were called **HOPE scholarships**.

The first HOPE scholarships were for two years of college. In 1994, the grant was expanded to four years of college. Students who earned at least a "B" average in their high school courses and attended a state school qualified. In April 2002, for the fifth year in a row, Georgia ranked first among the 50 states in academic-based student financial aid. By that time, more than 600,000 students had received HOPE scholarships.

In the next section, you will learn more about the issues facing Georgia and the nation.

Section 1 Assessment

1. TERMS & NAMES
Explain the significance of:
a. 1996 Olympic Games
b. Newt Gingrich
c. Contract with America
d. HOPE scholarships

2. TAKING NOTES
Use a time line like the one below to note the milestones in making Atlanta the site for the 1996 Olympic Games.

1986   1997

3. MAIN IDEAS
a. Describe the role of Billy Payne in bringing the Olympic Games to Atlanta.
b. How did Atlanta and the rest of Georgia benefit from the 1996 Olympic Games?
c. Describe Georgia's population in 2000 in terms of rural and urban sectors.

4. CRITICAL THINKING
Evaluating

If there is more demand for HOPE scholarships than there is money to fund them, how do you think Georgians should resolve that issue?

Think About
• more students qualifying for the scholarship

ACTIVITY -OPTIONS-   **Geography/Math** Create a color-coded **map** of Georgia's population density, or make a **pie chart** with the current population of its largest urban regions.

National Trends and Issues

MAIN IDEA	**WHY IT MATTERS NOW**	**TERMS & NAMES**
Globalization and acts of terrorism changed the world.	Americans must constantly adapt to changes in their daily lives as business and government respond to global issues.	information revolution globalization NAFTA terrorism

SETTING THE STAGE

Students born in the 1990s sometimes can't imagine life before cell phones, the Internet, and satellite communication. This technology gives you instant access to people, ideas, and products from all over the world. It brings the world closer together. Most Americans are eager to use the convenience of technology, but they probably never imagined some of the side effects. How has technology changed U.S. government, business, and the lives of its citizens?

▲ Cell phones, instant messaging, and the wireless Internet are changing the way we gather and use information.

Technology and Globalization

By the end of the twentieth century, most businesses depended on computers to perform certain tasks. The increased speed of communication and transfer of information changed the way business was conducted. Some people referred to the era as an **information revolution**.

Computers are not limited to businesses, however. In 2000, 51 percent of U.S. households owned one or more computers. The Internet provides nearly instant access to e-mail and information. Another tool that has changed communication is the cellular phone. By 2003, over 145 million people in the United States used cell phones.

A Global Economy Using the Internet, companies on different continents can do business as if they were in the same city. **Globalization** is the term used to describe the practice of making products and ideas available all over the world. Trade and investments among international companies grew in the 1990s. Corporations built factories and offices in other countries.

Taking Notes

Use your chart to summarize the effects of national trends and issues on Georgia.

CAUSE: GROWTH OF GEORGIA AND ATLANTA		
Effect		
Summary of Effects		

In 1993, Congress passed the North American Free Trade Agreement (**NAFTA**). NAFTA was designed to increase trade among the United States, Canada, and Mexico. Part of the agreement banned tariffs between the countries. Tariffs are taxes on goods from another country. Many Americans opposed NAFTA because they feared that companies would move jobs to Mexico where labor is cheaper and, under NAFTA, taxes would be cheaper. In some cases, that happened. Other people supported NAFTA because they thought it would be good for all economies. It would also help American companies to export their products.

Reading History

A. Making Inferences Why were many Americans afraid that jobs would be lost by NAFTA?

Dealing with Terrorism

In the 1990s, the United States began to experience acts of **terrorism** against its people. Terrorism is the threat or use of violence against individuals or property to intimidate or cause fear for political or social reasons. Some terrorists have been from foreign countries, whereas others have been U.S. citizens.

September 11, 2001 The most destructive act of terrorism against the United States occurred on September 11, 2001. Nineteen Islamic extremist terrorists hijacked four airplanes from airports on the East Coast. Two airplanes crashed into the World Trade Center towers in New

York City. The third plane crashed into the southwest side of the Pentagon, the headquarters of the American military in Washington, D.C. The fourth plane was possibly headed for the Capitol. However, courageous passengers apparently jumped the hijackers and kept them from reaching their target by crashing into an empty field in Pennsylvania. More than 3,000 people died in the combined attacks.

Confronting the Terrorists

President George W. Bush had been in office only nine months when he declared a "war on terrorism" because of the tragic events of September 11, 2001. Bush identified several countries as sponsors of terrorism, including Iran, Iraq, Afghanistan, Syria, Libya, Cuba, North Korea, and the Sudan.

Terrorist Attacks in the United States, 1993–2001

DATE	LOCATION	DEATHS / INJURIES	PEOPLE RESPONSIBLE
1993	under the World Trade Center, New York, NY	6 killed; 1,000 injured	convicted: Islamic terrorists
1995	Murrah Federal Building, Oklahoma City, OK	186 killed; 842 injured	convicted: Timothy McVeigh, U.S. citizen
1996	Olympic Games, Atlanta, GA	2 killed; 111 injured	charged: Eric Rudolph, U.S. citizen
1997	nightclub and women's clinic, Atlanta, GA	11 injured	
1998	women's clinic, Birmingham, AL	1 killed; 1 injured	
2001	World Trade Center, New York, NY	2,749 killed; 4,000 injured overall	19 Islamic terrorists, trained by Al-Qaeda
	Pentagon, Washington, D.C.	184 killed	
	Shanksville, PA	over 90 killed	

SKILLBUILDER Interpreting Charts

1. *Which bombings were carried out by U.S. citizens?*
2. *How many were killed or injured in the bombing of the Murrah Federal Building?*

Background

The terrorist organization Al-Qaeda is financed by a Saudi Arabian multimillionaire named Osama Bin Laden. He is now on the FBI's Most Wanted list and $25 million is offered as a reward for his capture.

Afghanistan   The United States focused first on Afghanistan, the home base of the terrorist organization, Al-Qaeda, which had planned the September 11 attacks. In October 2001, the United States began bombing airfields and command centers. This weakened Al-Qaeda by killing some members and driving others to flee to other countries. By December, the Afghani rulers were driven from power.

Iraq   In March 2003, the United States decided to send troops into Iraq to end the regime of Saddam Hussein. President Bush justified the invasion as part of the war on terrorism. On May 1, 2003, Hussein's regime fell. Hussein was finally captured on December 13, 2003.

Georgians in the Conflicts   Military personnel from across Georgia were involved in invasions of Afghanistan and Iraq. The 3rd Infantry Division of Fort Stewart lost many soldiers. President Bush visited Fort Stewart in September 2003, when the soldiers returned home.

Changes in America

Terrorist activities prompted changes in business, government, and the daily routines of most Americans.

Business   Many businesses suffered as a result of terrorism. People were afraid to return to "business as usual." Their fear affected their buying and spending habits. They spent less money, unemployment rose, and the economy dipped.

Government   President Bush asked Congress to add the Department of Homeland Security to the president's Cabinet. The department is responsible for protecting the nation from terrorist attacks. Each state has created its own homeland security measures. These plans are partly funded with money from the new federal department.

In October 2001, Congress passed the Patriot Act. This law gave the government new powers of oversight, including monitoring the telecommunications of suspected terrorists. It also led to closer federal supervision of thousands of immigrants.

Security in the United States   Americans were divided over the Patriot Act. Many thought the tightened security was good. But others felt that the Patriot Act and other restrictions threatened many civil liberties that Americans did not want to give up. For instance, they questioned whether the government should have the right to listen in on cell phone conversations and read private e-mail messages.

Increased security measures have made life safer, yet sometimes more difficult. Screening and random searches at airports and metal detectors at sports and other entertainment events have become routine. Americans will continue to struggle to find the right balance between the protection of personal privacy and property and the government's role of protecting all citizens. And Georgia will continue to protect its people and resources, as you will read in the next section.

Section 2 Assessment

1. TERMS & NAMES

Explain the significance of:

a. information revolution

b. globalization

c. NAFTA

d. terrorism

2. TAKING NOTES

Use a diagram like the one below to record the tools and systems of the information era of the late twentieth century.

3. MAIN IDEAS

a. How did globalization change the market of many businesses?

b. Why have several countries been singled out in the war on terrorism?

c. Summarize the ways that the war on terrorism has impacted American lives.

4. CRITICAL THINKING

Evaluating

Should the government respect civil rights as it wages a war against terrorism? Why or why not?

Think About
• why civil rights were originally created
• who is protected by civil rights
• under what conditions civil rights may be taken away

Technology/Drama   What do you think the United States will be like in 10 years? Design a **Web page** or write and perform a **skit** that presents your vision.

3

Georgia's Issues for the Future

MAIN IDEA

WHY IT MATTERS NOW

TERMS & NAMES

MAIN IDEA	WHY IT MATTERS NOW	TERMS & NAMES
Issues of a good water supply, clean air, and adequate transportation are challenges facing Georgians today.	The issues facing Georgia affect all of its citizens today and into the future.	water war Fall Line Freeway Smart Growth

SETTING THE STAGE

In the 2002 election, it seemed that rural Georgia had a stronger voice in government than it had experienced in the past. Sonny Perdue from Bonaire in rural Georgia was elected governor. The first Republican to be elected governor since Reconstruction, Governor Perdue appointed many people from rural areas to leadership positions. A governor and his staff cannot solve all of the problems and issues of the state. The citizens must be actively involved. What are some of the issues that you will face as an adult?

▲ Governor Sonny Perdue served in the Georgia Senate from 1990 to 2002.

Water

With all the rivers, lakes, and streams in Georgia, it's hard to believe that there could be a shortage of water. But there is, and a **"water war"** began in 1990 between Georgia, Florida, and Alabama.

Alabama, Florida, and Georgia share waters from several rivers. The Apalachicola-Chattahoochee-Flint basin flows from northwest Georgia south along the border of Alabama and empties into Florida's Apalachicola Bay. The Alabama-Coosa-Tallapoosa basin also begins in northwest Georgia and empties into Alabama's Mobile Bay.

Conflict Between States Georgia has the advantage because it is the "upstream user"; water flows through Georgia first and then travels south to streams in Alabama and Florida. Alabama and Florida are worried about the amount and quality of the water remaining for their use. Alabama contends that its growth potential will be limited if Atlanta keeps growing and using more and more water. Florida has a different concern. The Apalachicola Bay is known for its oyster industry. The oysters depend on a mixture of fresh water and ocean water.

Taking Notes

Use your chart to summarize the effects of Atlanta's growth on Georgia's future.

CAUSE: GROWTH OF GEORGIA AND ATLANTA		
Effect		
Summary of Effects		

Streams in the Chattahoochee National Forest are among the cleanest in the state.

If the freshwater supply is limited, the oyster industry could be harmed or destroyed.

Conflict Within Georgia   The rapid growth of metropolitan Atlanta has put an unexpected strain on the water supply. As the population grew, people built new houses without paying adequate attention to their impact on the limited water supply.

Farmers in South Georgia depend on irrigation systems for successful crops. They are some of the "downstream users" who fear that metropolitan Atlanta may be using more than its fair share of the water.

Looking for Answers   In 1990, Alabama sued the U.S. Army Corps of Engineers to stop them from building a reservoir to keep more water for the metropolitan Atlanta area. The lawsuit was postponed to give the states a chance to work out their own agreement.

Finding the solution is not easy. Because people representing the states cannot agree, negotiators will have to determine the most important uses for the water. The U.S. Supreme Court may get involved. Permanent outdoor watering restrictions may be one solution. Charging more for electricity generated by hydroelectric power plants is another option. In the near future, Georgians may have to decide between watering lawns and watering food crops.

Reading History

A. Finding Main Ideas   How do the states with conflicting water needs propose to resolve these issues?

Clean Air

In the summer of 2003, a federal court ruled that the quality of metro Atlanta's air had worsened and the danger posed by it should be rated as "severe" rather than "serious." The ruling could mean that some industries will have to either cut back on harmful emissions that pollute the air, or pay large fines.

Air pollution from cars, industries, and power plants is dangerous to humans and other living things. Atlanta's air quality is worse than other places because of the population density of the area, the amount of daily traffic, and the number of businesses in the area. Augusta, Columbus, and Macon could face similar problems if they do not address air quality issues as they grow.

Transportation

You learned in earlier chapters how transportation systems influenced the growth or decline of particular cities and regions. You have read in this chapter that too many vehicles contribute to poor air quality. Can a city have growth without a good transportation system? Can there be a good transportation system without air quality problems? These are issues that are facing Georgians.

Reading History

B. Making Inferences How will good transportation systems bring the "Two Georgias" together?

Some politicians and business leaders have proposed that one way to bring the "Two Georgias" together is to make sure that all counties have access to good transportation systems. In 1988, the state legislature adopted the Governor's Road Improvement Plan, or GRIP. The goal of GRIP is to connect most Georgia cities having a population of 2,500 or more to the interstate system via four-lane roads. Another part of the plan is to ensure that most Georgians are within two miles of a four-lane highway.

The Fall Line Freeway   One of the GRIP projects is the 215-mile **Fall Line Freeway** connecting Columbus and Augusta. This four-lane freeway will provide a quick and easy route for drivers traveling east or west across the middle of the state.

Solving Atlanta's Traffic Problem   Georgians need to make some decisions about how to solve Atlanta's growing traffic congestion and the pollution problems that come with it. One plan is called Mobility 2030, a plan to keep traffic moving as the region prepares for the estimated two million more people to move into the region by 2030.

"**Smart Growth**" may be one answer to Atlanta's problems—and to the issue of "Two Georgias." Smart Growth means using a plan to slow urban sprawl and to push investment into more rural areas. Smart Growth principles encourage the improvement of existing communities rather than starting new ones. That will be better for the environment. Georgia's leaders will have to ensure that other parts of the state are attractive to investors, so that areas outside of Atlanta grow as well.

▼ With no natural boundaries such as rivers or mountains, it is hard to contain the sprawl of Atlanta's expansion.

Georgia Demographics—The 2000 Census

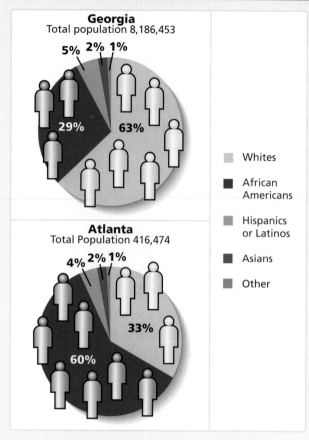

Georgia
Total population 8,186,453

5% 2% 1%

29%   63%

Atlanta
Total Population 416,474

4% 2% 1%

33%

60%

■ Whites

■ African Americans

■ Hispanics or Latinos

■ Asians

■ Other

SKILLBUILDER

Interpreting Charts

1. *How do the white and African-American populations in Atlanta compare to the state as a whole?*
2. *What percentage of Georgia's population is Hispanic?*

Citizenship Issues

Georgia's population has become more racially diverse since the 1960s. The table at the left shows how our state looked in the 2000 U.S. Census.

Atlanta has much greater racial and ethnic diversity than other Georgia cities. However, Georgia's Asian and Hispanic population is growing as people from Latin American and Asian countries are immigrating to many small towns across Georgia. We have many different religious and cultural beliefs. Rural, urban, and suburban residents can have varying goals. But we are all citizens of Georgia.

Citizen Involvement As Georgia's population becomes increasingly diverse, it is important that all individuals have a voice. Georgia's voter turnout rates continue to be low. If citizens want to have a voice in the future of the state, they must exercise the right to vote. They can express their opinions in other ways as well. Citizens may help in campaigns, write letters to elected officials, write letters to the local newspapers, and attend public meetings at which political decisions are discussed.

Even as a teenager, there are things that you can do now to contribute to the state and its future. Some of them are listed below.

- Get the best possible education for the work you want to do.
- Participate in school activities such as social studies fairs, mock elections, and Model United Nations.
- Stay informed of current affairs by watching the news, reading news magazines, and listening to community leaders.
- Volunteer in your community. Be a good role model for younger children.
- Learn the procedures for registering to vote, obtaining a driver's license, and other rights and privileges.

Georgia's Future Now that you have learned more about Georgia's past, spend some time thinking about Georgia's future. With imagination and creativity, Georgians can come together to make an ever-better place for us all to live. Georgia can be a good state, or it can be a great state. Its future is up to you—its future adult citizens.

▲ What kinds of changes would you like to see in Georgia? You can be part of making those changes happen.

Section 3 Assessment

1. TERMS & NAMES

Explain the significance of:

a. water war

b. Fall Line Freeway

c. Smart Growth

2. TAKING NOTES

Use a diagram like the one below to note each competing region's shared and individual need for the use of fresh water. What is Georgia's advantage?

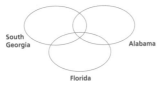

South Georgia

Alabama

Florida

3. MAIN IDEAS

a. What are some factors to consider in water resource distribution?

b. Why is air quality worse in Atlanta than in other cities?

c. How could "Smart Growth" decrease the problem of Two Georgias?

d. Why is voting important for citizens?

4. CRITICAL THINKING

Compare and Contrast

What are the advantages and disadvantages of each of these plans for Georgia's transportation needs: GRIP, Mobility 2030, and Smart Growth?

Think About
- the costs in money and pollution
- the growth of Georgia

ACTIVITY -OPTIONS- **Math/Geography** Survey students in your school about their ethnic background. Present your findings in a **graph** or create a **map**.

VISUAL SUMMARY

Entering the 21st Century

1990
- Atlanta is selected to host the Olympics.
- Georgia's "water war" begins.

1991
- Georgia governor establishes HOPE scholarships.

1992
- Bill Clinton is elected President.

1993
- Congress passes NAFTA.

1996
- Atlanta hosts Olympic Games.
- President Bill Clinton is re-elected.

- Georgia's population tops 8 million.
- George W. Bush is elected President.

2000

2001
- Terrorists attack the World Trade Center and Pentagon.
- U.S. bombs airfields in Afghanistan.
- President Bush establishes the Department of Homeland Security.
- Congress passes the Patriot Act.

2003
- U.S. invades Iraq.
- Court rules that Atlanta's air quality danger is "severe."

Baghdad ☆
IRAQ

TERMS & NAMES

Briefly explain the significance of the following.

1. 1996 Olympic Games
2. Newt Gingrich
3. Contract with America
4. HOPE Scholarships
5. information revolution
6. globalization
7. NAFTA
8. terrorism
9. water war
10. Fall Line Freeway

REVIEW QUESTIONS

Georgia on the National and International Scene (pages 513–516)

1. How did the 1996 Olympics bring new life to Atlanta?
2. How did the Contract with America affect government?
3. Why has the Georgia state legislature been willing to provide money to Atlanta?

National Trends and Issues (pages 517–520)

4. What is the purpose of NAFTA?
5. What countries are identified as sponsors of terrorism?
6. How has government responded to terrorism?
7. How has business responded to terrorism?

Georgia's Issues for the Future (pages 521–525)

8. What is the cause of Georgia's water war?
9. What is GRIP?
10. What is Smart Growth?

CRITICAL THINKING

1. USING YOUR NOTES: ANALYZING CAUSES AND RECOGNIZING EFFECTS

CAUSE: GROWTH OF GEORGIA AND ATLANTA			
Effect			
Summary of Effects			
Responses to Effects			

Using your completed chart, answer the questions below.

a. How has Atlanta's growth affected the state?
b. What are the possible results of Georgia's water war?

2. ANALYZING LEADERSHIP

How did Billy Payne's vision and leadership impact the city of Atlanta?

3. APPLYING CITIZENSHIP SKILLS

Why is active citizenship critical as diversity increases?

4. THEME: DEMOCRATIC IDEALS

The Patriot Act gave the government new powers of oversight. Is this law a threat to civil liberties or a necessity for our security?

5. FORMING AND SUPPORTING OPINIONS

Is it fair for state money to support the city of Atlanta? Why or why not?

INTERACT with HISTORY

Having read about the challenges facing your state, what steps will you take to be a more involved citizen?

Use the graphs and your knowledge of Georgia history to answer the questions.

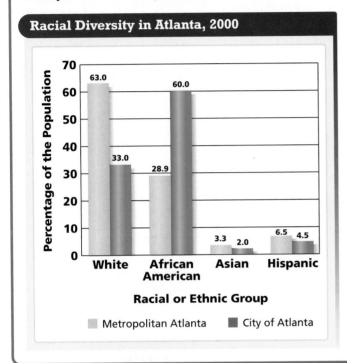

Racial Diversity in Atlanta, 2000

- Metropolitan Atlanta
- City of Atlanta

1. In 2000, what percentage of Metropolitan Atlanta's population was white?

   A. 63%
   B. 29%
   C. 6.5%
   D. 4.5%

2. In 2000, what percentage of the City of Atlanta's population was African American?

   A. 60%
   B. 28.9%
   C. 6.5%
   D. 3.3%

3. In 2000, what percentage of Metropolitan Atlanta's population was Hispanic?

   A. 63%
   B. 33%
   C. 6.5%
   D. 4.5%

TEST PRACTICE
CLASSZONE.COM

ALTERNATIVE ASSESSMENT

1. CONDUCTING AN INTERVIEW

Many challenges face your state and country today. Select an issue that's important to you. Then select an authority on that issue in your community. Research your issue, and prepare a list of questions for your authority. Then, interview your authority by phone, letter, or e-mail. Summarize the results of your interview.

2. COOPERATIVE LEARNING

Create your own Homeland Security Task Force. Research the security plans for terrorist attacks in your state and in your local community. Then work as a team to create a security plan for your school. What will administrators, teachers, and students do in the case of a terrorist attack?

INTEGRATED TECHNOLOGY ACTIVITY

DESIGNING A WEB PAGE

What do you think Georgia will be like in ten years? Design a Web page that presents your vision. Your Web page may include pictures and descriptions that portray your ideas. It should also include links to other sites that discuss technology, politics, and social issues. Draw a design of what the page will look like. Write your copy, and select the graphics and images you will include. Present your vision of Georgia to the class.

RESEARCH LINKS
CLASSZONE.COM

ARCTIC OCEAN

Baffin Bay

GREENLAND
(Den.)

Arctic Circle

RUSSIA

ALASKA

Yukon (U.S.)

Anchorage

ICELAND

FAROE IS.
(Den.)

Aleutian Islands

C A N A D A

Hudson Bay

IRELAND

Vancouver

Missouri

Newfoundland

Montréal

Ottawa

UNITED STATES

Chicago

New York
Washington D.C.

PORTUGAL

Azores
(Port.)

Los Angeles

Colorado

Casablanca

Houston

Mississippi

ATLANTIC

Canary
Islands
(Sp.)

MEXICO

Gulf of Mexico

BAHAMAS

W. SAHARA

MOR...

Tropic of Cancer

MIDWAY IS.
(U.S.)

CUBA

DOM. REP.

CAPE
VERDE

MAURITANIA

Hawaiian
Islands
(U.S)

Mexico City

HAITI

PUERTO RICO (U.S.)

SENEGAL

BELIZE

JAMAICA

Caribbean
Sea

GAMBIA

GUAT.

HOND.

GUINEA-BISSAU

GUINEA

PACIFIC

EL. SAL.

NIC.

SIERRA LEONE

Caracas

TRINIDAD AND TOBAGO

LIBERIA

COSTA
RICA

VENEZUELA

GUYANA

PANAMA

SURINAME

COLOMBIA

FRENCH GUIANA

Equator

Galapagos Islands
(Ecuador)

ECUADOR

Amazon

KIRIBATI

PERU

BRAZIL

Lima

O C E A N

O C E A N

SAMOA

AMERICAN
SAMOA

BOLIVIA

ST. HELENA
(U.K.)

COOK
ISLANDS (N.Z.)

TONGA

PARAGUAY

Tropic of Capricorn

FRENCH POLYNESIA

Rio de Janeiro

ARGENTINA

Easter Island
(Chile)

URUGUAY

Santiago

Buenos
Aires

N

CHILE

0   1000   2000 Miles

0   1000   2000   3000 Kilometers

Copyright by Rand McNally & Co.
Robinson Projection

FALKLAND IS.
(U.K.)

South
Georgia
(U.K.)

South
Orkney Is.
(U.K.)

Antarctic Circle

South
Shetland Is.
(U.K.)

Weddell
Sea

ARCTIC OCEAN

Franz Josef
Land

Novaya
Zemlya

75°

60°

bergen
or.)

15° 30° 45° 60° 75° 90° 105° 120° 135° 150° 165° 180°

FINLAND

SWEDEN
EST.
LAT.
LITH.

Moscow

Volga

Novosibirsk

R U S S I A

Yenisey

Ob.

Lena

Sea of Okhotsk

Bering
Sea

45°

DEN.

GERMANY
POLAND

BELARUS

UKRAINE

KAZAKHSTAN

MONGOLIA

NORTH
KOREA

Sea of Japan

JAPAN
Tokyo

CZ.
AUS.
SLVK.
HUNG.
SWITZ.
ROM.
MOLD.
UZBEKISTAN
KYRG.
Beijing
SOUTH
KOREA

ITALY
CRO.
BOS.
BUL.
Black Sea
GEO.
ARM.
AZER.
TURKMENISTAN
TAJIK.
C H I N A

Rome
ALB.
MA.
Caspian Sea
Shanghai

GREECE
TURKEY
SYRIA
IRAN
AFGHANISTAN
Chang Jiang
Yangtze
30°

Med.
CYPRUS
LEB.
ISRAEL
JORDAN
IRAQ
KUWAIT
PAKISTAN
NEPAL
Ganges
BHU.
Guangzhou
TAIWAN
PACIFIC

TUNISIA
Crete
Mediterranean Sea
Cairo
QATAR
U.A.E.
Kolkata
(Calcutta)
BNGL.
Tropic of Cancer

RIA
LIBYA
EGYPT
SAUDI
ARABIA
OMAN
Mumbai
(Bombay)
I N D I A
MYANMAR
LAOS
South China
NORTHERN
MARIANA ISLANDS
(U.S.)
WAKE ISLAND
(U.S.)

NIGER
CHAD
SUDAN
Red Sea
ERITREA
YEMEN
Arabian
Sea
Bay of
Bengal
THAILAND
VIETNAM
Sea
PHILIPPINES
GUAM (U.S.)
15°

Nile
DJIBOUTI
Bangkok
CAMBODIA
O C E A N

NGERIA
CENTRAL
AFRICAN
REPUBLIC
Addis
Ababa
ETHIOPIA
SRI LANKA
BRUNEI
PALAU
FED. STATES OF
MICRONESIA
MARSHALL
ISLANDS

agos
CAMEROON
SOMALIA
MALAYSIA

ORIAL
GABON
UGANDA
KENYA
MALDIVES
SINGAPORE
Borneo
New Guinea
Equator

P. OF
ongo
DEM. REP.
OF CONGO
RWANDA
BURUNDI
Sumatra
Jakarta
INDONESIA
PAPUA
NEW GUINEA
SOLOMON
ISLANDS

Congo
TANZANIA
Java
EAST TIMOR

ANGOLA
SEYCHELLES
I N D I A N
Darwin
Coral Sea
VANUATU

ZAMBIA
COMOROS
15°
NEW CALEDONIA
(Fr.)
FIJI

NAMIBIA
ZIMBABWE
MOZAMBIQUE
MADAGASCAR
MAURITIUS
Tropic of Capricorn

BOTSWANA
REUNION
(Fr.)
A U S T R A L I A

SWAZILAND
O C E A N
Perth
Darling
Sydney
30°

SOUTH
AFRICA
LESOTHO
Melbourne

Cape Town
Kerguelen
Islands
(Fr.)
Tasmania
NEW ZEALAND
Wellington

45°

60°

Antarctic Circle

75°

ANTARCTICA

15° 30° 45° 60° 75° 90° 105° 120° 135° 150° 165° 180°

INNESOTA

International Falls

St. Cloud

•Minneapolis ★St. Paul

Mankato• •Rochester

•Waterloo

IOWA

Des Moines ★

aha

•St. Joseph

Kansas City

opeka •Jefferson City

mporia

MISSOURI

•Springfield

Isa

•Muskogee

•Fort Smith

ARKANSAS

•Pine Bluff

•Texarkana

•Tyler

Sam yburn Res.

LOUISIANA

•Beaumont

■Houston

•Galveston

Lake of the Woods

D A

ONTARIO

Lake Nipigon

Isle Royale

Lake Superior

•Marquette

•Duluth

Sault Ste. Marie

Eau Claire

WISCONSIN

•Green Bay

Appleton•

OshKosh•

Milwaukee■

Madison• •Racine

•Rockford

Dubuque• Cedar Rapids•

Davenport•

Aurora• Chicago■

•Moline

Peoria•

•Bloomington

ILLINOIS

Springfield★ •Decatur

Columbia•

St. Louis★

Cape Girardeau•

Clarksville•

MICHIGAN

Traverse City

Lake Michigan

Grand Rapids•

Kalamazoo•

South Bend•

Gary•

INDIANA

Muncie•

Indianapolis★

Terre Haute•

Bloomington•

Evansville•

Owensboro•

KENTUCKY

Kentucky Lake

Georgian Bay

Lake Huron

Saginaw•

•Flint

•Lansing

Detroit■

Ann Arbor•

Toledo●

Lima•

OHIO

Dayton•

Columbus●

Springfield•

Cincinnati●

Louisville●

Frankfort★

Lexington•

QUÉBEC

Montréal★

Ottawa

Toronto★ Lake Ontario

Cleveland●

Akron•

Youngstown•

Pittsburgh●

Oil City•

PENNSYLVANIA

Harrisburg★

St. Lawrence

Watertown•

•Rochester

Buffalo■

Lake Erie

Erie•

Scranton•

Allentown•

NEW YORK

Binghamton•

Albany★

Hudson

Lake Champlain

Burlington•

Montpelier★

Concord★

MAINE

Moosehead Lake

•Bangor

Augusta★

NEW HAMPSHIRE

Manchester•

VERMONT

Portland•

Gulf of Maine

Worcester• Boston★

MASSACHUSETTS

CONNECTICUT

Hartford★ R.I. Providence★

Bridgeport• Long Island

Nantucket Island

New York■

Newark■

Trenton★

Philadelphia■

Wilmington•

NEW JERSEY

Dover★

DELAWARE

Delaware Bay

Annapolis★

Baltimore●

Washington D.C.★

MARYLAND

Susquehanna

WEST VIRGINIA

Huntington•

Charleston•

Ohio

Johnson City•

Roanoke•

Richmond•

VIRGINIA

Newport News•

Norfolk● ★Virginia Beach

Albemarle Sound

NORTH CAROLINA

Winston-Salem• Greensboro• Durham•

Raleigh★

Roanoke

Asheville•

Knoxville•

Chattanooga•

Nashville★

Clarksville•

Cumberland

TENNESSEE

Huntsville•

Memphis■

Fayetteville•

Jonesboro•

Arkansas

•Little Rock

Ouachita

Shreveport• •Monroe

MISSISSIPPI

•Jackson

Hattiesburg•

Baton Rouge•

New Orleans■

Lafayette•

Lake Charles•

Toledo Bend Res.

Red

Trinity

Mississippi

Tuscaloosa•

Birmingham★

ALABAMA

Montgomery★

Tombigbee

Dothan•

Mobile•

Gulfport•

Pensacola•

Columbus•

Macon•

Athens•

Atlanta★

Augusta•

GEORGIA

Albany•

Chattahoochee

Tallahassee★

Altamaha

Savannah•

Savannah

Columbia•

SOUTH CAROLINA

Greenville•

Charlotte●

Charleston•

•Wilmington

ATLANTIC

OCEAN

N

100   200   300 Miles

0   100 200 300 400 Kilometers

Copyright by Rand McNally & Co.
Alber's Conic Equal Area Projection

Jacksonville●

Gainesville•

Daytona Beach•

Orlando•

Tampa★ •Lakeland

St. Petersburg•

FLORIDA

Lake Okeechobee

Fort Myers•

West Palm Beach•

Fort Lauderdale•

Miami■

BAHAMAS

Nassau●

GULF OF MEXICO

Key West•

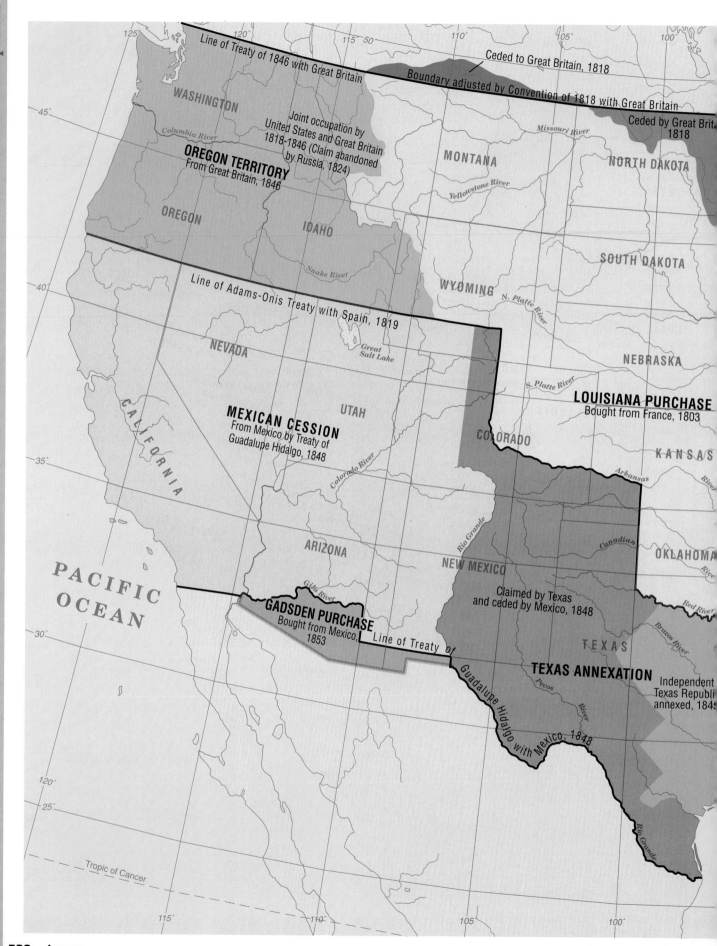

Line of Treaty of 1846 with Great Britain

Ceded to Great Britain, 1818

Boundary adjusted by Convention of 1818 with Great Britain

Ceded by Great Brita...
1818

WASHINGTON

Joint occupation by
United States and Great Britain
1818-1846 (Claim abandoned
by Russia, 1824)

Columbia River

OREGON TERRITORY
From Great Britain, 1846

MONTANA

Missouri River

NORTH DAKOTA

OREGON

IDAHO

Yellowstone River

Snake River

WYOMING

SOUTH DAKOTA

Line of Adams-Onis Treaty with Spain, 1819

N. Platte River

NEVADA

*Great
Salt Lake*

NEBRASKA

S. Platte River

LOUISIANA PURCHASE
Bought from France, 1803

MEXICAN CESSION
From Mexico by Treaty of
Guadalupe Hidalgo, 1848

UTAH

COLORADO

KANSAS

Arkansas

C A L I F O R N I A

Colorado River

*Arkansas
River*

ARIZONA

Rio Grande

NEW MEXICO

Canadian

OKLAHOMA

Red River

**PACIFIC
OCEAN**

Gila River

GADSDEN PURCHASE
Bought from Mexico,
1853

Line of Treaty of

Claimed by Texas
and ceded by Mexico, 1848

T E X A S

Brazos River

Guadalupe Hidalgo with Mexico, 1848

Pecos

TEXAS ANNEXATION

Independent
Texas Republi...
annexed, 184...

River

Rio Grande

Tropic of Cancer

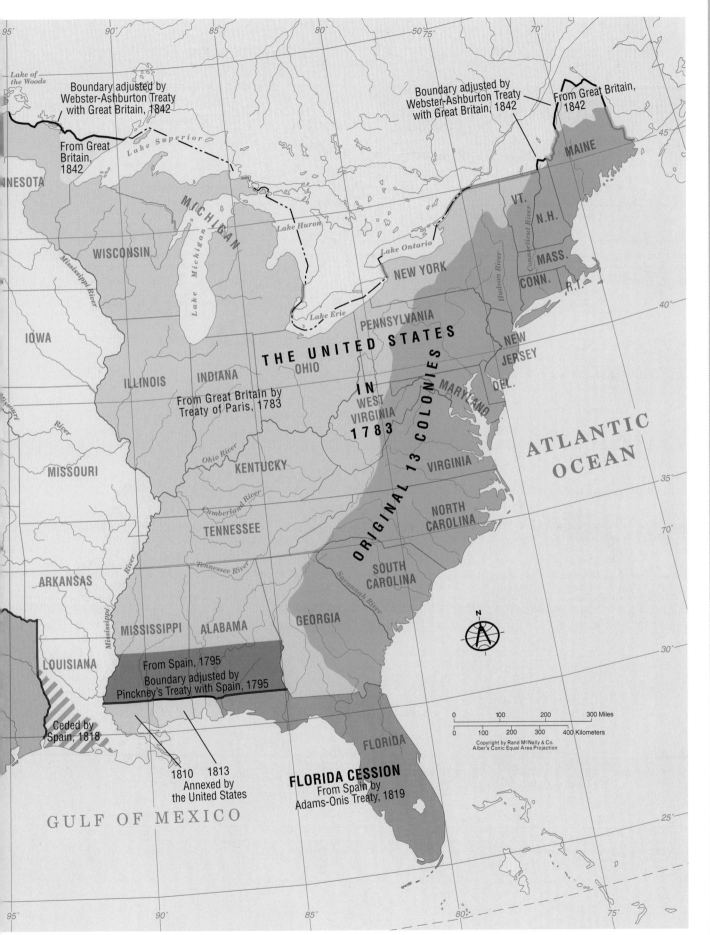

Lake of the Woods

Boundary adjusted by Webster-Ashburton Treaty with Great Britain, 1842

From Great Britain, 1842

Boundary adjusted by Webster-Ashburton Treaty with Great Britain, 1842

From Great Britain, 1842

MINNESOTA

Lake Superior

MAINE

MICHIGAN

WISCONSIN

Lake Huron

Lake Michigan

VT.

N.H.

Lake Ontario

MASS.

NEW YORK

CONN.

R.I.

IOWA

Mississippi River

Lake Erie

PENNSYLVANIA

NEW JERSEY

THE UNITED STATES

ILLINOIS

INDIANA

OHIO

DEL.

IN

WEST VIRGINIA

MARYLAND

ATLANTIC OCEAN

Missouri River

From Great Britain by Treaty of Paris, 1783

1783

MISSOURI

Ohio River

KENTUCKY

VIRGINIA

ORIGINAL 13 COLONIES

Cumberland River

NORTH CAROLINA

ARKANSAS

TENNESSEE

Tennessee River

SOUTH CAROLINA

Savannah River

River

Mississippi River

MISSISSIPPI

ALABAMA

GEORGIA

LOUISIANA

From Spain, 1795
Boundary adjusted by Pinckney's Treaty with Spain, 1795

Ceded by Spain, 1818

1810   1813
Annexed by the United States

FLORIDA

FLORIDA CESSION
From Spain by Adams-Onis Treaty, 1819

GULF OF MEXICO

0   100   200   300 Miles

0   100   200   300   400 Kilometers

Copyright by Rand McNally & Co.
Alber's Conic Equal Area Projection

RAND McNALLY

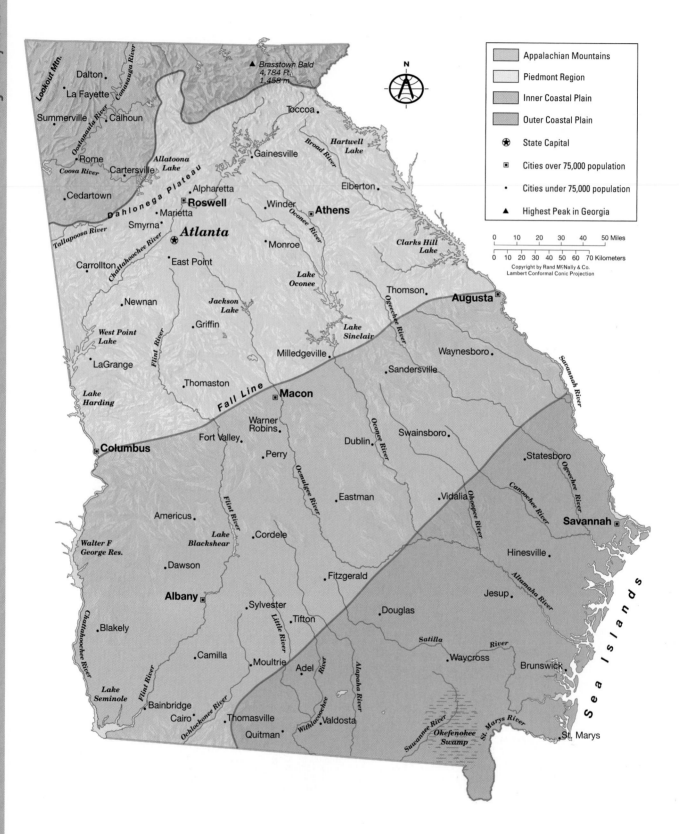

Legend:
- Appalachian Mountains
- Piedmont Region
- Inner Coastal Plain
- Outer Coastal Plain
- ✪ State Capital
- ▣ Cities over 75,000 population
- • Cities under 75,000 population
- ▲ Highest Peak in Georgia

0 10 20 30 40 50 Miles
0 10 20 30 40 50 60 70 Kilometers
Copyright by Rand McNally & Co.
Lambert Conformal Conic Projection

Lookout Mtn.
Dalton
La Fayette
Summerville
Rome
Cedartown
Cartersville
Calhoun
Conasauga River
Oostanaula River
Coosa River
Allatoona Lake
Dahlonega Plateau
Tallapoosa River
Chattahoochee River
Alpharetta
Roswell
Marietta
Smyrna
Atlanta
East Point
Carrollton
Newnan
Griffin
Jackson Lake
Flint River
West Point Lake
LaGrange
Thomaston
Lake Harding
Fall Line
Macon
Warner Robins
Fort Valley
Perry
Columbus
Americus
Lake Blackshear
Cordele
Dawson
Walter F George Res.
Albany
Sylvester
Blakely
Camilla
Moultrie
Adel
Lake Seminole
Bainbridge
Cairo
Thomasville
Quitman
Ochlockonee River
Chattahoochee River
Flint River
Little River
Withlacoochee
Alapaha River
River
Tifton
Fitzgerald
Eastman
Dublin
Ocmulgee River
Oconee River
Swainsboro
Vidalia
Ohoopee River
Douglas
Waycross
Satilla River
Okefenokee Swamp
Suwannee River
St. Marys River
St. Marys
Brunswick
Jesup
Altamaha River
Hinesville
Savannah
Canoochee River
Ogeechee River
Statesboro
Sandersville
Waynesboro
Savannah River
Augusta
Thomson
Clarks Hill Lake
Ogeechee River
Milledgeville
Lake Sinclair
Lake Oconee
Monroe
Winder
Athens
Oconee River
Clarks Hill Lake
Elberton
Hartwell Lake
Broad River
Gainesville
Toccoa
▲ Brasstown Bald 4,784 Ft. 1,458 m
Sea Islands

534 ATLAS

DADE
CATOOSA
WHITFIELD
WALKER
MURRAY
CHATTOOGA
GORDON
FLOYD
BARTOW
POLK
PAULDING
HARALSON
DOUGLAS
CARROLL
FULTON
COWETA
HEARD
TROUP
MERIWETHER
HARRIS
MUSCOGEE
CHATTAHOOCHEE
STEWART
QUITMAN
RANDOLPH
CLAY
EARLY
MILLER
SEMINOLE
DECATUR

FANNIN
UNION
TOWNS
RABUN
GILMER
WHITE
HABERSHAM
LUMPKIN
STEPHENS
PICKENS
DAWSON
FRANKLIN
HALL
BANKS
HART
CHEROKEE
FORSYTH
MADISON
ELBERT
JACKSON
BARROW
CLARKE
COBB
GWINNETT
OGLETHORPE
Atlanta
DE KALB
OCONEE
WILKES
LINCOLN
WALTON
ROCKDALE
MORGAN
GREENE
TALIAFERRO
COLUMBIA
CLAYTON
NEWTON
McDUFFIE
FAYETTE
HENRY
RICHMOND
WARREN
SPALDING
BUTTS
JASPER
PUTNAM
HANCOCK
GLASCOCK
PIKE
LAMAR
MONROE
JONES
BALDWIN
JEFFERSON
BURKE
UPSON
WASHINGTON
BIBB
TALBOT
CRAWFORD
WILKINSON
JENKINS
SCREVEN
TWIGGS
JOHNSON
TAYLOR
PEACH
EMANUEL
MARION
MACON
HOUSTON
BLECKLEY
LAURENS
TREUTLEN
CANDLER
BULLOCH
EFFINGHAM
SCHLEY
PULASKI
MONTGOMERY
DOOLY
DODGE
WHEELER
TOOMBS
EVANS
BRYAN
WEBSTER
SUMTER
TATTNALL
CHATHAM
WILCOX
TELFAIR
CRISP
JEFF DAVIS
APPLING
LIBERTY
TERRELL
LEE
TURNER
BEN HILL
LONG
CALHOUN
DOUGHERTY
IRWIN
COFFEE
BACON
WAYNE
McINTOSH
WORTH
TIFT
PIERCE
BAKER
GLYNN
BERRIEN
ATKINSON
WARE
BRANTLEY
MITCHELL
COLQUITT
COOK
LANIER
CLINCH
CHARLTON
CAMDEN
GRADY
THOMAS
BROOKS
LOWNDES
ECHOLS

★ State Capital
County Boundary

N

0   10   20   30   40   50 Miles
0   20   40   60   80 Kilometers
Copyright by Rand McNally & Co.
Lambert Conformal Conic Projection

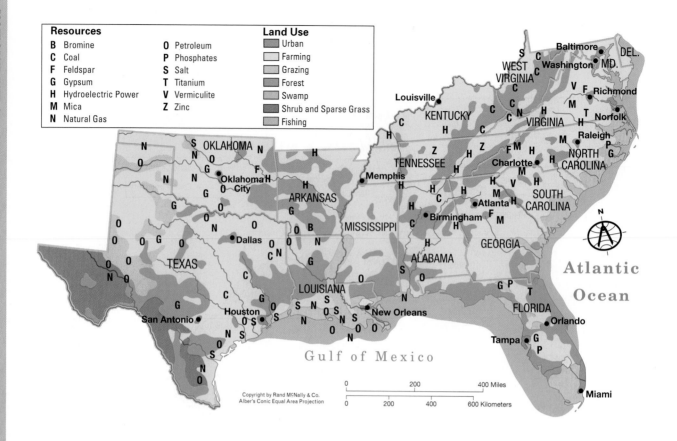

Resources

B Bromine
C Coal
F Feldspar
G Gypsum
H Hydroelectric Power
M Mica
N Natural Gas

O Petroleum
P Phosphates
S Salt
T Titanium
V Vermiculite
Z Zinc

Land Use

Urban
Farming
Grazing
Forest
Swamp
Shrub and Sparse Grass
Fishing

Copyright by Rand McNally & Co.
Alber's Conic Equal Area Projection

0	200	400 Miles
0	200	400	600 Kilometers

Gulf of Mexico

Atlantic

Ocean

Northeast
Middle West
South
West

Scale does not apply to Alaska and Hawaii.
Alber's Conic Equal Area Projection

Copyright by Rand McNally & Co.

0	200	400	600 Miles
0	200	400	600	800 Kilometers

Georgia Counties

COUNTY	DATE OF FORMATION	NAMED FOR	COUNTY SEAT	LAND AREA (SQ. MILES)	1990 POPULATION	2000 POPULATION
Appling	1818	Colonel Daniel Appling	Baxley	512	15,744	17,419
Atkinson	1917	Gov. William Atkinson	Pearson	344	6,213	7,609
Bacon	1917	Augustus Octavius Bacon	Alma	286	9,566	10,103
Baker	1825	Colonel John Baker	Newton	249	3,615	4,074
Baldwin	1806	Abraham Baldwin	Milledgeville	268	39,530	44,700
Banks	1858	Dr. Richard Banks	Homer	234	10,308	14,422
Barrow	1914	David Barrow	Winder	163	29,721	46,144
Bartow	1832	Colonel Francis Bartow	Cartersville	471	55,915	76,019
Ben Hill	1906	U.S. Senator Benjamin Hill	Fitzgerald	254	16,245	17,484
Berrien	1856	John Macpherson Berrien	Nashville	458	14,153	16,235
Bibb	1822	Dr. William Bibb	Macon	255	150,137	153,887
Bleckley	1912	Georgia Supreme Court Justice Logan Bleckley	Cochran	219	10,430	11,666
Brantley	1920	William or Benjamin Brantley	Nahunta	447	11,077	14,629
Brooks	1858	Preston Brooks	Quitman	498	15,398	16,450
Bryan	1793	Jonathan Bryan	Pembroke	455	15,438	23,417
Bulloch	1796	Provisional Gov. Archibald Bulloch	Statesboro	689	43,125	55,983
Burke	1777	Edmund Burke	Waynesboro	835	20,579	22,243
Butts	1825	Capt. Samuel Butts	Jackson	190	15,326	19,522
Calhoun	1854	U.S. Senator John Calhoun	Morgan	284	5,013	6,320
Camden	1777	Earl of Camden	Woodbine	783	30,167	43,664
Candler	1914	Gov. Allen Candler	Metter	249	7,744	9,577
Carroll	1825	Charles Carroll	Carrollton	504	71,422	87,268
Catoosa	1853	Catoosa Springs	Ringgold	163	42,464	53,282
Charlton	1854	U.S. Senator Robert Charlton	Folkston	783	8,496	10,282
Chatham	1777	William Pitt, Earl of Chatham	Savannah	646	216,774	232,048
Chattahoochee	1854	Chattahoochee River	Cusseta	251	16,934	14,882
Chattooga	1838	Chattooga River	Summerville	314	22,242	25,470

COUNTY	DATE OF FORMATION	NAMED FOR	COUNTY SEAT	LAND AREA (SQ. MILES)	1990 POPULATION	2000 POPULATION
Cherokee	1831	Cherokee Indians	Canton	434	90,204	141,903
Clarke	1801	Gen. Elijah Clarke	Athens	121	87,594	101,489
Clay	1854	U.S. Senator Henry Clay	Fort Gaines	217	3,364	3,357
Clayton	1858	Judge Augustin Clayton	Jonesboro	144	181,436	236,517
Clinch	1850	Gen. Duncan Clinch	Homerville	824	6,160	6,878
Cobb	1832	U.S. Senator Thomas Cobb	Marietta	345	447,745	607,751
Coffee	1854	Gen. John Coffee	Douglas	603	29,592	37,413
Colquitt	1856	U.S. Sen. Walter Colquitt	Moultrie	557	36,645	42,053
Columbia	1790	Christopher Columbus	Appling	308	66,031	89,288
Cook	1918	Gen. Philip Cook	Adel	233	13,456	15,771
Coweta	1825	Coweta Indians	Newnan	446	53,853	89,215
Crawford	1822	U.S. Senator William Crawford	Knoxville	327	8,991	12,495
Crisp	1905	U.S. Representative Charles Crisp	Cordele	281	20,011	21,996
Dade	1837	Maj. Francis Dade	Trenton	174	13,147	15,154
Dawson	1857	U.S. Senator William Dawson	Dawsonville	214	9,429	15,999
Decatur	1823	Commodore Stephen Decatur	Decatur	623	25,517	28,240
Dekalb	1822	Baron Johann DeKalb	Bainbridge	271	546,171	665,865
Dodge	1870	William Dodge	Eastman	503	17,607	19,171
Dooly	1821	Col. John Dooly	Vienna	398	9,901	11,525
Dougherty	1853	Judge Charles Dougherty	Albany	335	96,321	96,065
Douglas	1870	U.S. Senator Stephen Douglas	Douglasville	200	71,120	92,174
Early	1818	Judge Peter Early	Blakely	516	11,854	12,354
Echols	1858	Brig. Gen. Robert Echols	Statenville	421	2,334	3,754
Effingham	1777	Lord Effingham	Springfield	482	25,687	37,535
Elbert	1790	Gen. Samuel Elbert	Elberton	375	18,949	20,511
Emanuel	1812	Gov. David Emanuel	Swainsboro	690	20,546	21,837
Evans	1914	General Clement Evans	Claxton	187	8,724	10,495
Fannin	1854	Col. James Fannin	Blue Ridge	392	15,992	19,798
Fayette	1821	Marquis de Lafayette	Fayetteville	199	62,415	91,263
Floyd	1832	Gen. John Floyd	Rome	519	81,251	90,565

Georgia Counties, continued

COUNTY	DATE OF FORMATION	NAMED FOR	COUNTY SEAT	LAND AREA (SQ. MILES)	1990 POPULATION	2000 POPULATION
Forsyth	1832	Gov. John Forsyth	Cumming	247	44,083	98,407
Franklin	1784	Benjamin Franklin	Carnesville	266	16,650	20,285
Fulton	1853	Robert Fulton	Atlanta	535	648,779	816,006
Gilmer	1832	Gov. George Gilmer	Ellijay	432	13,368	23,456
Glascock	1857	Gen. Thomas Glascock	Gibson	145	2,357	2,556
Glynn	1777	John Glynn	Brunswick	583	62,496	67,568
Gordon	1850	William Washington Gordon	Calhoun	358	35,067	44,104
Grady	1905	Henry Grady	Cairo	460	20,279	23,659
Greene	1786	Maj. Gen. Nathanael Greene	Greensboro	406	11,793	14,406
Gwinnett	1818	Provisional Gov. Button Gwinnett	Lawrenceville	437	352,910	588,448
Habersham	1818	Joseph Habersham	Clarkesville	279	27,622	35,902
Hall	1818	Gov. Lyman Hall	Gainesville	429	95,434	139,277
Hancock	1793	John Hancock	Sparta	479	8,908	10,076
Haralson	1856	Gen. Hugh Haralson	Buchanan	283	21,966	25,690
Harris	1827	Charles Harris	Hamilton	473	17,788	23,695
Hart	1853	Nancy Hart	Hartwell	256	19,712	22,997
Heard	1830	Gov. Stephen Heard	Franklin	301	8,628	11,012
Henry	1821	Patrick Henry	McDonough	325	58,741	119,341
Houston	1821	Gov. John Houstoun	Perry	380	89,208	110,765
Irwin	1818	Gov. Jared Irwin	Ocilla	363	8,649	9,931
Jackson	1796	Gov. James Jackson	Jefferson	343	30,005	41,589
Jasper	1807	Sgt. William Jasper	Monticello	374	8,453	11,426
Jeff Davis	1905	Jefferson Davis	Hazlehurst	336	12,032	12,684
Jefferson	1796	President Thomas Jefferson	Louisville	530	17,408	17,266
Jenkins	1905	Gov. Charles Jenkins	Millen	353	8,247	8,575
Johnson	1858	Gov. Herschel Johnson	Wrightsville	307	8,329	8,560
Jones	1807	U.S. Representative James Jones	Gray	395	20,739	23,639
Lamar	1920	Lucius Quintus Cincinnatus Lamar	Barnesville	186	13,038	15,912
Lanier	1920	Poet Sidney Lanier	Lakeland	200	5,531	7,241
Laurens	1807	Col. John Laurens	Dublin	819	39,988	44,874

Georgia Counties, continued

COUNTY	DATE OF FORMATION	NAMED FOR	COUNTY SEAT	LAND AREA (SQ. MILES)	1990 POPULATION	2000 POPULATION
Lee	1825	Richard Henry Lee or Henry "Light Horse Harry" Lee	Leesburg	362	16,250	24,757
Liberty	1777	American independence	Hinesville	603	52,745	61,610
Lincoln	1796	Gen. Benjamin Lincoln	Lincolnton	257	7,442	8,348
Long	1920	Dr. Crawford Long	Ludowici	404	6,202	10,304
Lowndes	1825	William Lowndes	Valdosta	511	75,981	92,115
Lumpkin	1832	Gov. Wilson Lumpkin	Dahlonega	285	14,573	21,016
Mcduffie	1870	U.S. Senator George McDuffie	Oglethorpe	406	20,119	21,231
Mcintosh	1793	McIntosh family	Danielsville	286	8,634	10,847
Macon	1837	Nathaniel Macon	Buena Vista	368	13,114	14,074
Madison	1811	President James Madison	Thomson	266	21,050	25,730
Marion	1827	Gen. Francis "Swamp Fox" Marion	Darien	575	5,590	7,144
Meriwether	1827	David Meriwether	Greenville	505	22,411	22,534
Miller	1856	Andrew Miller	Colquitt	284	6,280	6,383
Mitchell	1857	Gen. Henry Mitchell	Camilla	514	20,275	23,932
Monroe	1821	President James Monroe	Forsyth	398	17,113	21,757
Montgomery	1793	Gen. Richard Montgomery	Mt. Vernon	247	7,379	8,270
Morgan	1807	Gen. Daniel Morgan	Madison	355	12,883	15,457
Murray	1832	Thomas Murray	Chatsworth	347	26,147	36,506
Muscogee	1825	Muscogee Indians	Columbus	221	179,280	186,291
Newton	1821	Sgt. John Newton	Covington	279	41,808	62,001
Oconee	1875	Oconee River	Watkinsville	186	17,618	26,225
Oglethorpe	1793	Gen. James Oglethorpe	Lexington	442	9,763	12,635
Paulding	1832	John Paulding	Dallas	315	41,611	81,678
Peach	1924	Georgia Peach	Fort Valley	152	21,189	23,668
Pickens	1853	Gen. Andrew Pickens	Jasper	233	14,432	22,983
Pierce	1857	President Franklin Pierce	Blackshear	344	13,328	15,636
Pike	1822	Gen. Zebulon Pike	Zebulon	220	10,224	13,688
Polk	1851	President James Polk	Cedartown	312	33,815	38,127
Pulaski	1808	Count Casimir Pulaski of Poland	Hawkinsville	250	8,108	9,588
Putnam	1807	Gen. Israel Putnam	Eatonton	361	14,137	18,812

Georgia Counties, continued

COUNTY	DATE OF FORMATION	NAMED FOR	COUNTY SEAT	LAND AREA (SQ. MILES)	1990 POPULATION	2000 POPULATION
Quitman	1858	Gen. John Quitman	Georgetown	161	2,210	2,598
Rabun	1819	Gov. William Rabun	Clayton	377	11,648	15,050
Randolph	1828	John Randolph	Cuthbert	431	8,023	7,791
Richmond	1777	Duke of Richmond, Charles Lenox	Augusta	329	189,719	199,775
Rockdale	1870	Rockdale Church	Conyers	132	54,091	70,111
Schley	1857	Gov. William Schley	Ellaville	168	3,590	3,766
Screven	1793	Brig. Gen. James Screven	Sylvania	656	13,842	15,374
Seminole	1920	Seminole Indians	Donalsonville	257	9,010	9,369
Spalding	1851	Thomas Spalding	Griffin	200	54,457	58,417
Stephens	1905	Alexander Stephens	Toccoa	184	23,436	25,435
Stewart	1830	Daniel Stewart	Lumpkin	463	5,654	5,252
Sumter	1831	Gen. Thomas Sumter	Americus	493	30,232	33,200
Talbot	1827	Gov. Matthew Talbot	Talbotton	395	6,524	6,498
Taliaferro	1825	Col. Benjamin Taliaferro	Crawfordville	196	1,915	2,077
Tattnall	1801	Josiah Tattnall	Reidsville	488	17,722	22,305
Taylor	1852	President Zachary Taylor	Butler	380	7,642	8,815
Telfair	1807	Gov. Edward Telfair	McRae	444	11,000	11,794
Terrell	1856	William Terrell	Dawson	338	10,653	10,970
Thomas	1825	Gen. Jett Thomas	Thomasville	552	38,943	42,737
Tift	1905	Nelson Tift	Tifton	269	34,998	38,407
Toombs	1905	Gen. Robert Toombs	Lyons	369	24,072	26,067
Towns	1856	Gov. George Towns	Hiawassee	172	6,754	9,319
Treutlen	1917	Gov. John Treutlen	Soperton	202	5,994	6,854
Troup	1825	Gov. George Troup	LaGrange	446	55,532	58,779
Turner	1905	Georgia Supreme Court Justice Henry Turner	Ashburn	290	8,703	9,504
Twiggs	1809	Gen. John Twiggs	Jeffersonville	363	9,806	10,590
Union	1832	Federal Union	Blairsville	329	11,993	17,289
Upson	1824	Stephen Upson	Thomaston	328	26,300	27,597
Walker	1833	U.S. Senator Freeman Walker	La Fayette	447	58,340	61,053
Walton	1818	Gov. George Walton	Monroe	330	38,586	60,687
Ware	1824	Sen. Nicholas Ware	Waycross	907	35,471	35,483
Warren	1793	Gen. Joseph Warren	Warrenton	287	6,078	6,336

COUNTY	DATE OF FORMATION	NAMED FOR	COUNTY SEAT	LAND AREA (SQ. MILES)	1990 POPULATION	2000 POPULATION
Washington	1794	President George Washington	Sandersville	684	19,112	21,176
Wayne	1830	Gen. "Mad" Anthony Wayne	Jesup	649	22,356	26,565
Webster	1853	Daniel Webster	Preston	210	2,263	2,390
Wheeler	1912	Gen. Joseph Wheeler	Alamo	300	4,903	6,179
White	1857	David White	Cleveland	242	13,006	19,944
Whitfield	1851	Evangelist George Whitefield	Dalton	291	72,462	83,525
Wilcox	1857	Gen. Mark Wilcox	Abbeville	383	7,008	8,577
Wilkes	1777	John Wilkes	Washington	474	10,597	10,687
Wilkinson	1803	Gen. James Wilkinson	Irwinton	453	10,228	10,220
Worth	1853	Maj. Gen. William Worth	Sylvester	575	19,744	21,967

Georgia Governors

GOVERNOR	TERM	BIRTHPLACE
John Adam Treutlen	1777–1778	Germany
John Houstoun	1778–1779	Georgia
John Wereat[1]	1779–1780	England
George Walton[1]	1779–1780	Virginia
Richard Howley[2]	1780	Savannah, Georgia
Stephen Heard[3]	1780–1781	Virginia
Nathan Brownson[3]	1781–1782	Connecticut
John Martin	1782–1783	Rhode Island
Lyman Hall	1783–1784	Connecticut
John Houstoun	1784–1785	Georgia
Samuel Elbert	1785–1786	South Carolina
Edward Telfair	1786–1787	Scotland
George Mathews	1787–1788	Virginia
George Handley	1788–1789	England
George Walton	1789–1790	Virginia
Edward Telfair	1790–1793	Scotland
George Mathews	1793–1796	Virginia
Jared Irwin	1796–1798	North Carolina
James Jackson	1798–1801	England
David Emanuel[3]	1801	Pennsylvania
Josiah Tattnall, Jr.	1801–1802	Savannah, Georgia
John Milledge	1802–1806	Savannah, Georgia
Jared Irwin	1806–1809	North Carolina
David B. Mitchell	1809–1813	Scotland
Peter Early	1813–1815	Virginia
David B. Mitchell	1815–1817	Scotland
William Rabun	1817–1819	North Carolina
Mathew Talbot[3]	1819	Virginia

1. Two patriot factions, one elected Wereat and the other elected Walton.

2. Howley was elected to both the governorship and to the Continental Congress. Served only a short time as governor before opting for the Continental Congress.

3. Others served for brief periods during these years, one for only two days.

Georgia Governors, continued

GOVERNOR	TERM	BIRTHPLACE
John Clark	1819–1823	North Carolina
George M. Troup	1823–1827	McIntosh Bluff, Georgia
John Forsyth	1827–1829	Virginia
George R. Gilmer	1829–1831	Wilkes County, Georgia (now Oglethorpe County)
Wilson Lumpkin	1831–1835	Virginia
William Schley	1835–1837	Maryland
George R. Gilmer	1837–1839	Wilkes County, Georgia (now Oglethorpe County)
Charles J. McDonald	1839–1843	South Carolina
George W. Crawford	1843–1847	Columbia County, Georgia
George W.B. Towns	1847–1851	Wilkes County, Georgia (now Oglethorpe County)
Howell Cobb	1851–1853	Cherry Hill, Georgia
Herschel V. Johnson	1853–1857	Burke County, Georgia
Joseph E. Brown	1857–1865	South Carolina
James Johnson [3, 4]	1865	North Carolina
Charles J. Jenkins [4]	1865–1868	South Carolina
Thomas H. Ruger [3, 5]	1868	New York
Rufus B. Bullock	1868–1871	New York
Benjamin Conley	1871–1872	New Jersey
James M. Smith	1872–1877	Twiggs County, Georgia
Alfred H. Colquitt	1877–1882	Walton County, Georgia
Alexander H. Stephens	1882–1883	Wilkes County, Georgia (now Oglethorpe County)
James S. Boynton [3]	1883	Henry County, Georgia
Henry D. McDaniel	1883–1886	Monroe, Georgia
John B. Gordon	1886–1890	Upson County, Georgia
William J. Northen	1890–1894	Jones County, Georgia
William Y. Atkinson	1894–1898	Oakland, Georgia
Allen D. Candler	1898–1902	Auraria, Georgia
Joseph M. Terrell	1902–1907	Greenville, Georgia
Hoke Smith [3]	1907–1909	North Carolina
Joseph M. Brown	1909–1911	Cherokee County, Georgia

4. provisional governor

5. U.S. military governor

Georgia Governors, continued

GOVERNOR	TERM	BIRTHPLACE
Hoke Smith	1911	North Carolina
John M. Slaton	1911–1912	Meriwether County, Georgia
Joseph M. Brown	1912–1913	Cherokee County, Georgia
John M. Slaton	1913–1915	Meriwether County, Georgia
Nathaniel E. Harris	1915–1917	Tennessee
Hugh M. Dorsey	1917–1921	Fayetteville, Georgia
Thomas W. Hardwick	1921–1923	Thomasville, Georgia
Clifford M. Walker	1923–1927	Monroe, Georgia
Lamartine G. Hardman	1927–1931	Harmony Grove, Georgia
Richard B. Russell, Jr.	1931–1933	Winder, Georgia
Eugene Talmadge	1933–1937	Forsyth, Georgia
Eurith D. Rivers	1937–1941	Arkansas
Eugene Talmadge	1941–1943	Forsyth, Georgia
Ellis G. Arnall	1943–1947	Newnan, Georgia
Herman E. Talmadge[6]	1947	Telfair County, Georgia
Melvin E. Thompson	1947–1948	Millen, Georgia
Herman E. Talmadge	1948–1955	Telfair County, Georgia
S. Marvin Griffin	1955–1959	Bainbridge, Georgia
S. Ernest Vandiver, Jr.	1959–1963	Canon, Georgia
Carl E. Sanders	1963–1967	Augusta, Georgia
Lester G. Maddox	1967–1971	Atlanta, Georgia
James E. Carter	1971–1975	Plains, Georgia
George Busbee	1975–1983	Vienna, Georgia
Joe Frank Harris	1983–1991	Bartow County, Georgia
Zell Miller	1991–1999	Young Harris, Georgia
Roy Barnes	1999–2003	Mableton, Georgia
George "Sonny" Perdue	2003–	Perry, Georgia

6. Claimed governorship when father died, but Georgia Supreme Court named Melvin Thompson governor instead.

Governor Terms by Various Constitutions of the State

YEAR ESTABLISHED	LENGTH OF TERM	CONSECUTIVE TERMS ALLOWED	OTHER RESTRICTIONS
1777	1 year	No	Not eligible for re-election until 2 years out of office
1789	2 years	Yes	No restrictions on re-election
1865	2 years	Yes—two	Not eligible for re-election until 4 years after second term
1868	4 years	Yes	No restrictions on re-election
1877	2 years	Yes—two	Not eligible for re-election until 4 years after second term
1941	4 years	No	Not eligible for re-election until 4 years from previous term
1977	4 years	Yes—two	Not eligible for re-election until 4 years from second term

State Symbols of Georgia

SYMBOL	CHOSEN	DESCRIPTION
bird	brown thrasher	a rich brown color with a long, curved bill and a very long tail
butterfly	tiger swallowtail	large yellow wings edged and striped with black
crop	peanut	Georgia produces 50 percent of the total United States peanut crop.
fish	largemouth bass	The world's biggest largemouth bass was taken from a Georgia stream.
flower	Cherokee rose	waxy white with a large golden center
fruit	peach	Georgia is known as the "Peach State" and its growers produce large quantities of the fruit.
gem	quartz	found in a wide variety of colors, including amethyst and clear white
insect	honeybee	produces honey and aids agriculture by cross-pollinating crops
marine mammal	right whale	Coastal waters are a calving area for the endangered right whale, which grows up to 50 feet long.
song	*Georgia on My Mind*	music by Hoagy Carmichael, lyrics by Stuart Gorrell, performed by Georgia-born recording artist Ray Charles
tree	live oak	flourishes along the coastal plains and on the islands where the first settlers made their homes
vegetable	vidalia sweet onion	While the granex seed produces a hot onion elsewhere, it grows into a sweet onion in Georgia's soil.
wildflower	azalea	vibrant colored flowers that bloom from March until August

Population of Georgia

YEAR	TOTAL	WHITE	BLACK OR AFRICAN-AMERICAN	ALL OTHERS
1790	82,548	53,284	29,264	*
1800	162,686	102,261	60,425	*
1810	252,433	145,414	107,019	*
1820	340,989	189,570	151,419	*
1830	516,823	296,806	220,017	*
1840	691,392	407,695	283,697	*
1850	906,185	521,572	384,613	*
1860	1,057,286	591,550	465,698	38
1870	1,184,109	638,926	545,142	41
1880	1,542,180	816,906	725,133	141
1890	1,837,353	978,357	858,815	181
1900	2,216,331	1,181,294	1,034,813	224
1910	2,609,121	1,431,802	1,176,987	332
1920	2,895,832	1,689,114	1,206,365	353
1930	2,908,506	1,836,974	1,071,125	407
1940	3,123,723	2,038,278	1,084,927	518
1950	3,444,578	2,380,577	1,062,762	1,239
1960	3,943,116	2,817,223	1,122,596	3,297
1970	4,589,575	3,391,242	1,187,149	11,184
1980	5,463,105	3,947,135	1,465,181	50,789
1990	6,478,216	4,636,431	1,751,179	90,606
2000	to come	to come	to come	to come

*Other ethnic groups were not separately counted until the 1860 census.

Skillbuilder **HANDBOOK**

Table of Contents

1.1 Finding Main Ideas

Defining the Skill

The **main idea** is a statement that summarizes the main point of a speech, an article, a section of a book, or a paragraph. The main idea of a paragraph is often stated in the first or last sentence. Other sentences in the paragraph provide details that support the main idea.

Applying the Skill

Use the following strategies to build your skills.

1 Identify what you think may be the main idea. Check the first and last sentences of the paragraph to see if either could be the main idea.

2 Identify details that support that idea. Some details explain the main idea. Others give examples of what is stated in the main idea.

Practicing the Skill

Turn to Chapter 16, page 363. Read the section titled "Georgia's Cities" and create a chart that identifies the main idea and the supporting details.

1.2 Taking Notes

Defining the Skill

When you **take notes,** you write down the important ideas and details of a paragraph, passage, or chapter. A chart or an outline can help you organize your notes to use in the future.

Applying the Skill

Use the following strategies to build your skills.

1 Look at the title to find the main topic of the passage. Identify the main ideas and details of the passage. Summarize these in your notes.

2 Identify and define key terms. In this book key terms are shown in boldface type and underlined.

3 In your notes, use abbreviations, such as *GA* for Georgia to save time and space.

Practicing the Skill

Turn to Chapter 23, page 513. Read the section titled "The 1996 Olympic Games" and use a chart to take notes on the passage.

1.3 Summarizing

Defining the Skill

When you **summarize,** you restate a paragraph, passage, or chapter in fewer words. You include only the main ideas and most important details. It is important to use your own words when summarizing.

Applying the Skill

Use the following strategies to build your skills.

1 Look for topic sentences stating the main idea. These are often at the beginning of a section or paragraph. Briefly restate each main idea—in your own words.

2 Include key facts and any numbers, dates, amounts, or percentages from the text.

3 After writing your summary, review it to see that you have included only the most important details.

Practicing the Skill

Turn to Chapter 1, page 15. Read the section titled "Rivers and Lakes" and write a paragraph summarizing the passage.

1.4 Sequencing Events

Defining the Skill

Sequence is the order in which events follow one another. By being able to follow the sequence of events through history, you can get an accurate sense of the relationship among events.

Applying the Skill

Use the following strategies to build your skills.

1 Look for specific dates provided in the text. If several months within a year are included, the year is usually not repeated.

2 Look for clues about time that allow you to order events according to sequence. Words such as *day, week, month,* or *year* may help to sequence the events.

Practicing the Skill

Turn to Chapter 21, page 471. Read the section titled "Vietnam" and make a time line showing the sequence of events in the passage.

1.5 Categorizing

Defining the Skill

To **categorize** is to sort people, objects, ideas, or other information into groups, called categories. Historians categorize information to help them identify and understand patterns in historical events.

Applying the Skill

Use the following strategies to build your skills.

❶ First, decide what kind of information needs to be categorized and how that information can be sorted into categories.

❷ Then decide what the categories will be. Look for clue words such as *some, other,* and *another.*

❸ Once you have chosen the categories, sort information into them.

Practicing the Skill

Turn to Chapter 19. Read Section 3, "Georgia's Growing Economy," and make a chart categorizing the changes in Georgia during this period.

1.6 Making Public Speeches

Defining the Skill

A speech is a talk given in public to an audience. Some speeches are given to persuade the audience to think or act in a certain way, or to support a cause. You can learn how to **make public speeches** effectively by analyzing great speeches in history.

Applying the Skill

Use the following strategies to build your skills.

❶ Choose one central idea or theme and organize your speech to support it.

❷ Use words or images that will win over your audience.

❸ Repeat words or images to drive home your main point—as if it is the "hook" of a pop song.

Practicing the Skill

Turn to Chapter 9, page 208. Read the section titled "Evaluating Indian Removal" and choose a topic, develop your outline, and write your speech.

1.7 Writing for Social Studies

Defining the Skill

Writing for social studies requires you to describe an idea, situation, or event. Often, social studies writing takes a stand on a particular issue or tries to make a specific point. To successfully describe an event or make a point, your writing needs to be clear, concise, and factually accurate.

Applying the Skill

Use the following strategies to build your skills.

❶ Focus on your topic. Be sure that you clearly state the main idea of your piece so that your readers know what you intend to say.

❷ Collect and organize your facts. Collect accurate information about your topic to support the main idea you are trying to make. Use your information to build a logical case to prove your point.

❸ To express your ideas clearly, use standard grammar, spelling, sentence structure, and punctuation when writing for social studies. Proofread your work to make sure it is well organized and grammatically correct.

Practicing the Skill

Read Chapter 8, Section 1, "Creating a New Government." Then use the strategies above to write your answer to Question 4 on page 152.

2.1 Analyzing Points of View

Defining the Skill

Analyzing points of view means looking closely at a person's arguments to understand the reasons behind that person's beliefs. This helps you understand a historical figure's thoughts and opinions about a topic.

Applying the Skill

Use the following strategies to build your skills.

❶ Look for statements that show you a person's view on an issue.

❷ Use information about people to validate them as sources and understand why they might disagree.

❸ Write a summary that explains why different people took different positions on the issue.

Practicing the Skill

Turn to Chapter 11, page 232. Read the section titled "Nullification Crisis." Make a chart to analyze points of view expressed by John C. Calhoun and Andrew Jackson.

2.2 Comparing and Contrasting

Defining the Skill

Comparing means looking at the similarities and differences between two or more things. **Contrasting** means examining only their differences.

Applying the Skill

Use the following strategies to build your skills.

❶ Look for two aspects of the subject that may be compared and contrasted.

❷ To contrast, look for clue words that show how two things differ. Clue words include *by contrast, however, except,* and *yet.* To find similarities, look for clue words indicating that two things are alike. Clue words include *both, like, as,* and *similarly.*

❸ Make a Venn diagram, listing the similarities in the overlapping area and the differences in the individual ovals.

Practicing the Skill

Turn to Chapter 2, page 25. Read the sections titled "The Archaic Period" and "The Woodland Period." Use a Venn diagram to compare and contrast these cultures.

2.3 Analyzing Causes; Recognizing Effects

Defining the Skill

A **cause** is an action that makes something happen. An **effect** is the event that is the result of the cause. A single event may have several causes and one cause may result in several effects. Cause-and-effect relationships help you understand why historical events took place.

Applying the Skill

Use the following strategies to build your skills.

❶ Ask why an action took place.

❷ Look for effects. Ask yourself, "What happened?" (the effect). Then ask, "Why did it happen?" (the cause). Look for clue words that signal causes, such as *cause* and *led to.*

❸ Use a diagram to list each cause in a box. Draw an arrow from the cause boxes to a box that lists the effect.

Practicing the Skill

Turn to Chapter 5, pages 81–84. Read the sections titled "Reasons for the Colony" and "New Rules for a New Colony." Make a diagram about the causes and effects of the new colony's organization.

2.4 Making Inferences

Defining the Skill

Inferences are ideas that the author has not directly stated. **Making inferences** involves reading between the lines to interpret the information you read. You can make inferences by studying what is stated and using your common sense and previous knowledge.

Applying the Skill

Use the following strategies to build your skills.

❶ Find statements of facts and ideas. These will give you a good basis for making inferences.

❷ Use your knowledge, logic, and common sense to make inferences that are based on facts.

❸ Make a chart stating facts in one column and inferences in the other column.

Practicing the Skill

Turn to Chapter 6, page 112. Read the section titled "Problems Within Georgia." Use a chart to identify facts; then make inferences about the Georgia colony.

2.5 Drawing Conclusions

Defining the Skill

Drawing conclusions means analyzing what you have read and forming an opinion about its meaning. You look at the facts and use your common sense and experience to decide what the facts mean.

Applying the Skill

Use the following strategies to build your skills.

❶ Identify and understand all the facts, or statements, that can be proven true.

❷ Use your own experiences and common sense to understand how the facts relate to each other.

❸ Make a diagram, listing the facts in boxes. Draw an arrow from the facts boxes to a box that lists the conclusions you have drawn.

Practicing the Skill

Turn to Chapter 3. Read Section 1, "Spanish Explorations in North America," and create a diagram to list facts and draw conclusions about the effects of the Renaissance on the world.

2.6 Making Decisions

Defining the Skill

Making decisions involves choosing between two or more options, or courses of action. Most decisions have consequences, or results. By understanding how historical figures made decisions, you can learn how to improve your decision-making skills.

Applying the Skill

Use the following strategies to build your skills.

❶ Identify a decision that needs to be made.

❷ Identify possible consequences of the decision.

❸ Identify the decision that was made.

❹ Identify actual consequences that resulted from the decision.

❺ Organize the information in a flow chart.

Practicing the Skill

Turn to Chapter 13. Read Section 1, "Reconstruction of the South Begins," and make a flow chart to identify a decision about Reconstruction and its consequences.

2.7 Recognizing Propaganda

Defining the Skill

Propaganda is communication that aims to influence people's opinions, emotions, or actions. Propaganda is not always factual. It uses one-sided language or striking symbols to sway emotions. By thinking critically, you will avoid being swayed by propaganda.

Applying the Skill

Use the following strategies to build your skills.

❶ Identify the aim, or purpose, of a piece of propaganda such as a cartoon, pamphlet, or poster.

❷ Identify images that viewers might respond to emotionally, and identify the emotions. Identify facts that have been ignored.

Practicing the Skill

Turn to Chapter 8, page 151, and look at the *Massachusetts Centinel* cartoon. Use a chart to identify the purpose, identify emotions, and note facts that have been ignored.

2.8 Identifying Facts and Opinions

Defining the Skill

Facts are events, dates, statistics, or statements that can be proved to be true. **Opinions** are the judgments, beliefs, and feelings of a writer or speaker. By identifying facts and opinions, you will be able to think critically when a person is trying to influence your opinion.

Applying the Skill

Use the following strategies to build your skills.

❶ Look for specific information that can be proved or checked for accuracy.

❷ Look for assertions, claims, and judgments that express opinions.

❸ Identify the facts and opinions in a three-column chart. Label the columns *Statement, Can It Be Proved?,* and *Fact or Opinion.*

Practicing the Skill

Turn to Chapter 17, page 376, and read the section titled "The 1932 Presidential Election: 'Try Something.'" Use a chart to analyze key statements. Are they facts or opinions?

2.9 Forming and Supporting Opinions

Defining the Skill

When you **form opinions,** you interpret and judge the importance of events and people in history. You should always **support your opinions** with facts, examples, and quotes.

Applying the Skill

Use the following strategies to build your skills.

1 Look for important information about the events.

2 Form an opinion about the event by asking yourself questions, such as How important was the event? What were its effects?

3 Support your opinions with facts, quotations, and examples. If the facts do not support the opinion, then revise your opinion so the facts support it.

Practicing the Skill

Turn to Chapter 11, page 235. Read the section titled "The Missouri Compromise." Create a chart to summarize your opinion of the Compromise with supporting facts.

2.10 Making Generalizations

Defining the Skill

To **make generalizations** means to make broad judgments based on information. When you make generalizations, you should gather information from several sources.

Applying the Skill

Use the following strategies to build your skills.

1 Look for information that the sources have in common.

2 Form a generalization that the sources would agree with. State your generalization in a sentence.

Practicing the Skill

Turn to Chapter 4. Read Section 1, "The English Establish 13 Colonies," and create a chart to make a generalization about how conditions in the colonies affected the growth of slavery.

2.11 Evaluating

Defining the Skill

To **evaluate** is to make a judgment about something. Historians evaluate the actions of people in history by examining the positives and negatives of a historical action, and then deciding which is stronger—the positive or the negative.

Applying the Skill

Use the following strategies to build your skills.

1 Before you evaluate a person's actions, determine what that person was trying to do.

2 Look for statements that show the positive or negative results of the person's actions.

3 Write an evaluation of the person's actions.

Practicing the Skill

Turn to Chapter 10. Read Section 1, "Southern Culture," and make a diagram to evaluate the positive and negative impacts of cotton on Southern culture.

2.12 Identifying and Solving Problems

Defining the Skill

Identifying problems means finding and understanding the difficulties faced by a particular group of people during a certain time. **Solving problems** means understanding how people tried to remedy those problems. By studying how people solved problems in the past, you can learn ways to solve problems today.

Applying the Skill

Use the following strategies to build your skills.

1 Look for the difficulties, or problems, people faced. Consider how the problem affected people with different points of view.

2 Look for solutions people tried to deal with a problem. Think about whether the solution was a good one for people with differing points of view.

3 Organize the information into a three-column chart. Label the columns *Problem, Differing Points of View,* and *Solution.*

Practicing the Skill

Turn to Chapter 20, page 449. Read the section titled "Federal Support for Civil Rights." Then make a chart that summarizes problems faced by the government and its solutions.

3.1 Using Primary and Secondary Sources

Defining the Skill

Primary sources are materials written or made by people who witnessed historical events. Primary sources can be letters, journal entries, speeches, autobiographies, or artwork. Other primary sources include government documents, census surveys, and financial records. **Secondary sources** are materials written by people who did not participate in an event. History books are secondary sources.

Applying the Skill

Use the following strategies to build your skills.

❶ Distinguish secondary sources from primary sources.

❷ Analyze the primary source and consider who the author was and why it was created.

Practicing the Skill

Turn to Chapter 7, page 129. Read the section titled "*Common Sense* Is Published." Make a chart to summarize the primary source and secondary source information.

3.2 Interpreting Graphs

Defining the Skill

Graphs present information visually. Bar graphs compare sets of numbers. Line graphs often show trends over time. Pie graphs show parts of a whole and often use percentages.

Applying the Skill

Use the following strategies to build your skills.

❶ Ask yourself what kinds of information the graph shows. For example, does it show chronological information, geographic distributions, or something else?

❷ Read the vertical and horizontal axes on bar and line graphs. Ask what each axis represents.

❸ Summarize the information shown in each part of the graph. Use the title to help you focus on what information the graph is presenting.

Practicing the Skill

Turn to Chapter 12, page 281. Look at the two graphs titled "Costs of the Civil War." Write a summary of the information you learn from the graphs.

3.3 Interpreting Charts

Defining the Skill

Charts, like graphs, present information in a visual form. Charts organize, summarize, and present information in an easy-to-understand format. Tables and diagrams are examples of commonly used charts.

Applying the Skill

Use the following strategies to build your skills.

❶ Ask yourself what kinds of information the chart shows. For example, does it show chronological information, geographic distributions, or something else?

❷ Read the labels to see how the information in the chart is organized.

❸ Study the data in the chart to understand the facts that the chart intends to show.

❹ Summarize the information shown in the chart. Use the title to help you focus on what information the chart is presenting.

Practicing the Skill

Turn to Chapter 7, page 141. Study the chart titled "Military Deaths in the American Revolution." Write a paragraph summarizing what you learn from the chart.

3.4 Interpreting Time Lines

Defining the Skill

A **time line** is a visual list of events and dates shown in the order in which they occurred. Time lines can be horizontal or vertical. On horizontal time lines, the earliest date is on the left. On vertical time lines, the earliest date is often at the top.

Applying the Skill

Use the following strategies to build your skills.

❶ Read the dates at the beginning and end of the time line to identify the period of history.

❷ Read the dates and events in sequential order, beginning with the earliest one. Pay particular attention to how the entries relate to each other. Think about which events caused later events.

❸ Summarize the main idea of the time line.

Practicing the Skill

Turn to Chapter 4, page 56, and write a summary of the information shown on the two time lines.

3.5 Reading a Map

Defining the Skill

Maps are representations of features on the earth's surface. Maps may also show political features or specialized information. By learning to use map elements, you can better understand how to read maps.

Applying the Skill

Use the following strategies to build your skills.

❶ Read the title to identify the main idea of the map.

❷ Read the map key to help you interpret the symbols or colors on the map.

❸ Use the scale and the pointer, or compass rose, to determine distance and direction. Use lines of latitude (horizontal) and longitude (vertical) to identify the location of the area on the earth.

❹ Summarize the information shown on the map.

Practicing the Skill

Turn to Chapter 3, page 40. Read the map titled "European Exploration of the Americas, 1500–1550." Make a chart to identify information on the map.

3.6 Creating a Map

Defining the Skill

Creating a map involves representing geographical information. It is easiest to use an existing map as a guide. You can show such things as geographical information, population trends, routes, or resources. Often, this data comes from a graph or a chart.

Applying the Skill

Use the following strategies to build your skills.

❶ Select a title that identifies the geographical area and the map's purpose.

❷ Create a key that shows the colors. Add the colors to the map to show information.

❸ Draw a compass rose and scale. Add lines of latitude and longitude, if needed, using short dashes.

Practicing the Skill

Turn to Chapter 23, page 515. Read the section titled "Georgia Continues to Grow." Use the statistics provided to create a map of Georgia showing the major metropolitan statistical areas with populations.

3.7 Interpreting Political Cartoons

Defining the Skill

Political cartoons are cartoons that use humor to make a serious point. They often express a point of view on an issue better than words do.

Applying the Skill

Use the following strategies to build your skills.

❶ Identify the subject by reading the title of the cartoon and looking at the cartoon as a whole.

❷ Identify important symbols and details.

❸ Write a sentence interpreting the message.

Practicing the Skill

Look at the cartoon on page 251 of Chapter 12. Use a chart to identify the subject, symbols and details, and message of the cartoon.

3.8 Creating a Model

Defining the Skill

When you **create a model,** you show an event or a situation in a visual way. Models include posters, diagrams, and dioramas.

Applying the Skill

Use the following strategies to build your skills.

❶ Gather the information you need to understand the situation or event.

❷ Visualize your model. Then make an actual sketch to plan how it might look.

❸ Since the model gives information in a visual way, think about ways you can use color, pictures, or other visuals to tell the story.

❹ Gather the supplies you will need and create the model.

❺ Write any supporting information, such as a title, to help people understand your model.

Practicing the Skill

Turn to Chapter 14. Read Section 3, "Urban and Rural Worlds of Georgia." Choose a crop, business, or industry of Georgia; and create a poster on the topic that shows related images, statistics, stories, etc.

4.1 Using an Electronic Card Catalog

Defining the Skill

An **electronic card catalog** will help you find information about the books and other materials in the library. You can use an electronic card catalog to create a bibliography (a list of books) on topics of interest.

Applying the Skill

Use the following strategies to build your skills.

❶ Begin searching by choosing either subject, title, or author.

❷ Select a book from the results of your search and identify the author, title, city, publisher, and date of publication.

❸ Locate the call number for the book. The call number indicates where you will find the book in the library.

Practicing the Skill

Turn to Chapter 5, and find an event or person that interests you. Use the SUBJECT search on an electronic card catalog to find books on your topic, and make a bibliography about the subject.

4.2 Creating a Database

Defining the Skill

A **database** is a collection of data for easy retrieval. Once an electronic database is set up, you can locate information without examining the entire database.

Applying the Skill

Use the following strategies to build your skills.

❶ Identify the topic of the database.

❷ Ask yourself what kind of data you need to include. Your choice of data will provide the column headings for your database.

❸ Identify the entries included under each column heading.

❹ Use the database to help you find information quickly.

Practicing the Skill

Use the information from your Chapter 2 notes (page 22) to create a database with information about prehistoric cultures. Identify lifestyle, technology, food, trade, and religion.

4.3 Using the Internet

Defining the Skill

Each location on the Internet has a home page with its own address, or URL (universal resource locator). The international collection of home pages, known as the World Wide Web, is a good source of current and historical information.

Applying the Skill

Use the following strategies to build your skills.

❶ Go directly to a Web page such as classzone.com. Then click on ClassZone and find the link to *Georgia History*.

❷ Explore the *Georgia History* links. Click on the links to find out more about a specific subject.

❸ You should confirm the information you find on the Internet. Web sites set up by universities, government agencies, and reputable news sources are more reliable than other sources.

Practicing the Skill

Turn to Chapter 15 and select a person or event that interests you. Gather information from three Web sites related to your topic.

4.4 Creating a Multimedia Presentation

Defining the Skill

Movies, CD-ROMs, television, and computer software are different kinds of media. To **create a multimedia presentation,** you need to collect information in different media and organize them into one presentation.

Applying the Skill

Use the following strategies to build your skills.

❶ Identify the topic of your presentation and decide which media are best.

❷ Research the topic in a variety of sources, selecting appropriate images or background music.

❸ Write the script to organize the presentation.

❹ Videotape the presentation, if possible, for future use.

Practicing the Skill

Turn to Chapter 18. Choose a topic from the chapter, and create a multimedia presentation about it.

GLOSSARY

A

abolition *n.* the movement to end slavery. (p. 236)

Acts of Trade *n.* trade and navigation laws. (p. 107)

Allied Powers *n.* an alliance of 28 countries, including the United States, that opposed the Central Powers during World War I (p. 352) and the Axis Powers during World War II. (p. 394)

Anaconda Plan *n.* a strategy by which the Union proposed to defeat the Confederacy in the Civil War. (p. 254)

Andersonville *n.* the location of the Confederate prison in Georgia during the Civil War; built to hold 10,000 Union prisoners, it eventually held 33,000. (p. 276)

antebellum *adj.* before the war. (p. 215)

anthropologist *n.* a scientist who studies human beings through their physical characteristics, culture, and environment. (p. 29)

Appalachian Mountains *n.* the mountain range that stretches from Canada to Alabama and is the highest and most rugged region of Georgia. (p. 9)

Appomattox Court House *n.* the village in Virginia where Lee surrendered to Grant on April 9, 1865, ending the Civil War. (p. 279)

apprentice *n.* a young boy who left his family to learn a trade from an experienced craftsman. (p. 71)

aquifer *n.* the gravel layer underground that collects water. (p. 15)

Archaic Indians *n.* the descendents of the Paleo-Indians who lived in North America from approximately 8000 B.C. to 1000 B.C. (p. 25)

archeologist *n.* a scientist who studies artifacts. (p. 23)

Articles of Confederation *n.* the document adopted by the Continental Congress in 1777 and all the states by 1781 that outlined the form of government in the new United States. (p. 146)

artifact *n.* an object from the past that contributes to our understanding of an earlier culture. (p. 23)

Atlanta Forward *n.* a national advertising campaign, started by the Atlanta Chamber of Commerce in 1925, promoting the growth of Atlanta. (p. 364)

atomic bomb *n.* an explosive weapon of great destructive power created by the rapid release of nuclear energy. (p. 402)

Augusta *n.* a fort, completed in 1738, built to serve as a secure settlement between the colonies of Savannah and Charles Town. (p. 89)

Axis Powers *n.* Germany, Italy, and their allies during World War II. (p. 393)

Azilia *n.* a proposed colony on the land between Spanish Florida and English Carolina. (p. 53)

B

B-29 *n.* an aircraft built by the Bell Aircraft Company in Georgia for World War II; also known as the B-29 Superfortress bomber. (p. 405)

baby boomer *n.* a term for a person born between 1946 and 1964, when the U.S. birthrate sharply increased following World War II. (p. 420)

Backcountry *n.* the region and settlements located in the inner, mountainous area in the South beginning at the Fall Line. (p. 66)

Battle of Antietam (an TEE tuhm) *n.* a Civil War battle in 1862 in which 23,000 men were killed or wounded. (p. 266)

Battle of Bloody Marsh *n.* a successful battle in 1742 against the Spanish troops by the early colonists of Georgia and their Native American allies. (p. 93)

Battle of Bull Run *n.* the first major battle in the Civil War, fought near Bull Run River, Virginia; it is known as the Battle of Manassas in the South. (p. 255)

Battle of Gettysburg *n.* an 1863 battle in the Civil War in which the Union defeated the Confederacy, ending hopes for a Confederate victory in the North. (p. 267)

Battle of Horseshoe Bend *n.* a battle of the U.S. military against the Red Sticks in 1814 in eastern Alabama; part of the War of 1812. (p. 164)

Battle of Shiloh *n.* an 1862 battle in which the Union forced the Confederacy to retreat in some of the fiercest fighting in the Civil War. (p. 264)

Bill of Rights *n.* the first ten amendments to the U.S. Constitution, added in 1791, and consisting of a formal list of citizens' rights and freedoms. (p. 152)

black code *n.* a law passed by Southern states that limited the freedom of former slaves. (p. 293)

Black Tuesday *n.* a name given to October 29, 1929, when stock prices fell sharply. (p. 371)

Board of Regents controversy *n.* the actions taken by Governor Eugene Talmadge in Georgia in 1941, to rid the state colleges of two professors whom he suspected of promoting desegregation. (p. 437)

boll weevil *n.* a beetle that lays its eggs in the cotton boll; the larvae eats the cotton boll, destroying the cotton harvest. (p. 365)

booster *n.* a Southerner who promoted the growth of his town in an effort for even more growth. (p. 315)

Boston Tea Party *n.* the dumping of 342 chests of tea into Boston Harbor by colonists protesting the Tea Act of 1733. (p. 114)

Bourbon (boor BON) Triumvirate *n.* John B. Gordon, Alfred Holt Colquitt, and Joseph E. Brown, who controlled the Democratic Party in Georgia from the 1870s to the 1890s. (p. 330)

Brain Trust *n.* a group of experts assembled by President Franklin D. Roosevelt to come up with programs and plans to fight the Depression. (p. 376)

Brown* v. *Board of Education *n.* a 1954 case in which the Supreme Court ruled that "separate but equal" education was unconstitutional. (p. 451)

C

California gold rush *n.* the large migration to California in 1849 after gold had been discovered there. (p. 238)

Camp David Accords *n.* a peace treaty in 1979 between Egypt and Israel that ended 30 years of conflict. (p. 492)

Camp Stewart *n.* a training camp for military personnel located near Savannah, Georgia. (p. 406)

carpetbagger *n.* an insulting term used to describe a Northerner who moved to the South after the Civil War. (p. 297)

cash crop *n.* a crop that is raised to be sold for money. (p. 62)

Central Powers *n.* an alliance of Austria-Hungary, Germany, the Ottoman Empire, and Bulgaria during World War I. (p. 352)

charter *n.* a written contract issued by a government giving the holder the right to establish a company. (p. 51)

checks and balances *n.* the ability of each branch of government to exercise checks, or controls, over the other branches. (p. 150)

Cherokee Constitution *n.* the document the Cherokee Nation wrote to establish their governing system and territory. (p. 201)

Cherokee *n.* the second largest group of Native Americans in early Georgia. (p. 32)

Cherokee Nation v. Georgia *n.* a law suit against Georgia brought by the Cherokee Nation; the Supreme Court ruled against the Cherokee. (p. 205)

Cherokee Phoenix *n.* the Cherokee newspaper, printed in English and Cherokee, started in 1828. (p. 200)

Civil Rights Act of 1964 *n.* an act that banned segregation in public places and created the Equal Employment Opportunity Commission. (p. 461)

civilization *n.* a form of culture characterized by city trade centers, specialized workers, organized forms of government and religion, systems of record keeping, and advanced tools. (p. 28)

clan *n.* a group of people with a common ancestor. (p. 31)

climate *n.* the average weather conditions over a long period. (p. 11)

Coastal Plain *n.* the southernmost geographic region in Georgia, consisting of the Outer Coastal Plain and the Inner Coastal Plain. (p. 6)

Cold War *n.* the state of hostility, without direct military conflict, that developed between the United States and the Soviet Union after World War II. (p. 424)

Colored Farmers' Alliance *n.* an organization created by African-American farmers in the late 1800s to try to get better wages for farm laborers. (p. 333)

committee of correspondence *n.* a group of colonists who exchanged letters on colonial affairs. (p. 112)

Commons House of Assembly *n.* a group of Georgia colonists elected to serve on the royal colonial legislature. (p. 96)

commonwealth *n.* a community in which people work together for the good of the whole. (p. 60)

Compact of 1802 *n.* an agreement whereby Georgia gave up all the land involved in the Yazoo Land Fraud to the U.S. and received $1.25 million and the promise to remove all Native Americans from Georgia. (p. 158)

Compromise of 1850 *n.* a series of Congressional laws intended to settle the major disagreements between free states and slave states. (p. 239)

concentration camp *n.* one of the places used by Germans to imprison and kill persecuted groups during World War II. (p. 401)

confederacy *n.* a group of people who band together for political or military strength. (p. 30)

conquistador (kon KEES tuh DOR) *n.* a Spanish explorer and conqueror who sought to destroy and take over existing culture in the Americas in the 1500s. (p. 40)

Constitutional Convention *n.* a meeting held in 1787 to consider changes to the Articles of Confederation; it resulted in the drafting of the Constitution. (p. 148)

containment *n.* the foreign policy of the United States following World War II, aimed at stopping the spread of communism. (p. 426, 471)

Contract with America *n.* the Republican Party's platform in 1994, developed by Newt Gingrich. (p. 515)

cotton gin *n.* a machine invented by Eli Whitney in 1793 for cleaning cotton. (p. 215)

county unit system *n.* the system used in Georgia between 1877 and 1963 that gave rural counties an advantage over urban counties in elections to the state legislature due to more representation per person. (p. 331)

Creek Confederacy *n.* the group of Mississippian tribes that banded together, becoming the largest group in the Southeast. (p. 30)

Creek War *n.* another name given to the War of 1812 by Southerners and Georgians who suspected Britain of supplying the Creek with weapons. (p. 163)

crop lien *n.* the legal right of the landowner to the crop of a tenant farmer who is in debt to him or her. (p. 317)

Cuban missile crisis *n.* the critical situation in 1962 in which the United States and the Soviet Union almost went to war because the Soviets had placed nuclear missiles in Cuba. (p. 428)

culture *n.* a way of life shared by people with similar arts, beliefs, and customs. (p. 23)

D

dame school *n.* a colonial school for young children taught by an older woman in her own home. (p. 72)

Daughters of Liberty *n.* a group of women colonists who persuaded other colonists to avoid British taxes by weaving their own cloth. (p. 110)

D-Day *n.* June 6, 1944, the day the Allies invaded France during World War II. (p. 400)

democratic republic *n.* a government based on the will of the people, in which the people choose representatives to govern for them. (p. 148, 498)

disfranchisement *n.* the withholding from a person of one of the rights of citizenship, such as the right to vote. (p. 336)

Dixie Highway *n.* the major highway, built between 1915 and 1927, that stretches from the Great Lakes to the Florida Keys. (p. 361)

Dixiecrat *n.* a political party created by Southern Democrats in 1948 in protest of the Democratic Party platform that included civil rights support. (p. 450)

draft *n.* a law requiring citizens to serve in the military when selected; the Confederacy passed the first draft in American history in April 1862. (p. 258)

Dred Scott v. Sandford *n.* an 1856 Supreme Court case in which a slave, Dred Scott, sued unsuccessfully for his freedom because he had been taken to live in territories where slavery was illegal. (p. 241)

E

Emancipation Proclamation *n.* an order issued by Abraham Lincoln on January 1, 1863, freeing the slaves in all regions rebelling against the Union. (p. 266)

Enlightenment *n.* an eighteenth-century cultural movement that emphasized reason and science. (p. 74)

executive branch *n.* the branch of government responsible for enforcing, or carrying out, the law. (p. 501)

Executive Order 8802 *n.* President Franklin Roosevelt's law that prohibited discrimination against defense workers because of race, creed, color, or national origin. (p. 449)

Exoduster (EKS suh duhs tuhr) *n.* one of the African Americans who left the South for the West and compared himself or herself to a Biblical Hebrew who left slavery in Egypt. (p. 328)

F

Fall Line Freeway *n.* a four-lane freeway connecting Columbus and Augusta. (p. 523)

fall zone *n.* the geographic zone that marks the transition from the Coastal Plain to the Piedmont. (p. 7)

fascism (FASH iz uhm) *n.* a political philosophy that advocates a strong, centralized, nationalistic government headed by a powerful dictator. (p. 393)

federalism *n.* a system of government where power is shared among the central (or federal) government and the states. (p. 150)

field hand *n.* an enslaved African-American worker on a plantation who plowed, hoed, and harvested the crops. (p. 224)

Field Order No. 120 *n.* Sherman's order to his troops to live off the land in their final march through Georgia during the "March to the Sea" in 1864. (p. 274)

Field Order No. 15 *n.* an order issued by Sherman in January 1865 that gave each household of freed slaves 40 acres of land along the coast. (p. 278)

Fifteenth Amendment *n.* an amendment to the U.S. Constitution, passed in 1870, stating that no male citizen could be stopped from voting "on account of race, color, or previous condition of servitude." (p. 300)

54th Massachusetts Colored Volunteers *n.* one of the first African-American regiments organized in the North during the Civil War. (p. 263)

First Continental Congress *n.* a meeting of delegates in 1774 from all the colonies except Georgia to uphold colonial rights. (p. 115)

food riot *n.* an angry reaction of Southern women to food shortages during the Civil War. (p. 261)

Fort Benning *n.* an army training facility in Columbus, Georgia. (p. 406)

Fort Pulaski *n.* a fort at the mouth of the Savannah River that the Confederacy lost to the Union in April 1862. (p. 256)

Fort Sumter *n.* a fort in South Carolina from which the first Confederate shots of the Civil War were fired. (p. 255)

Founding Fathers *n.* the group of influential men who made the greatest contributions to the establishment of the United States of America. (p. 145)

Fourteenth Amendment *n.* an amendment to the U.S. Constitution, passed in 1868, that made all persons born or naturalized in the United States—including former slaves—citizens of the country. (p. 294)

fourth branch (of the government) *n.* citizens of a democratic republic. (p. 507)

freedman *n.* a former slave. (p. 287)

Freedmen's Bureau *n.* a federal agency set up to help former slaves after the Civil War. (p. 289)

French and Indian War *n.* several small battles beginning in 1754 between the French (and their Native American allies) and British colonists over North American territory. (p. 103)

G

G.I. Bill *n.* the commonly used name for the Serviceman's Readjustment Act of 1944, which provided educational and economic help to veterans. (p. 419)

General Assembly *n.* the name of the legislative branch in Georgia. (p. 500)

globalization *n.* the practice of making products and ideas available all over the world. (p. 517)

governor *n.* the chief officer of the executive branch of state government. (p. 501)

Great Awakening *n.* a movement in the 1730s and 1740s that stirred up intense religious enthusiasm in the colonies. (p. 73)

Great Depression *n.* a period lasting from 1929 to 1941 during which the U.S. economy was in severe decline and millions of Americans were unemployed. (p. 372)

Great Migration *n.* a term used to describe the movement of 1.5 million Southern African Americans to cities in the North following World War I. (p. 358)

Great Society *n.* a program started by President Lyndon Johnson that provided help to the poor, the elderly, and women, and also promoted education and outlawed discrimination. (p. 474)

Great Wagon Road *n.* the main highway of the colonial Backcountry along the eastern edge of the Appalachians. (p. 67)

Gulf of Tonkin Resolution *n.* the Congressional resolution that gave President Lyndon B. Johnson power to use military force in Vietnam. (p. 471)

Gulf Stream *n.* a powerful ocean current that flows from the Gulf of Mexico north along the East Coast of North America before turning east toward Europe. (p. 41)

H

Harpers Ferry *n.* a federal arsenal in Virginia that was captured in 1859 during a slave revolt. (p. 242)

Hartsfield International Airport *n.* originally called Hartsfield Airport, Atlanta's airport was reconstructed in 1962 so that it could accommodate jet airplanes. (p. 481)

hazardous waste *n.* a chemically-based product which can be dangerous to people's health and the environment. (p. 15)

headright *n.* Georgia's system of land distribution in 1782, where each head of household was entitled to

200 acres of land, with an additional 50 acres of land per family member or slave, up to 1000 acres. (p. 155)

hierarchy *n.* the organization of people into different social rankings. (p. 28)

Homestead Act of 1862 *n.* the law which gave settlers 160 acres of land if they promised to live on that land for five years. (p. 328)

HOPE scholarships *n.* a Georgia program that grants college scholarships to deserving students, funded by a state lottery. (p. 516)

house slave *n.* an enslaved African-American worker who took care of the housework and child care of a plantation owner. (p. 224)

Huguenot (HYOOH gu not) *n.* a French Protestant of the sixteenth or seventeenth century who fled religious persecution. (p. 45)

Hundred Days *n.* President Franklin Roosevelt's first 100 days in office, in 1933, during which he sent Congress many new bills. (p. 377)

hurricane *n.* a very large spiraling wind system that forms above the ocean. (p. 12)

I

immigrant *n.* a person who settles in a new country. (p. 309)

indentured servant *n.* a person who sold his or her labor to a person in return for passage to the New World. (p. 51)

Indian Removal Act *n.* an 1830 act that called for the government to negotiate treaties that would require Native Americans to relocate in the West. (p. 204)

information revolution *n.* the era at the end of the twentieth century marked by increased speed of communication and the transfer of information. (p. 517)

Intolerable Acts *n.* a series of laws passed by Parliament in 1774 to punish Massachusetts colonists for the Boston Tea Party. (p. 114)

Iran hostage crisis *n.* an incident which started on November 4, 1979, when a group of Iranians overran the American embassy in Iran's capital of Tehran and took 52 Americans hostage. (p. 493)

iron curtain *n.* a term coined by British Prime Minister Winston Churchill for the Soviet Union's policy of shutting out the rest of the world following World War II. (p. 426)

island hopping *n.* a World War II strategy in which the Allies invaded islands that the Japanese weakly defended in order to stage further attacks and get closer to invading Japan. (p. 402)

J

Jim Crow laws *n.* a set of laws forcing the separation of white and black people in public places in the South. (p. 337)

joint-stock company *n.* a business project financed by investors who share in profits by owning stock in that company. (p. 51)

judicial branch *n.* the branch of government responsible for applying and interpreting the law, consisting of different levels of courts. (p. 501)

juvenile court system *n.* a court system that gives special consideration to people under 17 years of age. (p. 503)

K

kaolin (KAY uh lihn) *n.* a white clay found in Georgia that is used in making plastics, toothpaste, medicine, porcelain, paint, and paper coatings. (p. 363)

King Cotton Diplomacy *n.* a Southern policy of depending on the demand for cotton to win foreign support for the South during the Civil War. (p. 255)

Ku Klux Klan *n.* a group formed in 1866 to restore Democratic control of the South and keep former slaves powerless; the Klan used terror and violence to keep freedmen from exercising their civil rights. (p. 299)

L

laissez-faire (LES ay FAIR) *n.* a theory that business, if unregulated, acts in a way that will benefit the nation. (p. 308)

Lake Sidney Lanier *n.* a lake created in Georgia in the 1950s to supply the Atlanta area with water. (p. 436)

land lottery *n.* a lottery system Georgia used to distribute the newly acquired Native American lands. (p. 159)

legislative branch *n.* the branch of government responsible for making laws. (p. 500)

Lend-Lease Act *n.* a 1941 law that allowed the United States to ship arms and supplies, without immediate payment, to nations fighting the Axis Powers. (p. 397)

Lewis and Clark expedition *n.* a group led by Meriwether Lewis and William Clark to explore the lands of the Louisiana Purchase beginning in 1803. (p. 162)

Lexington and Concord *n.* the sites in Massachusetts of the first battles of the American Revolution. (p. 118)

Liberty Ship *n.* one of the transport ships built in Savannah and Brunswick, Georgia, for World War II. (p. 405)

Light Horse Guard *n.* the national police force of the Cherokee Nation, established in 1808. (p. 201)

linthead *n.* a term for a cotton mill worker because of the lint that stuck to his or her hair and clothes. (p. 312)

Lost Cause *n.* the term used for the belief some Southerners had that the "Old South" would return. (p. 311)

Louisiana Purchase *n.* the 1803 purchase of the Louisiana Territory from France. (p. 161)

Loyalist *n.* an American colonist who supported the British in the American Revolution. (p. 118)

lynching *n.* a murder by hanging or shooting, usually carried out by a mob. (p. 338)

M

Manifest Destiny *n.* the belief that the United States was destined to stretch across the continent from the Atlantic Ocean to the Pacific Ocean. (p. 165)

March on Washington *n.* a huge civil rights demonstration in Washington, D.C., in 1963. (p. 460)

March to the Sea *n.* the 60-mile-wide march of destruction between Atlanta and Savannah taken by Sherman's troops in 1864 in the Civil War. (p. 270)

market town *n.* a small town that grew in the improved economy of the New South, where farmers could trade, ship their crops, or purchase goods. (p. 315)

MARTA *n.* Metropolitan Atlanta Rapid Transit Authority; affordable public transportation via rail, established in 1971. (p. 479)

matrilineal *adj.* tracing ancestry through the mother's family. (p. 31)

mercantilism *n.* an economic theory in which government controls trade and attempts to transfer wealth from colonies to the parent country. (p. 49)

Military Reconstruction Acts *n.* a series of laws passed in 1867 that divided the previously Confederate states into military districts. (p. 295)

Milledgeville *n.* Georgia's state capital in 1860. (p. 244)

Mississippian culture *n.* the way of life among people living beside the Mississippi and Ohio rivers in the period following the Woodland period. (p. 27)

Missouri Compromise *n.* a series of laws enacted in 1820 to maintain the balance of power between slave states and free states. (p. 235)

monopoly *n.* a company that eliminates its competitors and controls an industry. (p. 52, 307)

Montgomery bus boycott *n.* an African-American boycott of the public buses in Montgomery, Alabama, in 1955 in response to the arrest of Rosa Parks, who refused to give up her seat to a white person. (p. 453)

N

NAACP *n.* National Association for the Advancement of Colored People, an organization founded in 1909 that worked to gain equal treatment for African-American citizens. (p. 447)

NAFTA *n.* the North American Free Trade Agreement, passed in 1993, creating a free trade bloc among the United States, Mexico, and Canada. (p. 518)

Nazi Party (NAHT see) *n.* the National Socialist German Workers' Party, which came to power under Adolf Hitler in the 1930s. (p. 394)

New Deal *n.* President Franklin Roosevelt's programs to fight the Great Depression. (p. 377)

New Echota *n.* the capital city of the Cherokee Nation, near what is today Calhoun, Georgia. (p. 200)

New France *n.* a French colony in North America with a population of 80,000. (p. 47)

New South *n.* the term used in the South to describe the new economy and expansion they hoped for after Reconstruction. (p. 310)

1996 Olympic Games *n.* the largest Olympics in history, held in Atlanta. (p. 513)

Nineteenth Amendment *n.* an amendment to the U.S. Constitution, ratified in 1920, which gave women full voting rights. (p. 358)

nuclear arms race *n.* the competition for atomic weapons between the Soviet Union and the United States following World War II. (p. 425)

nullify *v.* to invalidate a federal law. (p. 232)

O

one man, one vote *n.* the phrase used to describe the 1962 U.S. Supreme Court ruling that state legislatures could not give more representation to one group over another, which overturned the county unit system in Georgia. (p. 477)

OPEC *n.* Organization of Petroleum Exporting Countries, an organization of mainly Arab oil-producing nations. (p. 491)

Operation Dixie *n.* the name given to the effort by the Congress of Industrial Organizations to set up unions in the South after World War II. (p. 433)

overseer *n.* a man hired to manage the farming operation of a plantation in the absence of the owner. (p. 222)

ozone *n.* a gas made up of three atoms of oxygen that forms in the air when certain chemicals react with sunlight. (p. 13)

P

Paleo-Indians *n.* the inhabitants of North America who lived during a period approximately 10,000 years ago. (p. 24)

palisade *n.* a strong wooden wall built for defense around a settlement. (p. 87)

parish *n.* a district in Georgia similar to the counties of today, formed for religious and military organization rather than political organization. (p. 97)

Patriot *n.* an American colonist who sided with the rebels in the American Revolution. (p. 118)

Pearl Harbor *n.* an American naval base in Hawaii that was hit in a surprise attack by Japan on December 7, 1941, causing the U.S. to enter World War II. (p. 398)

Persian Gulf War *n.* a war in 1990–1991 between the United States and United Nations forces and Iraq, after Iraq had invaded Kuwait. (p. 495)

Piedmont *n.* the rolling, hilly plateau at the base of the Appalachian Mountains that divides Georgia's mountainous region from its coastal region. (p. 8)

Pilgrim *n.* a member of a religious group that wanted to separate from the Church of England in the early 1600s. (p. 59)

plantation economy *n.* the economic system of the very large farms in the Southern colonies, which produced everything needed for those who lived and worked there. (p. 64)

plantation *n.* a large farm in the South that extended over hundreds of acres. (p. 222)

planter *n.* one of Georgia's wealthy elite landowners, who owned 20 or more slaves to work on his plantation. (p. 222)

Plessy* v. *Ferguson *n.* an 1896 case in which the Supreme Court ruled that separation of the races in public accommodations was legal. (p. 337)

poll tax *n.* a fee required before a person could vote, used by Southern Democrats to prevent poor whites and African Americans from voting (c. 1908). (p. 336)

poor school system *n.* a public school system developed by Georgia's legislature in 1817. (p. 218)

popular sovereignty (SOV uhr in tee) *n.* a government in which the people rule; a system in which the residents vote to decide an issue. (p. 241)

Populist Party *n.* a political party formed in 1890 to represent the issues and needs of farmers and the working class. (p. 333)

prehistoric *adj.* relating to the time before written history. (p. 23)

Proclamation of 1763 *n.* an order by the British government forbidding American colonists to settle west of the Appalachians. (p. 105)

Progressive Movement *n.* an early twentieth-century reform movement seeking to return control of the government to the people, restore economic opportunities, and correct injustices in American life. (p. 341)

Prohibition *n.* the banning of the manufacture, sale, and possession of alcoholic beverages; the Eighteenth Amendment made it the law in 1920. (p. 358)

property tax *n.* a tax paid on the value of the land and buildings owned by people and businesses. (p. 506)

Public Works Administration (PWA) *n.* one of the relief programs of the New Deal, which created jobs by having people build low-cost housing, highways, bridges, and other public works. (p. 385)

Puritan *n.* a member of a religious group from England who wanted to "purify" the practices of the Church of England in the early 1600s. (p. 60)

Q

Quartering Act *n.* a law passed by Parliament in 1765 that required the colonists to house and supply British soldiers. (p. 109)

R

ration card *n.* the coupon book distributed by the government to Americans during World War II to limit their consumption of goods such as sugar, gasoline, cigarettes, and tires. (p. 410)

Redeemer *n.* one of the white politicians who took power after Georgia was readmitted to the Union in 1872. (p. 301)

region *n.* an area in which the climate, elevation, terrain, soils, and vegetations are similar. (p. 6)

Renaissance (REHN ih SAHNS) *n.* the European civilization from the 1300s to 1600 characterized by an increased interest in art and learning. (p. 39)

reservation *n.* a tract of land set aside by the U.S. government for a Native American tribe. (p. 328)

S

scalawag *n.* a white Southerner who worked with the Republican Party and the Reconstruction government after the Civil War. (p. 297)

SCLC *n.* the Southern Christian Leadership Conference, an organization established by ministers and civil rights leaders in Atlanta in 1957, with Martin Luther King, Jr., as president. (p. 454)

Scots Highlander *n.* a settler in early Georgia from one of the mountainous regions of Scotland. (p. 88)

secede *v.* to withdraw; to leave the Union. (p. 232)

sectionalism *n.* loyalty to the concerns of your own region or section of the country, rather than to the nation as a whole. (p. 231)

Selective Service Act *n.* a law passed in 1917 requiring all young men (ages 21–31, and later, ages 18–45) to register for the draft during World War I. (p. 353)

Seminole *n.* a tribe descended from the Mississippians that lived in Florida and some parts of Georgia territory. (p. 33)

settlement house *n.* an institution during the Progressive Movement that offered help to immigrants and people living in poverty, especially in large cities. (p. 343)

sharecropping *n.* the system in which landowners gave farm workers land, seed, and tools in return for a part of the crops they raised. (p. 291)

Sherman Antitrust Act *n.* a law passed in 1890 that made it illegal for corporations to gain control of industries by forming trusts. (p. 308)

Smart Growth *n.* the plan to slow urban sprawl and push investment to rural areas of Georgia. (p. 523)

SNCC *n.* the Student Non-Violent Coordinating Committee, formed in 1960 by young African Americans in Atlanta who wanted to participate in the civil rights movement. (p. 456)

Sons of Liberty *n.* a group of colonists who opposed British policies and pressured merchants not to sell taxed items. (p. 110)

Southern Farmers' Alliance *n.* an organization formed in Texas in the late 1870s to help the Southern farmers get better prices for crops. (p. 332)

Southern Manifesto *n.* an official declaration by 100 Southern members of Congress in 1956, indicating their resistance to desegregation. (p. 452)

Spanish influenza epidemic *n.* an outbreak of a highly contagious flu in 1918, which killed 675,000 Americans and 25 million people worldwide. (p. 356)

Stamp Act *n.* a law passed by Parliament in 1765 that required all legal and commercial documents to carry an official stamp showing a tax had been paid. (p. 109)

states' rights *n.* the privileges that states possess to govern themselves without interference from the federal government. (p. 232)

suburb *n.* a residential area outside a city. (p. 420)

Sugar Act *n.* a law passed in 1764 that included closer enforcement of merchants' sugar purchases. (p. 108)

Sunbelt *n.* a group of Southern states that stretches from the East Coast all the way to California. (p. 5)

supply-side economics *n.* the idea that lowering taxes will lead to increases in jobs, savings, investments, and government revenue. (p. 494)

T

Tariff of Abominations *n.* an 1828 law which placed a tax on foreign imports, brought about by Northern manufacturers against British goods and greatly disliked by Southerners. (p. 232)

Techwood Homes *n.* the public housing built for white tenants in Atlanta by the PWA in 1935. (p. 385)

Terminus *n.* the point at which the first stake of the Western and Atlantic Railroad was driven in 1837 marking the beginning of modern-day Atlanta. (p. 218)

terrorism *n.* the use, or threatened use, of violence against individuals or property to intimidate or cause fear for political or social reasons. (p. 518)

Tet Offensive *n.* a surprise attack in 1968 by the Viet Cong on U.S. military bases and cities and towns in South Vietnam during Tet, the Vietnamese celebration of the lunar New Year. (p. 472)

Thirteenth Amendment *n.* an amendment to the U.S. Constitution, adopted in 1865, banning slavery and involuntary servitude in the United States. (p. 289)

three governors controversy *n.* the confusion created when newly elected governor Eugene Talmadge died before taking office; three men each claimed to be the rightful governor of Georgia in 1946. (p. 440)

tornado *n.* a strong, fast wind that forms a tunnel-shaped spiral. (p. 12)

Townshend Acts *n.* a series of laws passed by Parliament in 1767 that established taxes on goods bought in the British colonies. (p. 110)

Trail of Tears *n.* the tragic journey of the Cherokee people from their homeland to Indian Territory between 1838 and 1839; thousands of Cherokee died. (p. 208)

transcontinental railroad *n.* the railroad that connected the East Coast of the U.S. with the West Coast, finished in 1869. (p. 328)

Treaty of Augusta *n.* an agreement negotiated by Governor Wright with the Creek that tripled the size of Georgia in 1763. (p. 106)

Treaty of New Echota *n.* an agreement formed between the Treaty Party and the U.S. government that gave up all Cherokee land in the Southeast in exchange for land in northeast Oklahoma. (p. 206)

Treaty of Paris *n.* an agreement between France and England that ended the Seven Years' War and ended French power in North America. (p. 104)

Treaty of Savannah *n.* an agreement signed by a group of Creek chiefs giving land to the new Georgia colony. (p. 85)

Treaty Party *n.* a small group of Cherokee formed by Major Ridge and others to negotiate land cessions to the federal government. (p. 206)

triangular trade *n.* a system of trade in which goods, including slaves, were exchanged between Europe, Africa, and the Americas. (p. 61)

trustee *n.* a man of prominence or wealth who holds property for the benefit of someone else. (p. 82)

20-slave exemption *n.* a system by which a Confederate, slaveholding man could avoid military service; for every 20 slaves on a plantation, one white man on the plantation was released from his requirement to serve in the military. (p. 258)

Twenty-Sixth Amendment *n.* an amendment to the U.S. Constitution in 1971, lowering the voting age from 21 to 18. (p. 473)

Two Georgias *n.* the term used by Georgians to describe the division of their state into two regions or cultures—one urban Georgia and one rural Georgia, or Atlanta and everything else. (p. 483)

U

Underground Railroad *n.* a series of escape routes used by slaves escaping the South. (p. 241)

Union League *n.* an organization formed by African Americans throughout the South after Reconstruction to protect their rights, especially to vote, run for office, and earn a living. (p. 298)

University Homes *n.* the public housing built for black tenants in Atlanta by the PWA in 1937. (p. 385)

Uprising of '34 *n.* the name given to a major textile worker strike across the South in 1934. (p. 380)

usage fee *n.* the small fee (amount of money) charged to use a county park. (p. 506)

V

V-E Day *n.* Victory in Europe Day, May 8, 1945, the day Germany surrendered. (p. 401)

victory garden *n.* a vegetable garden raised by an American during World War II so that farm produce could be shipped to the military. (p. 409)

V-J Day *n.* Victory in Japan Day, August 14, 1945, the end of fighting by Japan in World War II. (p. 402)

Voting Rights Act of 1965 *n.* a law banning literacy tests and other laws that kept African Americans from registering to vote. (p. 463)

W

War of 1812 *n.* a war Congress declared against Britain in response to its increasing interference in America's trade with France; *see Creek War.* (p. 163)

water war *n.* a conflict that started in 1990 between the states of Georgia, Florida, and Alabama over the use of shared water supplies. (p. 521)

Watergate *n.* the site of the Democratic National Committee headquarters in Washington, D.C.; a scandal resulting from the Nixon administration's attempt to cover up its involvement in a break-in there in 1972. (p. 474)

WAVES *n.* Women Appointed for Volunteer Emergency Service; the U.S. Navy service opportunity for women in World War II. (p. 408)

weather *n.* the condition and temperature of the atmosphere. (p. 11)

white primary *n.* another method by which Southern Democrats kept African Americans from voting by allowing only whites to vote in a primary. (p. 337)

Wilmot Proviso *n.* an 1846 proposal that outlawed slavery in any territory gained from the War with Mexico. (p. 237)

Woodland Indians *n.* the inhabitants of North America from approximately 1000 B.C. to A.D. 800. (p. 25)

Worcester v. Georgia *n.* a case brought to the Supreme court, which ruled that the Cherokee Nation was a distinct nation with its own laws and Georgia law was not valid in it. (p. 205)

Works Progress Administration *n.* a relief program in the New Deal in 1935 that put artists and writers to work on public projects and employed millions of other Americans in building bridges, roads, public buildings, public parks, and airports. (p. 383)

Wounded Knee *n.* the area of South Dakota in which U.S. soldiers massacred 300 unarmed Native Americans. (p. 328)

Y

Yamacraw Bluff *n.* the site chosen for the first town in the colony of Georgia, later named Savannah. (p. 84)

Yazoo Land Fraud *n.* the most widely known land fraud in U.S. history (1795) in which land companies bribed Georgia politicians to pass a law allowing them to buy large tracts of Georgia's western lands and sell smaller portions back to settlers for a profit. (p. 157)

yeoman farmer *n.* a white Georgia farmer who owned a few acres of land and grew crops on them. (p. 223)

INDEX

An *i* preceding a page reference in italics indicates that there is an illustration, and usually text information as well, on that page. An *m* or a *c* preceding an italic page reference indicates a map or a chart, as well as text information on that page.

ACKNOWLEDGMENTS

Cover

Georgia State Capitol Dome © Joseph Sohm/Visions of America/Corbis; Autumn trees © Stone/Getty Images; Asendorf House © Jim Schwabel/Index Stock Imagery; Atlanta skyline at dusk © Stone/Getty Images; *background* American flag © Stone/Getty Images.

Table of Contents

iv *top* Newman/Photo Network; **iv** *center* The Granger Collection, New York; **iv** *bottom* The Granger Collection, New York; **v** *top* © Bettmann/Corbis; **v** *center* The Granger Collection, New York; **v** *bottom* The Library of Congress; **vi** *top* The Granger Collection, New York; **vi** *center* Nativestock.com; **vi** *bottom* Illustration by Patrick Whelan; **vii** *top* © Tria Giovan/Corbis; **vii** *bottom* The Granger Collection, New York; **viii** *top* © Medford Historical Society Collection/Corbis; **viii** *bottom* The Granger Collection, New York; **ix** *top* The Granger Collection, New York; **ix** *center* © Bettmann/Corbis; **ix** *bottom* © Flip Schulke/Corbis; **x** *top* Time Life Pictures/Getty Images; **x** *bottom* © RonSherman.com—All Rights Reserved.

Geography Handbook

xvi © Jeff Greenberg/PhotoEdit; **1** *top* © Daniel Lainé/Corbis; **1** *bottom* Newman/Photo Network.

Unit 1

Chapter 1, 2–3 © RonSherman.com—All Rights Reserved; **4** © RonSherman.com—All Rights Reserved; **5** © Robert W. Ginn/PhotoEdit; **7** Newman/Photo Network; **8** Kelly Culpepper/TRANSPARENCIES, Inc.; **11** © RonSherman.com—All Rights Reserved; **13** © ALBANY HERALD/Corbis SYGMA; **14** © RonSherman.com—All Rights Reserved; **15** Getty Images.

Chapter 2, 20–21 AP Photo/The Daily Oklahoman, Chad Love; **20** *bottom left* Erich Lessing/Art Resource, NY; **20** *bottom center* Georgia Department of Industry, Trade, and Tourism; **21** *top* © RonSherman.com—All Rights Reserved; **21** *bottom* © The Newark Museum/Art Resource, NY; **22** Erich Lessing/Art Resource, NY; **24** *Mammoth Hunt* by Eric Mose. Courtesy of The Arizona State Museum, The University of Arizona; **25** © Aldo Tutino/Art Resource, NY; **26** © RonSherman.com—All Rights Reserved; **27** © William A. Blake/Corbis; **28** Georgia Department of Industry, Trade, and Tourism; **30** The Granger Collection, New York; **32** © Kevin Fleming/Corbis; **33** © Smithsonian American Art Museum, Washington, DC/Art Resource, NY.

Chapter 3, 36–37 Copyright © North Wind Picture Archives/North Wind Picture Archives—All rights reserved; **36** *bottom left* The Granger Collection, New York; **36** *bottom right* The Granger Collection, New York; **37** *bottom left* The Granger Collection, New York; **37** *bottom right* Getty Images; **38** Stock Montage, Inc.; **39** The Granger Collection, New York; **41** Stock Montage, Inc.; **43** The Granger Collection, New York; **45** Copyright © North Wind Picture Archives/North Wind Picture Archives—All rights reserved; **46** The Granger Collection, New York; **48** The Granger Collection, New York; **49** Sea Battle between the Spanish Armada and English Naval Forces (about 1600), Hendrik Corneliez Vroom. Oil on canvas, 91 cm x 153 cm. Landesmuseum Ferdinandeum, Innsbruck, Austria. Photo copyright © Erich Lessing/Art Resource, New York; **52** Stock Montage, Inc.; **53** Hargrett Rare Book and Manuscript Library/University of Georgia Libraries.

Unit 2

Chapter 4, 56–57 Courtesy of the Pilgrim Hall Museum, Plymouth, Massachusetts; **56** *bottom left* Stock Montage, Inc.; **56** *bottom right* Copyright © North Wind Picture Archives/North Wind Picture Archives—All rights reserved; **57** *bottom* The Granger Collection, New York; **58** Copyright © North Wind Picture Archives/North Wind Picture Archives—All rights reserved; **59** Stock Montage, Inc.; **60** The Granger Collection, New York;

63 © Robert Essel NYC/Corbis; **64** The Granger Collection, New York; **66** Getty Images; **69** The Granger Collection, New York; **71** *left* The Granger Collection, New York; **71** *right* Copyright © North Wind Picture Archives/North Wind Picture Archives—All rights reserved; **72** The Granger Collection, New York; **73** The Granger Collection, New York; **74** © Bettmann/Corbis.

Chapter 5, 78–79 The Granger Collection, New York; **78** *bottom left* Copyright © North Wind Picture Archives/North Wind Picture Archives—All rights reserved; **78** *bottom right* Copyright © North Wind Picture Archives/North Wind Picture Archives—All rights reserved; **79** *bottom left* The Georgia Historical Society, Savannah, Georgia, M.H. & D.B. Floyd Collection; **79** *bottom right* Copyright © North Wind Picture Archives/North Wind Picture Archives—All rights reserved; **80** Copyright © North Wind Picture Archives/Nancy Carter\North Wind Picture Archives—All rights reserved; **81** The Granger Collection, New York; **82** Brown Brothers; **84** Copyright © North Wind Picture Archives/Nancy Carter\North Wind Picture Archives—All rights reserved; **85** Copyright © North Wind Picture Archives/North Wind Picture Archives—All rights reserved; **87** The Granger Collection, New York; **88** The Granger Collection, New York; **89** *top* Copyright © North Wind Picture Archives/North Wind Picture Archives—All rights reserved; **89** *bottom* Copyright © North Wind Picture Archives/North Wind Picture Archives—All rights reserved; **91** The Granger Collection, New York; **92** Getty Images; **94** Copyright © North Wind Picture Archives/North Wind Picture Archives—All rights reserved; **96** The Georgia Historical Society, Savannah, Georgia, M.H. & D.B. Floyd Collection.

Chapter 6, 100–121 The Granger Collection, New York; **100** *bottom left* The Granger Collection, New York; **100** *bottom right* The Granger Collection, New York; **101** *bottom left* The Granger Collection, New York; **101** *bottom right* Copyright © North Wind Picture Archives/North Wind Picture Archives—All rights reserved; **102** The Granger Collection, New York; **103** Copyright © North Wind Picture Archives/North Wind Picture Archives—All rights reserved; **107** The Granger Collection, New York; **109** Copyright © Collection of The New-York Historical Society; **110** The Granger Collection, New York; **111** Copyright © North Wind Picture Archives/North Wind Picture Archives—All rights reserved; **112** *left* The Granger Collection, New York; **112** *right* The Granger Collection, New York; **113** *left* The Granger Collection, New York; **113** *right* John Adams (date unknown) John Trumbull, National Portrait Gallery, Smithsonian Institution/Art Resource, New York; **114** The Granger Collection, New York; **115** © Bettmann/Corbis; **116** Copyright © North Wind Picture Archives/North Wind Picture Archives—All rights reserved; **117** © Bettmann/Corbis; **118** The Granger Collection, New York.

Chapter 7, 122–123 The Granger Collection, New York; **122** *bottom left* Copyright © North Wind Picture Archives/North Wind Picture Archives—All rights reserved; **122** *bottom right* © Bettmann/Corbis; **123** *bottom left* Copyright © North Wind Picture Archives/North Wind Picture Archives—All rights reserved; **123** *bottom right* © Bettmann/Corbis; **124** The Library of Congress; **125** Copyright © Paul Mozell/Stock Boston; **126** Copyright © North Wind Picture Archives/North Wind Picture Archives—All rights reserved; **127** Detail of *The Death of General Warren at the Battle of Bunker's Hill, 17 June 1775* (date unknown), John Trumbull. Oil on canvas. Yale University Art Gallery, Trumbull Collection; **129** *top* The Granger Collection, New York; **129** *bottom* The Library of Congress; **130** © Corbis; **131** Detail of *The Declaration of Independence, 4 July 1776* (date unknown), John Trumbull. Oil of canvas. Yale University Art Gallery, Trumbull Collection; **133** *left* The Granger Collection, New York; **133** *right* The Granger Collection, New York; **134** © Michael Newman/PhotoEdit/PNI; **135** Library of Congress; **137** Culver Pictures, Inc.; **138** The Library of Congress.

Unit 3

Chapter 8, 142–143 Getty Images; **142** *bottom left* The Granger Collection, New York; **142** *bottom right* Copyright © North Wind

Picture Archives/North Wind Picture Archives—All rights reserved; **143** *bottom left* Getty Images; **143** *bottom right* Copyright © North Wind Picture Archives/North Wind Picture Archives—All rights reserved; **144** The Granger Collection, New York; **145** Copyright © North Wind Picture Archives/North Wind Picture Archives—All rights reserved; **147** The Granger Collection, New York; **148** The Granger Collection, New York; **149** © Joseph Sohm; ChromoSohm Inc./Corbis; **151** Courtesy of The New-York Historical Society, New York City; **153** The Granger Collection, New York; **154** The Granger Collection, New York; **155** Copyright © North Wind Picture Archives/North Wind Picture Archives—All rights reserved; **158** Culver Pictures Inc.; **159** The Granger Collection, New York; **160** The Granger Collection, New York; **162** *Lewis and Clark at Three Forks*, E.S. Paxson, Oil on Canvas, 1912, Courtesy of the Montana Historical Society. Photo by John Reddy; **163** Copyright © North Wind Picture Archives/North Wind Picture Archives—All rights reserved; **165** Copyright © North Wind Picture Archives/North Wind Picture Archives—All rights reserved.

Constitution Handbook, 177 AP Photo/White House, Cecil Stoughton; **183** © Bob Daemmrich/Corbis Sygma; **185** © David Young-Wolff/Photo Edit—All rights reserved; **187** *left* Getty Images; **187** *right* Copyright © Cynthia Johnson/Getty Images; **189** Franklin D. Roosevelt Library; **191** Copyright © Rock the Vote Inc.

Chapter 9, 194–195 Talmadge Davis–www.talmadge.net; **194** *top* The Granger Collection, New York; **194** *bottom* © Corbis; **195** *bottom left* Copyright © North Wind Picture Archives/North Wind Picture Archives—All rights reserved; **195** *bottom right* Nativestock.com; **196** The Granger Collection, New York; **197** © Corbis; **198** J. Pat Carter/Getty Images; **199** © Marilyn "Angel" Wynn; **200** *left* The Granger Collection, New York; **200** *bottom* The Granger Collection, New York; **201** Copyright © North Wind Picture Archives/North Wind Picture Archives—All rights reserved; **203** Nativestock.com; **204** Copyright © North Wind Picture Archives/North Wind Picture Archives—All rights reserved; **205** Copyright © North Wind Picture Archives/North Wind Picture Archives—All rights reserved; **206** The Granger Collection, New York.

Chapter 10, 212–213 © Scala/Art Resource, NY; **212** *bottom left* The Granger Collection, New York; **212** *bottom right* Putnam Museum of History and Natural Science, Davenport, Iowa © Don Milici; **213** *bottom left* NPS photograph by Jody Cook; **213** *bottom right* Stock Montage, Inc.; **214** The Granger Collection, New York; **215** © Richard Hamilton Smith/Corbis; **216** Illustration by Patrick Whelan; **218** NPS photograph by Jody Cook; **219** Courtesy, Georgia Division of Archives and History, Office of Secretary of State; **221** The Granger Collection, New York; **222** *top* © Joseph Sohm; ChromoSohm Inc./Corbis; **222** *bottom* © SEF/ Art Resource, NY; **223** Copyright © North Wind Picture Archives/ North Wind Picture Archives—All rights reserved; **224** © Corbis.

Unit 4

Chapter 11, 228–229 The Granger Collection, New York; **228** *bottom left* The Granger Collection, New York; **229** *bottom left* Copyright © North Wind Picture Archives/North Wind Picture Archives—All rights reserved; **229** *bottom right* The Granger Collection, New York; **230** © Bettmann/Corbis; **231** The Granger Collection, New York; **233** Museum of Confederacy, Richmond, Virginia. Photography by Katherine Wetzel; **234** Getty Images; **238** © Bettmann/Corbis; **239** Stock Montage, Inc.; **240** *left* The Granger Collection, New York; **240** *right* Copyright © North Wind Picture Archives/North Wind Picture Archives—All rights reserved; **241** The Granger Collection, New York; **242** The Granger Collection, New York; **244** © G.E. Kidder Smith/Corbis; **245** Stock Montage, Inc.

Chapter 12, 248–249 Hulton/Archive by Getty Images; **248** *bottom left* The Granger Collection, New York; **248** *bottom right* © Medford Historical Society Collection/Corbis; **249** *bottom left* © Scala/Art Resource, NY. *The Capture of Atlanta, Georgia, September 2, 1864;* **249** *bottom right* Library of Congress; **250** ©

Corbis; **251** © Corbis; **253** *left* Copyright © North Wind Picture Archives/North Wind Picture Archives—All rights reserved; **253** *right* The Granger Collection, New York; **255** The Granger Collection, New York; **256** Southern Museum of Civil War and Locomotive History; **257** The Granger Collection, New York; **258** *top* © Bettmann/Corbis; **258** *bottom* © Corbis; **260** © Tria Giovan/Corbis; **260–261** © Tria Giovan/Corbis; **260** *bottom left* Courtesy of the Collection of Joshua M. Landish/© Don Milici; **261** *bottom right* Courtesy of the Collection of Joshua M. Landish/ © Don Milici; **262** American Red Cross; **264** Copyright © North Wind Picture Archives/North Wind Picture Archives—All rights reserved; **265** *left* Library of Congress; **265** *right* Library of Congress; **267** © Bettmann/Corbis; **268** The Granger Collection, New York; **270** © Corbis; **272** © Medford Historical Society Collection/Corbis; **273** © Bettmann/Corbis; **274** © Bettmann/ Corbis; **276** *background* © Corbis; **276** *foreground* Massachusetts Commandery Military Order of the Loyal Legion and the U.S. Army Military History Institute; **277** © Corbis; **279** The Granger Collection, New York; **280** Tom Lovell, National Geographic Image Collection.

Chapter 13, 284–285 The Granger Collection, New York; **284** *bottom left* Copyright © North Wind Picture Archives/North Wind Picture Archives—All rights reserved; **284** *bottom right* Stock Montage Inc.; **285** *bottom left* Library of Congress; **285** *bottom right* Hulton/Archive by Getty Images; **286** © Bettmann/Corbis; **287** Stock Montage Inc.; **288** © Corbis; **289** Copyright © North Wind Picture Archives/North Wind Picture Archives—All rights reserved; **290** Courtesy, Georgia Division of Archives and History, Office of Secretary of State; **291** The Granger Collection, New York; **295** © Bettmann/Corbis; **297** The Granger Collection, New York; **298** © Corbis; **299** The Granger Collection, New York; **301** Atlanta History Center.

Unit 5

Chapter 14, 304–305 Courtesy, Georgia Division of Archives and History, Office of Secretary of State; **304** *bottom left* Copyright © North Wind Picture Archives/North Wind Picture Archives—All rights reserved; **304** *bottom right* © Bettmann/Corbis; **305** *bottom left* Courtesy, Georgia Division of Archives and History, Office of Secretary of State; **305** *bottom right* © Bettmann/ Corbis; **306** The Granger Collection, New York; **307** Special Collections Department, Georgia State University Library; **308** *left* The Granger Collection, New York; **308** *right* Courtesy of AT&T; **308** *background* U.S. Department of Commerce—Patent & Trademark Office, Washington, D.C.; **310** © Corbis; **311** © Bettmann/Corbis; **312** © David Young-Wolff/PhotoEdit; **313** Hulton/Archive by Getty Images; **314** The Granger Collection, New York; **315** Copyright © North Wind Picture Archives/North Wind Picture Archives—All rights reserved; **316** © Corbis; **317** © Bob Krist/Corbis; **318** Courtesy, Georgia Division of Archives and History, Office of Secretary of State; **319** *left* © Corbis; **319** *center* © Corbis; **319** *right* Courtesy, Georgia Division of Archives and History, Office of Secretary of State; **320** Whitfield Murray Historical Society; **321** Courtesy of the Herndon Foundation.

Chapter 15, 324–325 Copyright © North Wind Picture Archives/ North Wind Picture Archives—All rights reserved; **324** *bottom left* © Bettmann/Corbis; **324** *bottom right* © Corbis; **325** *bottom left* Atlanta University Photographs, Atlanta University Center, Robert W. Woodruff Library; **325** *bottom right* Getty Images; **326** Courtesy, Georgia Division of Archives and History, Office of Secretary of State; **327** State Historical Society of North Dakota, BO191; **328** The Last Spike (1869). William T. Garrett Foundry, San Francisco, 17 6/10 carat gold, alloyed with copper. 5 9/16" x 7/16" x 1/2" (shaft including head), 1/2" x 1 3/8" x 1 1/4". Iris & B. Gerald Cantor Center for Visual Arts at Stanford University. Gift of David Hewes, 1998; **329** Solomon D. Butcher Collection, Nebraska State Historical Society; **330** Courtesy, Georgia Division of Archives and History, Office of Secretary of State; **331** *left* © Corbis; **331** *center* Hulton/Archive by Getty Images; **331** *right* ©

Medford Historical Society Collection/Corbis; **332** Courtesy, Georgia Division of Archives and History, Office of Secretary of State; **333** Courtesy, Georgia Division of Archives and History, Office of Secretary of State; **335** © Bettmann/Corbis; **337** © Corbis; **338** The Granger Collection, New York; **339** *left* John Hope, Atlanta University Photographs, Atlanta University Center, Robert W. Woodruff Library. Photographer: Blackstone Studios, Inc.; **339** *right* Lugenia Burns Hope, Atlanta University Photographs, Atlanta University Center, Robert W. Woodruff Library. Photographer: Addison Scurlock Sr. Courtesy Scurlock Studio Records, Archives Center, National Museum of American History, Smithsonian Institution; **340** Library of Congress; **341** Atlanta History Center; **342** Reprinted with permission from National PTA; **343** © Corbis; **344** AP Photo.

Chapter 16, 348–349 © Corbis; **348** *bottom left* © Underwood & Underwood/Corbis; **348** *bottom right* National Infantry Museum; **349** *bottom* Atlanta History Center; **350** The Granger Collection, New York; **351** The Granger Collection, New York; **353** Stock Montage Inc.; **355** © Lake County Museum/Corbis; **357** The Granger Collection, New York; **358** Panel No. 1, "During the World War There Was a Great Migration of the Negro" from *The Migration of the Negro* mural series (1940–1941) by Jacob Lawrence. Tempera on masonite, 12" x 18". Acquired through Downtown Gallery, 1942. The Phillips Collection, Washington, D.C. © 2004 Gwendolyn Knight Lawrence/Artists Rights Society (ARS), New York. ; **359** © Underwood & Underwood/Corbis; **360** Courtesy, Georgia Division of Archives and History, Office of Secretary of State; **361** The Georgia Historical Society, Savannah, Georgia, J. Quattlebaum Collection; **362** © Underwood & Underwood/Corbis; **363** RonSherman.com—All Rights Reserved; **364** Atlanta History Center; **365** © George D. Lepp/Corbis.

Unit 6

Chapter 17, 368–369 AP Photo; **368** *bottom left* Stock Montage, Inc.; **368** *bottom right* Atlanta History Center; **369** *bottom left* © David Young-Wolff/Photo Edit—All rights reserved; **369** *bottom right* Atlanta History Center; **370** © Bettmann/Corbis; **371** Stock Montage, Inc.; **372** *The Atlanta Journal-Constitution*; **374** © Corbis; **375** © Bettmann/Corbis; **376** The Granger Collection, New York; **377** © Corbis; **378** Atlanta History Center; **379** *left* © Bettmann/Corbis; **379** *right* © Bettmann/Corbis; **380** Atlanta History Center; **382** © David Young-Wolff/Photo Edit—All rights reserved; **384** Courtesy, Georgia Division of Archives and History, Office of Secretary of State; **385** Atlanta History Center; **386** Atlanta History Center; **387** The Granger Collection, New York.

Chapter 18, 390–391 US Army Photo, Courtesy of Fort Stewart Museum; **390** *top* Atlanta History Center; **390** *bottom* AP Photo; **391** *bottom left* Getty Images; **391** *bottom right* © Bettmann/Corbis; **392** AP Photo; **393** Getty Images; **394** Corbis; **395** © Corbis; **397** AP Photo; **398** The Granger Collection, New York; **399** Getty Images; **400** National Archives; **401** Getty Images; **402** © Bettmann/Corbis; **404** Atlanta History Center; **405** *top* Atlanta History Center; **405** *bottom* Atlanta History Center; **407** © Bettmann/Corbis; **409** National Infantry Museum; **410** *background* Atlanta History Center; **410** *foreground* The Granger Collection, New York; **411** Getty Images; **412** Atlanta History Center.

Chapter 19, 416–417 Atlanta History Center; **416** *bottom left* AP Photo; **416** *bottom right* © Bettmann/Corbis; **417** *bottom left* The Granger Collection, New York; **417** *bottom right* Courtesy, Georgia Division of Archives and History, Office of Secretary of State; **418** Courtesy, Georgia Division of Archives and History, Office of Secretary of State; **419** © Bettmann/Corbis; **420–421** *background left* Getty Images; **420–421** *background center* © Bettmann/Corbis; **420–421** *background right* Getty Images; **420–421** *top left* © Bettmann/Corbis; **420–421** *bottom left* © H. Armstrong Roberts/Corbis; **420–421** *bottom right* AP Photo; **420–421** *top center* © William Gottlieb/Corbis;

420–421 *top right* Getty Images; **421** AP Photo; **422** *left* © Bettmann/Corbis; **422** *right* PETER GOULD/Time Life Pictures/Getty Images; **423** *top* AP Photo; **423** *bottom* The Granger Collection, New York; **424** The Granger Collection, New York; **425** © Bettmann/Corbis; **427** © Bettmann/Corbis; **428** The Granger Collection, New York; **429** © Bettmann/Corbis; **430** Robert Knudsen, White House/John Fitzgerald Kennedy Library, Boston; **431** Courtesy, Georgia Division of Archives and History, Office of Secretary of State; **432** Courtesy, Georgia Division of Archives and History, Office of Secretary of State; **434** Atlanta History Center; **436** Courtesy, Georgia Division of Archives and History, Office of Secretary of State; **437** Atlanta History Center; **438** GREY VILLET/Time Life Pictures/Getty Images; **439** © Bettmann/Corbis.

Chapter 20, 444–445 © Bettmann/Corbis; **444** *bottom left* Getty Images; **444** *bottom right* AP Photo/Horace Court; **445** *bottom* Time Life Pictures/Getty Images; **446** © Corbis; **447** © Bettmann/Corbis; **448** © Corbis; **449** © Bettmann/Corbis; **451** AP/Wide World Photos; **452** AP Photo/Horace Cort; **453** © Bettmann/Corbis; **454** © Flip Schulke/Corbis; **455** *left* Time Life Pictures/Getty Images; **455** *right* © Bettmann/Corbis; **456** © Bettmann/Corbis; **457** Atlanta History Center; **458** © Flip Schulke/Corbis; **459** © Bettmann/Corbis; **460** © Bettmann/Corbis; **461** © Bettmann/Corbis; **462** AP Photo/Dozier Mobley.

Unit 7

Chapter 21, 468–469 © RonSherman.com—All Rights Reserved; **468** *bottom* Courtesy of Hartsfield-Jackson Atlanta International Airport; **469** *bottom left* AP Photo; **469** *bottom right* Time Life Pictures/Getty Images; **470** Getty Images; **471** © Henry Diltz/Corbis; **472** © Bettmann/Corbis; **473** *left* © Bettmann/Corbis; **473** *right* Getty Images; **475** *The Atlanta Journal-Constitution*; **476** © Flip Schulke/Corbis; **477** © Bettmann/Corbis; **478** Time Life Pictures/Getty Images; **479** © Bettmann/Corbis; **480** © Bettmann/Corbis; **481** Courtesy of Hartsfield-Jackson Atlanta International Airport.

Chapter 22, 486–487 © Bettmann/Corbis; **486** *bottom left* © Bettmann/Corbis; **486** *bottom right* © Bettmann/Corbis; **487** *bottom* © Wally McNamee/Corbis; **488** © Dennis MacDonald/PhotoEdit; **489** AP Photo/Joe Holloway, Jr; **490** © Philip Gould/Corbis; **492** © Bettmann/Corbis; **493** AP Photo; **494** © Bettmann/Corbis; **495** AP Photo/Lionel Cironneau; **496** © RonSherman.com—All Rights Reserved; **497** © Wally McNamee/Corbis; **498** © Dennis MacDonald/PhotoEdit; **501** © RonSherman.com—All Rights Reserved; **503** © RonSherman.com—All Rights Reserved; **505** © Paul Conklin/PhotoEdit.

Chapter 23, 510–511 © RonSherman.com—All Rights Reserved; **510** *bottom left* © HAWKINS KEN/Corbis SYGMA; **510** *bottom right* © Kevin Fleming/Corbis; **511** *bottom left* © MARKOWITZ JEFFREY/Corbis SYGMA; **511** *bottom right* AP Photo/John Bazemore; **512** © Bob Krist/Corbis; **513** © John Van Hasselt/Corbis SYGMA; **514** © HAWKINS KEN/Corbis SYGMA; **515** © MARKOWITZ JEFFREY/Corbis SYGMA; **516** © RonSherman.com—All Rights Reserved; **517** © Charles Gupton/Corbis; **518** © Steve Sands/New York Newswire/Corbis; **521** AP Photo/John Bazemore; **522** © James Randklev/Corbis; **523** © Daniel Lainé/Corbis; **525** Getty Images.

Maps

Maps on pages **40, 55, 99, 104, 121, 161, 207, 236, 247, 283, 303, 347, 352, 396, 400, 415, 426,** and **463** created by Mapping Specialists.

Maps on pages **528–536** © Rand McNally & Company. All rights reserved.

All other maps created by MapQuest.